ALL·IN·ONE

CompTIA
Network+®

EXAM GUIDE
Fifth Edition

(Exam N10-005)

ABOUT THE AUTHOR

Michael Meyers is the industry's leading authority on CompTIA Network+ certification. He is the president and founder of Total Seminars, LLC, a major provider of PC and network repair seminars for thousands of organizations throughout the world, and a member of CompTIA.

Mike has written numerous popular textbooks, including the best-selling *Mike Meyers' CompTIA A+® Guide to Managing & Troubleshooting PCs*, *Mike Meyers' CompTIA A+® Guide to Essentials*, and *Mike Meyers' CompTIA A+® Guide to Operating Systems*.

About the Contributor

Scott Jernigan wields a mighty red pen as Editor in Chief for Total Seminars. With a Master of Arts degree in Medieval History, Scott feels as much at home in the musty archives of London as he does in the warm CRT glow of Total Seminars' Houston headquarters. After fleeing a purely academic life, he dove headfirst into IT, working as an instructor, editor, and writer.

Scott has written, edited, and contributed to dozens of books on computer literacy, hardware, operating systems, networking, and certification, including *Computer Literacy— Your Ticket to IC³ Certification*, and co-authoring with Mike Meyers the *All-in-One CompTIA Strata® IT Fundamentals Exam Guide*.

Scott has taught computer classes all over the United States, including stints at the United Nations in New York and the FBI Academy in Quantico. Practicing what he preaches, Scott is a CompTIA A+ and CompTIA Network+ certified technician, a Microsoft Certified Professional, a Microsoft Office User Specialist, and Certiport Internet and Computing Core Certified.

About the Technical Editor

Jonathan S. Weissman earned his master's degree in Computer and Information Science from Brooklyn College (CUNY), and holds nineteen industry certifications, including Cisco CCNA, CompTIA Security+, CompTIA i-Net+, CompTIA Network+, CompTIA A+, CompTIA Linux+, Novell CNE, Novell CNA, Microsoft Office Master, Microsoft MCAS Word, Microsoft MCAS PowerPoint, Microsoft MCAS Excel, Microsoft MCAS Access, Microsoft MCAS Outlook, and Microsoft MCAS Vista.

Jonathan is a tenured Assistant Professor of Computing Sciences at Finger Lakes Community College, in Canandaigua, NY, and also teaches graduate and undergraduate courses for the Department of Networking, Security, and Systems Administration at nearby Rochester Institute of Technology. In addition, Jonathan does computer, network, and security consulting for area businesses and individuals.

This textbook is just one of the many that Jonathan has edited for thoroughness and accuracy.

ALL·IN·ONE

CompTIA
Network+®

EXAM GUIDE
Fifth Edition

(Exam N10-005)

Mike Meyers

New York • Chicago • San Francisco • Lisbon
London • Madrid • Mexico City • Milan • New Delhi
San Juan • Seoul • Singapore • Sydney • Toronto

The *McGraw·Hill* Companies

Cataloging-in-Publication Data is on file with the Library of Congress

McGraw-Hill books are available at special quantity discounts to use as premiums and sales promotions, or for use in corporate training programs. To contact a representative, please e-mail us at bulksales@mcgraw-hill.com.

CompTIA Network+® All-in-One Exam Guide, Fifth Edition (Exam N10-005)

234567890 DOC DOC 109876543212

ISBN: Book p/n 978-0-07-178921-9 and CD p/n 978-0-07-178920-2
of set 978-0-07-178922-6

MHID: Book p/n 0-07-178921-9 and CD p/n 0-07-178920-0
of set 0-07-178922-7

Sponsoring Editor	**Technical Editor**	**Production Supervisor**
Timothy Green	*Jonathan S. Weissman*	*Jim Kussow*
Editorial Supervisor	**Copy Editor**	**Composition**
Jody McKenzie	*LeeAnn Pickrell*	*ContentWorks, Inc.*
Project Manager	**Proofreader**	**Illustration**
Molly Sharp	*Andrea Fox*	*ContentWorks, Inc.*
Acquisitions Coordinator	**Indexer**	**Art Director, Cover**
Stephanie Evans	*Jack Lewis, J & J Indexing*	*Jeff Weeks*

CompTIA Network+

The CompTIA Network+ certification ensures that the successful candidate has the important knowledge and skills necessary to manage, maintain, troubleshoot, install, operate, and configure basic network infrastructure; describe networking technologies and basic design principles; and adhere to wiring standards and use testing tools.

It Pays to Get Certified

In a digital world, digital literacy is an essential survival skill. Certification proves you have the knowledge and skill to solve business problems in virtually any business environment. Certifications are highly valued credentials that qualify you for jobs, increased compensation, and promotion.

CompTIA Network+ certification is held by many IT staffers across many organizations. 21% of IT staff within a random sampling of U.S. organizations within a cross section of industry verticals hold CompTIA Network+ certification.

- The CompTIA Network+ credential—proves knowledge of networking features and functions and is the leading vendor-neutral certification for networking professionals.

- Starting salary—the average starting salary of network engineers can be up to $70,000.

- Career pathway—CompTIA Network+ is the first step in starting a networking career, and is recognized by Microsoft as part of their MS program. Other corporations, such as Novell, Cisco, and HP also recognize CompTIA Network+ as part of their certification tracks.

- More than 325,000 individuals worldwide are CompTIA Network+ certified.

- Mandated/recommended by organizations worldwide—Apple, Cisco, HP, Ricoh, the U.S. State Department, and U.S. government contractors such as EDS, General Dynamics, and Northrop Grumman recommend or mandate CompTIA Network+.

How Certification Helps Your Career

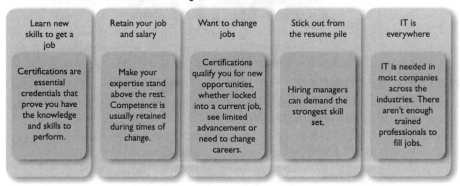

Learn new skills to get a job	Retain your job and salary	Want to change jobs	Stick out from the resume pile	IT is everywhere
Certifications are essential credentials that prove you have the knowledge and skills to perform.	Make your expertise stand above the rest. Competence is usually retained during times of change.	Certifications qualify you for new opportunities, whether locked into a current job, see limited advancement or need to change careers.	Hiring managers can demand the strongest skill set.	IT is needed in most companies across the industries. There aren't enough trained professionals to fill jobs.

CompTIA Career Pathway

CompTIA offers a number of credentials that form a foundation for your career in technology and that allow you to pursue specific areas of concentration. Depending on the path you choose, CompTIA certifications help you build upon your skills and knowledge, supporting learning throughout your career.

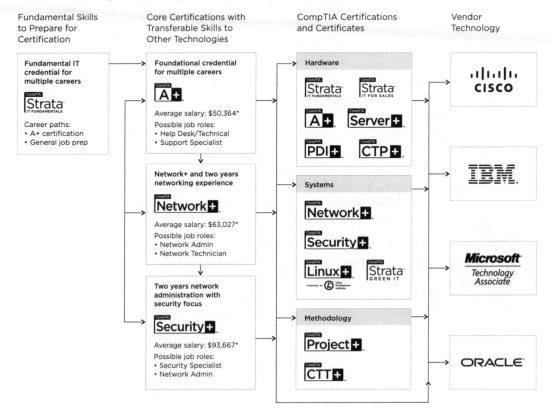

*Source: *Computerworld* Salary Survey 2010—U.S. salaries only

Steps to Getting Certified and Staying Certified

1. **Review exam objectives.** Review the certification objectives to make sure you know what is covered in the exam:
   www.comptia.org/certifications/testprep/examobjectives.aspx

2. **Practice for the exam.** After you have studied for the certification, take a free assessment and sample test to get an idea what type of questions might be on the exam:
   www.comptia.org/certifications/testprep/practicetests.aspx

3. **Purchase an exam voucher.** Purchase exam vouchers on the CompTIA Marketplace, which is located at: www.comptiastore.com

4. **Take the test!** Select a certification exam provider, and schedule a time to take your exam. You can find exam providers at the following link:
   www.comptia.org/certifications/testprep/testingcenters.aspx

5. **Stay certified!** Continuing education is required. Effective January 1, 2011, CompTIA Network+ certifications are valid for three years from the date of certification. There are a number of ways the certification can be renewed. For more information go to: http://certification.comptia.org/getCertified/steps_to_certification/stayCertified.aspx

Join the Professional Community

The free online IT Pro Community provides valuable content to students and professionals. Join the IT Pro Community:

http://itpro.comptia.org

Career IT job resources include:

- Where to start in IT
- Career assessments
- Salary trends
- U.S. job board

Join the IT Pro Community and get access to:

- Forums on networking, security, computing, and cutting-edge technologies
- Access to blogs written by industry experts
- Current information on cutting edge technologies
- Access to various industry resource links and articles related to IT and IT careers

 **AUTHORIZED**

Content Seal of Quality

This courseware bears the seal of CompTIA Approved Quality Content. This seal signifies this content covers 100 percent of the exam objectives and implements important instructional design principles. CompTIA recommends multiple learning tools to help increase coverage of the learning objectives.

Why CompTIA?

- **Global recognition**   CompTIA is recognized globally as the leading IT non-profit trade association and has enormous credibility. Plus, CompTIA's certifications are vendor-neutral and offer proof of foundational knowledge that translates across technologies.

- **Valued by hiring managers**   Hiring managers value CompTIA certification because it is vendor- and technology-independent validation of your technical skills.

- **Recommended or required by government and businesses**   Many government organizations and corporations (for example, Dell, Sharp, Ricoh, the U.S. Department of Defense, and many more) either recommend or require technical staff to be CompTIA certified.

- **Three CompTIA certifications ranked in the top 10**   In a study by DICE of 17,000 technology professionals, certifications helped command higher salaries at all experience levels.

How to Obtain More Information

- **Visit CompTIA online**   Go to www.comptia.org to learn more about getting CompTIA certified.

- **Contact CompTIA**   Please call 866-835-8020, ext. 5 or e-mail questions@comptia.org.

- **Join the IT Pro Community**   Go to http://itpro.comptia.org to join the IT community to get relevant career information.

- **Connect with CompTIA**   Find us on Facebook, LinkedIn, Twitter, and YouTube.

CAQC Disclaimer

CONTENTS AT A GLANCE

Chapter 1   CompTIA Network+in a Nutshell   1

Chapter 2   Network Models   11

Chapter 3   Cabling and Topology   55

Chapter 4   Ethernet Basics   81

Chapter 5   Modern Ethernet   107

Chapter 6   Installing a Physical Network   125

Chapter 7   TCP/IP Basics   177

Chapter 8   The Wonderful World of Routing   227

Chapter 9   TCP/IP Applications   275

Chapter 10   Network Naming   317

Chapter 11   Securing TCP/IP   359

Chapter 12   Advanced Networking Devices   401

Chapter 13   IPv6   433

Chapter 14   Remote Connectivity   459

Chapter 15   Wireless Networking   509

Chapter 16   Protecting Your Network   547

Chapter 17   Virtualization   575

Chapter 18   Network Management   601

Chapter 19   Building a SOHO Network   635

Chapter 20   Network Troubleshooting   657

Appendix A   Objectives Map: CompTIA Network+   683

Appendix B   About the CD-ROM   699

Glossary   703

Index   763

CONTENTS

Acknowledgments xxii

Chapter 1 CompTIA Network+ in a Nutshell 1
   Who Needs CompTIA Network+? I Just Want to Learn about Networks! . . . 2
   What Is CompTIA Network+ Certification? 2
      What Is CompTIA? 2
      The Current CompTIA Network+ Certification Exam Release 3
      How Do I Become CompTIA Network+ Certified? 3
   What Is the Exam Like? 4
      How Do I Take the Test? 5
      How Much Does the Test Cost? 5
   How to Pass the CompTIA Network+ Exam 6
      Obligate Yourself 6
      Set Aside the Right Amount of Study Time 6
      Study for the Test 7

Chapter 2 Network Models 11
   Historical/Conceptual 12
   Working with Models 12
      Biography of a Model 13
      Network Models 14
   The OSI Seven-Layer Model in Action 15
      Welcome to MHTechEd! 16
   Test Specific 17
   Let's Get Physical—Network Hardware and Layers 1–2 17
      The NIC 20
      The Two Aspects of NICs 28
   Beyond the Single Wire—Network Software and Layers 3–7 30
      IP—Playing on Layer 3, the Network Layer 31
      Packets Within Frames 33
      Assembly and Disassembly—Layer 4, the Transport Layer 35
      Talking on a Network—Layer 5, the Session Layer 37
      Standardized Formats, or Why Layer 6, Presentation, Has No Friends 40
      Network Applications—Layer 7, the Application Layer 42
   The TCP/IP Model 43
      The Link Layer 44
      The Internet Layer 45
      The Transport Layer 45

The Application Layer 48
Frames, Packets, and Segments, Oh My! 49
The Tech's Troubleshooting Tool 50
Chapter Review 51
Questions 51
Answers 53

Chapter 3 Cabling and Topology 55
Test Specific 55
Topology 55
Bus and Ring 56
Star 58
Hybrids 59
Mesh and Point-to-Multipoint 60
Point-to-Point 62
Parameters of a Topology 63
Cabling 63
Coaxial Cable 63
Twisted Pair 67
Fiber-Optic 71
Other Cables 73
Fire Ratings 75
Networking Industry Standards—IEEE 76
Chapter Review 78
Questions 78
Answers 79

Chapter 4 Ethernet Basics 81
Historical/Conceptual 82
Ethernet 82
Topology 83
Test Specific 84
Organizing the Data: Ethernet Frames 84
CSMA/CD 87
Early Ethernet Networks 89
10BaseT 89
10BaseFL 94
Extending and Enhancing Ethernet Networks 96
Connecting Ethernet Segments 96
Switched Ethernet 99
Troubleshooting Hubs and Switches 103
Chapter Review 104
Questions 104
Answers 105

Chapter 5 Modern Ethernet 107
    Test Specific 107
    100-Megabit Ethernet 107
        100BaseT 108
        100BaseFX 110
    Gigabit Ethernet 112
        1000BaseCX 113
        1000BaseSX 113
        1000BaseLX 114
        New Fiber Connectors 114
        Implementing Multiple Types of Gigabit Ethernet 115
    10 Gigabit Ethernet 116
        Fiber-based 10 GbE 117
        The Other 10 Gigabit Ethernet Fiber Standards 118
        Copper-based 10 GbE 119
        10 GbE Physical Connections 119
        Backbones 120
        Know Your Ethernets! 120
    Chapter Review 122
        Questions 122
        Answers 123

Chapter 6 Installing a Physical Network 125
    Historical/Conceptual 127
    Understanding Structured Cabling 127
        Cable Basics—A Star Is Born 127
    Test Specific 129
        Structured Cable Network Components 129
        Structured Cable—Beyond the Star 140
    Installing Structured Cabling 144
        Getting a Floor Plan 145
        Mapping the Runs 145
        Determining the Location of the Telecommunications Room 146
        Pulling Cable 147
        Making Connections 150
        Testing the Cable Runs 155
    NICs 162
        Buying NICs 163
        Link Lights 166
    Diagnostics and Repair of Physical Cabling 168
        Diagnosing Physical Problems 168
        Check Your Lights 168
        Check the NIC 169
        Cable Testing 170
        Problems in the Telecommunications Room 171
        Toners 172

Chapter Review 173
    Questions 173
    Answers 175

Chapter 7 TCP/IP Basics 177
    Historical/Conceptual 178
    Standardizing Networking Technology 178
    Test Specific 179
    The TCP/IP Protocol Suite 179
        Internet Layer Protocols 180
        Transport Layer Protocols 182
        Application Layer Protocols 183
    IP in Depth 185
        IP Addresses 186
        IP Addresses in Action 191
        Class IDs 200
    CIDR and Subnetting 202
        Subnetting 202
        CIDR: Subnetting in the Real World 211
    Using IP Addresses 212
        Static IP Addressing 212
        Dynamic IP Addressing 216
        Special IP Addresses 222
    Chapter Review 223
        Questions 223
        Answers 225

Chapter 8 The Wonderful World of Routing 227
    Historical/Conceptual 228
    How Routers Work 228
    Test Specific 230
    Routing Tables 230
        Freedom from Layer 2 237
        Network Address Translation 238
    Dynamic Routing 245
        Routing Metrics 246
        Distance Vector 247
        Link State 254
        EIGRP—the Lone Hybrid 259
        Dynamic Routing Makes the Internet 259
    Working with Routers 260
        Connecting to Routers 260
        Basic Router Configuration 267
        Router Problems 270
    Chapter Review 272
        Questions 272
        Answers 274

Chapter 9 TCP/IP Applications 275
   Historical/Conceptual 276
   Transport Layer and Network Layer Protocols 276
      How People Communicate 276
   Test Specific 277
      TCP 277
      UDP 278
      ICMP 279
      IGMP 280
   The Power of Port Numbers 280
      Registered Ports 282
      Connection Status 286
      Rules for Determining Good vs. Bad Communications 291
   Common TCP/IP Applications 291
      The World Wide Web 291
      Telnet 299
      E-mail 304
      FTP 309
      Internet Applications 313
   Chapter Review 314
      Questions 314
      Answers 315

Chapter 10 Network Naming 317
   Historical/Conceptual 318
   DNS 318
   Test Specific 320
      How DNS Works 320
      Name Spaces 321
      DNS Servers 336
      Troubleshooting DNS 346
   WINS 349
      Configuring WINS Clients 351
      Troubleshooting WINS 352
   Diagnosing TCP/IP Networks 352
   Chapter Review 355
      Questions 355
      Answers 357

Chapter 11 Securing TCP/IP 359
   Test Specific 360
   Making TCP/IP Secure 360
      Encryption 360
      Nonrepudiation 368
      Authentication 375
      Authorization 375

TCP/IP Security Standards 376
   Authentication Standards 376
   Encryption Standards 388
   Combining Authentication and Encryption 391
Secure TCP/IP Applications 394
   HTTPS 394
   SCP 395
   SFTP 396
   SNMP 396
   LDAP 397
   NTP 398
Chapter Review 398
   Questions 398
   Answers 400

Chapter 12 Advanced Networking Devices 401
Client/Server and Peer-to-Peer Topologies 402
Historical/Conceptual 402
   Client/Server 402
   Peer-to-Peer 404
Test Specific 405
   Client/Server and Peer-to-Peer Today 405
Virtual Private Networks 406
   PPTP VPNs 408
   L2TP VPNs 411
   SSL VPNs 411
Virtual LANs 412
   Trunking 413
   Configuring a VLAN-capable Switch 414
   Virtual Trunk Protocol 417
   InterVLAN Routing 417
Multilayer Switches 419
   Load Balancing 420
   QoS and Traffic Shaping 423
   Network Protection 424
Chapter Review 430
   Questions 430
   Answers 431

Chapter 13 IPv6 433
Test Specific 434
IPv6 Basics 434
   IPv6 Address Notation 434
   Link-Local Address 435
   IPv6 Subnet Masks 437
   The End of Broadcast 437

Global Address 439
Aggregation 441
Using IPv6 445
Enabling IPv6 445
NAT in IPv6 446
DHCP in IPv6 447
DNS in IPv6 449
Moving to IPv6 450
IPv4 and IPv6 450
Tunnels 451
IPv6 Is Here, Really! 456
Chapter Review 456
Questions 456
Answers 458

Chapter 14 Remote Connectivity 459
Historical/Conceptual 459
Telephony and Beyond 460
The Dawn of Long Distance 461
Test Specific 467
Digital Telephony 467
Copper Carriers: T1 and T3 468
Fiber Carriers: SONET/SDH and OC 472
Packet Switching 473
Real-World WAN 478
Alternative to Telephony WAN 479
The Last Mile 479
Dial-Up 480
DSL 486
Cable Modems 490
Satellite 492
Cellular WAN 492
Fiber 494
BPL 494
Which Connection? 495
Using Remote Access 495
Dial-Up to the Internet 496
Private Dial-Up 496
Dedicated Connection 499
Remote Terminal 501
Chapter Review 505
Questions 505
Answers 507

Chapter 15 Wireless Networking **509**
    Historical/Conceptual 509
    Test Specific 510
    Wi-Fi Standards 510
        802.11 511
        802.11b 519
        802.11a 519
        802.11g 520
        802.11n 520
        Wireless Networking Security 521
        Power over Ethernet 526
    Implementing Wi-Fi 526
        Performing a Site Survey 526
        Installing the Client 528
        Setting Up an Ad Hoc Network 528
        Setting Up an Infrastructure Network 529
        Extending the Network 538
        Verify the Installation 539
    Troubleshooting Wi-Fi 539
        Hardware Troubleshooting 540
        Software Troubleshooting 540
        Connectivity Troubleshooting 540
        Configuration Troubleshooting 542
    Chapter Review 543
        Questions 543
        Answers 545

Chapter 16 Protecting Your Network **547**
    Test Specific 548
    Common Threats 548
        System Crash/Hardware Failure 548
        Administrative Access Control 549
        Malware 550
        Social Engineering 552
        Man in the Middle 553
        Denial of Service 553
        Physical Intrusion 554
        Attacks on Wireless Connections 555
    Securing User Accounts 557
        Authentication 557
        Passwords 557
        Controlling User Accounts 559
    Firewalls 562
        Hiding the IPs 562
        Port Filtering 563
        Packet Filtering 565

MAC Filtering 567
Personal Firewalls 567
Network Zones 570
Vulnerability Scanners 571
Chapter Review 572
Questions 572
Answers 574

Chapter 17 Virtualization **575**
Historical/Conceptual 575
What Is Virtualization? 575
Meet the Hypervisor 577
Emulation vs. Virtualization 579
Sample Virtualization 580
Test Specific 586
Why Do We Virtualize? 586
Power Saving 586
Hardware Consolidation 586
System Recovery 586
System Duplication 587
Research 587
Virtualization in Modern Networks 588
Virtual Machine Managers 590
Hypervisors 592
Virtual Switches 593
Virtual PBX 595
Network as a Service 596
Chapter Review 597
Questions 597
Answers 599

Chapter 18 Network Management **601**
Test Specific 601
Network Configuration Management 601
Configuration Management Documentation 602
Change Management Documentation 609
Monitoring Performance and Connectivity 610
Performance Monitor 610
Logs and Network Traffic 618
Network Performance Optimization 620
Caching 621
Controlling Data Throughput 621
Keeping Resources Available 625
Chapter Review 632
Questions 632
Answers 633

Chapter 19 Building a SOHO Network 635
  Historical/Conceptual 635
  Test Specific 636
  Designing a SOHO Network 636
  Building the Network 637
    Define the Network Needs 638
    Network Design 638
    Compatibility Issues 640
    Internal Connections 641
    External Connections 645
    ISPs and MTUs 649
    Peripherals 651
  Security 652
  Chapter Review 654
    Questions 654
    Answers 656

Chapter 20 Network Troubleshooting 657
  Test Specific 658
  Troubleshooting Tools 658
    Hardware Tools 658
    Software Tools 663
  The Troubleshooting Process 669
    Identify the Problem 671
    Establish a Theory of Probable Cause 673
    Test the Theory to Determine Cause 673
    Establish a Plan of Action and Identify Potential Effects 673
    Implement and Test the Solution or Escalate as Necessary 674
    Verify Full System Functionality and Implement
      Preventative Measures 674
    Document Findings, Actions, and Outcomes 675
  Troubleshooting Scenarios 675
    "I Can't Log In!" 676
    "I Can't Get to This Web Site!" 676
    "Our Web Server Is Sluggish!" 676
    "I Can't See Anything on the Network!" 677
    "It's Time to Escalate!" 677
    Troubleshooting Is Fun! 679
  Chapter Review 680
    Questions 680
    Answers 682

Appendix A Objectives Map: CompTIA Network+ 683

Appendix B About the CD-ROM 699

Playing Mike Meyers Introduction Video 699

System Requirements 699

Installing and Running Total Tester 700

Total Tester 700

LearnKey Video Training 700

Mike's Cool Tools 700

Secure PDF Copy of the Book 701

Boson's NetSim Network Simulator 701

Technical Support 702

LearnKey Technical Support 702

Boson Technical Support 702

Glossary 703

Index 763

To Staci Lynne Davis, vegan chef and punk rocker: Thanks for showing me your world and, in the process, expanding mine.

ACKNOWLEDGMENTS

I'd like to acknowledge the many people who contributed their talents to make this book possible:

To Tim Green, my acquisitions editor at McGraw-Hill: Didn't think I'd get the book out this quickly, did you? Thanks for your superb support and encouragement, as always.

To my in-house Editor-in-Chief, Scott Jernigan: Didn't think we'd get the book out that fast, did you? How many 85s do you have now? Pelape still smokes them all in DPS.

To Jonathan Weissman, technical editor: Holy crap, you kicked my butt. Thanks for making my book dramatically better than it has ever been.

To LeeAnn Pickrell, copy editor: u made me write good, thx.

To Michael Smyer, Total Seminars' resident tech guru and photographer: Glad to see you staying focused. And your photos rocked as always!

To Ford Pierson, graphics maven and editor: Superb conceptual art? Check! Great editing? Check! Beating the boss in Unreal Tournament over and over again? Check, unfortunately.

To Aaron Verber, editor extraordinaire: Your quiet toils in the dark corner of the office have once again paid outstanding dividends!

To Dudley Lehmer, my partner at Total Seminars: As always, thanks for keeping the ship afloat while I got to play on this book!

To Stephanie Evans, acquisitions coordinator at McGraw-Hill: You are my favorite South African ambassador since the Springboks. Thanks for keeping track of everything and (gently) smacking Scott when *he* forgot things.

To Molly Sharp and Jody McKenzie, project editors: It was a joy to work with you, Molly, and again with you, Jody. I couldn't have asked for a better team! (Didn't think I could resist making the pun, did you?)

To Andrea Fox, proofreader: You did a super job, thank you

To Tom Sharp, compositor: The layout was excellent, thanks!

CompTIA Network+ in a Nutshell

In this chapter, you will gain essential knowledge
- Describe the importance of CompTIA Network+ certification
- Illustrate the structure and contents of the CompTIA Network+ certification exam
- Plan a strategy to prepare for the exam

By picking up this book, you've shown an interest in learning about networking. But be forewarned. The term *networking* describes a vast field of study, far too large for any single certification, book, or training course to cover. Do you want to configure routers and switches for a living? Do you want to administer a large Windows network at a company? Do you want to install wide area network connections? Do you want to set up Web servers? Do you want to secure networks against attacks?

If you're considering a CompTIA Network+ certification, you probably don't yet know exactly what aspect of networking you want to pursue, and that's okay! You're going to *love* preparing for the CompTIA Network+ certification.

Attaining CompTIA Network+ certification provides you with three fantastic benefits. First, you get a superb overview of networking that helps you decide what part of the industry you'd like to pursue. Second, it acts as a prerequisite toward other, more advanced certifications. Third, the amount of eye-opening information you'll gain just makes getting CompTIA Network+ certified plain old *fun*.

Nothing comes close to providing a better overview of networking than CompTIA Network+. The certification covers local area networks (LANs), wide area networks (WANs), the Internet, security, cabling, and applications in a wide-but-not-too-deep fashion that showcases the many different parts of a network and hopefully tempts you to investigate the aspects that intrigue you by looking into follow-up certifications.

The process of attaining CompTIA Network+ certification will give you a solid foundation in the whole field of networking. Mastering the competencies will help fill in gaps in your knowledge and provide an ongoing series of "a-ha!" moments of grasping the big picture that make being a tech so much fun.

Ready to learn a lot, grab a great certification, and have fun doing it? Then welcome to CompTIA Network+ certification!

Who Needs CompTIA Network+? I Just Want to Learn about Networks!

Whoa up there, amigo! Are you one of those folks who either has never heard of the CompTIA Network+ exam or just doesn't have any real interest in certification? Is your goal only to get a solid handle on the idea of networking and a jump start on the basics? Are you looking for that "magic bullet" book that you can read from beginning to end and then start installing and troubleshooting a network? Do you want to know what's involved with running network cabling in your walls or getting your new wireless network working? Are you tired of not knowing enough about what TCP/IP is and how it works? If these types of questions are running through your mind, then rest easy—you have the right book. Like every book with the Mike Meyers name, you'll get solid concepts without pedantic details or broad, meaning-less overviews. You'll look at real-world networking as performed by real techs. This is a book that understands your needs and goes well beyond the scope of a single certification.

If the CompTIA Network+ exam isn't for you, you can skip the rest of this chapter, shift your brain into learn mode, and dive into Chapter 2. But then, if you're going to have the knowledge, why *not* get the certification?

What Is CompTIA Network+ Certification?

CompTIA Network+ certification is an industry-wide, vendor-neutral certification program developed and sponsored by the Computing Technology Industry Association (CompTIA). The CompTIA Network+ certification shows that you have a basic competency in the physical support of networking systems and knowledge of the conceptual aspects of networking. To date, many hundreds of thousands of technicians have become CompTIA Network+ certified.

CompTIA Network+ certification enjoys wide recognition throughout the IT industry. At first, it rode in on the coattails of the successful CompTIA A+ certification program, but it now stands on its own in the networking industry and is considered the obvious next step after CompTIA A+ certification.

What Is CompTIA?

CompTIA is a nonprofit, industry trade association based in Oakbrook Terrace, Illi-nois, on the outskirts of Chicago. Tens of thousands of computer resellers, value-added resellers, distributors, manufacturers, and training companies from all over the world are members of CompTIA.

CompTIA was founded in 1982. The following year, CompTIA began offering the CompTIA A+ certification exam. CompTIA A+ certification is now widely recognized as a *de facto* requirement for entrance into the PC industry. Because the CompTIA A+ exam covers networking only lightly, CompTIA decided to establish a vendor-neutral test covering basic networking skills. So, in April 1999, CompTIA unveiled the CompTIA Network+ certification exam.

CompTIA provides certifications for a variety of areas in the computer industry, offers opportunities for its members to interact, and represents its members' interests to government bodies. CompTIA certifications include CompTIA A+, CompTIA Network+, and CompTIA Security+, to name a few. Check out the CompTIA Web site at www.comptia.org for details on other certifications.

CompTIA is *huge*. Virtually every company of consequence in the IT industry is a member of CompTIA: Microsoft, Dell, Cisco... Name an IT company and it's probably a member of CompTIA.

The Current CompTIA Network+ Certification Exam Release

CompTIA constantly works to provide exams that cover the latest technologies and, as part of that effort, periodically updates its certification objectives, domains, and exam questions. This book covers all you need to know to pass the N10-005 CompTIA Network+ exam released in 2011.

How Do I Become CompTIA Network+ Certified?

To become CompTIA Network+ certified, you simply pass one computer-based, multiple choice exam. There are no prerequisites for taking the CompTIA Network+ exam, and no networking experience is needed. You're not required to take a training course or buy any training materials. The only requirements are that you pay a testing fee to an authorized testing facility and then sit for the exam. Upon completion of the exam, you will immediately know whether you passed or failed.

Once you pass, you become CompTIA Network+ certified for three years. After three years, you'll need to renew your certification by retaking the current exam or completing approved Continuing Education activities. By completing these activities, you earn credits that (along with an annual fee) allow you to keep your CompTIA Network+ certification. For a full list of approved activities, check out CompTIA's Web site (www.comptia.org) and search for **CompTIA Continuing Education Program**.

Now for the details: CompTIA recommends that you have at least nine to twelve months of networking experience and CompTIA A+ knowledge, but this is not a requirement. Note the word "recommend." You may not need experience or CompTIA A+ knowledge, but they help! The CompTIA A+ certification competencies have a degree of overlap with the CompTIA Network+ competencies, such as types of connectors and how networks work.

As for experience, keep in mind that CompTIA Network+ is mostly a practical exam. Those who have been out there supporting real networks will find many of the questions reminiscent of the types of problems they have seen on LANs. The bottom line is that you'll probably have a much easier time on the CompTIA Network+ exam if you have some CompTIA A+ experience under your belt.

What Is the Exam Like?

The CompTIA Network+ exam contains 100 questions, and you have 90 minutes to complete the exam. To pass, you must score at least 720 on a scale of 100–900, at the time of this writing. Check the CompTIA Web site when you get close to testing to determine the current scale:

http://certification.comptia.org/getCertified/certifications/network.aspx

The exam questions are divided into five areas that CompTIA calls domains. This table lists the CompTIA Network+ domains and the percentage of the exam that each represents.

CompTIA Network+ Domain	Percentage
1.0 Network Technologies	21%
2.0 Network Installation and Configuration	23%
3.0 Network Media and Topologies	17%
4.0 Network Management	20%
5.0 Network Security	19%

The CompTIA Network+ exam is extremely practical. Questions often present real-life scenarios and ask you to determine the best solution. The CompTIA Network+ exam loves troubleshooting. Let me repeat: many of the test objectives deal with direct, *real-world troubleshooting*. Be prepared to troubleshoot both hardware and software failures and to answer both "What do you do next?" and "What is most likely the problem?" types of questions.

A qualified CompTIA Network+ certification candidate can install and configure a PC to connect to a network. This includes installing and testing a network card, configuring drivers, and loading all network software. The exam will test you on the different topologies, standards, and cabling.

Expect conceptual questions about the Open Systems Interconnection (OSI) seven-layer model. If you've never heard of the OSI seven-layer model, don't worry! This book will teach you all you need to know. While this model rarely comes into play during the daily grind of supporting a network, you need to know the functions and protocols for each layer to pass the CompTIA Network+ exam. You can also expect questions on most of the protocol suites, with heavy emphasis on the TCP/IP suite.

 NOTE CompTIA occasionally makes changes to the content of the exam, as well as the score necessary to pass it. Always check the Web site of my company, Total Seminars (www.totalsem.com), before scheduling your exam.

How Do I Take the Test?

To take the test, you must go to an authorized testing center. You cannot take the test over the Internet. Prometric and Pearson VUE administer the actual CompTIA Network+ exam. You'll find thousands of Prometric and Pearson VUE testing centers scattered across the United States and Canada, as well as in over 75 other countries around the world. You may take the exam at any testing center. To locate a testing center and schedule an exam, call Prometric at 888-895-6116 or Pearson VUE at 877-551-7587. You can also visit their Web sites at www.prometric.com and www.vue.com.

> **NOTE** Although you can't take the exam over the Internet, both Prometric and Pearson VUE provide easy online registration. Go to www.prometric.com or www.vue.com to register online.

How Much Does the Test Cost?

CompTIA fixes the price, no matter what testing center you use. The cost of the exam depends on whether you work for a CompTIA member. At press time, the cost for non-CompTIA members is US$246.

If your employer is a CompTIA member, you can save money by obtaining an exam voucher. In fact, even if you don't work for a CompTIA member, you can purchase a voucher from member companies and take advantage of significant member savings. You simply buy the voucher and then use the voucher to pay for the exam. Vouchers are delivered to you on paper and electronically via e-mail. The voucher number is the important thing. That number is your exam payment, so protect it from fellow students until you're ready to schedule your exam.

If you're in the United States or Canada, you can visit www.totalsem.com or call 800-446-6004 to purchase vouchers. As I always say, "You don't have to buy your voucher from us, but for goodness' sake, get one from somebody!" Why pay full price when you have a discount alternative?

You must pay for the exam when you schedule, whether online or by phone. If you're scheduling by phone, be prepared to hold for a while. Have your Social Security number (or the international equivalent) ready and either a credit card or a voucher number when you call or begin the online scheduling process. If you require any special accommodations, both Prometric and Pearson VUE will be able to assist you, although your selection of testing locations may be a bit more limited.

International prices vary; see the CompTIA Web site for international pricing. Of course, prices are subject to change without notice, so always check the CompTIA Web site for current pricing!

How to Pass the CompTIA Network+ Exam

The single most important thing to remember about the CompTIA Network+ certification exam is that CompTIA designed it to test the knowledge of a technician with as little as nine months of experience—so keep it simple! Think in terms of practical knowledge. Read this book, answer the questions at the end of each chapter, take the practice exams on the media accompanying this book, review any topics you missed, and you'll pass with flying colors.

Is it safe to assume that it's probably been a while since you've taken an exam? Consequently, has it been a while since you've had to study for an exam? If you're nodding your head yes, you'll probably want to read the next sections. They lay out a proven strategy to help you study for the CompTIA Network+ exam and pass it. Try it. It works.

Obligate Yourself

The first step you should take is to schedule the exam. Ever heard the old adage that heat and pressure make diamonds? Well, if you don't give yourself a little "heat," you might procrastinate and unnecessarily delay taking the exam. Even worse, you may end up not taking the exam at all. Do yourself a favor. Determine how much time you need to study (see the next section), and then call Prometric or Pearson VUE and schedule the exam, giving yourself the time you need to study—and adding a few extra days for safety. Afterward, sit back and let your anxieties wash over you. Suddenly, turning off the television and cracking open the book will become a lot easier! Keep in mind that Prometric and Pearson VUE let you schedule an exam only a few weeks in advance, at most. If you schedule an exam and can't make it, you must reschedule at least a day in advance or lose your money.

Set Aside the Right Amount of Study Time

After helping thousands of techs get their CompTIA Network+ certification, we at Total Seminars have developed a pretty good feel for the amount of study time needed to pass the CompTIA Network+ exam. Table 1.1 will help you plan how much study time you must devote to the exam. Keep in mind that these are averages. If you're not a great student or if you're a little on the nervous side, add another 10 percent. Equally, if you're the type who can learn an entire semester of geometry in one night, reduce the numbers by 10 percent. To use this table, just circle the values that are most accurate for you and add them up to get the number of study hours.

A complete neophyte will need at least 120 hours of study time. An experienced network technician already CompTIA A+ certified should only need about 24 hours.

Study habits also come into play here. A person with solid study habits (you know who you are) can reduce the number by 15 percent. People with poor study habits should increase that number by 20 percent.

The total hours of study time you need is _____.

Type of Experience	Amount of Experience			
	None	Once or Twice	On Occasion	Quite a Bit
Installing a SOHO wireless network	4	2	1	1
Installing an advanced wireless network (802.1X, RADIUS, etc.)	2	2	1	1
Installing structured cabling	3	2	1	1
Configuring a home router	5	3	2	1
Configuring a Cisco router	4	2	1	1
Configuring a software firewall	3	2	1	1
Configuring a hardware firewall	2	2	1	1
Configuring an IPv4 client	8	4	2	1
Configuring an IPv6 client	3	3	2	1
Working with a SOHO WAN connection (DSL, cable)	2	2	1	0
Working with an advanced WAN connection (Tx, OCx, ATM)	3	3	2	2
Configuring a DNS server	2	2	2	1
Configuring a DHCP server	2	1	1	0
Configuring a Web application server (HTTP, FTP, SSH, etc.)	4	4	2	1
Configuring a VLAN	3	3	2	1
Configuring a VPN	3	3	2	1
Configuring a dynamic routing protocol (RIP, EIGRP, OSPF)	2	2	1	1

Table 1-1   Determining How Much Study Time You Need

Study for the Test

Now that you have a feel for how long it's going to take to study for the exam, you need a strategy for studying. The following has proven to be an excellent game plan for cramming the knowledge from the study materials into your head.

This strategy has two alternate paths. The first path is designed for highly experienced technicians who have a strong knowledge of PCs and networking and want to concentrate on just what's on the exam. Let's call this group the Fast Track group. The second path, and the one I'd strongly recommend, is geared toward people like me: the ones who want to know why things work, those who want to wrap their arms completely around a concept, as opposed to regurgitating answers just to pass the CompTIA Network+ exam. Let's call this group the Brainiacs.

To provide for both types of learners, I have broken down most of the chapters into two parts:

- **Historical/Conceptual** Although not on the CompTIA Network+ exam, this knowledge will help you understand more clearly what is on the CompTIA Network+ exam.
- **Test Specific** These topics clearly fit under the CompTIA Network+ certification domains.

The beginning of each of these areas is clearly marked with a large banner that looks like the following.

Historical/Conceptual

If you consider yourself a Fast Tracker, skip everything but the Test Specific section in each chapter. After reading the Test Specific sections, jump immediately to the Chapter Review questions, which concentrate on information in the Test Specific sections. If you run into problems, review the Historical/Conceptual sections in that chapter. After going through every chapter as described, take the free practice exams on the media that accompanies the book. First, take them in practice mode, and then switch to final mode. Once you start scoring in the 80–85 percent range, go take the test!

Brainiacs should first read the book—the whole book. Read it as though you're reading a novel, starting on Page 1 and going all the way through. Don't skip around on the first read-through, even if you are a highly experienced tech. Because there are terms and concepts that build on each other, skipping around might confuse you, and you'll just end up closing the book and firing up your favorite PC game. Your goal on this first read is to understand concepts—to understand the whys, not just the hows.

Having a network available while you read through the book helps a lot. This gives you a chance to see various concepts, hardware, and configuration screens in action as you read about them in the book. Nothing beats doing it yourself to reinforce a concept or piece of knowledge!

TIP Be aware that you may need to return to previous chapters to get the Historical/Conceptual information you need for a later chapter.

NOTE We have active and helpful discussion groups at www.totalsem.com/ forums. You need to register to participate (though not to read posts), but that's only to keep the spammers at bay. The forums provide an excellent resource for answers, suggestions, and just socializing with other folks studying for the exam.

You will notice a lot of historical information—the Historical/Conceptual sections—that you may be tempted to skip. Don't! Understanding how some of the older stuff worked or how something works conceptually will help you appreciate the reason behind current networking features and equipment, as well as how they function.

After you have completed the first read-through, cozy up for a second. This time, try to knock out one chapter per sitting. Concentrate on the Test Specific sections. Get a highlighter and mark the phrases and sentences that make major points. Take a hard look at the pictures and tables, noting how they illustrate the concepts. Then, answer the end of chapter questions. Repeat this process until you not only get all the questions right, but also understand *why* they are correct!

Once you have read and studied the material in the book, check your knowledge by taking the practice exams included on the media accompanying the book. The exams can be taken in practice mode or final mode. In practice mode, you are allowed to check references in the book (if you want) before you answer each question, and each question is graded immediately. In final mode, you must answer all the questions before you are given a test score. In each case, you can review a results summary that tells you which questions you missed, what the right answer is, and where to study further.

Use the results of the exams to see where you need to bone up, and then study some more and try them again. Continue retaking the exams and reviewing the topics you missed until you are consistently scoring in the 80–85 percent range. When you've reached that point, you are ready to pass the CompTIA Network+ exam!

If you have any problems or questions, or if you just want to argue about something, feel free to send an e-mail to me at michaelm@totalsem.com or to my editor, Scott Jernigan, at scottj@totalsem.com.

For additional information about the CompTIA Network+ exam, contact CompTIA directly at its Web site: www.comptia.org.

Good luck!

—Mike Meyers

Network Models

The CompTIA Network+ certification exam expects you to know how to
- 1.1 Explain the function of common networking protocols (such as TCP/IP)
- 1.2 Classify how applications, devices, and protocols relate to the OSI model layers
- 1.3 Identify the following address formats (IPv4)
- 2.5 Given a scenario, troubleshoot common router and switch problems

To achieve these goals, you must be able to
- Describe how models such as the OSI seven-layer model and the TCP/IP model help technicians understand and troubleshoot networks
- Explain the major functions of networks with the OSI seven-layer model
- Describe the major functions of networks with the TCP/IP model

The CompTIA Network+ certification challenges you to understand virtually every aspect of networking—not a small task. Luckily for you, we use two methods to conceptualize the many parts of a network: the *Open Systems Interconnection (OSI) seven-layer model* and the *Transmission Control Protocol/Internet Protocol (TCP/IP) model*.

These models act as guidelines and break down how a network functions into discrete parts called layers. If you want to get into networking—and if you want to pass the CompTIA Network+ certification exam—you must understand both the OSI seven-layer model and the TCP/IP model in great detail.

These models provide two tools that make them critical for networking techs. First, the OSI and TCP/IP models provide powerful mental tools for diagnosing problems. Understanding the models enables a tech to determine quickly at what layer a problem can occur and helps him or her zero in on a solution without wasting a lot of time on false leads. Second, these models also provide a common language to describe networks—a way for us to communicate with each other about the functions of a network. Figure 2-1 shows a sample Cisco Systems Web page about configuring routing—a topic this book covers in detail later. A router operates at Layer 3 of the OSI seven-layer model, for example, so you'll hear techs (and Web sites) refer to it as a "Layer 3 switch."

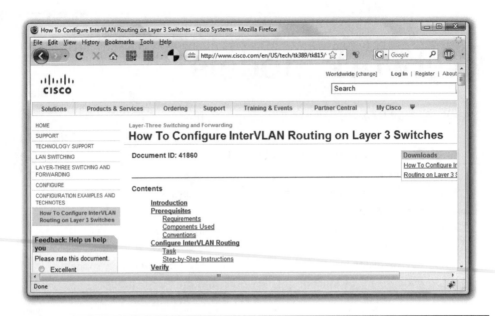

Figure 2-1 Using the OSI terminology—Layer 3—in a typical setup screen

NOTE The term "Layer 3 switch" has evolved over time and refers today to a variety of complex network boxes that I'll cover later in the book.

This chapter looks first at models in general and how models help conceptualize and troubleshoot networks. We'll then go into both the OSI seven-layer model and the TCP/IP model to see how they help clarify network architecture for techs.

Historical/Conceptual

Working with Models

Networking is hard. It takes a lot of pieces, both hardware and software, to get anything done. Just making Google appear in your Web browser requires millions of hours in research, development, and manufacturing. Whenever we encounter highly complex technologies, we need to simplify the overall process (making Google show up in your browser) by breaking it into discrete, simple, individual processes. We do this using models.

Modeling is critical to the networking world. We use models to understand and communicate with other techs about networks. Most beginning network techs, however, might have a very different idea of what modeling means.

Biography of a Model

What does the word "model" mean to you? Does the word make you think of a beautiful woman walking down a catwalk at a fashion show or some hunky guy showing off the latest style of blue jeans on a huge billboard? Maybe it makes you think of a plastic model airplane? What about those computer models that try to predict weather? We use the term "model" in a number of ways, but each use shares certain common themes.

All models are a simplified representation of the real thing. The human model ignores the many different types of body shapes, using only a single "optimal" figure. The model airplane lacks functional engines or the internal framework, and the computerized weather model might disregard subtle differences in wind temperatures or geology (Figure 2-2).

Figure 2-2   Types of models (images from left to right courtesy of NOAA, Mike Schinkel, and Michael Smyer)

Additionally, a model must have at least all the major functions of the real item, but what constitutes a major rather than a minor function is open to opinion. Figure 2-3 shows a different level of detail for a model. Does it contain all the major components of an airplane? There's room for argument that perhaps the model should have landing gear to go along with the propeller, wings, and tail.

Figure 2-3
Simple model
airplane

Network Models

Network models face similar challenges. What functions define all networks? What details can you omit without rendering the model inaccurate? Does the model retain its usefulness when describing a network that does not employ all the layers?

In the early days of networking, different manufacturers made unique types of networks that functioned fairly well. But each network had its own cabling, hardware, drivers, naming conventions, applications, and many other unique features. Back then, a single manufacturer provided everything for a customer whenever you purchased a network solution: cabling, NICs, hubs, drivers, and all the software in one complete and expensive package. Although these networks worked fine as stand-alone networks, the proprietary nature of the hardware and software made it difficult—to put it mildly—to connect networks of multiple manufacturers. To interconnect networks and improve networking as a whole, someone needed to create a guide, a model that described the functions of a network, so that people who made hardware and software could work together to make networks that worked together well.

The granddaddy of network models came from the International Organization for Standardization, known as ISO. Their model, known as the OSI seven-layer model, works for almost every type of network, even extremely old and long-obsolete ones. On the other hand, the TCP/IP model only works for networks that use the now-dominant TCP/IP protocol suite. (Don't worry about what TCP/IP means yet—most of this book's job is to explain that in great detail.) Since most of the world uses TCP/IP, the TCP/IP model supplanted the OSI model in many cases, though most discussion that involves the word "Layers" refers to the OSI model. A good tech can talk the talk of both models, and they are objectives on the CompTIA Network+ exam, so let's learn both.

 NOTE ISO may look like a misspelled acronym, but it's actually a word, derived from the Greek word *isos*, which means "equal." The International Organization for Standardization sets standards that promote *equality* among network designers and manufacturers, thus ISO.

The best way to learn the OSI and TCP/IP models is to see them in action. For this reason, I'll introduce you to a small network that needs to copy a file from one computer to another. This example goes through each of the OSI and TCP/IP layers needed to copy that file, and I explain each step and why it is necessary. By the end of the chapter, you should have a definite handle on using either of these models as a tool to conceptualize networks. You'll continue to build on this knowledge throughout the book and turn your OSI and TCP/IP model knowledge into a powerful troubleshooting tool.

I'll begin by discussing the OSI seven-layer model. After seeing this small network through the lens of the OSI seven-layer model, we'll repeat the process with the TCP/IP model.

The OSI Seven-Layer Model in Action

Each layer in the OSI seven-layer model defines an important function in computer networking, and the protocols that operate at that layer offer solutions to those functions. *Protocols* are sets of clearly defined rules, regulations, standards, and procedures that enable hardware and software developers to make devices and applications that function properly at a particular level. The OSI seven-layer model encourages modular design in networking, meaning that each layer has as little to do with the operation of other layers as possible. Think of it as an automobile assembly line. The guy painting the car doesn't care about the gal putting doors on the car—he expects the assembly line process to make sure the cars he paints have doors. Each layer on the model trusts that the other layers on the model do their jobs.

The OSI seven layers are:

- **Layer 7** Application
- **Layer 6** Presentation
- **Layer 5** Session
- **Layer 4** Transport
- **Layer 3** Network
- **Layer 2** Data Link
- **Layer 1** Physical

The OSI seven layers are not laws of physics—anybody who wants to design a network can do it any way he or she wants. Although many protocols fit neatly into one of the seven layers, others do not.

Now that you know the names of the layers, let's see what each layer does. The best way to understand the OSI layers is to see them in action. Let's see them at work at the fictional company of MHTechEd, Inc.

EXAM TIP Be sure to memorize both the name and the number of each OSI layer. Network techs use OSI terms such as "Layer 4" and "Transport layer" synonymously. Students have long used mnemonics for memorizing such lists. One of my favorites for the OSI seven-layer model is "Please Do Not Throw Sausage Pizza Away." Yum!

NOTE This section is a conceptual overview of the hardware and software functions of a network. Your network may have different hardware or software, but it will share the same functions!

Welcome to MHTechEd!

Mike's High-Tech Educational Supply Store and Post Office, or MHTechEd for short, has a small network of PCs running Windows, a situation typical of many small businesses today. Windows runs just fine on a PC unconnected to a network, but it also comes with all the network software it needs to connect to a network. All the computers in the MHTechEd network are connected by special network cabling.

As in most offices, virtually everyone at MHTechEd has his or her own PC. Figure 2-4 shows two workers, Janelle and Dana, who handle all the administrative functions at MHTechEd. Because of the kinds of work they do, these two often need to exchange data between their two PCs. At the moment, Janelle has just completed a new employee handbook in Microsoft Word, and she wants Dana to check it for accuracy. Janelle could transfer a copy of the file to Dana's computer by the tried-and-true Sneakernet method—saving the file on a thumb drive and walking it over to her—but thanks to the wonders of computer networking, she doesn't even have to turn around in her chair. Let's watch in detail each piece of the process that gives Dana direct access to Janelle's computer, so she can copy the Word document from Janelle's system to her own.

Figure 2-4

Janelle and Dana, hard at work

Long before Janelle ever saved the Word document on her system—when the systems were first installed—someone who knew what they were doing set up and configured all the systems at MHTechEd to be part of a common network. All this setup activity resulted in multiple layers of hardware and software that can work together behind the scenes to get that Word document from Janelle's system to Dana's. Let's examine the different pieces of the network, and then return to the process of Dana grabbing that Word document.

Test Specific

Let's Get Physical—Network Hardware and Layers 1–2

Clearly the network needs a physical channel through which it can move bits of data between systems. Most networks use a cable like the one shown in Figure 2-5. This cable, known in the networking industry as *unshielded twisted pair (UTP)*, usually contains four pairs of wires that can transmit and receive data.

Figure 2-5
UTP cabling

Another key piece of hardware the network uses is a special box-like device called a *hub* (Figure 2-6), often tucked away in a closet or an equipment room. Each system on the network has its own cable that runs to the hub. Think of the hub as being like one of those old-time telephone switchboards, where operators created connections between persons who called in wanting to reach other telephone users.

Figure 2-6
Typical hub

NOTE Readers with some networking experience know that hubs don't exist in modern networks, having been replaced with much better devices called *switches*. But the CompTIA Network+ exam expects you to know what hubs are; plus hubs make this modeling discussion simpler. I'll get to switches soon enough.

Layer 1 of the OSI model defines the method of moving data between computers, so the cabling and hubs are part of the *Physical layer* (Layer 1). Anything that moves data from one system to another, such as copper cabling, fiber optics, even radio waves, is part of the OSI Physical layer. Layer 1 doesn't care what data goes through; it just moves the data from one system to another system. Figure 2-7 shows the MHTechEd network in the OSI seven-layer model thus far. Note that each system has the full range of layers, so data from Janelle's computer can flow to Dana's computer.

Figure 2-7
The network so far, with the Physical layer hardware installed

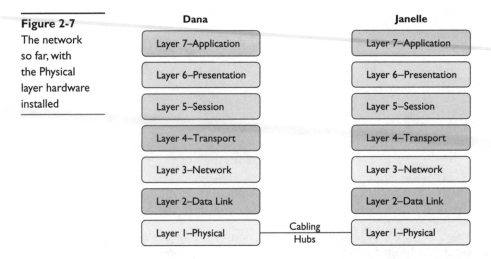

The real magic of a network starts with the *network interface card*, or *NIC* (pronounced "nick"), which serves as the interface between the PC and the network. While NICs come in a wide array of shapes and sizes, the ones at MHTechEd look like Figure 2-8.

Figure 2-8
Typical NIC

On older systems, a NIC truly was a separate card that snapped into a handy expansion slot, which is why they were called network interface *cards.* Even though they're now built into the motherboard, they are still called NICs.

When installed in a PC, the NIC looks like Figure 2-9. Note the cable running from the back of the NIC into the wall; inside that wall is another cable running all the way back to the hub.

Figure 2-9
NIC with cable connecting the PC to the wall jack

Cabling and hubs define the Physical layer of the network, and NICs provide the interface to the PC. Figure 2-10 shows a diagram of the network cabling system. I'll build on this diagram as I delve deeper into the network process.

Figure 2-10
The MHTechEd network

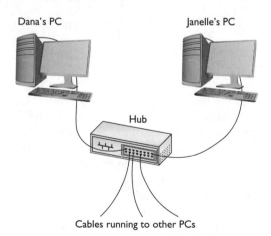

Dana's PC   Janelle's PC

Hub

Cables running to other PCs

You might be tempted to categorize the NIC as part of the Physical layer at this point, and you'd have a valid argument. The NIC clearly is necessary for the physical connection to take place. The CompTIA Network+ exam and many authors put the NIC in OSI Layer 2, the Data Link layer, though, so clearly something else is happening inside the NIC. Let's take a closer look.

The NIC

To understand networks, you must understand how NICs work. The network must provide a mechanism that gives each system a unique identifier—like a telephone number—so data is delivered to the right system. That's one of the NIC's most important jobs. Inside every NIC, burned onto some type of ROM chip, is special firmware containing a unique identifier with a 48-bit value called the *media access control address*, or *MAC address*.

No two NICs ever share the same MAC address—ever. Any company that makes NICs must contact the Institute of Electrical and Electronics Engineers (IEEE) and request a block of MAC addresses, which the company then burns into the ROMs on its NICs. Many NIC makers also print the MAC address on the surface of each NIC, as shown in Figure 2-11. Note that the NIC shown here displays the MAC address in hexadecimal notation. Count the number of hex characters—because each hex character represents 4 bits, it takes 12 hex characters to represent 48 bits.

Figure 2-11
MAC address

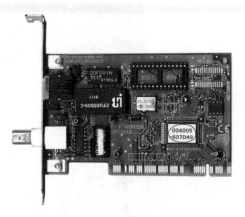

The MAC address in Figure 2-11 is 004005-607D49, although in print, we represent the MAC address as 00–40–05–60–7D–49. The first six digits, in this example 00–40–05, represent the number of the NIC manufacturer. Once the IEEE issues those six hex digits to a manufacturer—often referred to as the *organizationally unique identifier (OUI)*—no other manufacturer may use them. The last six digits, in this example 60–7D–49, are the manufacturer's unique serial number for that NIC; this portion of the MAC is often referred to as the *device ID*.

Would you like to see the MAC address for your NIC? If you have a Windows system, type **ipconfig /all** from a command prompt to display the MAC address (Figure 2-12). Note that ipconfig calls the MAC address the *physical address*, which is an important distinction, as you'll see a bit later in the chapter.

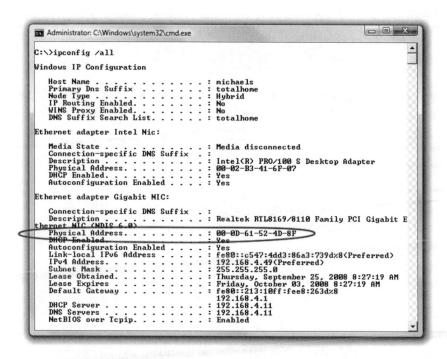

Figure 2-12 Output from `ipconfig /all`

 EXAM TIP The Institute of Electrical and Electronics Engineers (IEEE) forms MAC addresses from a numbering name space originally called *MAC-48*, which simply means that the MAC address will be 48 bits, with the first 24 bits defining the OUI, just as described here. The current term for this numbering name space is *EUI-48*. EUI stands for *Extended Unique Identifier*. (IEEE apparently went with the new term because they could trademark it.) Most techs just call them MAC addresses, as you should, but you might see MAC-48 or EUI-48 on the CompTIA Network+ exam.

Okay, so every NIC in the world has a unique MAC address, but how is it used? Ah, that's where the fun begins! Recall that computer data is binary, which means it's made up of streams of ones and zeroes. NICs send and receive this binary data as pulses of electricity, light, or radio waves. The NICs that use electricity to send and receive data are the most common, so let's consider that type of NIC. The specific process by which a NIC uses electricity to send and receive data is exceedingly complicated but, luckily for you, not necessary to understand. Instead, just think of a *charge* on the wire as a *one* and *no charge* as a *zero*. A chunk of data moving in pulses across a wire might look something like Figure 2-13.

Figure 2-13
Data moving
along a wire

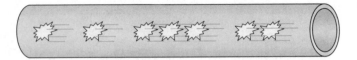

If you put an oscilloscope on the wire to measure voltage, you'd see something like Figure 2-14. An oscilloscope is a powerful tool that enables you to see electrical pulses.

Figure 2-14
Oscilloscope of
data

Now, remembering that the pulses represent binary data, visualize instead a string of ones and zeroes moving across the wire (Figure 2-15).

Figure 2-15
Data as ones and
zeroes

Once you understand how data moves along the wire, the next question is how does the network get the right data to the right system? All networks transmit data by breaking whatever is moving across the Physical layer (files, print jobs, Web pages, and so forth) into discrete chunks called frames. A *frame* is basically a container for a chunk of data moving across a network. The NIC creates and sends, as well as receives and reads, these frames.

I like to visualize an imaginary table inside every NIC that acts as a frame creation and reading station. I see frames as those pneumatic canisters you see when you go to a drive-in teller at a bank. A little guy inside the network card—named Nic, naturally!—builds these pneumatic canisters (the frames) on the table and then shoots them out on the wire to the hub (Figure 2-16).

Figure 2-16
Inside the NIC

NOTE A number of different frame types are used in different networks. All NICs on the same network must use the same frame type, or they will not be able to communicate with other NICs.

Here's where the MAC address becomes important. Figure 2-17 shows a representation of a generic frame. Even though a frame is a string of ones and zeroes, we often draw frames as a series of rectangles, each rectangle representing a part of the string of ones and zeroes. You will see this type of frame representation used quite often, so you should become comfortable with it (even though I still prefer to see frames as pneumatic canisters). Note that the frame begins with the MAC address of the NIC to which the data is to be sent, followed by the MAC address of the sending NIC. Then comes the data, followed by a special bit of checking information called the *frame check sequence (FCS)*. The FCS uses a type of binary math called a *cyclic redundancy check (CRC)* that the receiving NIC uses to verify that the data arrived intact.

Figure 2-17
Generic frame

Recipient's MAC address	Sender's MAC address	Data	FCS

So, what's inside the data part of the frame? You neither know nor care. The data may be a part of a file, a piece of a print job, or part of a Web page. NICs aren't concerned with content! The NIC simply takes whatever data is passed to it via its device driver and addresses it for the correct system. Special software will take care of *what* data gets sent and what happens to that data when it arrives. This is the beauty of imagining frames as little pneumatic canisters (Figure 2-18). A canister can carry anything from dirt to diamonds—the NIC doesn't care one bit (pardon the pun).

Figure 2-18
Frame as a
canister

To:
234a12f42b1c
From:
234a12r4er1ac

Like a canister, a frame can hold only a certain amount of data. Different networks use different sizes of frames, but a single frame holds about 1500 bytes of data.

This raises a new question: what happens when the data to be sent is larger than the frame size? Well, the sending system's software must chop the data up into nice, frame-sized chunks, which it then hands to the NIC for sending. As the receiving system begins to accept the incoming frames, the receiving system's software recombines the data chunks as they come in from the network. I'll show how this disassembling and reassembling is done in a moment—first, let's see how the frames get to the right system!

When a system sends a frame out on the network, the frame goes into the hub. The hub, in turn, makes an exact copy of that frame, sending a copy of the original frame to every other system on the network. The interesting part of this process is when the copy of the frame comes into all the other systems. I like to visualize a frame sliding onto the receiving NIC's "frame assembly table," where the electronics of the NIC inspect it. Here's where the magic takes place: only the NIC to which the frame is addressed will process that frame—the other NICs simply erase it when they see that it is not addressed to their MAC address. This is important to appreciate: *every* frame sent on a network is received by *every* NIC, but only the NIC with the matching MAC address will process that particular frame (Figure 2-19).

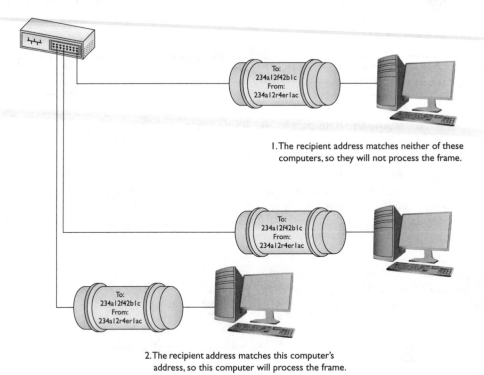

1. The recipient address matches neither of these computers, so they will not process the frame.

2. The recipient address matches this computer's address, so this computer will process the frame.

Figure 2-19   Incoming frame!

NOTE   Most FCSs are only 4 bytes long, yet the average frame carries around 1500 bytes of data. How can 4 bytes tell you if all 1500 bytes in the data are correct? That's the magic of the math of the CRC. Without going into the grinding details, think of the CRC as just the remainder of a division problem. (Remember learning remainders from division back in elementary school?) The NIC sending the frame does a little math to make the CRC. Using binary arithmetic, it works a division problem on the data using a divisor called a *key*. The result of this division is the CRC. When the frame gets to the receiving NIC, it divides the data by the same key. If the receiving NIC's answer is the same as the CRC, it knows the data is good.

Getting the Data on the Line

The process of getting data onto the wire and then picking that data off the wire is amazingly complicated. For instance, what happens to keep two NICs from speaking at the same time? Because all the data sent by one NIC is read by every other NIC on the network, only one system may speak at a time. Networks use frames to restrict the amount of data a NIC can send at once, giving all NICs a chance to send data over the network in a reasonable span of time. Dealing with this and many other issues requires sophisticated electronics, but the NICs handle these issues completely on their own without our help. Thankfully, the folks who design NICs worry about all these details, so we don't have to!

Getting to Know You

Using the MAC address is a great way to move data around, but this process raises an important question. How does a sending NIC know the MAC address of the NIC to which it's sending the data? In most cases, the sending system already knows the destination MAC address because the NICs had probably communicated earlier, and each system stores that data. If it doesn't already know the MAC address, a NIC may send a *broadcast* onto the network to ask for it. The MAC address of FF-FF-FF-FF-FF-FF is the *broadcast address*—if a NIC sends a frame using the broadcast address, every single NIC on the network will process that frame. That broadcast frame's data will contain a request for a system's MAC address. Without knowing the MAC address to begin with, the requesting computer will use an IP address or host name to pick the target computer out of the crowd. The system with the MAC address your system is seeking will read the request in the broadcast packet and respond with its MAC address.

The Complete Frame Movement

Now that you've seen all the pieces used to send and receive frames, let's put these pieces together and see how a frame gets from one system to another. The basic send/receive process is as follows.

First, the sending system's network operating system (NOS) software—such as Windows 7—hands some data to its NIC. The NIC builds a frame to transport that data to the receiving NIC (Figure 2-20).

Figure 2-20   Building the frame

After the NIC creates the frame, it adds the FCS, and then dumps it and the data into the frame (Figure 2-21).

Figure 2-21
Adding the data
and FCS to the
frame

Next, the NIC puts both the destination MAC address and its own MAC address onto the frame. It waits until no other NIC is using the cable, and then sends the frame through the cable to the network (Figure 2-22).

Figure 2-22
Sending the frame

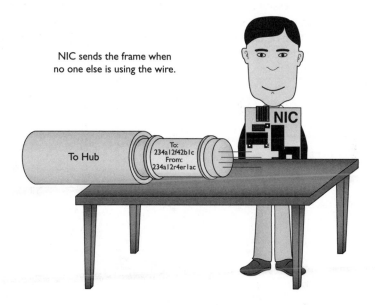

NIC sends the frame when no one else is using the wire.

The frame propagates down the wire into the hub, which creates copies of the frame and sends it to every other system on the network. Every NIC receives the frame and checks the MAC address. If a NIC finds that a frame is addressed to it, it processes the frame (Figure 2-23); if the frame is not addressed to it, the NIC erases it.

Figure 2-23
Reading an
incoming frame

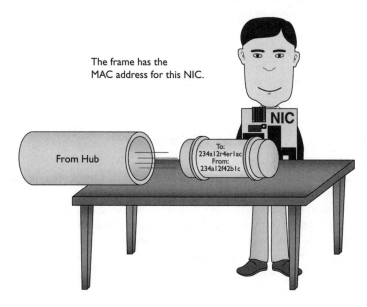

The frame has the MAC address for this NIC.

So, what happens to the data when it gets to the *correct* NIC? First, the receiving NIC uses the FCS to verify that the data is valid. If it is, the receiving NIC strips off all the framing information and sends the data to the software—the network operating system—for processing. The receiving NIC doesn't care what the software does with the data; its job stops the moment it passes on the data to the software.

Any device that deals with a MAC address is part of the OSI *Data Link layer*, or Layer 2 of the OSI model. Let's update the OSI model to include details about the Data Link layer (Figure 2-24).

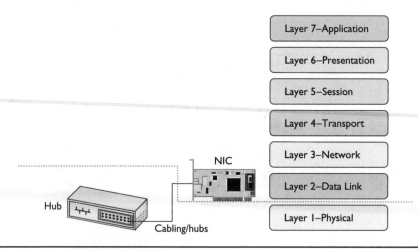

Figure 2-24 Layer 1 and Layer 2 are now properly applied to the network.

Note that the cabling and the hub are located in the Physical layer. The NIC is in the Data Link layer, but spans two sublayers.

 EXAM TIP The Data Link layer provides a service called *Data Link Control (DLC)*. The only reason to mention this is there's an ancient printing protocol with the same name. DLC might show up as an incorrect answer on the exam.

The Two Aspects of NICs

Consider how data moves in and out of a NIC. On one end, frames move into and out of the NIC's network cable connection. On the other end, data moves back and forth between the NIC and the network operating system software. The many steps a NIC performs to keep this data moving—sending and receiving frames over the wire, creating outgoing frames, reading incoming frames, and attaching MAC addresses—are classically broken down into two distinct jobs.

The first job is called the *Logical Link Control (LLC)*. The LLC is the aspect of the NIC that talks to the operating system, places data coming from the software into frames, and creates the CRC on each frame. The LLC is also responsible for dealing with incoming frames: processing those that are addressed to this NIC and erasing frames addressed to other machines on the network.

The second job is called the *Media Access Control (MAC)*, and I bet you can guess what it does! That's right—it remembers the NIC's own MAC address and attaches MAC addresses to the frames. Recall that each frame the LLC creates must include both the sender's and recipient's MAC addresses. The MAC also ensures that the frames, now complete with their MAC addresses, are then sent along the network cabling. Figure 2-25 shows the Data Link layer in detail.

Figure 2-25
LLC and MAC,
the two parts
of the Data
Link layer

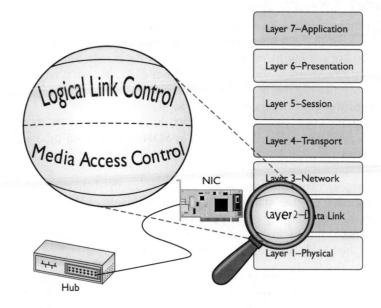

Layer 7–Application

Layer 6–Presentation

Layer 5–Session

Layer 4–Transport

Layer 3–Network

Layer 2–Data Link

Layer 1–Physical

NIC

Hub

 EXAM TIP The CompTIA Network+ exam tests you on the details of the OSI seven-layer model, so remember that the Data Link layer is the only layer that has any sublayers.

NIC and Layers

Most networking materials that describe the OSI seven-layer model put NICs squarely into the Data Link layer of the model. It's at the MAC sublayer, after all, that data gets encapsulated into a frame, destination and source MAC addresses get added to that frame, and error checking occurs. What bothers most students with placing NICs solely in the Data Link layer is the obvious other duty of the NIC—putting the ones and zeroes on the network cable. How much more physical can you get?

Many teachers will finesse this issue by defining the Physical layer in its logical sense—that it defines the rules for the ones and zeroes—and then ignore the fact that the data sent on the cable has to come from something. The first question when you hear a statement like that—at least to me—is, "What component does the sending?" It's the NIC, of course, the only device capable of sending and receiving the physical signal.

Network cards, therefore, operate at both Layer 2 and Layer 1 of the OSI seven-layer model. If cornered to answer one or the other, however, go with the more common answer, Layer 2.

Beyond the Single Wire—Network Software and Layers 3–7

Getting data from one system to another in a simple network (defined as one in which all the computers connect to one hub) takes relatively little effort on the part of the NICs. But one problem with simple networks is that computers need to broadcast to get MAC addresses. It works for small networks, but what happens when the network gets big, like the size of the entire Internet? Can you imagine millions of computers all broadcasting? No data could get through.

Equally important, data flows over the Internet using many technologies, not just Ethernet. These technologies, such as SONET, ATM, and others, don't know what to do with Ethernet MAC addresses. When networks get large, you can't use the MAC addresses anymore.

Large networks need a *logical addressing* method, like a postal code or telephone numbering scheme, that ignores the hardware and enables you to break up the entire large network into smaller networks called *subnets*. Figure 2-26 shows two ways to set up a network. On the left, all the computers connect to a single hub. On the right, however, the LAN is separated into two five-computer subnets.

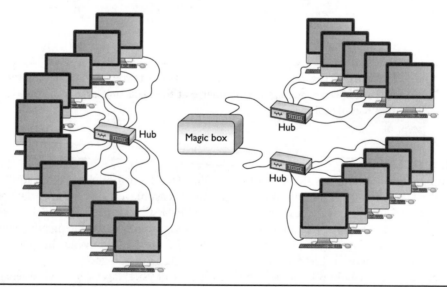

Figure 2-26   Large LAN complete (left) and broken up into two subnets (right)

To move past the physical MAC addresses and start using logical addressing requires some special software called a *network protocol*. Network protocols exist in every operating system. A network protocol not only has to create unique identifiers for each system, but also must create a set of communication rules for issues like how to handle data chopped up into multiple packets and how to ensure those packets get from one subnet to another. Let's take a moment to learn a bit about the most famous network protocol—TCP/IP—and its unique universal addressing system.

 EXAM TIP MAC addresses are also known as *physical addresses*.

To be accurate, TCP/IP is really several network protocols designed to work together—but two protocols, TCP and IP, do so much work that the folks who invented all these protocols named the whole thing TCP/IP. TCP stands for *Transmission Control Protocol*, and IP stands for *Internet Protocol*. IP is the network protocol I need to discuss first; rest assured, however, I'll cover TCP in plenty of detail later.

 NOTE TCP/IP dominates the networking universe. Almost every network in existence uses TCP/IP. Because it is more specific, a simpler model called the TCP/IP model was created to describe it. You'll learn all about this model later in the chapter.

IP—Playing on Layer 3, the Network Layer

At the *Network layer*, Layer 3, packets get created and addressed so they can go from one network to another. The *Internet Protocol* is the primary logical addressing protocol for TCP/IP. IP makes sure that a piece of data gets to where it needs to go on the network. It does this by giving each device on the network a unique numeric identifier called an *IP address*. An IP address is known as a *logical address* to distinguish it from the physical address, the MAC address of the NIC.

 NOTE Try to avoid using redundant expressions. Even though many techs will say "IP protocol," for example, you know that "IP" stands for "Internet Protocol." It wouldn't be right to say "Internet Protocol protocol" in English, so it doesn't work in network speak either.

Every network protocol uses some type of naming convention, but no two protocols use the same convention. IP uses a rather unique dotted decimal notation (sometimes referred to as a dotted-octet numbering system) based on four 8-bit numbers. Each 8-bit number ranges from 0 to 255, and the four numbers are separated by periods. (If you don't see how 8-bit numbers can range from 0 to 255, don't worry—by the end of this book, you'll understand these naming conventions in more detail than you ever believed possible!) A typical IP address might look like this:

192.168.4.232

No two systems on the same network share the same IP address; if two machines accidentally receive the same address, they won't be able to send or receive data. These IP addresses don't just magically appear—they must be configured by the end user (or the network administrator).

Take a look at Figure 2-26. What makes logical addressing powerful is the magic box—called a *router*—that connects each of the subnets. Routers use the IP address, not the MAC address, to forward data. This enables networks to connect across data lines that don't use Ethernet, like the telephone network. Each network type (such as Ethernet, SONET, ATM, and others that we'll discuss later in the book) uses a unique frame. Figure 2-27 shows a typical router.

Figure 2-27
Typical small
router

What's important here is for you to appreciate that in a TCP/IP network, each system has two unique identifiers: the MAC address and the IP address. The MAC address (the physical address) is literally burned into the chips on the NIC, whereas the IP address (the logical address) is simply stored in the system's software. MAC addresses come with the NIC, so you don't configure MAC addresses, whereas you must configure IP addresses using software. Figure 2-28 shows the MHTechEd network diagram again; this time with the MAC and IP addresses displayed for each system.

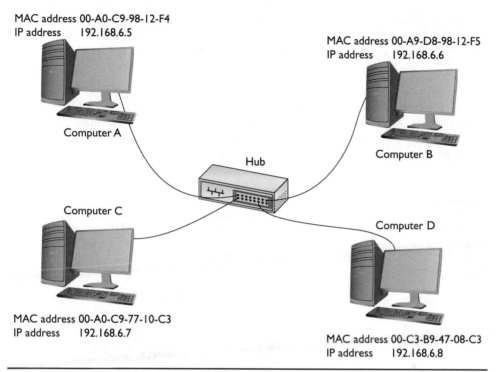

MAC address 00-A0-C9-98-12-F4
IP address   192.168.6.5

MAC address 00-A9-D8-98-12-F5
IP address   192.168.6.6

Computer A

Computer B

Hub

Computer C

Computer D

MAC address 00-A0-C9-77-10-C3
IP address   192.168.6.7

MAC address 00-C3-B9-47-08-C3
IP address   192.168.6.8

Figure 2-28   MHTechEd addressing

Packets Within Frames

For a TCP/IP network to send data successfully, the data must be wrapped up in two
distinct containers. A frame of some type enables the data to move from one device to
another. Inside that frame is both an IP-specific container that enables routers to determine where to send data—regardless of the physical connection type—and the data
itself. In TCP/IP, that inner container is called a *packet*.

Figure 2-29 shows a typical IP packet; notice the similarity to the frames you saw
earlier.

Figure 2-29
IP packet

Destination IP address	Source IP address	Data

NOTE This is a highly simplified IP packet. I am not including lots of little parts of the IP packet in this diagram because they are not important to what you need to understand right now—but don't worry, you'll see them later in the book!

But IP packets don't leave their PC home without any clothes on! Each IP packet is handed to the NIC, which then encloses the IP packet in a regular frame, creating, in essence, a *packet within a frame*. I like to visualize the packet as an envelope, with the envelope in the pneumatic canister frame (Figure 2-30). A more conventional drawing would look like Figure 2-31.

Figure 2-30
IP packet in
a frame
(as a canister)

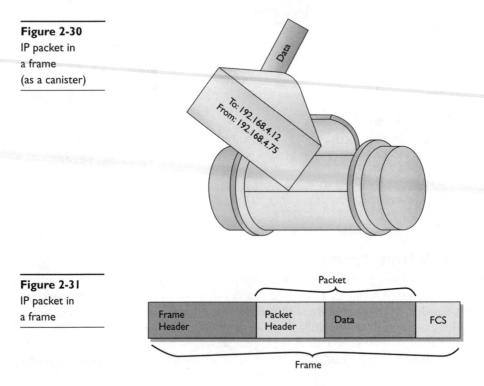

Figure 2-31
IP packet in
a frame

When you send data from one computer to another on a TCP/IP network such as the Internet, that data can go through many routers before it reaches its destination. Each router strips off the incoming frame, determines where to send the data according to the IP address in the packet, creates a new frame, and then sends the packet within a frame on its merry way. The new frame type will be the appropriate technology for whatever connection technology connects to the next router. That could be a cable or DSL network connection, for example (Figure 2-32). The IP packet, on the other hand, remains unchanged.

Figure 2-32
Router removing
network frame
and adding one
for the outgoing
connection

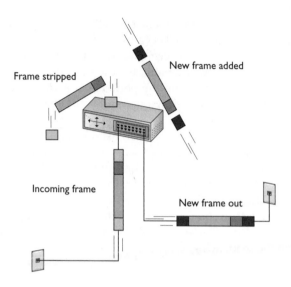

Frame stripped

New frame added

Incoming frame

New frame out

Once the packet reaches the destination subnet's router, that router will strip off the incoming frame—no matter what type—look at the destination IP address, and then add a frame with the appropriate destination MAC address that matches the destination IP address.

NOTE Keep in mind that not all networks are Ethernet networks. Ethernet may dominate, but IP packets fit in all sorts of other connectivity options. For example, cable modems use a type of frame called DOCSIS. T1 lines use a frame called DS1. The beauty of IP packets is that they can travel unchanged in each of these and many others. For more about these technologies, check out Chapter 14.

The receiving NIC strips away the Ethernet frame and passes the remaining packet off to the software. The networking software built into your operating system handles all the rest of the work. The NIC's driver software is the interconnection between the hardware and the software. The NIC driver knows how to communicate with the NIC to send and receive frames, but it can't do anything with the packet. Instead, the NIC driver hands the packet off to other programs that know how to deal with all the separate packets and turn them into Web pages, e-mail messages, files, and so forth.

The Network layer (Layer 3) is the last layer that deals directly with hardware. All the other layers of the OSI seven-layer model work strictly within software.

Assembly and Disassembly—Layer 4, the Transport Layer

Because most chunks of data are much larger than a single packet, they must be chopped up before they can be sent across a network. When a serving computer receives a request for some data, it must be able to chop the requested data into chunks that will fit into a packet (and eventually into the NIC's frame), organize the packets for the benefit of the receiving system, and hand them to the NIC for sending. The receiving system must be able to recognize a series of incoming packets as one data transmission, reassemble the packets correctly based on information included in the packets by the sending system, and verify that all the packets for that piece of data arrived in good shape.

This part is relatively simple—the transport protocol breaks up the data into packets and gives each packet some type of sequence number. I like to compare this process to the one that my favorite international shipping company uses. I receive boxes from UPS almost every day; in fact, some days I receive many, many boxes from UPS. To make sure I get all the boxes for one shipment, UPS puts a numbering system, like the one shown in Figure 2-33, on the label of each box. A computer sending data on a network does the same thing. Embedded into the data of each packet is a sequencing number. By reading the sequencing numbers, the receiving system knows both the total number of packets and how to put them back together.

Figure 2-33

Labeling the

boxes

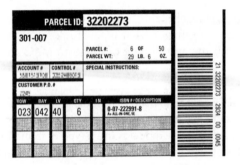

NOTE   I'm using the term "packets" here to refer to a generic container. Because the OSI model can be applied to many different network protocols, the terminology for this container changes. Almost all protocols split up data at the Transport layer and add sequencing numbers so the receiving computer can put them together in logical order. What happens at that point depends on the protocol suite. In TCP/IP, for example, the precisely named *IP packet* is created at the Network layer and other container types are created at the Transport layer.

I'll go into a lot more detail on this in the TCP/IP model section later in this book. That model, rather than the OSI model, makes more sense for TCP/IP network descriptions.

The MHTechEd network just keeps getting more and more complex, doesn't it? And the Word document still hasn't been copied, has it? Don't worry; you're almost there—just a few more pieces to go!

Layer 4, the *Transport layer* of the OSI seven-layer model, has a big job: it's the assembler/disassembler software. As part of its job, the Transport layer also initializes requests for packets that weren't received in good order (Figure 2-34).

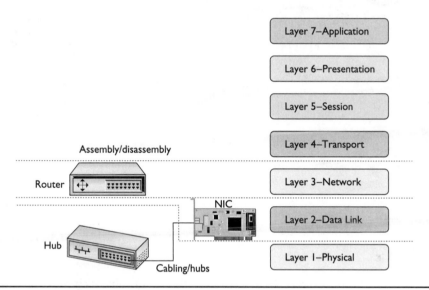

Figure 2-34 OSI updated

 NOTE A lot of things happen on a TCP/IP network at the Transport layer. I'm simplifying here because the TCP/IP model does a way better job explaining each thing than does the OSI model.

Talking on a Network—Layer 5, the Session Layer

Now that you understand that the system uses software to assemble and disassemble data packets, what's next? In a network, any one system may be talking to many other systems at any given moment. For example, Janelle's PC has a printer used by all the MHTechEd systems, so there's a better than average chance that, as Dana tries to access the Word document, another system will be sending a print job to Janelle's PC (Figure 2-35).

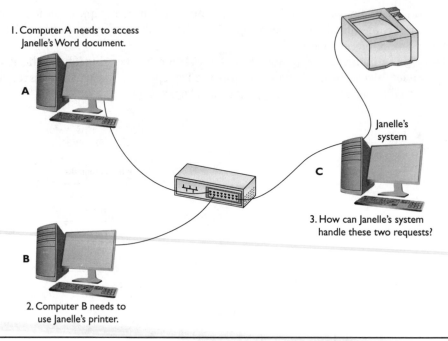

1. Computer A needs to access
   Janelle's Word document.

A

Janelle's
system

C

3. How can Janelle's system
   handle these two requests?

B

2. Computer B needs to
   use Janelle's printer.

Figure 2-35   Handling multiple inputs

Janelle's system must direct these incoming files, print jobs, Web pages, and so on, to the right programs (Figure 2-36). Additionally, the operating system must enable one system to make a connection to another system to verify that the other system can handle whatever operation the initiating system wants to perform. If Bill's system wants to send a print job to Janelle's printer, it first contacts Janelle's system to ensure that it is ready to handle the print job. The *session software* handles this part of networking, connecting applications to applications.

Layer 5, the *Session layer* of the OSI seven-layer model, handles all the sessions for a system (Figure 2-37). The Session layer initiates sessions, accepts incoming sessions, and opens and closes existing sessions. The Session layer also keeps track of computer naming conventions, such as calling your computer SYSTEM01 or some other type of name that makes more sense than an IP or MAC address.

NOTE   You can run the netstat program from a command prompt to see all of them. Open a command prompt and type `netstat -a` and then press the ENTER key to see your sessions. Don't worry about trying to interpret what you see—Chapter 9 covers netstat in detail. For now, simply appreciate that each line in the netstat output is a session. Count them!

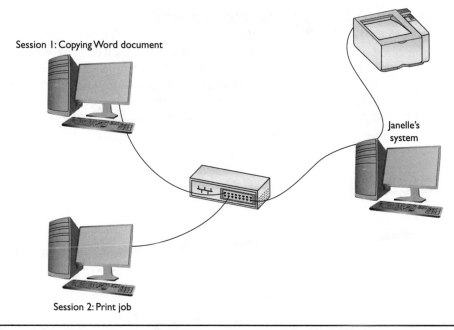

Session 1: Copying Word document

Janelle's system

Session 2: Print job

Figure 2-36 Each request becomes a session.

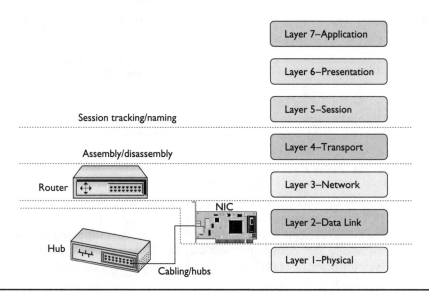

Figure 2-37 OSI updated

Standardized Formats, or Why Layer 6, Presentation, Has No Friends

One of the most powerful aspects of a network lies in the fact that it works with (almost) any operating system. Today's networks easily connect, for example, a Macintosh system to a Windows PC, despite the fact that these different operating systems use different formats for many types of data. Different data formats used to drive us crazy back in the days before word processors (like Microsoft Word) could import or export a thousand other word processor formats (Figure 2-38).

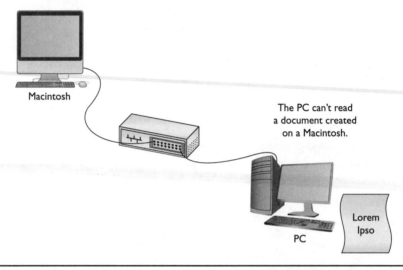

Figure 2-38   Different data formats were often unreadable between systems.

This issue motivated folks to create standardized formats that anyone—at least with the right program—could read from any type of computer. Specialized file formats, such as Adobe's popular Portable Document Format (PDF) for documents and PostScript for printing, provide standard formats that any system, regardless of operating system, can read, write, and edit (Figure 2-39).

NOTE   Adobe released the PDF standard to ISO in 2007 and PDF became the ISO 32000 open standard. Adobe Reader remains the premier application for reading PDF documents. Note that Adobe seems to be phasing out the Acrobat branding of PDF documents, but many techs still call PDF "Adobe Acrobat format."

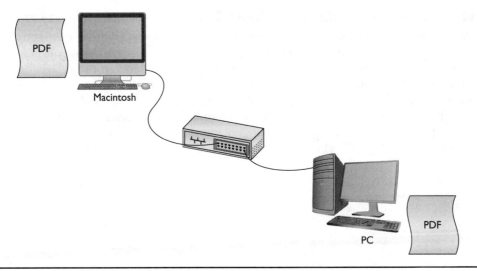

Figure 2-39 Everyone recognizes PDF files!

Layer 6, the *Presentation layer* of the OSI seven-layer model, handles the conversion of data into formats that are readable by the system. Of all the OSI layers, the high level of file format standardization has made the Presentation layer the least important and least used (Figure 2-40).

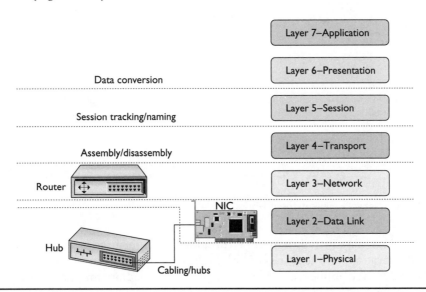

Figure 2-40 OSI updated

Network Applications—Layer 7, the Application Layer

The last and most visible part of any network is the software applications that use it. If you want to copy a file residing on another system in your network, you need an application like Network in Windows 7 (or My Network Places in earlier versions of Windows) that enables you to access files on remote systems. If you want to view Web pages, you need a Web browser like Internet Explorer or Mozilla Firefox. The people who use a network experience it through an application. A user who knows nothing about all the other parts of a network may still know how to open an e-mail application to retrieve mail (Figure 2-41).

Figure 2-41 Network applications at work

Applications may include a number of additional functions, such as encryption, user authentication, and tools to control the look of the data. But these functions are specific to the given applications. In other words, if you want to put a password on your Word document, you must use the password functions in Word to do so.

The *Application layer* is Layer 7 in the OSI seven-layer model. Keep in mind that the Application layer doesn't refer to the applications themselves. It refers to the code built into all operating systems that enables network-aware applications. All operating systems have *Application Programming Interfaces (APIs)* that programmers can use to make their programs network aware (Figure 2-42). An API, in general, provides a standard way for programmers to enhance or extend an application's capabilities.

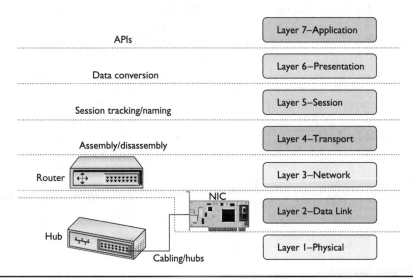

Figure 2-42   OSI updated

The TCP/IP Model

The OSI model was developed as a reaction to a world of hundreds, if not thousands, of different protocols made by different manufacturers that needed to play together. The ISO declared the OSI seven-layer model as the tool for manufacturers of networking equipment to find common ground between multiple protocols, enabling them to create standards for interoperability of networking software and hardware.

The OSI model is extremely popular and very well-known to all networking techs. Today's world, however, is a TCP/IP world. The complexity of the OSI model doesn't make sense in a world with one protocol suite. Given its dominance, the aptly named TCP/IP model shares equal popularity with the venerable OSI model.

The TCP/IP model consists of four layers:

- Application
- Transport
- Internet
- Link/Network Interface

It's important to appreciate that the TCP/IP model doesn't have a standards body to define the layers. Because of this, there are a surprising number of variations on the TCP/IP model.

A great example of this lack of standardization is the Link layer. Without a standardizing body, we can't even agree on the name. While "Link layer" is extremely common, the term "Network Interface layer" is equally popular. A good tech knows both of these terms and understands that they are interchangeable. Notice also that, unlike the OSI model, the TCP/IP model does not identify each layer with a number.

CompTIA has chosen one popular version of the TCP/IP model for the CompTIA Network+ competencies and exam. That's the version you'll learn right here. It's concise, having only four layers, and many important companies, like Cisco and Microsoft, use it, although with a few variations in names as just described. The TCP/IP model gives each protocol in the TCP/IP protocol suite a clear home in one of the four layers.

The clarity of the TCP/IP model shows the flaws in the OSI model. The OSI model couldn't perfectly describe all the TCP/IP protocols. In fact, the OSI model couldn't perfectly describe any of the now defunct alternative protocols, such as IPX/SPX and NetBIOS/NetBEUI. Network nerds have gotten into fistfights over a particular protocol's exact location in the OSI model.

The TCP/IP model fixes this ambiguity, at least for TCP/IP. Because of its tight protocol-to-layer integration, the TCP/IP model is a *descriptive* model, whereas the OSI seven-layer model is a *prescriptive* model.

The Link Layer

The TCP/IP model lumps together the OSI model's Layer 1 and Layer 2 into a single layer called the *Link layer* (or *Network Interface layer*), as seen in Figure 2-43. It's not that the Physical and Data Link layers are unimportant to TCP/IP, but the TCP/IP protocol suite really begins at Layer 3 of the OSI model. In essence, TCP/IP techs count on other techs to handle the physical connections in their networks. All of the pieces that you learned in the OSI model (cabling, hubs, physical addresses, and NICs) sit squarely in the Link layer.

Figure 2-43
TCP/IP Link layer compared to OSI Layers 1 and 2

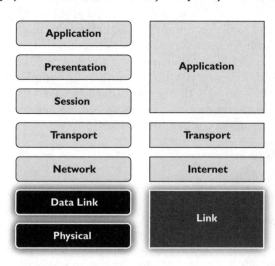

A nice way to separate layers in the TCP/IP model is to think about packets and frames. Any part of the network that deals with complete frames is in the Link layer. The moment the frame information is stripped away from an IP packet, we move out of the Link layer and into the Internet layer.

The Internet Layer

The *Internet layer* should really be called the "IP packet" layer (Figure 2-44). Any device or protocol that deals with pure IP packets—getting an IP packet to its destination—sits in the Internet layer. IP addressing itself is also part of the Internet layer, as are routers and the magic they perform to get IP packets to the next router. IP packets are created at this layer.

Figure 2-44
TCP/IP
Internet layer
compared to
OSI Layer 3

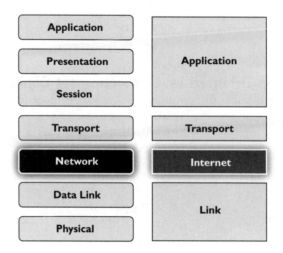

The Internet layer doesn't care about the type of data an IP packet carries, nor does it care whether the data gets there in good order or not. Those jobs are for the next layer: the Transport layer.

The Transport Layer

The *Transport layer* combines features of the OSI Transport and Session layers with a dash of Application layer just for flavor (Figure 2-45). While the TCP/IP model is certainly involved with the assembly and disassembly of data, it also defines other functions, such as connection-oriented and connectionless communication.

Figure 2-45
TCP/IP
Transport layer
compared to
OSI Layers 4, 5,
and part of 7

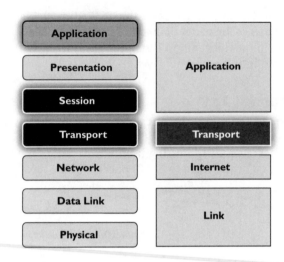

| Application |
| Presentation |
| Session |
| Transport |
| Network |
| Data Link |
| Physical |

| Application |
| Transport |
| Internet |
| Link |

Connection-Oriented vs. Connectionless Communication

Some protocols, like the popular Post Office Protocol (POP) used for sending e-mail messages, require that the e-mail client and server verify that they have a good connection before a message is sent (Figure 2-46). This makes sense because you don't want your e-mail message to be a corrupted mess when it arrives.

Figure 2-46
Connection
between e-mail
client and server

Alternatively, a number of TCP/IP protocols simply send data without first waiting to verify that the receiving system is ready (Figure 2-47). When using Voice over IP (VoIP), for example, the call is made without verifying first whether another device is there.

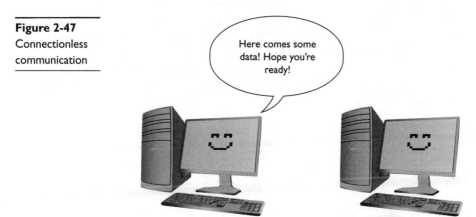

Figure 2-47
Connectionless
communication

The connection-oriented protocol is called *Transmission Control Protocol (TCP)*. The connectionless protocol is called *User Datagram Protocol (UDP)*.

NOTE Chapter 7 covers TCP, UDP, and all sorts of other protocols in detail.

Everything you can do on the Internet, from Web browsing to Skype phone calls to playing World of Warcraft, is predetermined to be either connection-oriented or connectionless. It's simply a matter of knowing your applications.

Segments Within Packets

To see the Transport layer in action, strip away the IP addresses from an IP packet. What's left is a chunk of data in yet another container called a *TCP segment*. TCP segments have many other fields that ensure the data gets to its destination in good order. These fields have names such as Checksum, Flags, and Acknowledgement. Chapter 7 goes into more detail on TCP segments, but, for now, just know that TCP segments have fields that ensure the connection-oriented communication works properly. Figure 2-48 shows a typical (although simplified) TCP segment.

Destination port	Source port	Sequence number	Checksum	Flags	Acknowledgement	Data

Figure 2-48 TCP segment

Data comes from the Application layer applications. The Transport layer breaks that data into chunks, adding port numbers and sequence numbers, creating the TCP segment. The Transport layer then hands the TCP segment to the Internet layer that, in turn, creates the IP packet.

Most traffic on a TCP/IP network uses TCP at the Transport layer, but like Yoda said, "There is another," and that's UDP. UDP also gets data from the Application layer programs and adds port and sequencing numbers to create a container called a *UDP datagram*. A UDP datagram lacks most of the extra fields found in TCP segments, simply because UDP doesn't care if the receiving computer gets its data. Figure 2-49 shows a UDP datagram.

Figure 2-49
UDP datagram

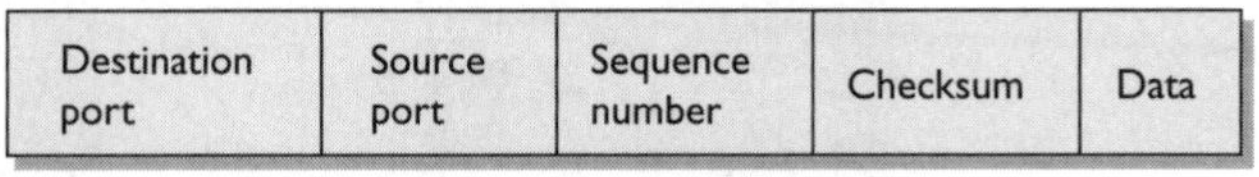

Destination port	Source port	Sequence number	Checksum	Data

The Application Layer

The TCP/IP *Application layer* combines features of the top three layers of the OSI model (Figure 2-50). Every application, especially connection-oriented applications, must know how to initiate, control, and disconnect from a remote system. No single method exists for doing this. Each TCP/IP application uses its own method.

Figure 2-50
TCP/IP
Application layer
compared to OSI
layers 5–7

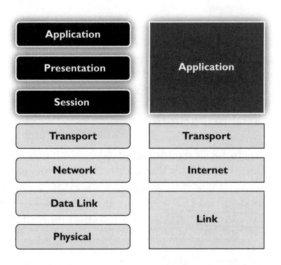

TCP/IP uses a unique port numbering system that gives each application a unique number between 1 and 65535. Some of these port numbers are very famous. The protocol that makes Web pages work, HTTP, uses port 80, for example.

Although we can say that the OSI model's Presentation layer fits inside the TCP/IP model's Application layer, no application requires any particular form of presentation as seen in the OSI model. Standard formats are part and parcel with TCP/IP protocols. For example, all e-mail messages use an extremely strict format called MIME. All e-mail servers and clients read MIME without exception.

In the OSI model, we describe the API—the smarts that make applications network-aware—as being part of the Application layer. While this is still true for the TCP/IP model, all applications designed for TCP/IP are, by definition, network-aware. There is no such thing as a "TCP/IP word processor" or a "TCP/IP image editor" that requires the added ability to know how to talk to a network—all TCP/IP applications can talk to the network, as long as they are part of a network. And every TCP/IP application must be a part of a network to function: Web browsers, e-mail clients, multiplayer games, and so on.

Don't think that the TCP/IP model is any simpler than the OSI model just because it only uses four layers. With the arguable exception of the Presentation layer, everything you saw in the OSI model is also found in the TCP/IP model (Figure 2-51).

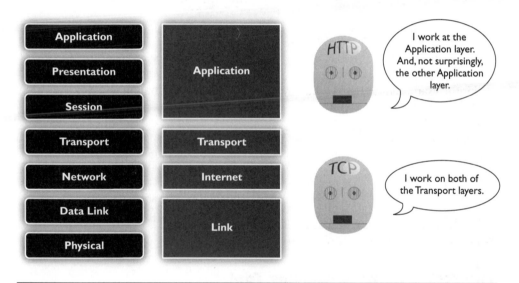

Figure 2-51   OSI model and TCP/IP model side by side

Frames, Packets, and Segments, Oh My!

The TCP/IP model shows its power in its ability to describe what happens at each layer to the data that goes from one computer to another. The Application layer programs create the data. The Transport layer breaks the data into chunks, putting those chunks into TCP segments or UDP datagrams. The Internet layer adds the IP addressing and creates the IP packets. The Link layer wraps the IP packet into a frame, with the MAC address information and a frame check sequence (FCS). Now the data is ready to hit the wire (or airwaves, if you're in a café). Figure 2-52 shows all this encapsulating goodness relative to the TCP/IP model.

Figure 2-52
Data
encapsulation
in TCP/IP

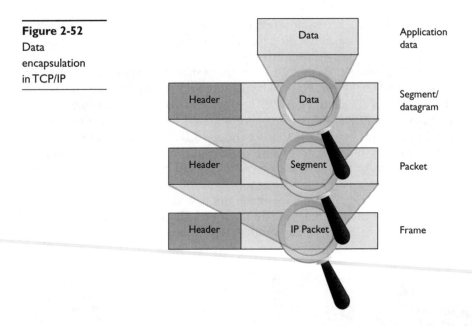

For the exam, remember at what layer each encapsulation happens. Table 2-1 shows the layers and the corresponding data structure.

TCP/IP Model Layer	Data Structure
Link	Frame
Internet	IP packet
Transport	TCP segment/UDP datagram
Application	(The data starts and ends here)

Table 2-1   TCP/IP Model Layers and Corresponding Data Structures

The Tech's Troubleshooting Tool

The OSI seven-layer model and TCP/IP model provide you with a way to conceptualize a network to determine what could cause a specific problem when the inevitable problems occur. Good techs always use a model to troubleshoot their networks.

If Jane can't print to the networked printer, for example, a model can help solve the problem. If her NIC shows activity, then, using the OSI model, you can set aside both the Physical layer (Layer 1) and Data Link layer (Layer 2). If you're a TCP/IP model tech, you can look at the same symptoms and eliminate the Link layer. In either case, you'll find yourself moving up the layer ladder to the OSI model's Network layer (Layer 3) or the TCP/IP model's Internet layer. If her computer has a proper IP address, then you can set that layer aside too, and you can move on up to check other layers to solve the problem.

Understanding both the OSI and TCP/IP models is important. Sure, they're on the CompTIA Network+ exam, but more importantly, they are your primary diagnostic tool for troubleshooting networks and a communication tool for talking to your fellow techs.

Chapter Review

Questions

1. Where does a hub send data?
   A. Only to the receiving system
   B. Only to the sending system
   C. To all the systems connected to the hub
   D. Only to the server

2. What uniquely identifies every NIC?
   A. IP address
   B. Media access control address
   C. ISO number
   D. Packet ID number

3. What Windows utility do you use to find the MAC address for a system?
   A. IPCONFIG
   B. IPCFG
   C. PING
   D. MAC

4. A MAC address is known as a(n) _____ address.
   A. IP
   B. Logical
   C. Physical
   D. OEM

5. A NIC sends data in discrete chunks called _____.

   A. Segments

   B. Sections

   C. Frames

   D. Layers

6. Which MAC address begins a frame?

   A. Receiving system

   B. Sending system

   C. Network

   D. Router

7. A frame ends with a special bit called the frame check sequence (FCS). What does the FCS do?

   A. Cycles data across the network

   B. Verifies that the MAC addresses are correct

   C. Verifies that the data arrived correctly

   D. Verifies that the IP address is correct

8. Which of the following is an example of a MAC address?

   A. 0–255

   B. 00–50–56–A3–04–0C

   C. SBY3M7

   D. 192.168.4.13

9. Which layer of the TCP/IP model controls the assembly and disassembly of data?

   A. Application layer

   B. Presentation layer

   C. Session layer

   D. Transport layer

10. Which layer of the OSI seven-layer model keeps track of a system's connections to send the right response to the right computer?

    A. Application layer

    B. Presentation layer

    C. Session layer

    D. Transport layer

Answers

1. **C.** Data comes into a hub through one wire and is then sent out through all the other wires. A hub sends data to all the systems connected to it.

2. **B.** The unique identifier on a network interface card is called the media access control (MAC) address.

3. **A.** All versions of Windows use ipconfig/all from the command line to determine the MAC address.

4. **C.** The MAC address is a physical address.

5. **C.** Data is sent in discrete chunks called frames. Networks use frames to keep any one NIC from hogging the wire.

6. **A.** The frame begins with the MAC address of the receiving NIC, followed by the MAC address of the sending NIC, followed, in turn, by the data and FCS.

7. **C.** The data is followed by a special bit of checking information called the frame check sequence, which the receiving NIC uses to verify that the data arrived correctly.

8. **B.** A MAC address is a 48-bit value, and no two NICs ever share the same MAC address—ever. 00–50–56–A3–04–0C is a MAC address. Answer D (192.168.4.13) is an IP address.

9. **D.** The Transport layer controls the assembly and disassembly of data.

10. **C.** The Session layer keeps track of a system's connections to ensure that it sends the right response to the right computer.

Cabling and Topology

The CompTIA Network+ certification exam expects you to know how to

- 3.1 Categorize standard media types and associated properties
- 3.2 Categorize standard connector types based on network media
- 3.5 Describe different network topologies

To achieve these goals, you must be able to

- Explain the different types of network topologies
- Describe the different types of network cabling
- Describe the IEEE networking standards

Every network must provide some method to get data from one system to another. In most cases, this method consists of some type of cabling (usually copper or fiber-optic) running between systems, although many networks skip wires and use wireless methods to move data. Stringing those cables brings up a number of critical issues you need to understand to work on a network. How do all these cables connect the computers? Does every computer on the network run a cable to a central point? Does a single cable snake through the ceiling, with all the computers on the network connected to it? These questions need answering! Furthermore, manufacturers need standards so they can make networking equipment that works well together. While we're talking about standards, what about the cabling itself? What type of cable? What quality of copper? How thick should it be? Who defines the standards for cables so they all work in the network?

This chapter answers these questions in three parts. First, you will learn about *network topology*—the way that cables and other pieces of hardware connect to one another. Second, you will tour the most common standardized cable types used in networking. Third, you will discover the IEEE committees that create network technology standards.

Test Specific

Topology

Computer networks employ many different *topologies*, or ways of connecting computers together. This section looks at both the historical topologies—bus, ring, and star—and the modern topologies—hybrid, mesh, point-to-multipoint, and point-to-point.

Bus and Ring

The first generation of wired networks used one of two topologies, both shown in Figure 3-1. A *bus topology* uses a single cable that connects all of the computers in a line. A *ring topology* connects all computers on the network with a ring of cable.

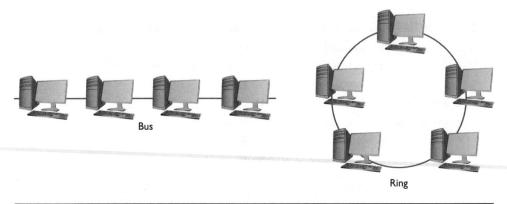

Bus

Ring

Figure 3-1   Bus and ring topologies

Note that topologies are diagrams, much like an electrical circuit diagram. Real network cabling doesn't go in perfect circles or perfect straight lines. Figure 3-2 shows a bus topology network that illustrates how the cable might appear in the real world.

Figure 3-2
Real-world
bus topology

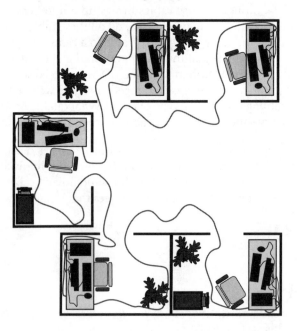

Data flows differently between bus and ring networks, creating different problems and solutions. In bus topology networks, data from each computer simply goes out on the whole bus. A network using a bus topology needs termination at each end of the cable to prevent a signal sent from one computer from reflecting at the ends of the cable, quickly bringing the network down (Figure 3-3).

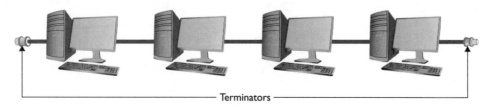

Terminators

Figure 3-3 Terminated bus topology

In a ring topology network, in contrast, data traffic moves in a circle from one computer to the next in the same direction (Figure 3-4). With no end to the cable, ring networks require no termination.

Figure 3-4
Ring topology
moving in a
certain direction

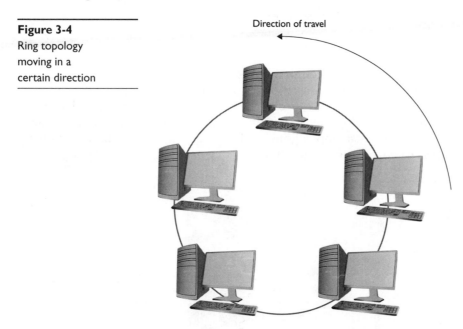

Direction of travel

Bus and ring topology networks work well but suffer from the same problem: the entire network stops working if the cable breaks at any point. The broken ends on a bus topology network aren't terminated, causing reflection between computers that are still connected. A break in a ring topology network simply breaks the circuit, stopping the data flow (Figure 3-5).

Figure 3-5
Nobody is
talking!

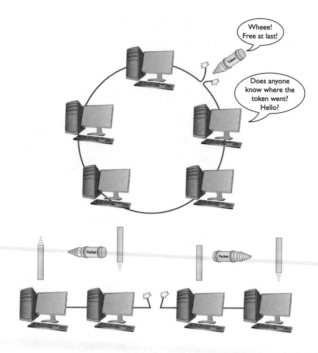

Star

The *star topology* uses a central connection box for all the computers on the network (Figure 3-6). Star topology has a huge benefit over ring and bus topologies by offering *fault tolerance*—if one of the cables breaks, all of the other computers can still communicate. Bus and ring topology networks were popular and inexpensive to implement, however, so the old-style star topology networks weren't very successful. Network hardware designers couldn't easily redesign their existing networks to use a star topology.

Figure 3-6
Star topology

Hybrids

Even though network designers couldn't easily use a star topology, the benefits of star topologies were overwhelming, motivating smart people to come up with a way to use star topologies without requiring a major redesign—and the way they did so was ingenious. The ring topology network designers struck first by taking the entire ring and shrinking it into a small box, as shown in Figure 3-7.

Figure 3-7
Shrinking the ring

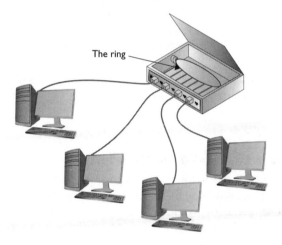

The ring

 NOTE The most successful of the star ring topology networks was called *Token Ring*, manufactured by IBM.

This was quickly followed by the bus topology folks who, in turn, shrunk their bus (better known as the *segment*) into their own box (Figure 3-8).

Figure 3-8
Shrinking the segment

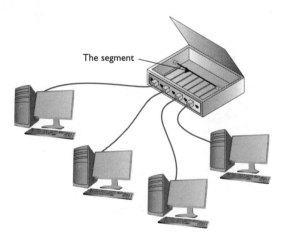

The segment

Physically, they looked like a star, but if you examined it as an electronic schematic, the signals acted like a ring or a bus. Clearly the old definition of topology needed a little clarification. When we talk about topology today, we separate how the cables physically look (the *physical topology*) from how the signals travel electronically (the *signaling topology* or *logical topology*).

Any form of networking technology that combines a physical topology with a signaling topology is called a *hybrid topology*. Hybrid topologies have come and gone since the earliest days of networking. Only two hybrid topologies, *star-ring topology* and *star-bus topology*, ever saw any amount of popularity. Eventually star-ring lost market share, and star-bus reigned as the undisputed king of topologies.

EXAM TIP Most techs refer to the signaling topology as the *logical topology* today. That's how you'll see it on the CompTIA Network+ exam as well.

Mesh and Point-to-Multipoint

Topologies aren't just for wired networks. Wireless networks also need topologies to get data from one machine to another, but using radio waves instead of cables involves somewhat different topologies. Almost all wireless networks use one of two different topologies: a mesh topology or a point-to-multipoint topology (Figure 3-9).

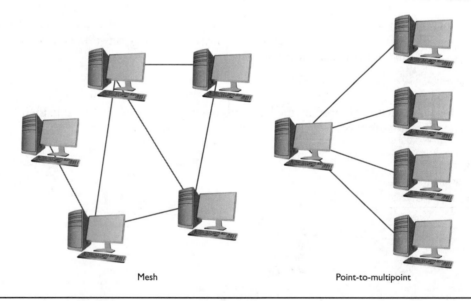

Mesh   Point-to-multipoint

Figure 3-9 Mesh and point-to-multipoint topologies

Mesh

In a *mesh topology* network, every computer connects to every other computer via two or more routes. Some of the routes between two computers may require traversing through another member of the mesh network.

There are two types of meshed topologies: partially meshed and fully meshed (Figure 3-10). In a *partially meshed topology* network, at least two machines have redundant connections. Every machine doesn't have to connect to every other machine. In a *fully meshed topology* network, every computer connects directly to every other computer.

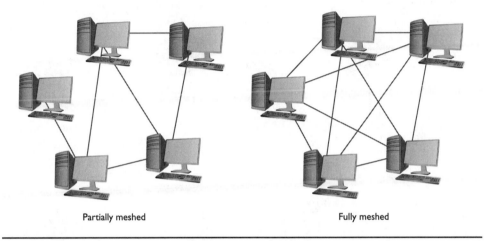

Partially meshed   Fully meshed

Figure 3-10 Partially and fully meshed topologies

If you're looking at Figure 3-10 and thinking that a mesh topology looks amazingly resilient and robust, it is—at least on paper. Because every computer connects to every other computer on the fully meshed network, even if half the PCs crash, the network still functions as well as ever (for the survivors). In a practical sense, however, implementing a fully meshed topology for a wired network would be an expensive mess. Even a tiny fully meshed network with 10 PCs, for example, would need 45 separate and distinct pieces of cable to connect every PC to every other PC. What a mesh mess! Because of this, mesh topologies have never been practical for a wired network.

Make sure you know the formula to calculate the number of connections needed to create a fully meshed network, given a certain number of computers. Here's the formula:

$$y = \text{number of computers}$$
$$\text{Number of connections} = y(y - 1)/2$$

So, if you have six computers, you need $6(6 - 1)/2 = 30/2 = 15$ connections to create a fully meshed network.

Point-to-Multipoint

In a *point-to-multipoint topology*, a single system acts as a common source through which all members of the point-to-multipoint network converse. If you compare a star topology to a slightly rearranged point-to-multipoint topology, you might be tempted to say they're the same thing. Granted, they're similar, but look at Figure 3-11. See what's in the middle? The subtle but important difference is that a point-to-multipoint topology requires an intelligent device in the center, whereas the device in the center of a star topology has little more to do than send or provide a path for a signal down all the connections.

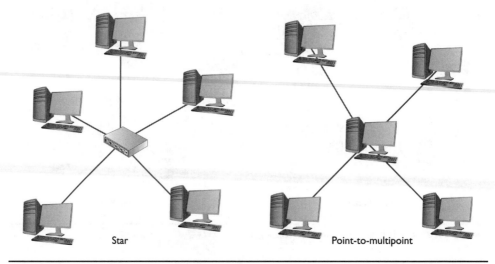

Star   Point-to-multipoint

Figure 3-11   Comparing star and point-to-multipoint topologies

You'll sometimes find mesh or point-to-multipoint topology used in wired networks, but they're rare. These two topologies are far more commonly seen in wireless networks.

Point-to-Point

In a *point-to-point topology* network, two computers connect directly together with no need for a central device of any kind. You'll find point-to-point topologies implemented in both wired and wireless networks (Figure 3-12).

Figure 3-12
Point-to-point
topology

Parameters of a Topology

Although a topology describes the method by which systems in a network connect, the topology alone doesn't describe all of the features necessary to enable those networks. The term *bus topology*, for example, describes a network that consists of some number of machines connected to the network via a single linear piece of cable. Notice that this definition leaves a lot of questions unanswered. What is the cable made of? How long can it be? How do the machines decide which machine should send data at a specific moment? A network based on a bus topology can answer these questions in a number of different ways—but it's not the job of the topology to define issues like these. A functioning network needs a more detailed standard.

Over the years, particular manufacturers and standards bodies have created several specific network technologies based on different topologies. A *network technology* is a practical application of a topology and other critical technologies that provides a method to get data from one computer to another on a network. These network technologies have names like 10BaseT, 1000BaseF, and 10GBaseLX. You will learn all about these in the next two chapters.

 EXAM TIP Make sure you know all your topologies: bus, ring, star, hybrid, mesh, point-to-multipoint, and point-to-point.

Cabling

The majority of networked systems link together using some type of cabling. Different types of networks over the years have used a number of different types of cables—and you need to learn about all these cables to succeed on the CompTIA Network+ exam! This section explores both the cabling types used in older networks and those found in today's networks.

All cables used in the networking industry can be categorized in three distinct groups: coaxial (coax), twisted pair, and fiber-optic. Let's look at all three.

Coaxial Cable

Coaxial cable contains a central conductor wire surrounded by an insulating material, which, in turn, is surrounded by a braided metal shield. The cable is referred to as coaxial (coax for short) because the center wire and the braided metal shield share a common axis or centerline (Figure 3-13).

Figure 3-13
Cutaway view
of coaxial cable

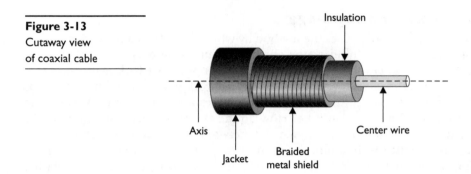

Insulation

Axis

Center wire

Jacket

Braided
metal shield

Coaxial cable shields data transmissions from *electromagnetic interference (EMI)*. Many devices in the typical office environment generate magnetic fields, including lights, fans, copy machines, and refrigerators. When a metal wire encounters these magnetic fields, electrical current is generated along the wire. This extra current—EMI—can shut down a network because it is easily misinterpreted as a signal by devices like NICs. To prevent EMI from affecting the network, the outer mesh layer of a coaxial cable shields the center wire (on which the data is transmitted) from interference (Figure 3-14).

Figure 3-14
Coaxial cable
showing braided
metal shielding

Early bus topology networks used coaxial cable to connect computers together. Back in the day, the most popular cable used special bayonet-style connectors called *BNC connectors* (Figure 3-15). Even earlier bus networks used thick cable that required vampire connections—sometimes called *vampire taps*—that literally pierced the cable.

Figure 3-15
BNC connector
on coaxial cable

 NOTE Techs all around the globe argue over the meaning of BNC. A solid percentage says with authority that it stands for "British Naval Connector." An opposing percentage says with equal authority that it stands for "Bayonet Neill-Concelman," after the stick-and-twist style of connecting and the purported inventors of the connector. The jury is still out, though this week I'm leaning toward Neill and Concelman and their bayonet-style connector.

You'll find coaxial cable used today primarily to enable a cable modem to connect to an *Internet service provider (ISP)*. Connecting a computer to the cable modem enables that computer to access the Internet. This cable is the same type used to connect televisions to cable boxes or to satellite receivers. These cables use an *F-connector* that screws on, making for a secure connection (Figure 3-16).

Figure 3-16
F-type connector
on coaxial cable

 EXAM TIP Coaxial cabling is also very popular with satellite, over-the-air antennas, and even some home video devices. This book covers cable and other Internet connectivity options in great detail in Chapter 14.

Cable modems connect using either RG-6 or, rarely, RG-59. RG-59 was used primarily for cable television rather than networking. Its thinness and the introduction of digital cable motivated the move to the more robust RG-6, the predominant cabling used today (Figure 3-17).

Figure 3-17
RG-6 cable

All coax cables have a *Radio Grade (RG) rating*. The U.S. military developed these ratings to provide a quick reference for the different types of coax. The only important measure of coax cabling is its *Ohm rating*, a relative measure of the resistance (or more precisely, characteristic impedance) on the cable. You may run across other coax cables that don't have acceptable Ohm ratings, although they look just like network-rated coax. Fortunately, most coax cable types display their Ohm ratings on the cables themselves (see Figure 3-18). Both RG-6 and RG-59 cables are rated at 75 Ohms.

Figure 3-18
Ohm rating
(on an older,
RG-58 cable used
for networking)

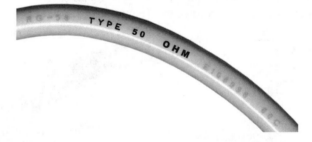

NOTE The Ohm rating of a particular piece of cable describes the impedance of that cable. Impedance describes a set of characteristics that define how much a cable resists the flow of electricity. This isn't simple resistance, though. Impedance also factors in things like how long it takes the wire to get a full charge—the wire's *capacitance*—and more.

Given the popularity of cable for television and Internet in homes today, you'll run into situations where people need to take a single coaxial cable and split it. Coaxial handles this quite nicely with coaxial splitters like the one shown in Figure 3-19. You can also connect two coaxial cables together easily using a barrel connector when you need to add some distance to a connection (Figure 3-20).

Figure 3-19
Coaxial splitter

Figure 3-20
Barrel connector

Twisted Pair

The most common type of cabling used in networks consists of twisted pairs of cables, bundled together into a common jacket. Twisted-pair cabling for networks is composed of multiple pairs of wires, twisted around each other at specific intervals. The twists reduce interference, called *crosstalk*: the more twists, the less crosstalk. Networks use two types of twisted-pair cabling: shielded twisted pair and unshielded twisted pair.

 NOTE Have you ever picked up a telephone and heard a distinct crackling noise? That's an example of crosstalk.

Shielded Twisted Pair

Shielded twisted pair (STP), as its name implies, consists of twisted pairs of wires surrounded by shielding to protect them from EMI. STP is pretty rare, primarily because there's so little need for STP's shielding. The shielding only really matters in locations with excessive electronic noise, such as a shop floor with lots of lights, electric motors, or other machinery that could cause problems for other cables. Figure 3-21 shows the most common STP type: the venerable IBM Type 1 cable used in Token Ring network technology.

Figure 3-21
Shielded twisted pair

Unshielded Twisted Pair

Unshielded twisted pair (UTP) is by far the most common type of network cabling used today. UTP consists of twisted pairs of wires surrounded by a plastic jacket (Figure 3-22). This jacket does not provide any protection from EMI, so when installing UTP cabling, you must be careful to avoid interference from fluorescent lights, motors, and so forth. UTP costs much less than STP but, in most cases, performs just as well.

Figure 3-22
Unshielded twisted pair

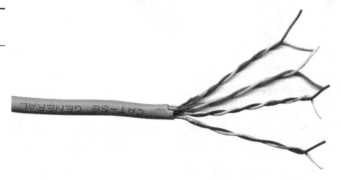

Although more sensitive to interference than coaxial or STP cable, UTP cabling provides an inexpensive and flexible means to cable networks. UTP cable isn't exclusive to networks. Many other technologies (such as telephone systems) employ the same cabling. This makes working with UTP a bit of a challenge. Imagine going up into a ceiling and seeing two sets of UTP cables: how would you determine which is for the telephones and which is for the network? Not to worry—a number of installation standards and tools exist to help those who work with UTP answer these types of questions.

Not all UTP cables are the same! UTP cabling has a number of variations, such as the number of twists per foot. To help network installers get the right cable for the right network technology, the cabling industry has developed a variety of grades called *category (CAT) ratings*. CAT ratings are officially rated in *megahertz (MHz)*, indicating the highest frequency the cable can handle. Table 3-1 shows the most common categories along with their status with the TIA/EIA (see the note following the table for more information).

CAT Rating	Max Frequency	Max Bandwidth	Status with TIA/EIA
CAT 1	< 1 MHz	Analog phone lines only	No longer recognized
CAT 2	4 MHz	4 Mbps	No longer recognized
CAT 3	16 MHz	16 Mbps	Recognized
CAT 4	20 MHz	20 Mbps	No longer recognized
CAT 5	100 MHz	100 Mbps	No longer recognized
CAT 5e	100 MHz	1000 Mbps	Recognized
CAT 6	250 MHz	10000 Mbps	Recognized

Table 3-1   CAT Ratings for UTP

NOTE   Several international groups set the standards for cabling and networking in general. Ready for alphabet soup? At or near the top is the International Organization for Standardization (ISO). The American National Standards Institute (ANSI) is both the official U.S. representative to the ISO and a major international player. ANSI checks the standards and accredits other groups, such as the Telecommunications Industry Association (TIA) and the Electronic Industries Alliance (EIA). The TIA and EIA together set the standards for UTP cabling, among many other things.

UTP cables are rated to handle a certain frequency or cycles per second, such as 100 MHz or 1000 MHz. You could take the frequency number in the early days of networking and translate that into the maximum throughput for a cable. Each cycle per second (or hertz) basically accounted for one bit of data per second. A 10 million cycle per second (10 MHz) cable, for example, could handle 10 million bits per second (10 Mbps). The maximum amount of data that goes through the cable per second is called the *bandwidth*.

For current networks, developers have implemented *bandwidth-efficient encoding schemes,* which means they can squeeze more bits into the same signal as long as the cable can handle it. Thus, the CAT 5e cable can handle a throughput of up to 1000 Mbps, even though it's rated to handle a frequency of only up to 100 MHz.

EXAM TIP The CompTIA Network+ exam is only interested in CAT 3, CAT 5, CAT 5e, and CAT 6 cables.

Because most networks can run at speeds of up to 1000 MHz, most new cabling installations use Category 5e (CAT 5e) cabling, although a large number of installations use CAT 6 to future-proof the network. CAT 5e cabling currently costs much less than CAT 6, although as CAT 6 gains in popularity, it's slowly dropping in price.

Make sure you can look at UTP and know its CAT rating. There are two places to look. First, UTP is typically sold in boxed reels, and the manufacturer will clearly mark the CAT level on the box (Figure 3-23). Second, look on the cable itself. The category level of a piece of cable is usually printed on the cable (Figure 3-24).

Figure 3-23
CAT level
marked on
box of UTP

Figure 3-24
CAT level on UTP

NOTE If you have a need for speed, the latest finalized update to the venerable UTP cable is Category 6a. This update doubles the bandwidth of CAT 6 to 500 MHz to accommodate 10-Gbps speeds up to 100 meters. Take that, fiber! (The 100-meter limitation, by the way, refers to the Ethernet standard, the major implementation of UTP in the networking world. Chapter 4 covers Ethernet in great detail.)

Other standards are in the works, however, so by the time you read this paragraph, CAT 6a might be old news. CAT 7 (600 MHz), CAT 7a (1000 MHz), and CAT 8 (1200 MHz) are just around the corner.

Anyone who's plugged in a telephone has probably already dealt with the *registered jack (RJ)* connectors used with UTP cable. Telephones use *RJ-11* connectors, designed to support up to two pairs of wires. Networks use the four-pair *RJ-45* connectors (Figure 3-25).

Figure 3-25
RJ-11 (left) and
RJ-45 (right)
connectors

Fiber-Optic

Fiber-optic cable transmits light rather than electricity, making it attractive for both high-EMI areas and long-distance transmissions. Whereas a single copper cable cannot carry data more than a few hundred meters at best, a single piece of fiber-optic cabling will operate, depending on the implementation, for distances of up to tens of kilometers. A fiber-optic cable has four components: the glass fiber itself (the *core*); the *cladding*, which is the part that makes the light reflect down the fiber; *buffer* material to give strength, and the *insulating jacket* (Figure 3-26).

Figure 3-26

Cross section of fiber-optic cabling

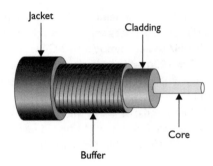

Fiber-optic cabling is manufactured with many different diameters of core and cladding. In a convenient bit of standardization, cable manufacturers use a two-number designator to define fiber-optic cables according to their core and cladding measurements. The most common fiber-optic cable size is 62.5/125 µm. Almost all network technologies that use fiber-optic cable require pairs of fibers. One fiber is used for sending, the other for receiving. In response to the demand for two-pair cabling, manufacturers often connect two fibers together like a lamp cord to create the popular duplex fiber-optic cabling (Figure 3-27).

Figure 3-27

Duplex fiber-optic cable

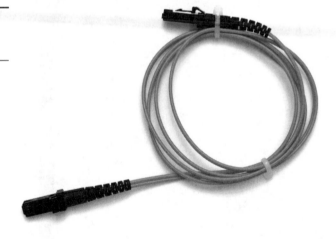

 NOTE For those of you unfamiliar with it, the odd little u-shaped symbol describing fiber cable size (µ) stands for *micro,* or 1/1,000,000.

Fiber cables are pretty tiny! Light can be sent down a fiber-optic cable as regular light or as laser light. The two types of light require totally different fiber-optic cables. Most network technologies that use fiber optics use LEDs (light emitting diodes) to send light signals. A fiber-optic cable that uses LEDs is known as *multimode fiber (MMF)*.

A fiber-optic cable that uses lasers is known as *single-mode fiber (SMF)*. Using laser light and single-mode fiber-optic cables prevents a problem unique to multimode fiber optics called *modal distortion* (signals sent at the same time don't arrive at the same time because the paths differ slightly in length) and enables a network to achieve phenomenally high transfer rates over incredibly long distances.

Fiber optics also define the wavelength of light used, measured in nanometers (nm). Almost all multimode cables transmit 850-nm wavelengths, whereas single-mode transmits either 1310 or 1550 nm, depending on the laser.

Fiber-optic cables come in a broad choice of connector types. There are over one hundred different connectors, but the three you need to know for the CompTIA Network+ exam are ST, SC, and LC (Figure 3-28). LC is unique because it is a duplex connector, designed to accept two fiber cables.

Figure 3-28
From left to right: ST, SC, and LC fiber-optic connectors

 NOTE Most technicians call common fiber-optic connectors by their initials—such as ST, SC, or LC—perhaps because there's no consensus about what words go with those initials. ST probably stands for *straight tip*, although some call it *snap twist*. But SC and LC? How about *subscriber connector, standard connector*, or *Siemon connector* for the former, and *local connector* or *Lucent connector* for the latter?

If you want to remember the connectors for the exam, try these: stick and twist for the bayonet-style ST connectors; stick and click for the straight push-in SC connectors; and little connector for the . . . little . . . LC connector.

Other Cables

Fiber-optic and UTP make up almost all network cabling, but a few other types of cabling may serve from time to time as alternatives to these two: the ancient serial and parallel cables from the earliest days of PCs and the modern high-speed serial connection, better known as FireWire. These cables are only used with quick-and-dirty temporary connections, but they do work, so they bear at least a quick mention.

Classic Serial

Serial cabling predates both networking and the personal computer. *RS-232*, the *recommended standard (RS)* upon which all serial communication takes place on your PC, dates from 1969 and hasn't substantially changed in around 40 years. When IBM invented the PC way back in 1980, serial connections were just about the only standard input/output technology available, so IBM included two serial ports on every PC. The most common serial port is a 9-pin, male D-subminiature (or DB-9) connector, as shown in Figure 3-29.

Figure 3-29
Serial port

Serial ports offer a poor option for networking, with very slow data rates—only about 56,000 bps—and only point-to-point connections. In all probability, copying something on a flash drive and just walking over to the other system is faster, but serial networking does work if needed. Serial ports are quickly fading away, however, and you no longer see them on new PCs.

Parallel

Parallel connections are as ancient as serial ports. Parallel can run up to around 2 Mbps, although when used for networking, they tend to be much slower. Parallel is also limited to point-to-point topology but uses a 25-pin female—rather than male—DB type connector (Figure 3-30). The *IEEE 1284* committee sets the standards for parallel communication. (See the section "Networking Industry Standards—IEEE," later in this chapter.)

Figure 3-30
Parallel connector

EXAM TIP   Concentrate on UTP—that's where the hardest CompTIA Network+ exam questions come into play. Don't forget to give coax, STP, and fiber-optic a quick pass, and make sure you understand the reasons for picking one type of cabling over another. Even though the CompTIA Network+ exam does not test too hard on cabling, this is important information that you will use in the real networking world.

FireWire

FireWire (based on the *IEEE 1394* standard) is the only viable alternative cabling option to fiber-optic or UTP. FireWire is also restricted to point-to-point connections, but it's very fast (currently the standard is up to 800 Mbps). FireWire has its own unique connector (Figure 3-31).

Figure 3-31
FireWire
connector

 NOTE   You cannot network computers using FireWire in Windows Vista or Windows 7.

Fire Ratings

Did you ever see the movie *The Towering Inferno*? Don't worry if you missed it—*The Towering Inferno* was one of the better disaster movies of the 1970s, although it was no *Airplane!* Anyway, Steve McQueen stars as the fireman who saves the day when a skyscraper goes up in flames because of poor-quality electrical cabling. The burning insulation on the wires ultimately spreads the fire to every part of the building. Although no cables made today contain truly flammable insulation, the insulation is made from plastic, and if you get any plastic hot enough, it will create smoke and noxious fumes. The risk of burning insulation isn't fire—it's smoke and fumes.

To reduce the risk of your network cables burning and creating noxious fumes and smoke, Underwriters Laboratories and the National Electrical Code (NEC) joined forces to develop cabling *fire ratings*. The two most common fire ratings are PVC and plenum. Cable with a *polyvinyl chloride (PVC)* rating has no significant fire protection. If you burn a PVC cable, it creates lots of smoke and noxious fumes. Burning *plenum*-rated cable creates much less smoke and fumes, but plenum-rated cable—often referred to simply as "plenum"—costs about three to five times as much as PVC-rated cable. Most city ordinances require the use of plenum cable for network installations. The bottom line? Get plenum!

The space between the acoustical tile ceiling in an office building and the actual concrete ceiling above is called the plenum—hence the name for the proper fire rating of cabling to use in that space. A third type of fire rating, known as *riser*, designates the proper cabling to use for vertical runs between floors of a building. Riser-rated cable provides less protection than plenum cable, though, so most installations today use plenum for runs between floors.

Networking Industry Standards—IEEE

The *Institute of Electrical and Electronics Engineers (IEEE)* defines industry-wide standards that promote the use and implementation of technology. In February 1980, a new committee called the 802 Working Group took over from the private sector the job of defining network standards. The IEEE 802 committee defines frames, speeds, distances, and types of cabling to use in a network environment. Concentrating on cables, the IEEE recognizes that no single cabling solution can work in all situations and, therefore, provides a variety of cabling standards.

IEEE committees define standards for a wide variety of electronics. The names of these committees are often used to refer to the standards they publish. The IEEE 1284 committee, for example, sets standards for parallel communication. Have you ever seen a printer cable marked "IEEE 1284–compliant," as in Figure 3-32? This means the manufacturer followed the rules set by the IEEE 1284 committee. Another committee you may have heard of is the IEEE 1394 committee, which controls the FireWire standard.

Figure 3-32
Parallel cable marked IEEE 1284–compliant

The IEEE 802 committee sets the standards for networking. Although the original plan was to define a single, universal standard for networking, it quickly became apparent that no single solution would work for all needs. The 802 committee split into smaller subcommittees, with names such as IEEE 802.3 and IEEE 802.5. Table 3-2 shows the currently recognized IEEE 802 subcommittees and their areas of jurisdiction. I've included the inactive subcommittees for reference. The missing numbers, such as 802.4 and 802.12, were used for committees long-ago disbanded. Each subcommittee is officially called a Working Group, except the few listed as a Technical Advisory Group (TAG) in the table.

 EXAM TIP Memorize the 802.3 and 802.11 standards. Ignore the rest.

Some of these committees deal with technologies that didn't quite make it, and the committees associated with those standards, such as IEEE 802.4, Token Bus, have become dormant. When preparing for the CompTIA Network+ exam, concentrate on the IEEE 802.3 and 802.11 standards. You will see these again in later chapters.

IEEE 802	LAN/MAN Overview & Architecture
IEEE 802.1	Higher Layer LAN Protocols
802.1s	Multiple Spanning Trees
802.1	Rapid Reconfiguration of Spanning Tree
802.1x	Port Based Network Access Control
IEEE 802.2	Logical Link Control (LLC); now inactive
IEEE 802.3	Ethernet
802.3ae	10 Gigabit Ethernet
IEEE 802.5	Token Ring; now inactive
IEEE 802.11	Wireless LAN (WLAN); specifications, such as Wi-Fi
IEEE 802.15	Wireless Personal Area Network (WPAN)
IEEE 802.16	Broadband Wireless Access (BWA); specifications for implementing Wireless Metropolitan Area Networks (Wireless MANs); referred to also as WiMAX
IEEE 802.17	Resilient Packet Ring (RPR)
IEEE 802.18	Radio Regulatory Technical Advisory Group
IEEE 802.19	Coexistence Technical Advisory Group
IEEE 802.20	Mobile Broadband Wireless Access (MBWA)
IEEE 802.21	Media Independent Handover
IEEE 802.22	Wireless Regional Area Networks

Table 3-2 IEEE 802 Subcommittees

Chapter Review

Questions

1. Which of the following topologies requires termination?
   A. Star
   B. Bus
   C. Mesh
   D. Ring

2. Star-bus is an example of a(n) _____ topology.
   A. Transitional
   B. System
   C. Hybrid
   D. Rampant

3. Of the topologies listed, which one is the most fault-tolerant?
   A. Point-to-point
   B. Bus
   C. Star
   D. Ring

4. What term is used to describe the interconnectivity of network components?
   A. Segmentation
   B. Map
   C. Topology
   D. Protocol

5. Coaxial cables all have a(n) _____ rating.
   A. Resistance
   B. Watt
   C. Speed
   D. Ohm

6. Which of the following is a type of coaxial cable?
   A. RJ-45
   B. RG-59

    C. BNC

    D. Barrel

7. Which network topology connects nodes with a ring of cable?

    A. Star

    B. Bus

    C. Ring

    D. Mesh

8. Which network topology is most commonly seen only in wireless networks?

    A. Star

    B. Bus

    C. Ring

    D. Mesh

9. Which of the following is a duplex fiber-optic connection?

    A. LC

    B. RJ-45

    C. ST

    D. SC

10. What is the most common category of UTP used in new cabling installations?

    A. CAT 5

    B. CAT 5e

    C. CAT 6

    D. CAT 6a

Answers

1. **B.** In a bus topology, all computers connect to the network via a main line. The cable must be terminated at both ends to prevent signal reflection.

2. **C.** Star-bus is a hybrid topology because it uses a star physical topology and a bus signal topology.

3. **C.** Of the choices listed, only star topology has any fault tolerance.

4. **C.** *Topology* is the term used to describe the interconnectivity of network components.

5. **D.** All coaxial cables have an Ohm rating. RG-59 and RG-6 both are rated at 75 Ohms.

6. **B.** RG-59 is a type of coaxial cable.

7. **C.** The aptly named ring topology connects nodes with a central ring of cable.

8. **D.** Mesh is, for the most part, unique to wireless networks.

9. **A.** Of the options given, only the LC connector is designed for duplex fiber-optic.

10. **B.** CAT 5e is the most common cabling category used today, although CAT 6 is gaining in popularity.

Ethernet Basics

The CompTIA Network+ certification exam expects you to know how to

- 1.2 Classify how applications, devices, and protocols relate to the OSI model layers: switch, bridge
- 1.4 Explain the purpose and properties of routing and switching: broadcast domain vs. collision domain
- 2.5 Given a scenario, troubleshoot common router and switch problems: switching loop, bad cables, port configuration
- 3.1 Categorize standard media types and associated properties: STP, crossover, media converters, distance and speed limitations
- 3.2 Categorize standard connector types based on network media: RJ-45, RJ-11
- 3.7 Compare and contrast different LAN technologies: Types: Ethernet, 10BaseT; Properties: CSMA/CD, broadcast, collision

To achieve these goals, you must be able to

- Define and describe Ethernet
- Explain early Ethernet implementations
- Describe ways to extend and enhance Ethernet networks

In the beginning, there were no networks. Computers were isolated, solitary islands of information in a teeming sea of proto-geeks who used clubs and wore fur pocket protectors. Okay, maybe it wasn't that bad, but if you wanted to move a file from one machine to another—and proto-geeks were as much into that as modern geeks—you had to use *Sneakernet*, which meant you saved the file on a disk, laced up your tennis shoes, and hiked over to the other system. All that walking no doubt produced lots of health benefits, but frankly, proto-geeks weren't all that into health benefits—they were into speed, power, and technological coolness in general. (Sound familiar?) It's no wonder, then, that geeks everywhere agreed on the need to replace Sneakernet with a faster and more efficient method of sharing data. The method they came up with is the subject of this chapter.

Historical/Conceptual

Ethernet

In 1973, Xerox answered the challenge of moving data without sneakers by developing *Ethernet*, a networking technology standard based on a bus topology. The Ethernet standard dominates today's networks and defines all of the issues involved in transferring data between computer systems. The original Ethernet used a single piece of coaxial cable in a bus topology to connect several computers, enabling them to transfer data at a rate of up to 3 Mbps. Although slow by today's standards, this early version of Ethernet was a huge improvement over Sneakernet methods and served as the foundation for all later versions of Ethernet.

Ethernet remained a largely in-house technology within Xerox until 1979, when Xerox decided to look for partners to help promote Ethernet as an industry standard. Xerox worked with Digital Equipment Corporation (DEC) and Intel to publish what became known as the Digital-Intel-Xerox (DIX) standard. Running on coaxial cable, the DIX standard enabled multiple computers to communicate with each other at a screaming 10 Mbps. Although 10 Mbps represents the low end of standard network speeds today, at the time it was revolutionary. These companies then transferred control of the Ethernet standard to the IEEE, which, in turn, created the *802.3 (Ethernet)* committee that continues to control the Ethernet standard to this day.

NOTE The source for all things Ethernet is but a short click away on the Internet. For starters, check out www.ieee802.org.

Given that Ethernet's been around for so long, we need to start at a common point. I've chosen to use 10BaseT, the earliest version of Ethernet designed to use UTP cabling. At this point, don't worry what 10BaseT means—this chapter will cover the definition. For right now, just get into the idea of how Ethernet works.

EXAM TIP There have been many versions of Ethernet over the years. The earliest versions, named 10Base5 and 10Base2, are long obsolete. As of 2009, CompTIA finally dropped these ancient technologies from the CompTIA Network+ exam. Rest in peace, 10Base5 and 10Base2!

Oddly, though, the official Network+ Acronym List refers to two analog technologies used in networks circa 1980s, *amplitude modulation (AM)* and *frequency modulation (FM)*. These were used to transmit multiple signals at the same time over cable. For the exam, note that these are not used in networks today.

Ethernet's designers faced the same challenges as the designers of any network: how to send data across the wire, how to identify the sending and receiving computers, and how to determine which computer should use the shared cable at what time. The engineers resolved these issues by using data frames that contain MAC addresses to identify computers on the network and by using a process called CSMA/CD (discussed shortly) to determine which machine should access the wire at any given time. You saw some of this in action in Chapter 2, but now I need to introduce you to a bunch of new terms, so let's look at each of these solutions.

NOTE   Ethernet is a standard for a family of network technologies that share the same basic bus topology, frame type, and network access method. Because the technologies share these essential components, you can communicate between them just fine. The implementation of the network might be different, but the frames remain the same. This is true for Ethernet running on a physical bus topology—the ancient 10Base5 and 10Base2—and a logical bus topology—10BaseT and later.

Topology

Every version of Ethernet invented since the early 1990s uses a hybrid star-bus topology. At the center of these early networks was a *hub*. A hub is nothing more than an electronic *repeater*—it interprets the ones and zeroes coming in from one port and repeats the same signal out to the other connected ports. Hubs do not send the same signal back down the port that originally sent it (Figure 4-1). Repeaters are not amplifiers! They read the incoming signal and send new copies of that signal out to every connected port on the hub.

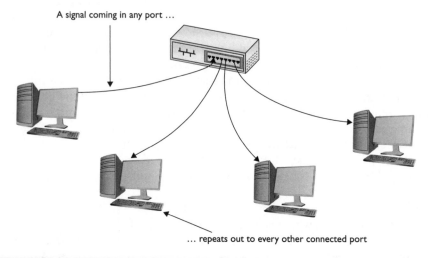

A signal coming in any port ...

... repeats out to every other connected port

Figure 4-1   Ethernet hub

Test Specific

Organizing the Data: Ethernet Frames

All network technologies break data transmitted between computers into smaller pieces called *frames*, as you'll recall from Chapter 2. Using frames addresses two networking issues. First, frames prevent any single machine from monopolizing the shared bus cable. Second, they make the process of retransmitting lost data more efficient.

 EXAM TIP The terms *frame* and *packet* are often used interchangeably, especially on exams! This book uses the terms more strictly. You'll recall from Chapter 2 that frames are based on MAC addresses; packets are generally associated with data assembled by the IP protocol at Layer 3 of the OSI seven-layer model.

The process you saw in Chapter 2 of transferring a word processing document between two computers illustrates these two issues. First, if the sending computer sends the document as a single huge frame, the frame will monopolize the cable and prevent other machines from using the cable until the entire file gets to the receiving system. Using relatively small frames enables computers to share the cable easily—each computer listens on the *segment*, sending a few frames of data whenever it detects that no other computer is transmitting. Second, in the real world, bad things can happen to good data. When errors occur during transmission, the sending system must retransmit the frames that failed to get to the receiving system in good shape. If a word processing document were transmitted as a single massive frame, the sending system would have to retransmit the entire frame—in this case, the entire document. Breaking the file up into smaller frames enables the sending computer to retransmit only the damaged frames. Because of these benefits—shared access and more efficient retransmission—all networking technologies use frames, and Ethernet is no exception to that rule.

In Chapter 2, you saw a generic frame. Let's take what you know of frames and expand on that knowledge by inspecting the details of an Ethernet frame. A basic Ethernet frame contains seven pieces of information: the preamble, the MAC address of the frame's recipient, the MAC address of the sending system, the type of the data, the data itself, a pad (if needed), and a frame check sequence, generically called a cyclic redundancy check (CRC). Figure 4-2 shows these components.

Preamble

All Ethernet frames begin with a *preamble*, a 64-bit series of alternating ones and zeroes that ends with 11. The preamble gives a receiving NIC time to realize a frame is coming and to know exactly where the frame starts. The preamble is added by the sending NIC.

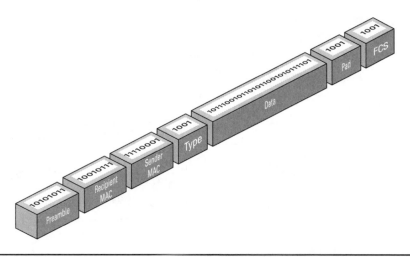

Figure 4-2 Ethernet frame

MAC Addresses

Each NIC, more commonly called a *node*, on an Ethernet network must have a unique identifying address. Ethernet identifies the NICs on a network using special 48-bit (6-byte) binary addresses known as *MAC addresses*.

 EXAM TIP The CompTIA Network+ exam might describe MAC addresses as 48-bit binary addresses or 6-byte binary addresses.

MAC addresses give each NIC a unique address. When a computer sends out a data frame, it goes into the hub that repeats an exact copy of that frame to every connected port, as shown in Figure 4-3. All the other computers on the network listen to the wire and examine the frame to see if it contains their MAC address. If it does not, they ignore the frame. If a machine sees a frame with its MAC address, it opens the frame and begins processing the data.

This system of allowing each machine to decide which frames it will process may be efficient, but because any device connected to the network cable can potentially capture any data frame transmitted across the wire, Ethernet networks carry a significant security vulnerability. Network diagnostic programs, commonly called *sniffers*, can order a NIC to run in *promiscuous mode*. When running in promiscuous mode, the NIC processes all the frames it sees on the cable, regardless of their MAC addresses. Sniffers are valuable troubleshooting tools in the right hands, but Ethernet provides no protections against their unscrupulous use.

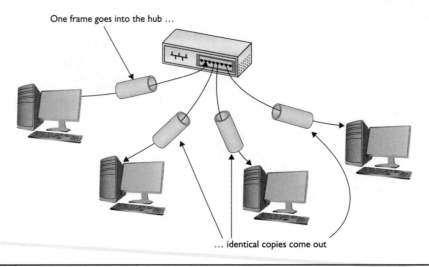

One frame goes into the hub ...

... identical copies come out

Figure 4-3   Frames propagating on a network

NOTE   There are many situations in which one computer might have two or more NICs, so one physical system might represent more than one node.

Type

An Ethernet frame may carry one of several types of data. The Type field helps the receiving computer interpret the frame contents at a very basic level. This way the receiving computer can tell if the frame contains IPv4 data, for example, or IPv6 data. (See Chapter 7 for more details on IPv4; I cover IPv6 in Chapter 13.)

The Type field does *not* tell you if the frame carries higher-level data, such as an e-mail message or Web page. You have to dig deeper into the data section of the frame to find that information.

Data

The data part of the frame contains whatever payload the frame carries. If the frame carries an IP packet, that packet will include extra information, such as the IP addresses of both systems, sequencing numbers, and other information.

Pad

The minimum Ethernet frame is 64 bytes in size, but not all of that has to be actual data. If an Ethernet frame has fewer than 64 bytes of data to haul, the sending NIC will automatically add extra data—a *pad*—to bring the data up to the minimum 64 bytes.

Frame Check Sequence

The *frame check sequence (FCS)*—Ethernet's term for the *cyclic redundancy check*—enables Ethernet nodes to recognize when bad things happen to good data. Machines on a network must be able to detect when data has been damaged in transit. To detect errors, the computers on an Ethernet network attach a special code to each frame. When creating an Ethernet frame, the sending machine runs the data through a special mathematical formula and attaches the result, the frame check sequence, to the frame. The receiving machine opens the frame, performs the same calculation, and compares its answer with the one included with the frame. If the answers do not match, the receiving machine asks the sending machine to retransmit that frame.

At this point, those crafty network engineers have solved two of the problems facing them: they've created frames to organize the data to be sent and put in place MAC addresses to identify machines on the network. But the challenge of determining which machine should send data at which time requires another solution: CSMA/CD.

CSMA/CD

Ethernet networks use a system called *carrier sense multiple access/collision detection (CSMA/CD)* to determine which computer should use a shared cable at a given moment. *Carrier sense* means that each node using the network examines the cable before sending a data frame (Figure 4-4). If another machine is using the network, the node detects traffic on the segment, waits a few milliseconds, and then rechecks. If it detects no traffic—the more common term is to say the cable is "free"—the node sends out its frame.

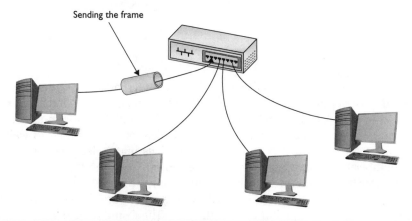

Figure 4-4   No one else is talking—send the frame!

EXAM TIP CSMA/CD is a network access method that maps to the IEEE 802.3 standard for Ethernet networks.

Multiple access means that all machines have equal access to the wire. If the line is free, any Ethernet node may begin sending a frame. From Ethernet's point of view, it doesn't matter what function the node is performing: it could be a desktop system running Windows XP or a high-end file server running Windows Server 2008 or Linux. As far as Ethernet is concerned, a node is a node is a node and access to the cable is assigned strictly on a first-come, first-served basis.

So what happens if two machines, both listening to the cable, simultaneously decide that it is free and try to send a frame? A collision occurs, and both of the transmissions are lost (Figure 4-5). A collision resembles the effect of two people talking at the same time: the listener hears a mixture of two voices and can't understand either one.

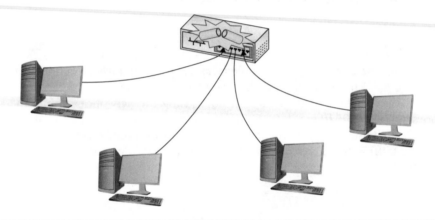

Figure 4-5 Collision!

It's easy for NICs to notice a collision. When two NICs send at the same time, the hub sends out the overlapping signals, and the NICs immediately know that a collision has occurred. When they detect a collision, both nodes immediately stop transmitting.

They then each generate a random number to determine how long to wait before trying again. If you imagine that each machine rolls its magic electronic dice and waits for that number of seconds, you wouldn't be too far from the truth, except that the amount of time an Ethernet node waits to retransmit is much shorter than one second (Figure 4-6). Whichever node generates the lowest random number begins its retransmission first, winning the competition to use the wire. The losing node then sees traffic on the wire and waits for the wire to be free again before attempting to retransmit its data.

Collisions are a normal part of the operation of an Ethernet network. Every Ethernet network wastes some amount of its available bandwidth dealing with these collisions. A properly running average Ethernet network has a maximum of 10 percent collisions. For every 20 frames sent, approximately 2 frames will collide and require a resend. Collision rates greater than 10 percent often point to damaged NICs or out-of-control software.

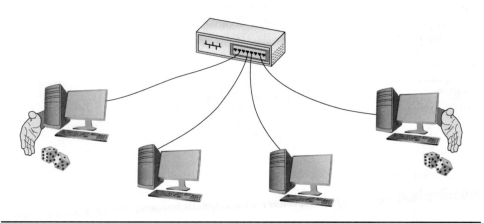

Figure 4-6   Rolling for timing

In an Ethernet network, a *collision domain* is a group of nodes that have the capability of sending frames at the same time as each other, resulting in collisions. A segment is certainly a collision domain, but there are ways to connect segments to create larger collision domains. If the collision domain gets too large, you'll start running into traffic problems that manifest as general network sluggishness. That's one of the reasons to break up networks into smaller groupings.

Early Ethernet Networks

Now we have the answers to many of the questions that faced those early Ethernet designers. MAC addresses identify each machine on the network. CSMA/CD determines when each machine should have access to the cable. But all this remains in the realm of theory—you still need to build the thing! Contemplating the physical network brings up numerous questions. What kind of cables should you use? What should they be made of? How long can they be? For these answers, turn to the IEEE 802.3 standard and two early implementations of Ethernet: 10BaseT and 10BaseFL.

10BaseT

In 1990, the IEEE 802.3 committee created a new version of Ethernet called *10BaseT* to modernize the first generations of Ethernet. Very quickly 10BaseT became the most popular network technology in the world, replacing competing and now long-gone competitors with names like Token Ring and AppleTalk. Over 99 percent of all networks use 10BaseT or one of its faster, newer, but very similar versions. The classic 10BaseT network consists of two or more computers connected to a central hub. The NICs connect with wires as specified by the 802.3 committee.

10BaseT hubs come in a variety of shapes and sizes to support different sizes of networks. The biggest differentiator between hubs is the number of *ports* (connections) that a single hub provides. A small hub might have only 4 ports, whereas a hub for a large network might have 48 ports. As you can imagine, the more ports on a hub, the more expensive the hub. Figure 4-7 shows two hubs. On the top is a small, 8-port hub for small offices or the home. It rests on a 12-port rack-mount hub for larger networks.

Figure 4-7
Two 10BaseT hubs

Regardless of size, all 10BaseT hubs need electrical power. Larger hubs will take power directly from a power outlet, whereas smaller hubs often come with an AC adapter. In either case, if the hub loses power, the entire segment will stop working.

 EXAM TIP If you ever run into a situation on a 10BaseT or later network in which none of the computers can get on the network, always check the hub first!

The name 10BaseT follows roughly the same naming convention used for earlier Ethernet cabling systems. The number *10* refers to the speed: 10 Mbps. The word *Base* refers to the signaling type: baseband. (*Baseband* means that the cable only carries one type of signal. Contrast this with *broadband*—as in cable television—where the cable carries multiple signals or channels.) The letter *T* refers to the type of cable used: twisted-pair.

 EXAM TIP The names of two earlier physical bus versions of Ethernet, 10Base5 and 10Base2, gave the maximum length of the bus. 10Base5 networks could be up to 500 meters long, for example, whereas 10Base2 could be almost 200 meters (though in practice, they topped out at 185 meters).

UTP

Officially, 10BaseT requires the use of CAT 3 (or higher), two-pair, *unshielded twisted-pair (UTP) cable*. One pair of wires sends data to the hub while the other pair receives data from the hub. Even though 10BaseT only requires two-pair cabling, everyone installs four-pair cabling to connect devices to the hub as insurance against the possible requirements of newer types of networking (Figure 4-8). Most UTP cables come with stranded Kevlar fibers to give the cable added strength, which, in turn, enables installers to pull on the cable without excessive risk of literally ripping it apart.

Figure 4-8

A typical four-pair CAT 5e unshielded twisted-pair cable

10BaseT also introduced the networking world to the *RJ-45 connector* (Figure 4-9). Each pin on the RJ-45 connects to a single wire inside the cable; this enables devices to put voltage on the individual wires within the cable. The pins on the RJ-45 are numbered from 1 to 8, as shown in Figure 4-10.

Figure 4-9

Two views of an RJ-45 connector

Figure 4-10

The pins on an RJ-45 connector are numbered 1 through 8.

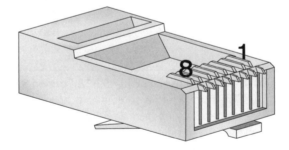

The 10BaseT standard designates some of these numbered wires for specific purposes. As mentioned earlier, although the cable has four pairs, 10BaseT uses only two of the pairs. 10BaseT devices use pins 1 and 2 to send data, and pins 3 and 6 to receive data. Even though one pair of wires sends data and another receives data, a 10BaseT device connected to a hub cannot send and receive simultaneously. The rules of CSMA/CD still apply: only one device can use the segment contained in the hub without causing a collision.

NICs that can communicate in only one direction at a time run in *half-duplex* mode. Later advances (as you'll see shortly) enabled NICs to send and receive at the same time, thus running in *full-duplex* mode.

An RJ-45 connector is usually called a *crimp*, and the act (some folks call it an art) of installing a crimp onto the end of a piece of UTP cable is called *crimping*. The tool used to secure a crimp onto the end of a cable is a *crimper*. Each wire inside a UTP cable must connect to the proper pin inside the crimp. Manufacturers color-code each wire within a piece of four-pair UTP to assist in properly matching the ends. Each pair of wires consists of a solid-colored wire and a striped wire: blue/blue-white, orange/orange-white, brown/brown-white, and green/green-white (Figure 4-11).

Figure 4-11
Color-coded
pairs

 NOTE The real name for RJ-45 is "8 Position 8 Contact (8P8C) modular plug." The name RJ-45 is so dominant, however, that nobody but the nerdiest of nerds calls it by its real name. Stick to RJ-45.

The Telecommunications Industry Association/Electronics Industries Alliance (TIA/EIA) defines the industry standard for correct crimping of four-pair UTP for 10BaseT networks. Two standards currently exist: *TIA/EIA 568A* and *TIA/EIA 568B*. Figure 4-12 shows the TIA/EIA 568A and TIA/EIA 568B color-code standards. Note that the wire pairs used by 10BaseT (1 and 2, 3 and 6) come from the same color pairs (green/green-white and orange/orange-white). Following an established color-code scheme, such as TIA/EIA 568A, ensures that the wires match up correctly at each end of the cable.

NOTE TIA/EIA 568C, the newest standard, includes the same wiring standards as TIA/EIA 568A and TIA/EIA 568B. It's all just wrapped up in a new name.

Figure 4-12
The TIA/EIA
568A and 568B
standards

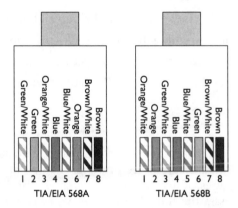

An easy trick to remembering the difference between 568A and 568B is the word "GO." The green and orange pairs are swapped between 568A and 568B, whereas the blue and brown pairs stay in the same place!

The ability to make your own Ethernet cables is a real plus for a network tech. With a reel of CAT 5e, a bag of RJ-45 connectors, a moderate investment in a crimping tool, and a little practice, you can kiss those mass-produced cables goodbye! You can make cables to your own length specifications, replace broken RJ-45 connectors that would otherwise mean tossing an entire cable—and, in the process, save your company or clients time and money.

 EXAM TIP For the CompTIA Network+ exam, you won't be tested on the TIA/EIA 568A or 568B color codes. Just know that they are industry-standard color codes for UTP cabling.

10BaseT Limits and Specifications

Like any other Ethernet cabling system, 10BaseT has limitations, both on cable distance and on the number of computers. The key distance limitation for 10BaseT is the distance between the hub and the computer. The twisted-pair cable connecting a computer to the hub may not exceed 100 meters in length. A 10BaseT hub can connect no more than 1024 computers, although that limitation rarely comes into play. It makes no sense for vendors to build hubs that large—or more to the point, that *expensive*—because excessive collisions can easily bog down Ethernet performance with far fewer than 1024 computers.

10BaseT Summary

- **Speed**   10 Mbps
- **Signal type**   Baseband
- **Distance**   100 meters between the hub and the node
- **Node limit**   No more than 1024 nodes per hub
- **Topology**   Star-bus topology: physical star, logical bus
- **Cable type**   CAT 3 or better UTP cabling with RJ-45 connectors

10BaseFL

Just a few years after the introduction of 10BaseT, a fiber-optic version, called *10BaseFL*, appeared. As you know from the previous chapter, fiber-optic cabling transmits data packets using pulses of light instead of using electrical current. Using light instead of electricity addresses the three key weaknesses of copper cabling. First, optical signals can travel much farther. The maximum length for a 10BaseFL cable is up to 2 kilometers, depending on how you configure it. Second, fiber-optic cable is immune to electrical interference, making it an ideal choice for high-interference environments. Third, the cable is much more difficult to tap into, making it a good choice for environments with security concerns. 10BaseFL uses *multimode* fiber-optic and employs either an SC or an ST connector.

NOTE   10BaseFL is often simply called "10BaseF."

Figure 4-13 shows a typical 10BaseFL card. Note that it uses two fiber connectors—one to send and one to receive. All fiber-optic networks use at least two fiber-optic cables. Although 10BaseFL enjoyed some popularity for a number of years, most networks today are using the same fiber-optic cabling to run far faster network technologies.

10BaseFL Summary

- **Speed**   10 Mbps
- **Signal type**   Baseband
- **Distance**   2000 meters between the hub and the node
- **Node limit**   No more than 1024 nodes per hub
- **Topology**   Star-bus topology: physical star, logical bus
- **Cable type**   Multimode fiber-optic cabling with ST or SC connectors

Figure 4-13
Typical 10BaseFL
card

So far you've seen two different flavors of Ethernet, 10BaseT and 10BaseFL. Even though these use different cabling and hubs, the actual packets are still Ethernet frames. As a result, interconnecting flavors of Ethernet is common. Because 10BaseT and 10BaseFL use different types of cable, you can use a *media converter* (Figure 4-14) to interconnect different Ethernet types.

Figure 4-14
Typical copper-
to-fiber Ethernet
media converter
(photo courtesy
of TRENDnet)

Extending and Enhancing Ethernet Networks

Once you have an Ethernet network in place, you can extend or enhance that network in several ways. You can install additional hubs to connect multiple local area networks, for example. A network bridge can connect two Ethernet segments, effectively doubling the size of a collision domain. You can also replace the hubs with better devices to reduce collisions.

Connecting Ethernet Segments

Sometimes, one hub is just not enough. Once an organization uses every port on its existing hub, adding more nodes requires adding hubs or a device called a bridge. Even fault tolerance can motivate an organization to add more hubs. If every node on the network connects to the same hub, that hub becomes a single point of failure—if it fails, everybody drops off the network. You can connect hubs in two ways: via an uplink port or a crossover cable. You can also connect Ethernet segments using a bridge.

Uplink Ports

Uplink ports enable you to connect two hubs using a *straight-through* cable. They're always clearly marked on the hub, as shown in Figure 4-15. To connect two hubs, insert one end of a cable to the uplink and the other cable to any one of the regular ports. To connect more than two hubs, you must daisy-chain your hubs by using one uplink port and one regular port. Figure 4-16 shows properly daisy-chained hubs. As a rule, you cannot daisy-chain more than four hubs together.

Figure 4-15
Typical uplink port

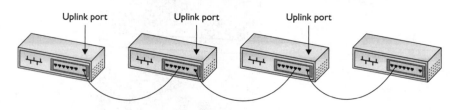

Figure 4-16   Daisy-chained hubs

You also cannot use a single central hub and connect multiple hubs to that single hub, as shown in Figure 4-17. It simply won't work.

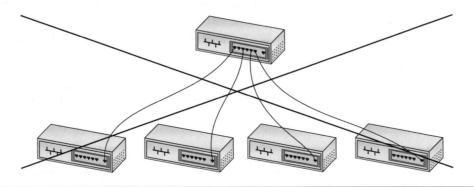

Figure 4-17   A hierarchical hub configuration will not work!

Working with uplink ports is sometimes tricky, so you need to take your time. Messing up and using a central hub is easy. Hub makers give their uplink ports many different names, such as crossover, MDI-X, and OUT. There are also tricks to using uplink ports. Refer to Figure 4-15 again. See the line connecting the uplink port and the port labeled 2X? You may use only one of those two ports, not both at the same time. Additionally, some hubs place a button for one of the ports; you press this button to make it either a regular port or an uplink port (Figure 4-18). Pressing the button electronically reverses the wires inside the hub.

Figure 4-18
Press-button port

When connecting hubs, remember the following:

- You can only daisy-chain hubs.
- Take time to figure out the uplink ports.
- If you plug hubs in incorrectly, no damage will occur—they just won't work.

 EXAM TIP   Two terms you might see on hubs and switches and, consequently, on the exam: MDI and MDIX (or MDI-X). A *media dependent interface (MDI)* is a regular port on a hub or switch. A *media dependent interface crossover (MDI-X)* is an uplink port.

Crossover Cables

Hubs can also connect to each other via special twisted-pair cables called crossover cables. A standard cable cannot be used to connect two hubs without using an uplink port because both hubs will attempt to send data on the second pair of wires (3 and 6) and will listen for data on the first pair (1 and 2). A *crossover cable* reverses the sending and receiving pairs on one end of the cable. One end of the cable is wired according to the TIA/EIA 568A standard, whereas the other end is wired according to the TIA/EIA 568B standard (Figure 4-19). With the sending and receiving pairs reversed, the hubs can hear each other; hence the need for two standards for connecting RJ-45 jacks to UTP cables.

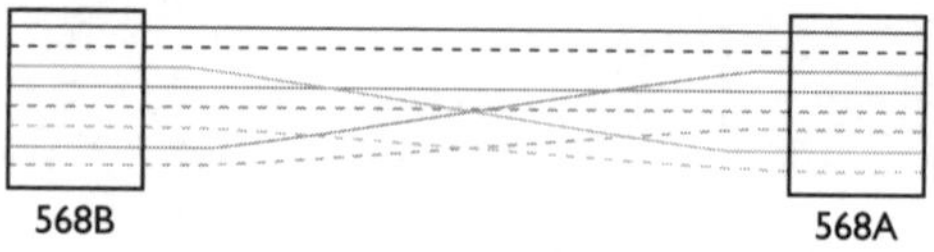

Figure 4-19

A crossover cable reverses the sending and receiving pairs.

568B   568A

A crossover cable connects to a regular port on each hub. Keep in mind that you can still daisy-chain even when you use crossover cables. Interestingly, many hubs, especially higher-end hubs, do not come with any uplink ports at all. In these cases, your only option is to use a crossover cable.

In a pinch, you can use a crossover cable to connect two computers together using 10BaseT NICs with no hub between them at all. This is handy for quickie connections, such as for a nice little home network or when you absolutely, positively must chase down a friend in a computer game!

Be careful about confusing crossover cables with uplink ports. First, never connect two hubs by their uplink ports with a straight-through cable. Take a straight-through cable; connect one end to the uplink port on one hub and the other end to any regular port on the other hub. Second, if you use a crossover cable, just plug each end into any handy regular port on each hub.

If you mess up your crossover connections, you won't cause any damage, but the connection will not work. Think about it. If you take a straight-through cable (that is, not a crossover cable) and try to connect two PCs directly, it won't work. Both PCs will try to use the same send and receive wires. When you plug the two PCs into a hub, the hub electronically crosses the data wires, so one NIC sends and the other can receive. If you plug a second hub to the first hub using regular ports, you essentially cross the cross and create a straight connection again between the two PCs! That won't work. Luckily, nothing gets hurt—except your reputation if one of your colleagues notes your mistake!

Bridges

The popularity and rapid implementation of Ethernet networks demanded solutions or workarounds for the limitations inherent in the technology. An Ethernet segment could only be so long and connect a certain number of computers. What if your network went beyond those limitations?

A *bridge* acts like a repeater or hub to connect two Ethernet segments, but it goes one step beyond—filtering and forwarding traffic between those segments based on the MAC addresses of the computers on those segments. This preserves precious bandwidth and makes a larger Ethernet network possible. To *filter* traffic means to stop it from crossing from one network to the next; to *forward* traffic means to pass traffic originating on one side of the bridge to the other.

 EXAM TIP   Because bridges work with MAC addresses, they operate at Layer 2, the Data Link layer, of the OSI networking model. They function in the Link/Network Interface layer of the TCP/IP model.

A newly installed Ethernet bridge initially behaves exactly like a repeater, passing frames from one segment to another. Unlike a repeater, however, a bridge monitors and records the network traffic, eventually reaching a point where it can begin to filter and forward. This capability makes the bridge more "intelligent" than a repeater. A new bridge usually requires only a few seconds to gather enough information to start filtering and forwarding.

Although bridges offer a good solution for connecting two segments and reducing bandwidth usage, these days you'll mainly find bridges used in wireless, rather than wired, networks. (I cover those kinds of bridges in Chapter 15.) Most networks have now turned to a different magic box—a switch—to extend and enhance an Ethernet network.

Switched Ethernet

As any fighter pilot will tell you, sometimes you just feel the need—the need for speed. While plain-vanilla 10BaseT Ethernet performed well enough for first-generation networks (which did little more than basic file and print sharing), by the early 1990s networks used more-demanding applications, such as Lotus Notes, SAP business management software, and Microsoft Exchange, which quickly saturated a 10BaseT network. Fortunately, those crazy kids over at the IEEE kept expanding the standard, giving the network tech in the trenches a new tool that provided additional bandwidth—the switch.

 NOTE   SAP originally stood for Systems Applications and Products when the company formed in the early 1970s. Like IBM, SAP is now just referred to by the letters.

The Trouble with Hubs

A classic 10BaseT network with a hub can only have one message on the wire at any time. When two computers send at the same time, the hub dutifully repeats both signals. The nodes recognize the collision and, following the rules of CSMA/CD, attempt to resend. Add in enough computers and the number of collisions increases, lowering the effective transmission speed for the whole network. A busy network becomes a slow network because all the computers share the same collision domain.

Switches to the Rescue

An Ethernet *switch* looks like a hub, because all nodes plug into it (Figure 4-20). But switches don't function like hubs inside. Switches come with extra smarts that enable them to take advantage of MAC addresses, effectively creating point-to-point connections between two conversing computers. This gives every conversation between two computers the full bandwidth of the network.

Figure 4-20
Hub (top) and
switch (bottom)
comparison

To see a switch in action, check out Figure 4-21. When you first turn on a switch, it acts exactly as though it were a hub, passing all incoming frames right back out to all the other ports. As it forwards all frames, however, the switch copies the source MAC addresses and quickly creates an electronic table of the MAC addresses of each connected computer. The table is called a *Source Address Table (SAT)*.

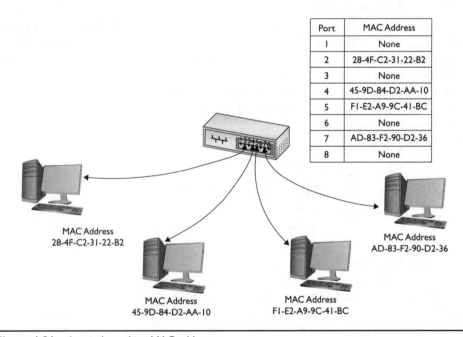

Port	MAC Address
1	None
2	28-4F-C2-31-22-B2
3	None
4	45-9D-84-D2-AA-10
5	F1-E2-A9-9C-41-BC
6	None
7	AD-83-F2-90-D2-36
8	None

MAC Address
28-4F-C2-31-22-B2

MAC Address
AD-83-F2-90-D2-36

MAC Address
45-9D-84-D2-AA-10

MAC Address
F1-E2-A9-9C-41-BC

Figure 4-21   A switch tracking MAC addresses

EXAM TIP One classic difference between a hub and a switch is in the repeating of frames during normal use. Although it's true that switches initially forward all frames, they filter by MAC address in regular use. Hubs never learn and always forward all frames.

As soon as this table is created, the switch begins to do something amazing. When a computer sends a frame into the switch destined for another computer on the same switch, the switch acts like a telephone operator, creating an on-the-fly connection between the two devices. While these two devices communicate, it's as though they are the only two computers on the network. Figure 4-22 shows this in action. Because the switch handles each conversation individually, each conversation runs at 10 Mbps.

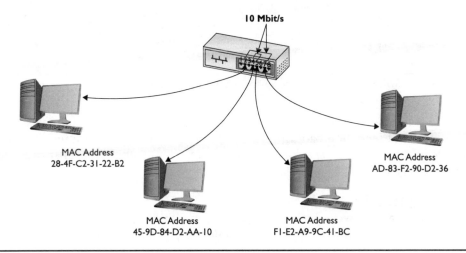

Figure 4-22 A switch making two separate connections

Each port on a switch is in its own collision domain, plus the switch can buffer incoming frames. That means that two nodes connected to the switch can send data at the same time and the switch will handle it without any collision.

With half-duplex switches, collisions can occur and the rules of CSMA/CD apply. These collisions can only happen between the switch and a node, not between two nodes, if the switch tries to send a frame to a node at the same time as the node tries to send a frame to the switch.

Network developers eventually figured out how to make switches and NICs run in full-duplex mode, so they could send and receive data at the same time. With full-duplex Ethernet, CSMA/CD is disabled and no collisions can occur. Each node will always get the full bandwidth of the network.

NOTE Because a switch filters traffic on MAC addresses (and MAC addresses run at Layer 2 of the OSI seven-layer model), they are sometimes called *Layer 2 switches*.

With full-duplex switched Ethernet, you can ignore the old rules about daisy-chaining that applied to hubs. Feel free to connect your switches pretty much any way you wish (Figure 4-23).

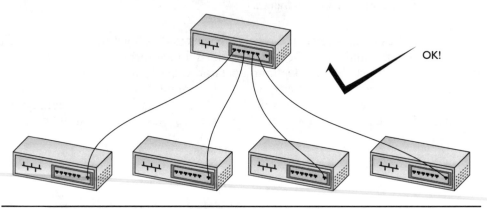

Figure 4-23   Switches are very commonly connected in a tree organization.

Unicast messages always go only to the intended recipient when you use a switch. The switch will send all broadcast messages to all the ports. You'll commonly hear a switched network called a *broadcast domain* to contrast it to a hub-based network with its *collision domain*.

Spanning Tree Protocol

Because you can connect switches together in any fashion, you can create redundant connections in a network. These are called *bridge loops* (Figure 4-24).

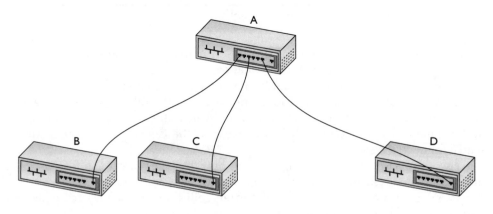

Figure 4-24   A bridge loop

EXAM TIP The CompTIA Network+ exam refers to bridge loops as *switching loops*. The terms mean the same thing, but bridge loop is more common. Be prepared for either term on the exam.

In the early days of switches, making a bridge loop in a network setup would bring the network crashing down. A frame could get caught in the loop, so to speak, and not reach its destination.

The Ethernet standards body adopted the *Spanning Tree Protocol (STP)* to eliminate the problem of accidental bridge loops. Switches with STP enabled can detect loops, communicate with other switches, and set the looped port's state to blocking.

STP-enabled switches use a frame called a *Bridge Protocol Data Unit (BPDU)* to communicate with each other to determine things like the distances between them and to keep track of changes on the network.

NOTE Switches today all have STP enabled and network designers create bridge loops in their networks to provide fault tolerance. Ports set as blocking still listen to the traffic on the network. If a link fails, the blocking port can become a forwarding port, thus enabling traffic to flow properly.

Troubleshooting Hubs and Switches

The hubs and simple switches described in this chapter generally function flawlessly for years without any need for a tech to do more than wipe dust off the top. Very occasionally you'll run into a hub or switch that has problems. These problems fall into three categories:

- Obvious physical damage
- Dead ports
- General flakiness

Diagnosing any of these problems follows a similar pattern. First, you'll recognize that a hub or switch might have problems because you've plugged a device in and the device can't connect to the network. Second, you should examine the switch for obvious damage. Third, look for link lights. If they're not flashing, try a different port. Fourth, don't forget to look at your cables. If anything looks bent, broken, or stepped on, you should replace it. A bad cable or improper cable type can lead to problems that point to a "failed" hub or switch when the true culprit is really the cable. Finally, use the tried and true method of replacing the hub or switch or the cable with a known good device.

NOTE When we get to modern higher-end switches in Chapter 12, you'll need to follow other procedures to do proper diagnostic work. We'll get there soon enough!

Chapter Review

Questions

1. Ethernet hubs take an incoming packet and _____ it out to the other connected ports.

    A. Amplify

    B. Repeat

    C. Filter

    D. Distort

2. What begins an Ethernet frame?

    A. MAC address

    B. Length

    C. Preamble

    D. CRC

3. What type of bus does 10BaseT use?

    A. Bus

    B. Ring

    C. Star bus

    D. Bus ring

4. What is the maximum distance that can separate a 10BaseT node from its hub?

    A. 50 meters

    B. 100 meters

    C. 185 meters

    D. 200 meters

5. When used for Ethernet, unshielded twisted pair uses what type of connector?

    A. RG-58

    B. RJ-45

    C. RJ-11

    D. RS-232

6. What is the maximum number of nodes that can be connected to a 10BaseT hub?

   A. 1024

   B. 500

   C. 100

   D. 185

7. Which of the following is not true of crossover cables?

   A. They are a type of twisted-pair cabling.

   B. They reverse the sending and receiving wire pairs.

   C. They are used to connect hubs.

   D. Both ends of a crossover cable are wired according to the TIA/EIA 568B standard.

8. Which of the following connectors are used by 10BaseFL cable? (Select two.)

   A. SC

   B. RJ-45

   C. RJ-11

   D. ST

9. Which networking devices can use the Spanning Tree Protocol (STP)?

   A. Hubs

   B. Media converters

   C. UTP cables

   D. Switches

10. What device directs packets based on MAC addresses?

   A. Router

   B. Hub

   C. Bridge

   D. Switch

Answers

1. **B.** Hubs are nothing more than multiport repeaters.

2. **C.** All Ethernet frames begin with a preamble.

3. **C.** 10BaseT uses a star-bus topology.

4. **B.** The maximum distance between a 10BaseT node and its hub is 100 meters.

5. **B.** UTP cable uses an RJ-45 connector when used for Ethernet. RG-58 is the type of coaxial cable used with 10Base2. RJ-11 is the standard four-wire connector used for regular phone lines. RS-232 is a standard for serial connectors.

6. **A.** A 10BaseT hub can connect no more than 1024 nodes (computers).

7. **D.** One end of a crossover cable is wired according to the TIA/EIA 568B standard; the other is wired according to the TIA/EIA 586A standard. This is what crosses the wire pairs and enables two hubs to communicate without colliding.

8. **A, D.** 10BaseFL uses two types of fiber-optic connectors called SC and ST connectors.

9. **D.** The Spanning Tree Protocol is unique to switches.

10. **C.** Any device that directs packets based on their MAC addresses is by definition a bridge.

Modern Ethernet

The CompTIA Network+ certification exam expects you to know how to

- 3.1 Categorize standard media types and associated properties: media converters, distance limitations
- 3.2 Categorize standard connector types based on network media: fiber
- 3.7 Compare and contrast different LAN technologies: 100BaseT, 100BaseTX, 100BaseFX, 1000BaseT, 1000BaseX, 10GBaseSR, 10GBaseLR, 10GBaseER, 10GBaseSW, 10GBaseLW, 10GBaseEW, and 10GBaseT

To achieve these goals, you must be able to

- Describe the varieties of 100-megabit Ethernet
- Discuss copper- and fiber-based Gigabit Ethernet
- Compare the competing varieties of 10 Gigabit Ethernet

Within a few years of its introduction, 10BaseT proved inadequate to meet the growing networking demand for speed. As with all things in the computing world, bandwidth is the key. Even with switching, the 10-Mbps speed of 10BaseT, seemingly so fast when first developed, quickly found a market clamoring for even faster speeds. This chapter looks at the improvements in Ethernet since 10BaseT. You'll read about 100-megabit standards and the several standards in Gigabit Ethernet. The chapter wraps up with the newest speed standards, 10 Gigabit Ethernet.

Test Specific

100-Megabit Ethernet

The quest to break 10-Mbps network speeds in Ethernet started in the early 1990s. By then, 10BaseT Ethernet had established itself as the most popular networking technology (although other standards, such as IBM's Token Ring, still had some market share). The goal was to create a new speed standard that made no changes to the actual Ethernet frames themselves. By doing this, the 802.3 committee ensured that different speeds of Ethernet could interconnect, assuming you had something that could handle the speed differences and a media converter if the connections were different.

100BaseT

If you want to make a lot of money in the technology world, create a standard and then get everyone else to buy into it. For that matter, you can even give the standard away and still make tons of cash if you have the inside line on making the hardware that supports the standard.

When it came time to come up with a new standard to replace 10BaseT, network hardware makers forwarded a large number of potential standards, all focused on the prize of leading the new Ethernet standard. As a result, two twisted-pair Ethernet standards appeared, *100BaseT4* and *100BaseTX*. 100BaseT4 used CAT 3 cable whereas 100BaseTX used CAT 5. By the late 1990s, 100BaseTX became the dominant 100-megabit Ethernet standard. 100BaseT4 disappeared from the market and today has been forgotten. As a result, we almost never say 100BaseTX, simply choosing to use the term *100BaseT*.

NOTE 100BaseT was at one time called *Fast Ethernet.* The term still sticks to the 100-Mbps standards—including 100BaseFX, which you'll read about in an upcoming section—even though there are now much faster versions of Ethernet.

100BaseTX (100BaseT) Summary

- **Speed** 100 Mbps
- **Signal type** Baseband
- **Distance** 100 meters between the hub and the node
- **Node limit** No more than 1024 nodes per hub
- **Topology** Star-bus topology: physical star, logical bus
- **Cable type** CAT 5e or better UTP or STP cabling with RJ-45 connectors

Upgrading a 10BaseT network to 100BaseT is not a small process. First, you need to make sure you have CAT 5 cable or better. This part isn't a big deal because almost all network cables installed in the past decade are at least CAT 5. Second, you must replace all the old 10BaseT NICs with 100BaseT NICs. Third, you need to replace the 10BaseT hub or switch with a 100BaseT hub or switch. Making this upgrade cost a lot in the early days of 100BaseT, so people clamored for a way to make the upgrade a little easier. This was accomplished via multispeed, auto-sensing NICs and hubs/switches.

Figure 5-1 shows a typical multispeed, auto-sensing 100BaseT NIC from the late 1990s. When this NIC first connects to a network, it starts to negotiate automatically with the hub or switch to determine the other device's highest speed. If they both do 100BaseT, then you get 100BaseT. If the hub or switch only does 10BaseT, then the NIC does 10BaseT. All of this happens automatically (Figure 5-2).

Figure 5-1
Typical 100BaseT
NIC

Figure 5-2
Auto-negotiation
in action

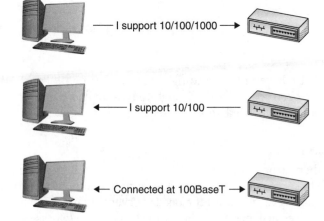

I support 10/100/1000 →

← I support 10/100

← Connected at 100BaseT →

NOTE If you want to sound like a proper tech, you need to use the right words. Techs don't actually say, "multispeed, auto-sensing," but rather "10/100." As in, "Hey, is that a 10/100 NIC you got there?" Now you're talking the talk!

Distinguishing a 10BaseT NIC from a 100BaseT NIC without close inspection is impossible. Look for something on the card to tell you its speed. Some NICs may have extra link lights to show the speed (see Chapter 6 for the scoop on link lights). Of course, you can always simply install the card, as shown in Figure 5-3, and see what the operating system says it sees!

Figure 5-3
Typical 100BaseT
NIC in Windows Vista

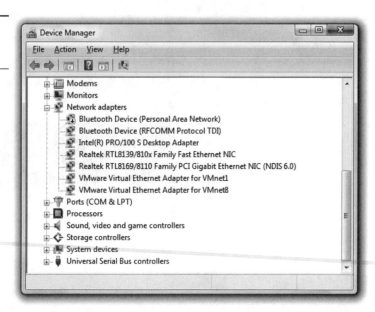

You'll also have trouble finding a true 10BaseT or 100BaseT NIC because multispeed NICs have been around long enough to have replaced any single-speed NIC. All modern NICs are multispeed and auto-sensing.

100BaseFX

Most Ethernet networks use UTP cabling, but quite a few use fiber-based networks instead. In some networks, using fiber simply makes more sense.

UTP cabling cannot meet the needs of every organization for three key reasons. First, the 100-meter distance limitation of UTP-based networks is inadequate for networks covering large buildings or campuses. Second, UTP's lack of electrical shielding makes it a poor choice for networks functioning in locations with high levels of electrical interference. Finally, the Maxwell Smarts and James Bonds of the world find UTP cabling (and copper cabling in general) easy to tap, making it an inappropriate choice for high-security environments. To address these issues, the IEEE 802.3 standard provides for a flavor of 100-megabit Ethernet using fiber-optic cable, called 100BaseFX.

EXAM TIP Installing networks in areas of high electrical interference used to require the use of *shielded twisted-pair (STP)* cabling rather than UTP. Even though you can still get STP cabling, its use is rare today. Most installations use fiber-optic cable in situations where UTP won't cut it. The exception to this rule is with relatively short cable runs through high-noise areas, like in a workshop. Swapping out a UTP cable with an STP cable is simpler and much less expensive than running fiber and changing NICs as well.

The *100BaseFX* standard saw quite a bit of interest for years, as it combined the high speed of 100-megabit Ethernet with the reliability of fiber optics. Outwardly, 100BaseFX looks exactly like 10BaseFL. Both use the same multimode fiber-optic cabling, and both use SC or ST connectors. 100BaseFX offers improved data speeds over 10BaseFL and equally long cable runs, supporting a maximum cable length of two kilometers.

NOTE Just as the old 10BaseFL was often called *10BaseF*, 100BaseFX is sometimes called simply *100BaseF*.

100BaseFX Summary

- **Speed**   100 Mbps
- **Signal type**   Baseband
- **Distance**   Two kilometers between the hub and the node
- **Node limit**   No more than 1024 nodes per hub
- **Topology**   Star-bus topology: physical star, logical bus
- **Cable type**   Multimode fiber-optic cabling with ST or SC connectors

NOTE The *Fiber Distributed Data Interface (FDDI)* flourished on college campuses during the 1990s because it could cover long distances and transfer data at the (then) blazing speed of 100 Mbps. FDDI used fiber-optic cables with a token bus network protocol over a ring topology. Fast Ethernet over UTP offered a much cheaper alternative when it became available, plus it was completely compatible with 10BaseT, so FDDI faded away.

Full-Duplex Ethernet

Early 100BaseT NICs, just like 10BaseT NICs, could send and receive data, but not at the same time—a feature called *half-duplex* (Figure 5-4). The IEEE addressed this characteristic shortly after adopting 100BaseT as a standard. By the late 1990s, most 100BaseT cards could auto-negotiate for full-duplex. With *full-duplex*, a NIC can send and receive at the same time, as shown in Figure 5-5.

Figure 5-4
Half-duplex: sending at the top, receiving at the bottom

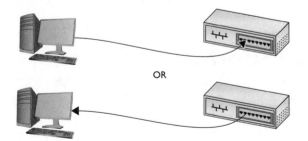

OR

Figure 5-5
Full-duplex

NOTE Full-duplex doesn't increase network speed, but it doubles network bandwidth. Imagine a one-lane road expanded to two lanes while keeping the speed limit the same. And if you recall from the previous chapter, going full-duplex disables CSMA/CD and eliminates collisions.

Almost all NICs today can go full-duplex. The NIC and the attached hub/switch determine full- or half-duplex during the auto-negotiation process. The vast majority of the time you simply let the NIC do its negotiation. Every operating system has some method to force the NIC to a certain speed/duplex, as shown in Figure 5-6.

Figure 5-6
Forcing speed
and duplex in
Windows 7

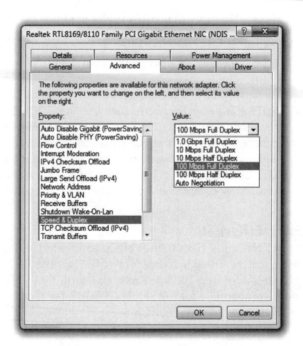

Gigabit Ethernet

By the end of the 1990s, the true speed junkie needed an even more powerful version of Ethernet. In response, the IEEE created *Gigabit Ethernet*, which today is the most common type of Ethernet found on new NICs.

The IEEE approved two different versions of Gigabit Ethernet. The most widely implemented solution, published under the IEEE *802.3ab* standard, is called *1000BaseT*. The other version, published under the *802.3z* standard and known as *1000BaseX*, is divided into a series of standards, with names such as 1000BaseCX, 1000BaseSX, and 1000BaseLX.

1000BaseT uses four-pair UTP or STP cabling to achieve gigabit performance. Like 10BaseT and 100BaseT, 1000BaseT has a maximum cable length of 100 meters on a segment. 1000BaseT connections and ports look exactly like the ones on a 10BaseT or 100BaseT network. 1000BaseT is the dominant Gigabit Ethernet standard.

NOTE The term *Gigabit Ethernet* is more commonly used than *1000BaseT*.

The 802.3z standards require a bit more discussion. Let's look at each of these solutions in detail to see how they work.

1000BaseCX

1000BaseCX uses a unique cable known as twinaxial cable (Figure 5-7). Most techs shorten the cable name to *twinax*. Twinaxial cables are special shielded 150-Ohm cables with a length limit of only 25 meters. 1000BaseCX has made little progress in the Gigabit Ethernet market.

Figure 5-7
Twinaxial cable

1000BaseSX

Many networks upgrading to Gigabit Ethernet use the *1000BaseSX* standard. 1000BaseSX uses multimode fiber-optic cabling to connect systems, with a generous maximum cable length of 220 to 500 meters; the exact length is left up to the various manufacturers. 1000BaseSX uses an 850-nm (nanometer) wavelength LED to transmit light on the fiber-optic cable. 1000BaseSX devices look similar to 100BaseFX devices, and although both standards can use several types of connectors, 1000BaseSX devices commonly use LC, while 100BaseFX devices frequently use SC. (See "New Fiber Connectors" later in the chapter for the scoop on LC connectors.)

1000BaseLX

1000BaseLX is the long-distance carrier for Gigabit Ethernet. 1000BaseLX uses single-mode (laser) cables to shoot data at distances up to 5 kilometers—and some manufacturers use special repeaters to increase that to distances as great as 70 kilometers! The Ethernet folks are trying to position this as the Ethernet backbone of the future, and already some large carriers are beginning to adopt 1000BaseLX. You may live your whole life and never see a 1000BaseLX device, but odds are good that you will encounter connections that use such devices in the near future. 1000BaseLX connectors look like 1000BaseSX connectors.

New Fiber Connectors

Around the time that Gigabit Ethernet first started to appear, two problems began to surface with ST and SC connectors. First, ST connectors are relatively large, twist-on connectors, requiring the installer to twist the cable when inserting or removing it. Twisting is not a popular action with fiber-optic cables, as the delicate fibers may fracture. Also, big-fingered techs have a problem with ST connectors if the connectors are too closely packed: they can't get their fingers around them. SC connectors snap in and out, making them much more popular than STs. SC connectors are also large, however, and the folks who make fiber networking equipment wanted to pack more connectors onto their boxes. This brought about two new types of fiber connectors, known generically as *Small Form Factor (SFF)* connectors. The first SFF connector—the *Mechanical Transfer Registered Jack (MT-RJ)*, shown in Figure 5-8—gained popularity with important companies like Cisco and is still quite common.

Figure 5-8
MT-RJ connector

You read about the second type of popular SFF connector, the *Local Connecter (LC)*, back in Chapter 3—it's shown in Figure 5-9. LC-type connectors are very popular, particularly in the United States, and many fiber experts consider the LC-type connector to be the predominant fiber connector.

Figure 5-9

LC-type connector

LC and MT-RJ are the most popular types of SFF fiber connectors, but many others exist, as outlined in Table 5-1. The fiber industry has no standard beyond ST and SC connectors, which means that different makers of fiber equipment may have different connections.

Standard	Cabling	Cable Details	Connectors	Length
1000BaseCX	Copper	Twinax	Twinax	25 m
1000BaseSX	Multimode fiber	850 nm	Variable, commonly LC	220–500 m
1000BaseLX	Single-mode fiber	1300 nm	Variable, commonly LC and SC	5 km
1000BaseT	CAT 5e/6 UTP	Four-pair/full-duplex	RJ-45	100 m

Table 5-1   Gigabit Ethernet Summary

Implementing Multiple Types of Gigabit Ethernet

Because Ethernet packets don't vary among the many flavors of Ethernet, network hardware manufacturers have long built devices capable of supporting more than one flavor right out of the box. Ancient hubs supported 10Base2 and 10BaseT at the same time, for example.

You can also use dedicated *media converters* to connect any type of Ethernet cabling together. Most media converters are plain-looking boxes with a port or dongle on either side. They come in all flavors:

- Single-mode fiber (SMF) to UTP/STP
- Multimode fiber (MMF) to UTP/STP
- Fiber to coaxial
- SMF to MMF

 EXAM TIP The CompTIA Network+ exam competencies erroneously describe some media converters as single-mode fiber to *Ethernet* and multi-mode fiber to *Ethernet*. It's all Ethernet! Don't be surprised if you get one of those terms on the exam, however. Now you'll know what they mean.

Finally, the Gigabit Ethernet folks created a standard for modular ports called a *gigabit interface converter (GBIC)*. With many Gigabit Ethernet switches and other hardware, you can simply pull out a GBIC module that supports one flavor of Gigabit Ethernet and plug in another. You can replace an RJ-45 port GBIC, for example, with an SC GBIC, and it'll work just fine. Electronically, the switch or other gigabit device is just that—Gigabit Ethernet—so the physical connections don't matter. Ingenious!

10 Gigabit Ethernet

The ongoing demand for bandwidth on the Internet means that the networking industry is continually reaching for faster LAN speeds. *10 Gigabit Ethernet (10 GbE)* is showing up in high-level LANs, with the anticipation that it will trickle-down to desktops in the near future.

 NOTE There are proposed Ethernet standards that go way beyond 10-Gbps speeds, including a 100 GbE proposal, but nothing is fully standardized as of this writing. Today, 10 GbE is the reigning king of network speeds.

Because 10 GbE is still a new technology, there are a large number of standards in existence. Over time some of these standards will certainly grow in popularity, but most will disappear. For now, though, the landscape is in flux. 10 GbE has a number of fiber standards and two copper standards. 10 GbE was first and foremost designed with fiber optics in mind. As a result, 10 GbE copper products have only been for sale since 2008.

Fiber-based 10 GbE

When the IEEE members sat down to formalize specifications on Ethernet running at 10 Gbps, they faced several challenges. First, they had to maintain the integrity of the Ethernet frame. Data is king, after all, and the goal was to create a network that could interoperate with any other Ethernet network. Second, they had to figure out how to transfer those frames at such blazing speeds. This second challenge had some interesting ramifications because of two factors. They could use the traditional Physical layer mechanisms defined by the Ethernet standard. But a perfectly usable ~10-Gbps fiber network, called *SONET*, was already in place and being used for wide area networking (WAN) transmissions. What to do?

NOTE Chapter 14 covers SONET in great detail. For now, think of it as a data transmission standard that's different from the LAN Ethernet standard.

The IEEE created a whole set of 10 GbE standards that could use traditional LAN Physical layer mechanisms, plus a set of standards that could take advantage of the SONET infrastructure and run over the WAN fiber. To make the 10-Gbps jump as easy as possible, the IEEE also recognized the need for different networking situations. Some implementations require data transfers that can run long distances over single-mode fiber, for example, whereas others can make do with short-distance transfers over multimode fiber. This led to a lot of standards for 10 GbE.

The 10 GbE standards are defined by several factors: the type of fiber used, the wavelength of the laser or lasers, and the Physical layer signaling type. These factors also define the maximum signal distance.

The IEEE uses specific letter codes with the standards to help sort out the differences so you know what you're implementing or supporting. All the standards have names in the following format: "10GBase" followed by two other characters, what I'll call *xy*. The *x* stands for the type of fiber (usually, though not officially) and the wavelength of the laser signal; the *y* stands for the Physical layer signaling standard. The *y* code is always either *R* for LAN-based signaling or *W* for SONET/WAN-based signaling. The *x* differs a little more, so let's take a look.

10GBaseS*y* uses a short-wavelength (850 nm) signal over multimode fiber. The maximum fiber length is 300 meters, although this length will vary depending on the type of multimode fiber used. *10GBaseSR* (Figure 5-10) is used for Ethernet LANs, and *10GBaseSW* is used to connect to SONET devices.

Standard	Fiber Type	Wavelength	Physical Layer Signaling	Maximum Signal Length
10GBaseSR	Multimode	850 nm	LAN	26–300 m
10GBaseSW	Multimode	850 nm	SONET/WAN	26–300 m

Figure 5-10
A 10GBaseSR NIC (photo courtesy of Intel Corporation)

10GBaseL*y* uses a long-wavelength (1310 nm) signal over single-mode fiber. The maximum fiber length is 10 kilometers, although this length will vary depending on the type of single-mode fiber used. *10GBaseLR* connects to Ethernet LANs and *10GBaseLW* connects to SONET equipment. 10GBaseLR is the most popular and least expensive 10 GbE media type.

Standard	Fiber Type	Wavelength	Physical Layer Signaling	Maximum Signal Length
10GBaseLR	Single-mode	1310 nm	LAN	10 km
10GBaseLW	Single-mode	1310 nm	SONET/WAN	10 km

10GBaseE*y* uses an extra-long-wavelength (1550 nm) signal over single-mode fiber. The maximum fiber length is 40 kilometers, although this length will vary depending on the type of single-mode fiber used. *10GBaseER* works with Ethernet LANs and *10GBaseEW* connects to SONET equipment.

Standard	Fiber Type	Wavelength	Physical Layer Signaling	Maximum Signal Length
10GBaseER	Single-mode	1550 nm	LAN	40 km
10GBaseEW	Single-mode	1550 nm	SONET/WAN	40 km

The 10 GbE fiber standards do not define the type of connector to use and instead leave that to manufacturers (see the upcoming section "10 GbE Physical Connections").

The Other 10 Gigabit Ethernet Fiber Standards

Manufacturers have shown, in these early days of 10 GbE implementation, both creativity and innovation in taking advantage of both existing fiber and the most cost-effective equipment. This has led to a variety of standards that are not covered by the CompTIA Network+ competencies, but that you should know about nevertheless. The top three as of this writing are 10GBaseL4, 10GBaseLRM, and 10GBaseZR.

The 10GBaseL4 standard uses four lasers at a 1300-nanometer wavelength over legacy fiber. On FDDI-grade multimode cable, 10GBaseL4 can support up to 300-meter transmissions. The range increases to 10 kilometers over single-mode fiber.

The 10GBaseLRM standard uses the long wavelength signal of 10GBaseLR but over legacy multimode fiber. The standard can achieve a range of up to 220 meters, depending on the grade of fiber cable.

Finally, some manufacturers have adopted the 10GBaseZR "standard," which isn't part of the IEEE standards at all (unlike 10GBaseL4 and 10GBaseLRM). Instead, the manufacturers have created their own set of specifications. 10GBaseZR networks use a 1550-nanometer wavelength over single-mode fiber to achieve a range of a whopping 80 kilometers. The standard can work with both Ethernet LAN and SONET/WAN infrastructure.

Copper-based 10 GbE

It took until 2006 for the IEEE to come up with a standard for 10 GbE running on twisted-pair cabling—called, predictably, 10GBaseT. *10GBaseT* looks and works exactly like the slower versions of UTP Ethernet. The only downside is that 10GBaseT running on CAT 6 has a maximum cable length of only 55 meters. The updated CAT 6a standard enables 10GBaseT to run at the standard distance of 100 meters. Table 5-2 summarizes the 10 GbE standards.

Standard	Cabling	Wavelength/Cable Details	Connectors	Length
10GBaseSR/SW	Multimode fiber	850 nm	Not defined	26–300 m
10GBaseLR/LW	Single-mode fiber	1310 nm	Variable, commonly LC	10 km
10GBaseER/EW	Single-mode fiber	1550 nm	Variable, commonly LC and SC	40 km
10GBaseT	CAT 6/6a UTP	Four-pair/full-duplex	RJ-45	55/100 m

Table 5-2   10 GbE Summary

10 GbE Physical Connections

This hodgepodge of 10 GbE types might have been the ultimate disaster for hardware manufacturers. All types of 10 GbE send and receive the same signal; only the physical medium is different. Imagine a single router that had to come out in seven different versions to match all these types! Instead, the 10 GbE industry simply chose not to define the connector types and devised a very clever, very simple concept called *multisource agreements (MSAs)*. An MSA transceiver plugs into your 10 GbE equipment, enabling you to convert from one media type to another by inserting the right transceiver. Unfortunately, there have been as many as four different competing MSA types in the past few years. Figure 5-11 shows a typical MSA called XENPAK.

For now, 10 GbE equipment is the exclusive domain of high-bandwidth LANs and WANs, including parts of the big-pipe Internet connections.

Figure 5-11
XENPAK MSA

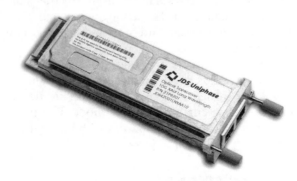

 NOTE Not all 10 GbE manufacturers use MSAs in their equipment.

Backbones

The beauty and the challenge of the vast selection of Ethernet flavors is deciding which one to use in your network. The goal is to give your users as fast a network response time as possible, combined with keeping costs at a reasonable level. To combine these two issues, most network administrators find that a multispeed Ethernet network works best. In a multispeed network, a series of high-speed (relative to the rest of the network) switches maintain a backbone network. No computers, other than possibly servers, attach directly to this backbone. Figure 5-12 shows a typical backbone network. Each floor has its own switch that connects to every node on the floor. In turn, each of these switches also has a separate high-speed connection to a main switch that resides in the office's computer room.

To make this work, you need switches with separate, dedicated, high-speed ports like the ones shown in Figure 5-13. The add-on ports on the switches run straight to the high-speed backbone switch.

Know Your Ethernets!

This single chapter is little more than a breakdown of the evolution of Ethernet since the old 10BaseT standard. Make sure you know the details of these Ethernet versions and take advantage of the summaries and tables to recognize the important points of each type.

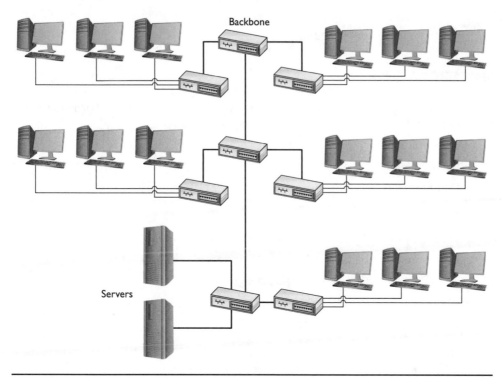

Figure 5-12 Typical network configuration showing backbone

Figure 5-13
Switches with
dedicated, high-
speed add-on ports

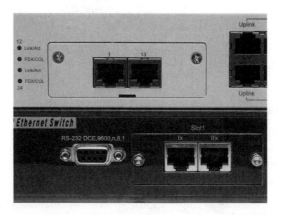

Additionally, keep in mind that you've only just begun to delve into the world of switching. The book has covered thus far only the functions of a basic switch. There is a lot more to know in terms of the capabilities of these powerful devices, but first you need to understand networking at a deeper level.

Chapter Review

Questions

1. With 100BaseT, what is the maximum distance between the hub (or switch) and the node?

   A. 1000 meters

   B. 400 meters

   C. 100 meters

   D. 150 meters

2. What type of cable and connector does 100BaseFX use?

   A. Multimode fiber with ST or SC connectors

   B. STP CAT 6 with RJ-45 connectors

   C. Single-mode fiber with MT-RJ connectors

   D. UTP CAT 5e with RJ-45 connectors

3. How many pairs of wires do 10BaseT and 100BaseT use?

   A. 4

   B. 1

   C. 3

   D. 2

4. What standard does IEEE 802.3ab describe?

   A. 1000BaseLX

   B. 1000BaseT

   C. 1000BaseCX

   D. 1000BaseSX

5. What is the big physical difference between 1000BaseSX and 100BaseFX?

   A. 1000BaseSX uses the SC connector exclusively.

   B. 1000BaseSX is single-mode, whereas 100BaseFX is multimode.

   C. 1000BaseSX uses the ST connector exclusively.

   D. There is no difference.

6. What is the maximum distance for 1000BaseLX without repeaters?

    A. 1 mile

    B. 2,500 meters

    C. 20,000 feet

    D. 5,000 meters

7. What is a big advantage to using fiber-optic cable?

    A. Fiber is common glass; therefore, it's less expensive.

    B. Fiber is not affected by EM interference.

    C. Making custom cable lengths is easier with fiber.

    D. All that orange fiber looks impressive in the network closet.

8. How many wire pairs does 1000BaseT use?

    A. 1

    B. 2

    C. 3

    D. 4

9. What is the standard connector for the 10 GbE fiber standard?

    A. ST

    B. SC

    C. MT-RJ

    D. There is no standard.

10. What is the maximum cable length of 10GBaseT on CAT 6?

    A. 55 meters

    B. 100 meters

    C. 20 meters

    D. 70 meters

Answers

1. **C.** The maximum distance is 100 meters.

2. **A.** 100BaseFX uses multimode fiber with either ST or SC connectors.

3. **D.** 10BaseT and 100BaseT use two wire pairs.

4. **B.** IEEE 802.3ab is the 1000BaseT standard (also known as Gigabit Ethernet).

5. **A.** While 1000BaseSX looks similar to 100BaseFX, the former does not allow the use of the ST connector.

6. **D.** 1000BaseLX can go for 5000 meters (5 kilometers).

7. **B.** Because fiber uses glass and light, it is not affected by EM interference.

8. **D.** 1000BaseT uses all four pairs of wires.

9. **D.** There is no standard connector; the 10 GbE committee has left this up to the manufacturers.

10. **A.** With CAT 6 cable, 10GBaseT is limited to 55 meters.

Installing a Physical Network

6

The CompTIA Network+ Certification exam expects you to know how to

- 3.2 Categorize standard connector types based on network media: patch panel, 110 block
- 3.6 Given a scenario, troubleshoot common physical connectivity problems
- 3.7 Compare and contrast different LAN technologies: bonding
- 3.8 Identify components of wiring distribution
- 4.2 Given a scenario, use appropriate hardware tools to troubleshoot connectivity issues

To achieve these goals, you must be able to

- Recognize and describe the functions of basic components in a structured cabling system
- Explain the process of installing structured cable
- Install a network interface card
- Perform basic troubleshooting on a structured cable network

Armed with the knowledge of previous chapters, it's time to start going about the business of actually constructing a physical network. This might seem easy; after all, the most basic network is nothing more than a switch with a number of cables snaking out to all of the PCs on the network (Figure 6-1).

Figure 6-1
What an orderly
looking network!

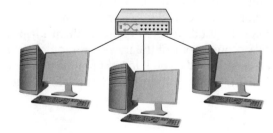

On the surface, such a network setup is absolutely correct, but if you tried to run a network using only a switch and cables running to each system, you'd have some serious practical issues. In the real world, you need to deal with physical obstacles like walls and ceilings. You also need to deal with those annoying things called *people*. People are incredibly adept at destroying physical networks. They unplug switches, trip over cables, and rip connectors out of NICs with incredible consistency unless you protect the network from their destructive ways. Although the simplified switch-and-a-bunch-of-cables type of network can function in the real world, the network clearly has some problems that need addressing before it can work safely and efficiently (Figure 6-2).

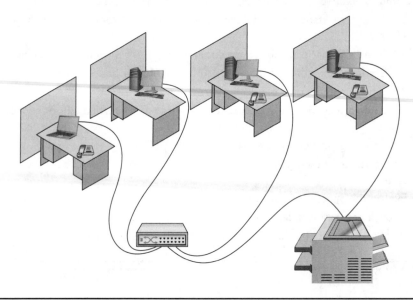

Figure 6-2 A real-world network

This chapter takes the abstract discussion of network technologies from previous chapters into the concrete reality of real networks. To achieve this goal, it marches you through the process of installing an entire network system from the beginning. The chapter starts by introducing you to *structured cabling*, the critical set of standards used all over the world to install physical cabling in a safe and orderly fashion. It then delves into the world of larger networks—those with more than a single switch—and shows you some typical methods used to organize them for peak efficiency and reliability. Next, you'll take a quick tour of the most common NICs used in PCs, and see what it takes to install them. Finally, you'll look at how to troubleshoot cabling and other network devices, including an introduction to some fun diagnostic tools.

Historical/Conceptual

Understanding Structured Cabling

If you want a functioning, dependable, real-world network, you need a solid under-standing of a set of standards, collectively called *structured cabling*. These standards, defined by the Telecommunications Industry Association/Electronic Industries Alliance (TIA/EIA)—yup, the same folks who tell you how to crimp an RJ-45 onto the end of a UTP cable—give professional cable installers detailed standards on every aspect of a cabled network, from the type of cabling to use to the position of wall outlets.

The CompTIA Network+ exam requires you to understand the basic concepts involved in designing a network and installing network cabling and to recognize the components used in a real network. The CompTIA Network+ exam does not, however, expect you to be as knowledgeable as a professional network designer or cable installer. Your goal is to understand enough about real-world cabling systems to communicate knowledgeably with cable installers and to perform basic troubleshooting. Granted, by the end of this chapter, you'll have enough of an understanding to try running your own cable (I certainly run my own cable), but consider that knowledge a handy bit of extra credit.

The idea of structured cabling is to create a safe, reliable cabling infrastructure for all of the devices that may need interconnection. Certainly this applies to computer net-works, but also to telephone, video—anything that might need low-power, distributed cabling.

 NOTE A structured cabling system is useful for more than just computer networks. You'll find structured cabling defining telephone networks and video conferencing setups, for example.

You should understand three issues with structured cabling. Cable basics start the picture, with switches, cabling, and PCs. You'll then look at the components of a net-work, such as how the cable runs through the walls and where it ends up. This section wraps up with an assessment of connections leading outside your network.

Cable Basics—A Star Is Born

This exploration of the world of connectivity hardware starts with the most basic of all networks: a switch, some UTP cable, and a few PCs—in other words, a typical physical star network (Figure 6-3).

Figure 6-3
A switch
connected by
UTP cable to
two PCs

No law of physics prevents you from installing a switch in the middle of your office and running cables on the floor to all the computers in your network. This setup works, but it falls apart spectacularly when applied to a real-world environment. Three problems present themselves to the network tech. First, the exposed cables running along the floor are just waiting for someone to trip over them, damaging the network and giving that person a wonderful lawsuit opportunity. Possible accidents aside, simply moving and stepping on the cabling will, over time, cause a cable to fail due to wires breaking or RJ-45 connectors ripping off cable ends. Second, the presence of other electrical devices close to the cable can create interference that confuses the signals going through the wire. Third, this type of setup limits your ability to make any changes to the network. Before you can change anything, you have to figure out which cables in the huge rat's nest of cables connected to the switch go to which machines. Imagine *that* troubleshooting nightmare!

"Gosh," you're thinking (okay, I'm thinking it, but you should be, too), "there must be a better way to install a physical network." A better installation would provide safety, protecting the star from vacuum cleaners, clumsy coworkers, and electrical interference. It would have extra hardware to organize and protect the cabling. Finally, the new and improved star network installation would feature a cabling standard with the flexibility to enable the network to grow according to its needs and then to upgrade when the next great network technology comes along.

As you have no doubt guessed, I'm not just theorizing here. In the real world, the people who most wanted improved installation standards were the ones who installed cable for a living. In response to this demand, the TIA/EIA developed standards for cable installation. The TIA/EIA 568 standards you learned about in earlier chapters are only part of a larger set of TIA/EIA standards all lumped together under the umbrella of structured cabling.

NOTE Installing structured cabling properly takes a startlingly high degree of skill. Thousands of pitfalls await inexperienced network people who think they can install their own network cabling. Pulling cable requires expensive equipment, a lot of hands, and the ability to react to problems quickly. Network techs can cost employers a lot of money—not to mention losing their good jobs—by imagining they can do it themselves without the proper knowledge. If you are interested in learning more details about structured cabling, an organization called BICSI (www.bicsi.org) provides a series of widely recognized certifications for the cabling industry.

Test Specific

Structured Cable Network Components

Successful implementation of a basic structured cabling network requires three essential ingredients: a telecommunications room, horizontal cabling, and a work area. Let's zero in on one floor of Figure 5-12 from the previous chapter. All the cabling runs from individual PCs to a central location, the *telecommunications room* (Figure 6-4). What equipment goes in there—a switch or a telephone system—is not the important thing. What matters is that all the cables concentrate in this one area.

Telecommunications room

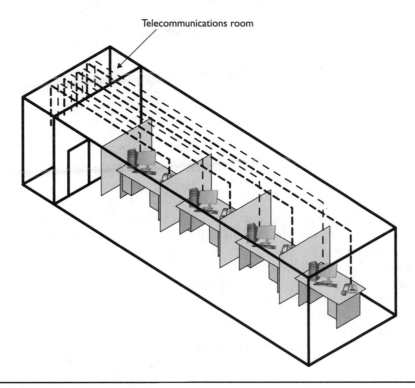

Figure 6-4   Telecommunications room

All cables run horizontally (for the most part) from the telecommunications room to the PCs. This cabling is called, appropriately, *horizontal cabling*. A single piece of installed horizontal cabling is called a *run*. At the opposite end of the horizontal cabling from the telecommunications room is the work area. The *work area* is often simply an office or cubicle that potentially contains a PC and a telephone. Figure 6-5 shows both the horizontal cabling and work areas.

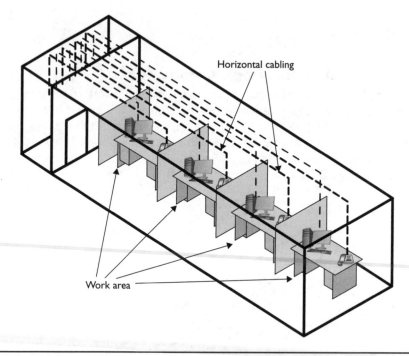

Figure 6-5   Horizontal cabling and work area

Each of the three parts of a basic star network—the telecommunications room, the horizontal cabling, and the work area(s)—must follow a series of strict standards designed to ensure that the cabling system is reliable and easy to manage. The cabling standards set by TIA/EIA enable techs to make sensible decisions on equipment installed in the telecommunications room, so let's tackle horizontal cabling first, and then return to the telecommunications room. We'll finish up with the work area.

Horizontal Cabling

A horizontal cabling run is the cabling that goes more or less horizontally from a work area to the telecommunications room. In most networks, this cable is a CAT 5e or better UTP, but when you move into structured cabling, the TIA/EIA standards define a number of other aspects of the cable, such as the type of wires, number of pairs of wires, and fire ratings.

EXAM TIP   A single piece of cable that runs from a work area to a telecommunications room is called a *run*.

Solid Core vs. Stranded Core

All UTP cables come in one of two types: solid core or stranded core. Each wire in *solid core* UTP uses a single solid wire. With *stranded core*, each wire is actually a bundle of tiny wire strands. Each of these cable types has its benefits and downsides. Solid core is a better conductor, but it is stiff and will break if handled too often or too roughly. Stranded core is not quite as good a conductor, but it will stand up to substantial handling without breaking. Figure 6-6 shows a close-up of solid and stranded core UTP.

Figure 6-6
Solid and
stranded
core UTP

TIA/EIA specifies that horizontal cabling should always be solid core. Remember, this cabling is going into your walls and ceilings, safe from the harmful effects of shoes and vacuum cleaners. The ceilings and walls enable you to take advantage of the better conductivity of solid core without the risk of cable damage. Stranded cable also has an important function in a structured cabling network, but I need to discuss a few more parts of the network before I talk about where to use stranded UTP cable.

Number of Pairs

Pulling horizontal cables into your walls and ceilings is a time-consuming and messy business, and not a process you want to repeat, if at all possible. For this reason, most cable installers recommend using the highest CAT rating you can afford. Many years ago, I would also mention that you should use four-pair UTP, but today, four-pair is assumed. Four-pair UTP is so common that it's difficult, if not impossible, to find two-pair UTP.

NOTE   Unlike previous CAT standards, TIA/EIA defines CAT 5e and later as four-pair-only cables.

You'll find larger bundled UTP cables in higher-end telephone setups. These cables hold 25 or even 100 pairs of wires (Figure 6-7).

Figure 6-7
25-pair UTP

Choosing Your Horizontal Cabling

In the real world, network people only install CAT 5e or CAT 6 UTP, although CAT 6a is also starting to show up as 10GBaseT begins to see acceptance. Installing higher-rated cabling is done primarily as a hedge against new network technologies that may require a more advanced cable. Networking *caveat emptor* (buyer beware): many network installers take advantage of the fact that a lower CAT level will work on most networks and bid a network installation using the lowest-grade cable possible.

The Telecommunications Room

The telecommunications room is the heart of the basic star. This room—technically called the *intermediate distribution frame (IDF)*—is where all the horizontal runs from all the work areas come together. The concentration of all this gear in one place makes the telecommunications room potentially one of the messiest parts of the basic star. Even if you do a nice, neat job of organizing the cables when they are first installed, networks change over time. People move computers, new work areas are added, network topologies are added or improved, and so on. Unless you impose some type of organization, this conglomeration of equipment and cables decays into a nightmarish mess.

 NOTE The telecommunications room is also known as an *intermediate distribution frame (IDF)*, as opposed to the main distribution frame (MDF), which we will discuss later in the chapter.

Fortunately, the TIA/EIA structured cabling standards define the use of specialized components in the telecommunications room that make organizing a snap. In fact, it might be fair to say that there are too many options! To keep it simple, we're going to stay with the most common telecommunications room setup and then take a short peek at some other fairly common options.

Equipment Racks

The central component of every telecommunications room is one or more equipment racks. An *equipment rack* provides a safe, stable platform for all the different hardware components. All equipment racks are 19 inches wide, but they vary in height from two- to three-foot-high models that bolt onto a wall (Figure 6-8) to the more popular floor-to-ceiling models (Figure 6-9).

Figure 6-8
A short
equipment rack

Figure 6-9
A floor-to-ceiling
rack

NOTE Equipment racks evolved out of the railroad signaling racks from the 19th century. The components in a rack today obviously differ a lot from railroad signaling, but the 19" width has remained the standard for well over a 100 years.

You can mount almost any network hardware component into a rack. All manufacturers make rack-mounted switches that mount into a rack with a few screws. These switches are available with a wide assortment of ports and capabilities. There are even rack-mounted servers, complete with slide-out keyboards, and rack-mounted uninterruptible power supplies (UPSs) to power the equipment (Figure 6-10).

Figure 6-10
A rack-mounted
UPS

All rack-mounted equipment uses a height measurement known simply as a *U*. A U is 1.75 inches. A device that fits in a 1.75-inch space is called a 1U; a device designed for a 3.5-inch space is a 2U; and a device that goes into a 7-inch space is called a 4U. Most rack-mounted devices are 1U, 2U, or 4U. The rack in Figure 6-9 is called a 42U rack to reflect the total number of Us it can hold.

Patch Panels and Cables

Ideally, once you install horizontal cabling, you should never move it. As you know, UTP horizontal cabling has a solid core, making it pretty stiff. Solid core cables can handle some rearranging, but if you insert a wad of solid core cables directly into your switches, every time you move a cable to a different port on the switch, or move the switch itself, you will jostle the cable. You don't have to move a solid core cable many times before one of the solid copper wires breaks, and there goes a network connection!

Luckily for you, you can easily avoid this problem by using a patch panel. A *patch panel* is simply a box with a row of female connectors (ports) in the front and permanent connections in the back, to which you connect the horizontal cables (Figure 6-11).

Figure 6-11
Typical patch
panels

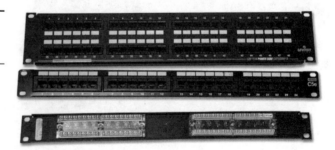

The most common type of patch panel today uses a special type of connecter called a *110 block*, or sometimes a *110-punchdown block*. UTP cables connect to a 110 block using a *punchdown tool*. Figure 6-12 shows a typical punchdown tool, and Figure 6-13 shows the punchdown tool punching down individual strands.

Figure 6-12
Punchdown tool

Figure 6-13
Punching down
a 110 block

The punchdown block has small metal-lined grooves for the individual wires. The punchdown tool has a blunt end that forces the wire into the groove. The metal in the groove slices the cladding enough to make contact.

 NOTE Make sure you insert the wires according to the same standard (TIA/EIA 568A or TIA/EIA 568B) on both ends of the cable. If you don't, you might swap the sending and receiving wires (known as *TX/RX reversed*) and inadvertently create a crossover cable.

At one time, the older 66-punchdown block patch panel, found in just about every commercial telephone installation (Figure 6-14), saw some use in PC networks. The 110 block introduces less crosstalk than 66 blocks, so most high-speed network installations use the former for both telephone service and PC LANs. Given their large installed base, it's still common to find a group of 66-block patch panels in a telecommunications room separate from the PC network's 110-block patch panels.

Figure 6-14
66-block patch panels

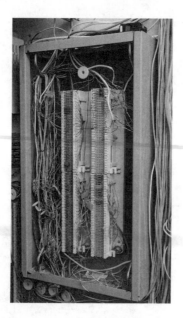

 EXAM TIP The CompTIA Network+ exam uses the terms *110 block* and *66 block* exclusively to describe the punchdown blocks common in telecommunication. In the field, in contrast, and in manuals and other literature, you'll see the punchdown blocks referred to as *110-punchdown blocks* and *66-punchdown blocks* as well. Some manufacturers even split punchdown into two words, i.e., punch down. Be prepared to be nimble in the field, but expect 110 block and 66 block on the exam.

Not only do patch panels prevent the horizontal cabling from being moved, but they are also your first line of defense in organizing the cables. All patch panels have space in the front for labels, and these labels are the network tech's best friend! Simply place a tiny label on the patch panel to identify each cable, and you will never have to experience that sinking feeling of standing in the telecommunications room of your nonfunctioning network, wondering which cable is which. If you want to be a purist, there is an official, and rather confusing, TIA/EIA labeling methodology called *TIA/EIA 606*, but a number of real-world network techs simply use their own internal codes (Figure 6-15).

Figure 6-15
Typical patch
panels with labels

NOTE The TIA/EIA 606 standard covers proper labeling and documentation of cabling, patch panels, and wall outlets. If you want to know how the pros label and document a structured cabling system (and you've got US$360 to blow), check out the TIA/EIA 606 standard hardcopy from TIA.

Patch panels are available in a wide variety of configurations that include different types of ports and numbers of ports. You can get UTP, STP, or fiber ports, and some manufacturers combine several different types on the same patch panel. Panels are available with 8, 12, 24, 48, or even more ports.

UTP patch panels, like UTP cables, come with CAT ratings, which you should be sure to check. Don't blow a good CAT 6 cable installation by buying a cheap patch panel—get a CAT 6 patch panel! A CAT 6 panel can handle the 250-MHz frequency used by CAT 6 and offers lower crosstalk and network interference. A higher-rated panel supports earlier standards, so you can use a CAT 6 or even CAT 6a rack with CAT 5e cabling. Most manufacturers proudly display the CAT level right on the patch panel (Figure 6-16).

Figure 6-16
CAT level on
patch panel

Once you have installed the patch panel, you need to connect the ports to the switch through *patch cables*. Patch cables are short (typically two- to five-foot) UTP cables. Patch cables use stranded rather than solid cable, so they can tolerate much more handling. Even though you can make your own patch cables, most people buy premade ones. Buying patch cables enables you to use different-colored cables to facilitate organization (yellow for accounting, blue for sales, or whatever scheme works for you). Most prefabricated patch cables also come with a reinforced (booted) connector specially designed to handle multiple insertions and removals (Figure 6-17).

Figure 6-17
Typical patch
cable

A telecommunications room doesn't have to be a special room dedicated to computer equipment. You can use specially made cabinets with their own little built-in equipment racks that sit on the floor or attach to a wall, or you can use a storage room as long as the equipment can be protected from the other items stored there. Fortunately, the demand for telecommunications rooms has been around for so long that most office spaces have premade telecommunications rooms, even if they are no more than closets in smaller offices.

At this point, the network is taking shape (Figure 6-18). The TIA/EIA horizontal cabling is installed and the telecommunications room is configured. Now it's time to address the last part of the structured cabling system: the work area.

The Work Area

From a cabling standpoint, a work area is nothing more than a wall outlet that serves as the termination point for horizontal network cables: a convenient insertion point for a PC and a telephone. (In practice, of course, the term "work area" includes the office or cubicle.) A wall outlet itself consists of one or two female jacks to accept the cable, a mounting bracket, and a face-plate. You connect the PC to the wall outlet with a patch cable (Figure 6-19).

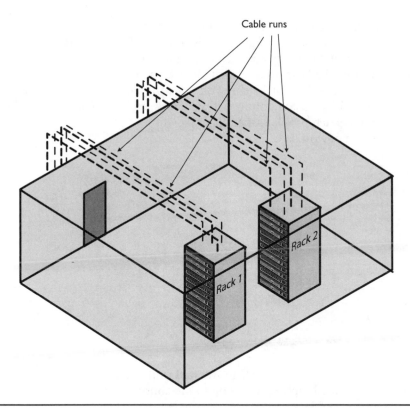

Cable runs

Rack 1

Rack 2

Figure 6-18   Network taking shape, with racks installed and horizontal cabling run

Figure 6-19

Typical work
area outlet

The female RJ-45 jacks in these wall outlets also have CAT ratings. You must buy CAT-rated jacks for wall outlets to go along with the CAT rating of the cabling in your network. In fact, many network connector manufacturers use the same connectors in the wall outlets that they use on the patch panels. These modular outlets significantly increase ease of installation. Make sure you label the outlet to show the job of each connector (Figure 6-20). A good outlet will also have some form of label that identifies its position on the patch panel. Proper documentation of your outlets will save you an incredible amount of work later.

Figure 6-20
Properly labeled
outlet

The last step is connecting the PC to the wall outlet. Here again, most folks use a patch cable. Its stranded cabling stands up to the abuse caused by moving PCs, not to mention the occasional kick.

You'll recall from Chapter 5 that 10/100/1000BaseT networks specify a limit of 100 meters between a hub or switch and a node. Interestingly, though, the TIA/EIA 568 specification allows only UTP cable lengths of 90 meters. What's with the missing 10 meters? Have you figured it out? Hint: the answer lies in the discussion we've just been having. Ding! Time's up! The answer is … the patch cables! Patch cables add extra distance between the switch and the PC, so TIA/EIA compensates by reducing the horizontal cabling length.

The work area may be the simplest part of the structured cabling system, but it is also the source of most network failures. When a user can't access the network and you suspect a broken cable, the first place to look is the work area.

Structured Cable—Beyond the Star

Thus far you've seen structured cabling as a single star topology on a single floor of a building. Let's now expand that concept to an entire building and learn the terms used by the structured cabling folks, such as the demarc and NIU, to describe this much more complex setup.

NOTE Structured cabling goes beyond a single building and even describes methods for interconnecting multiple buildings. The CompTIA Network+ certification exam does not cover interbuilding connections.

You can hardly find a building today that isn't connected to both the Internet and the telephone company. In many cases, this is a single connection, but for now, let's treat them as separate connections.

As you saw in the previous chapter, a typical building-wide network consists of a high-speed backbone that runs vertically through the building and connects to multispeed switches on each floor that, in turn, service the individual PCs on that floor. A dedicated telephone cabling backbone that enables the distribution of phone calls to individual telephones runs alongside the network cabling. While every telephone installation varies, most commonly you'll see one or more strands of 25-pair UTP cables running to the 66 block in the telecommunications room on each floor (Figure 6-21).

Figure 6-21
25-pair running
to local 66-block

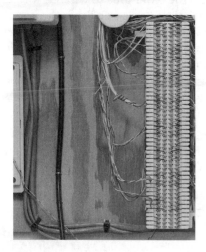

Demarc

Connections from the outside world—whether network or telephone—come into a building at a location called a *demarc*, short for *demarcation point*. The term "demarc" refers to the physical location of the connection and marks the dividing line of responsibility for the functioning of the network. You take care of the internal functioning; the person or company that supplies the upstream service to you must support connectivity and function on the far side of the demarc.

In a private home, the DSL or cable modem supplied by your ISP is a *network interface unit (NIU)* that serves as a demarc between your home network and your ISP, and most homes have a network interface box, like the one shown in Figure 6-22, that provides the connection for your telephone.

Figure 6-22
Typical home
network
interface box

 NOTE The terms used to describe the devices that often mark the demarcation point in a home or office get tossed about with wild abandon. Various manufacturers and technicians call them network interface units, network interface boxes, or network interface devices. (Some techs call them demarcs, just to muddy the waters further, but we won't go there.) By name or by initial—NIU, NIB, or NID—it's all the same thing, the box that marks the point where your responsibility begins on the inside.

In an office environment, the demarc is usually more complex, given that a typical building simply has to serve a much larger number of telephones and computers. Figure 6-23 shows the demarc for a midsized building, showing both Internet and telephone connections coming in from the outside.

Figure 6-23
Typical office
demarc

NOTE The best way to think of a demarc is in terms of responsibility. If something breaks on one side of the demarc, it's your problem; on the other side, it's the ISP/phone company's problem.

One challenge to companies that supply ISP/telephone services is the need to diagnose faults in the system. Most of today's NIUs come with extra "smarts" that enable the ISP or telephone company to determine if the customer has disconnected from the NIU. These special (and very common) NIUs are known as *smart jacks*. Smart jacks also have the very handy capability to set up a remote loopback—critical for loopback testing when you're at one end of the connection and the other connection is blocks or even miles away.

Connections Inside the Demarc

After the demarc, network and telephone cables connect to some type of box, owned by the customer, that acts as the primary distribution tool for the building. Any cabling that runs from the NIU to whatever box is used by the customer is the *demarc extension*. For telephones, the cabling might connect to a special box called a *multiplexer* and, on the LAN side, almost certainly to a powerful switch. This switch usually connects to a patch panel. This patch panel, in turn, leads to every telecommunications room in the building. This main patch panel is called a *vertical cross-connect*. Figure 6-24 shows an example of a fiber patch panel acting as a vertical cross-connect for a building.

Figure 6-24
LAN vertical
cross-connect

Telephone systems also use vertical cross-connects. Figure 6-25 shows a vertical cross-connect for a telephone system. Note the large number of 25-pair UTP cables feeding out of this box. Each 25-pair cable leads to a telecommunications room on a floor of the building.

Figure 6-25
Telephone
vertical cross-
connect

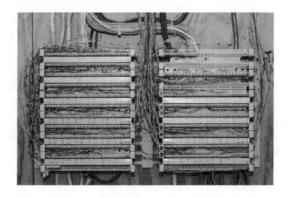

The combination of demarc, telephone cross-connects, and LAN cross-connects needs a place to live in a building. The room that stores all of this equipment is known as a *main distribution frame (MDF)* to distinguish it from the multiple IDF rooms (a.k.a. telecommunications rooms) that serve individual floors.

The ideal that every building should have a single demarc, a single MDF, and multiple IDFs is only that—an ideal. Every structured cabling installation is unique and must adapt to the physical constraints of the building provided. One building may serve multiple customers, creating the need for multiple NIUs each serving a different customer. A smaller building may combine a demarc, MDF, and IDF into a single room. With structured cabling, the idea is to appreciate the terms while, at the same time, appreciate that it's the actual building and the needs of the customers that determine the actual design of a structured cabling system.

Installing Structured Cabling

A professional installer always begins a structured cabling installation by first assessing your site and planning the installation in detail before pulling a single piece of cable. As the customer, your job is to work closely with the installer. That means locating floor plans, providing access, and even putting on old clothes and crawling along with the installer as he or she combs through your ceilings, walls, and closets. Even though you're not the actual installer, you must understand the installation process, so you can help the installer make the right decisions for your network.

Structured cabling requires a lot of planning. You need to know if the cables from the work areas can reach the telecommunications room—is the distance less than the 90-meter limit dictated by the TIA/EIA standard?

How will you route the cable? What path should each run take to get to the wall outlets? Don't forget that just because a cable looks like it will reach, there's no guarantee that it will. Ceilings and walls often include hidden surprises like firewalls—big, thick, concrete walls designed into buildings that require a masonry drill or a jackhammer to punch through. Let's look at the steps that go into proper planning.

Getting a Floor Plan

First, you need a blueprint of the area. If you ever contact an installer and he or she doesn't start by asking for a floor plan, fire them immediately and get one who does. The floor plan is the key to proper planning; a good floor plan shows you the location of closets that could serve as telecommunications rooms, alerts you to any firewalls in your way, and gives you a good overall feel for the scope of the job ahead.

If you don't have a floor plan—and this is often the case with homes or older buildings—you'll need to create your own. Go get a ladder and a flashlight—you'll need them to poke around in ceilings, closets, and crawl spaces as you map out the location of rooms, walls, and anything else of interest to the installation. Figure 6-26 shows a typical do-it-yourself floor plan, drawn out by hand.

Figure 6-26
Hand-drawn
network
floor plan

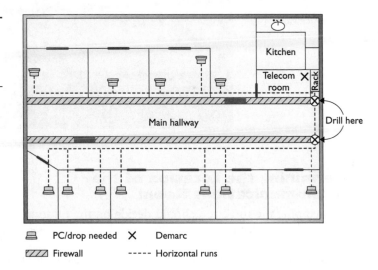

Mapping the Runs

Now that you have your floor plan, you need to map the cable runs. Here's where you run around the work areas, noting the locations of existing or planned systems to determine where to place each cable drop. A *cable drop* is the location where the cable comes out of the wall in the workstation. You should also talk to users, management, and other interested parties to try to understand their plans for the future. Installing a few extra drops now is much easier than installing them a year from now when those two unused offices suddenly find themselves with users who immediately need networked computers!

EXAM TIP Watch out for the word *drop*, as it has more than one meaning. A single run of cable from the telecommunications room to a wall outlet is often referred to as a "drop." The word "drop" is also used to define a new run coming through a wall outlet that does not yet have a jack installed.

At this point, cost first raises its ugly head. Face it: cables, drops, and the people who install them cost money! The typical price for a network installation is around US $150 per drop. Find out how much you want to spend and make some calls. Most network installers price their network jobs by quoting a per-drop cost.

While you're mapping your runs, you have to make another big decision: Do you want to run the cables in the walls or outside them? Many companies sell wonderful external *raceway* products that adhere to your walls, making for a much simpler, though less neat, installation than running cables in the walls (Figure 6-27). Raceways make good sense in older buildings or when you don't have the guts—or the rights—to go into the walls.

Figure 6-27
A typical raceway

Determining the Location of the Telecommunications Room

While mapping the runs, you should decide on the location of your telecommunications room. When deciding on this location, keep five issues in mind:

- **Distance**   The telecommunications room must be located in a spot that won't require cable runs longer than 90 meters. In most locations, keeping runs under 90 meters requires little effort, as long as the telecommunications room is placed in a central location.

- **Power**   Many of the components in your telecommunications room need power. Make sure you provide enough! If possible, put the telecommunications room on its own dedicated circuit; that way, when someone blows a circuit in the kitchen, it doesn't take out the entire network.

- **Humidity**   Electrical components and water don't mix well. (Remind me to tell you about the time I installed a rack in an abandoned bathroom and the toilet that later exploded.) Remember that dryness also means low humidity. Avoid areas with the potential for high humidity, such as a closet near a pool or the room where the cleaning people leave mop buckets full of water. Of course, any well air-conditioned room should be fine—which leads to the next big issue…

- **Cooling**   Telecommunications rooms tend to get warm, especially if you add a couple of server systems and a UPS. Make sure your telecommunications room has an air-conditioning outlet or some other method of keeping the room cool. Figure 6-28 shows how I installed an air-conditioning duct in my small equipment closet. Of course, I did this only after I discovered that the server was repeatedly rebooting due to overheating!

Figure 6-28
An A/C duct cooling a telecommunications room

- **Access**   Access involves two different issues. First, it means preventing unauthorized access. Think about the people you want and don't want messing around with your network, and act accordingly. In my small office, the equipment closet literally sits eight feet from me, so I don't concern myself too much with unauthorized access. You, on the other hand, may want to consider placing a lock on the door of your telecommunications room if you're concerned that unscrupulous or unqualified people might try to access it.

One other issue to keep in mind when choosing your telecommunications room is expandability. Will this telecommunications room be able to grow with your network? Is it close enough to be able to service any additional office space your company may acquire nearby? If your company decides to take over the floor above you, can you easily run vertical cabling to another telecommunications room on that floor from this room? While the specific issues will be unique to each installation, keep thinking "expansion" as you design—your network will grow, whether or not you think so now!

So, you've mapped your cable runs and established your telecommunications room—now you're ready to start pulling cable!

Pulling Cable

Pulling cable is easily one of the most thankless and unpleasant jobs in the entire networking world. It may not look that hard from a distance, but the devil is in the details. First of all, pulling cable requires two people if you want to get the job done quickly;

having three people is even better. Most pullers like to start from the telecommunications room and pull toward the drops. In an office area with a drop ceiling, pullers will often feed the cabling along the run by opening ceiling tiles and stringing the cable via hooks or *cable trays* that travel above the ceiling (Figure 6-29). Professional cable pullers have an arsenal of interesting tools to help them move the cable horizontally, including telescoping poles, special nylon pull ropes, and even nifty little crossbows and pistols that can fire a pull rope long distances!

Figure 6-29
Cable trays over
a drop ceiling

Cable trays are standard today, but a previous lack of codes or standards for handling cables led to a nightmare of disorganized cables in drop ceilings all over the world. Any cable puller will tell you that the hardest part of installing cables is the need to work around all the old cable installations in the ceiling (Figure 6-30).

Figure 6-30
Messy cabling
nightmare

Local codes, TIA/EIA, and the National Electrical Code (NEC) all have strict rules about how you pull cable in a ceiling. A good installer uses either hooks or trays, which provide better cable management, safety, and protection from electrical interference (Figure 6-31). The faster the network, the more critical good cable management becomes. You probably won't have a problem laying UTP directly on top of a drop ceiling if you just want a 10BaseT network, and you might even get away with this for 100BaseT—but forget about doing this with Gigabit or beyond. Cable installation companies are making a mint from all the CAT 5 and earlier network cabling installations that need to be redone to support Gigabit Ethernet.

Figure 6-31
Nicely run cables

Running cable horizontally requires relatively little effort, compared to running the cable down from the ceiling to a pretty faceplate at the work area, which often takes a lot of skill. In a typical office area with sheetrock walls, the installer first decides on the position for the outlet, generally using a stud finder to avoid cutting on top of a stud. Once the worker cuts the hole (Figure 6-32), most installers drop a line to the hole using a weight tied to the end of a nylon pull rope (Figure 6-33). They can then attach the network cable to the pull rope and pull it down to the hole. Once the cable is pulled through the new hole, the installer puts in an outlet box or a low-voltage *mounting bracket* (Figure 6-34). This bracket acts as a holder for the faceplate.

Figure 6-32
Cutting a hole

Figure 6-33
Locating a
dropped
pull rope

Figure 6-34
Installing a
mounting
bracket

Back in the telecommunications room, the many cables leading to each work area are consolidated and organized in preparation for the next stage: making connections. A truly professional installer takes great care in organizing the equipment closet. Figure 6-35 shows a typical installation using special cable guides to bring the cables down to the equipment rack.

Figure 6-35
End of cables
guided to rack

Making Connections

Making connections consists of connecting both ends of each cable to the proper jacks. This step also includes the most important step in the entire process: testing each cable run to ensure that every connection meets the requirements of the network that will use it. Installers also use this step to document and label each cable run—a critical step too often forgotten by inexperienced installers, and one you need to verify takes place!

Connecting the Work Areas

Let's begin by watching an installer connect a cable run. In the work area, that means the cable installer will now crimp a jack onto the end of the wire and mount the faceplate to complete the installation (Figure 6-36).

Figure 6-36
Crimping a jack

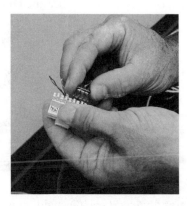

Note the back of the jack shown in Figure 6-36. This jack uses the popular 110-punchdown connection just like the one shown earlier in the chapter for patch panels. All 110 connections have a color code that tells you which wire to punch into which connection on the back of the jack.

Rolling Your Own Patch Cables

Although most people prefer simply to purchase premade patch cables, making your own is fairly easy. To make your own, use stranded UTP cable that matches the CAT level of your horizontal cabling. Stranded cable also requires specific crimps, so don't use crimps designed for solid cable. Crimping is simple enough, although getting it right takes some practice.

Figure 6-37 shows the two main tools of the crimping trade: an RJ-45 crimper with built-in stripper and a pair of wire snips. Professional cable installers naturally have a wide variety of other tools as well.

Figure 6-37
Crimper and snips

Here are the steps for properly crimping an RJ-45 onto a UTP cable. If you have some crimps, cable, and a crimping tool handy, follow along!

1. Cut the cable square using RJ-45 crimpers or scissors.
2. Strip off ½ inch of plastic jacket from the end of the cable (Figure 6-38).

Figure 6-38
Properly stripped
cable

3. Slowly and carefully insert each individual wire into the correct location according to either TIA/EIA 568A or B (Figure 6-39). Unravel as little as possible.

Figure 6-39
Inserting the
individual strands

4. Insert the crimp into the crimper and press (Figure 6-40). Don't worry about pressing too hard; the crimper has a stop to prevent you from using too much pressure.

Figure 6-40
Crimping the cable

Figure 6-41 shows a nicely crimped cable. Note how the plastic jacket goes into the crimp.

Figure 6-41
Properly
crimped cable

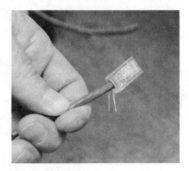

A good patch cable should include a boot. Figure 6-42 shows a boot being slid onto a newly crimped cable. Don't forget to slide each boot onto the patch cable *before* you crimp both ends!

Figure 6-42
Adding a boot

After making a cable, you need to test it to make sure it's properly crimped. Read the section on testing cable runs later in this chapter to see how to test them.

Connecting the Patch Panels

Connecting the cables to patch panels requires you to deal with three issues. The first issue is patch cable management. Figure 6-43 shows the front of a small network's equipment rack—note the complete lack of cable management!

Managing patch cables means using the proper cable management hardware. Plastic D-rings guide the patch cables neatly along the sides and front of the patch panel. Finger boxes are rectangular cylinders with slots in the front; the patch cables run into the open ends of the box, and individual cables are threaded through the fingers on their way to the patch panel, keeping them neatly organized.

Figure 6-43
Bad cable
management

Creativity and variety abound in the world of cable-management hardware—there are as many different solutions to cable management as there are ways to screw it up. Figure 6-44 shows a rack using good cable management—these patch cables are well secured using cable-management hardware, making them much less susceptible to damage from mishandling. Plus, it looks much nicer!

Figure 6-44
Good cable
management

The second issue to consider when connecting cables is the overall organization of the patch panel as it relates to the organization of your network. Organize your patch panel so it mirrors the layout of your network. You can organize according to the physical layout, so the different parts of the patch panel correspond to different parts of your office space—for example, the north and south sides of the hallway. Another popular way to organize patch panels is to make sure they match the logical layout of the network, so the different user groups or company organizations have their own sections of the patch panel.

Finally, proper patch panel cable management means documenting everything clearly and carefully. This way, any competent technician can follow behind you and troubleshoot connectivity problems. Good techs draw diagrams!

Testing the Cable Runs

Well, in theory, your horizontal cabling system is now installed and ready for a switch and some systems. Before you do this, though, you must test each cable run. Someone new to testing cable might think that all you need to do is verify that each jack has been properly connected. Although this is an important and necessary step, the interesting problem comes after that: verifying that your cable run can handle the speed of your network.

Before I go further, let me be clear: a typical network admin/tech cannot properly test a new cable run. TIA/EIA provides a series of incredibly complex and important standards for testing cable, requiring a professional cable installer. The testing equipment alone totally surpasses the cost of most smaller network installations. Advanced network testing tools easily cost over US$5,000, and some are well over US$10,000! Never fear, though—a number of lower-end tools work just fine for basic network testing.

 NOTE The test tools described here also enable you to diagnose network problems.

Most network admin types staring at a potentially bad cable want to know the following:

- How long is this cable? If it's too long, the signal will degrade to the point that it's no longer detectable on the other end.
- Are any of the wires broken or not connected in the crimp? If a wire is broken, it no longer has *continuity* (a complete, functioning connection).
- If there is a break, where is it? It's much easier to fix if the location is detectable.
- Are all of the wires terminated in the right place in the plug or jack?
- Is there electrical or radio interference from outside sources? UTP is susceptible to electromagnetic interference.
- Is the signal from any of the pairs in the same cable interfering with another pair?

To answer these questions you must verify that both the cable and the terminated ends are correct. Making these verifications requires a *cable tester*. Various models of cable testers can answer some or all of these questions, depending on the amount of money you are willing to pay. At the low end of the cable tester market are devices that only test for continuity. These inexpensive (under US$100) testers are often called *continuity testers* (Figure 6-45). Many of these testers require you to insert both ends of the cable into the tester. Of course, this can be a bit of a problem if the cable is already installed in the wall!

Figure 6-45
Continuity tester

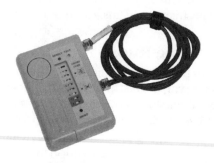

Better testers can run a *wiremap* test that goes beyond mere continuity, testing that all the wires on both ends of the cable connect to the right spot. A wiremap test will pick up shorts, crossed wires, and more.

 NOTE Many techs and network testing folks use the term *wiremap* to refer to the proper connectivity for wires, as in, "Hey Joe, check the wiremap!"

A multimeter works perfectly well to test for continuity, assuming you can place its probes on each end of the cable. Set the multimeter to its continuity setting if it has one (Figure 6-46) or to Ohms. With the latter setting, if you have a connection, you get zero Ohms, and if you don't have a connection, you get infinite Ohms.

Figure 6-46
Multimeter

NOTE If you have a multimeter with probes too large to connect to individual contacts on an RJ-45, you can use an old tech trick to finesse the problem. Take a patch cable and cut off about two feet, so you have a short cable with one end bare. Strip an inch of the cladding away from the bare end to expose the wires. Strip a little of the sheath off each wire and plug the cable into the jack. Now you can test continuity by putting the probes directly onto the wire!

Medium-priced testers (~US$400) certainly test continuity and wiremap and include the additional capability to determine the length of a cable; they can even tell you where a break is located on any of the individual wire strands. This type of cable tester (Figure 6-47) is generically called a *time domain reflectometer (TDR)*. Most medium-priced testers come with a small loopback device to insert into the far end of the cable, enabling the tester to work with installed cables. This is the type of tester you want to have around!

Figure 6-47

A typical medium-priced TDR called a Microscanner

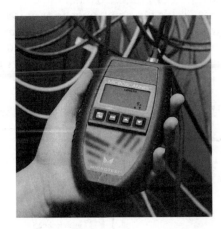

If you want a device that fully tests a cable run to the very complex TIA/EIA standards, the price shoots up fast. These higher-end testers can detect things the lesser testers cannot, such as crosstalk and attenuation.

Crosstalk poses a threat to properly functioning cable runs. Today's UTP cables consist of four pairs of wires, all squished together inside a plastic tube. When you send a signal down one of these pairs, the other pairs pick up some of the signal, as shown in Figure 6-48. This is called *crosstalk*.

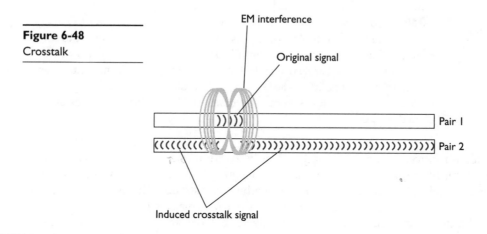

Figure 6-48
Crosstalk

Every piece of UTP in existence generates crosstalk. Worse, when you crimp the end of a UTP cable to a jack or plugs, crosstalk increases. A poor-quality crimp creates so much crosstalk that a cable run won't operate at its designed speed. To detect crosstalk, a normal-strength signal is sent down one pair of wires in a cable. An electronic detector, connected on the same end of the cable as the end emanating the signal, listens on the other three pairs and measures the amount of interference, as shown in Figure 6-49. This is called *near-end crosstalk (NEXT)*.

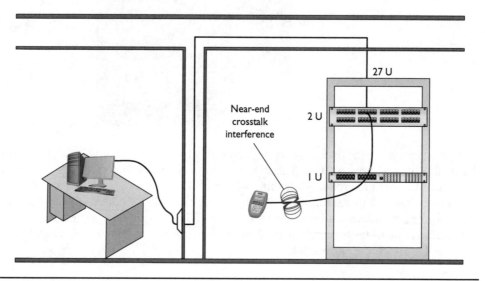

Figure 6-49   Near-end crosstalk

If you repeat this test, sending the signal down one pair of wires, but this time listening on the other pairs on the far end of the connection, you test for *far-end crosstalk (FEXT)*, as shown in Figure 6-50.

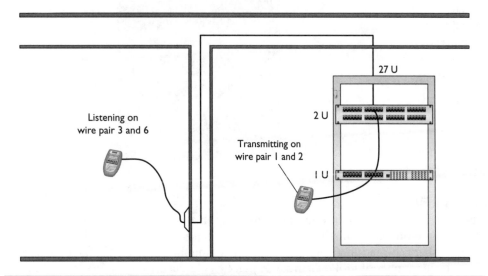

Figure 6-50 Far-end crosstalk

 NOTE Both NEXT and FEXT are measured in decibels (db).

As if that's not bad enough, as a signal progresses down a piece of wire, it becomes steadily weaker: this is called *attenuation*. As a cable run gets longer, the attenuation increases, and the signal becomes more susceptible to crosstalk. A tester must send a signal down one end of a wire, test for NEXT and FEXT on the ends of every other pair, and then repeat this process for every pair in the UTP cable.

This process of verifying that every cable run meets the exacting TIA/EIA standards requires very powerful testing tools, generally known as *cable certifiers* or just certifiers. Cable certifiers can both do the high-end testing and generate a report that a cable installer can print out and hand to a customer to prove that the installed cable runs pass TIA/EIA standards. Figure 6-51 shows an example of this type of scanner made by Fluke (www.fluke.com) in its Microtest line. Most network techs don't need these advanced testers, so unless you have some deep pockets or find yourself doing serious cable testing, stick to the medium-priced testers.

Figure 6-51
A typical cable certifier—a Microtest OMNIScanner (photo courtesy of Fluke Networks)

Testing Fiber

Fiber-optic cabling is an entirely different beast in terms of termination and testing. The classic termination method requires very precise stripping, polishing the end of the tiny fiber cable, adding epoxy glue, and inserting the connector. A fiber technician uses a large number of tools (Figure 6-52) and an almost artistic amount of skill. Over the years, easier terminations have been developed, but putting an ST, SC, LC, or other connector on the end of a piece of fiber is still very challenging.

Figure 6-52
Older fiber termination kit

A fiber-optic run has problems that are both similar to and different from those of a UTP run. Fiber-optic runs don't experience crosstalk or interference (as we usually think of it) because they use light instead of an electrical current.

Fiber-optic cables still break, however, so a good tech always keeps an *optical time domain reflectometer (OTDR)* handy (Figure 6-53). OTDRs determine continuity and, if there's a break, tell you exactly how far down the cable to look for the break.

Figure 6-53
An optical
time domain
reflectometer
(photo courtesy
of Fluke
Networks)

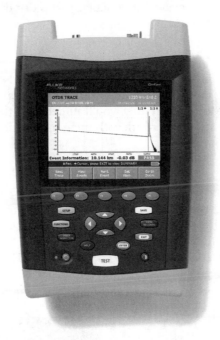

TIA/EIA has very complex requirements for testing fiber runs, and the cabling industry sells fiber certifiers to make sure a fiber will carry its designed signal speed.

The three big issues with fiber are attenuation, light leakage, and modal distortion. The amount of light propagating down the fiber cable diffuses over distance, which causes attenuation or *dispersion* (when the light signal spreads). If you bend a fiber-optic cable too much you get *light leakage*, as shown in Figure 6-54. Every type of fiber cabling has a very specific maximum bend radius. Modal distortion is unique to multimode fiber-optic cable. As the light source illuminates, it sends out light in different modes. Think of a mode as a slightly different direction. Some light shoots straight down the fiber; other modes bounce back and forth at a sharp angle.

Figure 6-54
The arrows show
the light leaking
out at the bends.

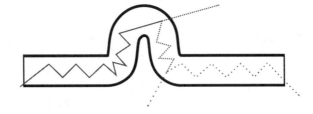

NOTE *Attenuation* is the weakening of a signal as it travels long distances. *Dispersion* is when a signal spreads out over long distances. Both attenuation and dispersion are caused when wave signals travel too far without help over fiber-optic media. The confusing part is that dispersion can cause attenuation and vice versa.

The process of installing a structured cabling system is rather involved, requires a great degree of skill, and should be left to professionals. By understanding the process, however, you can tackle most of the problems that come up in an installed structured cabling system. Most importantly, you'll understand the lingo used by the structured cabling installers so you can work with them more efficiently.

NICs

Now that the network is completely in place, it's time to turn to the final part of any physical network: the NICs. A good network tech must recognize different types of NICs by sight and know how to install and troubleshoot them. Let's begin by reviewing the differences between UTP and fiber-optic NICs.

All UTP Ethernet NICs use the RJ-45 connector. The cable runs from the NIC to a hub or a switch (Figure 6-55). It is impossible to tell one from the other simply by looking at the connection.

Figure 6-55
Typical UTP NIC

NOTE It's a rare motherboard these days that doesn't include an onboard NIC. This, of course, completely destroys the use of the acronym "NIC" for network interface card because no card is actually involved. But heck, we're nerds and, just as we'll probably never stop using the term "RJ-45" when the correct term is "8P8C," we'll keep using the term "NIC." I know! Let's just pretend it stands for *network interface connection*!

Fiber-optic NICs come in a wide variety; worse, manufacturers use the same connector types for multiple standards. You'll find a 100BaseFX card designed for multimode cable with an SC connector, for example, and an identical card designed for single-mode cable, also with an SC connector. You simply must see the documentation that comes with the two cards to tell them apart. Figure 6-56 shows a typical fiber-optic network card.

Figure 6-56
Typical fiber NIC
(photo courtesy
of 3Com Corp.)

Buying NICs

Some folks may disagree with me, but I always purchase name-brand NICs. For NICs, I recommend sticking with big names, such as 3Com or Intel. The NICs are better made, have extra features, and are easy to return if they turn out to be defective.

Plus, replacing a missing driver on a name-brand NIC is easy, and you can be confident the drivers work well. The type of NIC you purchase depends on your network. Try to think about the future and go for multispeed cards if your wallet can handle the extra cost. Also, where possible, try to stick with the same model of NIC. Every different model you buy means another set of driver discs you need to haul around in your tech bag. Using the same model of NIC makes driver updates easier, too.

NOTE Many people order desktop PCs with NICs simply because they don't take the time to ask if the system has a built-in NIC. Take a moment and ask about this!

Physical Connections

I'll state the obvious here: If you don't plug the NIC into the computer, the NIC won't work! Many users happily assume some sort of quantum magic when it comes to computer communications, but as a tech, you know better. Fortunately, most PCs come with built-in NICs, making physical installation a nonissue. If you're buying a NIC, physically inserting the NIC into one of the PC's expansion slots is the easiest part of the job. Most PCs today have two types of expansion slots. The older, but still common, expansion slot is the Peripheral Component Interconnect (PCI) type (Figure 6-57).

Figure 6-57
PCI NIC

The newer PCI Express (PCIe) expansion slots are now more widely adopted by NIC suppliers. PCIe NICs usually come in either one-lane (×1) or two-lane (×2) varieties (Figure 6-58).

Figure 6-58
PCIe NIC

If you're not willing to open a PC case, you can get NICs with USB or PC Card connections. While convenient, USB 2.0 (the most common version available) has a maximum speed of 480 Mbps—slower than Gigabit Ethernet, and PC Card is only a laptop solution (Figure 6-59). If, however, you manage to find a USB 3.0 NIC, which can handle speeds up to 5 Gbps, you shouldn't have a problem. USB NICs are handy to keep in your toolkit. If you walk up to a machine that might have a bad NIC, test your suspicions by inserting a USB NIC and moving the network cable from the potentially bad NIC to the USB one. (Don't forget to bring your driver disc along!)

Figure 6-59
USB NIC

Figure 6-59
USB NIC

Drivers

Installing a NIC's driver into a Windows, Mac, or Linux system is easy: just insert the driver CD when prompted by the system. Unless you have a very offbeat NIC, the operating system will probably already have the driver preinstalled, but there are benefits to using the driver on the manufacturer's CD. The CDs that comes with many NICs, especially the higher-end, brand-name ones, include extra goodies such as enhanced drivers and handy utilities, but you'll only be able to access them if you install the driver that comes with the NIC.

Every operating system has some method to verify that the computer recognizes the NIC and is ready to use it. Windows systems have the Device Manager, Ubuntu Linux users have the Network applet under the Administration menu, and your Macintosh has the Network utility in System Preferences. Actually, most operating systems have multiple methods to show that the NIC is in good working order. Learn the various ways to verify the NIC for your OS as this is the ultimate test of a good NIC installation.

Bonding

Most switches enable you to use multiple NICs for a single machine, a process called *bonding* or *link aggregation*. Bonding effectively doubles (or more) the speed between a machine and a switch. In preparing for this book, for example, I found that the connection between my graphics development computer and my file server was getting pounded by my constant sending and receiving of massive image files, slowing down everyone else's file access. Rather than upgrading the switches and NICs from Gigabit to 10-Gigabit Ethernet—still fairly expensive at this writing—I found that simply doubling the connections among those three machines—graphics computer, switch, and file server—increased performance all around. If you want to add link aggregation to your network to increase performance, use identical NICs and switches from the same companies to avoid the hint of incompatibility.

EXAM TIP *The Link Aggregation Control Protocol (LACP)* controls how multiple network devices send and receive data as a single connection.

Link Lights

All UTP NICs made today have some type of light-emitting diodes (LEDs) that give information about the state of the NIC's link to whatever's on the other end of the connection. Even though you know the lights are actually LEDs, get used to calling them *link lights*, as that's the term all network techs use. NICs can have between one and four different link lights, and the LEDs can be any color. These lights give you clues about what's happening with the link and are one of the first items to check whenever you think a system is disconnected from the network (Figure 6-60).

Figure 6-60
Mmmm, pretty lights!

A link light tells you that the NIC is connected to a hub or switch. Hubs and switches also have link lights, enabling you to check the connectivity at both ends of the cable. If a PC can't access a network and is acting disconnected, always check the link lights first. Multispeed devices usually have a link light that tells you the speed of the connection. In Figure 6-61, the light for port 2 in the top photo is orange, signifying that the other end of the cable is plugged into either a 10BaseT or 100BaseT NIC. The same port connected to a Gigabit NIC—that's the lower picture—displays a green LED.

A properly functioning link light is on and steady when the NIC is connected to another device. No flickering, no on and off, just on. A link light that is off or flickering indicates a connection problem.

Another light is the *activity light*. This little guy turns on when the card detects network traffic, so it intermittently flickers when operating properly. The activity light is a lifesaver for detecting problems, because in the real world, the connection light will sometimes lie to you. If the connection light says the connection is good, the next step is to try to copy a file or do something else to create network traffic. If the activity light does not flicker, there's a problem.

Figure 6-61

Multispeed lights

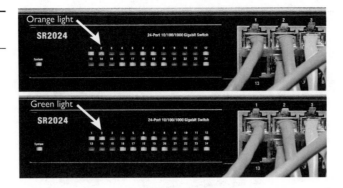

You might run into yet another light on some much older NICs, called a collision light. As you might suspect from the name, the *collision light* flickers when it detects collisions on the network. Modern NICs don't have these, but you might run into this phrase on the CompTIA Network+ certification exam.

Keep in mind that the device on the other end of the NIC's connection has link lights, too! Figure 6-62 shows the link lights on a modern switch. Most switches have a single LED per port to display connectivity and activity.

Figure 6-62

Link lights on
a switch

No standard governs how NIC manufacturers use their lights, and, as a result, they come in an amazing array of colors and layouts. When you encounter a NIC with a number of LEDs, take a moment to try to figure out what each one means. Although different NICs have various ways of arranging and using their LEDs, the functions are always the same: link, activity, and speed.

Many fiber-optic NICs don't have lights, making diagnosis of problems a bit more challenging. Nevertheless, most physical connection issues for fiber can be traced to the connection on the NIC itself. Fiber-optic cabling is incredibly delicate; the connectors that go into NICs are among the few places that anyone can touch fiber optics, so the connectors are the first thing to check when problems arise. Those who work with fiber always keep around a handy optical tester to enable them to inspect the quality of the connections. Only a trained eye can use such a device to judge a good fiber connection from a bad one—but once you learn how to use it, this kind of tester is extremely handy (Figure 6-63).

Figure 6-63
Optical
connection
tester

Diagnostics and Repair of Physical Cabling

"The network's down!" is easily the most terrifying phrase a network tech will ever hear. Networks fail for many reasons, and the first thing to know is that good-quality, professionally installed cabling rarely goes bad. Chapter 20 covers principles of network diagnostics and support that apply to all networking situations, but let's take a moment now to discuss what to do when you think you've got a problem with your physical network.

Diagnosing Physical Problems

Look for errors that point to physical disconnection. A key clue that you may have a physical problem is that a user gets a "No server is found" error, or tries to use the operating system's network explorer utility (like Network in Windows 7) and doesn't see any systems besides his or her own. First, try to eliminate software errors: if one particular application fails, try another. If the user can browse the Internet, but can't get e-mail, odds are good that the problem is with software, not hardware—unless someone unplugged the e-mail server!

Multiple systems failing to access the network often points to hardware problems. This is where knowledge of your network cabling helps. If all the systems connected to one switch suddenly no longer see the network, but all the other systems in your network still function, you not only have a probable hardware problem, but also you have a suspect—the switch.

Check Your Lights

If you suspect a hardware problem, first check the link lights on the NIC and switch. If they're not lit, you know the cable isn't connected somewhere. If you're not physically at the system in question (if you're on a tech call, for example), you can have the user check his or her connection status through the link lights or through software. Every operating system has some way to tell you on the screen if it detects the NIC is disconnected. The network status icon in the Notification Area in Windows 7, for example, will display a little red × when a NIC is disconnected (Figure 6-64). A user who's unfamiliar with link lights (or who may not want to crawl under his or her desk) will have no problem telling you if the icon says "Not Connected."

Figure 6-64
Disconnected
NIC in Windows 7

If your problem system is clearly not connecting, eliminate the possibility of a failed switch or other larger problem by checking to make sure other people can access the network, and that other systems can access the shared resource (server) that the problem system can't see. Make a quick visual inspection of the cable running from the back of the PC to the outlet. Finally, if you can, plug the system into a known good outlet and see if it works. A good network tech always keeps a long patch cable for just this purpose. If you get connectivity with the second outlet, you should begin to suspect the structured cable running from the first outlet to the switch. Assuming the cable is installed properly and has been working correctly before this event, a simple continuity test will confirm your suspicion in most cases.

Check the NIC

Be warned that a bad NIC can also generate this "can't see the network" problem. Use the utility provided by your OS to verify that the NIC works. If you've got a NIC with diagnostic software, run it—this software will check the NIC's circuitry. The NIC's female connector is a common failure point, so NICs that come with diagnostic software often include a special test called a *loopback test*. A loopback test sends data out of the NIC and checks to see if it comes back. Some NICs perform only an internal loopback, which tests the circuitry that sends and receives, but not the actual connecting pins. A true external loopback requires a *loopback plug* inserted into the NIC's port (Figure 6-65). If a NIC is bad, replace it—preferably with an identical NIC so you don't have to reinstall drivers!

Figure 6-65
Loopback plug

NOTE Onboard NICs on laptops are especially notorious for breaking due to constant plugging and unplugging. On some laptops, the NICs are easy to replace; others require a motherboard replacement.

Cable Testing

The vast majority of network disconnect problems occur at the work area. If you've tested those connections, though, and the work area seems fine, it's time to consider deeper issues.

With the right equipment, diagnosing a bad horizontal cabling run is easy. Anyone with a network should own a midrange tester with TDR such as the Fluke MicroScanner.

With a little practice, you can easily determine not only whether a cable is disconnected but also where the disconnection takes place. Sometimes patience is required, especially if you've failed to label your cable runs, but you will find the problem.

When you're testing a cable run, always include the patch cables as you test. This means unplugging the patch cable from the PC, attaching a tester, and then going to the telecommunications room. Here you'll want to unplug the patch cable from the switch and plug the tester into that patch cable, making a complete test, as shown in Figure 6-66.

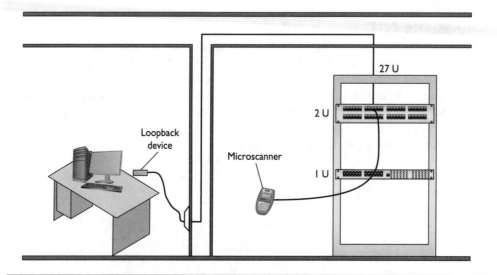

Figure 6-66 Loopback plug in action

Testing in this manner gives you a complete test from the switch to the system. In general, a broken cable must be replaced. A bad patch cable is easy, but what happens if the horizontal cable is to blame? In these cases, I get on the phone and call my local installer. If a cable's bad in one spot, the risk of it being bad in another is simply too great to try anything other than total replacement.

Problems in the Telecommunications Room

Even a well-organized telecommunications room is a complex maze of equipment racks, switches, and patch panels. The most important issue to remember as you work is to keep your diagnostic process organized and documented. For example, if you're testing a series of cable runs along a patch panel, start at one end and don't skip connections. Place a sticker as you work to keep track of where you are on the panel.

Your biggest concerns in the telecommunications room are power and environmental issues.

All those boxes in the rack need good-quality power. Even the smallest rack should run off of a good *uninterruptible power supply (UPS)*, a battery backup that plugs into the wall. Make sure you get one that can handle the amount of wattage used by all the equipment in the rack.

NOTE You can purchase two different types of UPSs—online and standby. An *online UPS* continuously charges a battery that, in turn, powers the computer components. If the telecommunications room loses power, the computers stay powered up without missing a beat, at least until the battery runs out.

A *standby power supply (SPS)* also has a big battery but doesn't power the computer unless the power goes out. Circuitry detects the power outage and immediately kicks on the battery.

But what if the UPS reports lots of times when it's kicking on? Don't assume the power coming from your physical plant (or power company) is okay. If your UPS comes on too often, it might be time to install a voltage event recorder (Figure 6-67). As its name implies, a *voltage event recorder* plugs into your power outlet and tracks the voltage over time. These devices often reveal interesting issues. For example, a small network was having trouble sending an overnight report to a main branch—the uploading servers reported that they were not able to connect to the Internet. Yet, in the morning, the report could be run manually with no problems. After placing a voltage event recorder in the telecommunications room, we discovered that the building management was turning off the power as a power-saving measure. This would have been hard to determine without the proper tool.

The temperature in the telecommunications room should be maintained and monitored properly. If you lose the air conditioning, for example, and leave systems running, the equipment will overheat and shut down—sometimes with serious damage. To prevent this, all serious telecommunications rooms should have *temperature monitors*.

Likewise, you need to control the level of humidity in a telecommunications room. You can install *environmental monitors* that keep a constant watch on humidity, temperature, and more, for just a few hundred dollars. The devices cost little in comparison to the equipment in the telecommunications room that you're protecting.

Figure 6-67
An excellent
voltage event
recorder (photo
courtesy of Fluke
Networks)

Toners

It would be nice to say that all cable installations are perfect and that over the years they won't tend to grow into horrific piles of spaghetti-like, unlabeled cables. In the real world, though, you might eventually find yourself having to locate or *trace* cables. Even in the best-planned networks, labels fall off ports and outlets, mystery cables appear behind walls, new cable runs are added, and mistakes are made counting rows and columns on patch panels. Sooner or later, most network techs will have to be able to pick out one particular cable or port from a stack.

When the time comes to trace cables, network techs turn to a device called a toner for help. *Toner* is the generic term for two separate devices that are used together: a tone generator and a tone probe. The *tone generator* connects to the cable using alligator clips, tiny hooks, or a network jack, and it sends an electrical signal along the wire at a certain frequency. The *tone probe* emits a sound when it is placed near a cable connected to the tone generator (Figure 6-68). These two devices are often referred to by the brand-name Fox and Hound, a popular model of toner made by the Triplett Corporation.

Figure 6-68
Fox and Hound

EXAM TIP You'll see a tone probe referred to on the CompTIA Network+ exam as a *toner probe*.

To trace a cable, connect the tone generator to the known end of the cable in question, and then position the tone probe next to the other end of each of the cables that might be the right one. The tone probe makes a sound when it's placed next to the right cable. Some toners have one tone probe that works with multiple tone generators. Each generator emits a separate frequency, and the probe sounds a different tone for each one. Even good toners are relatively inexpensive (US$75); although inexpensive toners can cost less than US$25, they don't tend to work well, so spending a little more is worthwhile. Just keep in mind that if you have to support a network, you'd do best to own a decent toner.

More advanced toners include phone jacks, enabling the person manipulating the tone generator to communicate with the person manipulating the tone probe: "Jim, move the tone generator to the next port!" These either come with their own headset or work with a *butt set*, the classic tool used by telephone repair technicians for years (Figure 6-69).

A good, medium-priced cable tester and a good toner are the most important tools for folks who must support, but not install, networks. A final tip: be sure to bring along a few extra batteries—there's nothing worse than sitting on the top of a ladder holding a cable tester or toner that has just run out of juice!

Figure 6-69
Technician with
a butt set

Chapter Review

Questions

1. Which of the following cables should never be used in a structured cabling installation?

    A. UTP

    B. STP

    C. Fiber-optic

    D. Coax

2. Which of the following enables you to use multiple NICs in a computer to achieve a much faster network speed?

    A. Bonding

    B. Linking

    C. SLI

    D. Xing

3. How many pairs of wires are in a CAT 5e-rated cable?

    A. 2

    B. 4

    C. 8

    D. It doesn't specify.

4. A(n) _____ organizes and protects the horizontal cabling in the telecommunications room.

    A. Rack

    B. Patch panel

    C. Outlet

    D. 110 jack

5. Which of the following would never be seen in an equipment rack?

    A. Patch panel

    B. UPS

    C. PC

    D. All of the above may be seen in an equipment rack.

6. What are patch cables used for? (Select two.)

    A. To connect different telecommunications rooms.

    B. To connect the patch panel to the hub.

    C. They are used as crossover cables.

    D. To connect PCs to outlet boxes.

7. Which of the following network technologies use UTP cabling in a star topology? (Select two.)

   A. 10Base2

   B. Fiber optics

   C. 10BaseT

   D. 100BaseT

8. Jane needs to increase network throughput on a 10BaseT network that consists of 1 hub and 30 users. Which of the following hardware solutions would achieve this most inexpensively?

   A. Add a fiber backbone.

   B. Upgrade the network to 100BaseT.

   C. Replace the hub with a switch.

   D. Add a router.

9. What two devices together enable you to pick a single cable out of a stack of cables? (Select two.)

   A. Tone aggregator

   B. Tone binder

   C. Tone generator

   D. Tone probe

10. Rack-mounted equipment has a height measured in what units?

    A. Mbps

    B. MBps

    C. Inches

    D. U

Answers

1. **D.** Coax cable should not be used in structured cabling networks.

2. **A.** Bonding, or link aggregation, is the process of using multiple NICs as a single connection, thus increasing speed.

3. **B.** The CAT 5e rating requires four pairs of wires.

4. **B.** The patch panel organizes and protects the horizontal cabling in the telecommunications room.

5. **D.** All these devices may be found in equipment racks.

6. **B** and **D**. Patch cables are used to connect the hub to the patch panel and the PCs to the outlet boxes.

7. **C** and **D**. 10BaseT and 100BaseT use UTP cabling in a star topology. 10Base2 is an older, dying technology that doesn't use UTP in a star. Fiber-optic networking uses a star topology, but the name is a dead giveaway that it doesn't use UTP!

8. **C**. Upgrading to 100BaseT will work, but replacing the hub with a switch is much less expensive.

9. **C** and **D**. A tone generator and tone probe work together to enable you to pick a single cable out of a stack of cables.

10. **D**. Rack-mounted equipment uses a height measurement known simply as a U.

TCP/IP Basics

The CompTIA Network+ certification exam expects you to know how to

- 1.3 Explain the purpose and properties of IP addressing
- 1.5 Identify common TCP and UDP default ports: DHCP
- 1.6 Explain the function of common networking protocols: TCP/IP suite, DHCP, ARP
- 2.1 Given a scenario, install and configure routers and switches: IP addressing
- 2.3 Explain the purpose and properties of DHCP
- 4.3 Given a scenario, use appropriate software tools to troubleshoot connectivity issues: arp

To achieve these goals, you must be able to

- Describe how the TCP/IP protocol suite works
- Explain CIDR and subnetting
- Describe the functions of static and dynamic IP addresses

The mythical MHTechEd network (remember that from Chapter 2?) provided an overview of how networks work. At the bottom of every network, at OSI Layers 1 and 2 (the Link/Network Interface layer of the TCP/IP model), resides the network hardware: the wires, network cards, switches, and more that enable data to move physically from one computer to another. Above the Physical and Data Link layers, the "higher" layers of the model—such as Network and Transport—work with the hardware to make the network magic happen.

Chapters 3 through 6 provided details of the hardware at the Physical and Data Link layers of the OSI model and the Link/Network Interface layer of the TCP/IP model. You learned about the network protocols, such as Ethernet, that create uniformity within networks so that the data frame created by one NIC can be read properly by another NIC.

This chapter begins a fun journey into the software side of networking. You'll learn the details about the IP addressing scheme that enables computers on one network to communicate with each other and computers on other networks. You'll get the full story on how TCP/IP networks divide into smaller units—subnets—to make management of a large TCP/IP network easier. And you won't just get it from a conceptual standpoint. This chapter provides the details you've undoubtedly been craving—it teaches you how to set up a network properly. The chapter finishes with an in-depth discussion on implementing IP addresses.

Historical/Conceptual

Standardizing Networking Technology

The early days of networking software saw several competing standards that did not work well together. Novell NetWare, Microsoft Windows, and Apple Macintosh ran networking software to share folders and printers, while the UNIX/Linux world did crazy things like sharing terminals—handy for the UNIX/Linux users, but it made no sense to the Windows folks—and then there was this new thing called e-mail (like that was ever going to go anywhere). The Internet had just been opened to the public. The World Wide Web was merely a plaything for programmers and scientists. All of these folks made their own software, interpreting (or totally ignoring) the OSI model in various ways, and all trying (arguably) to become *the way* the whole world networked computers. It was an unpleasant, ugly world for guys like me who had the audacity to try to make, for example, a UNIX box work with a Windows computer.

The problem was that no one agreed on how a network should run. Everyone's software had its own set of Rules of What a Network Should Do and How to Do It. These sets of rules—and the software written to follow these rules—were broken down into individual rules called *protocols*. Each set of rules had many protocols lumped together under the term *protocol suite*. Novell NetWare called its protocol suite IPX/SPX; Microsoft's was called NetBIOS/NetBEUI; Apple used AppleTalk; and the UNIX folks used this wacky protocol suite called TCP/IP.

 EXAM TIP Even in the old days companies created methods to connect different operating systems together. Microsoft created software to enable a Windows client to connect to a NetWare server, for example. This software, called the *Microsoft IPX/SPX Protocol* or *NWLINK*, shows up as a possible answer on the CompTIA Network+ exam. Because NWLINK is long gone, don't assume it's going to be the *correct* answer!

Well, TCP/IP won. Sure, you may find the occasional network still running one of these other protocol suites, but they're rare these days. To get ahead in today's world, to get on the Internet, and to pass the CompTIA Network+ exam, you only need to worry about TCP/IP. Novell, Microsoft, and Apple no longer actively support anything but TCP/IP. You live in a one-protocol-suite world, the old stuff is forgotten, and you kids don't know how good you got it!

Test Specific

The TCP/IP Protocol Suite

Chapter 2 introduced you to the TCP/IP model. Let's take a second look and examine some of the more critical protocols that reside at each layer. I'll also explore and develop the IP packet in more detail to show you how it organizes all of these protocols. Remember, TCP/IP is so powerful because IP packets can exist in almost any type of network technology. The Link layer, therefore, counts on technologies outside the TCP/IP protocol suite (like Ethernet, cable modem, or DSL) to get the IP packets from one system to the next (Figure 7-1).

Figure 7-1
The Link layer
is important, but
it's not part of
the TCP/IP
protocol suite.

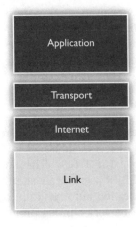

When discussing the software layers of the TCP/IP protocol suite, let's focus on only the three top layers in the TCP/IP model: Internet, Transport, and Application (Figure 7-2). I'll revisit each of these layers and add representative protocols from the protocol suite so you gain a better understanding of "who's who" in TCP/IP.

Figure 7-2
The TCP/IP
model
redux

NOTE The TCP/IP protocol suite consists of thousands of different protocols doing thousands of different things. For the most part, the rest of this book discusses TCP/IP protocols. Right now, my goal is to give you an idea of which protocols go where in the TCP/IP protocol suite.

If you look at an IP packet, certain parts of that packet fit perfectly into layers of the TCP/IP model. The parts consist of a series of nested headers with data. The header for a higher layer is part of the data for a lower layer. The packet's payload, for example, can be a TCP segment that consists of data from layers above and a sequence number (Figure 7-3). The higher you go up the model, more headers are stripped away until all you have left is the data delivered to the application that needs it.

Figure 7-3

IP packet showing headers

Internet Layer Protocols

The *Internet Protocol (IP)* works at the Internet layer, taking data chunks from the Transport layer, adding addressing, and creating the final IP packet. The Internet Protocol software then hands the IP packet to Layer 2 for encapsulation into a frame. Let's look at the addressing in more depth.

I think it's safe to assume that most folks have seen IP addresses before. Here's a typical example:

192.168.1.115

This type of address—four values ranging from 0 to 255, separated by three periods—is known officially as an *Internet Protocol version four (IPv4)* address.

This chapter introduces you to IPv4 addresses. You should understand the correct name for this older type of address because the world is moving to a newer, longer type of IP address called IPv6. Here's an example of an IPv6 address:

2001:0:4137:9e76:43e:2599:3f57:fe9a

IPv4 and IPv6 addresses aren't the only protocols that work at the Internet layer. A number of applications test basic issues at this layer, such as "Is there a computer with the IP address of 192.168.1.115?" These applications use the *Internet Control Message Protocol (ICMP)*. TCP/IP users rarely start a program that uses ICMP. For the most part, ICMP features are called automatically by applications as needed without your ever knowing. There is one very famous program that runs under ICMP, however: the venerable ping utility. Run ping from a command prompt to query if a host is reachable. Ping will show the *round trip time (RTT)*—some call this the *real transfer time*—for the ICMP packet, usually in seconds. If ping can't find the host, the packet will time out and ping will show you that information too.

When thinking about the Internet layer, remember the following three protocols:

- IPv4 (sometimes you just say IP)
- IPv6
- ICMP

 NOTE The TCP/IP model's Internet layer corresponds roughly to the OSI model's Network layer.

Figure 7-4 shows a highly simplified IP header.

Figure 7-4
Simplified IP header

The full IP packet header has 14 different fields. As you would expect, the destination and source IP addresses are part of the Network/Internet layer. Other fields include version, header length, and more. Dissecting the entire set of fields isn't important, but here are a few descriptions just to whet your appetite:

- **Version** The version (Ver) field defines the IP address type: 4 for IPv4, 6 for IPv6.
- **Header Length** The total size of the IP portion of the packet in words (32-bits) is displayed in the header length field.
- **Differentiated Services Code Point (DSCP)** The DSCP field contains data used by bandwidth-sensitive applications like Voice over IP. (Network techs with long memories will note that this field used to be called the *Type of Service* field.)
- **Time to Live** Routers on the Internet are not perfect and sometimes create loops. The Time to Live (TTL) field prevents an IP packet from indefinitely spinning through the Internet by using a counter that decrements by one every time a packet goes through a router. This number cannot start higher than 255; many applications start at 128.
- **Protocol** In the vast majority of cases, the protocol field is either TCP or UDP. See the next section for more information.

Transport Layer Protocols

When moving data from one system to another, the TCP/IP protocol suite needs to know if the communication is connection-oriented or connectionless. When you want to be positive that the data moving between two systems gets there in good order, use a connection-oriented application. If it's not a big deal for data to miss a bit or two, then connectionless is the way to go. The connection-oriented protocol used with TCP/IP is called the *Transmission Control Protocol (TCP)*. The connectionless one is called the *User Datagram Protocol (UDP)*.

Let me be clear: you don't *choose* TCP or UDP. The people who developed the applications decide which protocol to use. When you fire up your Web browser, for example, you're using TCP because Web browsers use an Application layer protocol called HTTP. HTTP is built on TCP.

TCP

Over 95 percent of all TCP/IP applications use TCP—that's why we call the protocol suite "TCP/IP" and not "UDP/IP." TCP gets an application's data from one machine to another reliably and completely. As a result, TCP comes with communication rules that require both the sending and receiving machines to acknowledge the other's presence and readiness to send and receive data. We call this process ACK/NACK or just ACK (Figure 7-5). TCP also chops up data into *segments*, gives the segments a sequencing number, and then verifies that all sent segments were received. If a segment goes missing, the receiving system must request the missing segments.

Figure 7-5
ACK in action

Figure 7-6 shows a simplified TCP header. Notice the source port and the destination port. Port numbers are values ranging from 1 to 65535 and are used by systems to determine what application needs the received data. Each application is assigned a specific port number. Web servers use port 80 (HTTP), for example, whereas port 110 is used to receive e-mail messages from e-mail servers (POP3). The client uses the source port number to remember which client application requested the data. The rest of this book dives much deeper into ports. For now, know that the TCP or UDP headers of an IP packet store these values.

Figure 7-6 TCP header

Ports aren't the only items of interest in the TCP header. The header also contains these fields:

- **Sequence number**   This value is used to assemble/disassemble data.
- **ACK number**   This value tracks the readiness of the two communicating systems to send/receive data.
- **Flags**   These individual bits give both sides detailed information about the state of the connection.
- **Checksum**   The checksum checks the TCP header for errors.

UDP is the "fire and forget" missile of the TCP/IP protocol suite. As you can see in Figure 7-7, a UDP *datagram* doesn't possess any of the extras you see in TCP to make sure the data is received intact. UDP works best when you have a lot of data that doesn't need to be perfect or when the systems are so close to each other that the chances of a problem occurring are too small to bother worrying about. A few dropped frames on a Voice over IP call, for example, won't make much difference in the communication between two people. So there's a good reason to use UDP: it's smoking fast compared to TCP.

Figure 7-7 UDP header

 NOTE You saw this back in Chapter 2, but I'll mention it again here. Data gets chopped up into chunks at the Transport layer. The chunks are called *segments* with TCP and *datagrams* with UDP.

Application Layer Protocols

TCP/IP applications use TCP/IP protocols to move data back and forth between servers and clients. Because every application has different needs, I can't show you a generic application header. Instead, we'll look at one sample header from one function of possibly the most popular application protocol of all: HTTP.

As mentioned previously, Web servers and Web browsers use HTTP to communicate. Figure 7-8 shows a sample header for HTTP. Specifically, this header is a response segment from the Web server telling the remote system that the last set of data transfers is complete. This header begins with the value "HTTP/1.1" and the number "200" followed by "OK\r\n," which means "OK, go to the next line." The data (the contents of the Web page) begins below the header.

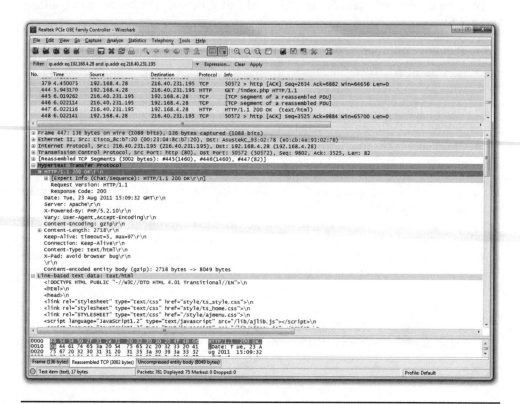

Figure 7-8   HTTP header

 NOTE   I'm simplifying the call and response interaction between a Web server and a Web client. The explanation here is only the first part of the process in accessing a Web page.

Super! Now that you're comfortable with how the TCP/IP protocols fit into clear points on the TCP/IP model, let's head back to the Internet layer and explore IP addressing.

IP in Depth

TCP/IP supports simple networks and complex networks. You can use the protocol suite to connect a handful of computers to a switch and create a local area network (LAN). TCP/IP also enables you to interconnect multiple LANs into a wide area network (WAN).

At the LAN level, all the computers use Ethernet, and this creates a hurdle for WAN-wide communication. For one computer to send a frame to another computer, the sending computer must know the MAC address of the destination computer. This begs the question: How does the sender get the recipient's MAC address?

In a small network, this is easy. The sending computer simply *broadcasts* by sending a frame to MAC address FF-FF-FF-FF-FF-FF, the universal MAC address for broadcast. Figure 7-9 shows a computer broadcasting for another computer's MAC address.

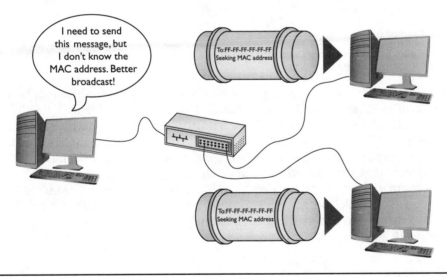

Figure 7-9 PC broadcasting for a MAC address

Broadcasting takes up some of the network bandwidth, but in a small network, the amount is acceptably small. But what would happen if the entire Internet used broadcasting (Figure 7-10)? In this case, the whole Internet would come to a grinding halt.

Figure 7-10   Broadcasting won't work for the entire Internet!

TCP/IP networks use *IP addressing* to overcome the limitations inherent in Ethernet networks. IP addresses provide several things. First, every machine on a TCP/IP network—small or large—gets a unique IP address that identifies the machine on that network. Second, IP addresses group together sets of computers into logical networks, so you can, for example, distinguish one LAN from another. Finally, because TCP/IP network equipment understands the IP addressing scheme, computers can communicate with each other *between* LANs, in a WAN, and without broadcasting for MAC addresses (other than for the default gateway). Chapter 2 touched on IP addresses briefly, but network techs need to understand them intimately. Let's look at the structure and function of the IP addressing scheme.

IP Addresses

The most common type of IP address (officially called IPv4, but usually simplified to just "IP") consists of a 32-bit value. Here's an example of an IP address:

11000000101010000000010000000010

Whoa! IP addresses are just strings of 32 binary digits? Yes, they are, but to make IP addresses easier for humans to use, the 32-bit binary value is broken down into four groups of eight, separated by periods or *dots* like this:

11000000.10101000.00000100.00000010

Each of these 8-bit values is, in turn, converted into a decimal number between 0 and 255. If you took every possible combination of eight binary values and placed them in a spreadsheet, it would look something like the list in the left column. The right column shows the same list with a decimal value assigned to each.

00000000	00000000 = 0
00000001	00000001 = 1
00000010	00000010 = 2
00000011	00000011 = 3
00000100	00000100 = 4
00000101	00000101 = 5
00000110	00000110 = 6
00000111	00000111 = 7
00001000	00001000 = 8
(skip a bunch in the middle)	*(skip a bunch in the middle)*
11111000	11111000 = 248
11111001	11111001 = 249
11111010	11111010 = 250
11111011	11111011 = 251
11111100	11111100 = 252
11111101	11111101 = 253
11111110	11111110 = 254
11111111	11111111 = 255

Converted, the original value of 11000000.10101000.00000100.00000010 is displayed as 192.168.4.2 in IPv4's *dotted decimal notation* (also referred to as the *dotted-octet numbering system*). Note that dotted decimal is simply a shorthand way for people to discuss and configure the binary IP addresses computers use.

NOTE When you type an IP address into a computer, the computer ignores the periods and immediately converts the decimal numbers into binary. People need dotted decimal notation, but computers do not.

People who work on TCP/IP networks must know how to convert dotted decimal to binary and back. You can convert easily using any operating system's calculator. Every OS has a calculator (UNIX/Linux systems have about 100 different ones to choose from) that has a scientific or programmer mode like the one shown in Figure 7-11.

Figure 7-11
Mac OS X
Calculator in
Programmer mode

To convert from decimal to binary, just go to decimal view, type in the value, and then switch to binary view to get the result. To convert to decimal, just go into binary view, enter the binary value, and switch to decimal view to get the result. Figure 7-12 shows the result of Windows 7's Calculator converting the decimal value 47 into binary. Notice the result is 101111—the leading two zeroes do not appear. When you work with IP addresses you must always have eight digits, so just add two more to the left to get 00101111.

NOTE   Using a calculator utility to convert to and from binary/decimal is a critical skill for a network tech. Later on you'll do this again, but by hand!

Figure 7-12
Converting
decimal to binary
with Windows 7's
Calculator

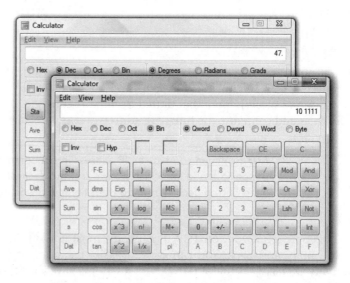

Just as every MAC address must be unique on a network, every IP address must be unique as well. For logical addressing to work, no two computers on the same network

may have the same IP address. In a small network running TCP/IP, every computer has
both an IP address and a MAC address (Figure 7-13).

Figure 7-13
A small network
with both IP and
MAC addresses

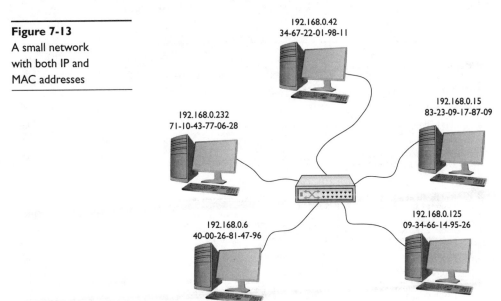

Every operating system comes with a utility (usually more than one utility) to display
a system's IP address and MAC address. Figure 7-14 shows a Mac OS X system's Network
utility. Note the MAC address (00:14:51:65:84:a1) and the IP address (192.168.4.57).

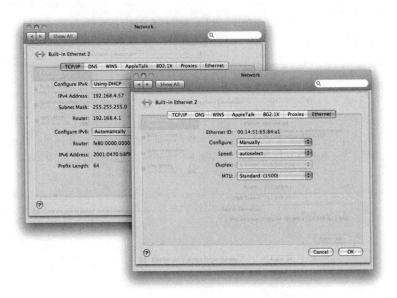

Figure 7-14 Mac OS X Network utility

Every operating system also has a command-line utility that gives you this information. In Windows, for example, you can use *ipconfig* to display the IP and MAC addresses. Run **ipconfig /all** to see the results shown in Figure 7-15.

```
Administrator: Command Prompt

Microsoft Windows [Version 6.0.6001]
Copyright (c) 2006 Microsoft Corporation.  All rights reserved.

C:\Users\scottj.TOTALHOME>ipconfig /all

Windows IP Configuration

    Host Name . . . . . . . . . . . . : scott-vista
    Primary Dns Suffix  . . . . . . . : totalhome
    Node Type . . . . . . . . . . . . : Hybrid
    IP Routing Enabled. . . . . . . . : No
    WINS Proxy Enabled. . . . . . . . : No
    DNS Suffix Search List. . . . . . : totalhome

Ethernet adapter Local Area Connection 2:

    Media State . . . . . . . . . . . : Media disconnected
    Connection-specific DNS Suffix  . :
    Description . . . . . . . . . . . : NVIDIA nForce Networking Controller #2
    Physical Address. . . . . . . . . : 00-15-F2-F4-AE-15
    DHCP Enabled. . . . . . . . . . . : Yes
    Autoconfiguration Enabled . . . . : Yes

Ethernet adapter Local Area Connection:

    Connection-specific DNS Suffix  . :
    Description . . . . . . . . . . . : NVIDIA nForce Networking Controller
    Physical Address. . . . . . . . . : 00-15-F2-F4-AE-14
    DHCP Enabled. . . . . . . . . . . : Yes
    Autoconfiguration Enabled . . . . : Yes
    IPv6 Address. . . . . . . . . . . : 2001:470:b8f9:1:1584:889a:269f:887(Deprec
ated)
    Temporary IPv6 Address. . . . . . : 2001:470:b8f9:1:4476:46b2:648c:ecdc(Depre
cated)
    Link-local IPv6 Address . . . . . : fe80::1584:889a:269f:887%8(Preferred)
    IPv4 Address. . . . . . . . . . . : 192.168.4.60(Preferred)
    Subnet Mask . . . . . . . . . . . : 255.255.255.0
    Lease Obtained. . . . . . . . . . : Monday, February 02, 2009 9:51:44 AM
    Lease Expires . . . . . . . . . . : Tuesday, February 10, 2009 9:51:13 AM
    Default Gateway . . . . . . . . . : fe80::223:4ff:fe8c:b720%8
                                        192.168.4.1
    DHCP Server . . . . . . . . . . . : 192.168.4.11
    DNS Servers . . . . . . . . . . . : 192.168.4.11
    NetBIOS over Tcpip. . . . . . . . : Enabled
```

Figure 7-15   Results from running ipconfig /all in Windows

In the UNIX/Linux/Mac OS X world, you can run the very similar *ifconfig* command. Figure 7-16, for example, shows the result of an ifconfig ("eth0" is the NIC) in Ubuntu.

EXAM TIP   Make sure you know that ipconfig and ifconfig provide a tremendous amount of information regarding a system's TCP/IP settings.

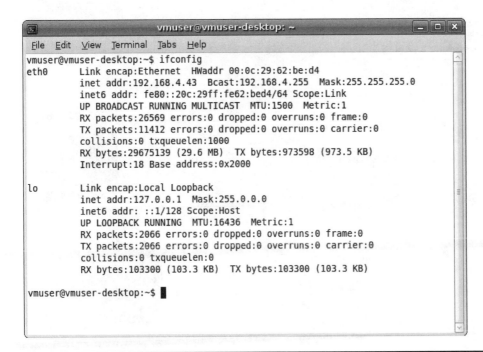

Figure 7-16   Results from running ifconfig in Ubuntu

IP Addresses in Action

IP addresses support both LANs and WANs. This can create problems in some circumstances, such as when a computer needs to send data both to computers in its own network and to computers in other networks. How can this be accomplished?

To make all this work, IP must do three things:

- Create some way to use IP addresses so that each LAN has its own identification.

- Interconnect all of the LANs using routers and give those routers some way to use the network identification to send packets to the right network.

- Give each computer on the network some way to recognize if a packet is for the LAN or for a computer on the WAN so it knows how to handle the packet.

Network IDs

To differentiate LANs from one another, each computer on a single LAN must share a very similar IP address. Some parts of the IP address will match all the others on the LAN. Figure 7-17 shows a LAN where all of the computers share the first three numbers of the IP address, with only the last number being unique on each system.

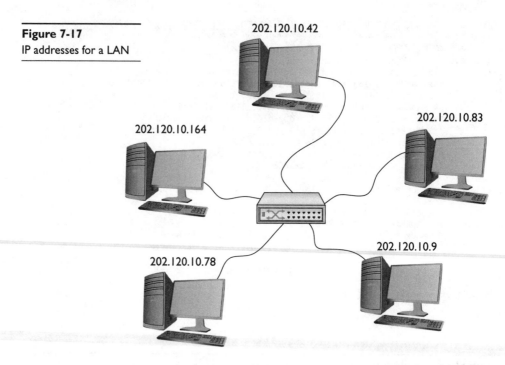

Figure 7-17
IP addresses for a LAN

202.120.10.42

202.120.10.164

202.120.10.83

202.120.10.78

202.120.10.9

In this example, every computer has an IP address of 202.120.10.*x*. That means the *network ID* is 202.120.10.0. The *x* part of the IP address is the *host ID*. Combine the network ID (after dropping the ending 0) with the host ID to get an individual system's IP address. No individual computer can have an IP address that ends with 0 because that is reserved for network IDs.

NOTE The network ID and the host ID are combined to make a system's IP address.

Interconnecting

To organize all those individual LANs into a larger network, every TCP/IP LAN that wants to connect to another TCP/IP LAN must have a router connection. There is no exception to this critical rule. A router, therefore, needs an IP address on the LANs that it serves (Figure 7-18), so it can correctly route packets.

That router is known as the *default gateway*. When configuring a client to access the network beyond the router, you use the IP address for the default gateway.

Most network administrators give the LAN-side NIC on the default gateway the lowest host address in the network, usually the host ID of 1.

Figure 7-18
LAN with router

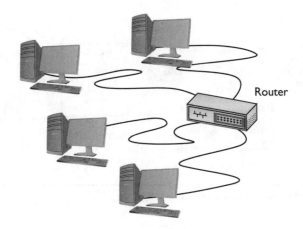

Routers use network IDs to determine network traffic. Figure 7-19 shows a diagram for a small, two-NIC router similar to the ones you see in many homes. Note that one port (202.120.10.1) connects to the LAN and the other port connects to the Internet service provider's network (14.23.54.223). Built into this router is a *routing table*, the actual instructions that tell the router what to do with incoming packets and where to send them.

Figure 7-19
Router diagram

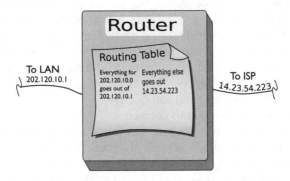

NOTE Routing tables are covered in more detail in Chapter 8.

Now let's add in the LAN and the Internet (Figure 7-20). When discussing networks in terms of network IDs, by the way, especially with illustrations in books, the common practice is to draw circles around stylized networks. Here, you should concentrate on the IDs—not the specifics of the networks.

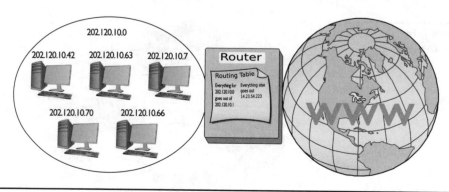

Figure 7-20   LAN, router, and the Internet

Network IDs are very flexible, as long as no two interconnected networks share the same network ID. If you wished, you could change the network ID of the 202.120.10.0 network to 202.155.5.0, or 202.21.8.0, just as long as you can guarantee no other LAN on the WAN shares the same network ID. On the Internet, powerful governing bodies carefully allocate network IDs to ensure no two LANs share the same network ID. I'll talk more about how this works later in the chapter.

So far you've only seen examples of network IDs where the last value is zero. This is common for small networks, but it creates a limitation. With a network ID of 202.120.10.0, for example, a network is limited to IP addresses from 202.120.10.1 to 202.120.10.254. (202.120.10.255 is a broadcast address used to talk to every computer on the LAN.) This provides only 254 IP addresses: enough for a small network, but many organizations need many more IP addresses. No worries! You can simply use a network ID with more zeroes, such as 170.45.0.0 (for a total of 65,534 hosts) or even 12.0.0.0 (for around 16.7 million hosts).

Network IDs enable you to connect multiple LANs into a WAN. Routers then connect everything together, using routing tables to keep track of which packets go where. So that takes care of the second task: interconnecting the LANs using routers and giving those routers a way to send packets to the right network.

Now that you know how IP addressing works with LANs and WANs, let's turn to how IP enables each computer on a network to recognize if a packet is going to a computer on the LAN or to a computer on the WAN. The secret to this is something called the subnet mask.

Subnet Mask

Picture this scenario. Three friends sit at their computers—Computers A, B, and C—and want to communicate with each other. Figure 7-21 illustrates the situation. You can tell from the drawing that Computers A and B are in the same LAN, whereas Computer C is on a completely different LAN. The IP addressing scheme can handle this communication, so let's see how it works.

Figure 7-21
The three amigos, separated by walls or miles

LAN 1

LAN 2

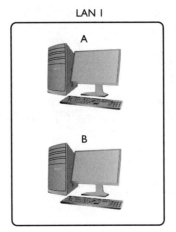

The process to get a packet to a local computer is very different from the process to get a packet to a faraway computer. If one computer wants to send a packet to a local computer, it must send a broadcast to get the other computer's MAC address, as you'll recall from earlier in the chapter and Figure 7-9. (It's easy to forget about the MAC address, but remember that the network uses Ethernet and *must* have the MAC address to get the packet to the other computer.) If the packet is for some computer on a faraway network, the sending computer must send the packet to the default gateway (Figure 7-22).

Figure 7-22
Sending a packet remotely

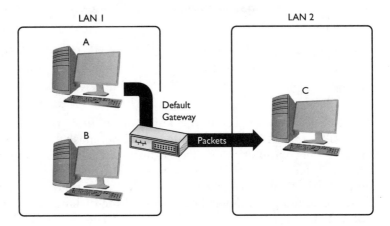

In the scenario illustrated in Figure 7-21, Computer A wants to send a packet to Computer B. Computer B is on the same LAN as Computer A, but that begs a question: How does Computer A know this? Every TCP/IP computer needs a tool to tell the sending computer whether the destination IP address is local or long distance. This tool is the subnet mask.

A *subnet mask* is nothing more than a string of ones followed by some number of zeroes, always totaling exactly 32 bits, typed into every TCP/IP host. Here's an example of a typical subnet mask:

11111111111111111111111100000000

For the courtesy of the humans reading this (if any computers are reading this book, please call me—I'd love to meet you!), let's convert this to dotted decimal. First, add some periods:

11111111.11111111.11111111.00000000

Then convert each octet into decimal (use a calculator):

255.255.255.0

When you line up an IP address with a corresponding subnet mask in binary, the portion of the IP address that aligns with the ones of the subnet mask is the network ID portion of the IP address. The portion that aligns with the zeroes is the host ID. With simple IP addresses, you can see this with dotted decimal, but you'll want to see this in binary for a true understanding of how the computers work.

The IP address 192.168.5.23 has a subnet mask of 255.255.255.0. Convert both numbers to binary and then compare the full IP address to the ones and zeroes of the subnet mask:

	Dotted Decimal	Binary
IP address	192.168.5.23	11000000.10101000.00000101.00010111
Subnet mask	255.255.255.0	11111111.11111111.11111111.00000000
Network ID	192.168.5.0	11000000.10101000.00000101.x
Host ID	x.x.x.23	x.x.x.00010111

Before a computer sends out any data, it first compares the destination IP address to its own IP address using the subnet mask. If the destination IP address matches the computer's IP wherever there's a 1 in the subnet mask, then the sending computer knows the destination is local. The network IDs match. If even one bit of the destination IP address where the 1s are on the subnet mask is different, then the sending computer knows it's a long-distance call. The network IDs do not match.

NOTE The explanation about comparing an IP address to a subnet mask simplifies the process, leaving out how the computer uses its routing table to accomplish the goal. We'll get to routing and routing tables in Chapter 8. For now, stick with the concept of the node using the subnet mask to determine the network ID.

EXAM TIP At this point, you should memorize that 0 = 00000000 and 255 = 11111111. You'll find knowing this very helpful throughout the rest of the book.

Let's head over to Computer A and see how the subnet mask works. Computer A's IP address is 192.168.5.23. Convert that into binary:

11000000.10101000.00000101.00010111

Now drop the periods because they mean nothing to the computer:

11000000101010000000010100010111

Let's say Computer A wants to send a packet to Computer B. Computer A's subnet mask is 255.255.255.0. Computer B's IP address is 192.168.5.45. Convert this address to binary:

11000000101010000000010100101101

Computer A compares its IP address to Computer B's IP address using the subnet mask, as shown in Figure 7-23. For clarity, I've added a line to show you where the ones end and the zeroes begin in the subnet mask. Computers certainly don't need the line!

Figure 7-23
Comparing addresses

A-ha! Computer A's and Computer B's network IDs match! It's a local call. Knowing this, Computer A can now send out an ARP request, which is a broadcast, as shown in Figure 7-24, to determine Computer B's MAC address. The *Address Resolution Protocol (ARP)* is how a TCP/IP network figures out the MAC address based on the destination IP address.

Figure 7-24
Sending an ARP
request

The addressing for the ARP frame looks like Figure 7-25. Note that Computer A's IP address and MAC address are included.

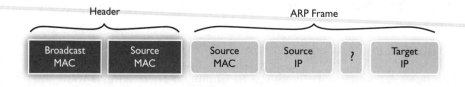

Figure 7-25 Simplified ARP frame

Computer B responds to the ARP request by sending Computer A an ARP response (Figure 7-26). Once Computer A has Computer B's MAC address, it starts sending packets.

Figure 7-26
Computer B
responds.

 EXAM TIP The long-dead *Reverse Address Resolution Protocol (RARP)* was used to get a Layer 3 address when the computer's MAC address was known, thus, the reverse of an ARP. You'll see this sometimes as an incorrect answer on the CompTIA Network+ exam.

But what happens when Computer A wants to send a packet to Computer C? First, Computer A compares Computer C's IP address to its own using the subnet mask

(Figure 7-27). It sees that the IP addresses do not match in the 1s part of the subnet mask—meaning the network IDs don't match; therefore, this is a long-distance call.

Figure 7-27
Comparing
addresses again

NOTE To show Windows' current ARP table, open a command line and type:

```
arp -a.
```

You should see results similar to this:

```
Interface: 192.168.4.71 --- 0x4

Internet Address  Physical Address  Type

192.168.4.76  00-1d-e0-78-9c-d5  dynamic
192.168.4.81  00-1b-77-3f-85-b4  dynamic
```

Whenever a computer wants to send to an IP address on another LAN, it knows to send the packet to the default gateway. It still sends out an ARP request, but this time to the default gateway (Figure 7-28). Once Computer A gets the default gateway's MAC address, it then begins to send packets.

Figure 7-28
Sending an
ARP request
to the
gateway

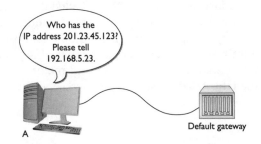

Subnet masks are represented in dotted decimal like IP addresses—just remember that both are really 32-bit binary numbers. All of the following (shown in both binary and dotted decimal formats) can be subnet masks:

11111111111111111111111100000000 = 255.255.255.0
11111111111111110000000000000000 = 255.255.0.0
11111111000000000000000000000000 = 255.0.0.0

Most network folks represent subnet masks using special shorthand: a / character followed by a number equal to the number of ones in the subnet mask. Here are a few examples:

11111111111111111111111100000000 = /24 (24 ones)
11111111111111110000000000000000 = /16 (16 ones)
11111111000000000000000000000000 = /8 (8 ones)

An IP address followed by the / and number tells you the IP address and the subnet mask in one statement. For example, 201.23.45.123/24 is an IP address of 201.23.45.123 with a subnet mask of 255.255.255.0. Similarly, 184.222.4.36/16 is an IP address of 184.222.4.36 with a subnet mask of 255.255.0.0.

Fortunately, computers do all of this subnet filtering automatically. Network administrators need only to enter the correct IP address and subnet mask when they first set up their systems, and the rest happens without any human intervention.

 NOTE By definition, all computers on the same network have the same subnet mask and network ID.

If you want a computer to work in a routed internetwork (like the Internet), you absolutely must have an IP address that's part of its network ID, a subnet mask, and a default gateway. No exceptions!

Class IDs

The Internet is by far the biggest and the most complex TCP/IP internetwork. Numbering over half a billion computers way back in 2009, it has grown so quickly that now it's nearly impossible to find an accurate number. The single biggest challenge for the Internet is to make sure no two devices share the same public IP address. To support the dispersion of IP addresses, an organization called the *Internet Assigned Numbers Authority (IANA)* was formed to track and disperse IP addresses to those who need them. Initially handled by a single person (the famous Jon Postel) until 1998, the IANA has grown dramatically and now oversees a number of Regional Internet Registries (RIRs) that parcel out IP addresses to large ISPs and major corporations. The RIR for North America is called the *American Registry for Internet Numbers (ARIN)*. The vast majority of end users get their IP addresses from their respective ISPs. IANA passes out IP addresses in contiguous chunks called *class licenses*, which are outlined in the following table:

	First Decimal Value	Addresses	Hosts per Network ID
Class A	1–126	1.0.0.0–126.255.255.255	16,277,214
Class B	128–191	128.0.0.0–191.255.255.255	65,534
Class C	192–223	192.0.0.0–223.255.255.255	254
Class D	224–239	224.0.0.0–239.255.255.255	Multicast
Class E	240–254	240.0.0.0–254.255.255.255	Experimental

A typical Class A license, for example, has a network ID that starts between 1 and 126; hosts on that network have only the first octet in common, with any numbers for the other three octets. Having three octets to use for hosts means you have an enormous number of possible hosts, over 16 million different number combinations. The subnet mask for Class A licenses is 255.0.0.0, which means you have 24 bits for host IDs.

Do you remember binary math? $2^{24} = 16,277,216$. Because the host can't use all zeroes or all ones (those are reserved for the network ID and broadcast IP, respectively), you subtract two from the final number to get the available host IDs.

NOTE The Internet Corporation for Assigned Names and Numbers (ICANN) manages the IANA.

A Class B license, with a subnet mask of 255.255.0.0, uses the first two octets to define the network ID. This leaves two octets to define host IDs, which means each Class B network ID can have up to 65,534 different hosts.

A Class C license uses the first three octets to define only the network ID. All hosts in network 192.168.35.0, for example, would have all three first numbers in common. Only the last octet defines the host IDs, which leaves only 254 possible unique addresses. The subnet mask for Class C licenses is 255.255.255.0.

Multicast class licenses are used for one-to-many communication, such as in streaming video conferencing. There are three ways to send a packet: a *broadcast*, which is where every computer on the LAN hears the message; a *unicast*, where one computer sends a message directly to another user; and a *multicast*, where a single computer sends a packet to a group of interested computers. Multicast is often used when routers talk to each other.

Experimental addresses are reserved and never used except for occasional experimental reasons. These were originally called reserved addresses.

EXAM TIP Make sure you memorize the IP class licenses! You should be able to look at any IP address and know its class license. Here's a trick to help: The first binary octet of a Class A address always begins with a 0 (0*xxxxxxx*);

for Class B, it begins with a 10 (10*xxxxxx*); for Class C, with 110 (110*xxxxx*); for Class D, with 1110 (1110*xxxx*); and for Class E, it begins with 1111 (1111*xxxx*).

IP class licenses worked well for the first few years of the Internet but quickly ran into trouble due to the fact that they didn't quite fit for everyone. Early on, IANA gave away IP class licenses rather generously, perhaps too generously. Over time, unallocated IP addresses became scarce. Additionally, the IP class licenses concept didn't scale well. If an organization needed 2,000 IP addresses, for example, it either had to take a single Class B license (wasting 63,000 addresses) or eight Class C licenses. As a result, a new method of generating blocks of IP addresses, called *Classless Inter-Domain Routing (CIDR)*, was developed.

CIDR and Subnetting

CIDR is based on a concept called *subnetting*: taking a single class of IP addresses and chopping it up into multiple smaller groups. CIDR and subnetting are virtually the same thing. Subnetting is done by an organization—it is given a block of addresses and then breaks the single block of addresses into multiple subnets. CIDR is done by an ISP—it is given a block of addresses, subnets the block into multiple subnets, and then passes out the smaller individual subnets to customers. Subnetting and CIDR have been around for quite a long time now and are a critical part of all but the smallest TCP/IP networks. Let's first discuss subnetting and then visit CIDR.

Subnetting

Subnetting enables a much more efficient use of IP addresses compared to class licenses. It also enables you to separate a network for security (separating a bank of public access computers from your more private computers) and for bandwidth control (separating a heavily used LAN from one that's not so heavily used).

 EXAM TIP You need to know how to subnet to pass the CompTIA Network+ exam.

The cornerstone to subnetting lies in the subnet mask. You take an existing /8, /16, or /24 subnet and extend the subnet mask by adding more ones (and taking away the corresponding number of zeroes). For example, let's say you have an Internet café with about 50 computers, 40 of which are for public use and 10 of which are used in the back office for accounting and such (Figure 7-29). Your network ID is 192.168.4.0/24. You want to prevent people using the public systems from accessing your private machines, so you decide to create subnets. You also have wireless Internet and want to separate wireless clients (never more than 10) on their own subnet.

You need to keep two things in mind about subnetting. First, start with the given subnet mask and move it to the right until you have the number of subnets you need. Second, forget the dots. They no longer define the subnets.

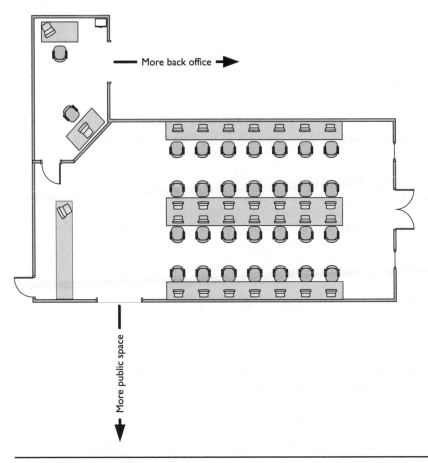

More back office ➡

More public space

Figure 7-29 Layout of the network

Never try to subnet without first converting to binary. Too many techs are what I call "victims of the dots." They are so used to working only with class licenses that they forget there's more to subnets than just /8, /16, and /24 networks. There is no reason network IDs must end on the dots. The computers, at least, think it's perfectly fine to have subnets that end at points between the periods, such as /26, /27, or even /22. The trick here is to stop thinking about network IDs and subnet masks just in their dotted decimal format and instead return to thinking of them as binary numbers.

NOTE Many authors will drop the trailing zeroes when using CIDR notation. I always do this when teaching because it's faster to write. So you might see a network ID like 192.168.4/24. The last octet of zero is *implied* by the /24. Either way works.

Let's begin subnetting the café's network of 192.168.4/24. Start by changing a zero to a one on the subnet mask so the /24 becomes a /25 subnet:

11111111111111111111111110000000

Calculating Hosts

Before going even one step further, you need to answer this question: On a /24 network, how many hosts can you have? Well, if you used dotted decimal notation you might say

192.168.4.1 to 192.168.4.254 = 254 hosts

But do this from the binary instead. In a /24 network, you have eight zeroes that can be the host ID:

00000001 to 11111110 = 254

There's a simple piece of math here: $2^x - 2$, where x represents the number of zeroes in the subnet mask.

$2^8 - 2 = 254$

If you remember this simple formula, you can always determine the number of hosts for a given subnet. This is critical! Memorize this!

If you have a /16 subnet mask on your network, what is the maximum number of hosts you can have on that network?

1. Because a subnet mask always has 32 digits, a /16 subnet means you have 16 zeroes left after the 16 ones.

2. $2^{16} - 2 = 65,534$ total hosts.

If you have a /26 subnet mask on your network, what is the maximum number of hosts you can have on that network?

1. Because a subnet mask always has 32 digits, a /26 subnet means you have 6 zeroes left after the 26 ones.

2. $2^6 - 2 = 62$ total hosts.

Excellent! Knowing how to determine the number of hosts for a particular subnet mask will help you tremendously in a moment.

Your First Subnet

Let's now make a subnet. All subnetting begins with a single network ID. In this scenario, you need to convert the 192.168.4/24 network ID for the café into three network IDs: one for the public computers, one for the private computers, and one for the wireless clients.

 NOTE You cannot subnet without using binary!

The primary tool for subnetting is the existing subnet mask. Write it out in binary. Place a line at the end of the ones, as shown in Figure 7-30.

Figure 7-30
Step 1 in subnetting

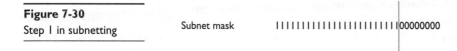
Subnet mask   IIIIIIIIIIIIIIIIIIIIIIII|00000000

Now draw a second line one digit to the right, as shown in Figure 7-31. You've now separated the subnet mask into three areas that I call (from left to right) the default subnet mask (DSM), the network ID extension (NE), and the hosts (H). These are not industry terms so you won't see them on the CompTIA Network+ exam, but they're a handy Mike Trick that makes the process of subnetting a lot easier.

Figure 7-31
Organizing the
subnet mask

Subnet mask   IIIIIIIIIIIIIIIIIIIIIIIII|00000000

DSM   NE H

You now have a /25 subnet mask. At this point, most people first learning how to subnet start to freak out. They're challenged by the idea that a subnet mask of /25 isn't going to fit into one of the three pretty subnets of 255.0.0.0, 255.255.0.0, or 255.255.255.0. They think, "That can't be right! Subnet masks are made out of only 255s and 0s." That's not correct. A subnet mask is a string of ones followed by a string of zeroes. People only convert it into dotted decimal to enter things into computers. So convert /25 into dotted decimal. First write out 25 ones, followed by seven zeroes. (Remember, subnet masks are *always* 32 binary digits long.)

11111111111111111111111110000000

Insert the periods in between every eight digits:

11111111.11111111.11111111.10000000

Then convert them to dotted decimal:

255.255.255.128

Get used to the idea of subnet masks that use more than 255s and 0s. Here are some examples of perfectly legitimate subnet masks. Try converting these to binary to see for yourself.

255.255.255.224
255.255.128.0
255.248.0.0

Calculating Subnets

When you subnet a network ID, you need to follow the rules and conventions dictated by the good folks who developed TCP/IP to ensure that your new subnets can interact properly with each other and with larger networks. All you need to remember for subnetting is this: start with a beginning subnet mask and extend the subnet extension until you have the number of subnets you need. The formula for determining how many subnets you create is 2^y, where y is the number of bits you add to the subnet mask.

Let's practice this a few times. Figure 7-32 shows a starting subnet of 255.255.255.0. If you move the network ID extension over one, it's only a single digit, 2^1.

Figure 7-32

Organizing the subnet mask

Starting subnet: 255.255.255.0

Subnet mask   IIIIIIIIIIIIIIIIIIIIIIIII00000000

Moving over one digit

That single digit is only a zero or a one, which gives you two subnets. You have only one problem—the café needs three subnets, not just two! So let's take /24 and subnet it down to /26. Extending the network ID by two digits creates four new network IDs, $2^2 = 4$. To see each of these network IDs, first convert the original network ID—192.168.4.0—into binary. Then add the four different network ID extensions to the end, as shown in Figure 7-33.

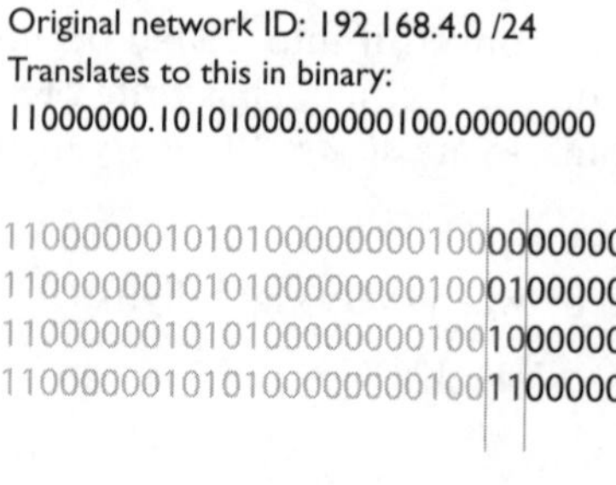

Figure 7-33

Creating the new network IDs

Original network ID: 192.168.4.0 /24
Translates to this in binary:
11000000.10101000.00000100.00000000

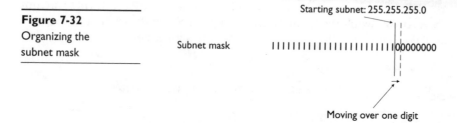

11000000101010000000010000000000
11000000101010000000010001000000
11000000101010000000010010000000
11000000101010000000010011000000

Figure 7-34 shows a sample of the IP addresses for each of the four new network IDs.

Figure 7-34
New network
ID address ranges

```
11000000101010000000001000000001
11000000101010000000001000000010
11000000101010000000001000000011
11000000101010000000001000000100

11000000101010000000001001000001
11000000101010000000001001000010
11000000101010000000001001000011
11000000101010000000001001000100

11000000101010000000001010000001
11000000101010000000001010000010
11000000101010000000001010000011
11000000101010000000001010000100

11000000101010000000001011000001
11000000101010000000001011000010
11000000101010000000001011000011
11000000101010000000001011000100
```

Now convert these four network IDs back to dotted decimal:

Network ID	Host Range
192.168.4.0/26	(192.168.4.1 – 192.168.4.62)
192.168.4.64/26	(192.168.4.65 – 192.168.4.126)
192.168.4.128/26	(192.168.4.129 – 192.168.4.190)
192.168.4.192/26	(192.168.4.193 – 192.168.4.254)

Congratulations! You've just taken a single network ID, 192.168.4.0/24, and subnetted it into four new network IDs! Figure 7-35 shows how you can use these new network IDs in a network.

You may notice that the café only needs three subnets, but you created four—you're wasting one. Because subnets are created by powers of two, you will often create more subnets than you need—welcome to subnetting.

NOTE   If wasting subnets seems contrary to the goal of efficient use, keep in mind that subnetting has two goals: efficiency and making multiple network IDs from a single network ID. This example is geared more toward the latter goal.

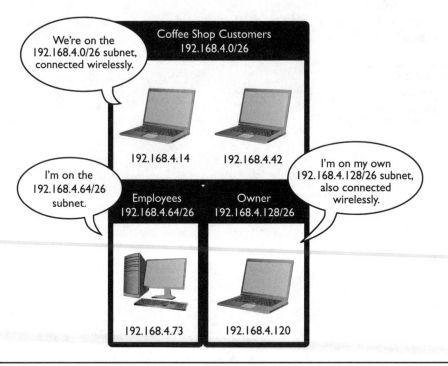

Figure 7-35 Three networks using the new network IDs

For a little more subnetting practice, let's create eight subnets on a /27 network. First, move the NE over three digits (Figure 7-36).

Figure 7-36

Moving the network ID extension three digits

Subnet mask	11111111111111111111111100000000
192.168.4.0	11000000101010000000010000000000
Add 000	11000000101010000000010000000000
Add 001	11000000101010000000010000100000
Add 010	11000000101010000000010001000000
Add 011	11000000101010000000010001100000
Add 100	11000000101010000000010010000000
Add 101	11000000101010000000010010100000
Add 110	11000000101010000000010011000000
Add 111	11000000101010000000010011100000

To help you visualize the address range, I'll calculate two of the subnets—using 001 and 011 (Figure 7-37). Please do the other six for practice.

Figure 7-37

Two of the eight network ID address ranges

```
11000000101010000000010000100000
11000000101010000000010000100001
11000000101010000000010000100010
                        ⋮
11000000101010000000010000111101
11000000101010000000010000111110
11000000101010000000010000111111


11000000101010000000010001100000
11000000101010000000010001100001
11000000101010000000010001100010
                        ⋮
11000000101010000000010001111101
11000000101010000000010001111110
11000000101010000000010001111111
```

Note that in this case you only get $2^5 - 2 = 30$ hosts per network ID! These better be small networks!

Converting these to dotted decimal, you get:

192.168.4.0/27 (192.168.4.1 – 192.168.4.30)
192.168.4.32/27 (192.168.4.33 – 192.168.4.62)
192.168.4.64/27 (192.168.4.65 – 192.168.4.94)
192.168.4.96/27 (192.168.4.97 – 192.168.4.126)
192.168.4.128/27 (192.168.4.129 – 192.168.4.158)
192.168.4.160/27 (192.168.4.161 – 192.168.4.190)
192.168.4.192/27 (192.168.4.193 – 192.168.4.222)
192.168.4.224/27 (192.168.4.225 – 192.168.4.254)

These two examples began with a Class C address. However, you can begin with any starting network ID. Nothing changes about the process you just learned.

NOTE If you order real, unique, ready-for-the-Internet IP addresses from your local ISP, you'll invariably get a classless set of IP addresses. More importantly, when you order them for clients, you need to be able to explain why their subnet mask is 255.255.255.192, when all the books they read tell them it should be 255.255.255.0!

All this assumes you can get an IPv4 address by the time you're reading this book. See Chapter 13 for the scoop on IPv6, the addressing scheme of the future.

Manual Dotted Decimal to Binary Conversion

The best way to convert from dotted decimal to binary and back is to use a calculator. It's easy, fast, and accurate. There's always a chance, however, that you may find yourself in a situation where you need to convert without a calculator. Fortunately, manual conversion, although a bit tedious, is also fairly easy. You just have to remember a single number: 128.

Take a piece of paper and write the number **128** in the top-left corner. Now, what is half of 128? That's right, 64. Write **64** next to 128. Now keep dividing the previous number in half until you get to the number 1. The result will look like this:

```
128   64   32   16   8   4   2   1
```

Notice that you have eight numbers. Each of these numbers corresponds to a position of one of the eight binary digits. To convert an 8-bit value to dotted decimal, just take the binary value and put the numbers under the corresponding eight digits. Wherever there's a 1, add that decimal value.

Let's take the binary value 10010110 into decimal. Write down the numbers as shown, and then write the binary values underneath each corresponding decimal number:

```
128   64   32   16   8   4   2   1


 1    0    0    1   0   1   1   0
```

Add the decimal values that have a 1 underneath:

$$128 + 16 + 4 + 2 = 150$$

Converting from decimal to binary is a bit more of a challenge. You still start with a line of decimal numbers starting with 128, but this time, you place the decimal value above. If the number you're trying to convert is greater than or equal to the number underneath, subtract it and place a 1 underneath that value. If not, then place a 0 under it and move the number to the next position to the right. Let's give this a try by converting 221 to binary. Begin by placing 221 over the 128:

```
221
128   64   32   16   8   4   2   1
 93
  1
```

Now place the remainder, 93, over the 64:

```
      93
128   64   32   16   8   4   2   1
      29
  1    1
```

Place the remainder, 29, over the 32. The number 29 is less than 32, so place a 0 underneath the 32 and move to 16:

```
                29
128   64   32   16   8   4   2   1
                13
  1    1    0    1
```

Then move to the 8:

```
                    13
128   64   32   16   8   4   2   1
                     5
  1    1    0    1   1
```

Then the 4:

```
                      5
128   64   32   16   8    4    2    1
                          1
 1    1    0    1    1    1
```

Then the 2. The number 1 is less than 2, so drop a 0 underneath and move to 1:

```
                          1
128   64   32   16   8    4    2    1
 1    1    0    1    1    1    0    1
```

Finally, the 1; 1 is equal to 1, so put a 1 underneath and you're done. The number 221 in decimal is equal to 11011101 in binary.

EXAM TIP   Make sure you can manually convert decimal to binary and binary to decimal.

CIDR: Subnetting in the Real World

I need to let you in on a secret—there's a better than average chance that you'll never have to do subnetting in the real world. That's not to say that subnetting isn't important. It's a critical part of the Internet's structure. Subnetting most commonly takes place in two situations: ISPs that receive class licenses from IANA and then subnet those class licenses for customers, and very large customers that take subnets (sometimes already subnetted class licenses from ISPs) and make their own subnets. Even if you'll never make a working subnet in the real world, there are a number of reasons to learn subnetting.

First and most obvious, the CompTIA Network+ exam expects you to know subnetting. For the exam, you need to be able to take any existing network ID and break it down into a given number of subnets. You need to know how many hosts the resulting network IDs possess. You need to be able to calculate the IP addresses and the new subnet masks for each of the new network IDs.

Second, even if you never do your own subnetting, you will most likely contact an ISP and get CIDR addresses. You can't think about subnet masks in terms of dotted decimal. You need to think of subnets in terms of CIDR values like /8, /22, /26, and so on.

Third, there's a better than average chance you'll look to more advanced IT certifications. Most Cisco, many Microsoft, and a large number of other certifications assume you understand subnetting. Subnetting is a competency standard that everyone who's serious about networking understands in detail—it's a clear separation between those who know networks and those who do not.

You've done well, my little padawan. Subnetting takes a little getting used to. Go take a break. Take a walk. Play some World of Warcraft. Or fire up your Steam client and see if I'm playing Counter-Strike or Left 4 Dead (player name "desweds"). After a good mental break, dive back into subnetting and *practice*. Take any old network ID and practice making multiple subnets—lots of subnets!

Using IP Addresses

Whew! After all that subnetting, you've reached the point where it's time to start actually using some IP addresses. That is, after all, the goal of going through all that pain. There are two ways to give a computer an IP address, subnet mask, and default gateway: either by typing in all the information (called *static addressing*) or by having a server program running on a system that automatically passes out all the IP information to systems as they boot up on or connect to a network (called *dynamic addressing*). Additionally, you must learn about a number of specialty IP addresses that have unique meanings in the IP world to make this all work.

Static IP Addressing

Static addressing means typing all of the IP information into each of your clients. But before you type in anything, you have to answer two questions: What are you typing in and where do you type it? Let's visualize a four-node network like the one shown in Figure 7-38.

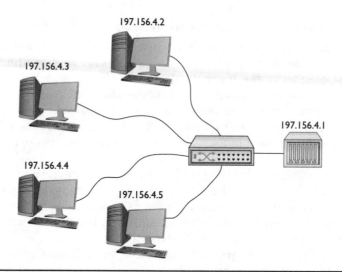

Figure 7-38   A small network

To make this network function, each computer must have an IP address, a subnet mask, and a default gateway. First, decide what network ID to use. In the old days, your ISP gave you a block of IP addresses to use. Assume that's still the method and you've been allocated a Class C license for 197.156.4/24. The first rule of Internet addressing is ... no one talks about Internet addressing. Actually, we can maul the *Fight Club* reference and instead say, "The first rule of Internet addressing is that you can do whatever you want with your own network ID." There are no rules other than to make sure every computer gets a legit IP address and subnet mask for your network ID and make sure every IP address is unique. You don't have to use the numbers in order, you don't have to give the default gateway the 192.156.4.1 address—you can do it any way you want. That said, most networks follow a common set of principles:

1. Give the default gateway the first IP address in the network ID.

2. Try to use the IP addresses in some kind of sequential order.

3. Try to separate servers from clients. For example, servers could have the IP addresses 197.156.4.10 to 197.156.4.19, whereas the clients range from 197.156.4.200 to 197.156.4.254.

4. Write down whatever you choose to do so the person who comes after you understands.

These principles have become unofficial standards for network techs, and following them will make you very popular with whoever has to manage your network in the future.

Now you can give each of the computers an IP address, subnet mask, and default gateway.

Every operating system has some method for you to enter in the static IP information. In Windows, you use the Internet Protocol Version 4 (TCP/IPv4) Properties dialog, as shown in Figure 7-39.

Figure 7-39

Entering static IP information in Windows Internet Protocol Version 4 (TCP/IPv4) Properties

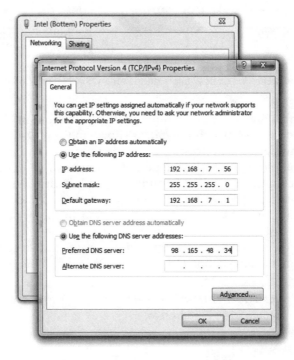

In Mac OS X, run the Network utility in System Preferences to enter in the IP information (Figure 7-40).

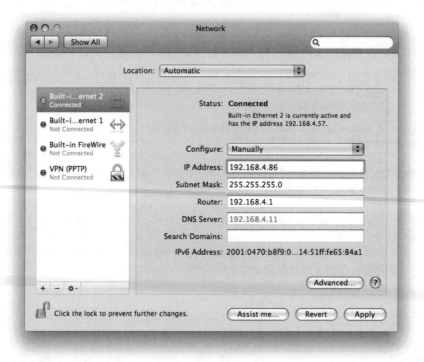

Figure 7-40 Entering static IP information in the OS X Network utility

The only universal tool for entering IP information on UNIX/Linux systems is the command-line ifconfig command, as shown in Figure 7-41. A warning about setting static IP addresses with ifconfig: any address entered will not be permanent and will be lost on reboot. To make the new IP permanent, you need to find and edit your network configuration files. Fortunately, modern distributions (distros) make your life a bit easier. Almost every flavor of UNIX/Linux comes with some handy graphical program, such as Network Configuration in the popular Ubuntu Linux distro (Figure 7-42).

Once you've added the IP information for at least two systems, you should always verify using the ping command, as shown in Figure 7-43.

CAUTION Always verify with `ping`—it's too easy to make a typo when you enter static IP addresses.

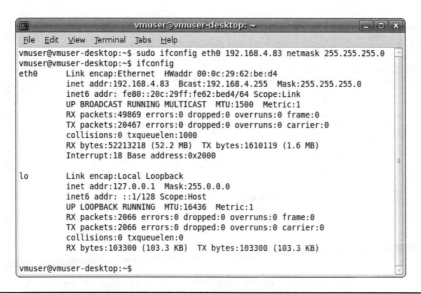

Figure 7-41 Using the ifconfig command to set static IP addresses

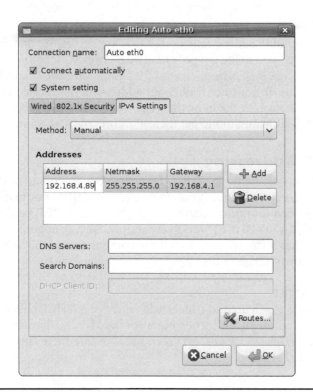

Figure 7-42 Ubuntu's Network Configuration utility

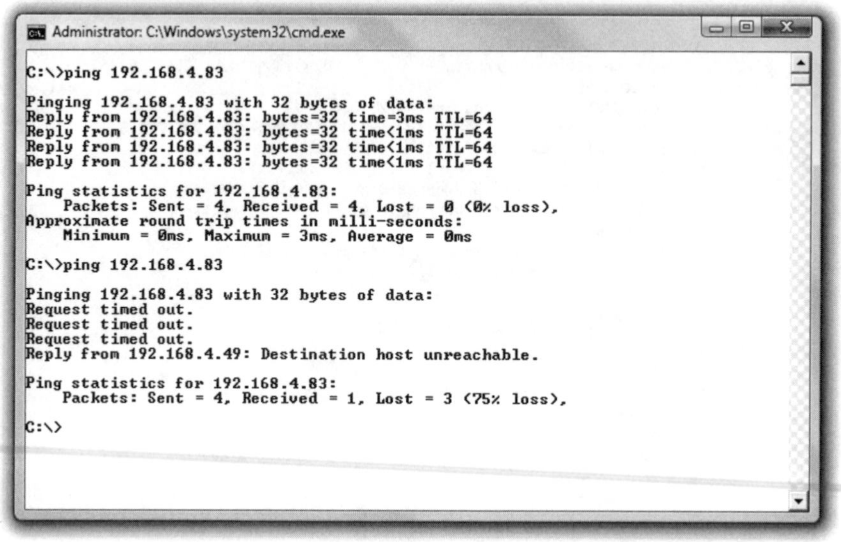

Figure 7-43 Two pings (successful ping on top, unsuccessful ping on bottom)

If you've entered an IP address and your ping is not successful, first check your IP settings. Odds are good you made a typo. Otherwise, check your connections, driver, and so forth. Static addressing has been around for a long time and is still heavily used for more critical systems on your network. Static addressing poses one big problem, however: making any changes to the network is a serious pain. Most systems today use a far easier and more flexible method to get their IP information: dynamic IP addressing.

Dynamic IP Addressing

Dynamic IP addressing, better known as *Dynamic Host Configuration Protocol (DHCP)* or the older (and long vanished) *Bootstrap Protocol (BOOTP)*, automatically assigns an IP address whenever a computer connects to the network. DHCP (and BOOTP, though for simplicity I'll just say DHCP) works very simply. First, configure a computer to use DHCP. Every OS has some method to tell the computer to use DHCP, as in the Windows example shown in Figure 7-44.

How DHCP Works

Once a computer is configured to use DHCP, we call it a DHCP client. When a DHCP client boots up, it automatically sends out a special DHCP Discover packet using the broadcast address. This DHCP Discover message asks "Are there any DHCP servers out there?" (See Figure 7-45.)

Figure 7-44   Setting up for DHCP

Figure 7-45
Computer
sending out a
DHCP Discover
message

For DHCP to work, one system on the LAN must be running special DHCP server software. This server is designed to respond to DHCP Discover requests with a DHCP Offer. The DHCP server is configured to pass out IP addresses from a range (called a *DHCP scope*) and a subnet mask (Figure 7-46). It also passes out other information, known generically as options, that cover an outrageously large number of choices, such as your default gateway, DNS server, Network Time server, and so on.

Server Settings (DHCP)

DHCP Server: ⦿ **Enable** ○ **Disable** ○ **DHCP Relay**

DHCP Server: [ ] . [ ] . [ ] . [ ]

Starting IP Address: 192.168.1. [100]

Maximum Number of DHCP Users: [50]

Client Lease Time: [0] minutes (0 means one day)

Static DNS 1: [ ] . [ ] . [ ] . [ ]

Static DNS 2: [ ] . [ ] . [ ] . [ ]

Static DNS 3: [ ] . [ ] . [ ] . [ ]

WINS: [ ] . [ ] . [ ] . [ ]

Figure 7-46 DHCP server main screen

EXAM TIP DHCP servers can be set up to reserve addresses for specific machines through what's called, appropriately, *DHCP reservations.* You use these for servers inside your network, for example, so if you had to change their IP addresses for some reason, you could do it from a central location. The other option is to use static IPs, but then you'd need to log in to each server to change the IP addresses.

Figure 7-47 shows the configuration screen from the popular DHCP Server that comes with Windows Server 2008. Note the single scope. Figure 7-48 shows the same DHCP Server tool, in this case, detailing the options screen. At this point, you're probably not sure what any of these options are for. Don't worry. I'll return to these topics in later chapters.

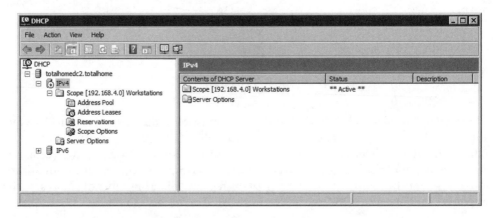

Figure 7-47 DHCP Server configuration screen

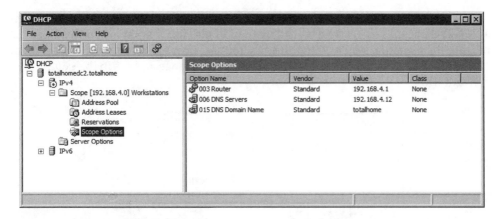

Figure 7-48   DHCP Server options screen

The DHCP client sends out a DHCP Request—a poor name choice as it is really accepting the offer. The DHCP server then sends a DHCP Acknowledge and lists the MAC address as well as the IP information given to the DHCP client in a database (Figure 7-49).

Figure 7-49   i-cap Request and Acknowledge

The acceptance from the DHCP client of the DHCP server's data is called a *DHCP lease*. A DHCP lease is set for a fixed amount of time, generally five to eight days. Near the end of the lease time, the DHCP client simply makes another DHCP Discover message. The DHCP server looks at the MAC address information and, unless another computer has taken the lease, always gives the DHCP client the same IP information, including the same IP address.

Living with DHCP

DHCP is very convenient and, as such, very popular. It's so popular that you'll very rarely see a user's computer on any network using static addressing.

You should know how to deal with DHCP problems. The single biggest issue is when a DHCP client tries to get a DHCP address and fails. You'll know when this happens because the operating system will post some form of error telling you there's a problem (Figure 7-50) and the DHCP client will have a rather strange address in the 169.254/16 network ID.

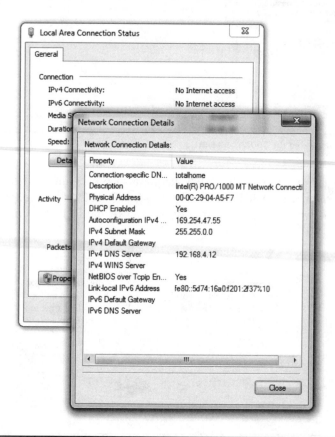

Figure 7-50 DHCP error in Windows 7

This special IP address is generated by *Automatic Private IP Addressing (APIPA)*. All DHCP clients are designed to generate an APIPA address automatically if they do not receive a response to a DHCP Discover message. The client only generates the last two octets of an APIPA address. This enables the dynamic clients on a single network to continue to communicate with each other because they are on the same network ID.

Unfortunately, APIPA cannot issue a default gateway, so you'll never get on the Internet using APIPA. That provides a huge clue to a DHCP problem: you can communicate with other computers on your network, but you can't get to the Internet.

EXAM TIP Systems that use static IP addressing can never have DHCP problems.

If you can't get to the Internet, use whatever tool your OS provides to check your IP address. If it's an APIPA address, you know instantly that you have a DHCP problem. First of all, try to reestablish the lease manually. Every OS has some way to do this. In Windows, you can type the following command:

```
ipconfig /renew
```

On a Mac, go to System Preferences and use the Network utility (Figure 7-51).

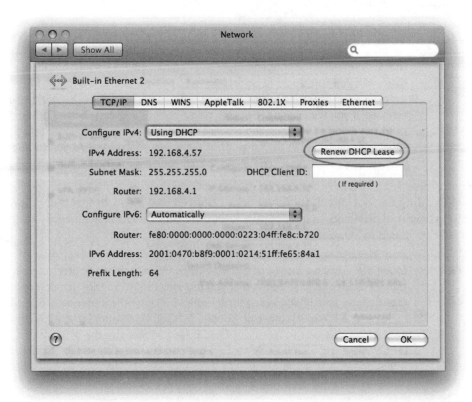

Figure 7-51 Network utility in System Preferences

 EXAM TIP CompTIA loves TCP and UDP port numbers, so make sure you know that DHCP and BOOTP servers use UDP ports 67 and 68. You'll also see the term BOOTPS on the exam, which simply refers to a BOOTP server (as opposed to BOOTPC for a BOOTP client).

Sometimes you might find yourself in a situation where your computer gets confused and won't grab an IP address no matter what you try. In these cases, you should first force the computer to release its lease. In Windows, get to a command prompt and type these two commands; follow each by pressing ENTER:

```
ipconfig /release
ipconfig /renew
```

In UNIX/Linux and Mac OS X, use the ifconfig command to release and renew a DHCP address. Here's the syntax to release:

```
sudo ifconfig eth0 down
```

And here's the syntax to renew:

```
sudo ifconfig eth0 up
```

NOTE With UNIX, Linux, and Mac OS X command-line commands, case matters. If you run `sudo ifconfig eth0 down` all in lowercase, for example, your Ethernet connection will drop as the DHCP or BOOTP lease is released. If you try running the same command in uppercase, on the other hand, the Linux et al. command prompt will look at you quizzically and then snort with derision. "What's this SUDO of which you speak?" And then give you a prompt for a "real" command. Watch your case with UNIX/Linux/OS X!

Depending on your distribution, you may not need to type **sudo** first, but you will need to have root privileges to use ifconfig. Root privileges are Linux's version of administrative privileges in Windows.

EXAM TIP Make sure you know how to configure your computers to use static IP addressing and know that you use ping to ensure they can communicate. For dynamic IP addressing, make sure you know the common protocol—DHCP—and the much older protocol—BOOTP. Understand that each client must have some way to "turn on" DHCP. Also understand the concept of a DHCP client and a DHCP server. Last but not least, be comfortable with APIPA and releasing and renewing a lease on a client.

Special IP Addresses

The folks who invented TCP/IP created a number of special IP addresses you need to know about. The first special address is 127.0.0.1—the *loopback address*. When you tell a device to send data to 127.0.0.1, you're telling that device to send the packets to itself. The loopback address has a number of uses. One of the most common is to use it with the ping command. I use the command `ping 127.0.0.1` to test a NIC's capability to send and receive packets.

EXAM TIP Even though, by convention, you use 127.0.0.1 as the loopback address, the entire 127.0.0.0/8 subnet is reserved for loopback addresses. You can use any address in the 127.0.0.0/8 subnet as a loopback address.

Lots of folks use TCP/IP in networks that either aren't connected to the Internet or want to hide their computers from the rest of Internet. Certain groups of IP addresses, known as *private IP addresses,* are available to help in these situations. All routers destroy private IP addresses. Those addresses can never be used on the Internet, making them a handy way to hide systems. Anyone can use these private IP addresses, but they're useless for systems that need to access the Internet—unless you use the mysterious and powerful NAT, which I'll discuss in the next chapter. (Bet you're dying to learn about NAT now!) For the moment, however, let's just look at the ranges of addresses that are designated as private IP addresses:

- 10.0.0.0 through 10.255.255.255 (1 Class A license)
- 172.16.0.0 through 172.31.255.255 (16 Class B licenses)
- 192.168.0.0 through 192.168.255.255 (256 Class C licenses)

All other IP addresses are public IP addresses.

 EXAM TIP Make sure you can quickly tell the difference between a private and a public IP address for the CompTIA Network+ exam.

Chapter Review

Questions

1. How many bits does an IPv4 address consist of?

   A. 16

   B. 32

   C. 64

   D. 128

2. Identify the network ID section of the following IP address and subnet mask: 10.14.12.43–255.255.255.0.

   A. 10.14

   B. 43

   C. 10.14.12

   D. 14.12.43

3. Which of the following is a proper subnet mask?

   A. 11111111111111111111111100000000

   B. 00000000000000000000000011111111

   C. 10101010101010101010101011111111

   D. 01010101010101010101010100000000

4. What does ARP stand for?

   A. Address Reconciliation Process

   B. Automated Ranking Protocol

   C. Address Resolution Protocol

   D. Advanced Resolution Protocol

5. Identify the class of the following IP address: 146.203.143.101.

   A. Class A

   B. Class B

   C. Class C

   D. Class D

6. Which of the following are valid subnet masks? (Select two.)

   A. 11111111.11111111.11100000.00000000

   B. 11111111.11111111.11111111.00000000

   C. 11111111.00000000.11111111.00000000

   D. 00000000.00000000.11111111.11111111

7. What is the maximum number of hosts in a /19 subnet?

   A. 254

   B. 8,192

   C. 16,382

   D. 8,190

8. What is the number 138 in binary?

   A. 10001010

   B. 10101010

   C. 10000111

   D. 11001010

9. When DHCP Discover fails, what process will the client use to generate an address for itself?

 A. ATAPI (Automatic Temporary Address Program Initiator)

 B. APIPA (Automatic Private IP Addressing)

 C. ATIPA (Automatic Temporary IP Address)

 D. APFBA (Automatic Programmable Fall Back Address)

10. Which of the following is a valid loopback address?

 A. 128.0.0.1

 B. 127.0.0.0

 C. 128.0.0.255

 D. 127.24.0.1

Answers

1. **B.** An IPv4 address consists of 32 bits.

2. **C.** The network ID is the first three octets when using the specified subnet.

3. **A.** A subnet is all ones followed by zeroes.

4. **C.** Address Resolution Protocol.

5. **B.** The address is Class B.

6. **A and B.** Subnet masks, when written in binary, consist of a string of ones followed by a string of zeroes.

7. **D.** The total number of hosts is 8,190 ($2^{13} - 2$).

8. **A.** 10001010.

9. **B.** APIPA (Automatic Private IP Addressing).

10. **D.** 127.24.0.1. Any address in the 127.0.0.0/8 subnet will work as a loopback.

The Wonderful World of Routing

The CompTIA Network+ certification exam expects you to know how to

- 1.4 Explain the purpose and properties of routing and switching
- 2.1 Given a scenario, install and configure routers and switches: routing tables, NAT, PAT
- 2.5 Given a scenario, troubleshoot common router and switch problems

To achieve these goals, you must be able to

- Explain how routers work
- Describe dynamic routing technologies
- Install and configure a router successfully

The true beauty and amazing power of TCP/IP lies in one word: routing. Routing enables us to interconnect individual LANs into WANs. Routers, the magic boxes that act as the interconnection points, have all the built-in smarts to inspect incoming packets and forward them toward their eventual LAN destination. Routers are, for the most part, automatic. They require very little in terms of maintenance once their initial configuration is complete because they can talk to each other to determine the best way to send IP packets. The goal of this chapter is to take you into the world of routers and show you how they do this.

The chapter discusses how routers work, including an in-depth look at different types of Network Address Translation (NAT), and then dives into an examination of various dynamic routing protocols. You'll learn about distance vector protocols, including Routing Information Protocol (RIP) and Border Gateway Protocol (BGP), among others. The chapter finishes with the nitty-gritty details of installing and configuring a router successfully.

Not only will you understand how routers work, you should be able to set up a basic home router and diagnose common router issues by the end of this chapter.

Historical/Conceptual

How Routers Work

A *router* is any piece of hardware that forwards packets based on their destination IP address. Routers work, therefore, at the Network layer of the OSI model and at the Internet layer of the TCP/IP model.

Classically, routers are dedicated boxes that contain at least two connections, although many routers contain many more connections. In a business setting, for example, you might see a Cisco 2600 Series device, one of the most popular routers ever made. These routers are a bit on the older side, but Cisco builds their routers to last. With occasional software upgrades, a typical router will last for many years. The 2611 router shown in Figure 8-1 has two connections (the other connections are used for maintenance and configuration). The two "working" connections are circled. One port leads to one network; the other leads to another network. The router reads the IP addresses of the packets to determine where to send the packets. (I'll elaborate on how that works in a moment.)

Figure 8-1   Cisco 2611 router

Most techs today get their first exposure to routers with the ubiquitous home routers that enable PCs to connect to a DSL modem or a cable modem (Figure 8-2). The typical home router, however, serves multiple functions, often combining a router, a switch, and other features like a firewall (for protecting your network from intruders), a DHCP server, and much more into a single box.

Figure 8-2
Business end of
a typical home
router

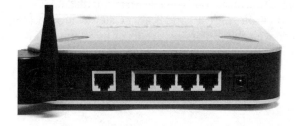

NOTE See Chapter 16 for an in-depth look at firewalls and other security options.

Figure 8-3 shows the electronic diagram for a two-port Cisco router, whereas Figure 8-4 shows the diagram for a Linksys home router.

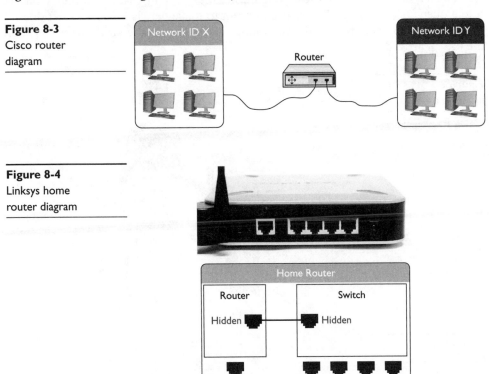

Figure 8-3
Cisco router
diagram

Figure 8-4
Linksys home
router diagram

Note that both boxes connect two networks. The big difference is that the LAN side of the Linksys home router connects immediately to the built-in switch. That's convenient! You don't have to buy a separate switch to connect multiple computers to the cable modem or DSL receiver. Many users and even some new techs look at that router, though, and say, "It has five ports so it'll connect to five different networks," when in reality it can connect only two networks. The extra physical ports belong to the built-in switch.

All routers—big and small, plain or bundled with a switch—examine packets and then send the packets to the proper destination. Let's take a look at that process in more detail now.

Test Specific

Routing Tables

Routing begins as packets come into the router for handling (Figure 8-5). The router immediately strips off any of the Layer 2 information and drops the resulting IP packet into a queue (Figure 8-6). The important point to make here is that the router doesn't care where the packet originated. Everything is dropped into the same queue based on the time it arrived.

Figure 8-5
Incoming packets

Figure 8-6
All incoming packets stripped of Layer 2 data and dropped into a common queue

The router inspects each packet's destination IP address and then sends the IP packet out the correct port. To perform this inspection, each router comes with a *routing table* that tells the router exactly where to send the packets. Figure 8-7 shows the simple routing table for a typical home router. This router has only two ports internally: one that connects to whichever type of service provider you use to bring the Internet into your home (cable/DSL/fiber or whatever)—labeled as WAN in the Interface column of the table—and another one that connects to a built-in four-port switch—labeled LAN in the table. Figure 8-8 is a diagram for the router. Let's inspect this router's routing table; this table is the key to understanding and controlling the process of forwarding packets to their proper destination.

Figure 8-7

Routing table
from a home
router

Routing Table Entry List			Refresh
Destination LAN IP	Subnet Mask	Gateway	Interface
10.12.14.0	255.255.255.0	0.0.0.0	LAN
76.30.4.0	255.255.254.0	0.0.0.0	WAN
0.0.0.0	0.0.0.0	76.30.4.1	WAN
			Close

Figure 8-8

Electronic
diagram of
the router

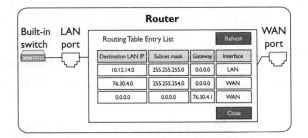

Each row in this little router's simple routing table defines a single route. Each column identifies specific criteria. Reading Figure 8-7 from left to right shows the following:

- **Destination LAN IP**   A defined network ID. Every network ID directly connected to one of the router's ports is always listed here.

- **Subnet Mask**   To define a network ID, you need a subnet mask (described in Chapter 7).

Your router uses the combination of the destination LAN IP and subnet mask to see if a packet matches that route. For example, if you had a packet with the destination 10.12.14.26 coming into the router, the router would check the network ID and subnet mask. It would quickly determine that the packet matches the first route shown in Figure 8-7. The other two columns in the routing table then tell the router what to do with the packet:

- **Gateway**   The IP address for the *next hop* router; in other words, where the packet should go. If the outgoing packet is for a network ID that's not directly connected to the router, the Gateway column tells the router the IP address of a router to which to send this packet. That router then handles the packet and your router is done (you count on well-configured routers to make sure your packet will get to where it needs to go!). If the network ID is directly connected, then you don't need a gateway. Based on what's needed, this is set to 0.0.0.0 or to the IP address of the directly connected port.

- **Interface** Tells the router which of its ports to use. On this router, it uses the terms "LAN" and "WAN." Other routing tables use the port's IP address or some other type of abbreviation. Cisco routers, for example, use f0/0, f0/1, and so on.

The router compares the destination IP address on a packet to every listing in the routing table and then sends the packet out.

The router reads every line and then decides what to do. Some routers compare a packet to the routing table by starting from the top down and other routers read from the bottom up. The direction the router chooses to read the routing table isn't important because the router must compare the destination IP address to every route in the routing table. The most important trick to reading a routing table is to remember that a zero (0) means "anything." For example, in Figure 8-7, the first route's destination LAN IP is 10.12.14.0. You can compare that to the subnet mask (255.255.255.0) to confirm that this is a /24 network. This tells you that any value (between 1 and 254) is acceptable for the last value in the 10.12.14/24 network ID.

Routing tables tell you a lot about the network connections. From just this single routing table, for example, the diagram in Figure 8-9 can be drawn.

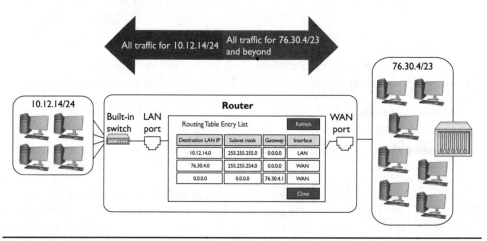

Figure 8-9 The network based on the routing table in Figure 8-7

So how do I know the 76.30.4.1 port connects to another network? The third line of the routing table shows the default route for this router, and every router has one. (There's one exception to this. See the Note that follows.) This line says

(*Any destination address*) (*with any subnet mask*) (*forward it to* 76.30.4.1) (*using my* WAN port)

Destination LAN IP	Subnet Mask	Gateway	Interface
0.0.0.0	0.0.0.0	76.30.4.1	WAN

The default route is very important because this tells the router exactly what to do with every incoming packet *unless* another line in the routing table gives another route. Excellent! Interpret the other two lines of the routing table in Figure 8-7 in the same fashion:

(Any packet for the 10.12.14.0) (/24 network ID) (don't use a gateway) (just ARP on the LAN interface to get the MAC address and send it directly to the recipient)

Destination LAN IP	Subnet Mask	Gateway	Interface
10.12.14.0	255.255.255.0	0.0.0.0	LAN

(Any packet for the 76.30.4.0) (/23 network ID) (don't use a gateway) (just ARP on the WAN interface to get the MAC address and send it directly to the recipient)

Destination LAN IP	Subnet Mask	Gateway	Interface
76.30.4.0	255.255.254.0	0.0.0.0	WAN

I'll let you in on a little secret. Routers aren't the only devices that use routing tables. In fact, every node (computer, printer, TCP/IP-capable soda dispenser, whatever) on the network also has a routing table.

At first, this may seem silly—doesn't every computer only have a single Ethernet connection and, therefore, all data traffic has to go out that port? First of all, many computers have more than one NIC. (These are called *multihomed computers*. See the following Note for more details.) But even if your computer has only a single NIC, how does it know what to do with an IP address like 127.0.01? Second, every packet sent out of your computer uses the routing table to figure out where the packet should go, whether directly to a node on your network or to your gateway.

Here's an example of a routing table in Windows. This machine connects to the home router described earlier, so you'll recognize the IP addresses it uses.

```
C:\>route print
===========================================================================
Interface List
0x1 ......................... MS TCP Loopback interface
```

```
0x2 ...00 11 d8 30 16 c0 ...... NVIDIA nForce Networking Controller
===========================================================================
===========================================================================
Active Routes:
Network Destination        Netmask         Gateway       Interface  Metric
0.0.0.0                    0.0.0.0       10.12.14.1    10.12.14.201      1
10.12.14.0           255.255.255.0     10.12.14.201   10.12.14.201      1
10.12.14.201       255.255.255.255       127.0.0.1      127.0.0.1       1
10.12.14.255       255.255.255.255     10.12.14.201   10.12.14.201      1
127.0.0.0              255.0.0.0         127.0.0.1      127.0.0.1       1
169.254.0.0          255.255.0.0       10.12.14.201   10.12.14.201     20
224.0.0.0              240.0.0.0        10.12.14.201   10.12.14.201      1
255.255.255.255    255.255.255.255     10.12.14.201   10.12.14.201      1
Default Gateway:        10.12.14.1
===========================================================================
Persistent Routes:
None
C:\>
```

Unlike the routing table for the typical home router you saw in Figure 8-7, this one seems a bit more complicated, if for no other reason than it has a lot more routes. My PC has only a single NIC, though, so it's not quite as complicated as it might seem at first glance. Take a look at the details. First note that my computer has an IP address of 10.12.14.201/24 and 10.12.14.1 as the default gateway.

 NOTE Every modern operating system gives you tools to view a computer's routing table. Most techs use the command line or terminal window interface—often called simply *terminal*—because it's fast. To see your routing table in Windows, Linux, or in Mac OS X, for example, type this command at a terminal: `netstat -r`. In Windows, try this command as an alternative: `route print`.

You should note two differences in the columns from what you saw in the previous routing table. First, the interface has an actual IP address—10.12.14.201, plus the loopback of 127.0.0.1—instead of the word "LAN." Second—and this is part of the magic of routing—is something called the metric.

A *metric* is just a relative value that defines the "cost" of using this route. The power of TCP/IP is that a packet can take more than one route to get to the same place. Figure 8-10 shows a networked router with two routes to the same place. The router has a route to Network B with a metric of 1 using Route 1, and a second route to Network B using Route 2 with a metric of 10.

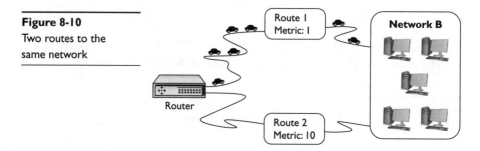

Figure 8-10

Two routes to the same network

NOTE When a router has more than one route to the same network, it's up to the person in charge of that router to assign a different metric for each route. With dynamic routing protocols (discussed in detail later in the chapter in "Dynamic Routing"), the routers determine the proper metric for each route.

Lowest routes always win. In this case, the router will always use the route with the metric of 1, unless that route suddenly stopped working. In that case, the router would automatically switch to the route with the 10 metric (Figure 8-11). This is the cornerstone of how the Internet works! The entire Internet is nothing more than a whole bunch of big, powerful routers connected to lots of other big, powerful routers. Connections go up and down all the time, and routers (with multiple routes) constantly talk to each other, detecting when a connection goes down and automatically switching to alternate routes.

Figure 8-11
When a route
no longer works,
the router
automatically
switches.

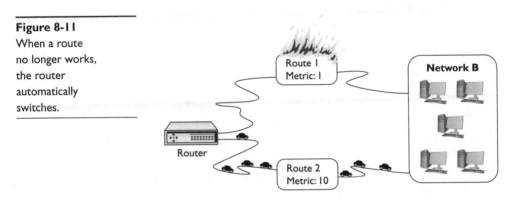

I'll go through this routing table one line at a time. Remember, every address is compared to every line in the routing table before it goes out, so it's no big deal if the default route is at the beginning or the end. Windows machines read from bottom up, going through all local addresses before going out to the router, so that's how I'll go through it here.

The bottom line defines the default IP broadcast. If you send out an IP broadcast (255.255.255.255), your NIC knows to send it out to the local network.

Network Destination	Netmask	Gateway	Interface	Metric
255.255.255.255	255.255.255.255	10.12.14.201	10.12.14.201	1

The next line up is the multicast address range. Odds are good you'll never need it, but most operating systems put it in automatically.

Network Destination	Netmask	Gateway	Interface	Metric
224.0.0.0	240.0.0.0	10.12.14.201	10.12.14.201	1

The next route says that any addresses in the 169.254/16 network ID are part of the LAN (remember, whenever the gateway and interface are the same, the connection is local). If your computer uses Dynamic Host Configuration Protocol (DHCP) and can't get an IP address, this route would enable you to communicate with other computers on the network that are also having the same DHCP problem. Note the high metric.

Network Destination	Netmask	Gateway	Interface	Metric
169.254.0.0	255.255.0.0	10.12.14.201	10.12.14.201	20

This next line is another loopback, but examine it carefully. Earlier you learned that only 127.0.0.1 is the loopback, but according to this route, any 127/8 address is the loopback.

Network Destination	Netmask	Gateway	Interface	Metric
127.0.0.0	255.0.0.0	127.0.0.1	127.0.0.1	1

The next line up is the directed broadcast. Occasionally your computer needs to send a broadcast to the other computers on the same network ID. That's what this row signifies. This difference between a directed broadcast and a full broadcast is the former goes only to the targeted subnet, not the full broadcast domain.

Network Destination	Netmask	Gateway	Interface	Metric
10.12.14.255	255.255.255.255	0.12.14.201	10.12.14.201	1

Okay, on to the next line. This one's easy. Anything addressed to this machine should go right back to it through the loopback (127.0.0.1).

Network Destination	Netmask	Gateway	Interface	Metric
10.12.14.201	255.255.255.255	127.0.0.1	127.0.0.1	1

The next line defines the local connection: (*Any packet for the* 10.12.14.0) (*/24 network ID*) (*don't use a gateway*) (*just ARP on the LAN interface to get the MAC address and send it directly to the recipient*) (*Cost of* 1 *to use this route*).

Network Destination	Netmask	Gateway	Interface	Metric
10.12.14.0	255.255.255.0	10.12.14.201	10.12.14.201	1

So, if a gateway of 10.12.14.201 here means "don't use a gateway," why put a number in at all? Local connections don't use the default gateway, although every routing table has a gateway column. The Microsoft folks had to put *something* there, thus they put the IP address of the NIC. That's why the gateway address is the same as the interface address. The NIC is the gateway between the local PC and the destination. Just pass it out the NIC and the destination will get it.

This is how Windows XP displays the gateway on this line. In Windows Vista and Windows 7, the gateway value for local connections just says "on-link"—a clear description! Part of the joy of learning routing tables is getting used to how different operating systems deal with issues like these.

The top line defines the default route: (*Any destination address*) (*with any subnet mask*) (*forward it to my default gateway*) (*using my NIC*) (*Cost of* 1 *to use this route*). Anything that's not local goes to the router and from there out to the destination (with the help of other routers).

Network Destination	Netmask	Gateway	Interface	Metric
0.0.0.0	0.0.0.0	10.12.14.1	10.12.14.201	1

Just for fun, let's add one more routing table; this time from my old Cisco 2811, which is still connecting me to the Internet after all these years! I access the Cisco router remotely from my Windows 7 system using a tool called PuTTY (you'll see more of PuTTY throughout this book), log in, and then run this command:

```
show ip route
```

Don't let all the text confuse you. The first part, labeled Codes, is just a help screen to let you know what the letters at the beginning of each row mean:

```
Gateway#show ip route

Codes: C - connected, S - static, R - RIP, M - mobile, B - BGP
       D - EIGRP, EX - EIGRP external, O - OSPF, IA - OSPF inter area
       N1 - OSPF NSSA external type 1, N2 - OSPF NSSA external type 2
       E1 - OSPF external type 1, E2 - OSPF external type 2
       i - IS-IS, su - IS-IS summary, L1 - IS-IS level-1, L2 - IS-IS level-2
       ia - IS-IS inter area, * - candidate default, U - per-user static route
       o - ODR, P - periodic downloaded static route

Gateway of last resort is 208.190.121.38 to network 0.0.0.0

C     208.190.121.0/24 is directly connected, FastEthernet0/1
C     192.168.4.0/24 is directly connected, FastEthernet0/0
S*    0.0.0.0/0 [1/0] via 208.190.121.38
```

These last three lines are the routing table. The router has two Ethernet interfaces called FastEthernet0/1 and FastEthernet0/0. This is how Cisco names router interfaces.

Reading from the top, you see that FastEthernet0/1 is directly connected (the C at the beginning of the line) to the network 208.190.121.0/24. Any packets that match 208.190.121.0/24 go out on FastEthernet0/1. Equally, any packets for the connected 192.168.4.0/24 network go out on FastEthernet0/0. The last route gets an S for static because I entered it in manually. The asterisk (*) shows that this is the default route.

In this section, you've seen three different types of routing tables from three different types of devices. Even though these routing tables have different ways to list the routes and different ways to show the categories, they all perform the same job: moving IP packets to the correct interface to ensure they get to where they need to go.

Freedom from Layer 2

Routers enable you to connect different types of network technologies. You now know that routers strip off all of the Layer 2 data from the incoming packets, but thus far you've only seen routers that connect to different Ethernet networks—and that's just fine with routers. But routers can connect to almost anything that stores IP packets. Not to take away from some very exciting upcoming chapters, but Ethernet is not the only networking technology out there. Once you want to start making long-distance connections, Ethernet disappears, and technologies with names like Data-Over-Cable Service Interface Specification (DOCSIS) (cable modems), Frame Relay, and Asynchronous Transfer Mode (ATM) take over. These technologies are not Ethernet, and they all work very differently than Ethernet. The only common feature of these technologies is they all carry IP packets inside their Layer 2 encapsulations.

Most serious (that is, not home) routers enable you to add interfaces. You buy the router and then snap in different types of interfaces depending on your needs. Note the Cisco router in Figure 8-12. Like most Cisco routers, it comes with removable modules.

If you're connecting Ethernet to ATM, you buy an Ethernet module and an ATM module. If you're connecting Ethernet to a DOCSIS (cable modem) network, you buy an Ethernet module and a DOCSIS module.

Figure 8-12
Modular
Cisco router

Network Address Translation

The ease of connecting computers together using TCP/IP and routers creates a rather glaring security risk. If every computer on a network must have a unique IP address, and TCP/IP applications enable you to do something on a remote computer, what's to stop a malicious programmer from writing a program that does things on your computer that you don't want done? All he or she would need is the IP address for your computer and the attacker could target you from anywhere on the network. Now expand this concept to the Internet. A computer sitting in Peoria can be attacked by a program run from Bangkok as long as both computers connect directly to the Internet. And this happens all the time.

Security is one problem. The other is a deal breaker—the IANA assigned the last of the IPv4 addresses as of February 2011. Although you can still get an IP address from an ISP, the days of easy availability are over. Routers running some form of *Network Address Translation (NAT)* hide the IP addresses of computers on the LAN but still enable those computers to communicate with the broader Internet. NAT extended the useful life of IPv4 addressing on the Internet for many years. NAT is extremely common and heavily in use, so learning how it works is important. Note that many routers offer NAT as a feature *in addition to* the core capability of routing. NAT is not routing, but a separate technology. With that said, you are ready to dive into how NAT works to protect computers connected by router technology and conserve IP addresses as well.

The Setup

Here's the situation. You have a LAN with eight computers that need access to the Internet. With classic TCP/IP and routing, several things have to happen. First, you need to get a block of legitimate, unique, expensive IP addresses from an Internet service provider (ISP). You could call up an ISP and purchase a network ID, say 1.2.3.136/29. Second, you assign an IP address to each computer and to the LAN connection on the router. Third, you assign the IP address for the ISP's router to the WAN connection on the local router, such as 1.2.4.1. After everything is configured, the network looks like Figure 8-13. All of the clients on the network have the same default gateway (1.2.3.137). This router, called a *gateway router* (or simply a *gateway*), acts as the default gateway for a number of client computers.

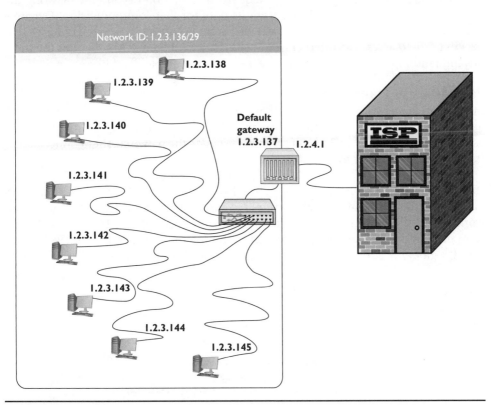

Figure 8-13   Network setup

This style of network mirrors how computers in LANs throughout the world connected to the Internet for the first 20 years, but the major problems of security and a finite number of IP addresses worsened as more and more computers connected.

NAT solved both of these issues for many years. NAT is a simple concept: The router replaces the source IP address of a computer with its outside interface address on outgoing packets. The simplest NAT, called *basic NAT*, does exactly that, translating the private or internal IP address to a global IP address on a one-to-one basis.

 EXAM TIP NAT replaces the source IP address of a computer with the source IP address from the outside router interface on outgoing packets. NAT is performed by NAT-capable routers.

With *dynamic NAT*, in contrast, many computers can share a pool of routable IP addresses that number fewer than the computers. The NAT might have 10 routable IP addresses, for example, to serve 40 computers on the LAN. LAN traffic uses the internal, private IP addresses. When a computer requests information beyond the network, the NAT doles out a routable IP address from its pool for that communication. Dynamic NAT is also called *Pooled NAT*. This works well enough—unless you're the unlucky 11th person to try to access the Internet from behind the company NAT—but has the obvious limitation of still needing many true, expensive, routable IP addresses.

Port Address Translation

Most internal networks today don't have one machine, of course, nor do most IT departments want to pay for many routable IP addresses. Instead, internal networks use a block of private IP addresses for the hosts inside the network. They connect to the Internet through one or more public IP addresses.

The most common form of NAT that handles this one-to-many connection—called *Port Address Translation (PAT)*—uses port numbers to map traffic from specific machines in the network. Let's use a simple example to make the process clear. John has a network at his office that uses the private IP addressing space of 192.168.1.0/24. All the computers in the private network connect to the Internet through a single PAT router with the global IP address of 208.190.121.12/24. See Figure 8-14.

Figure 8-14
John's network setup

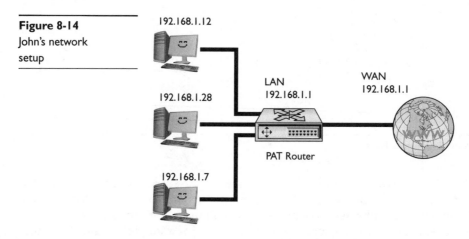

When an internal machine initiates a session with an external machine, such as a Web browser accessing a Web site, the source and destination IP addresses and port numbers for the TCP segment or UDP datagram are recorded in the PAT's translation table, and the private IP address is swapped for the public IP address on each packet. Plus, the port number used by the internal computer for the session is also translated into a unique port number and the router records this as well. See Figure 8-15.

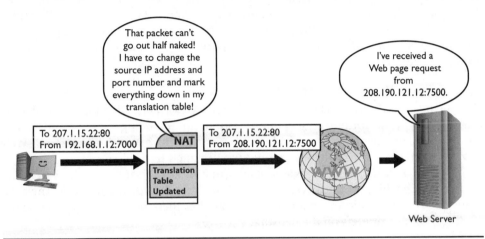

Figure 8-15 PAT in action—changing the source IP address and port number to something usable on the Internet

Table 8-1 shows a sample of the translation table inside the PAT router. Note that more than one computer translation has been recorded.

Source	Translated Source	Destination
192.168.1.12:7000	208.190.121.12:7500	
192.168.1.24:13245	208.190.121.12:15000	17.5.85.11:80

Table 8-1 Sample NAT Translation Table

When the receiving system sends the packet back, it reverses the IP addresses and ports. The PAT router compares the incoming destination port and source IP address to the entry in the *NAT translation table* to determine which IP address to put back on the packet. It then sends the packet to the correct computer on the network.

This mapping of internal IP address and port number to a translated IP address and port number enables perfect tracking of packets out and in. PAT can handle many internal computers with a single public IP address because the TCP/IP port number space is big, as you'll recall from Chapter 7, with values ranging from 1 to 65535. Some of those port numbers are used for common protocols, but many thousands are available for PAT to work its magic.

NOTE Chapter 9 goes into port numbers in great detail.

PAT takes care of all of the problems facing a network exposed to the Internet. You don't have to use legitimate Internet IP addresses on the LAN and the IP addresses of the computers behind the routers are invisible and protected from the outside world.

Since the router is revising the packets and recording the IP address and port information already, why not enable it to handle ports more aggressively? Enter port forwarding, stage left.

Port Forwarding

The obvious drawback to relying exclusively on PAT for network address translation is that it only works for outgoing communication, not incoming communication. For traffic originating *outside* the network to access an *internal* machine, such as a Web server hosted inside your network, you need to use other technologies.

Static NAT (SNAT) maps a single routable (that is, not private) IP address to a single machine, enabling you to access that machine from outside the network. The NAT keeps track of the IP address or addresses and applies them permanently on a one-to-one basis with computers on the network.

EXAM TIP Despite the many uses in the industry of the acronym SNAT, the CompTIA Network+ exam uses SNAT for Static NAT exclusively.

With *port forwarding*, you can designate a specific local address for various network services. Computers outside the network can request a service using the public IP address of the router and the port number of the desired service. The port-forwarding router would examine the packet, look at the list of services mapped to local addresses, and then send that packet along to the proper recipient.

You can use port forwarding to hide a service hosted inside your network by changing the default port number for that service. To hide an internal Web server, for example, you could change the request port number to something other than port 80, the default for HTTP traffic. The router in Figure 8-16, for example, is configured to forward all port 8080 packets to the internal Web server at port 80.

To access that internal Web site from outside your local network, you would have to change the URL in the Web browser by specifying the port request number. Figure 8-17 shows a browser that has :8080 appended to the URL, which tells the browser to make the HTTP request to port 8080 rather than port 80.

NOTE Most browsers require you to write out the full URL, including HTTP://, when using a nondefault port number.

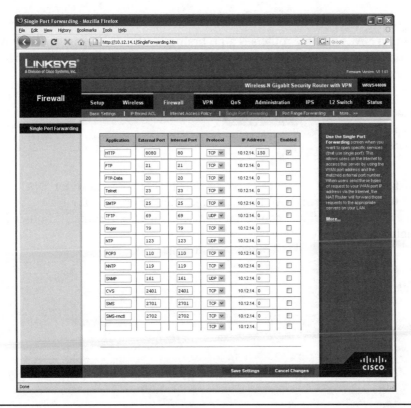

Figure 8-16   Setting up port forwarding on a home router

Figure 8-17
Changing the
URL to access
a Web site
using a
nondefault
port number

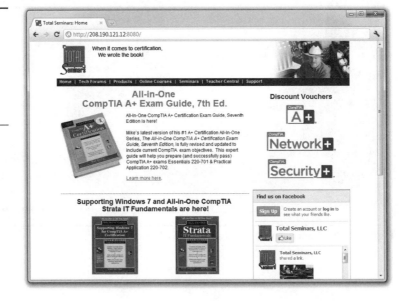

Configuring NAT

Configuring NAT on home routers is a no-brainer as these boxes invariably have NAT turned on automatically. Figure 8-18 shows the screen on my home router for NAT. Note the radio buttons that say Gateway and Router.

Figure 8-18
NAT setup on
home router

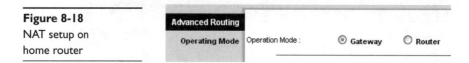

By default, the router is set to Gateway, which is Linksys-speak for "NAT is turned on." If I wanted to turn off NAT, I would set the radio button to Router.

Figure 8-19 shows a router configuration screen on a Cisco router. Commercial routers enable you to do a lot more with NAT.

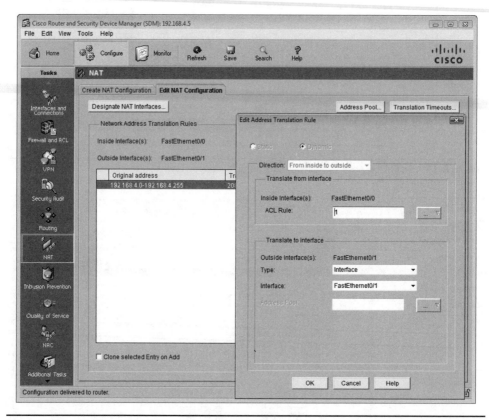

Figure 8-19   Configuring NAT on a commercial-grade router

Dynamic Routing

Based on what you've read up to this point, it would seem that routes in your routing tables come from two sources: either they are manually entered or they are detected at setup by the router. In either case, a route seems to be a static beast, just sitting there and never changing. And based on what you've seen so far, that is absolutely true. Routers have *static routes*. But most routers also have the capability to update their routes *dynamically*, assuming they're provided with the extra smarts in the form of *dynamic routing* protocols.

If you've been reading carefully, you might be tempted at this point to say, "Why do I need this dynamic routing stuff? Don't routers use metrics so I can add two or more routes to another network ID in case I lose one of my routes?" Yes, but metrics really only help when you have direct connections to other network IDs. What if your routers look like Figure 8-20?

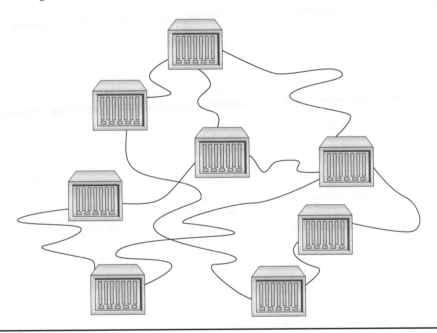

Figure 8-20　Lots of routers

Do you really want to try to set up all these routes statically? What happens when something changes? Can you imagine the administrative nightmare? Why not just give routers the brainpower to talk to each other so they know what's happening not only to the other directly connected routers but also to routers two or more routers away? A *hop* is defined as each time a packet goes through a router. Let's talk about hops for a moment. Figure 8-21 shows a series of routers. If you're on a computer in Network ID

X and you ping a computer in Network ID Y, you go one hop. If you ping a computer in Network ID Z, you go two hops.

Figure 8-21
Hopping through
a WAN

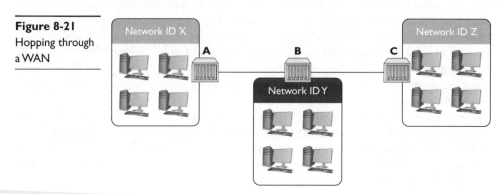

Routing protocols have been around for a long time, and, like any technology, there have been a number of different choices and variants over those years. CompTIA Network+ competencies break these many types of routing protocols into three distinct groups: distance vector, link state, and hybrid. CompTIA obsesses over these different types of routing protocols, so this chapter does too!

Routing Metrics

Earlier in the chapter, you learned that routing tables contain a factor called a *metric*. A metric is a relative value that routers use when they have more than one route to get to another network. Unlike the gateway routers in our homes, a more serious router will often have multiple connections to get to a particular network. This is the beauty of routers combined with dynamic protocols. If a router suddenly loses a connection, it has alternative routes to the same network. It's the role of the metric setting for the router to decide which route to use.

NOTE If a routing table has two or more valid routes for a particular IP address destination, it always chooses the route with the lowest value.

There is no single rule to set the metric value in a routing table. The various types of dynamic protocols use different criteria. Here are the most common criteria for determining a metric.

- **Maximum Transmission Unit** Better known by the abbreviation MTU, this determines the largest frame a particular technology can handle. Ethernet likes to use 1,500-byte frames. Other technologies use smaller or larger frames. If an IP packet is too big for a particular technology, that packet is broken into pieces to fit into the network protocol in what is called *fragmentation*. Fragmentation is bad because it slows down the movement of IP packets (see "Latency"). By setting the optimal MTU size before IP packets are sent, you avoid or at least reduce fragmentation.

- **Costs** Connecting to the Internet isn't free. Some connections *cost* more than others, and some incur costs based on usage.

- **Bandwidth** Some connections handle more data than others. An old dial-up connection moves at best 64 Kbps. A cable modem easily handles many millions of bits per second.

- **Latency** Say you have a race car that has a top speed of 200 miles per hour, but it takes 25 minutes to start the car. If you press the gas pedal, it takes 15 seconds to start accelerating. If the engine runs for more than 20 minutes, the car won't go faster than 50 miles per hour. These issues prevent the car from doing what it should be able to do: go 200 miles per hour. Latency is like that. Hundreds of issues occur that slow down network connections between routers. These issues are known collectively as *latency*. A great example is a satellite connection. The distance between the satellite and the antenna causes a delay that has nothing to do with the speed of the connection.

Different dynamic routing protocols use one or more of these routing metrics to calculate their own routing metric. As you learn about these protocols, you will see how each of these calculates their own metrics differently.

Distance Vector

Distance vector routing protocols were the first to appear in the TCP/IP routing world. The cornerstone of all distance vector routing protocols is some form of total cost. The simplest total cost sums the hops (the hop count) between a router and a network, so if you had a router one hop away from a network, the cost for that route would be 1; if it were two hops away, the cost would be 2.

All network connections are not equal. A router might have two, one-hop routes to a network—one using a fast connection and the other using a slow connection. Administrators set the metric of the routes in the routing table to reflect the speed. The slow single-hop route, for example, might be given the metric of 10 rather than the default of 1 to reflect the fact that it's slow. The total cost for this one-hop route is 10, even though it's only one hop. Don't assume a one-hop route always has a cost of 1.

Distance vector routing protocols calculate the total cost to get to a particular network ID and compare that cost to the total cost of all the other routes to get to that same network ID. The router then chooses the route with the lowest cost.

For this to work, routers using a distance vector routing protocol transfer their entire routing table to other routers in the WAN. Each distance vector routing protocol has a maximum number of hops that a router will send its routing table to keep traffic down.

Assume you have four routers connected as shown in Figure 8-22. All of the routers have static routes set up between each other with the metrics shown. You add two new networks, one that connects to Router A and the other to Router D. For simplicity, call them Network ID X and Network ID Y. A computer on one network wants to send packets to a computer on the other network, but the routers in between Routers A and D don't yet know the two new network IDs. That's when distance vector routing protocols work their magic.

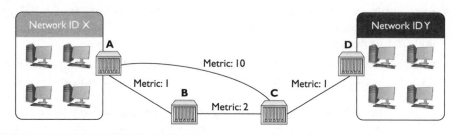

Figure 8-22   Getting a packet from Network ID X to Network ID Y? No clue!

Because all of the routers use a distance vector routing protocol, the problem gets solved quickly. At a certain defined time interval (usually 30 seconds or less), the routers begin sending each other their routing tables (the routers each send their entire routing table, but for simplicity just concentrate on the two network IDs in question). On the first iteration, Router A sends its route to Network ID X to Routers B and C. Router D sends its route to Network ID Y to Router C (Figure 8-23).

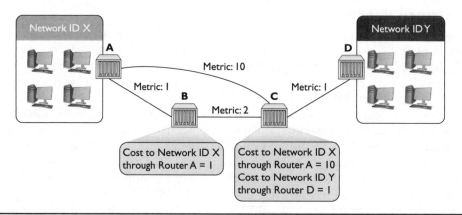

Figure 8-23   Routes updated

This is great—Routers B and C now know how to get to Network ID X, and Router C can get to Network ID Y. There's still no complete path, however, between Network ID X and Network ID Y. That's going to take another interval. After another set amount of time, the routers again send their now updated routing tables to each other, as shown in Figure 8-24.

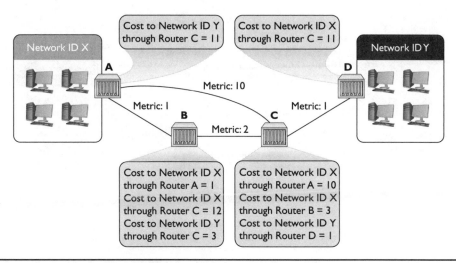

Figure 8-24   Updated routing tables

Router A knows a path now to Network ID Y, and Router D knows a path to Network ID X. As a side effect, Router B and Router C have two routes to Network ID X. Router B can get to Network ID X through Router A and through Router C. Similarly, Router C can get to Network ID X through Router A and through Router B. What to do? In cases where the router discovers multiple routes to the same network ID, the distance vector routing protocol deletes all but the route with the lowest total cost (Figure 8-25).

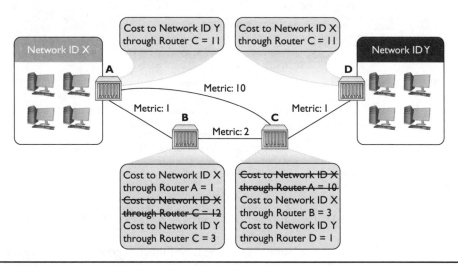

Figure 8-25   Deleting higher-cost routes

On the next iteration, Routers A and D get updated information about the lower total-cost hops to connect to Network IDs X and Y (Figure 8-26).

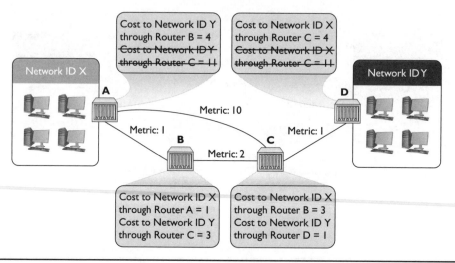

Figure 8-26 Argh! Multiple routes!

Just as Routers B and C only kept the routes with the lowest costs, Routers A and D keep only the lowest-cost routes to the networks (Figure 8-27).

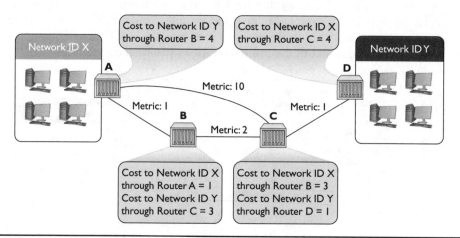

Figure 8-27 Last iteration

Now Routers A and D have a lower-cost route to Network IDs X and Y. They've removed the higher-cost routes and begin sending data.

At this point, if routers were human they'd realize that each router has all the information about the network and stop sending each other routing tables. Routers using distance vector routing protocols, however, aren't that smart. The routers continue to send their complete routing tables to each other, but because the information is the same, the routing tables don't change.

At this point, the routers are in *convergence* (also called *steady state*), meaning the updating of the routing tables for all the routers has completed. Assuming nothing changes in terms of connections, the routing tables will not change. In this example, it takes three iterations to reach convergence.

So what happens if the route between Routers B and C breaks? The routers have deleted the higher-cost routes, only keeping the lower-cost route that goes between Routers B and C. Does this mean Router A can no longer connect to Network ID Y and Router D can no longer connect to Network ID X? Yikes! Yes, it does. At least for a while.

Routers that use distance vector routing protocols continue to send to each other their entire routing table at regular intervals. After a few iterations, Routers A and D will once again know how to reach each other, although they will connect through the once-rejected slower connection.

Distance vector routing protocols work fine in a scenario such as the previous one that has only four routers. Even if you lose a router, a few minutes later the network returns to convergence. But imagine if you had tens of thousands of routers (the Internet). Convergence could take a very long time indeed. As a result, a pure distance vector routing protocol works fine for a network with a few (less than 10) routers, but it isn't good for large networks.

Routers can use one of three distance vector routing protocols: RIPv1, RIPv2, or BGP.

RIPv1

The granddaddy of all distance vector routing protocols is the *Routing Information Protocol (RIP)*. The first version of RIP—called *RIPv1*—dates from the 1980s, although its predecessors go back all the way to the beginnings of the Internet in the 1960s. RIP has a maximum hop count of 15 so your router will not talk to another router more than 15 routers away. This ended up being a problem because a routing table request could literally loop all the way around back to the initial router.

RIPv1 sent out an update every 30 seconds. This also turned into a big problem because every router on the network would send its routing table at the same time, causing huge network overloads.

As if these issues weren't bad enough, RIPv1 didn't know how to use *variable-length subnet masking (VLSM)*, where networks connected through the router used different subnet masks. Plus RIPv1 routers had no authentication, leaving them open to hackers sending false routing table information. RIP needed an update.

RIPv2

RIPv2, adopted in 1994, is the current version of RIP. It works the same way as RIPv1, but fixes many of the problems. VLSM has been added, and authentication is built into the protocol. (The maximum hop count of 15 continues to apply to RIPv2.)

Most routers still support RIPv2, but RIP's many problems, especially the time to convergence for large WANs, makes it obsolete for all but small, private WANs that consist of a few routers. The growth of the Internet demanded a far more robust dynamic routing protocol. That doesn't mean RIP rests in peace! RIP is both easy to use and simple for manufacturers to implement in their routers, so most routers, even home routers, have the ability to use RIP (Figure 8-28). If your network consists of only two, three, or four routers, RIP's easy configuration often makes it worth putting up with slower convergence.

Figure 8-28
Setting RIP in a home router

BGP

The explosive growth of the Internet in the 1980s required a fundamental reorganization in the structure of the Internet itself and one big part of this reorganization was the call to make the "big" routers use a standardized dynamic routing protocol. Implementing this was much harder than you might think because the entities that govern how the Internet works do so in a highly decentralized fashion. Even the organized groups, such as the Internet Society (ISOC), the Internet Assigned Numbers Authority (IANA), and the Internet Engineering Task Force (IETF), are made up of many individuals, companies, and government organizations from across the globe. This decentralization made the reorganization process take time and many meetings.

What came out of the reorganization eventually was a multitiered structure. At the top of the structure sit many Autonomous Systems. An *Autonomous System (AS)* is one or more networks that are governed by a single dynamic routing protocol within that AS. Figure 8-29 illustrates the central structure of the Internet.

Figure 8-29
The Internet

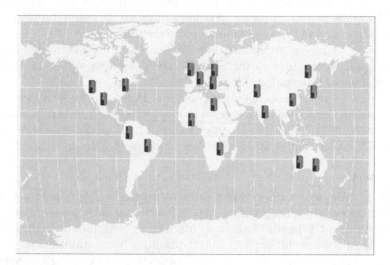

Autonomous Systems do not use IP addresses, but rather use a special globally unique Autonomous System Number (ASN) assigned by the IANA. Originally a 16-bit number, the current ASNs are 32 bits, displayed as two 16-bit numbers separated by a dot. So, 1.33457 would be a typical ASN. Just as you would assign an IP address to a router, you would configure the router to use or be the ASN assigned by the IANA. See Figure 8-30.

Figure 8-30	```Router2811(config)#router bgp ?```
Configuring a Cisco	`  <1-65535>  Autonomous system number`
router to use an ASN	`Router2811(config)#router bgp 1902`

Autonomous Systems communicate with each other using a protocol, called generically an *Exterior Gateway Protocol (EGP)*. The network or networks within an AS communicate with protocols as well; these are called generically *Interior Gateway Protocols (IGPs)*.

Let me repeat this to make sure you understand the difference between EGP and IGP. Neither EGP nor IGP are dynamic routing protocols; rather these are terms used by the large Internet service providers to separate their interconnected routers using ASNs from other interconnected networks that are not part of this special group of companies. The easy way to keep these terms separate is to appreciate that although many protocols are used *within* Autonomous Systems, such as RIP, the Internet has settled on one protocol for communication between each AS: the *Border Gateway Protocol (BGP-4)*. BGP is the glue of the Internet, connecting all of the Autonomous Systems. Other dynamic routing protocols such as RIP are, by definition, IGP. The current version of BGP is BGP-4.

NOTE You can see the AS for most Web sites by using this handy little Firefox add-on: www.asnumber.networx.ch. It doesn't work for every Web site, but it's still interesting.

The CompTIA Network+ exam objectives list BGP as a distance vector routing protocol, but it's really somewhat different. BGP doesn't have the same type of routing table as you've seen so far. Instead, BGP routers are manually configured (these types of connections aren't the type that go down very often!) and advertise information passed to them from different Autonomous Systems' *edge routers*—that's what the AS-to-AS routers are called. BGP forwards these advertisements that include the ASN and other very non-IP items.

BGP also knows how to handle a number of situations unique to the Internet. If a router advertises a new route that isn't reliable, most BGP routers will ignore it. BGP also supports policies for limiting which and how other routers may access an ISP.

BGP is an amazing and powerful dynamic routing protocol, but unless you're working deep in the router room of an AS, odds are good you'll never see it in action. Those who need to connect a few routers together usually turn to a family of dynamic routing protocols that work very differently from distance vector routing protocols.

> **NOTE** You can use BGP within an AS to connect networks, so you can and do run into situations where BGP is both the interior and exterior protocol for an AS. To distinguish between the two uses of the protocol, network folks refer to the BGP on the interior as the *internal BGP (iBGP)*; the exterior connection then becomes the *exterior BGP (eBGP)*.

Link State

The limitations of RIP motivated the demand for a faster protocol that took up less bandwidth on a WAN. The basic idea was to come up with a dynamic routing protocol that was more efficient than routers that simply sent out their entire routing table at regular intervals. Why not instead simply announce and forward individual route changes as they appeared? That is the basic idea of a *link state* dynamic routing protocol. There are only two link state dynamic routing protocols: OSPF and IS-IS.

> **NOTE** Please remember that in the earlier general distance vector routing example, I chose not to show that every update was an entire routing table! I only showed the changes, but trust me, the entire routing table is transmitted roughly every 30 seconds (with some randomization).

OSPF

Open Shortest Path First (OSPF) is the most commonly used IGP on the Internet. Most large Internet users (as opposed to ISPs) use OSPF on their internal networks. Even an AS, while still using BGP on its edge routers, will use OSPF internally because OSPF was designed from the ground up to work within a single AS. OSPF converges dramatically faster and is much more efficient than RIP. Odds are good that if you are using dynamic routing protocols, you're using OSPF.

Before you see OSPF in action, I need to warn you that OSPF is a complex protocol for routers. You won't find OSPF on inexpensive home routers because making it work takes a lot of computational firepower. But OSPF's popularity and CompTIA's coverage make this an important area for you to understand. The description here, although more than enough to get you through the CompTIA Network+ exam successfully, is still only a light touch on the fascinating world of OSPF.

Let's head back to the four-router setup used to explain RIP, but this time replace RIP with OSPF. Because OSPF is designed to work with the Internet, let's give Router B an upstream connection to the organization's ISP. When you first launch OSPF-capable routers, they send out *link state advertisements (LSAs)*, called *Hello packets*, looking for other OSPF routers (Figure 8-31).

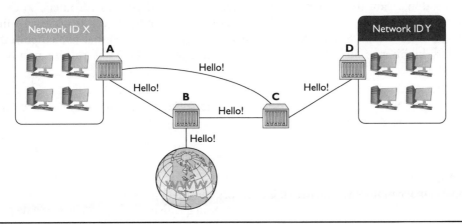

Figure 8-31 Hello!

A new router sends a lot of LSAs when it first starts. This is called *flooding*.

One of the big differences between OSPF and RIP is the hop cost. Whereas single hops in RIP have a cost of 1 unless manually changed, the cost in OSPF is based on the speed of the link. The formula is

```
100,000,000/bandwidth in bps
```

A 10BaseT link's OSPF cost is 100,000,000/10,000,000 = 10. The faster the bandwidth, the lower the cost. You can override this manually if you wish.

To appreciate the power of OSPF, look at Figure 8-32. When OSPF routers send LSA Hellos, they exchange this information and update their link state databases.

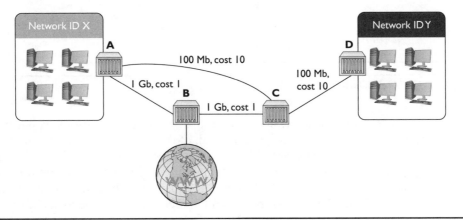

Figure 8-32 Link states

These LSA Hellos are forwarded to every OSPF router in the network. Every router knows the link state for every other router. This happens in a few seconds.

You don't want the routers to flood anywhere beyond your own routers, so every router is assigned an *Area ID*. Area IDs (unfortunately, in my opinion) look exactly like IP addresses. Every OSPF router is designed to accept an Area ID that you enter in the routers. In this case, all of the routers are given the Area ID of 0.0.0.0. This is commonly called *Area 0*.

NOTE   Even though OSPF Area IDs look like IP addresses, they have nothing to do with IP!

Area 0 is rather important in the world of OSPF. If your network gets more complex, you can make multiple areas. Area 0 is the most important area, however, and, therefore, is called the backbone. In this example, all of the routers are part of Area 0 (Figure 8-33).

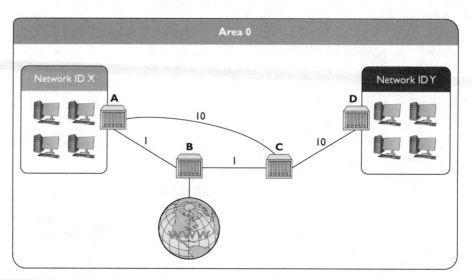

Figure 8-33   Area defined

Areas are very important for OSPF. To minimize router traffic, every area has one "El Supremo" router that relays information to all of the other routers in the area. This router is called the *designated router (DR)*. A second router is called the *backup designated router (BDR)* in case the DR isn't available. As the routers first begin to communicate, a DR and BDR election automatically begins. The router with the lowest total priority wins. In this case, Router B becomes the DR and Router A becomes the BDR. This election actually takes place during the initial Hello packet exchange (Figure 8-34). In most cases, you simply let the routers decide, but you can manually set a router as the DR and BDR if you desire (which is rare).

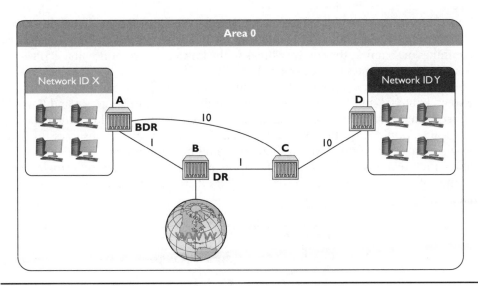

Figure 8-34 DR and BDR

Once the elections take place, it's finally time to distribute some routes across the area. Routers A and B send a separate LSA telling all routers in the area that they are connected to Network IDs X and Y, respectively. These are *not* the entire routing tables, but rather only a single route that is almost instantly dispersed across the routers in the OSPF area (Figure 8-35).

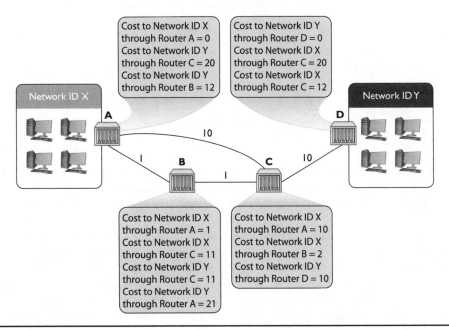

Figure 8-35 All routers updated

As you can see, OSPF areas almost instantly gain convergence compared to RIP. Once convergence is reached, all of the routers in the area send each other Hello LSAs every 30 minutes or so unless they detect a break in the link state. Also notice that OSPF routers keep alternate routes to the same network ID.

So what happens when something changes? For example, what if the connection between Routers A and B were to disconnect? In that case, both Routers A and B would almost instantly detect the break (as traffic between the two would suddenly stop). Each router would first attempt to reconnect. If reconnecting was unsuccessful (over a few seconds), the routers would then send out an LSA announcing the connection between the two was broken (Figure 8-36). Again, we're talking about a single route, not the entire routing table. Each router updates its routing table to remove the route that no longer works.

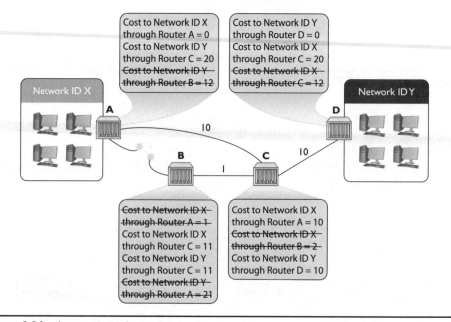

Figure 8-36   Announcing a disconnect

OSPF isn't popular by accident. It scales to large networks quite well and is supported by all but the most basic routers. By the way, did I forget to mention that OSPF also supports authentication and that the shortest-path-first method, by definition, prevents loops?

Why would anyone use anything else? Well, OSPF had one problem that wasn't repaired until fairly recently: support for something called IPv6 (see Chapter 13 for details on IPv6). Not to preempt Chapter 13, but IPv6 is a new addressing system for IP that dumps the old 32-bit address, replacing it with a 128-bit address. IPv6 is quickly gaining popularity and will one day replace 32-bit IP addressing. Just for the record, I've been predicting the end of 32-bit IP addressing for so long I'm now afraid to predict anymore when it's going to happen—but it will eventually.

EXAM TIP   OSPF corrects link failures and creates convergence almost immediately, making it the routing protocol of choice in most large enterprise networks. OSPF Version 2 is used for IPv4 networks, and OSPF Version 3 includes updates to support IPv6.

IS-IS

If you want to use a link state dynamic routing protocol and you don't want to use OSPF, your only other option is *Intermediate System to Intermediate System (IS-IS)*. IS-IS is extremely similar to OSPF. It uses the concept of areas and send-only updates to routing tables. IS-IS was developed at roughly the same time as OSPF and had the one major advantage of working with IPv6 from the start. IS-IS has some adoption with ISPs, but, for the most part, plays a distant second to the popularity of OSPF. Make sure you know that IS-IS is a link state dynamic routing protocol, and if you ever see two routers using it, call me as I've never seen IS-IS in action.

EIGRP—the Lone Hybrid

There is exactly one protocol that doesn't really fit into either the distance vector or link state camp: Cisco's proprietary *Enhanced Interior Gateway Routing Protocol (EIGRP)*. Back in the days when RIP was dominant, there was a huge outcry for an improved RIP, but OSPF wasn't yet out. Cisco, being the dominant router company in the world (a crown it still wears to this day), came out with the Interior Gateway Routing Protocol (IGRP), which was quickly replaced with EIGRP.

EIGRP has aspects of both distance vector and link state protocols, placing it uniquely into its own "hybrid" category. EIGRP is (arguably) fading away in the face of nonproprietary IGP protocols, especially OSPF.

Dynamic Routing Makes the Internet

Without dynamic routing, the complex, self-healing Internet we all enjoy today couldn't exist. So many routes come and go so often that manually updating static routes would be impossible. Review Table 8-2 to familiarize yourself with the differences among the different types of dynamic routing protocols.

Protocol	Type	IGP or BGP?	Notes
RIPv1	Distance vector	IGP	Old; only used variable subnets within an AS
RIPv2	Distance vector	IGP	Supports VLSM and discontiguous subnets
BGP-4	Distance vector	BGP	Used on the Internet, connects Autonomous Systems
OSPF	Link state	IGP	Fast, popular, uses Area IDs (Area 0/ backbone)
IS-IS	Link state	IGP	Alternative to OSPF
EIGRP	Hybrid	IGP	Cisco proprietary

Table 8-2   Dynamic Routing Protocols

Working with Routers

Understanding the different ways routers work is one thing. Actually walking up to a router and making it work is a different animal altogether. This section examines practical router installation. Physical installation isn't very complicated. With a home router, you give it power and then plug in connections. With a business-class router, you insert it into a rack, give it power, and plug in connections.

The complex part of installation comes with the specialized equipment and steps to connect to the router and configure it for your network needs. This section, therefore, focuses on the many methods and procedures used to access and configure a router.

The single biggest item to keep in mind here is that although there are many different methods for connecting, hundreds of interfaces, and probably millions of different configurations for different routers, the functions are still the same. Whether you're using an inexpensive home router or a hyper-powerful Internet backbone router, you are always working to do one main job: connect different networks.

Also keep in mind that routers, especially gateway routers, often have a large number of other features that have nothing to do with routing. Because gateway routers act as a separator between the computers and "The Big Scary Rest of the Network," they are a convenient place for all kinds of handy features like DHCP, protecting the network from intrusion (better known as firewalls), and NAT.

Connecting to Routers

When you take a new router out of the box, it's not good for very much. You need to somehow plug into that shiny new router and start telling it what you want to do. There are a number of different methods, but one of the oldest (yet still very common) methods is using a special serial connection. This type of connection is almost completely unique to Cisco-brand routers, but Cisco's massive market share makes understanding this type of connection a requirement for anyone who wants to know how to configure routers. Figure 8-37 shows the classic Cisco console cable, more commonly called a *rollover* or *Yost cable*.

Figure 8-37
Cisco console cable

NOTE   The term *Yost cable* comes from its creator's name, Dave Yost. For more information visit http://yost.com/computers/RJ45-serial.

At this time, I need to make an important point: switches as well as routers often have some form of configuration interface. Granted, you have nothing to configure on a basic switch, but in later chapters, you'll discover a number of network features that you'll want to configure more advanced switches to use. Both routers and these advanced switches are called *managed devices*. In this section, I use the term *router,* but it's important for you to appreciate that all routers and many better switches are all managed devices. The techniques shown here work for both!

When you first unwrap a new Cisco router, you plug the rollover cable into the console port on the router (Figure 8-38) and a serial port on a PC. If you don't have a serial port, then buy a USB-to-serial adapter.

Figure 8-38
Console port

Once you've made this connection, you need to use a terminal emulation program to talk to the router. The two most popular programs are PuTTY (www.chiark.greenend. org.uk/~sgtatham/putty) and HyperTerminal (www.hilgraeve.com/hyperterminal-trial). Using these programs requires that you to know a little about serial ports, but these basic settings should get you connected:

- 9600 baud
- 8 data bits
- 1 stop bit
- No parity

NOTE Much initial router configuration harkens back to the methods used in the early days of networking when massive mainframe computers were the computing platform available. Researchers used *dumb terminals*—machines that were little more than a keyboard, monitor, and network connection—to connect to the mainframe and interact. You connect to and configure many modern routers using software that enables your PC to pretend to be a dumb terminal. These programs are called *terminal emulators*; the screen you type into is called a *console*.

Every terminal emulator has some way for you to configure these settings. Figure 8-39 shows these settings using PuTTY.

Figure 8-39
Configuring PuTTY

Now it's time to connect. Most Cisco products run *Cisco IOS*, Cisco's proprietary operating system. If you want to configure Cisco routers, you must learn IOS. Learning IOS in detail is a massive job and outside the scope of this book. No worries, Cisco provides a series of certifications to support those who wish to become "Cisco People." Although the CompTIA Network+ exam won't challenge you in terms of IOS, it's important to get a taste of how this amazing operating system works.

NOTE IOS used to stand for *Internetwork Operating System*, but it's just IOS now with a little trademark symbol.

Once you've connected to the router and started a terminal emulator, you should see the initial router prompt, as shown in Figure 8-40. (If you plugged in and then started the router, you can actually watch the router boot up first.)

This is the IOS user mode prompt—you can't do too much here. To get to the fun, you need to enter privileged exec mode. Type **enable**, press ENTER, and the prompt changes to

```
Router#
```

NOTE A new Cisco router often won't have a password, but all good admins know to add one.

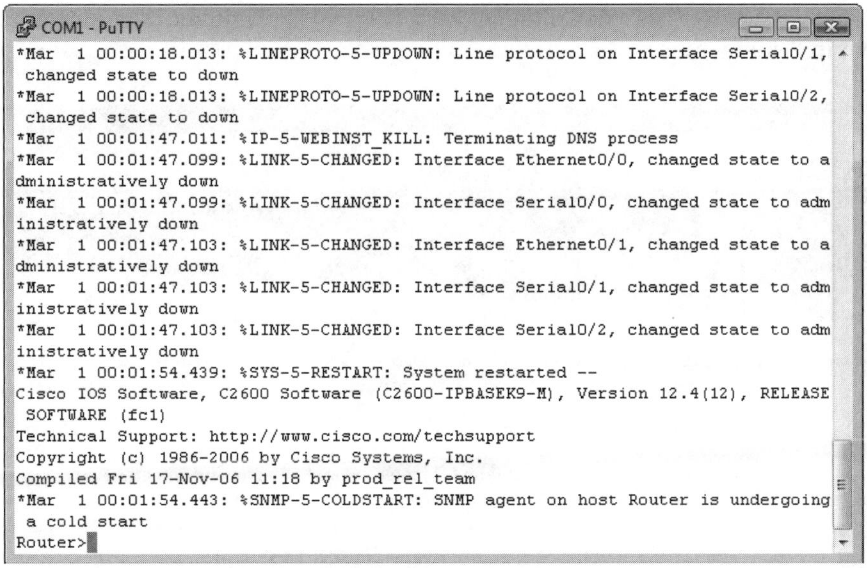

```
COM1 - PuTTY                                                    [_][□][×]
*Mar  1 00:00:18.013: %LINEPROTO-5-UPDOWN: Line protocol on Interface Serial0/1,
 changed state to down
*Mar  1 00:00:18.013: %LINEPROTO-5-UPDOWN: Line protocol on Interface Serial0/2,
 changed state to down
*Mar  1 00:01:47.011: %IP-5-WEBINST_KILL: Terminating DNS process
*Mar  1 00:01:47.099: %LINK-5-CHANGED: Interface Ethernet0/0, changed state to a
dministratively down
*Mar  1 00:01:47.099: %LINK-5-CHANGED: Interface Serial0/0, changed state to adm
inistratively down
*Mar  1 00:01:47.103: %LINK-5-CHANGED: Interface Ethernet0/1, changed state to a
dministratively down
*Mar  1 00:01:47.103: %LINK-5-CHANGED: Interface Serial0/1, changed state to adm
inistratively down
*Mar  1 00:01:47.103: %LINK-5-CHANGED: Interface Serial0/2, changed state to adm
inistratively down
*Mar  1 00:01:54.439: %SYS-5-RESTART: System restarted --
Cisco IOS Software, C2600 Software (C2600-IPBASEK9-M), Version 12.4(12), RELEASE
 SOFTWARE (fc1)
Technical Support: http://www.cisco.com/techsupport
Copyright (c) 1986-2006 by Cisco Systems, Inc.
Compiled Fri 17-Nov-06 11:18 by prod_rel_team
*Mar  1 00:01:54.443: %SNMP-5-COLDSTART: SNMP agent on host Router is undergoing
 a cold start
Router>█
```

Figure 8-40   Initial router prompt

From here, IOS gets very complex. For example, the commands to set the IP address for one of the router's ports look like this:

```
Router#configure terminal
Router(config)#interface Ethernet 0/0
Router(config-if)#ip address 192.168.4.10 255.255.255.0
Router(config-if)#^Z
Router#copy run start
```

Cisco has long appreciated that initial setup is a bit of a challenge, so a brand-new router will show you the following prompt:

```
Would you like to enter the initial configuration dialog?
[yes/no]?
```

Simply follow the prompts and the most basic setup is handled for you.

You will run into Cisco equipment as a network tech, and you will need to know how to use the console from time to time. For the most part, though, you'll access a router—especially one that's already configured—through Web access or network management software.

Web Access

Most routers come with a built-in Web interface that enables you to do everything you need on your router and is much easier to use than Cisco's command-line IOS. For a Web interface to work, however, the router must have a built-in IP address from the factory, or you have to enable the Web interface after you've given the router an IP address. Bottom line? If you want to use a Web interface, you have to know the router's

IP address. If a router has a default IP address, you will find it in the documentation, as shown in Figure 8-41.

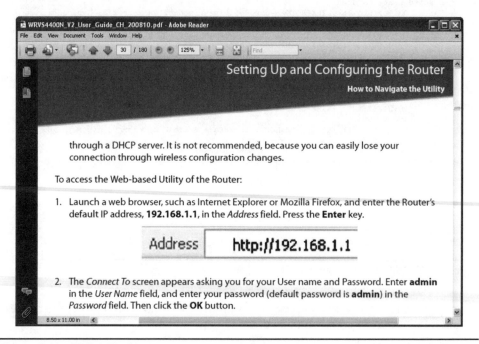

Figure 8-41   Default IP address

Never plug a new router into an existing network! There's no telling what that router might start doing. Does it have DHCP? You might now have a rogue DHCP server. Are there routes on that router that match up to your network addresses? Then you see packets disappearing into the great bit bucket in the sky. Always fully configure your router before you place it online.

Most router people use a laptop and a crossover cable to connect to the new router. To get to the Web interface, first set a static address for your computer that will place your PC on the same network ID as the router. If, for example, the router is set to 192.168.1.1/24 from the factory, set your computer's IP address to 192.168.1.2/24. Then connect to the router (some routers tell you exactly where to connect, so read the documentation first), and check the link lights to verify you're properly connected. Open up your Web browser and type in the IP address, as shown in Figure 8-42.

Figure 8-42

Entering the IP address

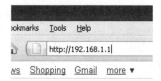

NOTE Many routers are also DHCP servers, making the initial connection much easier. Check the documentation to see if you can just plug in without setting an IP address on your PC.

Assuming you've done everything correctly, you almost always need to enter a default user name and password, as shown in Figure 8-43.

Figure 8-43
User name and password

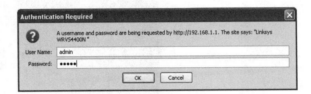

The default user name and password come with the router's documentation. If you don't have that information, plenty of Web sites list this data. Do a Web search on **"default user name password"** to find one.

NOTE Every brand of router tends to use the same default user name and password. Just about every Linksys router, for example, uses a blank user name and the password "admin." An admin who fails to change the default password is asking to get hacked!

Once you've accessed the Web interface, you're on your own to poke around to find the settings you need. There's no standard interface—even between different versions of the same router make and model. When you encounter a new interface, take some time and inspect every tab and menu to learn about the router's capabilities. You'll almost always find some really cool features!

Network Management Software

The idea of a "Web-server-in-a-router" works well for single routers, but as a network grows into lots of routers, administrators need more advanced tools that describe, visualize, and configure their entire network. These tools, known as *Network Management Software (NMS)*, know how to talk to your routers, switches, and even your computers to give you an overall view of your network. In most cases, NMS manifests as a Web site where administrators may inspect the status of the network and make adjustments as needed.

I divide NMS into two camps: proprietary tools made by the folks who make managed devices (OEM) and third-party tools. OEM tools are generally very powerful and easy to use, but only work on that OEM's devices. Figure 8-44 shows an example of Cisco Network Assistant, one of Cisco's NMS applications. Others include the Security Device Manager and CiscoWorks, their enterprise-level tool.

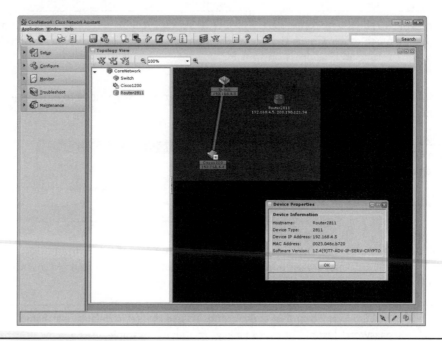

Figure 8-44 Cisco Network Assistant

A number of third-party NMS tools are out there as well; you can even find some pretty good freeware NMS options. These tools are invariably harder to configure and must constantly be updated to try to work with as many devices as possible.

They usually lack the amount of detail you see with OEM NMS and lack interactive graphical user interfaces. For example, CiscoWorks enables you to change the IP address of a port, whereas third-party tools will only let you see the current IP settings for that port. Figure 8-45 shows OpenNMS, a popular open source NMS.

Unfortunately, no single NMS tool works perfectly. Network administrators are constantly playing with this or that NMS tool in an attempt to give themselves some kind of overall picture of their networks.

Other Connection Methods

Be aware that most routers have even more ways to connect. Many home routers come with USB ports and configuration software. More powerful routers may enable you to connect using the ancient Telnet protocol or its newer and safer equivalent Secure Shell (SSH). These are terminal emulation protocols that look exactly like the terminal emulators seen earlier in this chapter but use the network instead of a serial cable to connect (see Chapter 9 for details on these protocols).

NOTE The PuTTY utility works with the old-style terminal emulation as well as Telnet and SSH.

Figure 8-45   OpenNMS

Basic Router Configuration

A router, by definition, must have at least two connections. When you set up a router, you must configure every port on the router properly to talk to its connected network IDs, and you must make sure the routing table sends packets to where you want them to go. As a demonstration, Figure 8-46 uses an incredibly common setup: a single gateway router used in a home or small office that's connected to an ISP.

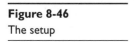

Figure 8-46

The setup

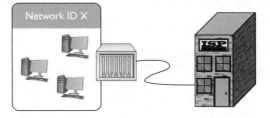

Step 1: Set Up the WAN Side

To start, you need to know the network IDs for each side of your router. The WAN side invariably connects to an ISP, so you need to know what the ISP wants you to do. If you bought a static IP address, type it in now. However—brace yourself for a crazy fact—most home Internet connections use DHCP! That's right, DHCP isn't just for your PC.

You can set up your router's WAN connection to use it too. DHCP is by far the most common connection to use for home routers. Access your router and locate the WAN connection setup. Figure 8-47 shows the setup for my home router set to DHCP.

Figure 8-47
WAN router setup

NOTE I'm ignoring a number of other settings here for the moment. I'll revisit most of these in later chapters.

But what if I called my ISP and bought a single static IP address? This is rarely done anymore, but virtually every ISP will gladly sell you one (although you will pay three to four times as much for the connection). If you use a static IP, your ISP will tell you what to enter, usually in the form of an e-mail message like the following:

```
Dear Mr. Meyers,
Thank you for requesting a static IP address from
totalsem.com!
Here's your new static IP information:
IP address: 1.151.35.55
Default Gateway: 1.151.32.132
Subnet Mask: 255.255.128.0

Installation instructions can be found at:
http://totalsem.com/setup/

Support is available at:
http://helpdesk.totalsem.com or by calling (281)922-4166.
```

In such a case, I would need to change the router setting to Static IP (Figure 8-48). Note how changing the drop-down menu to Static IP enables me to enter the information needed.

Figure 8-48
Entering a static IP

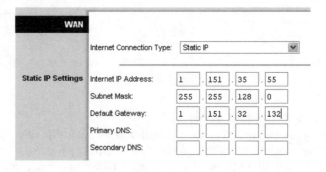

Once you've set up the WAN side, it's time to head over to set up the LAN side of the router.

Step 2: Set Up the LAN

Unlike the WAN side, you usually have total control on the LAN side of the router. You need to choose a network ID, almost always some arbitrarily chosen private range unless you do not want to use NAT. This is why so many home networks have network IDs of 192.168.1/24, 192.168.0/24, and so forth. Once you decide on your LAN-side network ID, you need to assign the correct IP information to the LAN-side NIC. Figure 8-49 shows the configuration for a LAN NIC on my home router.

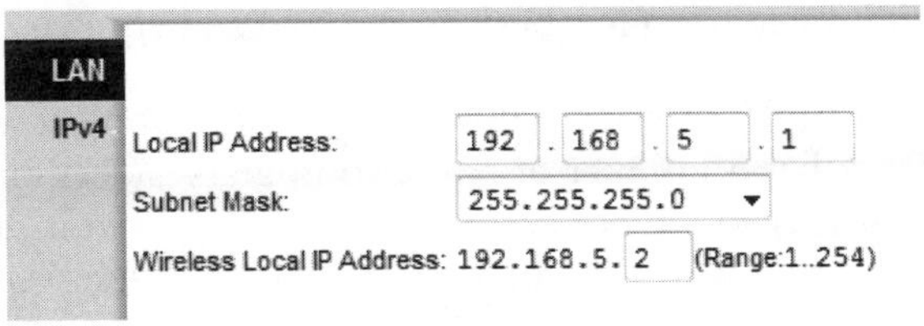

Figure 8-49
Setting up an IP address for the LAN side

Step 3: Establish Routes

Most routers are pretty smart and use the information you provided for the two interfaces to build a routing table automatically. If you need to add more routes, every router provides some method to add routes. The following shows the command line entered on a Cisco router to add a router to one of its NICs. The term "fa0/0" is used here to describe Ethernet NICs in its device software. It is short for FastEthernet, which you may remember as being the common name for 100BaseTX. Can you guess what Cisco calls gigabit ports or even ancient 10BaseT ports?

```
ip route 192.168.100.0 255.255.255.0 fa0/0 192.168.1.10
```

Step 4 (Optional): Configure a Dynamic Protocol

The rules to using any dynamic routing protocol are fairly straightforward. First, dynamic routing protocols are tied to individual NICs, not the entire router. Second, when you connect two routers together, make sure those two NICs are configured to use the same dynamic routing protocol. Third, unless you're in charge of two or more routers, you're probably not going to use any dynamic routing protocol.

The amazing part of a dynamic routing protocol is how easy it is to set up. In most cases you just figure out how to turn it on and that's about it. It just starts working.

Document and Back Up

Once you've configured your routes, take some time to document what you've done. A good router works for years without interaction, so by that time in the future when it goes down, odds are good you've forgotten why you added the routes. Last, take some time to back up the configuration. If a router goes down, it will most likely forget everything and you'll need to set it up all over again. Every router has some method to back up the configuration, however, so you can restore it later.

Router Problems

The CompTIA Network+ exam will challenge you on some basic router problems. All of these questions should be straightforward for you as long as you do the following:

- Consider other issues first because routers don't fail very often.
- Keep in mind what your router is supposed to do.
- Know how to use a few basic tools that can help you check the router.

Any router problem starts with someone not connecting to someone else. Even a small network has a number of NICs, computers, switches, and routers between you and whatever it is you're not connecting to. Compared to most of these, a router is a pretty robust device and shouldn't be considered as the problem until you've checked out just about everything else first.

In their most basic forms, routers route traffic. Yet you've seen in this chapter that routers can do more than just plain routing—for example, NAT. As this book progresses, you'll find that the typical router often handles a large number of duties beyond just routing. Know what your router is doing and appreciate that you may find yourself checking a router for problems that don't really have anything to do with routing at all.

Be aware that routers have some serious but rare potential problems. One place to watch is your routing table. For the most part, today's routers automatically generate directly connected routes, and dynamic routing takes care of itself leaving one type of route as a possible suspect: the static routes. This is the place to look when packets aren't getting to the places you expect them to go. Look at the following sample static route:

Net Destination	Netmask	Gateway	Interface	Metric
22.46.132.0	255.255.255.255	22.46.132.1	22.46.132.11	1

No incoming packets for network ID are getting out on interface 22.46.132.11. Can you see why? Yup, the Netmask is set to 255.255.255.255, and there are no computers that have exactly the address 22.46.132.0. Entering the wrong network destination, subnet mask, gateway, and so on, is very easy. If a new static route isn't getting the packets moved, first assume you made a typo.

Make sure to watch out for missing routes. These usually take place due to you forgetting to add them (if you're entering static routes) or, more commonly, there is a convergence problem in the dynamic routing protocols. For the CompTIA Network+ exam, be ready to inspect a routing table to recognize these problems.

When it comes to tools, the networking world comes with so many utilities and magic devices that it staggers the imagination. Some, like good old ping and route, you've already seen, but let's add two more tools: traceroute and MTR.

The *traceroute* tool, as its name implies, records the route between any two hosts on a network. On the surface, traceroute is something like ping in that it sends a single packet to another host, but as it progresses, it returns information about every router between them.

Every operating system comes with traceroute, but the actual command varies among them. In Windows, the command is `tracert` and looks like this (I'm running a traceroute to the router connected to my router—a short trip):

```
C:\>tracert 96.165.24.1

Tracing route to 96.165.24.1 over a maximum of 30 hops:

  1     1 ms     1 ms     1 ms    10.12.14.1
  2    10 ms    10 ms     8 ms    96.165.24.1
Trace complete.
```

The UNIX/Linux command is `traceroute` and looks like this:

```
michaelm@ubuntu:~$ traceroute 96.165.24.1
traceroute to 96.165.24.1 (96.165.24.1), 30 hops max, 40 byte
packets
1    10.12.14.1 (10.12.14.1)  0.763 ms 0.432 ms  0.233 ms
2    96.165.24.1 (96.165.24.1) 12.233 ms 11.255 ms 14.112 ms
michaelm@ubuntu:~$
```

The traceroute tool is handy, not so much for what it tells you when everything's working well, but for what it tells you when things are not working. Take a look at the following:

```
:\>tracert 96.165.24.1

Tracing route to 96.165.24.1 over a maximum of 30 hops
  1     1 ms     1 ms     1 ms   10.12.14.1
  2      *        *        *      Request timed out
  3   96.165.24.1  reports: Destination host unreachable.
```

If this traceroute worked in the past but now no longer works, you know that something is wrong between your router and the next router upstream. You don't know what's wrong exactly. The connection may be down; the router may not be working; but at least traceroute gives you an idea where to look for the problem and where not to look.

My traceroute (mtr) is very similar to traceroute, but it's dynamic, continually updating the route that you've selected (Figure 8-50). You won't find mtr in Windows; mtr is a Linux tool. Instead, Windows users can use pathping. This utility will ping each node on the route just like mtr, but instead of showing the results of each ping in real time, the pathping utility computes the performance over a set time and then shows you the summary after it has finished.

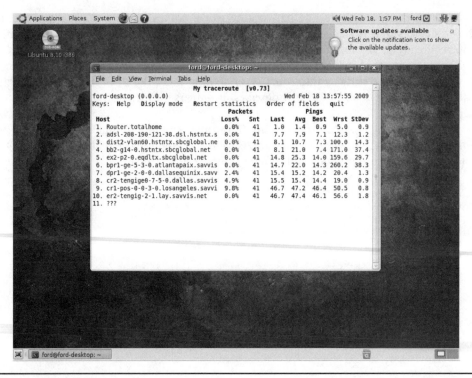

Figure 8-50   mtr in action

Chapter Review

Questions

1. What is a router?

   A. A piece of hardware that forwards packets based on IP address

   B. A device that separates your computers from the Internet

   C. A piece of hardware that distributes a single Internet connection to multiple computers

   D. A synonym for a firewall

2. Routers must use the same type of connection for all routes, such as Ethernet to Ethernet or ATM to ATM.

   A. True

   B. False

3. What technology allows you to share a single public IP address with many computers?

   A. Static Address Translation

   B. Natural Address Translation

   C. Computed Public Address Translation

   D. Port Address Translation

4. Given the following routing table:

Destination LAN IP	Subnet Mask	Gateway	Interface
10.11.12.0	255.255.255.0	0.0.0.0	LAN
64.165.5.0	255.255.255.0	0.0.0.0	WAN
0.0.0.0	0.0.0.0	64.165.5.1	WAN

   Where would a packet with the address 64.165.5.34 be sent?

   A. To the default gateway on interface WAN.

   B. To the 10.11.12.0/24 network on interface LAN.

   C. To the 64.165.5.0/24 network on interface WAN.

   D. Nowhere; the routing table does not have a route for that address.

5. Distance vector routing protocols such as RIP rely on what metric to determine the best route?

   A. Hop count.

   B. Link speed.

   C. Ping time.

   D. Routes are chosen at random.

6. What are two big advantages to using OSPF over RIP or BGP? (Select two.)

   A. OSPF is a modern protocol that does not have legacy problems.

   B. OSPF chooses routes based on link speed, not hop count.

   C. OSPF runs on all routers, big and small.

   D. OSPF sends only routing table changes, reducing network traffic.

7. What is Area 0 called in OSPF?

   A. Local Area

   B. Primary Zone

   C. Trunk

   D. Backbone

8. What is the name of the cable that you use to connect to the console port on Cisco routers?

   A. Router console cable

   B. Yost cable

   C. That funny blue Cisco cable

   D. Null modem cable

9. When you are first setting up a new router, you should never plug it into an existing network.

   A. True

   B. False

10. The traceroute utility is useful for

    A. Configuring routers remotely

    B. Showing the physical location of the route between you and the destination

    C. Discovering information about the routers between you and the destination address

    D. Fixing the computer's local routing table

Answers

1. **A.** A router is a piece of hardware that forwards packets based on IP address.

2. **B.** False; a router can interconnect different Layer 2 technologies.

3. **D.** Port Address Translation, commonly known as PAT, enables you to share a single public IP address with many computers.

4. **C.** It would be sent to the 64.165.5.0/24 network on interface WAN.

5. **A.** Distance vector routing protocols use hop count to determine the best route.

6. **B** and **D.** OSPF bases routes on speed and sends only route changes to minimize traffic.

7. **D.** Area 0 is called the backbone.

8. **B.** Yost cable, which was invented to standardize the serial console interface.

9. **A.** True; never plug a new router into an existing network.

10. **C.** Discovering information about the routers between you and the destination address.

TCP/IP Applications

The CompTIA Network+ Certification exam expects you to know how to

- 1.5 Identify common TCP and UDP default ports: SMTP, HTTP, HTTPS, FTP, Telnet, IMAP, SSH
- 1.6 Explain the function of common networking protocols: TCP, FTP, UDP, TFTP, HTTPS, HTTP, SSH, POP3, IMAP4, Telnet, SMTP, ICMP, IGMP

To achieve these goals, you must be able to

- Describe common Transport layer and Network layer protocols
- Explain the power of port numbers
- Define common TCP/IP applications such as HTTP, HTTPS, Telnet, e-mail (SMTP, POP3, and IMAP4), and FTP

We network to get work done. Okay, sometimes that "work" involves a mad gaming session in which I lay some smack down on my editors, but you know what I mean. Thus far in the book, everything you've read about networking involves connecting computers together. This chapter moves further up the OSI seven-layer model and the TCP/IP model to look at applications such as Web browsers, e-mail messaging, and more.

To understand the applications that use TCP/IP networks, a tech needs to know the structures *below* those applications that make them work. Have you ever opened multiple Web pages on a single computer? Have you ever run multiple Internet programs, such as a Web browser, an e-mail client, and a chat program, all at the same time? Clearly, a lot of data is moving back and forth between your computer and many other computers. With packets coming in from two, three, or more computers, there has to be a mechanism or process that knows where to send and receive that data.

In this chapter, you'll discover the process used by TCP/IP networks to ensure the right data gets to the right applications on your computer. This process uses very important Transport and Network layer protocols—TCP, UDP, and ICMP—and port numbering. When used together, TCP and UDP along with port numbers enable you to get work done on a network.

Transport Layer and Network Layer Protocols

I hate to tell you this, but you've been lied to. Not by me. Even though I've gone along with this Big Lie, I need to tell you the truth.

There is no such thing as TCP/IP. *TCP over IP* is really many other things, such as *HTTP, DHCP, POP,* and about 500 more terms over *TCP,* plus *UDP* and *ICMP* over *IP.* Given that this overly complex but much more correct term is too hard to use, the people who invented this network protocol stack decided to call it *TCP/IP,* even though that term is way too simplistic to cover all the functionality involved.

 NOTE There is a strong movement toward using the term *Internet Protocol* instead of the term *TCP/IP.* This movement has not yet reached the CompTIA Network+ certification.

So you can appreciate how TCP/IP applications work, this chapter breaks down the many unmentioned protocols and shows how they help make applications work. To start this process, let's consider how human beings communicate; you'll see some very interesting commonalities between computers and people.

How People Communicate

Imagine you walk into a school cafeteria to get some lunch. You first walk up to the guy making custom deli sandwiches (this is a great cafeteria!) and say, "Hello!" He says, "How may I help you?" You say, "I'd like a sandwich please." He says, "What kind of sandwich would you like?" and you order your sandwich. After you get your sandwich, you say, "Thanks!" and he says, "You're welcome." What a nice guy! In the networking world, we would call this a *connection-oriented* communication. Both you and the lunch guy first acknowledge each other. You then conduct your communication; finally, you close the communication.

While you're in line, you see your friend Janet sitting at your usual table. The line is moving fast so you yell out, "Janet, save me a seat!" before you rush along in the line. In this case, you're not waiting for her to answer; you just yell to her and hope she hears you. We call this a *connectionless* communication. There is no acknowledgment or any closing. You just yell out your communication and hope she hears it.

In the networking world, any single communication between a computer and another computer is called a *session.* When you open a Web page, you make a session. When you text chat with your buddy, you create a session. All sessions must begin and eventually end.

Test Specific

TCP

The *Transmission Control Protocol (TCP)* enables connection-oriented communication in networks that use the TCP/IP protocol suite. TCP is by far the most common type of session on a typical TCP/IP network. Figure 9-1 shows two computers. One computer (Server) runs a Web server and the other (Client) runs a Web browser. When you enter a computer's address in the browser running on Client, it sends a single SYN (synchronize) packet to the Web server. If Server gets that packet, it returns a single SYN, ACK (synchronize, acknowledge) packet. Client then sends Server a single ACK packet and immediately requests that Server begin sending the Web page. This process is called the *TCP three-way handshake*.

Figure 9-1

A connection-oriented session starting

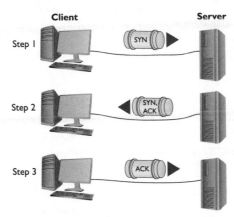

Once Server finishes sending the Web page, it sends a FIN, ACK (finished, acknowledge) packet. Client responds with an ACK (acknowledge) packet and then sends its own FIN, ACK packet. The server then responds with an ACK; now both parties consider the session closed (Figure 9-2).

Figure 9-2

A connection-oriented session ending

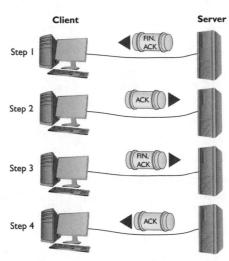

Most TCP/IP applications use TCP because connection-oriented sessions are designed to check for errors. If a receiving computer detects a missing packet, it just asks for a repeat as needed.

UDP

User Datagram Protocol (UDP) runs a distant second place to TCP in terms of the number of applications that use it, but that doesn't mean UDP is not important. UDP is perfect for the types of sessions that don't require the overhead of all that connection-oriented stuff.

DHCP

Probably the best example of an application that uses UDP is the Dynamic Host Configuration Protocol (DHCP). DHCP can't assume another computer is ready on either side of the session, so each step of a DHCP session just sends the information for that step without any confirmation (Figure 9-3). As you learned in Chapter 7, DHCP uses two port numbers. DHCP clients use port 67 for sending data to the DHCP server and DHCP servers use port 68 for sending data to DHCP clients.

NTP/SNTP

Two popular applications that use UDP are Network Time Protocol (NTP) and his lightweight little brother, Simple Network Time Protocol (SNTP). These protocols synchronize the clocks of devices on a network. Computers need to use the same time so things like Kerberos authentication work properly. If a device requires NTP/SNTP, you will be able to enter the IP address for an NTP/SNTP server. NTP/SNTP uses port 123.

Figure 9-3
DHCP steps

TFTP

You might also be tempted to think that UDP wouldn't work for any situation in which a critical data transfer takes place—untrue! *Trivial File Transfer Protocol (TFTP)* enables you to transfer files from one machine to another. TFTP, using UDP, doesn't have any data protection, so you would never use TFTP between computers across the Internet. TFTP is popular for moving files between computers on the same LAN, where the chances of losing packets is very small. TFTP uses port 69.

ICMP

While TCP and UDP differ dramatically—the former connection-oriented and the latter connectionless—both manage and modify packets in the classic sense with a destination IP address, source IP address, destination port numbers, and source port numbers. A single session might be one packet or a series of packets.

On the other hand, sometimes applications are so simple that they're always connectionless and never need more than a single packet. The *Internet Control Message Protocol (ICMP)* works at Layer 3 to deliver connectionless packets. ICMP handles mundane issues such as disconnect messages (host unreachable) that applications use to let the other side of a session know what's happening.

Good old ping is one place where you'll see ICMP in action. Ping is an ICMP application that works by sending a single ICMP packet called an *echo request* to an IP address you specify. All computers running TCP/IP (assuming no firewall is involved) respond to echo requests with an *echo reply,* as shown in Figure 9-4.

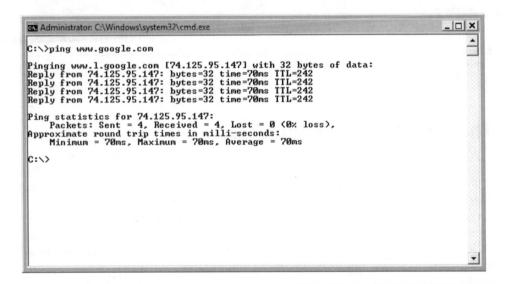

Figure 9-4   Ping in action

   NOTE   A *firewall* is a device or software that filters all the packets between two computers (or groups of computers) and acts like a club bouncer deciding who gets in and who gets blocked. Firewalls are vital for securing modern networks and will be discussed in Chapter 16.

IGMP

Do you remember the idea of IP multicast addresses, described in Chapter 7? The challenge of multicasting is determining who wants to receive the multicast and who does not. The *Internet Group Management Protocol (IGMP)* enables routers to communicate with hosts to determine a "group" membership. As you might remember from Chapter 7, multicast is in the Class D range (224/4). Multicast addresses only use a small subnet of the Class D range; specifically, they are assigned the network ID of 224.0.0.0/4. Multicast doesn't, however, assign IP addresses to individual hosts in the same manner as you've seen thus far. Instead, a particular multicast (called an *IGMP group*) is assigned to a 224.0.0.0/4 address, and those who wish to receive this multicast must tell their upstream router or switch (which must be configured to handle multicasts) that they wish to receive it. To do so, they join the IGMP group (Figure 9-5).

Figure 9-5 IGMP in action

The Power of Port Numbers

If you want to understand the power of TCP/IP, you have to get seriously into port numbers. If you want to pass the CompTIA Network+ exam, you need to know how TCP/IP uses port numbers and you have to memorize a substantial number of common port numbers. As you saw in the previous chapter, port numbers make NAT work. As you progress through this book, you'll see a number of places where knowledge of port numbers is critical to protect your network, make routers work better, and address a zillion other issues. There is no such thing as a network administrator who isn't deeply into the magic of port numbers and who cannot manipulate them for his or her network's needs.

Let's review and expand on what you learned about port numbers in the previous chapter. Thus far, you know that every TCP/IP application requires a server and a client. Clearly defined port numbers exist for every popular or *well-known* TCP/IP application. A port number is a 16-bit value between 0 and 65535. Web servers, for example, use port number 80. Port numbers from 0 to 1023 are called *well-known port numbers* and are reserved for specific TCP/IP applications.

EXAM TIP TCP/IP port numbers between 0 and 1023 are the well-known port numbers. You'll find them at every party.

When a Web client (let's say your computer running Firefox) sends an HTTP ACK to a Web server to request the Web page, your computer's IP packet looks like Figure 9-6.

Figure 9-6
HTTP ACK packet

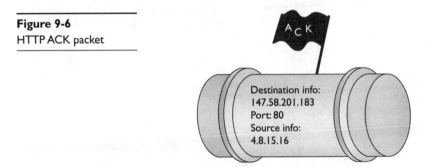

As you can see, the destination port number is 80. The computer running the Web server reads the destination port number, telling it to send the incoming packet to the Web server program (Figure 9-7).

Figure 9-7 Dealing with the incoming packet

The Web client's source port number is generated pseudo-randomly by the Web client computer. This value varies by operating system, but generally falls within the values 1024–5000—the port numbers classically assigned as *ephemeral port numbers*—and 49152–65535—the *dynamic* or *private port numbers*.

In the early days of the Internet, only ports 1024–5000 were used, but modern computers can use up all of those. More port numbers were added later. The Internet Assigned Numbers Authority (IANA) today recommends using only ports 49152–65535 as ephemeral port numbers. That's what current versions of Windows use as well. Let's redraw Figure 9-6 to show the more complete packet (Figure 9-8).

Figure 9-8
A more complete
IP packet

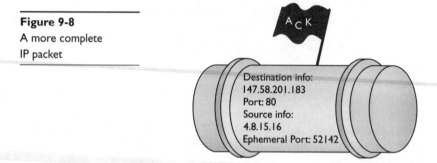

When the serving system responds to the Web client, it uses the ephemeral port number as the destination port to get the information back to the Web client running on the client computer (Figure 9-9).

Figure 9-9   Returning the packet

Registered Ports

The port numbers from 1024 to 49151 are called *registered ports*. Less-common TCP/IP applications can register their ports with the IANA. Unlike well-known ports, anyone can use these port numbers for their servers or for ephemeral numbers on clients. Most operating systems steer away (or are in the process of steering away) from using these port numbers for ephemeral ports, opting instead for the dynamic/private port numbers. Here's the full list of ports:

0–1023	Well-known port numbers
1024–49151	Registered ports
49152–65535	Dynamic or private ports

Each computer on each side of a session must keep track of the status of the communication. In the TCP/IP world, the session information (a combination of the IP address and port number) stored in RAM is called a *socket* or *endpoint*. When discussing the data each computer stores about the connection between two computers' TCP/IP applications, the term to use is *socket pairs* or *endpoints*. A *session* or *connection* refers to the connection in general, rather than anything specific to TCP/IP. Many people still use the term *session*, however. Here's a summary of the terms used:

- Terms for the connection data stored on a single computer—*socket* or *endpoint*
- Terms for the connection data stored on two computers about the same connection—*socket pairs* or *endpoints*
- Terms for the whole interconnection—*connection* or *session*

As two computers begin to communicate, they store the information about the session—the endpoints—so they know where to send and receive data. At any given point in time, your computer probably has a large number of communications going on. If you want to know who your computer is communicating with, you need to see this list of endpoints. As you'll recall from Chapter 8, Windows, Linux, and Mac OS X come with *netstat*, the universal "show me the endpoint" utility. The netstat utility works at the command line, so open one up and type **netstat -n** to see something like this:

```
C:\>netstat -n
Active Connections
   Proto  Local Address          Foreign Address        State
   TCP    192.168.4.27:57913     209.29.33.25:80        ESTABLISHED
   TCP    192.168.4.27:61707     192.168.4.10:445       ESTABLISHED
C:\>
```

 NOTE Even though almost all operating systems use netstat, there are subtle differences in options and output among the different versions.

When you run `netstat -n` on a typical computer, you'll see many more than just two connections! The preceding example is simplified for purposes of discussing the details. It shows two connections: My computer's IP address is 192.168.4.27. The top connection is an open Web page (port 80) to a server at 209.29.33.25. The second connection is an open Windows Network browser (port 445) to my file server (192.168.4.10). Looking on my Windows Desktop, you would certainly see at least these two windows open (Figure 9-10).

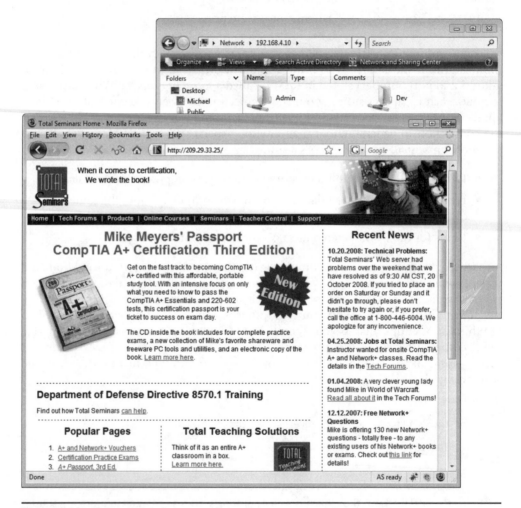

Figure 9-10   Two open windows

Don't think that a single open application always means a single connection. The following example shows what `netstat -n` looks like when I open the well-known www.microsoft.com Web site (I took out the connections that were not involved with the Web browser's connections to www.microsoft.com):

```
C:\>netstat -n
Active Connections
   Proto  Local Address          Foreign Address      State
   TCP    192.168.4.27:50015     80.12.192.40:80      ESTABLISHED
   TCP    192.168.4.27:50016     80.12.192.40:80      ESTABLISHED
   TCP    192.168.4.27:50017     80.12.192.40:80      ESTABLISHED
   TCP    192.168.4.27:50018     80.12.192.40:80      ESTABLISHED
   TCP    192.168.4.27:50019     80.12.192.40:80      ESTABLISHED
   TCP    192.168.4.27:50020     80.12.192.51:80      ESTABLISHED
   TCP    192.168.4.27:50021     80.12.192.40:80      ESTABLISHED
   TCP    192.168.4.27:50022     80.12.192.40:80      ESTABLISHED
   TCP    192.168.4.27:50023     80.12.192.40:80      ESTABLISHED
   TCP    192.168.4.27:50024     80.12.192.40:80      ESTABLISHED
   TCP    192.168.4.27:50025     80.12.192.51:80      ESTABLISHED
   TCP    192.168.4.27:50027     80.12.192.40:80      ESTABLISHED
   TCP    192.168.4.27:50028     80.12.192.40:80      ESTABLISHED
   TCP    192.168.4.27:50036     80.12.192.75:80      ESTABLISHED
```

A single simple Web page needs only a single connection, but this Web page is very complex. Different elements in the Web page, such as advertisements, each have their own connection.

 EXAM TIP The netstat utility enables you to see active TCP/IP connections at a glance.

You will see the powerful netstat tool used throughout this book. The CompTIA Network+ exam also tests your netstat skills. On the other hand, connections come and go constantly on your computer and netstat, being a command-line utility, can't update to reflect changes automatically. All of the cool, hip, network techs use graphical endpoint tools. Take a moment right now and download the popular, powerful, and completely free TCPView, written by Mark Russinovich, the Guru of Windows utilities. Just type **TCPView** into your search engine to find it or try going here:

http://technet.microsoft.com/en-us/sysinternals/default.aspx

Click the **Networking Utilities** icon to get the latest copy. Figure 9-11 shows TCPView in action. Note the red and green bars: red is for closing connections and green shows new connections as they appear.

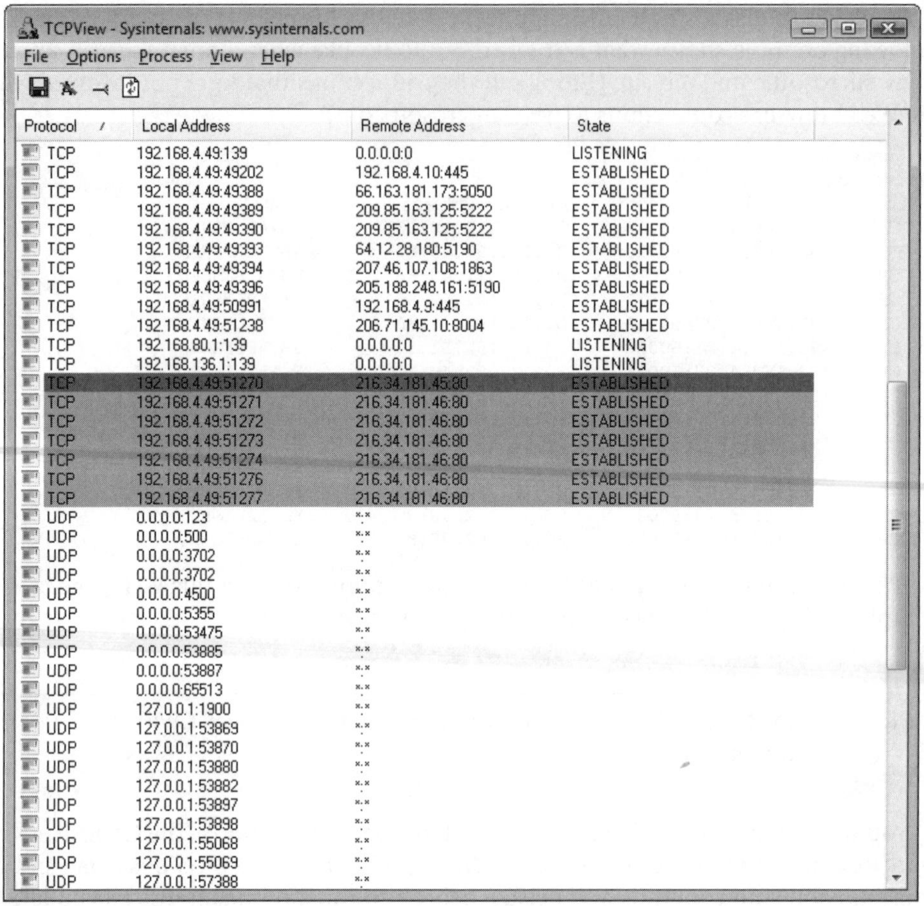

Figure 9-11   TCPView in action

TCPView won't work on anything but Windows, but other operating systems have equivalent programs. Linux folks often use the popular Net Activity Viewer (Figure 9-12). You can grab a copy of this program here:

http://netactview.sourceforge.net

Connection Status

Connection states change continually and it's helpful when using tools such as netstat or TCPView to understand their status at any given moment. Let's look at the status of connections so you understand what each means—this information is useful for determining what's happening on networked computers.

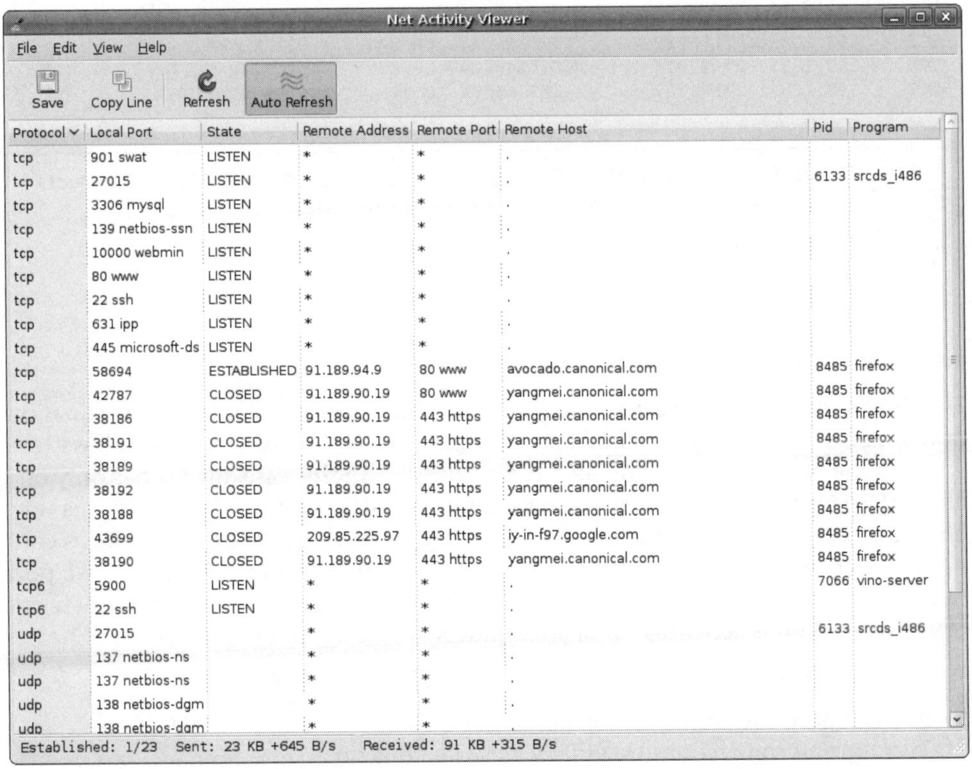

Figure 9-12   Net Activity Viewer in action

A socket that is prepared to respond to any IP packets destined for that socket's port number is called an *open port* or *listening port*. Every serving application has an open port. If you're running a Web server on a computer, for example, it will have an open port 80. That's easy enough to appreciate, but you'll be amazed at the number of open ports on just about *any* computer. Fire up a copy of netstat and type **netstat -an** to see all of your listening ports. Running netstat -an gives a lot of information, so let's just look at a small amount:

```
C:\>netstat -an
Active Connections
   Proto  Local Address          Foreign Address        State
   TCP    0.0.0.0:7              0.0.0.0:0              LISTENING
   TCP    0.0.0.0:135            0.0.0.0:0              LISTENING
   TCP    0.0.0.0:445            0.0.0.0:0              LISTENING
   TCP    0.0.0.0:912            0.0.0.0:0              LISTENING
   TCP    0.0.0.0:990            0.0.0.0:0              LISTENING
   TCP    127.0.0.1:27015        0.0.0.0:0              LISTENING
   TCP    127.0.0.1:52144        127.0.0.1:52145        ESTABLISHED
   TCP    127.0.0.1:52145        127.0.0.1:52144        ESTABLISHED
   TCP    127.0.0.1:52146        127.0.0.1:52147        ESTABLISHED
   TCP    127.0.0.1:52147        127.0.0.1:52146        ESTABLISHED
```

```
TCP    192.168.4.27:139         0.0.0.0:0                LISTENING
TCP    192.168.4.27:52312       74.125.47.108:80         TIME_WAIT
TCP    192.168.4.27:57913       63.246.140.18:80         CLOSE_WAIT
TCP    192.168.4.27:61707       192.168.4.10:445         ESTABLISHED
```

 NOTE The -a switch tells netstat to show all used ports. The -n instructs netstat to show raw port numbers and IP addresses.

First, look at this line:

```
TCP    0.0.0.0:445              0.0.0.0:0                LISTENING
```

This line shows a listening port ready for incoming packets that have a destination port number of 445. Notice the local address is 0.0.0.0. This is how Windows tells you that the open port works on all NICs on this PC. In this case, my PC has only one NIC (192.168.4.27), but even if you have only one NIC, netstat still shows it this way. This computer is sharing some folders on the network. At this moment, no one is connected, so netstat shows the Foreign Address as 0.0.0.0. Incoming requests use port number 445 to connect to those shared folders. If another computer on my network (192.168.4.83) was accessing the shared folders, this line would look like

```
TCP    192.168.4.27:445         192.168.4.83:1073        ESTABLISHED
```

Established ports are active, working endpoint pairs.

Over time all connections eventually close like this one:

```
TCP    192.168.4.27:57913       63.246.140.18:80         CLOSE_WAIT
```

This line shows a Web browser making a graceful closure, meaning each side of the conversation sees the session closing normally.

Not all connections close gracefully. The following line shows a Web browser that has lost the connection to the other side and is waiting a defined amount of time:

```
TCP    192.168.4.27:52312       74.125.47.108:80         TIME_WAIT
```

This is called a timeout period. Most Web browsers time out in approximately two minutes.

If data's going to move back and forth between computers, some program must always be doing the sending and/or receiving. Take a look at this line from netstat -an:

```
TCP    192.168.4.27:52312       74.125.47.108:80         ESTABLISHED
```

You see the 80 and might assume the connection is going out to a Web server. But what program on the computer is sending it? Enter the command **netstat -ano** (the -o switch tells netstat to show the process ID). Although you'll see many lines, the one for this connection looks like this:

```
Proto  Local Address         Foreign Address      State         PID
TCP    192.168.4.27:52312    74.125.47.108:80     ESTABLISHED   112092
```

Every running program on your computer gets a process ID (PID), a number used by the operating system to track all the running programs. Numbers aren't very helpful to you, though, because you want to know the name of the running program. In most operating systems, finding this out is fairly easy to do. In Windows, type **netstat –b**:

```
Proto       Local Address       Foreign Address        State
TCP         127.0.0.1:43543     Sabertooth:43544       ESTABLISHED
[firefox.exe]
```

In Linux, you can use the `ps` command:

```
michaelm@ubuntu:~$ ps
PID TTY        TIME CMD
3225 pts/1    00:00:00 bash
3227 pts/1    00:00:00 ps
```

If you want to find out the PID of a process, you can use the trusty Task Manager. The PIDs are hidden, by default, in modern versions of Windows, but they are easy to enable. Simply fire up Task Manager, select the **Processes** tab, select the **View** menu, and click the **Select Columns...** option. The first option in the list will be PID (Process Identifier). Check the box and then click **OK**. Task Manager will now show you the PID for all running programs.

Another great tool for discovering a process PID (and a whole lot more) is Mark Russinovich's Process Explorer; it is a perfect tool for this (Figure 9-13). The figure shows Process Explorer scrolled down to the bottom so you can see the program using PID 112092—good old Firefox!

 NOTE To get Process Explorer, enter **Process Explorer** in your search engine to find it or try going here: http://technet.microsoft.com/en-us/sysinternals/default.aspx Click the **Process Utilities** icon to get the latest copy.

You might be tempted to say "Big whoop, Mike—what else would use port 80?" Then consider the possibility that you run netstat and see a line like the one just shown, but *you don't have a browser open!* You determine the PID and discover the name of the process is "Evil_Overlord.exe." Something is running on your computer that should not be there.

Understanding how TCP/IP uses ports is a base skill for any network tech. To pass the CompTIA Network+ exam, you need to memorize a number of different well-known ports and even a few of the more popular registered ports. You must appreciate how the ports fit into the process of TCP/IP communications and know how to use netstat and other tools to see what's going on inside your computer.

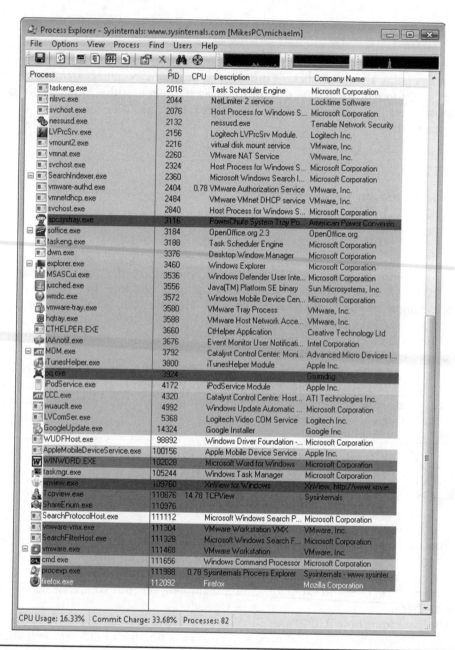

Figure 9-13 Process Explorer

The biggest challenge is learning what's supposed to be running and what's not. No one on Earth can run a netstat command and instantly recognize every connection and why it's running, but a good network tech should know most of them. For those connections that a tech doesn't recognize, he or she should know how to research them to determine what they are.

Rules for Determining Good vs. Bad Communications

Here is the general list of rules I follow for determining good versus bad communications (as far as networking goes, at least!):

1. Memorize a bunch of known ports for common TCP/IP applications. The next section in this chapter will get you started.

2. Learn how to use netstat to see what's happening on your computer. Learn to use switches such as –a, –n, –o, and –b to help you define what you're looking for.

3. Take the time to learn the ports that normally run on your operating system. When you see a connection using ports you don't recognize, figure out the process running the connection using a utility such as Linux's ps or Process Explorer for Windows.

4. Take the time to learn the processes that normally run on your operating system. Most operating systems have their own internal programs (such as Windows' SVCHOST.EXE) that are normal and important processes.

5. When you see a process you don't recognize, just enter the filename of the process in a Web search. Hundreds of Web sites are dedicated to researching mystery processes that will tell you what the process does.

6. Get rid of bad processes.

Common TCP/IP Applications

Finally! You now know enough about the Transport layer, port numbering, and sockets to get into some of the gritty details of common TCP/IP applications. There's no pretty way to do this, so let's start with the big daddy of them all, the Web.

The World Wide Web

Where would we be without the World Wide Web? If you go up to a non-nerd and say "Get on the Internet," most of them will automatically open a Web browser, because to them the Web *is* the Internet. The Internet is the infrastructure that enables the Web to function, but it's certainly more than just the Web. I think it's safe to assume you've used the Web, firing up your Web browser to surf to one cool site after another, learning new things, clicking links, often ending up somewhere completely unexpected . . . it's all fun! This section looks at the Web and the tools that make it function, specifically the protocols that enable communication over the Internet.

The Web is composed of servers that store specially formatted documents using a language called Hypertext Markup Language (HTML). Figure 9-14 shows the Web interface built into my router.

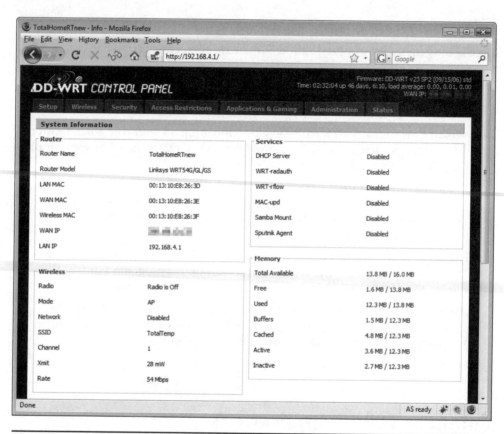

Figure 9-14 My router's Web page

HTML has been around for a long time and, as a result, has gone through many versions. Today many pages are being written in an updated HTML version called HTML 5, though the specification has not been finalized as of this writing. See Figure 9-15.

 EXAM TIP HTML is the most well-known markup language, but many others roam the Web today. Expect to see the *Extensible Markup Language (XML)* on the exam as well. XML provides the basic format or language for everything from application programming interfaces (APIs) to Microsoft Office documents.

Figure 9-15 HTML 5 source code

Web browsers are designed to request HTML pages from Web servers and then open them. To access a Web page, you enter **http://** plus the IP address of the Web server. When you type the address of a Web server, such as **http://192.168.4.1**, you tell the browser to go to 192.168.4.1 and ask for a Web page. All Web servers have a default Web page that they open unless you enter something more complex like **http://192.168.4.1/status**.

NOTE Most Web browsers are pretty forgiving. If you only type in **192.168.4.1**, forgetting the "http://" part, they just add it for you.

Granted, most people don't enter IP addresses into browsers, but rather enter text like www.totalsem.com or www.google.com. Memorizing text addresses is much easier than memorizing IP addresses. Web site text addresses use a naming protocol called Domain Name System (DNS), which you will learn about in the next chapter. For now, just enter the IP address as shown.

HTTP

The *Hypertext Transfer Protocol (HTTP)* is the underlying protocol used by the Web, and it runs, by default, on TCP port 80. When you enter **http://** at the beginning of a Web server's IP address, you are identifying how messages are formatted and transmitted, requesting and responding to the transfer of HTML-formatted files. HTTP defines what actions Web servers and browsers should take in response to various commands.

HTTP has a general weakness in its handling of Web pages: it relays commands executed by users without reference to any commands previously executed. The problem with this is that Web designers continue to design more complex and truly interactive Web pages. HTTP is pretty dumb when it comes to remembering what people have done on a Web site. Luckily for Web designers everywhere, other technologies exist to help HTTP relay commands and thus support more-interactive, intelligent Web sites. These technologies include JavaScript/AJAX, server-side scripting, Adobe Flash, and cookies.

 EXAM TIP Before connections to the Web became fast, many people used a completely different Internet service for swapping information, ideas, and files. *USENET* enjoyed great popularity for some years, though it barely survives today. Clients used the *Network News Transfer Protocol (NNTP)* to access USENET over TCP port 119. It might show up as an incorrect answer on the exam.

Publishing Web Pages

Once you've designed and created an HTML document, you can share it with the rest of the world. To do so, you find a Web server that will "host" the page. You most certainly can install a Web server on a computer, acquire a public IP address for that computer, and host the Web site yourself. Self-hosting is a time-consuming and challenging project, though, so most people use other methods. Most Internet service providers (ISPs) provide Web servers of their own, or you can find relatively inexpensive Web hosting service companies. The price of Web hosting usually depends on the services and drive space offered. Web hosts typically charge around US$10 a month for simple Web sites.

One option that has been available for a while is free Web hosting. Usually the services are not too bad, but free Web hosts have limitations. Nearly all free Web hosts insist on the right to place ads on your Web page. Third-party ads are not as much of an issue if you are posting a basic blog or fan Web page, but if you do any sort of business with your Web site, ads can be most annoying to your customers. The worst sort of free Web host services place pop-up ads *over* your Web page. Beyond annoying!

Once you have uploaded your HTML pages to your Web host, the Web server takes over. What's a Web server? I'm glad you asked!

Web Servers and Web Clients

A Web server is a computer that delivers (or *serves up*) Web pages. Web servers listen on port 80, fetching requested HTML pages and sending them to browsers. You can turn any computer into a Web server by installing server software and connecting the machine to the Internet, but you need to consider the operating system and Web server program you'll use to serve your Web site. Microsoft pushes *Internet Information Services (IIS)*, shown in Figure 9-16.

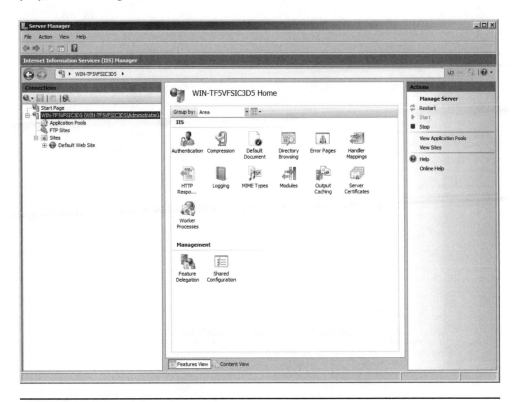

Figure 9-16   IIS in action

IIS enables you to set a maximum connection limit on your Web server based on available bandwidth and memory. This enables you to protect your network against an overwhelming number of requests due to a particularly popular page or a type of malicious attack called a Denial of Service (DoS) attack. (More on the latter in Chapter 16.)

Microsoft builds an artificial 20-connection limit into Windows XP, Windows Vista, and Windows 7 so you should only run IIS on Server versions of Windows (unless you don't expect too many people to visit your Web site at one time).

UNIX/Linux-based operating systems run *Apache HTTP Server*. As of this writing, Apache serves over 50 percent of the Web sites on the Internet. Apache is incredibly popular, runs on multiple operating systems (including Windows), and, best of all, is *free!* In comparison, even with the weight of Microsoft behind it, IIS still only commands about 25 percent market share.

Apache is nothing more than an executable program and a bunch of text files, so it isn't much to look at. To ease configuration, most Web administrators use add-on graphical user interfaces (GUIs) such as Webmin that make administering Apache a breeze. Figure 9-17 illustrates the wonderful simplicity that is Webmin.

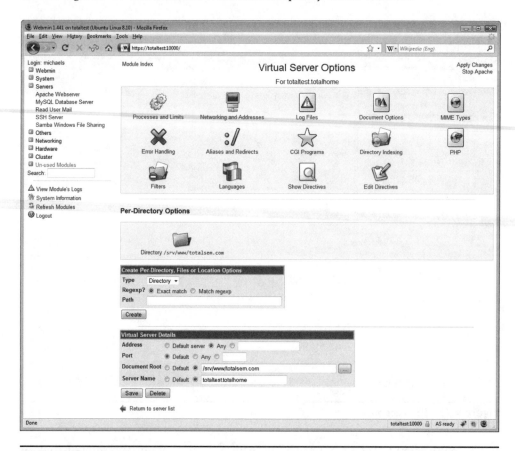

Figure 9-17 Webmin Apache module

IIS and Apache are by far the most common Web servers on the Internet. In third place is Google Web Server (GWS). GWS, used only by Google's servers, has about 5 percent of the total Web server market! After those three, there are literally hundreds of other Web servers, but you'll rarely see them outside of small personal Web sites.

NOTE In early 2009, China released numbers for a Chinese-only Web server called QZHTTP server and, as with anything to do with China and population, the numbers for hosted sites are staggeringly large. If accurate and sustained, QZHTTP would supplant GWS as the third most popular Web server software.

Web clients are the programs used to surf the Web. A client program (a Web browser) reads Web pages supplied by the Web server. To access a server, type either an IP address or, more commonly, the complete name of the Web server in the address bar. The complete name is often referred to as the *uniform resource locator (URL)*.

Most browsers handle multiple functions, from reading HTML documents to offering FTP services, and even serving as e-mail or newsgroup readers. (You'll learn all about these functions later in the chapter.) The most popular Web browsers are Microsoft Internet Explorer, Mozilla Firefox, Apple Safari, Opera, and Google Chrome.

NOTE Most Windows users just use Internet Explorer since it comes with Windows by default.

Secure Sockets Layer and HTTPS

HTTP is not a secure protocol. Any nosy person who can plug into a network can see and read the HTTP packets moving between a Web server and a Web client. Less than nice people can easily create a fake Web site to trick people into thinking it's a legitimate Web site and then steal their user names and passwords. For an Internet application to be secure, it must have

- **Authentication**   user names and passwords
- **Encryption**   stirring up the data so others can't read it
- **Nonrepudiation**   source not able to deny a sent message

While all of Chapter 11 is dedicated to these concepts, I can't mention HTTP without at least touching on its secure counterpart, HTTPS. The Web has blossomed into a major economic player, requiring serious security for those who wish to do online transactions (e-commerce). In the early days of e-commerce, people feared that a simple credit card transaction on a less-than-secure Web site could transform their dreams of easy online buying into a nightmare of being robbed blind and ending up living in a refrigerator box. I can safely say that it was *never* as bad as all that. And nowadays, many safeguards exist that can protect your purchases *and* your anonymity. One such safeguard is called *Secure Sockets Layer (SSL)*. SSL is a protocol developed by Netscape for transmitting private documents over the Internet. SSL works by using a public key to encrypt communication. This encrypted communication is sent over an SSL connection and then decrypted at the receiving end using a private key. All the popular Web browsers and Web servers support SSL, and many Web sites use the protocol to obtain confidential user information, such as credit card numbers. One way to tell if a site is using SSL is by looking at the Web page address. By convention, Web pages that use an SSL connection start with *https* instead of *http*.

HTTPS stands for *Hypertext Transfer Protocol over SSL*. HTTPS uses TCP port 443. You can also look for a small lock icon in the lower-right corner of your browser window. Figure 9-18 shows a typical secure Web page. The *https:* in the address and the lock icon are circled.

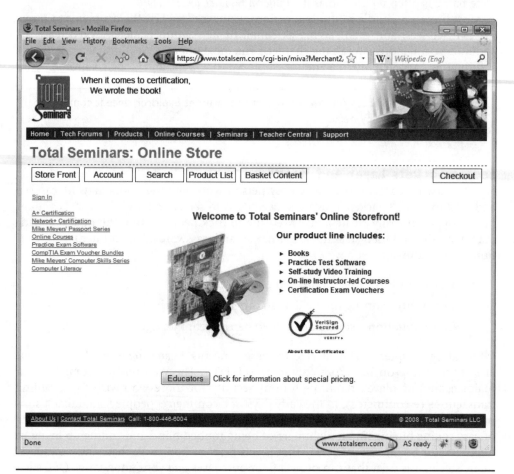

Figure 9-18   Secure Web page

EXAM TIP Many techs refer to HTTPS as Hypertext Transfer Protocol *Secure*, probably because it's easier to explain to non-techs that way. Don't be surprised to see it listed this way on the CompTIA Network+ exam.

The last few years have seen SSL replaced with the more powerful *Transport Layer Security* (*TLS*). Your secure Web page still looks the same as with SSL, so only the folks setting this up really care. Just make sure you know that SSL and TLS are functionally the same with Web pages. Read Chapter 11 for more details on SSL and TLS.

EXAM TIP HTTP enables you to access the Web, but HTTPS gets you there securely. HTTPS uses TLS to provide the security.

Telnet

Roughly one billion years ago, there was no such thing as the Internet or even networks... Well, maybe it was only about 40 years ago, but as far as nerds like me are concerned, a world before the Internet was filled with brontosauruses and palm fronds. The only computers were huge monsters called mainframes and to access them required a dumb terminal like the one shown in Figure 9-19.

Figure 9-19
Dumb terminal
(photo courtesy
of DVQ)

Operating systems didn't have windows and pretty icons. The interface to the mainframe was a command line, but it worked just fine for the time. Then the cavemen who first lifted their heads up from the computer ooze known as mainframes said to themselves, "Wouldn't it be great if we could access each other's computers from the comfort of our own caves?" That was what started the entire concept of a network. Back then, the idea of sharing folders or printers or Web pages hadn't been considered yet. The entire motivation for networking was so people could sit at their dumb terminals and, instead of accessing only their local mainframes, access totally different mainframes. The protocol to do this was called the *Telnet Protocol* or simply *Telnet*.

Even though PCs have replaced mainframes for the most part, Telnet still exists as the way to connect remotely to another computer via the command line (Figure 9-20). Telnet runs on TCP port 23, enabling you to connect to a Telnet server and run commands on that server as if you were sitting right in front of it.

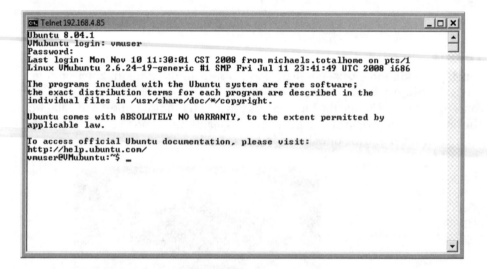

Figure 9-20   Telnet client

This way, you can remotely administer a server and communicate with other servers on your network. As you can imagine, this is sort of risky. If you can remotely control a computer, what is to stop others from doing the same? Thankfully, Telnet does not allow just *anyone* to log on and wreak havoc with your network. You must enter a user name and password to access a Telnet server. Unfortunately, Telnet does not have any form of encryption. If someone intercepted the conversation between a Telnet client and Telnet server, he or she would see all of the commands you type as well as the results from the Telnet server. As a result, Telnet is rarely used on the Internet and has been replaced with *Secure Shell (SSH)*, a terminal emulation program that looks exactly like Telnet but encrypts the data.

NOTE   Telnet only enables command-line remote access; it does not enable GUI access. If you want to access another computer's desktop remotely, you need another type of program.

Even though Telnet is less common than SSH, Telnet is a popular second option to connect to almost anything on a trusted TCP/IP network. Most routers have Telnet access capability (although many router admins turn it off for security). Almost every operating system has a built-in Telnet client and most operating systems—though not all Windows operating systems—come with built-in Telnet servers. Almost every type of server application has some way for you to access it with Telnet. It was once quite common, for example, to administer Apache-based Web servers through Telnet.

Telnet Servers and Clients

The oldest Telnet server, found on UNIX and Linux systems, is the venerable telnetd. Like most UNIX/Linux servers, telnetd isn't much to look at, so let's move over to the Windows world. Since the halcyon days of Windows NT, Windows has come with a basic Telnet server. It is disabled, by default, in modern Windows systems, and for good reason: Telnet is a gaping security hole. The built-in server is very limited and Microsoft discourages its use. I prefer to use this great little third-party server called freeSSHd (Figure 9-21). Note the name—freeSSHd, not "freeTelnet." As Telnet fades away and SSH becomes more dominant, finding a Telnet-only server these days is hard. All of the popular Telnet servers are also SSH servers.

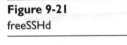

Figure 9-21
freeSSHd

A Telnet client is the computer from which you log onto the remote server. Most operating systems have a built-in Telnet client that you run from a command prompt. Figure 9-22 shows the Telnet client built into Ubuntu Linux. Just open a terminal window and type **telnet** and the IP address of the Telnet server.

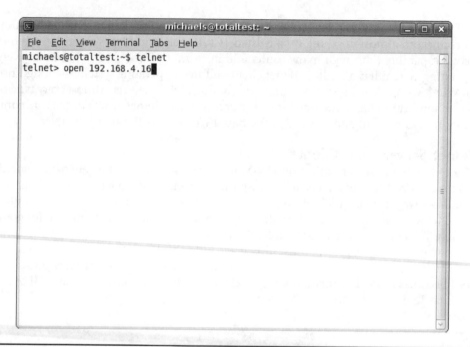

Figure 9-22 Ubuntu Telnet

NOTE Some versions of Windows Server came with a rather poor Telnet server that only allowed a maximum of two client connections.

Command-prompt Telnet clients lack a number of handy features. They can't, for example, remember the IP addresses, user names, or passwords for Telnet servers, so every time you use Telnet, you have to enter all that information again. Third-party Telnet clients, such as the very popular PuTTY, which you saw in Chapter 8, store all this information and much more (Figure 9-23).

Configuring a Telnet Client

When you configure a Telnet client, you must provide the host name, your user login name, and the password. As I mentioned previously, you must have permission to access the server to use Telnet. A *host name* is the name or IP address of the computer to which you want to connect. For instance, you might connect to a Web server with the host name websrv.mhteched.com. The user *login name* you give Telnet should be the same login name you'd use if you logged into the server at its location. Some computers, usually university libraries with online catalogs, have open systems that enable you to log in with Telnet. These sites either display a banner before the login prompt that tells you what login name to use, or they require no login name at all. As with the login name, you use the same password for a Telnet login that you'd use to log into the server directly. It's that simple. Computers with open access either tell you what password to use when they tell you what login name to use, or they require no login name/password at all.

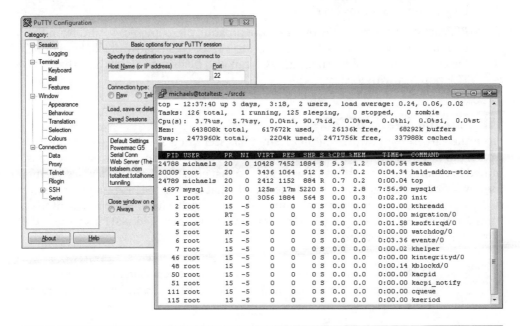

Figure 9-23 PuTTY

 EXAM TIP Telnet enables you to control a remote computer from a local computer over a network.

Rlogin, RSH, and RCP

The CompTIA Network+ exam tests you on *rlogin*, *RSH*, and *RCP*. These are three old-school programs in the UNIX world. The *R* stands for *remote*, and, like Telnet and SSH, these programs provide remote access and control of servers. Also like Telnet, they do not encrypt data and thus should not be used across the Internet. Here is a quick breakdown of the suite:

- *Remote Login (rlogin)* works very similarly to Telnet. You simply run the program with the host name of the server, and you can connect and run commands just like with Telnet. Rlogin has one very nice advantage over Telnet in that you can configure it to log in automatically without needing to enter a user name and password. It only connects to UNIX hosts, unlike Telnet. Rlogin works over TCP port 513.

- *Remote Shell (RSH)* enables you to send single commands to the remote server. Whereas rlogin is designed to be used interactively, RSH can be easily integrated into a script. RSH runs over TCP port 514 by default.

- *Remote Copy Protocol (RCP)* provides the capability to copy files to and from the remote server without needing to resort to FTP or NFS (Network File System, the UNIX form of folder sharing). RCP can also be used in scripts and shares TCP port 514 with RSH.

SSH and the Death of Telnet

From the earliest days of the Internet, Telnet has seen long and heavy use in the TCP world, but it suffers from lack of any security. Telnet passwords as well as data are transmitted in cleartext and are thus easily hacked. To that end, SSH has now replaced Telnet for any serious terminal emulation. In terms of what it does, SSH is extremely similar to Telnet in that it creates a terminal connection to a remote host. Every aspect of SSH, however, including both login and data transmittal, is encrypted. SSH also uses TCP port 22 instead of Telnet's port 23.

 EXAM TIP   SSH enables you to control a remote computer from a local computer over a network, just like Telnet. Unlike Telnet, SSH enables you to do it securely!

E-mail

Electronic mail (e-mail) has been a major part of the Internet revolution and not just because it has streamlined the junk mail industry. E-mail provides an extremely quick way for people to communicate with one another, letting you send messages and attachments (like documents and pictures) over the Internet. It's normally offered as a free service by ISPs. Most e-mail client programs provide a rudimentary text editor for composing messages, but many can be configured to let you edit your messages using more sophisticated editors.

E-mail consists of e-mail clients and e-mail servers. When a message is sent to your e-mail address, it is normally stored in an electronic mailbox on your e-mail server until you tell the e-mail client to download the message. Most e-mail client programs can be configured to signal you in some way when a new message has arrived or to download e-mails automatically as they come to you. Once you read an e-mail message, you can archive it, forward it, print it, or delete it. Most e-mail programs are configured to delete messages from the e-mail server automatically when you download them to your local machine, but you can usually change this configuration option to suit your circumstances.

E-mail programs use a number of application-level protocols to send and receive information. Specifically, the e-mail you find on the Internet uses SMTP to send e-mail, and either POP3 or IMAP4 to receive e-mail.

SMTP, POP3, and IMAP4, Oh My!

The following is a list of the different protocols that the Internet uses to transfer and receive mail:

SMTP The *Simple Mail Transfer Protocol (SMTP)* is used to send e-mail. SMTP travels over TCP port 25 and is used by clients to send messages.

POP3 *Post Office Protocol version 3 (POP3)* is one of the two protocols that receive e-mail from SMTP servers. POP3 uses TCP port 110. Most e-mail clients use this protocol, although some use IMAP4.

IMAP4 *Internet Message Access Protocol version 4 (IMAP4)* is an alternative to POP3. Like POP3, IMAP4 retrieves e-mail from an e-mail server. IMAP4 uses TCP port 143 and supports some features that are not supported in POP3. For example, IMAP4 enables you to search through messages on the mail server to find specific keywords and select the messages you want to download onto your machine. IMAP4 also supports the concept of folders that you can place on the IMAP4 server to organize your e-mail. Some POP3 e-mail clients have folders, but that's not a part of POP3, just a nice feature added to the client.

Alternatives to SMTP, POP3, and IMAP4

Although SMTP, POP3, and IMAP4 are by far the most common and most traditional tools for sending and receiving e-mail, two other options are widely popular: Web-based e-mail and proprietary solutions. Web-based mail, as the name implies, requires a Web interface. From a Web browser, you simply surf to the Web-mail server, log in, and access your e-mail. The cool part is that you can do it from anywhere in the world where you find a Web browser and an Internet hookup! You get the benefit of e-mail without even needing to own a computer. Some of the more popular Web-based services are Google's Gmail (Figure 9-24), Microsoft's Windows Live Hotmail, and Yahoo!'s Yahoo! Mail.

The key benefits of Web-based e-mail services are as follows:

- You can access your e-mail from anywhere.
- They're free.
- They're handy for throw-away accounts (like when you're required to give an e-mail address to download something, but you know you're going to get spammed if you do).

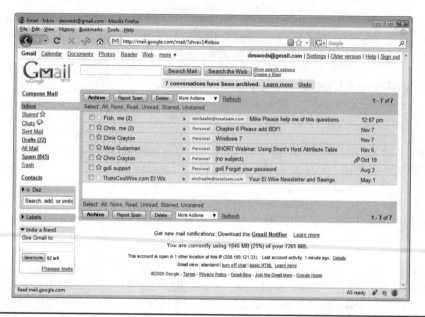

Figure 9-24   Gmail in action

E-mail Servers

The e-mail server world is much more fragmented than the Web server world. The current leader is *sendmail* used on Linux and UNIX operating systems. Like Apache, sendmail doesn't really have an interface, but many different third-party interfaces are available to help configure sendmail, such as Webmin shown in Figure 9-25.

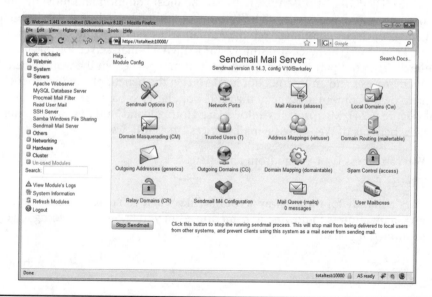

Figure 9-25   Webmin with the sendmail module

Sendmail controls about 20 percent of all e-mail servers but only uses SMTP. You must run a POP3 or IMAP4 server program to support e-mail clients. Programs like Eudora's Qpopper handle sending mail to POP3 e-mail clients. Microsoft, of course, has its own e-mail server, Microsoft Exchange Server, and like IIS, it only runs on Windows (Figure 9-26). Exchange Server is both an SMTP and a POP3 server in one package.

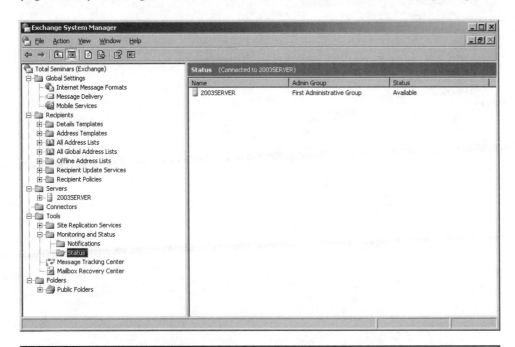

Figure 9-26 Microsoft Exchange Server

E-mail servers accept incoming mail and sort out the mail for recipients into individual storage area mailboxes. These *mailboxes* are special separate holding areas for each user's e-mail. An e-mail server works much like a post office, sorting and arranging incoming messages, and kicking back those messages that have no known recipient.

E-mail servers are difficult to manage. E-mail servers store user lists, user rights, and messages, and are constantly involved in Internet traffic and resources. Setting up and administering an e-mail server takes a lot of planning, although it's getting easier. Most e-mail server software runs in a GUI, but even the command-line-based interface of e-mail servers is becoming more intuitive.

E-mail Client An *e-mail client* is a program that runs on a computer and enables you to send, receive, and organize e-mail. The e-mail client program communicates with the SMTP e-mail server to send mail and communicates with the IMAP or POP e-mail server to download the messages from the e-mail server to the client computer.

There are hundreds of e-mail programs, some of the most popular of which are Microsoft Outlook, Microsoft's Windows Mail (Figure 9-27), Mozilla Thunderbird, and Qualcomm's Eudora.

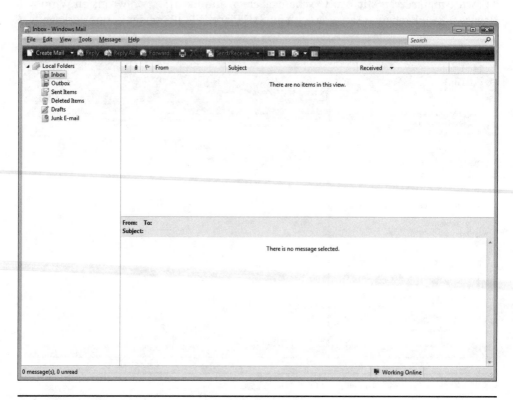

Figure 9-27 Windows Mail

Configuring an E-mail Client   Configuring a client is an easy matter. Your mail administrator will give you the server's domain name and your mailbox's user name and password. You need to enter the POP3 or IMAP4 server's domain name and the SMTP server's domain name to the e-mail client (Figure 9-28). Every e-mail client has a different way to add the server domain names or IP addresses, so you may have to poke around, but you'll find the option there somewhere! In many cases, this may be the same name or address for both the incoming and outgoing servers—the folks administering the mail servers will tell you. Besides the e-mail server domain names or addresses, you must also enter the user name and password of the e-mail account the client will be managing.

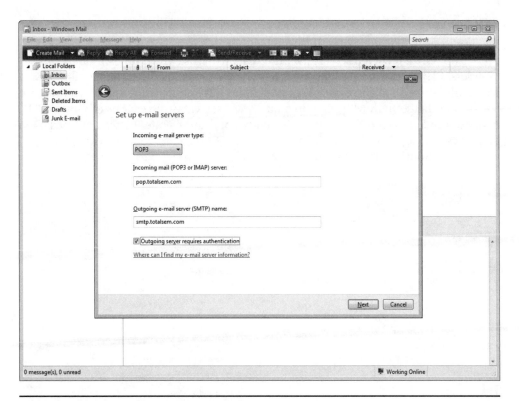

Figure 9-28   Entering server information in Windows Mail

FTP

File Transfer Protocol (FTP) is the original protocol used on the Internet for transferring files. Although HTTP can be used to transfer files as well, the transfer is often not as reliable or as fast as with FTP. In addition, FTP can do the transfer with security and data integrity. FTP uses TCP ports 21 and 20 by default, although passive FTP only uses port 21 for a default. See the discussion on active versus passive FTP later in this chapter.

FTP sites are either anonymous sites, meaning that anyone can log on, or secured sites, meaning that you must have a user name and password to access the site and transfer files. A single FTP site can offer both anonymous access and protected access, but you'll see different resources depending on which way you log in.

FTP Servers and FTP Clients

The FTP server does all the real work of storing the files, accepting incoming connections and verifying user names and passwords, and transferring the files. The client logs onto the FTP server (either from a Web site, a command line, or a special FTP application) and downloads the requested files onto the local hard drive.

FTP Servers

We don't set up servers for Internet applications nearly as often as we set up clients. I've set up only a few Web servers over the years whereas I've set up thousands of Web browsers. FTP servers are the one exception, as we nerds like to exchange files. If you have a file you wish to share with a lot of people (but not the entire Internet), there are few options better than whipping up a quick FTP server. Most versions of Linux/UNIX have built-in FTP servers, but many third-party applications offer better solutions. One of the best, especially for those "let me put up an FTP server so you guys can get a copy" type of situations, is Mozilla's FileZilla Server (Figure 9-29).

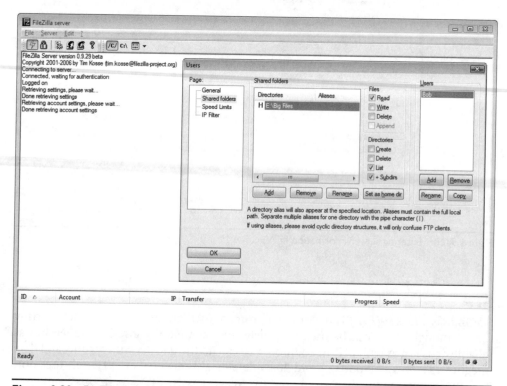

Figure 9-29 FileZilla Server

 NOTE Most Web servers are also FTP servers. These bundled versions of FTP servers are robust but do not provide all the options one might want.

FTP is not very secure because data transfers are not encrypted, so you don't want to use FTP for sensitive data. But you can add user names and passwords to prevent all but the most serious hackers from accessing your FTP server. I avoid using the anonymous login because unscrupulous people could use the server for exchanging illegal software.

Another thing to check when deciding on an FTP server setup is the number of clients you want to support. Most anonymous FTP sites limit the number of users who may download at any one time to around 500. This protects you from a sudden influx of users flooding your server and eating up all your Internet bandwidth.

FTP Clients FTP clients, as noted before, can access an FTP server through a Web site, a command line, or a special FTP application. Usually special FTP applications offer the most choices for accessing and using an FTP site.

NOTE Every operating system has a command-line FTP client. I avoid using them unless I have no other choice because they lack important features like the ability to save FTP connections to use again later.

You have many choices when it comes to FTP clients. For starters, some Web browsers handle FTP as well as HTTP, although they lack a few features. For example, Firefox only supports an anonymous login. To use your Web browser as an FTP client, type **ftp://** followed by the IP address or domain name of the FTP server (Figure 9-30).

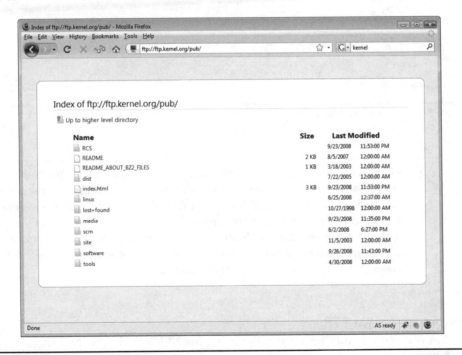

Figure 9-30 FTP in a Web browser

The best way to use FTP is to use a dedicated FTP client. So many good ones are available that I find myself using a different one all the time. FileZilla comes in a client version, but these days, I'm using an add-on to Firefox called FireFTP (Figure 9-31).

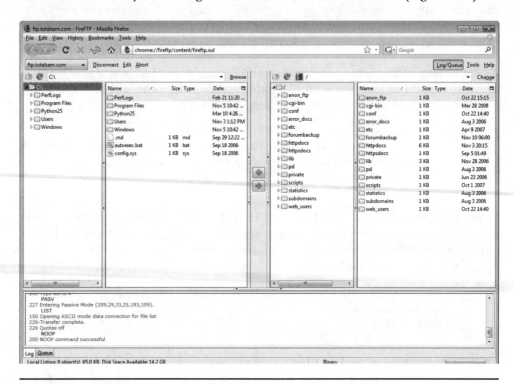

Figure 9-31 FireFTP hard at work

NOTE Firefox enables programmers to create add-ons, small programs that extend the capabilities of the browser with some pretty impressive results. Are you unfamiliar with Firefox add-ons? Start Firefox. Click **Firefox/Add-ons (or Tools/Add-ons** in older versions), and a whole new world will open for you. A couple of my favorites are Mouse Gestures—where you can flick the mouse left or right to navigate through windows and Web sites you've visited—and Speed Dial—quick access to your favorite sites.

Passive vs. Active FTP

FTP has two ways to transfer data: *active* and *passive* FTP. Traditionally, FTP uses the active process—let's see how this works. Remember that FTP uses TCP ports 20 and 21? Well, when your client sends an FTP request, it goes out on port 21. When your FTP server responds, however, it sends the data back using an ephemeral destination port and port 20 as a source port.

Active FTP works great unless your client uses NAT. Since your client didn't initiate the incoming port 20, your NAT router has no idea where to send this incoming packet. Additionally, any good firewall sees this incoming connection as something evil because it doesn't have anything inside the network that started the link on port 20. No problem! Good FTP clients all support passive FTP. With passive FTP, the server doesn't use port 20. Instead, the client sends an FTP request on port 21, just like active FTP. But then the server sends back a random port number, telling the client which port it's listening on for data requests. The client, in turn, sends data to the port specified by the FTP server. Because the client initiates all conversations, the NAT router knows where to send the packet.

The only trick to passive FTP is that the client needs to expect this other incoming data. When you configure an FTP client for passive, you're telling it to expect these packets.

NOTE Trivial File Transfer Protocol (TFTP) is used for transferring files and has a similar-sounding name to FTP, but beyond that it is very different. TFTP uses UDP port 69 and does not use user names and passwords, although you can usually set some restrictions based on the client's IP address. TFTP is not at all secure, so never use it on any network that's less than trustworthy.

Internet Applications

Use this table as a review tool to help you remember each Internet application:

Application	TCP/UDP	Port	Notes
HTTP	TCP	80	The Web
HTTPS	TCP	443	The Web, securely
Telnet	TCP	23	Terminal emulation
SSH	TCP	22	Secure terminal emulation
SMTP	TCP	25	Sending e-mail
POP3	TCP	110	E-mail delivery
IMAP4	TCP	143	E-mail delivery
FTP	TCP	20/21 (active), 21 (passive)	File transfer
TFTP	UDP	69	File transfer

Chapter Review

Questions

1. The protocol developed by Netscape for transmitting private documents over the Internet is known as

   A. SSS

   B. SSA

   C. SSL

   D. NSSL

2. Which of the following are key benefits of Web-based mail? (Select two.)

   A. You can use a third-party application, like Microsoft Outlook, to download your e-mail.

   B. You can access your e-mail from anywhere in the world using a Web browser and an Internet connection.

   C. It is completely spam-free.

   D. It is great for creating throw-away accounts.

3. An SSL URL connection starts with which prefix?

   A. HTTP

   B. WWW

   C. FTP

   D. HTTPS

4. Which statements about SSH and Telnet are true? (Select two.)

   A. Windows comes with preinstalled SSH and Telnet clients.

   B. SSH is more secure than Telnet because it encrypts data.

   C. Telnet is a command-line tool, whereas SSH is a GUI tool.

   D. SSH uses port 22, and Telnet uses port 23.

5. Why might you use the netstat utility?

   A. To see the route an IP packet takes across multiple routers

   B. To see your IP address and configuration details

   C. To see the endpoints of your sessions

   D. To issue commands to a remote server

6. Why might you use a Telnet client?

   A. To see the route an IP packet takes across multiple routers

   B. To see your IP address and configuration details

   C. To see the endpoints of your sessions

   D. To issue commands to a remote server

7. Port 110 (POP) is what kind of port?

   A. Well-known

   B. Registered

   C. Ephemeral

   D. Reserved

8. What ports does FTP use? (Select two.)

   A. 20

   B. 21

   C. 23

   D. 25

9. Which of the following protocols are used to receive e-mail from servers? (Select two.)

   A. IMAP

   B. ICMP

   C. IGMP

   D. POP

10. Which statements about netstat switches (in Windows) are true? (Select three.)

    A. -a shows all used ports.

    B. -n shows raw port numbers and IP addresses.

    C. -o shows the process ID.

    D. -s shows the application name.

Answers

1. **C.** Secure Sockets Layer (SSL) is a protocol developed by Netscape for transmitting private documents over the Internet. SSL works by using a public key to encrypt sensitive data.

2. **B and D.** You can access a Web-based e-mail account from any browser on any machine connected to the Internet. These accounts are great for creating throwaway e-mail addresses.

3. **D.** URLs that use an SSL connection start with HTTPS instead of HTTP.

4. **B** and **D.** SSH encrypts data and is more secure than Telnet. Also, SSH uses port 22, whereas Telnet uses port 23.

5. **C.** Use netstat to see the endpoints of your sessions.

6. **D.** Telnet is used to issue commands to a remote server.

7. **A.** Ports 0–1023 are well-known ports.

8. **A** and **B.** FTP uses ports 20 and 21.

9. **A** and **D.** IMAP and POP are used to receive e-mail.

10. **A, B,** and **C.** -a shows all used ports; -n shows raw port numbers and IP addresses; and -o shows the process ID.

Network Naming

The CompTIA Network+ certification exam expects you to know how to

- 1.5 Identify common TCP and UDP default ports: DNS
- 1.6 Explain the function of common networking protocols: DNS
- 1.7 Summarize DNS concepts and its components
- 2.3 Explain the purpose and properties of DHCP: options (DNS servers, suffixes)
- 2.5 Given a scenario, troubleshoot common router and switch problems: wrong DNS
- 4.3 Given a scenario, use appropriate software tools to troubleshoot connectivity issues: ping, dig, ipconfig/ifconfig, nslookup, arp, nbtstat, netstat

To achieve these goals, you must be able to

- Describe the function and capabilities of DNS
- Configure and troubleshoot WINS
- Use common TCP/IP utilities to diagnose problems with DNS and WINS

Did the last chapter seem a bit IP address-heavy to you? When you open a Web page, for example, do you normally type something like http://192.168.4.1, or do you usually type something like www.totalsem.com? Odds are good you normally do the latter and only rarely the former. Why? People are terrible at memorizing numbers, but are pretty good at memorizing words. This creates an interesting dilemma.

Although computers use IP addresses to communicate with each other over a TCP/IP network, people prefer easy-to-remember names over IP addresses. To solve this problem, TCP/IP developers created a process called *name resolution* to convert names to IP addresses (and *vice versa*) to make it easier for people to communicate with computers (Figure 10-1).

Like any process that's been around for a long time, name resolution has gone through a number of evolutions over the years: some dramatic and some subtle. Entire TCP/IP applications have been written, only to be supplanted (but never totally abandoned) by newer name resolution protocols.

Today, we use a single major name resolution protocol called *Domain Name System (DNS)*, but your brand-new system running the latest version of whatever operating system you prefer still fully supports a number of much older name resolution protocols! Name resolution in today's networking world is like a well-run home that's also full of ghosts that can do very strange things if you don't understand how those ghosts think.

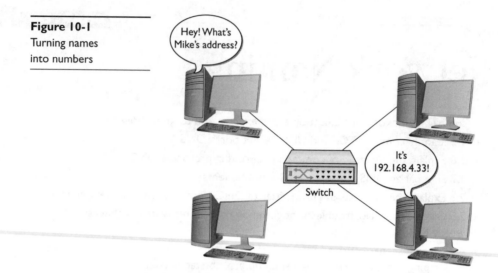

Figure 10-1

Turning names
into numbers

In this chapter, you'll take an in-depth tour of name resolution, starting with a discussion of DNS. After DNS, the chapter looks at one of the scariest ghosts running around inside your computer: an ancient and theoretically abandoned name resolution protocol invented by Microsoft called *Windows Internet Name Service (WINS)*. Despite what Microsoft claims, the ghost of WINS still lingers, not only on Windows computers but also on Linux and Mac OS X systems; as these folks discovered, if you don't respect these ghosts, you won't be able to do name resolution when you connect to a Windows computer.

Odds are good you have a system that is connected—or at least can connect—to the Internet. If I were you, I'd fire up that system because the vast majority of the programs you're going to learn about here come free with every operating system. Finding them may be a challenge on some systems, but don't worry—I'll show you where they all hang out.

Historical/Conceptual

DNS

When the Internet was very young and populated with only a few hundred computers, name resolution was pretty simple. The original TCP/IP specification implemented name resolution using a special text file called HOSTS. A copy of this file was stored on every computer system on the Internet. The *HOSTS file* contained a list of IP addresses for every computer on the Internet, matched to the corresponding system names. Remember, not only was the Internet a lot smaller then, but also there weren't yet rules about how to compose Internet names, such as that they must end in .com or .org, or start with www or ftp. Anyone could name their computer pretty much anything they wanted (there were a few restrictions on length and allowable characters) as long as nobody else had snagged the name first. Part of an old HOSTS file might look something like this:

```
192.168.2.1     fred
201.32.16.4     school2
123.21.44.16    server
```

If your system wanted to access the system called fred, it looked up the name fred in its HOSTS file and then used the corresponding IP address to contact fred. Every HOSTS file on every system on the Internet was updated every morning at 2 A.M. This worked fine when the Internet was still the province of a few university geeks and some military guys, but when the Internet grew to about 5000 systems, it became impractical to make every system use and update a HOSTS file. This created the motivation for a more scalable name resolution process, but the HOSTS file did not go away.

Believe it or not, the HOSTS file is still alive and well in every computer. You can find the HOSTS file in the \WinNT\System32\Drivers\Etc folder in Windows 2000, and in \Windows\System32\Drivers\Etc in Windows XP/2003/Vista/7. On OS X and Linux systems, you usually find it in the /etc/ folder. The HOSTS file is just a text file that you can open with any text editor. Here are a few lines from the default HOSTS file that comes with Windows.

```
# Additionally, comments (such as these) may be inserted on individual
# lines or following the machine name denoted by a '#' symbol.
#
# For example:
#
#           102.54.94.97    rhino.acme.com    # source server
#           38.25.63.10     x.acme.com        # x client host
127.0.0.1               localhost
```

See the # signs? Those are remark symbols that designate lines as comments (for humans to read) rather than code. Windows ignores any line that begins with #. Remove the # and Windows will read the line and try to act on it. Although all operating systems continue to support the HOSTS file, it is rarely used in the day-to-day workings of most TCP/IP systems.

Even though the HOSTS file is rarely used, *every* operating system always looks first in the HOSTS file before anything else when attempting to resolve a name. To see the power of the HOSTS file, follow these steps.

1. Go to a command prompt and type **ping www.totalsem.com**. You may or may not be successful with the ping utility, but you will get the IP address for my Web site. (You may get a different IP address from the one shown in this example.)

```
C:\>ping www.totalsem.com
Pinging www.totalsem.com [209.29.33.25] with 32 bytes of data:
Reply from 209.29.33.25: bytes=32 time=60ms TTL=51
Reply from 209.29.33.25: bytes=32 time=60ms TTL=51
```

```
Reply from 209.29.33.25: bytes=32 time=60ms TTL=51
Reply from 209.29.33.25: bytes=32 time=60ms TTL=51
Ping statistics for 209.29.33.25:
    Packets: Sent = 4, Received = 4, Lost = 0 (0% loss),
Approximate round trip times in milli-seconds:
    Minimum = 60ms, Maximum = 60ms, Average = 60ms
```

2. Open your HOSTS file using any text editor and add this line (keep in mind you may have a different IP address from the one shown in this example). Just press the SPACEBAR a few times to separate the IP address from the word "timmy."

```
209.29.33.25  timmy
```

3. Save the HOSTS file and close the text editor.

4. Open your Web browser and type **timmy**. You can also type **http://timmy** if you'd like. What happens?

The step-by-step example uses a Web browser, but keep in mind that a name in a HOSTS file resolves names for *every* TCP/IP application on that system. Go to a command prompt and type **ping timmy**. It works for ping too.

HOSTS files still have their place in today's world. Many people place shortcut names in a HOSTS file to avoid typing long names in some TCP/IP applications. Yet even though HOSTS still has some use, for the most part, you use the vastly more powerful DNS.

Test Specific

How DNS Works

The Internet folks, faced with the task of replacing HOSTS, first came up with the idea of creating one supercomputer that did nothing but resolve names for all the other computers on the Internet. There was one problem with that idea: even now, no computer is big enough or powerful enough to handle the job alone. So they fell back on that time-tested bureaucratic solution: delegation! The top-dog DNS system would delegate parts of the job to subsidiary DNS systems that, in turn, would delegate part of their work to other systems, and so on, potentially without end. These systems run a special DNS server program and are called, amazingly enough, *DNS servers*.

This is all peachy, but it raises another issue: they needed some way to decide how to divvy up the work. Toward this end, the Internet folks created a naming system designed to facilitate delegation. The top-dog DNS server is actually a bunch of powerful computers dispersed around the world. They work as a team and are known collectively as the *DNS root servers* (or simply as the *DNS root*). The Internet name of this computer team is "."—that's right, just "dot." Sure, it's weird, but it's quick to type, and they had to start somewhere.

 EXAM TIP   DNS servers primarily use UDP port 53 and sometimes TCP port 53.

NOTE The DNS root for the entire Internet consists of 13 powerful DNS server clusters scattered all over the world. Go to http://www.root-servers.org to see exactly where all the root servers are located.

DNS root has the complete definitive name resolution table, but most name resolution work is delegated to other DNS servers. Just below the DNS root in the hierarchy is a set of DNS servers—called the *top-level domain servers*—that handle what are known as the *top-level domain (TLD) names*. These are the famous com, org, net, edu, gov, mil, and int names (although many TLDs have been added since 2001). The top-level DNS servers delegate to thousands of second-level DNS servers; these servers handle the millions of names like totalsem.com and whitehouse.gov that have been created within each of the top-level domains. Second-level DNS servers support individual computers. For example, stored on the DNS server controlling the totalsem.com domain is a listing that looks like this:

```
www   209.29.33.25
```

EXAM TIP The original top-level domain names were com, org, net, edu, gov, mil, and int.

This means the totalsem.com domain has a computer called *www* with the IP address of 209.29.33.25. Only the DNS server controlling the totalsem.com domain stores the actual IP address for *www*.totalsem.com. The DNS servers above this one have a hierarchical system that enables any other computer to find the DNS server that controls the totalsem.com domain.

NOTE The *Internet Corporation for Assigned Names and Numbers (ICANN)* has the authority to create new TLDs. Since 2001, they've added many TLDs, such as .biz for businesses, .info for informational sites, and .pro for accountants, engineers, lawyers, and physicians in several Western countries.

Name Spaces

What does *hierarchical* mean in terms of DNS? Well, the DNS *hierarchical name space* is an imaginary tree structure of all possible names that could be used within a single system. By contrast, a HOSTS file uses a *flat name space*—basically just one big undivided list containing all names, with no grouping whatsoever. In a flat name space, all names must be absolutely unique—no two machines can ever share the same name under any circumstances. A flat name space works fine on a small, isolated network, but not so well for a large organization with many interconnected networks. To avoid naming conflicts, all its administrators would need to keep track of all the names used throughout the entire corporate network.

NOTE The Internet DNS names are usually consistent with this three-tier system, but if you want to add your own DNS server(s), you can add more levels, allowing you to name a computer www.houston.totalsem.com if you wish. The only limit is that a DNS name can have a maximum of only 255 characters.

A hierarchical name space offers a better solution, permitting a great deal more flexibility by enabling administrators to give networked systems longer, more fully descriptive names. The personal names people use every day are an example of a hierarchical name space. Most people address our town postman, Ron Samuels, simply as Ron. When his name comes up in conversation, people usually refer to him as Ron. The town troublemaker, Ron Falwell, and Mayor Jones's son, Ron, who went off to Toledo, obviously share first names with the postman. In some conversations, people need to distinguish between the good Ron, the bad Ron, and the Ron in Toledo (who may or may not be the ugly Ron). They could use a medieval style of address and refer to the Rons as Ron the Postman, Ron the Blackguard, and Ron of Toledo, or they could use the modern Western style of address and add their surnames: "That Ron Samuels—he is such a card!" "That Ron Falwell is one bad apple." "That Ron Jones was the homeliest child I ever saw." You might visualize this as the People name space, illustrated in Figure 10-2. Adding the surname creates what you might fancifully call a *Fully Qualified Person Name*—enough information to prevent confusion among the various people named Ron.

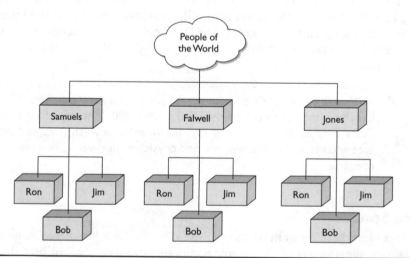

Figure 10-2   Our People name space

A name space most of you are already familiar with is the hierarchical file name space used by hard drive volumes. Hard drives formatted using one of the popular file formats, like Window's NTFS or Linux's ext3, use a hierarchical name space; you can create as many files named Data.txt as you want, as long as you store them in different parts of the file tree. In the example shown in Figure 10-3, two different files named

Data.txt can exist simultaneously on the same system, but only if they are placed in different directories, such as C:\Program1\Current\Data.txt and C:\Program1\Backup\Data.txt. Although both files have the same basic filename—Data.txt—their fully qualified names are different: C:\Program1\Current\Data.txt and C:\Program1\Backup\Data.txt.Additionally, multiple subfolders can use the same name. Having two subfolders that use the name Data is no problem, as long as they reside in different folders. Any Windows file system will happily let you create both C:\Program1\Data and C:\Program2\Data folders. Folks like this because they often want to give the same name to multiple folders doing the same job for different applications.

Figure 10-3
Two Data.txt files in different directories on the same system

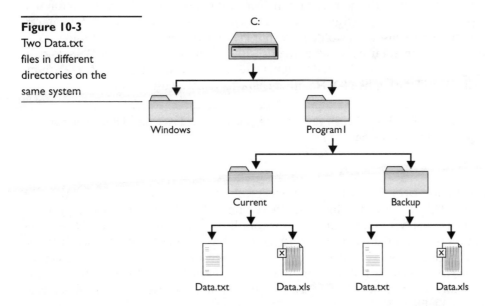

In contrast, imagine what would happen if your computer's file system didn't support folders/directories. Windows would have to store all the files on your hard drive in the root directory! This is a classic example of a flat name space. Because all your files would be living together in one directory, each one would have to have a unique name. Naming files would be a nightmare! Software vendors would have to avoid sensible descriptive names like Readme.txt because they would almost certainly have been used already. You'd probably have to do what the Internet does for IP addresses: An organization of some sort would assign names out of the limited pool of possible filenames. With a hierarchical name space, on the other hand, which is what all file systems use (thank goodness!), naming is much simpler. Lots of programs can have files called Readme.txt because each program can have its own folder and subfolders.

NOTE As hard as this may be to believe, some early file systems used a flat name space. Back in the late 1970s and early 1980s, operating systems such as CP/M and the early versions of DOS did not have the capability to use directories, creating a flat name space where all files resided on a single drive.

The DNS name space works in a manner extremely similar to how your computer's file system works. The DNS name space is a hierarchy of *DNS domains* and individual computer names organized into a tree-like structure that is called, rather appropriately, a *tree*. Each domain is like a folder—a domain is not a single computer, but rather a holding space into which you can add computer names. At the top of a *DNS tree* is the root. The *root* is the holding area to which all domains connect, just as the root directory in your file system is the holding area for all your folders. Individual computer names—more commonly called *host names* in the DNS naming convention—fit into domains. On a PC, you can place files directly into the root directory. The DNS world also enables us to add computer names to the root, but with the exception of a few special computers (described in a moment), this is rarely done. Each domain can have subdomains, just as the folders on your PC's file system can have subfolders. You separate each domain from its subdomains with a period. Characters for DNS domain names and host names are limited to uppercase and lowercase letters (A–Z, a–z), numbers (0–9), and the hyphen (-). No other characters may be used.

 NOTE Even though you may use uppercase or lowercase, DNS does not differentiate between them.

Don't think DNS is only for computers on the Internet. If you want to make your own little TCP/IP network using DNS, that's fine, although you will have to set up at least one DNS server as the root server for your little private *intranet*. Every DNS server program can be configured as a root server; just don't connect that DNS server to the Internet because it won't work outside your little network. Figure 10-4 shows a sample DNS tree for a small TCP/IP network that is not attached to the Internet. In this case, there is only one domain: ABCDEF. Each computer on the network has a host name, as shown in the figure.

Figure 10-4
Private DNS
network

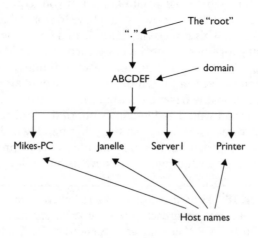

When you write out the complete path to a file stored on your PC, the naming convention starts with the root directory on the left, followed by the first folder, then any subfolders (in order), and finally the name of the file—for example, C:\Sounds\Thunder\mynewcobra.wav.

The DNS naming convention is *exactly the opposite*. A complete DNS name, including the host name and all of its domains (in order), is called a *fully qualified domain name (FQDN)*, and it's written with the root on the far right, followed by the names of the domains (in order) added to the left of the root, and the host name on the far left. Figure 10-4 shows the FQDNs for two systems in the ABCDEF domain. Note the period for the root is on the far *right* of each FQDN!

> Mikes-PC.ABCDEF.
> Janelle.ABCDEF.

Given that every FQDN will always have a period on the end to signify the root, it is commonplace to drop the final period when writing out FQDNs. To make the two example FQDNs fit into common parlance, therefore, you'd skip the last period:

> Mikes-PC.ABCDEF
> Janelle.ABCDEF

If you're used to seeing DNS names on the Internet, you're probably wondering about the lack of ".com," ".net," or other common DNS domain names. Those conventions are needed for computers that are visible on the Internet, such as Web servers, but they're not required on a private TCP/IP network. As long as you make a point never to make these computers visible on the Internet, you can use any naming convention you want!

NOTE Don't get locked into thinking FQDNs always end with names like ".com" or ".net." True, DNS names on the Internet must always end with them, but private TCP/IP networks can (and often do) ignore this and use whatever naming scheme they want with their DNS names.

Let's look at another DNS name space example, but make it a bit more complex. This network is not on the Internet, so I can use any domain I want. The network has two domains, Houston and Dallas, as shown in Figure 10-5. Note that each domain has a computer called Server1.

Figure 10-5
Two DNS domains

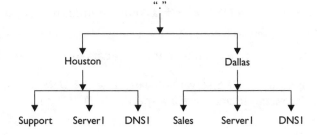

Because the network has two different domains, it can have two systems (one on each domain) with the same host name, just as you can have two files with the same name in different folders on your PC. Now, let's add some subdomains to the DNS tree, so that it looks like Figure 10-6.

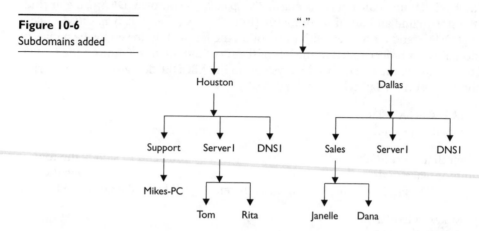

Figure 10-6

Subdomains added

You write out the FQDN from left to right, starting with the host name and moving up to the top of the DNS tree, adding all domains until you get to the top of the DNS tree:

Mikes-PC.Support.Houston
Tom.Server1.Houston
Janelle.Sales.Dallas
Server1.Dallas

EXAM TIP The DNS naming convention allows for DNS names up to 255 characters, including the separating periods.

Name Servers

So where does this naming convention reside and how does it work? The power of DNS comes from its incredible flexibility. DNS works as well on a small, private network as it does on the biggest network of all time—the Internet. Let's start with three key players:

- **DNS server** A *DNS server* is a computer running DNS server software.
- **Zone** A *zone* is a container for a single domain that gets filled with records.
- **Record** A *record* is a line in the zone data that maps an FQDN to an IP address.

Systems running DNS server software store the DNS information. When a system needs to know the IP address for a specific FQDN, it queries the DNS server listed in its TCP/IP configuration. Assuming the DNS server stores the zone for that particular FQDN, it replies with the computer's IP address.

A simple network usually has one DNS server for the entire network. This DNS server has a single zone that lists all the host names on the domain and their corresponding IP addresses. It's known as the *authoritative DNS server* for the domain (also called *Start of Authority*, or *SOA*).

If you've got a powerful computer, you can put lots of zones on a single DNS server and let that server support them all without a problem. A single DNS server, therefore, can act as the authoritative DNS server for one domain or many domains (Figure 10-7).

Figure 10-7
A single SOA can support one or more domains.

Equally, a single DNS domain may have a single authoritative DNS server but a number of other DNS servers, known simply as *name servers* (folks use the abbreviation "NS"), that are subordinate to the authoritative DNS server but all support the same domain, as shown in Figure 10-8. The SOA is a name server as well.

Figure 10-8 DNS flexibility

Note that every DNS server, whether it's the SOA or just an NS, knows the name and address of the SOA as well as every other NS server in the domain. The SOA's job is to make sure that all the other name servers are updated for changes. Let's say you add to the totalsem.com domain a new computer called ftp.totalsem.com with the IP address 192.168.4.22. As an administrator, you typically add this data to the SOA DNS server. The SOA then automatically distributes this information to the other name servers in the domain (Figure 10-9). This DNS feature is critical—you'll see more of this in detail later on in the "DNS Servers" section in this chapter. For now, appreciate that you can have multiple DNS servers for a single domain.

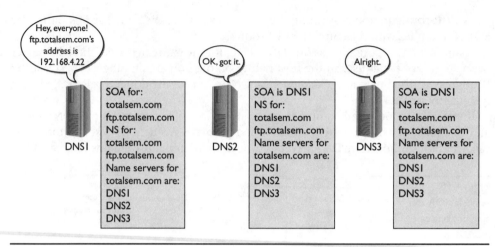

Figure 10-9   New information passed out

Now let's see how root servers work in DNS. What if Mikes-PC.Support.Houston needs the IP address of Server1.Dallas? Refer to Figure 10-10 for the answer. The network has two DNS servers: DNS1.Houston and DNS1.Dallas. DNS1.Dallas is the authoritative DNS server for all of the Dallas domains and DNS1.Houston is in charge of all the Houston domains. DNS1.Houston is also the root server for the entire network. (DNS servers may act as both a root server and an SOA at the same time—a very common practice in private networks.) As a root server, the Houston server has a listing for the SOA in the Dallas domain. This does *not* mean it knows the IP address for every system in the Dallas network. As a root server, it only knows that if any system asks for an IP address from the Dallas side, it will tell that system the IP address of the Dallas server. The requesting system will then ask the Dallas DNS server (DNS1.Dallas) for the IP address of the system it needs. That's the beauty of DNS root servers—they don't know the IP addresses for all of the computers, but they know where to send the requests!

NOTE   In the early days of DNS, you had to enter manually into your DNS server the host name and IP address of every system on the network. See "Dynamic DNS," later in this chapter, for the way it's done today.

The hierarchical aspect of DNS has a number of benefits. For example, the vast majority of Web servers are called www. If DNS used a flat name space, only the first organization that created a server with the name www could use it. Because DNS naming appends domain names to the server names, however, the servers www.totalsem.com and www.microsoft.com can both exist simultaneously. DNS names like www.microsoft.com must fit within a worldwide hierarchical name space, meaning that no two machines should ever have the same FQDN.

Figure 10-10
Root server in action

EXAM TIP Just because most Web servers are named www doesn't mean they must be named www! Naming a Web server www is etiquette, not a requirement.

Figure 10-11 shows the host named accounting with an FQDN of accounting.texas .totalsem.com.

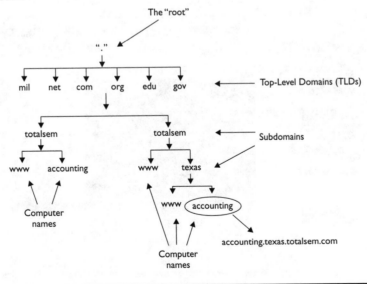

Figure 10-11 DNS domain

NOTE Technically, the texas.totalsem.com domain shown in Figure 10-11 is a subdomain of totalsem.com. Don't be surprised to see the terms "domain" and "subdomain" used interchangeably, as it's a common practice.

These domain names must be registered for Internet use with ICANN (www.icann .org). They are arranged in the familiar "second level.top level" domain name format, where the top level is com, org, net, and so on, and the second level is the name of the individual entity registering the domain name.

Name Resolution

You don't have to use DNS to access the Internet, but it sure makes life easier! Browsers like Internet Explorer accept names such as www.google.com as a convenience to the end user, but they use the IP address that corresponds to that name to create a connection. If you know the IP address of the system you want to talk to, you don't need DNS at all. Figure 10-12 shows Internet Explorer displaying the same Web page when given the straight IP address as it does when given the DNS name www.microsoft.com. In theory, if you knew the IP addresses of all the systems you wanted to access, you could avoid DNS completely. I guess you could also start a fire using a bow and drill too, but most people wouldn't make a habit of it if there were a more efficient alternative. In this case, DNS is much more efficient! I have no trouble keeping hundreds of DNS names in my head, but IP addresses? Forget it! Without DNS, I might as well not even try to use the Internet, and I'd wager that's true of most people.

Figure 10-12 Any TCP/IP-savvy program accepts either an IP address or an FQDN.

When you type in a Web address, your browser must resolve that name to the Web server's IP address to make a connection to that Web server. It can resolve the name in three ways: by broadcasting, by consulting the locally stored HOSTS text file, or by contacting a DNS server.

To *broadcast* for name resolution, the host sends a message to all the machines on the network, saying something like, "Hey! If your name is JOESCOMPUTER, please respond with your IP address." All the networked hosts receive that packet, but only JOESCOMPUTER responds with an IP address. Broadcasting works fine for small networks, but it is limited because it cannot provide name resolution across routers. Routers do not forward broadcast messages to other networks, as illustrated in Figure 10-13.

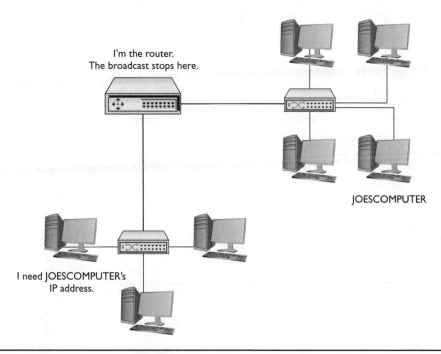

I'm the router.
The broadcast stops here.

JOESCOMPUTER

I need JOESCOMPUTER's
IP address.

Figure 10-13 Routers don't forward broadcasts!

As discussed earlier, a HOSTS file functions like a little black book, listing the names and addresses of machines on a network, just like a little black book lists the names and phone numbers of people. A typical HOSTS file would look like this:

```
109.54.94.197      stephen.totalsem.com
138.125.163.17     roger.totalsem.com
127.0.0.1          localhost
```

NOTE Notice that the name *localhost* appears in the HOSTS file as an alias for the loopback address, 127.0.0.1.

The final way to resolve a name to an IP address is to use DNS. Let's say you type **www.microsoft.com** in your Web browser. To resolve the name www.microsoft.com, the host contacts its DNS server and requests the IP address, as shown in Figure 10-14.

Figure 10-14

A host contacts its local DNS server.

Client

Client's DNS server

1. The client asks its DNS server for the www.microsoft.com IP address.

2. The DNS server doesn't know the IP address, so it asks the root DNS server.

To request the IP address of www.microsoft.com, your PC needs the IP address of its DNS server. You must enter DNS information into your system. DNS server data is part of the critical basic IP information such as your IP address, subnet mask, and default gateway, so you usually enter it at the same time as the other IP information. You configure DNS in Windows Vista/7 using the Internet Protocol Version 4 (TCP/IPv4) Properties dialog box. Figure 10-15 shows the DNS settings for my system. Note that I have more than one DNS server setting; the second one is a backup in case the first one isn't working. Two DNS settings is not a rule, however, so don't worry if your system shows only one DNS server setting, or perhaps more than two.

Figure 10-15

DNS information in Windows

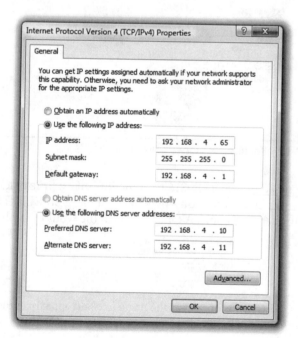

Every operating system has a way for you to enter DNS server information. In Linux, you can directly edit the /etc/resolv.conf file using a text editor. Just about every version of Linux has some form of graphical editor as well to make this an easy process. Figure 10-16 shows Ubuntu's Network Configuration utility.

Figure 10-16
Entering DNS information in Ubuntu

Every operating system also comes with a utility you can use to verify the DNS server settings. The tool in Windows, for example, is called *ipconfig*. You can see your current DNS server settings in Windows by typing **ipconfig /all** at the command prompt (Figure 10-17). In UNIX/Linux, type the following: **cat /etc/ resolv.conf.**

NOTE Remember, the ipconfig command gives you a ton of useful IP information.

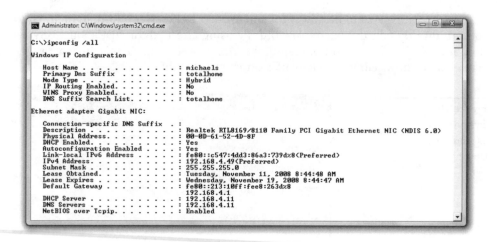

Figure 10-17   The ipconfig /all command showing DNS information in Windows

Now that you understand how your system knows the DNS server's IP address, let's return to the DNS process.

The DNS server receives the request for the IP address of www.microsoft.com from your client computer. At this point, your DNS server checks a cache of previously resolved FQDNs to see if www.microsoft.com is there (Figure 10-18). In this case, www.microsoft.com is not in the cache.

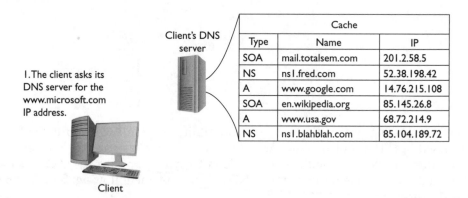

Figure 10-18   Checking the DNS cache

Now your DNS server needs to get to work. The local DNS server may not know the address for www.microsoft.com, but it does know the addresses of the DNS root servers. The root servers, maintained by 12 root name server operators, know all the addresses of the top-level domain DNS servers. The root servers don't know the address of www.microsoft.com, but they do know the address of the DNS servers in charge of all .com addresses. The root servers send your DNS server an IP address for a .com server (Figure 10-19).

Figure 10-19

Talking to a
root server

Client's DNS
server

Root DNS
server

 NOTE Yes, the 13 root name servers are maintained by 12 root name server operators. VeriSign, the company that handles security for a lot of the e-commerce on the Internet, maintains two root name server clusters.

The .com DNS server also doesn't know the address of www.microsoft.com, but it knows the IP address of the microsoft.com DNS server. It sends that IP address to your root server (Figure 10-20).

Figure 10-20

Talking to the
.com server

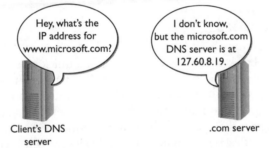

Client's DNS
server

.com server

The microsoft.com server does know the IP address of www.microsoft.com and can send that information back to the local DNS server. Figure 10-21 shows the process of resolving an FQDN into an IP address.

Figure 10-21

Talking to the
microsoft.com
DNS server

Client's DNS
server

microsoft.com
DNS server

Now that your DNS server has the IP address for www.microsoft.com, it stores a copy in its cache and sends the IP information to your PC. Your Web browser then begins the HTTP request to get the Web page.

Your computer also keeps a cache of recently resolved FQDNs. In Windows, for example, open a command prompt and type **ipconfig /displaydns** to see them. Here's a small part of the results of typing **ipconfig /displaydns**:

```
gizmodo.com
_____

    Record Name . . . . . : gizmodo.com
    Record Type . . . . . : 1
    Time To Live  . . . . : 70639
    Data Length . . . . . : 4
    Section . . . . . . . : Answer
    A (Host) Record . . . : 69.60.7.199
ftp.totalsem.com
_____

    Record Name . . . . . : ftp.totalsem.com
    Record Type . . . . . : 1
    Time To Live  . . . . : 83733
    Data Length . . . . . : 4
    Section . . . . . . . : Answer
    A (Host) Record . . . : 209.29.33.25
C:\>
```

DNS Servers

I've been talking about DNS servers for so long, I feel I'd be untrue to my vision of an All-in-One book unless I gave you at least a quick peek at a DNS server in action. Lots of operating systems come with built-in DNS server software, including Windows Server 2008 and just about every version of UNIX/Linux. A number of third-party DNS server programs are also available for virtually any operating system. I'm going to use the DNS server program that comes with Microsoft Windows Server 2008, primarily because (1) it takes the prettiest screen snapshots and (2) it's the one I use here at the office. You access the Windows DNS server by selecting **Start** | **Administrative Tools** | **DNS**. When you first open the DNS server, you won't see much other than the name of the server itself. In this case, Figure 10-22 shows a server, imaginatively named TOTALHOMEDC1.

 EXAM TIP The most popular DNS server tool used in UNIX/Linux systems is called BIND.

The DNS server has (at least) three folder icons visible: Cached Lookups, Forward Lookup Zones, and Reverse Lookup Zones. Depending on the version of Windows Server you're running and the level of customization, your server might have more than three folder icons. Let's look at the three that are important for this discussion.

When you open the tree on a Windows DNS server, the first folder you see is called Cached Lookups. Every DNS server keeps a list of *cached lookups*—that is, all the IP addresses it has already resolved—so it won't have to re-resolve an FQDN it has already checked. The cache has a size limit, of course, and you can also set a limit on how long the DNS server holds cache entries. Windows does a nice job of separating these cached addresses by placing all cached lookups in little folders that share the first name of the top-level domain with subfolders that use the second-level domain (Figure 10-23). This sure makes it easy to see where folks have been Web browsing!

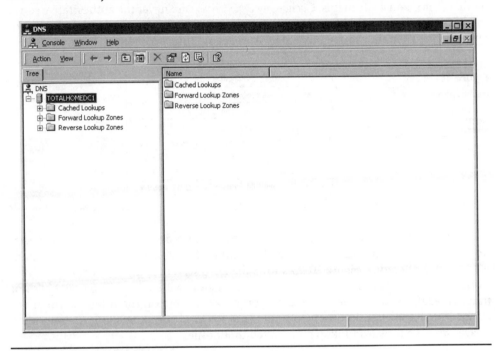

Figure 10-22   DNS server main screen

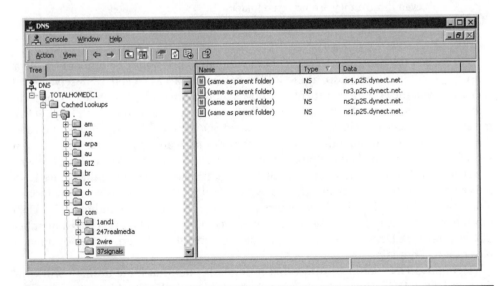

Figure 10-23   Inspecting the DNS cache

Now let's watch an actual DNS server at work. Basically, you choose to configure a DNS server to work in one of two ways: as an authoritative DNS server or as a cache-only DNS server. Authoritative DNS servers store IP addresses and FQDNs of systems for a particular domain or domains. *Cache-only DNS servers* are never the authoritative server for a domain. They are only used to talk to other DNS servers to resolve IP addresses for DNS clients. Then they cache the FQDN to speed up future lookups (Figure 10-24).

Figure 10-24
Authoritative
vs. cache-only
DNS server

Cache		
Type	Name	IP
SOA	mail.totalsem.com	201.2.58.5
NS	ns1.fred.com	52.38.198.42
A	www.google.com	14.76.215.108
SOA	en.wikipedia.org	85.145.26.8
A	www.usa.gov	68.72.214.9
NS	ns1.blahblah.com	85.104.189.72

Authoritative   Cache-only

The IP addresses and FQDNs for the computers in a domain are stored in special storage areas called *forward lookup zones*. Forward lookup zones are the most important part of any DNS server. Figure 10-25 shows the DNS server for my small corporate network. My domain is called "totalhome." I can get away with a domain name that's not Internet legal because none of these computers are visible on the Internet. The totalhome domain only works on my local network for local computers to find each other. I have created a forward lookup zone called totalhome.

 NOTE Microsoft DNS servers use a folder analogy to show lookup zones even though they are not true folders.

Let's look at the contents of the totalhome domain. First, notice a number of folders: _msdcs, _sites, _tcp, and _udp. These folders are unique to Microsoft DNS servers, and you'll see what they do in a moment. For now, ignore them and concentrate on the individual computer listings. Every forward lookup zone requires a Start of Authority (SOA), the single DNS server in charge. The record called SOA in the folder totalhome indicates that my server is the authoritative DNS server for a domain called totalhome. You can even see a few of the systems in that domain (note to hackers: these are fake, so don't bother). A tech looking at this would know that totalhomedc1.totalhome is the authoritative DNS server for the totalhome domain. The *NS records* are all of the DNS servers for totalhome. Note that totalhome has two DNS servers: totalhomedc1.totalhome and tera. The DNS server named tera is not a member of the totalhome domain. In fact, tera isn't a member of *any* domain. A DNS server does not have to be a member of a domain to be a name server for that domain.

Having two DNS servers ensures that if one fails, the totalhome domain will continue to have a DNS server. The *A records* in the folder are the IP addresses and names of all the systems on the totalhome domain.

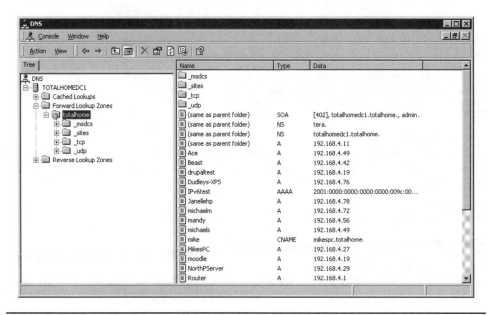

Figure 10-25 Forward lookup zone totalhome

Every DNS forward lookup zone will have one SOA and at least one NS record. In the vast majority of cases, a forward lookup zone will have some number of A records. But you may or may not see a number of other records in your standard DNS server. Look at Figure 10-26 for these less common types of DNS records: CNAME, MX, and AAAA.

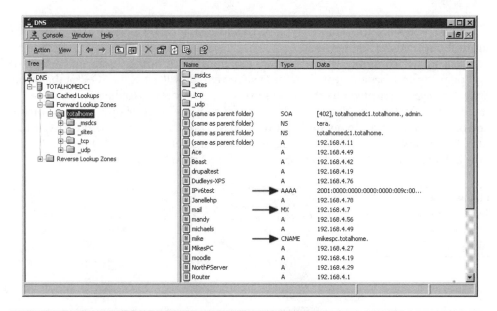

Figure 10-26 Less common DNS record types

A *canonical name (CNAME)* record acts like an alias. My computer's name is mikespc.totalhome, but you can also now use mike.totalhome to reference that computer. A ping of mike.totalhome returns the following:

```
C:\>ping mike.totalhome
Pinging mikespc.totalhome [192.168.4.27] with 32 bytes of data:
Reply from 192.168.4.27: bytes=32 time=2ms TTL=128
Reply from 192.168.4.27: bytes=32 time<1ms TTL=128
```

(rest of ping results deleted)

If your computer is a member of a domain and you are trying to access another computer in that domain, you can even skip the domain name, because your PC will simply add it back:

```
C:\>ping mike
Pinging mikespc.totalhome [192.168.4.27] with 32 bytes of data:
Reply from 192.168.4.27: bytes=32 time<1ms TTL=128
Reply from 192.168.4.27: bytes=32 time<1ms TTL=128
```

(rest of ping results deleted)

MX records are used exclusively by SMTP servers to determine where to send mail. I have an in-house SMTP server on a computer I cleverly called mail. If other SMTP servers wanted to send mail to mail.totalhome (although they can't because the SMTP server isn't connected to the Internet and lacks a legal FQDN), they would use DNS to locate the mail server.

 NOTE MX stands for Mail eXchanger.

AAAA records are for a newer type of IP addressing called IPv6. You'll learn a lot more about IPv6 in Chapter 13.

There are two common types of forward lookup zones: a primary zone and a secondary zone. *Primary zones* are created on the DNS server that will act as the SOA for that zone. *Secondary zones* are created on other DNS servers to act as backups to the primary zone. It's standard practice to have at least two DNS servers for any forward lookup zone: one primary and one secondary. Even in my small network, I have two DNS servers: TOTALDNS1, which runs the primary zone, and TOTALDNS2, which runs a secondary zone (Figure 10-27). Any time a change is placed on TOTALDNS1, TOTALDNS2 is quickly updated.

Figure 10-27
Two DNS servers
with updating
taking place

I've got updates for the primary lookup zone.

Okay, send them over to me.

TOTALDNS1   TOTALDNS2

NOTE If you're looking at a Windows server and adding a new forward lookup zone, you'll see a third type called an Active Directory–integrated forward lookup zone. I'll cover those in just a moment.

A *reverse lookup zone* (Figure 10-28) enables a system to determine an FQDN by knowing the IP address; that is, it does the exact reverse of what DNS normally does! Reverse lookup zones take a network ID, reverse it, and add the term "in-addr-arpa" to create the zone. The record created is called a *pointer record (PTR)*; PTRs point to canonical names.

A few low-level functions (like mail) and some security programs use reverse lookup zones, so DNS servers provide them. In most cases, the DNS server asks you if you want to make a reverse lookup zone when you make a new forward lookup zone. When in doubt, make one. If you don't need it, it won't cause any trouble.

Figure 10-28
Reverse
lookup zone

Microsoft added some wrinkles to DNS servers with the introduction of Windows 2000 Server, and each subsequent version of Windows Server retains the wrinkles. Windows Server can do cached lookups, primary and secondary forward lookup zones, and reverse lookup zones, just like UNIX/Linux DNS servers. But Windows Server also has a Windows-only type of forward lookup zone called an Active Directory–integrated zone.

Enter Windows

DNS works beautifully for any TCP/IP application that needs an IP address for another computer, but it has one glaring weakness: you need to add A records to the DNS server manually. Adding these can be a problem, especially in a world where you have many DHCP clients whose IP addresses may change from time to time. Interestingly, it was a throwback to an old Microsoft Windows protocol that fixed this and a few other problems all at the same time.

Even though TCP/IP was available back in the 1980s, Microsoft popularized another networking protocol called *NetBIOS/NetBEUI*. NetBIOS/NetBEUI was pretty simplistic compared to TCP/IP. It had a very simple naming convention (the NetBIOS part) that used broadcasts. When a computer booted up, it just told the world its name (Figure 10-29). NetBIOS/NetBEUI was suitable only for small networks. It provided no logical addressing like IP addresses; you had to remember the NetBIOS name and the MAC address. NetBIOS/NetBEUI was almost exclusively used to share folders and printers. There was no such thing as Telnet or the Web with NetBIOS/NetBEUI, but it worked well for what it did at the time.

Figure 10-29
NetBIOS
broadcast

By the mid-1990s, Microsoft realized that the world was going to TCP/IP, and it needed to switch too. Instead of dumping NetBIOS/NetBEUI entirely, Microsoft designed a new TCP/IP protocol that enabled it to keep using the NetBIOS names but dump the ancient NetBEUI protocol and instead run NetBIOS on top of TCP/IP with a protocol called *NetBT (NetBIOS over TCP/IP)*. In essence, Microsoft created its own name resolution protocol that had nothing to do with DNS!

Microsoft managed to crowbar the NetBIOS naming system into DNS basically by making the NetBIOS name the DNS name. Technically, NetBIOS no longer exists, but the overlying protocol that used it to share folders and printers is still very much alive. This protocol was originally called *Server Message Block (SMB)*, but the current version is called *Common Internet File System (CIFS)*.

Microsoft has used DNS names with the SMB/CIFS protocol to provide folder and printer sharing in small TCP/IP networks. SMB/CIFS is so popular that other operating systems have adopted support for SMB/CIFS. UNIX/Linux systems (including Mac OS X) come with the very popular Samba, the most popular tool for making non-Windows systems act like Windows computers (Figure 10-30).

Figure 10-30
Samba on Ubuntu
(it's so common
that the OS
doesn't even use
the term in the
dialog)

Living with the Legacy of CIFS   CIFS makes most small networks live in a two-world name resolution system. When your computer wants to access another computer's folders or files, it uses a simple CIFS broadcast to get the name. If that same computer wants to do anything "Internety," it uses its DNS server. Both CIFS and DNS live together perfectly well and, although many alternatives are available for this dual name resolution world, the vast majority of us are happy with this relationship.

Well, except for one little item, we're almost happy: CIFS organizes your computers into groups. There are three types of groups: workgroup, Windows domain, and Active Directory. A *workgroup* is just a name that organizes a group of computers. A computer running Windows (or another operating system running Samba) joins a workgroup, as shown in Figure 10-31. When a computer joins a workgroup, all the computers in the Network/My Network Places folder are organized, as shown in Figure 10-32.

Figure 10-31

Joining a workgroup

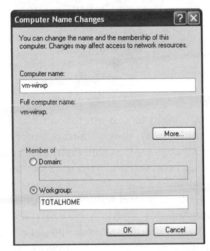

A Windows domain is a group of computers controlled by a computer running Windows Server. This Windows Server computer is configured as a domain controller. You then have your computers join the domain.

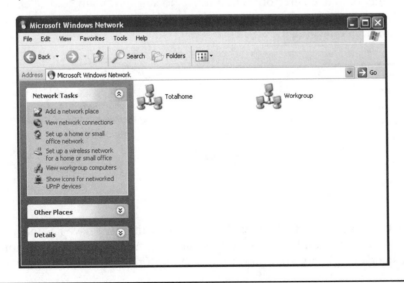

Figure 10-32   Two workgroups in the Network folder

All the computers within a domain authenticate to the domain controller when they log in. Windows gives you very powerful control over who can access what on your network (Figure 10-33).

Figure 10-33
Logging into the domain

Primary domain controller

Note that a Windows domain is not the same as a DNS domain. In the early days, a Windows domain didn't even have a naming structure that resembled the DNS hierarchically organized structure. Microsoft eventually revamped its domain controllers to work as part of DNS, however, and Windows domains now use DNS for their names. A Windows domain must have a true DNS name. DNS domains that are not on the Internet should use the top-level name .local (although you can cheat, as I do on my totalhome network, and not use it).

On a bigger scale, a Windows network can get complicated, with multiple domains connecting over long distances. To help organize this, Windows uses a type of super domain called Active Directory. An *Active Directory* is an organization of related computers that shares one or more Windows domains. Windows domain controllers are also *DNS servers*.

The beauty of Active Directory is that it has no single domain controller: all of the domain controllers are equal partners, and any domain controller can take over if one domain controller fails (Figure 10-34).

Figure 10-34
If one domain controller goes down, another automatically takes over.

Primary domain controller   Primary domain controller

Active Directory–Integrated Zones Now that you have an understanding of Windows domains and Active Directory, let's return to forward lookup zones and DNS. A standard primary zone stores the DNS information in text files on the DNS server. You then use secondary zones on other DNS servers to back up that server. If the primary DNS server goes down, the secondary servers can resolve FQDNs, but you can't add any new records. Nothing can be updated until the primary DNS server comes back up.

In an Active Directory–integrated zone, all of the domain controllers (which are all also DNS servers) are equal and the whole DNS system is not reliant on a single DNS server. The DNS servers store their DNS information in a data structure called the Active Directory. The Active Directory is stored across the servers in the domain. All Active Directory–enabled DNS servers automatically send DNS information to each other, updating every machine's DNS information to match the others.

Dynamic DNS

In the early days of TCP/IP networks, DNS servers required manual updates of their records. This was not a big deal until the numbers of computers using TCP/IP exploded in the 1990s. Then every office had a network and every network had a DNS server to update. DHCP helped to some extent. You could add a special option to the DHCP server, which is generally called the *DNS suffix*. This way the DHCP clients would know the name of the DNS domain to which they belonged. It didn't help the manual updating of DNS records, but clients don't need records. No one accesses the clients! The DNS suffix helps the clients access network resources more efficiently.

 NOTE All DHCP servers provide an option called *DNS server* that tells clients the IP address of the DNS server or servers.

Today, manual updating of DNS records is still the norm for most Internet serving systems like Web servers and e-mail servers. DNS has moved beyond Internet servers; even the smallest Windows networks that run Active Directory use it. Whereas a popular Web server might have a phalanx of techs to adjust DNS settings, small networks in which most of the computers run DHCP need an alternative to old-school DNS. Luckily, the solution was worked out over a decade ago.

The TCP/IP folks came up with a new protocol called *Dynamic DNS (DDNS)* in 1997 that enabled DNS servers to get automatic updates of IP addresses of computers in their forward lookup zones, mainly by talking to the local DHCP server. All modern DNS servers support DDNS, and all but the most primitive DHCP servers support Dynamic DNS as well.

Windows leans heavily on DDNS. For years, Windows networks used DDNS for the DHCP server to talk to the DNS server. Although all Windows DHCP servers offer this function, all current (Vista, Windows 7, and later) Windows client machines report to the DNS server as soon as they receive a new or changed IP address. The server then updates its A records accordingly. DDNS simplifies setting up and maintaining a LAN tremendously. If you need to force a DNS server to update its records, use the `ipconfig /registerdns` command from the command prompt.

DNS Security Extensions

If you think about what DNS does, you can appreciate that it can be a big security issue. Simply querying a DNS server gives you a list of every computer name and IP address that it serves. This isn't the kind of information we want bad guys to have. It's easy to tell a DNS server not to respond to queries such as nslookup or dig, but DNS by definition is a public protocol that requires one DNS server to respond to another DNS server.

The big fix is called *DNS Security Extensions (DNSSEC)*. DNSSEC is a set of authentication and authorization specifications designed to prevent bad guys from impersonating legitimate DNS servers. It's implemented through *extension mechanisms for DNS (EDNS)*, a specification that expands several parameter sizes, but maintains backward compatibility with DNS servers that don't use it.

Dynamic DNS on the Web

The proliferation of dedicated high-speed Internet connections to homes and business has led many people to use those connections for more than surfing the Web from inside the local network. Why not have a Web server in your network, for example, that you can access from anywhere on the Web? You could use Windows Remote Desktop to take control of your home machine. (See Chapter 14 for more details on Remote Desktop.)

The typical high-speed Internet connection presents a problem in making this work. Most folks have a cable or DSL modem connected to a router. The router has a DHCP server inside and that's what dishes out private IP addresses to computers on the LAN. The router also has an external IP address that it gets from the ISP, usually via DHCP. That external address can change unless you pay extra for a static IP address. Most people don't.

Several companies promote a service called *dynamic DNS* that maps a home or office router to a domain name. Each time the router's external address changes, the router contacts the dynamic DNS service and reports the change. The service updates its records. When you want to access your desktop remotely, you would type in the domain name rather than an IP address that might have changed. The domain name can be one you've purchased through GoDaddy or Joker.com, for example, or one obtained from the dynamic DNS service provider.

The most widely used provider of this service is TZO, formerly dynamicdns.org. Its current Web site is www.tzo.com.

Troubleshooting DNS

As I mentioned earlier, most DNS problems result from a problem with the client systems. This is because DNS servers rarely go down, and if they do, most clients have a secondary DNS server setting that enables them to continue to resolve DNS names. DNS servers have been known to fail, however, so knowing when the problem is the client system, and when you can complain to the person in charge of your DNS server, is important. All of the tools you're about to see come with every operating system that supports TCP/IP, with the exception of the ipconfig commands, which I'll mention when I get to them.

So how do you know when to suspect DNS is causing the problem on your network? Well, just about everything you do on an IP network depends on DNS to find the right system to talk to for whatever job the application does. E-mail clients use DNS to find their e-mail servers; FTP clients use DNS for their servers; Web browsers use DNS to find Web servers; and so on. The first clue something is wrong is generally when a user calls, saying he's getting a "server not found" error. Server not found errors look different depending on the application, but you can count on something being there that says in effect "server not found." Figure 10-35 shows how this error appears in an FTP client.

Figure 10-35
DNS error

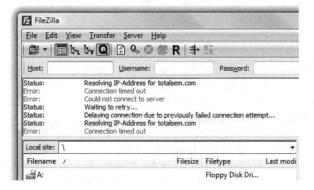

Before you start testing, you need to eliminate any DNS caches on the local system. If you're running Windows, run the `ipconfig /flushdns` command now. In addition, most Web browsers also have caches, so you can't use a Web browser for any testing. In such cases, it's time to turn to the *ping* command.

Your best friend when testing DNS is ping. Run ping from a command prompt, followed by the name of a well-known Web site, such as `ping www.microsoft.com`. Watch the output carefully to see if you get an IP address. You may get a "request timed out" message, but that's fine; you just want to see if DNS is resolving FQDNs into IP addresses (Figure 10-36).

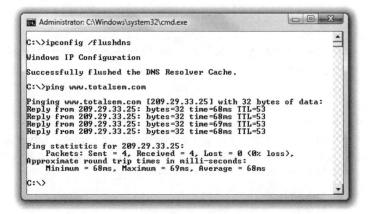

Figure 10-36 Using ping to check DNS

If you get a "server not found" error, you need to ping again using just an IP address. Most network techs keep the IP address of a known server in their heads. If you don't have one memorized, try 74.125.95.99 (Google). If ping works with the IP address but not with the Web site name, you know you have a DNS problem.

 EXAM TIP When troubleshooting, ping is your friend. If you can ping an IP address but not the name associated with that address, check DNS.

Once you've determined that DNS is the problem, check to make sure your system has the correct DNS server entry. Again, this information is something you should keep around. I can tell you the DNS server IP address for every Internet link I own—two in the office, one at the house, plus two dial-ups I use on the road. You don't have to memorize the IP addresses, but you should have all the critical IP information written down. If that isn't the problem, run `ipconfig /all` to see if those DNS settings are the same as the ones in the server; if they aren't, you may need to refresh your DHCP settings. I'll show you how to do that next.

If you have the correct DNS settings for your DNS server and the DNS settings in `ipconfig /all` match those settings, you can assume the problem is with the DNS server itself. The *nslookup* (name server lookup) command enables DNS server queries. All operating systems have a version of nslookup.

You run nslookup from a command prompt. With nslookup, you can (assuming you have the permission) query all types of information from a DNS server and change how your system uses DNS. Although most of these commands are far outside the scope of the CompTIA Network+ exam, you should definitely know nslookup. For instance, just running `nslookup` alone from a command prompt shows you some output similar to the following:

```
C:\>nslookup
Default Server:  totalhomedc2.totalhome
Address:  192.168.4.155
>
```

 EXAM TIP Make sure you know how to use nslookup to determine if a DNS server is active!

Running nslookup gives me the IP address and the name of my default DNS server. If I got an error at this point, perhaps a "server not found" error, I would know that either my primary DNS server is down or I might not have the correct DNS server information in my DNS settings. I can attach to any DNS server by typing **server**, followed by the IP address or the domain name of the DNS server:

```
> server totalhomedc1
Default Server:  totalhomedc1.totalhome
Addresses:  192.168.4.157, 192.168.4.156
```

This new server has two IP addresses; it has two multihomed NICs to ensure there's a backup in case one NIC fails. If I get an error on one DNS server, I use nslookup to check for another DNS server. I can then switch to that server in my TCP/IP settings as a temporary fix until my DNS server is working again.

Those using UNIX/Linux have an extra DNS tool called *domain information groper (dig)*. The dig tool is very similar to nslookup, but it runs noninteractively. In nslookup, you're in the command until you type **exit**; nslookup even has its own prompt. The dig tool, on the other hand, is not interactive—you ask it a question, it answers the question, and it puts you back at a regular command prompt. When you run dig, you tend to get a large amount of information. The following is a sample of a dig command run from a Linux prompt:

```
[mike@localhost]$dig -x 13.65.14.4
; <<>> DiG 8.2 <<>> -x
;; res options: init recurs defnam dnsrch
;; got answer:
;; ->>HEADER<<- opcode: QUERY, status: NOERROR, id: 4
;; flags: qr aa rd ra; QUERY: 1, ANSWER: 1, AUTHORITY: 2,
ADDITIONAL: 2
;; QUERY SECTION:
;;   4.14.65.13.in-addr.arpa, type = ANY, class = IN
;; ANSWER SECTION:
4.14.65.13.in-addr.arpa.   4H IN PTR
server3.houston.totalsem.com.
;; AUTHORITY SECTION:
65.14.4.in-addr.arpa.   4H IN NS   kernel.risc.uni-linz.ac.at.
65.14.4.in-addr.arpa.   4H IN NS   kludge.risc.uni-linz.ac.at.
;; ADDITIONAL SECTION:
kernel.risc.uni-linz.ac.at.   4H IN A   193.170.37.225
kludge.risc.uni-linz.ac.at.   4H IN A   193.170.37.224
;; Total query time: 1 msec
;; FROM: kernel to SERVER: default — 127.0.0.1
;; WHEN: Thu Feb 10 18:03:41 2000
;; MSG SIZE  sent: 44  rcvd: 180
[mike@localhost]$
```

WINS

Even though current versions of Windows use either DNS or CIFS names, NetBIOS names can still appear in older versions of Windows like Windows 9*x* or some versions of Windows 2000. A Windows NetBIOS system claims a NetBIOS name for itself simply by broadcasting out to the rest of the network. As long as no other system is already using that name, it works just fine. Of course, broadcasting can be a bit of a problem for routers and such, but this example presumes a single network on the same wire, so it's okay in this context.

NetBIOS was invented way back in the early 1980s. Microsoft had a big investment in NetBIOS and had to support a large installed base of systems, so even after NetBEUI began to lose market share to TCP/IP, Microsoft had to continue to support NetBIOS or incur the wrath of millions of customers. What happened next seems, in retrospect, more a comedy than the machinations of the most powerful software company in the world. Microsoft did something that should not have been possible: it redesigned Net-BIOS to work with TCP/IP. Eventually, Microsoft came up with CIFS, as you know from earlier in the chapter, and made NetBIOS DNS-compatible. But Microsoft tried a couple of things first. Let's look at some of the strategies and techniques Microsoft used to make NetBIOS and TCP/IP coexist on the same network.

One early strategy Microsoft came up with to reduce the overhead from NetBIOS broadcasts was to use a special text file called LMHOSTS. *LMHOSTS* contains a list of the NetBIOS names and corresponding IP addresses of the host systems on the network. Sound familiar? Well, it should—the LMHOSTS file works exactly the same way as the DNS HOSTS file. Although Microsoft still supports LMHOSTS file usage, and every Windows system has an LMHOSTS file for backward compatibility, networks that still need NetBIOS support will usually run Windows Internet Name Service (WINS) servers for name resolution. WINS servers let NetBIOS hosts register their names with just the one server, eliminating the need for broadcasting and thereby reducing NetBIOS overhead substantially. Figure 10-37 shows the copy of the WINS server that comes with Windows 2000 Server. Note that some of the PCs on this network have registered their names with the WINS server.

 NOTE You can find an LMHOSTS.SAM file on your Windows system. Use Notepad to open the file and inspect its contents.

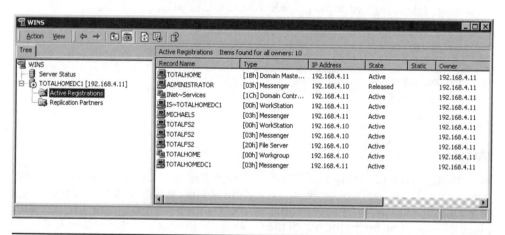

Figure 10-37 WINS server

There are only two good reasons to use a WINS server: (1) to reduce overhead from broadcasts and (2) to enable NetBIOS name resolution across routers. What does a WINS server have to do with routers, you ask? Just this: the WINS server enables NetBIOS to function in a routed network. IP routers are programmed to *kill* all broadcasts, remember? While newer Windows clients will simply register directly with the

WINS server, older (pre-Win95) Windows systems will still try to broadcast. To get around this problem, you can configure a system to act as a *WINS proxy agent*, forwarding WINS broadcasts to a WINS server on the other side of the router (Figure 10-38).

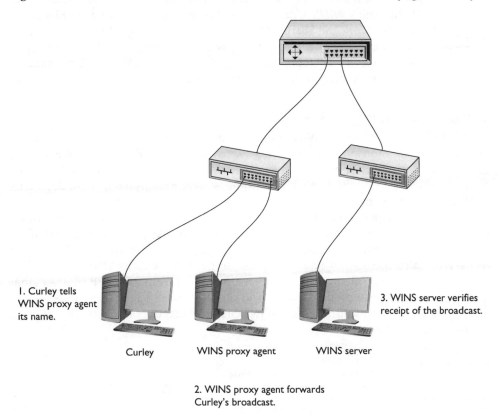

I. Curley tells WINS proxy agent its name.

3. WINS server verifies receipt of the broadcast.

Curley   WINS proxy agent   WINS server

2. WINS proxy agent forwards Curley's broadcast.

Figure 10-38   Proxy agent

The bottom line with WINS servers is this: larger or routed networks that run Net-BIOS still need them. As long as Windows NT and Windows 9*x* systems are out there running NetBIOS, don't be surprised to find that some system somewhere is running a WINS server.

Configuring WINS Clients

You don't need to do much to get a Windows client to use WINS. In fact, you only need to configure the IP address of a WINS server in its WINS settings under Network Properties. From then on, the Windows system will look for a WINS server to register its NetBIOS name. If it finds a WINS server, it will register its NetBIOS name to the WINS server; if it doesn't, it will automatically start broadcasting its NetBIOS name. You can add WINS information to DHCP if necessary, so unless you're running static

IP addresses, you may never have to enter anything into your Windows clients to get WINS to work.

NOTE Think WINS is dead? Open **Manage network connections** in your Network and Sharing Center. Drill down through the **Local Area Connection properties | IPv4 properties | Advanced** button to open the Advanced TCP/IP Settings dialog box. You'll see a WINS tab for backward compatibility with older computers on the network.

Troubleshooting WINS

Most WINS problems are not WINS problems at all. They are NetBIOS problems. By far, the most common problem is having two systems share the same name. In that case, you get a pretty clear error. It looks different in the various versions of Windows, but it usually says about the same thing: another system has this name. How do you fix it? Change the name of the system!

You can use the *nbtstat* program to help deal with NetBIOS problems. The nbtstat program will do a number of jobs, depending on the switches you add to the end of the command. The −c switch, for example, tells nbtstat to check the current NetBIOS name cache (yup, NetBIOS caches names just like some systems cache DNS names). The NetBIOS name cache contains the NetBIOS names and corresponding IP addresses that have been resolved by a particular host. You can use nbtstat to see if the WINS server has supplied inaccurate addresses to a WINS client. Here's an example of the `nbtstat` `−c` command and its results:

```
C:\ >nbtstat -c
Node IpAddress: [192.168.43.5] Scope Id: []
                NetBIOS Remote Cache Name Table
Name             Type        Host Address      Life [sec]

WRITERS     <1B>  UNIQUE     192.168.43.13       420
SCOTT       <20>  UNIQUE     192.168.43.3        420
VENUSPDC    <00>  UNIQUE     192.168.43.13       120
MIKE        <20>  UNIQUE     192.168.43.2        420
NOTES01     <20>  UNIQUE     192.168.43.4        420
```

Diagnosing TCP/IP Networks

I've dedicated all of Chapter 20 to network diagnostic procedures, but TCP/IP has a few little extras that I want to talk about here. TCP/IP is a pretty tough protocol, and in good networks, it runs like a top for years without problems. Most of the TCP/IP problems you'll see come from improper configuration, so I'm going to assume you've run into problems with a new TCP/IP install, and I'll show you some classic screw-ups common in this situation. I want to concentrate on making sure you can ping anyone you want to ping.

I've done thousands of IP installations over the years, and I'm proud to say that, in most cases, they worked right the first time. My users jumped on the newly configured systems, fired up their My Network Places/Network, e-mail software, and Web browsers, and were last seen typing away, smiling from ear to ear. But I'd be a liar if I didn't also admit that plenty of setups didn't work so well. Let's start with the hypothetical case of a user who can't see something on the network. You get a call: "Help!" he cries. The first troubleshooting point to remember here: it doesn't matter *what* he can't see. It doesn't matter if he can't see other systems in his network or can't see the home page on his browser—you go through the same steps in any event.

Remember to use common sense wherever possible. If the problem system can't ping by DNS name, but all the other systems can, is the DNS server down? Of course not! If something—*anything*—doesn't work on one system, *always* try it on another one to determine whether the problem is specific to one system or affects the entire network.

One thing I always do is check the network connections and protocols. I'm going to cover those topics in greater detail later in the book, so, for now, assume the problem systems are properly connected and have good protocols installed. Here are some steps to take:

1. *Diagnose the NIC.* First, use ping with the loopback address to determine if the system can send and receive packets. Specifically, type **ping 127.0.0.1** or **ping localhost** (remember the HOSTS file?). If you're not getting a good response, your NIC has a problem! Check your NIC's driver and replace it if necessary.

2. *Diagnose locally.* If the NIC's okay, diagnose locally by pinging a few neighboring systems, both by IP address and DNS name. If you're using NetBIOS, use the net view command to see if the other local systems are visible (Figure 10-39). If you can't ping by DNS, check your DNS settings. If you can't see the network using net view, you may have a problem with your NetBIOS settings.

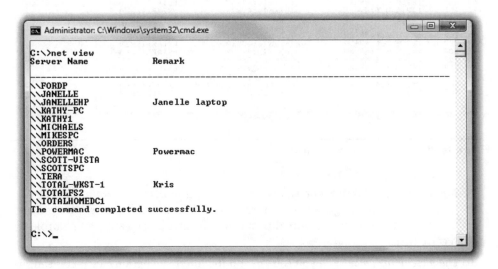

Figure 10-39 The net view command in action

3. *Check IP address and subnet mask.* If you're having a problem pinging locally, make sure you have the right IP address and subnet mask. Oh, if I had a nickel for every time I entered those incorrectly! If you're on DHCP, try renewing the lease—sometimes that does the trick. If DHCP fails, call the person in charge of the server.

 NOTE A good testing trick is to use the net send command to try sending messages to other systems. Not all versions of Windows support net send.

4. *Run netstat.* At this point, another little handy program comes into play called *netstat.* The netstat program offers a number of options. The two handiest ways to run netstat are with no options at all and with the -s option. Running netstat with no options shows you all the current connections to your system. Look for a connection here that isn't working with an application—that's often a clue to an application problem, such as a broken application or a sneaky application running in the background. Figure 10-40 shows a netstat program running.

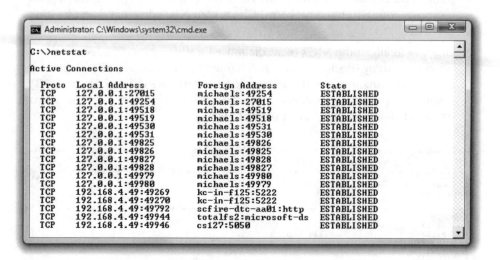

```
Administrator: C:\Windows\system32\cmd.exe

C:\>netstat

Active Connections

  Proto  Local Address          Foreign Address        State
  TCP    127.0.0.1:27015        michaels:49254         ESTABLISHED
  TCP    127.0.0.1:49254        michaels:27015         ESTABLISHED
  TCP    127.0.0.1:49518        michaels:49519         ESTABLISHED
  TCP    127.0.0.1:49519        michaels:49518         ESTABLISHED
  TCP    127.0.0.1:49530        michaels:49531         ESTABLISHED
  TCP    127.0.0.1:49531        michaels:49530         ESTABLISHED
  TCP    127.0.0.1:49825        michaels:49826         ESTABLISHED
  TCP    127.0.0.1:49826        michaels:49825         ESTABLISHED
  TCP    127.0.0.1:49827        michaels:49828         ESTABLISHED
  TCP    127.0.0.1:49828        michaels:49827         ESTABLISHED
  TCP    127.0.0.1:49979        michaels:49980         ESTABLISHED
  TCP    127.0.0.1:49980        michaels:49979         ESTABLISHED
  TCP    192.168.4.49:49269     kc-in-f125:5222        ESTABLISHED
  TCP    192.168.4.49:49270     kc-in-f125:5222        ESTABLISHED
  TCP    192.168.4.49:49792     scfire-dtc-aa01:http   ESTABLISHED
  TCP    192.168.4.49:49944     totalfs2:microsoft-ds  ESTABLISHED
  TCP    192.168.4.49:49946     cs127:5050             ESTABLISHED
```

Figure 10-40 The netstat program in action

5. *Run netstat –s.* Running netstat with the -s option displays several statistics that can help you diagnose problems. For example, if the display shows you are sending but not receiving, you almost certainly have a bad cable with a broken receive wire.

6. *Diagnose to the gateway.* If you can't get on the Internet, check to see if you can ping the router. Remember, the router has two interfaces, so try both: first the local interface (the one on your subnet) and then the one to the Internet. You *do* have both of those IP addresses memorized, don't you? You should! If you can't

ping the router, either it's down or you're not connected to it. If you can only ping the near side, something in the router itself is messed up, like the routing table.

7. *Diagnose to the Internet.* If you can ping the router, try to ping something on the Internet. If you can't ping one address, try another—it's always possible that the first place you try to ping is down. If you still can't get through, you can try to locate the problem using the *tracert* (trace route) command. Run tracert to mark out the entire route the ping packet traveled between you and whatever you were trying to ping. It may even tell you where the problem lies (see Figure 10-41).

```
Administrator: C:\Windows\system32\cmd.exe

C:\>tracert 216.40.231.194

Tracing route to server.threethirty3.com [216.40.231.194]
over a maximum of 30 hops:

  1     1 ms     1 ms    <1 ms   Router.totalhome [192.168.4.1]
  2     8 ms     8 ms     8 ms   adsl-208-190-121-38.dsl.hstntx.swbell.net [208.190.121.38]
  3     9 ms     8 ms     8 ms   dist1-vlan50.hstntx.sbcglobal.net [151.164.11.126]
  4     8 ms     8 ms     9 ms   ppp-151-164-38-132.rcsntx.swbell.net [151.164.38.132]
  5    67 ms    70 ms    64 ms   70.245.63.206
  6    64 ms    64 ms    64 ms   64.208.110.109
  7    62 ms    62 ms    62 ms   the-planet.gigabitethernet7-3.ar2.dal2.gblx.net [64.208.170.198]
  8    87 ms    68 ms    67 ms   et1-1.ibr02.hstntx1.theplanet.com [70.87.253.54]
  9    69 ms    67 ms    68 ms   po2.car01.hstntx1.theplanet.com [207.218.245.2]
 10    68 ms    69 ms    80 ms   server.threethirty3.com [216.40.231.194]

Trace complete.

C:\>
```

Figure 10-41 Using tracert

Chapter Review

Questions

1. NetBIOS uses what type of name space?

   A. Hierarchical name space

   B. People name space

   C. DNS name space

   D. Flat name space

2. The DNS root directory is represented by what symbol?

   A. . (dot)

   B. / (forward slash)

   C. \ (back slash)

   D. $ (dollar sign)

3. What command do you use to see the DNS cache on a Windows system?

   A. `ping /showdns`

   B. `ipconfig /showdns`

   C. `ipconfig /displaydns`

   D. `ping /displaydns`

4. The users on your network haven't been able to connect to the server for 30 minutes. You check and reboot the server, but you're unable to ping either its own loopback address or any of your client systems. What should you do?

   A. Restart the DHCP server.

   B. Restart the DNS server.

   C. Replace the NIC on the server because it has failed.

   D. Have your users ping the server.

5. A user calls to say she can't see the other systems on the network when she looks in My Network Places. You are not using NetBIOS. What are your first two troubleshooting steps? (Select two.)

   A. Ping the address of a known Web site.

   B. Ping the loopback address to test her NIC.

   C. Ping several neighboring systems using both DNS names and IP addresses.

   D. Ping the IP addresses of the router.

6. What is checked first when trying to resolve an FQDN to an IP address?

   A. HOSTS file

   B. LMHOSTS file

   C. DNS server

   D. WINS server

7. Which type of DNS record is used by mail servers to determine where to send e-mail?

   A. A record

   B. CNAME record

   C. MX record

   D. SMTP record

8. Which command enables you to eliminate DNS cache?

   A. `ipconfig`

   B. `ipconfig /all`

   C. `ipconfig /dns`

   D. `ipconfig /flushdns`

9. Which tool enables you to query the functions of a DNS server?

   A. ipconfig

   B. nslookup

   C. ping

   D. xdns

10. Where does a DNS server store the IP addresses and FQDNs for the computers within a domain?

   A. Forward lookup zone

   B. Canonical zone

   C. MX record

   D. SMTP record

Answers

1. **D.** NetBIOS uses a flat name space whereas DNS servers use a hierarchical name space.

2. **A.** The DNS root directory is represented by a dot (.).

3. **C.** To see the DNS cache on a Windows system, run the command `ipconfig / displaydns` at a command prompt.

4. **C.** You should replace the server's NIC because it's bad. It doesn't need either DNS or DHCP to ping its loopback address. Having the users ping the server is also pointless, as you already know they can't connect to it.

5. **B and C.** Your first two troubleshooting steps are to ping the loopback address to check the client's NIC and then to ping neighboring systems. If the NIC and the local network check out, then you might try pinging the router and a Web site, but those are later steps.

6. **A.** The HOSTS file is checked first when trying to resolve an FQDN to IP address.

7. **C.** The MX record is used by mail servers to determine where to send e-mail.

8. **D.** The command `ipconfig /flushdns` eliminates the DNS cache.

9. **B.** The tool to use for querying DNS server functions is nslookup.

10. **A.** A DNS server stores the IP addresses and FQDNs for the computers within a domain in the forward lookup zone.

Securing TCP/IP

The CompTIA Network+ certification exam expects you to know how to

- 1.2 Classify how applications, devices, and protocols relate to the OSI model layers: encryption devices
- 1.6 Explain the function of common networking protocols: HTTPS, NTP, SNMP 2/3, and SSH
- 4.4 Given a scenario, use the appropriate network monitoring resource to analyze traffic: SNMP, SNMPv2, and SNMPv3
- 5.2 Explain the methods of network access security: IPsec, ISAKMP, TLS, TLS2.0, PPP, and SSH
- 5.3 Explain methods of user authentication: PKI, Kerberos, AAA, network access control, CHAP, MS-CHAP, and EAP

To achieve these goals, you must be able to

- Discuss the standard methods for securing TCP/IP networks
- Compare TCP/IP security standards
- Implement secure TCP/IP applications

If you want to enter the minds of the folks who invented TCP/IP, Vint Cerf and Bob Kahn, look at TCP/IP from a security perspective. No part of TCP/IP has any real security. Oh sure, you can put user names and passwords on FTP, Telnet, and other TCP/IP applications, but everything else is wide open. Cerf and Kahn must have thought that the intent of the Internet was openness.

Sadly, today's world reveals a totally different perspective. Every device with a public IP address on the Internet is constantly bombarded with malicious code trying to gain some level of access to our precious data. Even data moving between two hosts is relatively easily intercepted and read. Bad guys make millions by stealing our data in any of a thousand different ways, and TCP/IP in its original form is all but powerless to stop them.

This chapter takes you on a tour of the many ways smart people have improved TCP/IP to protect our data from those who wish to do evil things to it. It's an interesting story of good intentions, knee-jerk reactions, dead ends, and failed attempts that luckily ends with a promise of easy-to-use protocols that protect our data.

This chapter examines the ways to make TCP/IP data and networks secure. I'll first give you a look at security concepts and then turn to specific standards and protocols used to implement security. The chapter wraps with a discussion on secure TCP/IP applications and their methods.

Test Specific

Making TCP/IP Secure

I break down TCP/IP security into four areas: encryption, nonrepudiation, authentication, and authorization. *Encryption* means to scramble, mix up, or change the data in such a way that bad guys can't read it. Of course, this scrambled-up data must also be descrambled by the person receiving the data.

Nonrepudiation is the process that guarantees that the data is the same as originally sent and that it came from the source you think it should have come from. Nonrepudiation is designed to cover situations in which someone intercepts your data on-the-fly and makes changes, or someone pretends to be someone they are not.

Authentication means to verify that whoever accesses the data is the person you want accessing that data. The most classic form of authentication is the user name and password combination, but there are plenty more ways to authenticate.

Authorization defines what a person accessing the data can do with that data. Different operating systems provide different schemes for authorization, but the classic scheme for Windows is to assign permissions to a user account. An administrator, for example, can do a lot more after being authenticated than a limited user can do.

Encryption, nonrepudiation, authentication, and authorization may be separate issues, but in the real world of TCP/IP security, they overlap a lot. If you send a user name and password over the Internet, wouldn't it be a good idea to encrypt the user name and password so others can't read it? Equally, if you send someone a "secret decoder ring" over the Internet so he or she can unscramble the encryption, wouldn't it be a good idea for the recipient to know that the decoder ring actually came from you? In TCP/IP security, you have protocols that combine encryption, nonrepudiation (sometimes), authentication, and authorization to create complete security solutions for one TCP/IP application or another.

Encryption

All data on your network is nothing more than ones and zeroes. Identifying what type of data the strings of ones and zeroes in a packet represent usually is easy. A packet of data on the Internet always comes with a port number, for example, so a bad guy quickly knows what type of data he's reading.

All data starts as *plaintext*, a somewhat misleading term that simply means the data is in an easily read or viewed industry-wide standard format. Plaintext, often also referred to as *cleartext*, implies that all data starts off as text—untrue! Data often is text, but it also might be a binary file such as a photograph or an executable program. Regardless of the type of data, it all starts as plaintext. I'll use the image in Figure 11-1 as a universal figure for a piece of plaintext.

Figure 11-1
Plaintext

If you want to take some data and make figuring out what it means difficult for other people, you need a cipher. A *cipher* is a series of complex and hard-to-reverse mathematics—called an *algorithm*—you run on a string of ones and zeroes to make a new set of seemingly meaningless ones and zeroes. A cipher and the method used to implement that cipher is commonly called the *complete algorithm*. (I know that's a mouthful of new terms— check the following Note for details.)

NOTE The terms *cipher*, *algorithm*, and *complete algorithm* lend themselves to a lot of confusion, especially because most people in the IT industry use them interchangeably. Here's the scoop: A cipher is a general term for a way to encrypt data. The *algorithm* is the mathematical formula that underlies the cipher. The *complete algorithm* is both the cipher and the implementation of that cipher. The problem with the terms is compounded by the lack of a third, distinct term. Most people drop the word "complete" from "complete algorithm," for example, thus the meanings of the three terms become muddied.

Let's say you have a string of ones and zeroes that looks like this:

```
01001101010010010100101101000101
```

This string may not mean much to you, but if it was part of an HTTP segment, your Web browser would instantly know that this is Unicode—that is, numbers representing letters and other characters—and convert it into text:

```
01001101 01001001 01001011 01000101
M        I        K        E
```

So let's create a cipher to encrypt this cleartext. All binary encryption requires some interesting binary math. You could do something really simple such as add 1 to every value (and ignore carrying the 1):

```
0 + 1 = 1 and 1 + 1 = 0 10110010101101101011010010111010
```

No big deal; that just reversed the values. Any decent hacker would see the pattern and break this code in about three seconds. Let's try something harder to break by bringing in a second value (a key) of any eight binary numbers (let's use 10101010 for this example) and doing some math to every eight binary values using this algorithm:

If cleartext is...	And key value is...	Then the result is...
0	0	0
0	I	I
I	0	I
I	I	0

This is known as a binary *XOR (eXclusive OR)*. Line up the key against the first eight values in the cleartext:

```
10101010
010011010100100101000101101000101
11100111
```

Then do the next eight binary values:

```
1010101010101010
010011010100100101000101101000101
1110011111100011
```

Then the next eight:

```
101010101010101010101010
010011010100100101000101101000101
111001111110001111100001
```

Then the final eight:

```
10101010101010101010101010101010
010011010100100101000101101000101
11100111111000111110000111101111
```

If you want to decrypt the data, you need to know the algorithm and the key. This is a very simple example of how to encrypt binary data. At first glance, you might say this is good encryption, but the math is simple, and a simple XOR is easy for someone to decrypt.

An XOR works with letters as well as numbers. See if you can crack the following code:

```
WKH TXLFN EURZQ IRA MXPSV RYHU WKH ODCB GRJ
```

This is a classic example of the Caesar cipher. You just take the letters of the alphabet and transpose them:

```
Real Letter: ABCDEFGHIJKLMNOPQRSTUVWXYZ
Code letter: DEFGHIJKLMNOPQRSTUVWXYZABC
```

Caesar ciphers are very easy to crack by using word patterns, frequency analysis, or brute force. The code "WKH" shows up twice, which means it's the same word (*word patterns*). The letters *W* and *H* show up fairly often too. Certain letters of the alphabet are used more than others, so a code-breaker can use that to help decrypt the code (*frequency analysis*). Assuming that you know this is a Caesar cipher, a computer can quickly go through every different code possibility and determine the answer (*brute force*). Incredibly, even though it's not as obvious, binary code also suffers from the same problem.

In computing, you need to make a cipher hard for anyone to break except the people you want to read the data. Luckily, computers do more complex algorithms very quickly (it's just math), and you can use longer keys to make the code much harder to crack.

Okay, let's take the information above and generate some more symbols to show this process. When you run cleartext through a cipher algorithm using a key, you get what's called *ciphertext* (Figure 11-2).

Figure 11-2
Encryption process

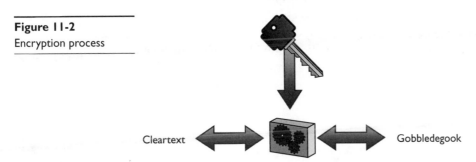

Cleartext ⟷ ⟷ Gobbledegook

Over the years, computing people have developed hundreds of different complete algorithms for use in encrypting binary data. Of these, only a few were or still are commonly used in the TCP/IP world. The math behind all of these complete algorithms is incredibly complex and way beyond the scope of the CompTIA Network+ exam, but all of them have two items in common: a complex algorithm underlying the cipher and a key or keys used to encrypt and decrypt the text.

Any encryption that uses the same key for both encryption and decryption is called symmetric-key encryption or a *symmetric-key algorithm*. If you want someone to decrypt what you encrypt, you have to make sure they have some tool that can handle the algorithm and you have to give them the key. This is a potential problem I will address later in this chapter. Any encryption that uses different keys for encryption and decryption is called asymmetric-key encryption or an *asymmetric-key algorithm*. Let's look at symmetric-key encryption first, and then turn to asymmetric-key encryption.

Symmetric-Key Algorithm Standards

There is one difference among symmetric-key algorithms. Most algorithms are called *block ciphers* because they encrypt data in single "chunks" of a certain length at a time. Let's say you have a 100,000-byte Microsoft Word document you want to encrypt. One type of encryption will take 128-bit chunks and encrypt each one separately (Figure 11-3). Block ciphers work well when data comes in clearly discrete chunks. Most data crossing wired networks comes in IP packets, for example, so block ciphers are very popular with these sorts of packets.

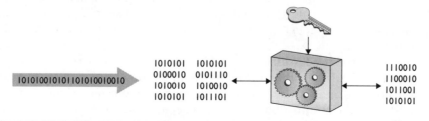

Figure 11-3   Block cipher

The alternative is a *stream cipher*, which takes a single bit at a time and encrypts on-the-fly (Figure 11-4). Stream ciphers are very popular whenever your data comes in long streams (such as with older wireless networks or cell phones).

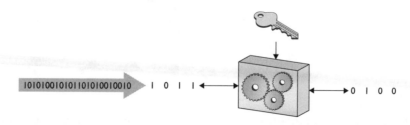

Figure 11-4   Stream cipher

The granddaddy of all TCP/IP symmetric-key algorithms is the *Data Encryption Standard (DES)*. DES was developed by the United States government in the late 1970s and was in widespread use in a variety of TCP/IP applications. DES used a 64-bit block and a 56-bit key. Over time, the 56-bit key made DES susceptible to brute-force attacks. The computing world came up with a number of derivatives of DES to try to address this issue, with names such as 3DES, International Data Encryption Algorithm (IDEA), and Blowfish.

On the streaming side, the only symmetric-key algorithm you'll probably ever see is *Rivest Cipher 4 (RC4)* stream cipher. RC4 was invented in the late 1980s by Ron Rivest, cryptographer and arguably the most famous of all inventors of TCP/IP security algorithms. RC4 is used in a number of TCP/IP applications. Over the years improvements in computing power made both DES and RC4 vulnerable to attacks in certain circumstances. As a result, almost all TCP/IP applications have moved to *Advanced Encryption Standard (AES)*. AES is a block cipher created in the late 1990s. It uses a 128-bit block size and 128-, 192-, or 256-bit key size. AES is incredibly secure, practically uncrackable (for now at least), and is so fast that even applications that traditionally used stream ciphers are switching to AES.

Not at all limited to TCP/IP, you'll find AES used for many applications from file encryption to wireless networking to some Web sites. Given that AES is still somewhat new, many TCP/IP applications are still in the process of moving toward adoption.

EXAM TIP When in doubt on a question about encryption algorithms, always pick AES. You'll be right most of the time.

Asymmetric-Key Algorithm Standards

Symmetric-key encryption has one serious weakness: anyone who gets a hold of the key can encrypt or decrypt data with it. The nature of symmetric-key encryption forces us to send the key to the other person in one way or another, making it a challenge to use symmetric-key encryption safely. As a result, folks have been strongly motived to create a methodology that allows the encrypter to send a key to the decrypter without fear of interception (Figure 11-5).

Sending...

Figure 11-5 How do we safely deliver the key?

The answer to the problem of key sharing came in the form of using two different keys—one to encrypt and one to decrypt, thus, an asymmetric-key algorithm. Three men in the late 1970s—Whitfield Diffie, Martin Hellman, and Ralph Merkle—introduced what became known as *public-key cryptography*, with which keys could be exchanged securely.

NOTE The public-key cryptography introduced by Diffie, Hellman, and Merkle became known as the *Diffie-Hellman key exchange*. Hellman, on the other hand, has insisted that if the scheme needs a name, it should be called the Diffie-Hellman-Merkle key exchange.

Ron Rivest (along with Adi Shamir and Leonard Adleman) came up with some improvements to the Diffie-Hellman method of public-key cryptography by introducing a fully functional algorithm called *Rivest Shamir Adleman (RSA)* that enabled secure digital signatures. Here's how public-key cryptography works.

Imagine two people, Mike and Melissa, who wish to send each other encrypted e-mail messages (Figure 11-6). SMTP doesn't have any (popular) form of encryption, so Mike and Melissa must come up with some program that encrypts their messages. They will then send the encrypted messages as regular e-mail.

Figure 11-6   Mike and Melissa, wanting to send encrypted e-mail messages

 EXAM TIP   Public-key cryptography is the most popular form of e-mail encryption.

Before Melissa can send an encrypted e-mail to Mike, he first generates *two* keys. One of these keys is kept on his computer (the *private* key), and the other key is sent to anyone from whom he wants to receive encrypted e-mail (the *public* key). These two keys—called a *key pair*—are generated at the same time and are designed to work together. He sends a copy of the public key to Melissa (Figure 11-7).

Figure 11-7   Sending a public key

A public-key cryptography algorithm works by encrypting data with a public key and then decrypting data with a private key. The public key of the key pair encrypts the data, and only the associated private key of the key pair can decrypt the data. Since Melissa has Mike's public key, Melissa can encrypt and send a message to Mike that only Mike's private key can decrypt. Mike can then decrypt the message (Figure 11-8).

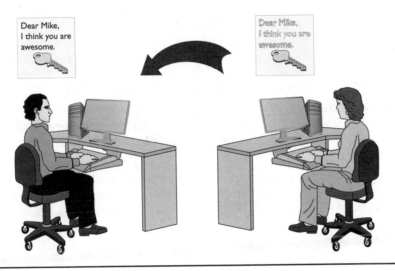

Figure 11-8   Decrypting a message

If Melissa wants Mike to send encrypted e-mail to her, she must generate her own key pair and send Mike the public key. In a typical public-key cryptography setup, everyone has their own private key plus a copy of the public keys for anyone with whom they wish to communicate securely (Figure 11-9).

Figure 11-9   Lots of keys

The only problem with all these keys is the chance that someone pretending to be someone else might pass out a public key. Therefore, the recipients have a strong desire to know who is passing out a key. This issue falls under the banner of nonrepudiation.

Encryption and the OSI Model

The process of encryption varies dramatically depending on what you want to encrypt. To make life a bit easier, let's look at how you encrypt using the OSI seven-layer model:

- **Layer 1**   No common encryption done at this layer.

- **Layer 2**   A common place for encryption using proprietary encryption devices. These boxes scramble all of the data in an Ethernet frame except the MAC address information. Devices or programs encode and decode the information on-the-fly at each end.

- **Layer 3**   Only one common protocol encrypts at Layer 3: IPsec. IPsec is typically done via software that takes the IP packet and encrypts everything inside the packet, leaving only the IP addresses and a few other fields unencrypted.

- **Layer 4**   Neither TCP nor UDP offers any encryption methods, so little happens security-wise at Layer 4.

- **Layers 5 and 6**   Not common layers for encryption.

- **Layer 7**   Many applications use their own encryption, placing them squarely in Layer 7. There are Layer 7 standards, with SSL/TLS being very common.

Nonrepudiation

Within networking, nonrepudiation simply means that the receiver of information has a very high degree of confidence that the sender of a piece of information truly is who the receiver thinks he or she or it should be. Nonrepudiation takes place all over a network. Is this truly the person who sent in the user name and password to log into my Windows domain? Is this really the eBay.com Web site I'm entering my credit card number into? Did this public key really come from Mike Meyers? As a result, nonrepudiation comes in a number of forms, but most of them use a very clever little bit of mathematical magic called a hash.

Hash

In computer security, a *hash* (or more accurately, a *cryptographic hash function*) is a mathematical function that you run on a string of binary digits of any length that results in a value of some fixed length (often called a *checksum* or a *digest*). A cryptographic hash function is a one-way function. One-way means the hash is practically irreversible. You should not be able to re-create the data, even if you know the hashing algorithm and the checksum. A cryptographic hash function should also have a unique checksum for any two different input streams (Figure 11-10).

Figure 11-10
A hash at work

Cryptographic hash functions have a huge number of uses, but one of the most common is for files. Let's say I'm sharing a file on my Web site. I'm worried an evil hacker might alter that file, so I run a hash on the file and supply you with both the file and the checksum. *Message-Digest Algorithm version 5*—everybody just calls it *MD5*—is arguably the most popular hashing function for this type of work. Figure 11-11 shows an example of this, a program called Net.MD5.

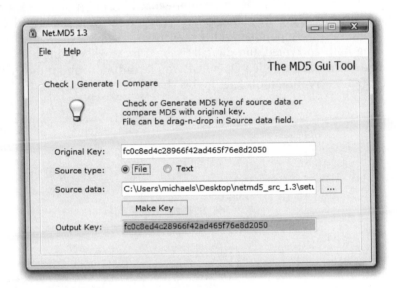

Figure 11-11   File and MD5

MD5 is a very popular cryptographic hash, but it's not the only one. The other hash you'll see from time to time is called *Secure Hash Algorithm (SHA)*. There are two versions of SHA: SHA-1 and SHA-2.

Many encryption and authentication schemes also use hashes. Granted, you won't actually see the hashes as they're used, but trust me: hashes are everywhere. For example, some SMTP servers use a special form of MD5, called *Challenge-Response Authentication Mechanism-Message Digest 5 (CRAM-MD5)*, as a tool for server authentication. (See the discussion of CHAP later in the "Authentication Standards" section for details on how challenge-response works.) Now that you understand hashes, let's return to public-key cryptography and see how digital signatures make public-key cryptography even more secure.

EXAM TIP   Look for CRAM-MD5 to show up on the CompTIA Network+ exam as a tool for server authentication.

Digital Signatures

As mentioned earlier, public-key cryptography suffers from the risk that you might be getting a message or a public key from someone who isn't who they say they are. To avoid this problem, you add a digital signature. A *digital signature* is another string of ones and zeroes that can only be generated by the sender, usually by doing something mathematically complex (part of the algorithms always includes some hashing) to the message and the private key. The person with the matching public key does something to the digital signature using the public key to verify it came from the intended sender. Digital signatures are very popular with e-mail users. Figure 11-12 shows an e-mail message being both encrypted and digitally signed in Mozilla Thunderbird using a special Thunderbird add-on called OpenPGP. You'll read more about the PGP family of authentication/encryption tools later in this chapter.

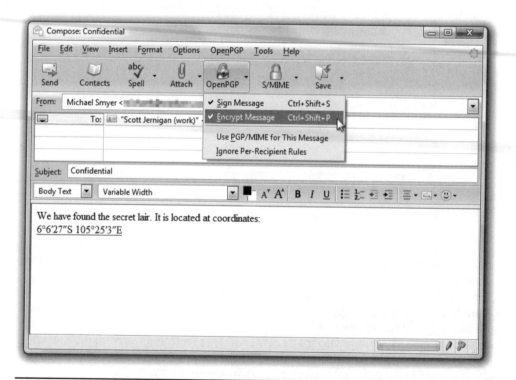

Figure 11-12   Digitally signed

PKI

Digital signatures are great, but what happens when you want to do business with someone you do not know? Before you enter a credit card number to buy that new USB 3.0 Blu-ray Disc player, wouldn't you like to know that the Web site you are doing business with truly is eBay? To address that need the industry came up with the idea of certificates. A *certificate* is a standardized type of digital signature that includes the digital signature of a third party, a person or a company that guarantees that who is passing out this certificate truly is who they say they are. As you might imagine, certificates are incredibly common with secure Web pages. When you go to eBay to sign in, your browser redirects to a secure Web page. These are easy to identify by the lock icon at the bottom of the screen or in the address bar (Figure 11-13) or the https:// used (instead of http://) in the address bar.

Figure II-13   Secure Web page

 EXAM TIP   If you see https:// or a small lock icon, you are most likely on a secure Web site.

In the background, several actions take place (all before the secure Web page loads). First, the Web server automatically sends a copy of its certificate. Built into that certificate is the Web server's public key and a signature from the third party that guarantees this is really eBay. Go to your national version of eBay (I'm in the United States, so I'll use eBay.com) and click **Sign In** (you don't even need an eBay account to do this). Now look at the certificate for the current session. Depending on the Web browser you use, you'll see it in different ways. Try clicking the little lock icon at the bottom of the page or in the address bar as this usually works. Figure 11-14 shows the certificate for this session.

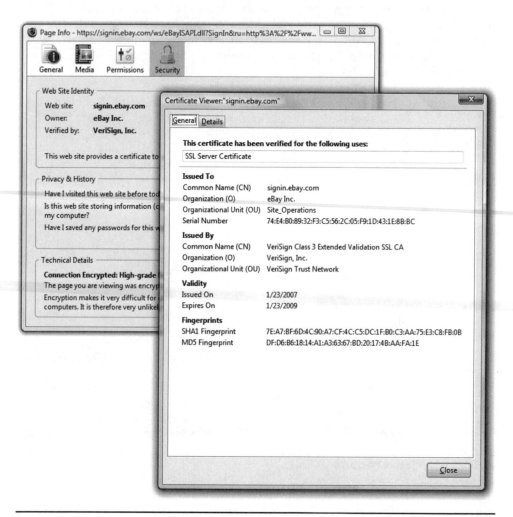

Figure 11-14   eBay sign-in certificate

So a company called VeriSign issued this certificate. That's great, but how does your computer check all this? VeriSign is a certificate authority. Every Web browser keeps a list of certificate authority certificates that it checks against when it receives a digital certificate. Figure 11-15 shows the certificate authority certificates stored on my system.

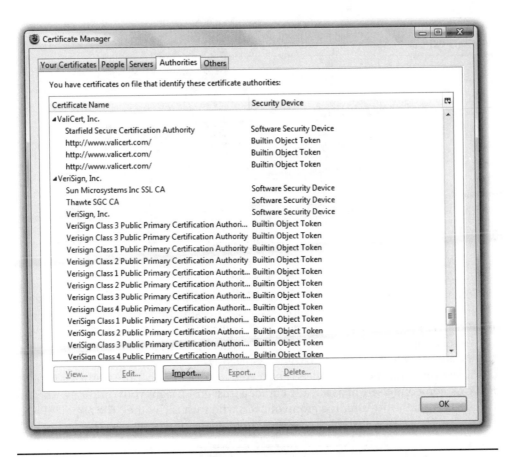

Figure 11-15 Certificate authority certificates on a system

> **NOTE** Becoming a root certificate authority with enough respect to have Web browsers install your certificate is very difficult!

When someone wants to create a secure Web site, he or she buys a certificate signed by a certificate authority, such as VeriSign (the biggest player in the market and the one I'll use for this example). VeriSign acts as the root, and the new Web site's certificate contains VeriSign's signature. For more advanced situations, VeriSign includes an intermediate certificate authority between VeriSign's root certificate authority and the user's certificate. This creates a tree of certificate authorization, with the root authorities at the top and issued certificates at the bottom. You can also have intermediate authorities although these are not as heavily used. Together, this organization is called a *public-key infrastructure (PKI)* (Figure 11-16).

Figure 11-16

VeriSign's PKI tree

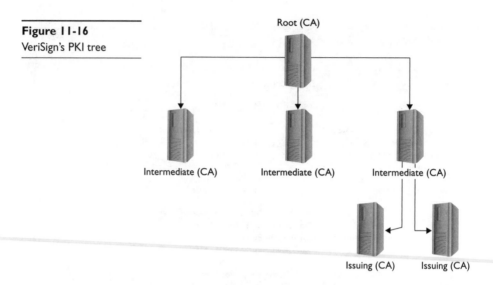

You don't have to use PKI to use certificates. First, you can create your own unsigned certificates. These are perfectly fine for lower-security situations (e-mail among friends, personal Web page, and so forth), but don't expect anyone to buy products on a Web site or send highly sensitive e-mail without a signed certificate from a well-known certificate authority like VeriSign, Thawte, or GoDaddy.

Finally, many certificate providers offer a Web-of-trust option, primarily for e-mail. In this case, someone else who is already part of a trust group signs your certificate. There is no certificate authority, simply a group of peers who trust each other. The popular Pretty Good Privacy (PGP) encryption program, among many others, uses such a trust model.

NOTE Almost all e-mail clients support encryption—you just need to get a certificate. If you want to start playing with e-mail encryption and signing, grab a free personal e-mail certificate from a number of different providers. Check out Secorio at www.secorio.com/index.php?S_MIME_Email_Certificates, or Comodo at www.instantssl.com/ssl-certificate-products/free-email-certificate.html. Instructions for certificate generation and installation are on the respective Web sites.

Digital certificates and asymmetric cryptography are closely linked because digital certificates are almost always used to verify the exchange of public keys. In many cases, this exchange takes place behind the scenes of e-mail, Web pages, and even in some very secure wireless networks. Though you may not see certificates in action very often, you now know that they are there.

NOTE Fans of software licensed under the GNU public license can try *GNU Privacy Guard (GPG)*, an alternative to the PGP suite. Check it out here: www.gnupg.org.

Authentication

You most likely have dealt with authentication at some level. Odds are good you've at least had to type in a user name and password on a Web site. Maybe your computer at work or school requires you to log on to the network. Whatever the case, the first exposure to authentication for most users is a request to enter a user name and password. A network technician should understand not only how different authentication methods control user names and passwords, but also some of the authentication standards used in today's TCP/IP networks.

Passwords offer significant security challenges. What happens after you type in a user name and password? How is this data transferred? Who or what reads this? What is the data compared to? A series of TCP/IP security standards that use combinations of user names, passwords, and sometimes certificates, all handled in a usually secure manner, address these issues, as described in the upcoming section "TCP/IP Security Standards."

Authorization

A large part of the entire networking process involves one computer requesting something from another computer. A Web client might ask for a Web page, for example, or a Common Internet File System (CIFS) client might ask a file server for access to a folder. A computer far away might ask another computer for access to a private network. Whatever the case, you should carefully assign levels of access to your resources. This is authorization. To help define how to assign levels of access, you use an access control list.

 EXAM TIP The "Network+ Acronym List" includes a term called *Network Access Control (NAC)*. NAC defines a newer series of protection applications that combine the features of what traditionally was done by separate applications. There is no perfect single definition for NAC. There are, however, certain functions that a NAC often does. A NAC usually prevents computers lacking antimalware and patches from accessing the network. NACs also create policies (their own policies, not Windows policies) that define what individual systems can do on the network, including network access, segregation of portions of the network, etc.

An *access control list (ACL)* is nothing more than a clearly defined list of permissions that specify what an authenticated user may perform on a shared resource. Over the years the way to assign access to resources has changed dramatically. To help you to understand these changes, the security industry likes to use the idea of *ACL access models*. There are three types of ACL access models: mandatory, discretionary, and role based.

In a *mandatory access control (MAC)* security model, every resource is assigned a label that defines its security level. If the user lacks that security level, he or she does not get access. MAC is used in many operating systems to define what privileges programs have to other programs stored in RAM. The MAC security model is the oldest and least common of the three.

Discretionary access control (DAC) is based on the idea that a resource has an owner who may at his or her discretion assign access to that resource. DAC is considered much more flexible than MAC.

Role-based access control (RBAC) is the most popular model used in file sharing. RBAC defines a user's access to a resource based on the roles the user plays in the network environment. This leads to the idea of creating groups. A group in most networks is nothing more than a name that has clearly defined accesses to different resources. User accounts are placed into various groups. A network might have a group called "Sales" on a Web server that gives any user account that is a member of the Sales group access to a special Web page that no other groups can see.

Keep in mind that these three types of access control are models. Every TCP/IP application and operating system has its own set of rules that sometimes follows one of these models, but in many cases does not. But do make sure you understand these three models for the CompTIA Network+ exam!

TCP/IP Security Standards

Now that you have a conceptual understanding of encryption, nonrepudiation, authentication, and authorization, it's time to see how the TCP/IP folks have put it all together to create standards so you can secure just about anything in TCP/IP networks.

TCP/IP security standards are a rather strange mess. Some are authentication standards, some are encryption standards, and some are so unique to a single application that I'm not even going to talk about them in this section and instead will wait until the "Secure TCP/IP Applications" discussion at the end of this chapter. There's a reason for all this confusion: TCP/IP was never really designed for security. As you read through this section, you'll discover that almost all of these standards either predate the whole Internet, are slapped-together standards that have some serious issues, or, in the case of the most recent standards, are designed to combine a bunch of old, confusing standards. So hang tight—it's going to be a bumpy ride!

Authentication Standards

Authentication standards are some of the oldest standards used in TCP/IP. Many are so old they predate the Internet itself. Once upon a time, nobody had fiber-optic, cable, or DSL connections to their ISPs. For the most part, if you wanted to connect to the Internet you had a choice: go to the computer center or use dial-up.

Dial-up, using telephone lines for the most part, predates the Internet, but the nerds of their day didn't want just anybody dialing into their computers. To prevent unauthorized access, they developed some excellent authentication methods that TCP/IP adopted for itself. A number of authentication methods were used back in these early days, but, for the most part, TCP/IP authentication started with something called the Point-to-Point Protocol.

PPP

The *Point-to-Point Protocol (PPP)* enables two point-to-point devices to connect, authenticate with a user name and password, and negotiate the network protocol the two devices will use. Today that network protocol is almost always TCP/IP.

Note that point-to-point and dial-up are not Ethernet, but still can support TCP/IP. Many network technologies don't need Ethernet, such as telephone, cable modem, microwave, and wireless (plus a bunch more you won't even see until Chapter 14). In fact, once you leave a LAN, most of the Internet is just a series of point-to-point connections.

If you're nerdy enough to pull up RFC (Request for Comment) 1661, the RFC that defines how PPP works, you'll see there are five distinct phases to a PPP connection.

1. **Link dead** This is a nice way to say there isn't a link yet. The modem is turned off; no one is talking. This phase is when all PPP conversations begin. The main player at this (and later phases) is the *Link Control Protocol (LCP)*. The LCP's job is to get the connection going. As he starts up, we move into the...

2. **Link establishment** The LCP communicates with the LCP on the other side of the PPP link, determining a good link, which, in turn, opens the...

3. **Authentication** Here is where the authentication takes place. In most cases, authentication is performed by entering a simple user name/password. I'll go into more detail in the next section. For now, once the authentication is complete and successful, the PPP connection goes into...

4. **Network layer protocol** PPP works with a number of OSI Layer 3 network protocols. Today everyone uses TCP/IP, but PPP still supports long-dead protocols such as NetWare IPX/SPX and Microsoft NetBEUI. The LCP uses yet another protocol called *Network Control Protocol (NCP)* to make the proper connections for that protocol. You now have a good connection. To shut down, the LCP initiates a...

5. **Termination** When done nicely, the two ends of the PPP connection send each other a few termination packets and the link is closed. If one person is cut off, the LCP will wait for a certain timeout and then terminate on its own side.

PPP provided the first common method to get a server to request a user name and password. In such a point-to-point connection, the side asking for the connection is called the *initiator*, whereas the other side, which has a list of user names and passwords, is called the *authenticator* (Figure 11-17).

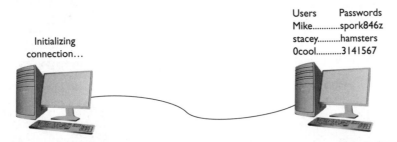

Initializing
connection...

Users   Passwords
Mike............spork846z
stacey..........hamsters
0cool...........3141567

Figure 11-17   A point-to-point connection

PPP came with two methods to authenticate a user name and password. The original way—called *Password Authentication Protocol (PAP)*—simply transmits the user name and password over the connection in plaintext. Unfortunately, that means anyone who can tap the connection can learn the user name and password (Figure 11-18).

Figure 11-18 PAP in action

Fortunately, PPP also includes the safer *Challenge Handshake Authentication Protocol (CHAP)* to provide a more secure authentication routine. CHAP relies on hashes based on a shared secret, usually a password that both ends of the connection know. When the initiator of the connection makes the initial connection request, the authenticator creates some form of challenge message. The initiator then makes a hash using the password and sends that to the authenticator. The authenticator, in turn, compares that value to its own hash calculation based on the password. If they match, the initiator is authenticated (Figure 11-19).

Once the connection is up and running, CHAP keeps working by periodically repeating the entire authentication process. This prevents man-in-the-middle attacks, where a third party inserts an independent connection, intercepts traffic, reads or alters it, and then forwards it on without either the sender or recipient being aware of the intrusion.

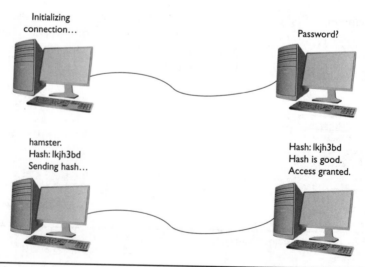

Figure 11-19 CHAP in action

CHAP works nicely because it never sends the actual password over the link. The CHAP standard leaves a number of issues undefined, however, like "If the hash doesn't match, what do I do?" The boom in dial-up connections to the Internet in the 1990s led Microsoft to invent a more detailed version of CHAP called *MS-CHAP*. The current version of MS-CHAP is called MS-CHAPv2. MS-CHAPv2 is still the most common authentication method for the few of us using dial-up connections. Believe it or not, dial-up is still being used, and even the latest operating systems support it. Figure 11-20 shows the dial-up connection options for Vista.

 NOTE   Yes, I still have a dial-up connection account that I use when nothing else is available.

 EXAM TIP   If you get a question on PAP, CHAP, and MS-CHAP on the CompTIA Network+ exam, remember that MS-CHAP offers the most security.

Figure 11-20
MS-CHAP is
alive and well.

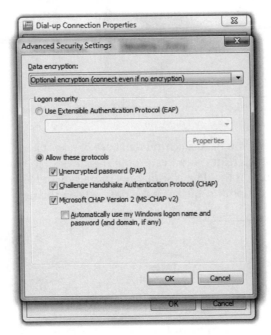

AAA

PPP does a great job of handling authentication for point-to-point connections, but it has some limitations. The biggest problem is that, in many cases, a network might have more than one point for an initiator to enter. PPP assumes that the authenticator at the endpoint has all the user name and password information, but that's not necessarily true. In traditional modem communication, for example, an Internet service provider

(ISP) has a large bank of modems to support any number of users. When a user dials in, the modem bank provides the first available connection, but that means that any modem in the bank has to support any of the users. You can't put the database containing all user names and passwords on every modem (Figure 11-21).

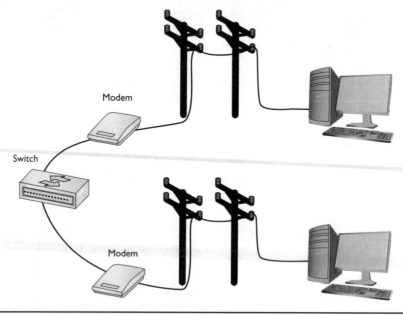

Figure 11-21 Where do you put the user names and passwords?

In this case, you need a central database of user names and passwords. That's simple enough, but it creates another problem—anyone accessing the network can see the passwords unless the data is somehow protected and encrypted. (Figure 11-22). PPP is good at the endpoints, but once the data gets on the network, it's unencrypted.

Figure 11-22
Central servers are
prone to attack.

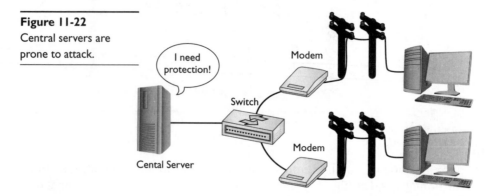

Thus, the folks overseeing central databases full of user names and passwords needed to come up with standards to follow to protect that data. They first agreed upon a philosophy called *Authentication, Authorization, and Accounting (AAA)*. AAA is designed for the idea of port authentication—the concept of allowing remote users authentication to a particular point-of-entry (a port) to another network.

- **Authentication** A computer that is trying to connect to the network must present some form of credential for access to the network. This credential is most commonly a user name and password, but it might also be a security token such as a smart card, retinal scan, or digital certificate. It might even be a combination of some of these. The authentication gives the computer the right to access the network.

- **Authorization** Once authenticated, the computer determines what it can or cannot do on the network. It might only be allowed to use a certain amount of bandwidth. It might be limited to working only certain times of day or might be limited to using only a certain set of applications.

- **Accounting** The authenticating server should do some form of accounting such as recording the number of times a user logs on and logs off. It might track unsuccessful logon attempts. It may track what services or resources the client system accessed. The number of items to be accounted is massive.

Once the idea of AAA took shape, those smart Internet folks developed two standards: RADIUS and TACACS+. Both standards offer authentication, authorization, and accounting.

RADIUS *RADIUS Remote Authentication Dial-In User Service (RADIUS)* is the better known of the two AAA standards and, as its name implies, was created to support ISPs with hundreds if not thousands of modems in hundreds of computers to connect to a single central database. RADIUS consists of three devices: the RADIUS server that has access to a database of user names and passwords, a number of *Network Access Servers (NASs)* that control the modems, and a group of systems that dial into the network (Figure 11-23).

 EXAM TIP NAS stands for either *Network Access Server* or *Network Attached Storage*. The latter is a type of dedicated file server used in many networks. Make sure you read the question to see which NAS it's looking for!

To use RADIUS, you need a RADIUS server. The most popular choice for Microsoft environments is *Internet Authentication Service (IAS)*. IAS comes built in with most versions of Microsoft Windows Server operating systems. For the UNIX/Linux crowd, the popular (yet, in my opinion, hard to set up) *FreeRADIUS* is the best choice. If you prefer a more prepackaged server, you might look at Juniper Network's Steel-Belted RADIUS—a very powerful and somewhat easy-to-set-up option that many people feel is well worth the roughly $3,000 price tag.

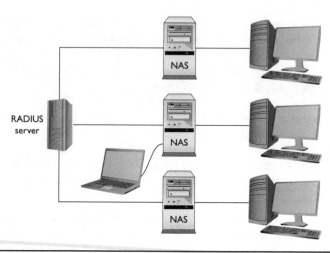

Figure 11-23   RADIUS setup

A single RADIUS server can support multiple NASs and provide a complete PPP connection from the requesting system, through the NAS, all the way to the RADIUS server. Like any PPP connection, the RADIUS server supports PAP, CHAP, and MS-CHAP. Even if you use PAP, RADIUS hashes the password so at no time is the user name/password exposed. Newer versions of RADIUS support even more authentication methods, as you will soon see. RADIUS performs this authentication on either UDP ports 1812 and 1813 or UDP ports 1645 and 1646.

TACACS+   Routers and switches need administration. In a simple network, you can access the administration screen for each router and switch by entering a user name and password for each device. When a network becomes complex, with many routers and switches, logging into each device separately starts to become administratively messy. The answer is to make a single server store the ACL for all the devices in the network. To make this secure, you need to follow the AAA principles.

Terminal Access Controller Access Control System Plus (TACACS+) is a proprietary protocol developed by Cisco to support AAA in a network with many routers and switches. TACACS+ is very similar to RADIUS in function, but uses TCP port 49 by default and separates authorization, authentication, and accounting into different parts. TACACS+ uses PAP, CHAP, and MD5 hashes, but can also use something called Kerberos as part of the authentication scheme.

Kerberos

Up to this point almost all the authentication schemes I've discussed either are based on PPP or at least take the idea of PPP and expand upon it. Of course, every rule needs an exception and Kerberos is the exception here.

Kerberos is an authentication protocol that has no connection to PPP. Twenty years ago, some Internet folks began to appreciate that TCP/IP was not secure and thus designed Kerberos. Kerberos is an authentication protocol for TCP/IP networks with many clients all connected to a single authenticating server—no point-to-point here! Kerberos works nicely in a network, so nicely that Microsoft adopted it as the authentication protocol for all Windows networks using a domain controller.

NOTE Kerberos uses UDP or TCP port 88 by default

The cornerstone of Kerberos is the *Key Distribution Center (KDC)*, which has two processes: the *Authentication Server (AS)* and the Ticket-Granting Service (TGS). In Windows server environments, the KDC is installed on the domain controller (Figure 11-24).

Figure 11-24 Windows Kerberos setup

When your client logs onto the domain, it sends a request that includes a hash of the user name and password to the AS. The AS compares the results of that hash to its own hash (as it also stores the user name and password) and, if they match, sends a *Ticket-Granting Ticket (TGT)* and a timestamp (Figure 11-25). The ticket has a default lifespan in Windows of ten hours. The client is now authenticated but not yet authorized.

Figure 11-25 AS sending a TGT back to client

NOTE The TGT is sometimes referred to as *Ticket to Get Ticket.*

The client then sends the timestamped TGT to the TGS for authorization. The TGS sends a timestamped service ticket (also called a *token* or *access token*) back to the client (Figure 11-26).

Client

AS
TGS

Figure 11-26 TGS sending token to client

This token is the key that the client uses to access any single resource on the entire domain. This is where authorization takes place. The token authorizes the user to access resources without reauthenticating. Any time the client attempts to access a folder, printer, or service anywhere in the domain, the server sharing that resource uses the token to see exactly what access the client may have to that resource. If you try to access some other feature under Windows, for example, retrieving your e-mail via Microsoft Exchange Server, you won't need to log in again.

> **NOTE** In Windows, the security token is called a Security Identifier (SID).

Timestamping is important for Kerberos because it forces the client to request a new token every eight hours. This prevents third parties from intercepting the tokens and attempting to crack them. Kerberos tokens can be cracked, but it's doubtful this can be done in under eight hours.

Kerberos is very popular, but has some serious weaknesses. First, if the KDC goes down, no one has access. That's why Microsoft and other operating systems that use Kerberos always stress the importance of maintaining a backup KDC. In Windows, it is standard practice to have at least two domain controllers. Second, timestamping requires that all the clients and servers synchronize their clocks. This is fairly easy to do in a wired network (such as a Windows domain or even a bunch of connected routers using TACACS+), but it adds an extra level of challenge in dispersed networks (such as those connected across the country).

EAP

One of the great challenges to authentication is getting the two ends of the authentication process to handle the many different types of authentication options. Even though PPP pretty much owned the user name/password authentication business, proprietary forms of authentication using smart cards/tokens, certificates, and so on, began to show up on the market, threatening to drop the entire world of authentication into a huge mess of competing standards.

The *Extensible Authentication Protocol (EAP)* was developed to create a single standard to allow two devices to authenticate. Despite the name, EAP is not a protocol in the classic sense, but rather it is a PPP wrapper that EAP-compliant applications can use to accept one of many types of authentication. Although EAP is a general-purpose authentication wrapper, its only substantial use is in wireless networks. (See Chapter 15 to see where EAP is used.) EAP comes in various types, but currently only six types are in common use:

- **EAP-PSK** Easily the most popular form of authentication used in wireless networks today, EAP-PSK (Personal Shared Key) is nothing more than a shared secret code that's stored on both the wireless access point and the wireless client, encrypted using the powerful AES encryption (Figure 11-27). See Chapter 15 for the scoop on wireless access points and EAP.

Figure 11-27
EAP-PSK in action

Password: Eggs

Wireless client   Wireless Access Point

- **EAP-TLS** EAP with Transport Layer Security (TLS) defines the use of a RADIUS server as well as mutual authentication, requiring certificates on both the server and every client. On the client side, a smart card may be used in lieu of a certificate. EAP-TLS is very robust, but the client-side certificate requirement is an administrative challenge. Even though it's a challenge, the most secure wireless networks all use EAP-TLS. EAP-TLS is only used on wireless networks, but TLS is used heavily on secure Web sites (see the section "SSL/TLS" later in this chapter). Figure 11-28 shows a typical EAP-TLS setup for a wireless network.

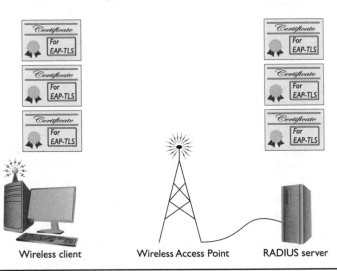

Wireless client   Wireless Access Point   RADIUS server

Figure 11-28 EAP-TLS

- **EAP-TTLS** EAP-TTLS (Tunneled TLS) is similar to EAP-TLS but only uses a single server-side certificate. EAP-TTLS is very common for more secure wireless networks (Figure 11-29).

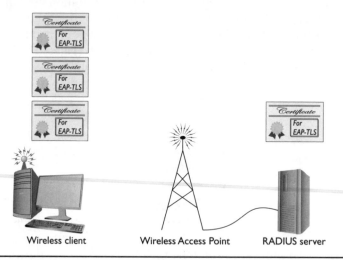

Figure 11-29 EAP-TTLS

- **EAP-MS-CHAPv2** More commonly known as *Protected Extensible Authentication Protocol (PEAP)*, EAP-MS-CHAPv2 uses a password function based on MS-CHAPv2 with the addition of an encrypted TLS tunnel similar to EAP-TLS.

- **EAP-MD5** This is a very simple version of EAP that uses only MD5 hashes for transfer of authentication credentials. EAP-MD5 is weak and the least used of all the versions of EAP described.

- **LEAP** *Lightweight Extensible Authentication Protocol (LEAP)* is a proprietary EAP authentication used almost exclusively by Cisco wireless products. LEAP is an interesting combination of MS-CHAP authentication between a wireless client and a RADIUS server.

802.1X

EAP was a huge success and almost overnight gave those who needed point-to-point authentication a one-stop-shop methodology to do so. EAP was so successful that there was a cry to develop an EAP solution for Ethernet networks. This solution is called 802.1X. Whereas traditional EAP is nothing more than an authentication method wrapped in PPP, 802.1X gets rid of the PPP (Ethernet is not a point-to-point protocol!) and instead puts the EAP information inside an Ethernet frame.

802.1X is a port-authentication network access control mechanism for networks. In other words, it's a complete authentication standard designed to force devices to go through a full AAA process to get anywhere past the interface on a gateway system. Before 802.1X, a system on a wired network could always access another system's port.

Granted, an attacker wouldn't be able to do much until he gave a user name/password or certificate, but he could still send packets to any computer on the network. This wasn't good because it enabled attackers to get to the systems to try to do evil things. 802.1X prevented them from even getting in the door until they were authenticated and authorized.

The interesting part is that you already know about most of the parts of 802.1X because the standard worked hard to use existing technologies. From a distance, 802.1X looks a lot like a RADIUS AAA setup. 802.1X changes the names of some of the components, as shown in Figure 11-30. Compare this to Figure 11-23 to get the new names (the jobs don't change).

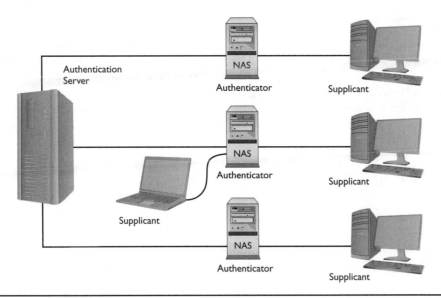

Figure 11-30 802.1X components

802.1X combines the RADIUS-style AAA with EAP versions to make a complete authentication solution. The folks who developed 802.1X saw it as a total replacement for every other form of authentication (even Kerberos), but the reality is that most people don't like changing something that already works. To that end, only wireless networking broadly adopted 802.1X.

 NOTE Technically, wireless networks don't use EAP. They use 802.1X, which, in turn, uses EAP.

I'm not done with authentication and authorization, but at least you now understand the basics of the popular authentication and authorization protocols and standards. You have more protocols to learn, but all of them are rather specialized for specific uses and thus are covered at various places throughout the book.

Encryption Standards

The Internet had authentication long before it had encryption. As a result, almost all encryption came out as a knee-jerk reaction to somebody realizing that his or her TCP/IP application wasn't secure. For years, there were new secure versions of just about every protocol in existence. New versions of all the classics started to appear, almost all starting with the word "Secure": Secure FTP, Secure SMTP, and even Secure POP were developed. They worked, but there were still hundreds of not-yet-secured protocols and the specter of redoing all of them was daunting. Fortunately, some new, all-purpose encryption protocols were developed that enabled a client to connect to a server in a secure way while still using their older, unsecure protocols—and it all started because of Telnet.

SSH

The broad adoption of the Internet by the early 1990s motivated programmers to start securing their applications. Telnet had a big problem. It was incredibly useful and popular, but it was completely insecure. It clearly needed to be fixed. As the story goes, Tatu Ylonen of the Helsinki University of Technology, reacting to an attack that intercepted Telnet user names and passwords on his network, invented a new secure replacement for Telnet called *Secure Shell (SSH)*. You've already seen SSH in action (in Chapter 9) as a secure version of Telnet, but now that you know more about security, let's look at SSH in detail.

 NOTE   SSH servers listen on TCP port 22.

SSH servers use PKI in the form of an RSA key. The first time a client tries to log into an SSH server, the server sends its public key to the client (Figure 11-31).

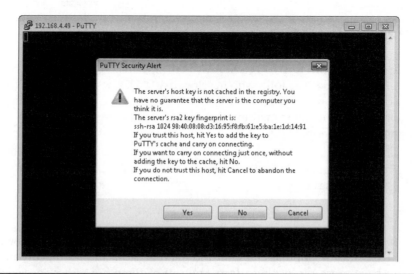

Figure 11-31   PuTTY getting an RSA key

After the client receives this key, it creates a session ID, encrypts it using the public key, and sends it back to the server. The server decrypts this session ID and uses it in all data transfers going forward. Only the client and the server know this session ID. Next, the client and server negotiate the type of encryption to use for the session. These days, AES is popular, but older symmetric-key ciphers such as 3DES may still be used. The negotiation for the cipher is automatic and invisible to the user.

Using RSA and a cipher makes a very safe connection, but the combination doesn't tell the server who is using the client. All SSH servers, therefore, add user names and passwords to authenticate the client (Figure 11-32). Once a user logs in with a user name and password, he or she has access to the system.

Figure 11-32

Users on an SSH server

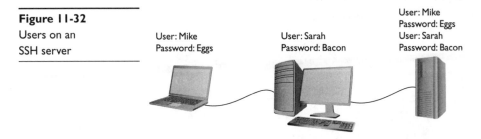

User: Mike
Password: Eggs

User: Sarah
Password: Bacon

User: Mike
Password: Eggs
User: Sarah
Password: Bacon

In addition to using a password for authentication, SSH also can use public keys to identify clients. This opens up some interesting possibilities such as noninteractive logins. You can also turn off password login altogether, hardening your server even further. To use public/private keys for authentication, you must first generate a pair of RSA or Digital Signature Algorithm (DSA) keys with a tool such as PuTTYgen (Figure 11-33). The public key is then copied to the server, and the private key is kept safe on the client.

Figure 11-33

Generated keys in PuTTYgen

When you connect to the server, your client generates a signature using its private key and sends it to the server. The server then checks the signature with its copy of the public key, and if everything checks out, you will be authenticated with the server.

If SSH stopped here as a secure replacement for Telnet, that would be fantastic, but SSH has another trick up its sleeve: the capability to act as a *tunnel* for *any* TCP/IP application. Let's see what tunnels are and how they work.

Tunneling

Simply, a *tunnel* is an encrypted link between two programs on two separate computers. Let's take a look at an SSH link between a server and a client. Once established, anything you enter into the client application is encrypted, sent to the server, decrypted, and then acted upon (Figure 11-34).

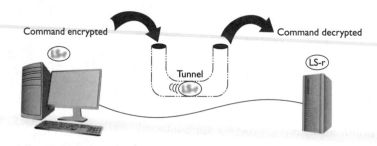

Figure 11-34 SSH in action

The nature of SSH is such that it took very little to extend the idea of SSH to accept input from any source, even another program (Figure 11-35). As long as the program can redirect to the SSH client and then the SSH server redirect to the server application, anything can go through an SSH connection encrypted. This is an SSH tunnel.

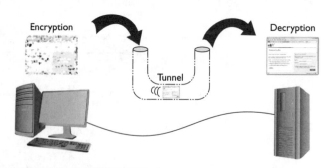

Figure 11-35 Encrypting a Web client

SSH tunnels are wildly popular and fairly easy to set up. Equally, all of the popular SSH clients and servers are designed to go into tunnel mode, usually with no more than a simple click of a check box (Figure 11-36).

Figure 11-36 Turning on tunneling in freeSSHd server

Many tunneling protocols and standards are used in TCP/IP. SSH is one of the simplest types of tunnels so it's a great first exposure to tunneling. As the book progresses, you'll see more tunneling protocols, and you'll get the basics of tunneling. For now, make sure you understand that a tunnel is an encrypted connection between two endpoints. Any packet that enters the encrypted tunnel, including a packet with unencrypted data, is automatically encrypted, goes through the tunnel, and is decrypted on the other endpoint.

SSH may be popular, but it's not the only option for encryption. All of the other encryption standards are built into combined authentication/encryption standards, as covered in the next section.

Combining Authentication and Encryption

The rest of the popular authentication and encryption standards are combined to include both authentication and encryption in a single standard. Lumping together authentication and encryption into the same standard does not make it weaker than the standards already discussed. These are some of the most popular standards on the Internet today, because they offer excellent security.

SSL/TLS

The introduction and rapid growth of e-commerce on the World Wide Web in the mid-1990s made it painfully obvious that some form of authentication and encryption was needed. Netscape Corporation took the first shot at a new standard. At the time, the dominant Web browser was Netscape Navigator. Netscape created a standard called *Secure Sockets Layer (SSL)*. SSL requires a server with a certificate. When a client requests access to an SSL-secured server, the server sends to the client a copy of the certificate. The SSL client checks this certificate (all Web browsers come with an exhaustive list of CA root certificates preloaded), and if the certificate checks out, the server is authenticated and the client negotiates a symmetric-key cipher for use in the session (Figure 11-37). The session is now in a very secure encrypted tunnel between the SSL server and the SSL client.

Figure 11-37

SSL at work

NOTE SSL/TLS also supports mutual authentication, but this is relatively rare.

The *Transport Layer Security (TLS)* protocol was designed as an upgrade to SSL. TLS is very similar to SSL, working in almost the same way. TLS is more robust and flexible and works with just about any TCP application. SSL is limited to HTML, FTP, SMTP, and a few older TCP applications. TLS has no such restrictions and is used in securing Voice over IP (VoIP) and virtual private networks (VPNs), but it is still most heavily used in securing Web pages. Every Web browser today uses TLS for HTTPS-secured Web sites, and EAP-TLS is common for more-secure wireless networks.

EXAM TIP Developers have continued to refine TLS since the release of TLS 1.0 (SSL 3.1) in 1999. Each of the TLS versions is considered an upgrade from SSL 3.0, so you'll see both numbers listed. TLS 1.1 (SSL 3.2) was released in 2006. The most recent version is TLS 1.2 (SSL 3.3), released in 2008 and modified in 2011.

IPsec

Every authentication and encryption protocol and standard you've learned about so far works *above* the Network layer of the OSI seven-layer model. *Internet Protocol Security (IPsec)* is an authentication and encryption protocol suite that works at the Internet/Network layer and should become the dominant authentication and encryption protocol suite as IPv6 continues to roll out and replace IPv4. (See Chapter 13 for details on IPv6.)

 NOTE The *Internet Engineering Task Force (IETF)* specifies the IPsec protocol suite, managing updates and revisions. One of those specifications regards the acronym for the protocol suite, calling it *IPsec* with a lowercase "s" rather than IPS or IPSec, which you might imagine to be the initials or acronym. Go figure.

IPsec works in two different modes: Transport mode and Tunnel mode. In Transport mode, only the actual payload of the IP packet is encrypted: the destination and source IP addresses and other IP header information are still readable. In Tunnel mode, the entire IP packet is encrypted and then placed into an IPsec endpoint where it is encapsulated inside another IP packet. The mode you use depends on the application (Figure 11-38). IPv6 will use the IPsec Transport mode by default.

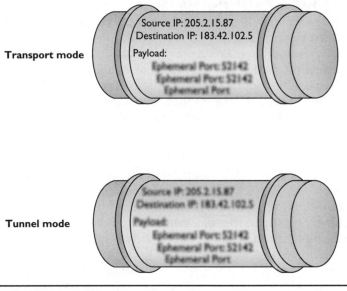

Figure 11-38 IPsec's two modes

The IPsec protocol suite uses many open source protocols to provide both tight authentication and robust encryption. You do not need to know how each of the protocols works for the CompTIA Network+ exam, but you should recognize which protocols function within IPsec. Here are the main protocols:

- *Authentication Header (AH)* for authentication
- *Encapsulating Security Payload (ESP)* for implementing authentication and encryption
- *Internet Security Association and Key Management Protocol (ISAKMP)* for establishing security associations (SAs) that define things like the protocol used for exchanging keys
- *Internet Key Exchange (IKE and IKEv2)* and *Kerberized Internet Negotiation of Keys (KINK)*, two widely used key exchanging protocols

Plus, IPsec can encrypt data using any number of encryption algorithms, such as MD5 and SHA that you read about earlier in this chapter.

IPsec is an incredibly powerful authentication/encryption protocol suite, but until IPv6 is widely implemented, its only common current use is creating secure tunnels between two computers: a job it performs very well. Keep an eye out for IPsec!

Secure TCP/IP Applications

I've covered quite a few TCP/IP security standards and protocols thus far in the chapter, but I really haven't put anything to work yet. Now is the time to talk about actual applications that use these tools to make secure connections. As mentioned earlier, this is in no way a complete list, as there are thousands of secure TCP applications; I'll stick to ones you will see on the CompTIA Network+ exam. Even within that group, I've saved discussion of some of the applications for other chapters that deal more directly with certain security aspects (such as remote connections).

HTTPS

You've already seen HTTPS back in Chapter 9, so let's do a quick review and then take the coverage a bit deeper. You know that HTTPS documents are unique pages that traditionally start with https:// and that most browsers also show a small lock icon in the lower-right corner or in the address bar. You also know that HTTPS uses SSL/TLS for the actual authentication and encryption process. In most cases, all of this works very well, but what do you do when HTTPS has trouble?

Since you won't get an HTTPS connection without a good certificate exchange, the most common problems are caused by bad certificates. When a certificate comes in from an HTTPS Web site, your computer checks the expiration date to verify the certificate is still valid and checks the Web site's URL to make sure it's the same as the site you are on. If either of these is not correct, you get an error such as the one shown in Figure 11-39.

Figure 11-39   Certificate problem

If you get one of these errors, you need to decide what to do. Good certificates do go bad (this even happened on my own Web site once) and sometimes the URLs on the certificates are not exactly the same as the site using them. When in doubt, stop. On the other hand, if the risk is low (for example, you're not entering a credit card number or other sensitive information) and you know and trust the site, proceeding is safe in most cases. A courtesy e-mail or phone call to the Web site administrator notifying him or her about the invalid certificate is usually greatly appreciated.

Invalid certificates aren't the only potential problems. After this basic check, the browser checks to see if the certificate has been revoked. Root authorities, like VeriSign, generate Certificate Revocation Lists (CRLs) that a Web browser can check against. Certificates are revoked for a number of reasons, but most of the time the reasons are serious, such as a hacked certificate. If you get a revoked certificate error, it's better to stay away from the site until they fix the problem.

SCP

One of the first SSH-enabled programs to appear after the introduction of SSH was *Secure Copy Protocol (SCP)*. SCP was one of the first protocols used to transfer data securely between two hosts and thus might have replaced FTP. SCP works well but lacks features such as a directory listing. SCP still exists, especially with the well-known UNIX scp command-line utility, but it has, for the most part, been replaced by the more powerful SFTP.

SFTP

Secure FTP (SFTP), also called *SSH FTP*, was designed as a replacement for FTP after many of the inadequacies of SCP (such as the inability to see the files on the other computer) were discovered. Although SFTP and FTP have similar names and perform the same job of transferring files, the way in which they do that job differs greatly.

The introduction of SSH made it easy to secure most TCP applications just by running them in an SSH tunnel. But FTP was a different case. FTP, at least active FTP, uses two ports, 20 and 21, creating a two-session communication. This makes FTP a challenge to run in its original form over SSH because SSH can only handle one session per tunnel. To fix this, a group of programmers from the OpenBSD organization developed a series of secure programs known collectively as *OpenSSH*. SFTP was one of those programs. SFTP looks like FTP, with servers and clients, but relies on an SSH tunnel. If you are on Windows and would like to connect with an SFTP server, WinSCP and FileZilla are two great client options.

SNMP

Simple Network Management Protocol (SNMP) is a very popular method for querying the state of SNMP-capable devices. SNMP can tell you a number of settings like CPU usage, network utilization, and detailed firewall hits. SNMP uses *agents* (special client programs) to collect network information from a *Management Information Base (MIB)*, SNMP's version of a server. To use SNMP, you need SNMP-capable devices and some tool to query them. One tool is Cacti (www.cacti.net), shown in Figure 11-40. Cacti, like most good SNMP tools, enables you to query an SNMP-capable device for hundreds of different types of information.

SNMP is a useful tool for network administrators, but the first version, SNMPv1, sent all data, including the passwords, unencrypted over the network. SNMPv2 had good encryption but was rather challenging to use. SNMPv3 is the standard version used today and combines solid, fairly easy-to-use authentication and encryption.

 NOTE SNMP runs on UDP port 161.

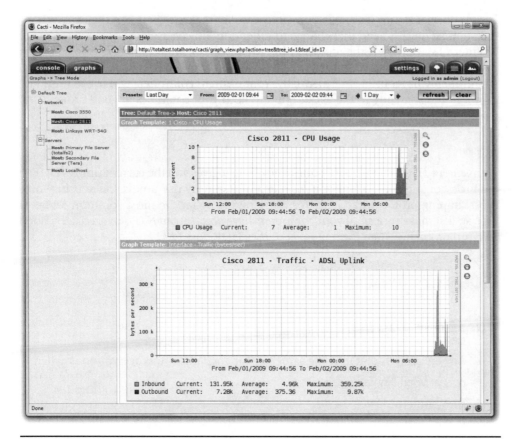

Figure 11-40   Cacti at work

LDAP

The *Lightweight Directory Access Protocol (LDAP)* is the tool that programs use to query and change a database used by the network. The network world is full of many different databases that are used in many different ways. I'm not talking about databases used by normal people to enter sales calls or to inventory trucks! These are databases used to track who is logged into the network, how many DHCP clients are currently DHCP active, or the location of all the printers in the local network.

One of the most complex and also most used databases is Windows Active Directory. Active Directory is the power behind single sign-on and network information (where's the closest printer to me?) and is the cornerstone of Windows' DNS implementation. Every Windows domain controller stores a copy of the Active Directory.

If a domain controller fails, another domain controller can and must instantly take over. To do this, every domain controller must have an identical copy of the Active

Directory. That means if a single domain controller makes a change to the Active Directory, it must quickly send that change to other domain controllers.

Enter LDAP. LDAP is the tool used in virtually every situation where one computer needs to access another computer's database for information or to make an update. You will probably never use LDAP manually. Your domain controllers will use it automatically and transparently in the background to keep your databases in good order. LDAP uses TCP port 389 by default.

NTP

The *Network Time Protocol (NTP)* does one thing: it gives you the current time. NTP is an old protocol and isn't in and of itself much of a security risk unless you're using some timestamping protocol like Kerberos. Windows is by far the most common Kerberos user, so just make sure all of your computers have access to an NTP server so users don't run into problems when logging in. NTP uses UDP port 123.

Chapter Review

Questions

1. Any encryption that uses the same key for encryption and decryption is called
   A. Encoded key
   B. Symmetric key
   C. Single key
   D. Synthetic key

2. RC4 is a(n) _____ cipher.
   A. Block
   B. Forwarding
   C. Stream
   D. Asymmetric

3. In a PKI encryption method, which key encrypts the data?
   A. Public
   B. Private
   C. Both
   D. Depends on who sends the data

4. The process of verifying with a high degree of confidence that the sender is who the receiver thinks he or she should be is called

   A. PKI

   B. Authentication

   C. Locking

   D. Nonrepudiation

5. A hash function is by definition

   A. A complex function

   B. A PKI function

   C. A one-way function

   D. A systematic function

6. Which of the following is a common hash function?

   A. MD5

   B. RC4

   C. AES

   D. BMX

7. In order to have a PKI infrastructure you must have a(n)

   A. Web server

   B. Web of trust

   C. Root authority

   D. Unsigned certificate

8. Which type of access control requires a label to define its sensitivity?

   A. MAC

   B. DAC

   C. RBAC

   D. VAC

9. If you saw some traffic running on UDP ports 1812 and 1813, what AAA standard would you know was running?

   A. PPP

   B. RADIUS

   C. MS-CHAP

   D. TACACS+

10. Which authentication standard is highly time sensitive?

   A. PAP

   B. RADIUS

   C. 802.1X

   D. Kerberos

Answers

1. **B.** Symmetric-key encryption uses the same key.

2. **C.** RC4 is a stream cipher.

3. **A.** You send someone a public key that he or she, in turn, encrypts. The private key decrypts it.

4. **D.** This is the definition of nonrepudiation.

5. **C.** Hash functions must be one-way. They should be complex but complexity is not a requirement.

6. **A.** Of the choices listed, only MD5 is a hash function.

7. **C.** A PKI infrastructure must have a root authority.

8. **A.** Mandatory access control must use a label to define sensitivity.

9. **B.** RADIUS uses UDP ports 1812 and 1813.

10. **D.** All Kerberos tickets are timestamped.

Advanced Networking Devices

The CompTIA Network+ certification exam expects you to know how to

- 1.2 Classify how applications, devices, and protocols relate to the OSI model layers: multilayer switch
- 1.4 Explain the purpose and properties of routing and switching: VLAN, port mirroring
- 2.1 Given a scenario, install and configure routers and switches: VLAN, managed vs. unmanaged, traffic filtering, VTP, QoS, port mirroring
- 2.5 Given a scenario, troubleshoot common router and switch problems: port configuration, VLAN assignment
- 3.5 Describe different network topologies: peer to peer, client/server
- 4.2 Explain the purpose and features of various network appliances: load balancer, proxy server, content filter, VPN concentrator
- 5.2 Explain the methods of network access security: SSL VPN, VPN, L2TP, PPTP, site-to-site, client-to-site
- 5.6 Categorize different types of network security appliances and methods: IDS and IPS

To achieve these goals, you must be able to

- Discuss client/server and peer-to-peer topologies
- Describe the features and functions of VPNs
- Configure and deploy VLANs
- Implement advanced switch features

So far in this book we've looked at simple network topologies and single-function devices. Ethernet networks employ a hybrid star-bus topology, for example, with a physical star and a logical bus. You have hubs humming along at Layer 1, switches at Layer 2, and routers at Layer 3, each performing heroic service. You have protocols functioning at the upper layers, enabling things like the Web and FTP.

When you zoom out from the network to the 30,000-foot view, network components take on one of several aspects. You have servers that dish out data and clients that access those servers. You have computers on networks that both serve and access data;

these are called peer-to-peer networks. You have connections between networks and connections from outside to inside a network.

This chapter starts with connection concepts, looking at classic and current uses of terms like client, server, and peer. The chapter then turns to virtual private networks, how businesses handle telecommuting, traveling employees, and multiple locations. The third part examines switches that can segment a network into multiple virtual networks. The chapter finishes with a discussion about multilayer switches—the boxes that do it all.

Client/Server and Peer-to-Peer Topologies

To share data and services, networks place computers or services into the category of *server*, the provider of such things. Other computers act as *clients*, the users of services. Many networks today blend the two roles, meaning each computer can both serve and request. Let's look at classic usage of client/server and peer-to-peer topologies, and then examine how the terms have changed in modern networking.

Historical/Conceptual

Client/Server

The earliest networks used a *client/server* model. In that model, certain systems acted as dedicated servers. Dedicated servers were called "dedicated" because that's all they did. You couldn't go up to a dedicated server and run Word or Solitaire. Dedicated servers ran powerful server network operating systems that offered up files, folders, Web pages, and so on to the network's client systems. Client systems on a client/server network never functioned as servers. One client system couldn't access shared resources on another client system. Servers served and clients accessed, and never the twain . . . crossed over . . . in the old days of client/server!

Figure 12-1 shows a typical client/server network. As far as the clients are concerned, the only system on the network is the server system. The clients can neither see each other, nor share data with each other directly. They must save the data on the server, so that other systems can access it.

Figure 12-1
A simple client/server network

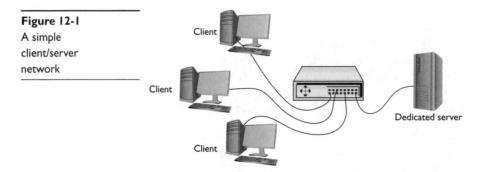

Client

Client

Client

Dedicated server

Back in the old days there was an operating system called Novell NetWare. Novell NetWare servers were true dedicated servers. You couldn't go up to a Novell NetWare server and write yourself a resume. There were no Windows or even user applications. The only thing Novell NetWare servers knew how to do was share their own resources, but they shared those resources extremely well! The Novell NetWare operating system was unique. It wasn't anything like Windows, Macintosh, or Linux. It required you to learn an entirely different set of installation, configuration, and administration commands. Figure 12-2 shows a screen from Novell NetWare. Don't let the passing resemblance to Windows fool you—it was a completely different operating system!

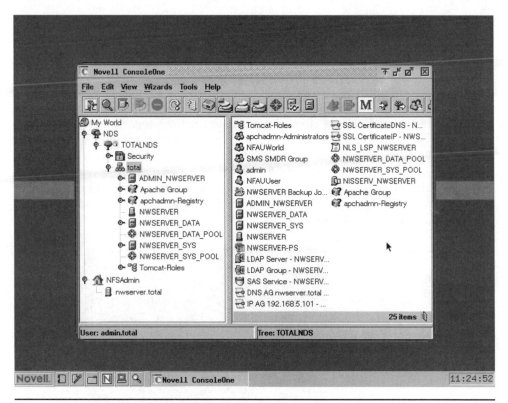

Figure 12-2 Novell NetWare in action

Dedicated servers enabled Novell to create an entire feature set not seen before on personal computers. Each dedicated server had its own database of user names and passwords. You couldn't access any of the resources on the server without logging in. The server's administrator would assign "permissions" to a specific user account, such as Write (add files to a directory), File Scan (see the contents of a directory), and Erase (delete files).

By keeping the server functionality separate from the client systems, the Novell folks made very powerful, dedicated servers without overwhelming the client computers with tons of software. This was, after all, in the early days of personal computers and they didn't have anything near the power of a modern PC.

NetWare servers had tremendous power and great security because the only thing they did was run server software. In the early days of networking, client/ server was king!

NOTE Novell NetWare as marketed today is a form of SUSE Linux. It is no longer a unique server-only operating system.

Peer-to-Peer

Novell NetWare was the first popular way to network PCs, but it wasn't too many years later that Microsoft introduced the first versions of network-capable Windows. The way in which these versions of Windows looked at networking, called peer-to-peer, was completely different from the client/server view of networking. In a *peer-to-peer* network, any system can act as a server, a client, or both, depending on how you configure that system. PCs on peer-to-peer networks frequently act as both clients and servers. One of the most common examples of a peer-to-peer network is the venerable Windows 9x series of operating systems. Figure 12-3 shows the sharing options for the ancient Windows 98 operating system, providing options to share a folder and thus turn that computer into a server.

Figure 12-3

Sharing options in Windows 98

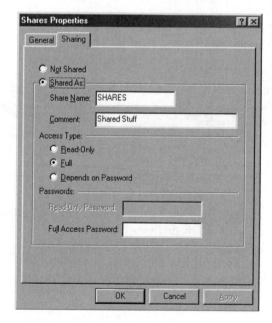

At first glance, it would seem that peer-to-peer is the way to go—why create a network that doesn't allow the clients to see each other? Wouldn't it make more sense to give users the freedom to allow their systems both to share and access any resource? The problem was a lack of security.

The early Windows systems did not have user accounts and the only permissions were Read Only and Full Control. So they made it easy to share but hard to control access to the shared resources. People wanted the freedom of peer-to-peer with the security of client/server.

 EXAM TIP The "old school" client/server model means dedicated servers with strong security. Clients see only the server. In the peer-to-peer model, any system is a client, server, or both, but at the cost of lower security and additional demands on the system resources of each peer.

Test Specific

Client/Server and Peer-to-Peer Today

In response to demand, every modern operating system has dumped the classic client/server or peer-to-peer label. Windows, Linux, and OS X all have the capability to act as a server or a client while also providing robust security through user accounts, permissions, and the like.

Since the widespread adoption of TCP/IP and the Internet, client/server and peer-to-peer have taken on new or updated definitions and refer more to *applications* than to network operating systems. Consider e-mail for a moment. For traditional e-mail to work, you need an e-mail client like Microsoft Outlook. But you also need an e-mail server program like Microsoft Exchange to handle the e-mail requests from your e-mail client. Outlook is a *dedicated client*—you cannot use the Outlook client as a mail-serving program. Likewise, you cannot use Microsoft Exchange as an e-mail client. Exchange is a *dedicated server* program.

Peer-to-peer applications, often referred to simply as *P2P*, act as both client and server. The best examples of these applications are the now infamous file-sharing applications based on special TCP/IP protocols. The applications, with names like BitTorrent, LimeWire, and DC++, act as both clients and servers, enabling a user to share files and access shared files. BitTorrent is actually an entire protocol, not just a particular application. Many different applications use the BitTorrent standard. Figure 12-4 shows one such program, μTorrent, in the process of simultaneously uploading and downloading files.

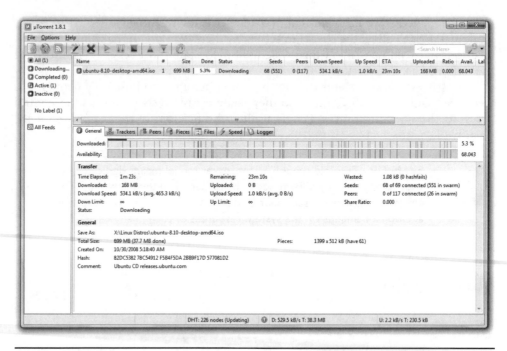

Figure 12-4   µTorrent downloading

The terms *server, client,* and *peer* manifest in another way when discussing connecting to a local network from a remote site or connecting two networks together so they function as if they're one network. Let's turn now to a technology that makes these connection types possible: *virtual private networks.*

Virtual Private Networks

Remote connections have been around for a long time, even before the Internet existed. The biggest drawback to remote connections was the cost to connect. If you were on one side of the continent and had to connect to your LAN on the other side of the continent, the only connection option was a telephone. Or if you needed to connect two LANs across the continent, you ended up paying outrageous monthly charges for a private connection. The introduction of the Internet gave people wishing to connect to their home networks a very inexpensive connection option, but there was one problem—the whole Internet was (and is) open to the public. People wanted to stop using dial-up and expensive private connections and use the Internet instead, but they wanted to be able to do it securely.

If you read the previous chapter, you might think you could use some of the tools for securing TCP/IP to help and you would be correct. Several standards use encrypted tunnels between a computer or a remote network and a private network through the Internet (Figure 12-5), resulting in what is called a *virtual private network (VPN)*.

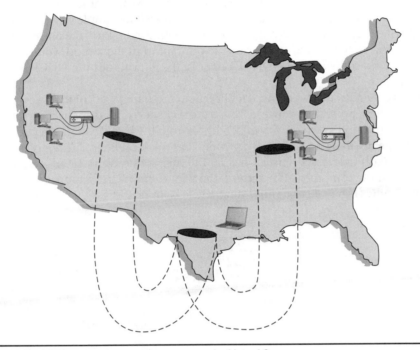

Figure 12-5 VPN connecting computers across the United States

As you saw in the previous chapter, an encrypted tunnel requires *endpoints*—the ends of the tunnel where the data is encrypted and decrypted. In the tunnels you've seen thus far, the client for the application sits on one end and the server sits on the other. VPNs do exactly the same thing. Either some software running on a computer or, in some cases, a dedicated box must act as an endpoint for a VPN (Figure 12-6).

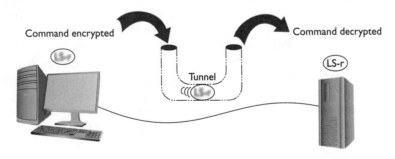

Figure 12-6 Typical tunnel

The key with the VPN is that all of the computers should be on the same network—and that means they must all have the same network ID. For example, you would want the laptop that you are using in an airport lounge to have the same network ID as all of the computers in your LAN back at the office. But there's no simple way to do this. If it's a single client trying to access a network, that client is going to take on the IP address from its local DHCP server. In the case of your laptop in the airport, your network ID and IP address come from the DHCP server in the airport, not the DHCP server back at the office.

To make the VPN work, you need a VPN client program protocol that uses one of the many tunneling protocols available. This remote client connects to the local LAN via its Internet connection, querying for an IP address from the local DHCP server. In this way, the VPN client will be on the same network ID as the local LAN. The remote computer now has two IP addresses. First, it has its Internet connection's IP address, obtained from the remote computer's ISP. Second, the VPN client creates a tunnel endpoint that acts like a NIC (Figure 12-7). This virtual NIC has an IP address that connects it to the local LAN.

Figure 12-7

Endpoints must have their own IP addresses.

Clever network engineers have come up with many ways to make this work, and those implementations function at different layers of the TCP/IP model. PPTP and L2TP, for example, work at the Link layer. Many VPNs use IPsec at the Internet layer to handle encryption needs. SSL VPNs work at the Application layer.

PPTP VPNs

So how do you make IP addresses appear out of thin air? What tunneling protocol have you learned about that has the smarts to query for an IP address? That's right! Good old PPP! Microsoft got the ball rolling with the *Point-to-Point Tunneling Protocol (PPTP)*, an advanced version of PPP that handles this right out of the box. The only trick is the endpoints. In Microsoft's view, a VPN is intended for individual clients to connect to a private network, so Microsoft places the PPTP endpoints on the client and the server. The server endpoint is a special remote access server program, originally only available on Windows Server, called *Routing and Remote Access Service (RRAS)* on the server—see Figure 12-8.

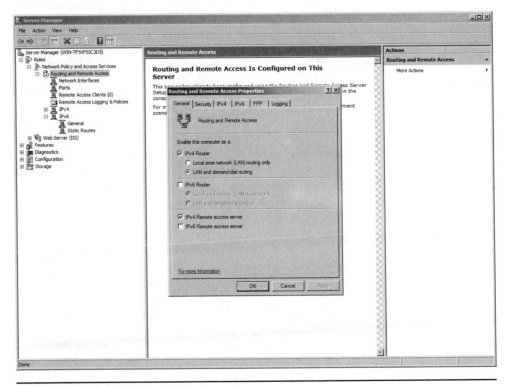

Figure 12-8 RRAS in action

On the Windows client side, you run **Create a New Connection**. This creates a virtual NIC that, like any other NIC, does a DHCP query and gets an IP address from the DHCP server on the private network (Figure 12-9).

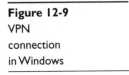

Figure 12-9
VPN
connection
in Windows

EXAM TIP A system connected to a VPN looks as though it's on the local network, but performs much slower than if the system was connected directly back at the office because it's not local at all.

When your computer connects to the RRAS server on the private network, PPTP creates a secure tunnel through the Internet back to the private LAN. Your client takes on an IP address of that network, as if your computer is directly connected to the LAN back at the office, even down to the default gateway. If you open your Web browser, your client will go across the Internet to the local LAN and then use the LAN's default gateway to get to the Internet! Using a Web browser will be much slower when you are on a VPN. Every operating system comes with some type of built-in VPN client that supports PPTP (among others). Figure 12-10 shows Network, the Mac OS X VPN connection tool.

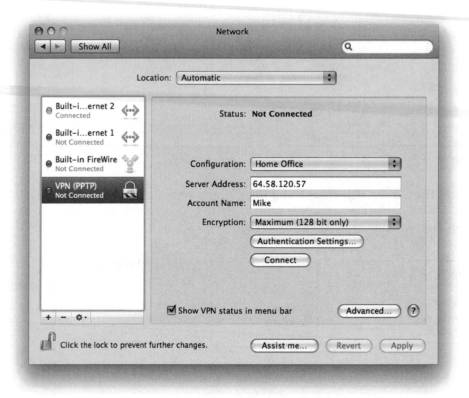

Figure 12-10 VPN on a Macintosh OS X system

This type of VPN connection, where a single computer logs into a remote network and becomes, for all intents and purposes, a member of that network, is commonly called a *client-to-site* connection.

L2TP VPNs

Microsoft pushed the idea of a single client tunneling into a private LAN using software. Cisco, being the router king that it is, came up with its own VPN protocol called *Layer 2 Tunneling Protocol (L2TP)*. L2TP took all the good features of PPTP and L2F and added support to run on almost any type of connection possible, from telephones to Ethernet to ultra-high-speed optical connections. Cisco also moved the endpoint on the local LAN from a server program to a VPN-capable router, called a *VPN concentrator*, such as the Cisco 2811 Integrated Services Router shown in Figure 12-11.

 EXAM TIP   Cisco made hardware that supported PPP traffic using a proprietary protocol called *Layer 2 Forwarding (L2F)*. L2F did not come with encryption capabilities, so it was replaced by L2TP a long time ago. You'll sometimes see the term on the CompTIA Network+ exam as an incorrect answer.

Figure 12-11
Cisco 2811
Integrated
Services Router

Cisco provides free client software to connect a single faraway PC to a Cisco VPN. This creates a typical client-to-site connection. Network people often directly connect two Cisco VPN concentrators to connect two separate LANs permanently. It's slow, but inexpensive, compared to a dedicated high-speed connection between two faraway LANs. This kind of connection enables two separate LANs to function as a single network, sharing files and services as if in the same building. This is called a *site-to-site* VPN connection.

L2TP differs from PPTP in that it has no authentication or encryption. L2TP generally uses IPsec for all security needs. Technically, you should call an L2TP VPN an "L2TP/IPsec" VPN. L2TP works perfectly well in the single-client-connecting-to-a-LAN world, too. Every operating system's VPN client fully supports L2TP/IPsec VPNs.

 NOTE   The years have seen plenty of crossover between Microsoft and Cisco. Microsoft RRAS supports L2TP, and Cisco routers support PPTP.

SSL VPNs

Cisco has made a big push for companies to adopt VPN hardware that enables VPNs using Secure Sockets Layer (SSL). These types of VPN work at the Application layer and offer an advantage over Link- or Internet-based VPNs because they don't require any special client software. Clients connect to the VPN server using a standard Web browser, with the traffic secured using SSL. The two most common types of *SSL VPNs* are SSL portal VPNs and SSL tunnel VPNs.

NOTE Many VPN connections use the terms *client* and *server* to denote the functions of the devices that make the connection. You'll also see the terms *host* and *gateway* to refer to the connections, such as a *host-to-gateway tunnel.*

With SSL portal VPNs, a client accesses the VPN and is presented with a secure Web page. The client gains access to anything linked on that page, be it e-mail, data, links to other pages, and so on.

With tunnel VPNs, in contrast, the client Web browser runs some kind of active control, such as Java or Flash, and gains much greater access to the VPN-connected network. SSL tunnel VPNs create a more typical client-to-site connection than SSL portal VPNs, but the user must have sufficient permissions to run the active browser controls.

NOTE There are other VPN options to PPTP, L2TP, and SSL, and some of them are quite popular. First is OpenVPN, which, like the rest of what I call "OpenXXX" applications, uses Secure Shell (SSH) for the VPN tunnel. Second is IPsec. The tech world is now seeing some pure (no L2TP) IPsec solutions that use IPsec tunneling for VPNs, such as Cisco Easy VPN.

Virtual LANs

Today's LANs are complex places. It's rare to see any serious network that doesn't have remote incoming connections, public Web or e-mail servers, wireless networks, as well as the basic string of connected switches. Leaving all of these different features on a single broadcast domain creates a tremendous amount of broadcast traffic and creates a security nightmare. You could separate the networks with multiple switches and put routers in between, but that's very inflexible and hard to manage. What if you could segment the network using the switches you already own? You can, and that's what a *virtual local area network (VLAN)* enables you to do.

To create a VLAN, you take a single physical broadcast domain and chop it up into multiple virtual broadcast domains. VLANs require special switches loaded with extra programming to create the virtual networks. Imagine a single switch with a number of computers connected to it. Up to this point, a single switch is always a single broadcast domain, but that's about to change. You've decided to take this single switch and turn it into two VLANs. VLANs typically get the name "VLAN" plus a number, like VLAN1 or VLAN275. The devices usually start at 1 although there's no law or rules on the numbering. In this example, I'll configure the ports on my single switch to be in one of two VLANs—VLAN1 or VLAN2 (Figure 12-12). I promise to show you how to configure ports for different VLANs shortly, but I've got a couple of other concepts to hit first.

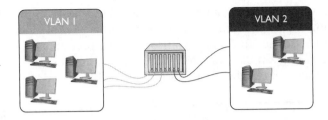

Figure 12-12

Switch with
two VLANs

 NOTE There is a VLAN0. This is the default VLAN. When you buy a new VLAN-capable switch and plug it in, every port on that switch is preset to VLAN0.

Figure 12-12 shows a switch configured to assign individual ports to VLANs. But there's another way to use VLANs that's supported by most VLAN-capable switches. Instead of assigning ports to a VLAN, you can assign MAC addresses to determine VLAN membership. A computer in this type of VLAN is always a member of the same VLAN no matter which port you plug the computer into on the switch.

A single switch configured into two VLANs is the simplest form of VLAN possible. More serious networks usually have more than one switch. Let's say you added a switch to a simple network. You'd like to keep VLAN1 and VLAN2 but use both switches. You can configure the new switch to use VLAN1 and VLAN2, but you've got to enable data to flow between the two switches, regardless of VLAN. That's where trunking comes into play.

Trunking

Trunking is the process of transferring VLAN traffic between two or more switches. Imagine two switches, each configured with a VLAN1 and a VLAN2, as shown in Figure 12-13.

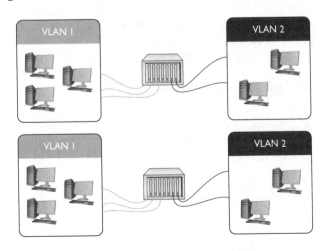

Figure 12-13

Two switches,
each with a
VLAN1 and
a VLAN2

You want all of the computers connected to VLAN1 on one switch to talk to all of the computers connected to VLAN1 on the other switch. Of course, you want to do this with VLAN2 also. To do this, you configure a port on each switch as a trunk port. A *trunk port* is a port on a switch configured to carry all traffic, regardless of VLAN number, between all switches in a LAN (Figure 12-14).

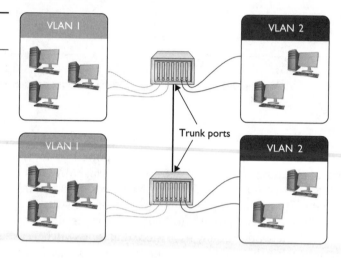

Figure 12-14
Trunk ports

In the early days of VLANs, every switch manufacturer had its own way to make VLANs work. Cisco, for example, had a proprietary form of trunking called Inter-Switch Link (ISL), which most Cisco switches still support. Today, every Ethernet switch prefers the IEEE 802.1Q trunk standard that enables you to connect switches from different manufacturers.

Configuring a VLAN-capable Switch

If you want to configure a VLAN-capable switch, you need a method to perform that configuration. One method uses a serial (console) port like the one described in Chapter 3, but the most common method is to access the switch with a Web browser interface, like the one shown in Figure 12-15. Catalyst is a model name for a series of popular Cisco routers with advanced switching features. Any switch that you can access and configure is called a *managed switch*.

NOTE The simple switches you've seen prior to this haven't had any configuration capability (aside from giving you a button to enable or disable an uplink port). These simple switches are called *unmanaged switches*.

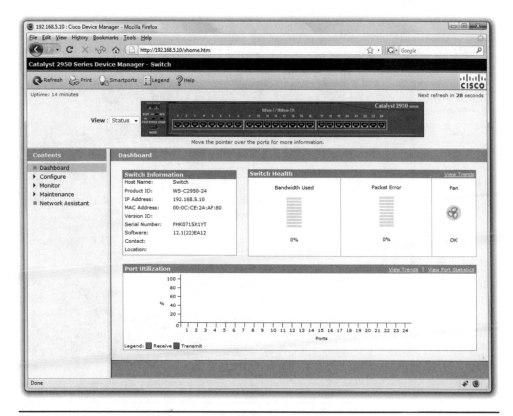

Figure 12-15 Catalyst 2950 Series Device Manager

So if you're giving the switch a Web interface, that means the switch needs an IP address—but don't switches use MAC addresses? They do, but managed switches also come with an IP address for configuration. A brand-new managed switch out of the box invariably has a preset IP address similar to the preset, private IP addresses you see on routers. This IP address isn't for any of the individual ports, but rather is for the whole switch. That means no matter where you physically connect to the switch, the IP address to get to the configuration screen is the same.

Every switch manufacturer has its own interface for configuring VLANs, but the interface shown in Figure 12-16 is a classic example. This is Cisco Network Assistant, a very popular tool that enables you to configure multiple devices through the same interface. Note that you first must define your VLANs.

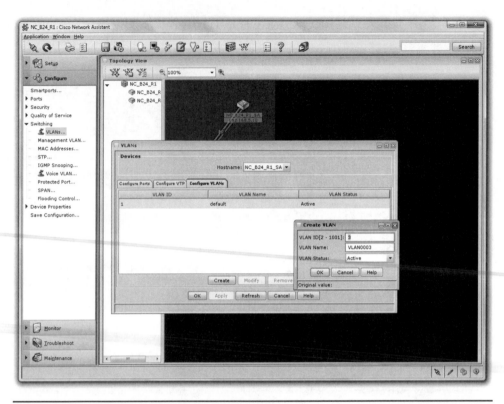

Figure 12-16   Defining VLANs in Cisco Network Assistant

After you create the VLANs, you usually either assign computers' MAC addresses to VLANs or assign ports to VLANs. Assigning MAC addresses means that no matter where you plug in a computer, it is always part of the same VLAN—a very handy feature for mobile users! Assigning each port to a VLAN means that whatever computer plugs into that port, it will always be a member of that port's VLAN. Figure 12-17 shows a port being assigned to a particular VLAN.

 NOTE   VLANs based on ports are the most common type of VLAN and are commonly known as *static VLANs*. VLANs based on MAC addresses are called *dynamic VLANs*.

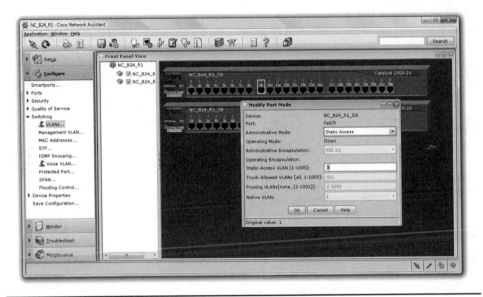

Figure 12-17   Assigning a port to a VLAN

Virtual Trunk Protocol

A busy network with many VLAN switches can require periods of intensive work to update. Imagine the work required to redo all the VLAN switches if you changed the VLAN configuration by adding or removing a VLAN. You'd have to access every switch individually, changing the port configuration to alter the VLAN assignment, and so on. The potential for errors is staggering. What if you missed updating one switch? Joe in Sales might wrongly have access to a sensitive accounting server or Phyllis in accounting might not be able to get her job done on time.

Cisco uses a proprietary protocol called *Virtual Trunk Protocol (VTP)* to automate the updating of multiple VLAN switches. With VTP, you put each switch into one of three states: server, client, or transparent. When you make changes to the VLAN configuration of the server switch, all the connected client switches update their configurations within minutes. The big job of changing every switch manually just went away.

When you set a VLAN switch to transparent, you tell it not to update but to hold onto its manual settings. You would use a transparent mode VLAN switch in circumstances where the overall VLAN configuration assignments did not apply.

InterVLAN Routing

Once you've configured a switch to support multiple VLANs, each VLAN is its own broadcast domain, just as if the two VLANs were on two completely separate switches and networks. There is no way for data to get from one VLAN to another unless you use a router. The process of making a router work between two VLANs is called *interVLAN routing*. In the early days of interVLAN routing, you commonly used a router with multiple ports as a backbone for the network. Figure 12-18 shows one possible way to connect two VLANs with a single router. Note that the router has one port connected to VLAN 100 and another connected to VLAN 200. Devices on VLAN 100 may now communicate with devices on VLAN 200.

Figure 12-18
One router connecting multiple VLANs

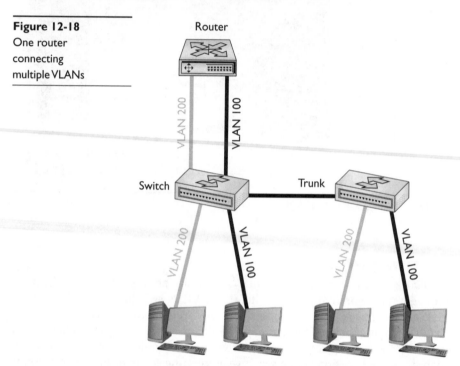

Adding a physical router like this isn't a very elegant way to connect VLANs. This forces almost all traffic to go through the router, and it's not a very flexible solution if you want to add more VLANs in the future. As a result, all but the simplest VLANs have at least one very special switch that has the ability to make virtual routers. Figure 12-19 shows an older but very popular interVLAN routing–capable switch, the Cisco 3550.

Figure 12-19
Cisco 3550

From the outside, the Cisco 3550 looks like any other switch. On the inside, it's an incredibly powerful and flexible device that not only supports VLANs, but also enables you to create virtual routers to interconnect these VLANs. Figure 12-20 shows the configuration screen for the 3550's interVLAN routing between two VLANs.

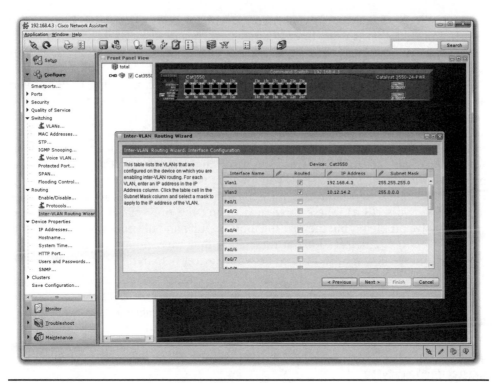

Figure 12-20 Setting up interVLAN routing

If the Cisco 3550 is a switch but also has built-in routers, on what layer of the OSI seven-layer model does it operate? If it's a switch, then it works at Layer 2. But it also has the capability to create virtual routers, and routers work at Layer 3. This isn't an ordinary switch. The Cisco 3550 works at both Layers 2 and 3 at the same time.

Multilayer Switches

The Cisco 3550 is an amazing box in that it seems to defy the entire concept of a switch because of its support of interVLAN routing. Up to this point, I've said a switch works at Layer 2 of the OSI model, but now you've just seen a very powerful (and expensive) switch that clearly also works at Layer 3. The Cisco 3550 is one example of what we call a *multilayer switch*.

At this point you must stop thinking that a switch always works at Layer 2. Instead, think of the idea that any device that forwards traffic based on anything inside a given packet is a switch. A Layer 2 switch forwards traffic based on MAC addresses, whereas a Layer 3 switch (also called a router) forwards traffic based on IP addresses. From here on out, I will carefully address at what layer of the OSI seven-layer model a switch operates.

The challenge to multilayer switches comes with the ports. On a classic Layer 2–only switch, individual ports don't have IP addresses. They don't need them. On a router, however, every port must have an IP address because the routing table uses the IP address to determine where to send packets.

A multilayer switch needs some option or feature for configuring ports to work at Layer 2 or Layer 3. Cisco uses the terms *switchport* and *router port* to differentiate between the two types of port. You can configure any port on a multilayer switch to act as a switchport or a router port, depending on your needs. Multilayer switches are incredibly common and support a number of interesting features, clearly making them part of what I call "advanced networking devices" and what CompTIA calls "specialized network devices." I'm going to show you three areas where multilayer switches are very helpful: load balancing, quality of service, and network protection (each term is defined in its respective section). These three areas aren't the only places where multilayer switches solve problems, but they are the most popular and the ones that the CompTIA Network+ exam covers. Let's look at these areas that are common to more advanced networks and see how more advanced network devices help in these situations.

NOTE Any device that works at multiple layers of the OSI seven-layer model, providing more than a single service, is called a *multifunction network device*.

Load Balancing

Popular Internet servers are exactly that—popular. So popular that a single system cannot possibly support the thousands, if not millions, of requests per day that bombard them. But from what you've learned thus far about servers, you know that a single server has a single IP address. Put this to the test. Go to a command prompt and type **ping www.google.com**.

```
C:\>ping www.google.com

Pinging www.1.google.com [74.125.95.147] with 32 bytes of data:
Reply from 74.125.95.147: bytes=32 time=71ms TTL=242
Reply from 74.125.95.147: bytes=32 time=71ms TTL=242
Reply from 74.125.95.147: bytes=32 time=70ms TTL=242
Reply from 74.125.95.147: bytes=32 time=70ms TTL=242
```

Getting a definite number is somewhat difficult, but by poking around on a few online analysis Web sites like Alexa (www.alexa.com), it seems that www.google.com receives around 130 to 140 million requests per day; that's about 1600 requests per second. Each request might require the Web server to deliver thousands of HTTP segments. A single, powerful, dedicated Web server (arguably) handles at best 2000 requests/second. A busy Web site often needs more than one Web server to handle all the requests. Let's say a Web site needs three servers to handle the traffic. How does that one Web site, using three different servers, use a single IP address? The answer is found in something called *load balancing*.

NOTE Coming to a consensus on statistics like the number of requests/day or how many requests a single server can handle is difficult. Just concentrate on the concept. If some nerdy type says your numbers are way off, nicely agree and walk away. Just don't invite them to any parties.

Load balancing means making a bunch of servers look like a single server, creating a *server cluster*. Not only do you need to make them look like one server, you need to make sure that requests to these servers are distributed evenly so no one server is bogged down while another is idle. There are a few ways to do this, as you are about to see. Be warned, not all of these methods require an advanced network device called a *load balancer*, but it's common to use one. Employing a device designed to do one thing really well is always much faster than using a general-purpose computer and slapping on software.

DNS Load Balancing

Using DNS for load balancing is one of the oldest and still very common ways to support multiple Web servers. In this case, each Web server gets its own (usually) public IP address. Each DNS server for the domain has multiple "A" DNS records, each with the same fully qualified domain name (FQDN). The DNS server then cycles around these records so the same domain name resolves to different IP addresses. Figure 12-21 shows a Windows DNS server with multiple A records for the same FQDN.

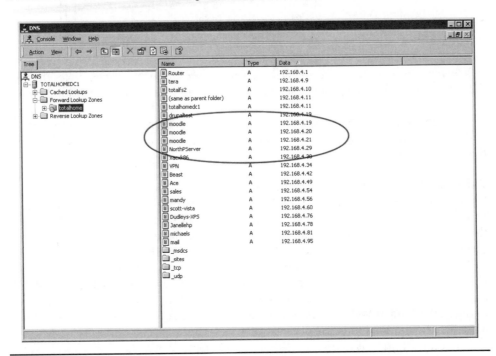

Figure 12-21   Multiple IP addresses, same name

Now that the A records have been added, you need to tell the DNS server to cycle around these names. With Windows DNS Server, you'll select a check box to do this, as shown in Figure 12-22.

Figure 12-22

Enabling round robin

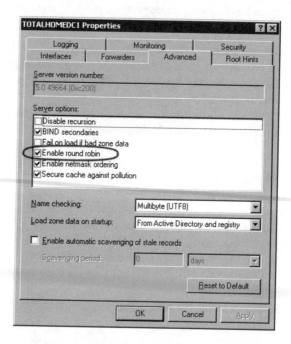

When a computer comes to the DNS server for resolution, the server cycles through the DNS A records, giving out first one and then the next in a cyclic (round robin) fashion.

The popular BIND DNS server has a very similar process but adds even more power and features such as weighting one or more servers more than others or randomizing the DNS response.

Using a Multilayer or Content Switch

DNS is an easy way to load balance, but it still relies on multiple DNS servers, each with its own IP address. As Web clients access one DNS server or another, they cache that DNS server's IP address. The next time they access the server, they go directly to the cached DNS server and skip the round robin, reducing its effectiveness.

To hide all of your Web servers behind a single IP, you have two popular choices. First is to use a special multilayer switch that works at Layers 3 and 4. This switch is really just a router that performs NAT and port forwarding, but also has the capability to query the hidden Web servers continually and send HTTP requests to a server that has a lighter workload than the other servers.

The second option is to use a *content switch*. Content switches always work at Layer 7 (Application layer). Content switches designed to work with Web servers, therefore, are able to read the incoming HTTP and HTTPS requests. With this, you can perform very advanced actions, such as handling SSL certificates and cookies, on the content switch, removing the workload from the Web servers. Not only can these devices load balance in the ways previously described, but their HTTP savvy can actually pass a cookie to HTTP requesters—Web browsers—so the next time that client returns, it is sent to the same server (Figure 12-23).

Figure 12-23 Layer 7 content switch	

 EXAM TIP The CompTIA Network+ exam refers to a content switch as a *content filter* network appliance.

QoS and Traffic Shaping

Just about any router you buy today has the capability to block packets based on port number or IP address, but these are simple mechanisms mainly designed to protect an internal network. What if you need to control how much of your bandwidth is used for certain devices or applications? In that case, you need *quality of service (QoS)* policies to prioritize traffic based on certain rules. These rules control how much bandwidth a protocol, PC, user, VLAN, or IP address may use (Figure 12-24).

On many advanced routers and switches, you can implement QoS through bandwidth management, such as *traffic shaping* where you control the flow of packets into or out of the network according to the type of packet or other rules.

 EXAM TIP The CompTIA Network+ exam uses the generic term *traffic filtering*, which means *traffic shaping*—the filtering of traffic based on type of packet or other rules.

Traffic shaping is very important when you must guarantee a device or application a certain amount of bandwidth and/or latency, such as with VoIP or video. Traffic shaping is also very popular in places such as schools, where IT professionals need to control user activities, such as limiting HTTP usage or blocking certain risky applications such as peer-to-peer file sharing.

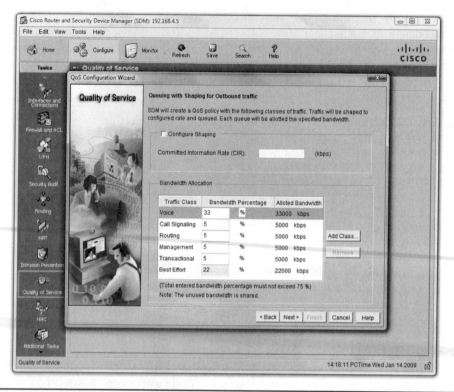

Figure 12-24 QoS configuration on a router

 EXAM TIP The term *bandwidth shaping* is synonymous with *traffic shaping*. The routers and switches that can implement traffic shaping are commonly referred to as *shapers*. The CompTIA Network+ exam refers to such devices as *bandwidth shapers*.

Network Protection

The last area where you're likely to encounter advanced networking devices is network protection. *Network protection* is my term to describe four different areas that CompTIA feels fit under the term *specialized network devices*:

- Intrusion protection/intrusion detection
- Port mirroring
- Proxy serving
- Port authentication

Intrusion Detection/Intrusion Prevention

Intrusion detection and intrusion prevention are very similar to the processes used to protect networks from intrusion and to detect that something has intruded into a network. Odds are good you've heard the term *firewall.* Firewalls are hardware or software tools that block traffic based on port number or IP address. A traditional firewall is a static tool: it cannot actually detect an attack. An *intrusion detection system (IDS)* is an application (often running on a dedicated IDS box) that inspects incoming packets, looking for active intrusions. A good IDS knows how to find attacks that no firewall can find, such as viruses, illegal logon attempts, and other well-known attacks. An IDS always has some way to let the network administrators know if an attack is taking place: at the very least the attack is logged, but some IDSs offer a pop-up message, an e-mail, or even a text message to your phone.

Third-party IDS tools, on the other hand, tend to act in a much more complex and powerful way. You have two choices with a real IDS: network based or host based. A *network-based IDS (NIDS)* consists of multiple sensors placed around the network, often on one or both sides of the gateway router. These sensors report to a central application that, in turn, reads a signature file to detect anything out of the ordinary (Figure 12-25).

Figure 12-25

Diagram of network-based IDS

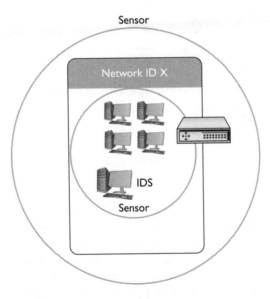

A *host-based IDS (HIDS)* is software running on individual systems that monitors for events such as system file modification or registry changes (Figure 12-26). More expensive third-party system IDSs do all this and add the ability to provide a single reporting source—very handy when one person is in charge of anything that goes on throughout a network.

Figure 12-26 OSSEC HIDS

A well-protected network uses both a NIDS and a HIDS. A NIDS monitors the incoming and outgoing traffic from the Internet whereas the HIDS monitors the individual computers.

 EXAM TIP The CompTIA Network+ exam can refer to an IDS system by either its location on the network—thus NIDS or HIDS—or by what the IDS system does in each location. The network-based IDS scans using signature files, thus it is a *signature-based IDS*. A host-based IDS watches for suspicious behavior on systems, thus it is a *behavior-based IDS*.

An *intrusion prevention system (IPS)* is very similar to an IDS, but an IPS adds the capability to react to an attack. Depending on what IPS product you choose, an IPS can block incoming packets on-the-fly based on IP address, port number, or application type. An IPS might go even further, literally fixing certain packets on-the-fly. As you might suspect, you can roll out an IPS on a network and it gets a new name: a *network intrusion prevention system (NIPS)*.

EXAM TIP The CompTIA Network+ exam refers to intrusion detection and prevention systems collectively by their initials, *IDS/IPS*.

Port Mirroring

Hubs may be obsolete, but they had one aspect that made them awfully handy: you could plug into a hub and see everybody's traffic. With switches now the way to connect, you no longer have a way to see any traffic other than traffic directed at the NIC and broadcasts. But if you have the right switch, you can get this capability back.

IDS/IPS often takes advantage of something called *port mirroring*. Many advanced switches have the capability to mirror data from any or all physical ports on a switch to a single physical port. It's as though you make a customized, fully configurable promiscuous port. Port mirroring is incredibly useful for any type of situation where an administrator needs to inspect packets coming to or from certain computers.

Proxy Serving

A *proxy server* sits in between clients and external servers, essentially pocketing the requests from the clients for server resources and making those requests itself. The client computers never touch the outside servers and thus stay protected from any unwanted activity. A proxy server usually *does something* to those requests as well. Let's see how proxy servers work using HTTP, one of the oldest uses of proxy servers.

Since proxy serving works by redirecting client requests to a proxy server, you first must tell the Web client not to use the usual DNS resolution to determine the Web server and instead to use a proxy. Every Web client comes with a program that enables you to set the IP address of the proxy server, as shown in the example in Figure 12-27.

Figure 12-27
Setting a proxy server in Mozilla Firefox

Once the proxy server is configured, HTTP requests move from the client directly to the proxy server. Built into every HTTP request is the URL of the target Web server, so the Web proxy knows where to get the requested data once it gets the request. In the simplest format, the proxy server simply forwards the requests using its own IP address and then forwards the returning packets to the client (Figure 12-28).

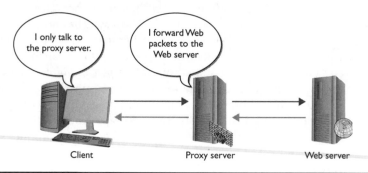

Client   Proxy server   Web server

Figure 12-28   Web proxy at work

This simple version of using a proxy server prevents the Web server from knowing where the client is located—a handy trick for those who wish to keep people from knowing where they are coming from, assuming you can find a public proxy server that accepts your HTTP requests (there are plenty!). There are many other good reasons to use a proxy server. One big benefit is caching. A proxy server keeps a copy of the served resource, giving clients a much faster response.

NOTE   If a proxy server caches a Web page, how does it know if the cache accurately reflects the real page? What if the real Web page was updated? In this case, a good proxy server uses querying tools to check the real Web page to update the cache.

A proxy server might inspect the contents of the resource, looking for inappropriate content, viruses/malware, or just about anything else the creators of the proxy might desire it to identify.

HTTP proxy servers are the most common type of proxy server, but any TCP application can take advantage of proxy servers. Numerous proxy serving programs are available, such as Squid, shown in Figure 12-29. Proxy serving takes some substantial processing, so many vendors sell proxy servers in a box, such as the Blue Coat ProxySG 510.

Port Authentication

The last place where you see advanced networking devices is in port authentication. We've already covered the concept in the previous chapter: *port authentication* is a critical component for any AAA authentication method, in particular RADIUS, TACACS+, and 802.1X. When you make a connection, you must have something at the point of connection to make the authentication, and that's where advanced networking devices come into play. Many switches, and almost every wireless access point, come with feature sets to support port authentication. A superb example is my own Cisco 2811 router. It supports RADIUS and 802.1X port authentication, as shown in Figure 12-30.

Figure 12-29   Squid Proxy Server software

Figure 12-30   802.1X configuration on a Cisco 2811

Chapter Review

Questions

1. Which of the following operating systems was designed for a pure client/server environment?

   A. Microsoft Windows NT

   B. NeXTSTEP

   C. Novell NetWare

   D. Linux

2. BitTorrent is an example of what kind of logical network topology?

   A. Peer-to-peer

   B. Client/server

   C. Multinode

   D. Server-to-server

3. Which of the following is a protocol popular with Cisco VPNs?

   A. PPTP

   B. L2TP

   C. IPsec

   D. PPPoE

4. A static VLAN assigns VLANs to

   A. IP addresses

   B. MAC addresses

   C. Ports

   D. Trunks

5. Which of the following is the most common trunking protocol used in today's VLANs?

   A. 802.1Q

   B. 802.1X

   C. 802.1t

   D. 802.1z

6. A content switch always works at least at which layer of the OSI model?

   A. 2

   B. 3

   C. 4

   D. 7

7. When the network is very busy, VoIP calls start to sound badly clipped. What solution might improve the quality of the VoIP calls?

   A. 802.1z

   B. Traffic shaping

   C. DNS

   D. Content switching

8. What is the main difference between an IDS and an IPS?

   A. An IPS documents intrusion.

   B. An IPS is always a stand-alone box.

   C. An IPS reacts to an attack.

   D. An IPS uses port mirroring.

9. What are the benefits of caching on a Web proxy? (Select two.)

   A. Response time

   B. Virus detection

   C. Tracking

   D. Authentication

10. 802.1X is a great example of

   A. Encryption

   B. Content switching

   C. Port authentication

   D. VLAN trunking

Answers

1. **C.** The venerable NetWare defined the original concept of client/server.

2. **A.** BitTorrent uses a peer-to-peer logical network topology.

3. **B.** Cisco invented and champions the L2TP VPN protocol.

4. **C.** Static VLANs assign VLANs to physical ports.

5. **A.** The 802.1Q standard is almost universal for VLAN trunking.

6. **D.** Content switches usually work at Layers 4 through 7, but they must work at least at Layer 7.

7. **B.** Traffic shaping will provide extra bandwidth to the VoIP applications, improving sound quality.

8. **C.** An IPS reacts to an attack. An IDS does not.

9. **A and B.** Cached Web pages can be sent to clients quickly. The contents can also be checked for viruses.

10. **C.** 802.1X uses port authentication.

IPv6

The CompTIA Network+ certification exam expects you to know how to

- 1.2 Classify how applications, devices, and protocols relate to the OSI model layers: EUI-64
- 1.3 Explain the purpose and properties of IP addressing: IPv4 vs. IPv6

To achieve these goals, you must be able to

- Discuss the fundamental concepts of IPv6
- Describe IPv6 practices
- Implement IPv6 in a TCP/IP network

The Internet developers wanted to make a networking protocol that had serious longevity, so they had to define a large enough IP address space to last well beyond the foreseeable future. They had to determine how many computers might exist in the future and then make the IP address space even bigger. But how many computers would exist in the future? Keep in mind that TCP/IP development took place in the early 1970s. There were less than 1000 computers in the entire world at the time, but that didn't keep the IP framers from thinking big! They decided to go absolutely crazy (as many people considered at the time) and around 1979 created the *Internet Protocol version 4 (IPv4)* 32-bit IP address space, creating about 4 billion IP addresses. That should have held us for the foreseeable future!

It hasn't. First, the TCP/IP folks wasted huge chunks of IP addresses due to classful addressing and a generally easygoing, wasteful method of parceling out IP addresses. Second, the Internet reached a level of popularity way beyond the original framers' imagination. By the mid-1980s, the rate of consumption for IP addresses started to worry the Internet people and the writing was on the wall for IPv4's 32-bit addressing. As a result, the Internet Engineering Task Force (IETF) developed a new IP addressing scheme called *Internet Protocol version 6 (IPv6)*, which is slowly replacing IPv4. IPv6 extends the 32-bit IP address space to 128 bits, allowing up to 2^{128} (that's close to 3.4×10^{38}) addresses. Take all the grains of sand on earth and that will give you an idea of how big a number that is! That should hold us for the foreseeable future!

 NOTE If you really want to know how many IP addresses IPv6 provides, here's your number: 340,282,366,920,938,463,463,374, 607,431,768,211,456.

But IPv6 isn't just about expanding the IP address space. IPv6 also improves security by making the Internet Protocol Security (IPsec) protocol support a standard part of every IPv6 stack. That doesn't mean you actually have to use IPsec, just that manufacturers must support it. If you use IPsec, every packet sent from your system is encrypted, opening the possibility that IPv6 would eliminate most (but not all) of the many encryption methods currently in use today.

IPv6 also provides a more efficient routing scheme. Taking advantage of aggregation (see the section "Aggregation," later in this chapter), routing tables should shrink dramatically, enabling fast routing.

It's taking a while, but IPv6 is finally gaining traction. You must learn and use IPv6, both for the CompTIA Network+ exam and for the real world. This chapter breaks the process into three parts. First, you need the basic concepts, such as how the numbers work. Second, you need to learn how to enable or apply IPv6 in a variety of technologies, such as NAT and DHCP. Finally, you need answers on how to deploy IPv6 in an IPv4 world.

Test Specific

IPv6 Basics

Although they achieve the same function—enabling computers on IP networks to send packets to each other—IPv6 and IPv4 differ a lot when it comes to implementation. The addressing numbers work differently, for example, and don't look alike. IPv6 uses link-local addressing, a concept not present in IPv4. Subnetting works differently as well. You also need to understand the concepts of multicast, global addresses, and aggregation. Let's look at all six topics.

IPv6 Address Notation

The 32-bit IPv4 addresses are written as 197.169.94.82, using four octets. Well, IPv6 has 128 bits, so octets are gone. IPv6 addresses are written like this:

```
2001:0000:0000:3210:0800:200C:00CF:1234
```

IPv6 uses a colon as a separator, instead of the period used in IPv4's dotted decimal format. Each group is a hexadecimal number between 0000 and FFFF.

 NOTE For those who don't play with hex regularly, one hexadecimal character (for example, F) represents 4 bits, so four hexadecimal characters make a 16-bit group.

A complete IPv6 address always has eight groups of four hexadecimal characters. If this sounds like you're going to type in really long IP addresses, don't worry, IPv6 offers a number of shortcuts.

First, leading zeroes can be dropped from any group, so 00CF becomes CF and 0000 becomes 0. Let's rewrite that IPv6 address using this shortcut:

```
2001:0:0:3210:800:200C:CF:1234
```

To write IPv6 addresses containing strings of zeroes, you can use a pair of colons (::) to represent a string of consecutive groups with a value of zero. For example, using the :: rule, you can write the IPv6 address

```
2001:0:0:3210:800:200C:CF:1234
```

as

```
2001::3210:800:200C:CF:1234
```

Double colons are very handy, but you have to be careful when you use them. Take a look at this IPv6 address:

```
FEDC:0000:0000:0000:00CF:0000:BA98:1234
```

If I convert it to

```
FEDC::CF:0:BA98:1234
```

I may not use a second :: to represent the third-to-last group of four zeroes—only one :: is allowed per address! There's a good reason for this rule. If more than one :: was used, how could you tell how many sets of zeroes were in each group? Answer: you couldn't.

Here's an example of a very special IPv6 address that takes full advantage of the double colon, the IPv6 loopback address:

```
::1
```

Without using the double-colon nomenclature, this IPv6 address would look like this:

```
0000:0000:0000:0000:0000:0000:0000:0001
```

NOTE The unspecified address (all zeroes) can never be used, and neither can an address that contains all ones (all Fs in IPv6 notation).

IPv6 still uses subnet masks, but you won't find a place to type in 255s anywhere. IPv6 uses the "/x" Classless Inter-Domain Routing (CIDR) nomenclature. Here's how to write an IP address and subnet for a typical IPv6 host:

```
FEDC::CF:0:BA98:1234/64
```

Link-Local Address

The folks who created IPv6 worked hard to make it powerful and easy to use, but you pretty much have to forget all the rules you learned about IPv4 addressing. The biggest item to wrap your mind around is that you no longer have a single IP address unless your network isn't connected to a router. When a computer running IPv6 first boots up, it gives itself a *link-local address*. Think of a link-local address as IPv6's equivalent to IPv4's APIPA address. The first 64 bits of a link-local address are always FE80::/64. That means every address always begins with FE80:0000:0000:0000. If your operating system supports IPv6 and IPv6 is enabled, you can see this address. Figure 13-1 is a screenshot of Linux's ifconfig command, showing the link-local address.

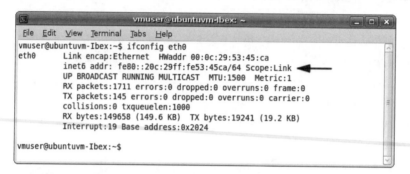

Figure 13-1   Link-local address

Take a close look at the IP address and compare it to the MAC address. The last 64 bits of the IPv6 address, collectively called the *Extended Unique Identifier, 64-bit (EUI-64),* are taken from the MAC address, placing the EUI-64 at Layer 2 of the OSI model. MAC addresses only contain 48 bits, so your system creates the EUI-64 as follows:

1. Remove the dashes from the MAC address and split it in half:
   000C29   5345CA

2. Add "FFFE" in the middle:
   000C29FFFE5345CA

3. This step requires a little binary knowledge. You convert the second hexadecimal digit, in this example the second 0, into binary: 0 in hex = 0000 in binary. You take the third binary digit and complement it, which means that if it's a 0, as in this example, you make it a 1, and if it's a 1, you make it a 0. Then convert it back to hexadecimal: 0010 = 2 in hexadecimal.

4. Put that value back in the second position:
   020C29FFFE5345CA

5. Break it into standard IPv6 format:
   020C:29FF:FE53:45CA

6. Add it to the first 64 bits and drop leading zeroes:
   FE80::20C:29FF:FE53:45CA

Don't worry about how to make your own EUI-64: just understand how your system comes up with this value. Every operating system, with the exception of Windows Vista and Windows 7, creates link-local addresses using EUI-64 by default. Microsoft adds a lot of extra steps in Vista, but the big difference is that the last 64 bits of the link-local addresses are generated randomly. I think Microsoft uses randomization for privacy. If your link-local address ties directly to a real MAC address, in theory, some bad guy might use this against you. No other operating system, not even Windows XP or Windows Server, does this randomized link-local numbering (Figure 13-2).

NOTE You can reconfigure Vista to use EUI-64 for link-local addresses by typing this at a command prompt:

```
netsh interface ipv6 set globalrandomizeidentifiers=disabled
```

Figure 13-2   Link-local address in Windows Vista

The link-local address does all the hard work in IPv6, and, as long as you don't need an Internet connection, it's all you need. The old concepts of static and DHCP addressing don't really make much sense in IPv6 unless you have dedicated servers (even in IPv6, servers generally still have static IP addresses). Link-local addressing takes care of all your local network needs!

IPv6 Subnet Masks

IPv6 subnet masks function the same as IPv4 subnet masks, in that systems use them to determine whether to ARP for a local MAC address or to ARP the default gateway to send the packets out to the Internet. But you need to know two new rules:

- The last 64 bits of an IPv6 address are generated by the NIC, leaving a maximum of 64 bits for the subnet. Therefore, no subnet is ever longer than /64.

- IANA passes out /32 subnets to big ISPs and end users who need large allotments. ISPs and others may pass out /48 and /64 subnets to end users. Therefore, the vast majority of IPv6 subnets are between /48 and /64.

You will never type in a subnet mask. With link-local addressing the subnet mask is defined as /64. Other types of IPv6 addresses get the subnet information automatically from their routers (described next).

The End of Broadcast

A system's IPv6 link-local address is a *unicast address*, a unique address that is exclusive to that system. IPv4 also relies on unicast addresses. But IPv6 completely drops the idea of broadcast addresses, replacing it with the idea of *multicast*.

Multicast isn't some new idea introduced with IPv6. Multicast addressing has been around for a long time and works well in IPv4 and IPv6. A *multicast address* is a set of reserved addresses designed to go only to certain systems. As you've learned in previous chapters, any IPv4 address that starts with 224.0.0.0/4 (the old Class D network addresses) are reserved for multicast. Within that reserved range, individual addresses are assigned to specific applications that wish to use multicast. For example, if a system is configured to use the *Network Time Protocol (NTP)*, it will listen on multicast address 224.0.1.1 for time information.

Multicast works the same for IPv6, but brings in a number of IPv6-only multicast addresses to get specific jobs done. If an IPv6 system sends out a multicast to the address FF02::2, for example, only routers read the message while everyone else ignores it (Figure 13-3).

Multicast packets are encapsulated into Ethernet frames just like any other packet. Ethernet reserves the address 01-00-5E-*xx-xx-xx* for IPv4 multicast frame destination addresses. The Ethernet address 33-33-*xx-xx-xx-xx* is used on Ethernet frames that encapsulate IPv6 multicast packets.

Figure 13-3
Multicast to
routers

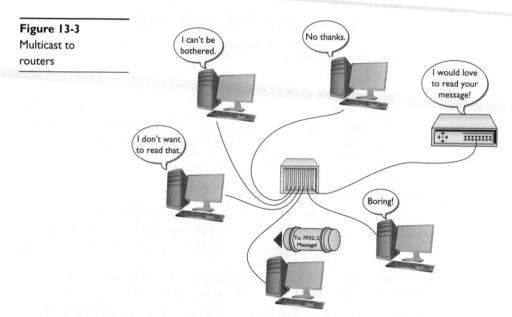

Every computer sees the multicast frame, but only the computers specifically set up to process the frame process it. Table 13-1 shows some of the more useful IPv6 multicast addresses. You've just seen FF02::2; I'll explain the rest later in this chapter.

Table 13-1
IPv6 Multicast
Addresses

Address	Function
FF02::1	All Nodes Address
FF02::2	All Routers Address
FF02::1:FFXX:XXXX	Solicited-Node Address

Looking at the first listing, FF02::1, you might ask: "How is that different from a broadcast?" The answer lies more in the definition of multicast than in what really takes place. A computer must be configured as a member of a particular group to read a particular multicast. In this case, if a computer is a member of "All Nodes," then it reads the message.

Beyond unicast and multicast, IPv6 uses a third type of addressing called *anycast*. An anycast address is a bit of a strange animal, so it's helpful to know why you need an anycast address before you try to understand what one is. The best place to learn how anycast works and why it is needed is the one place where its use is very common: DNS.

You learned in Chapter 10 that the top of the DNS root structure consists of a number of root DNS servers. Every DNS server on the Internet keeps the IP addresses of the root servers in a file called *root hints*. Here's one part of the root hints file from my own DNS server:

```
                              NS    F.ROOT-SERVERS.NET.
F.ROOT-SERVERS.NET.           A     192.5.5.241
F.ROOT-SERVERS.NET.           AAAA  2001:500:2f::f
```

At first glance, you might think that this root server is a single physical box because it only has a single IPv4 address and a single IPv6 address. It's not. It is roughly 20 groups of server clusters strategically placed all over the world. Back in Chapter 12, you saw how DNS can make a cluster of computers act as a single server, but none of those solutions can make a bunch of clusters all over the world act as a single server in an efficient way to make sure the DNS queries are answered as quickly as possible. To do this, we need anycasting.

Anycasting starts by giving a number of computers (or clusters of computers) the same IP address. Then routers (in the case of DNS, only the biggest, tier-one Internet routers) use the Border Gateway Protocol (BGP) to determine which of the many computers with the same IP address are closest. When that router gets a packet addressed to that IP address, it sends it only to the closest root DNS server, even though it may know where others are located. That is an anycast address.

An anycast address looks like a unicast address, and, in most cases, the computer sending the packet doesn't know or care to know that the address is anycast and not unicast. The only device that knows (and cares) is the top-tier router that has the smarts to send the packet only to the closest root DNS server.

Global Address

To get on the Internet, your system needs a second IPv6 address called a *global unicast address*, usually shortened to "global address." The only way to get a global address is from your default gateway, which must be configured to pass out global IPv6 addresses. When your computer boots up, it sends out a router solicitation message on multicast address FF02::2 looking for a router. Your router hears this message and tells your computer your network ID and subnet (together called the prefix). See Figure 13-4.

Figure 13-4
Getting a global
address

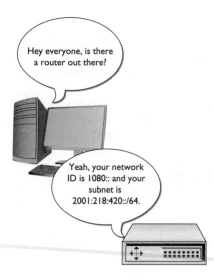

Once you have your prefix, your computer generates the rest of the global address. It uses the MAC address to create the last 64 bits, just as it does to create the last 64 bits of a link-local address. You now have a legitimate public IP address as well as your link-local address. Figure 13-5 shows the IPv6 information on a Mac running OS X 10.5.

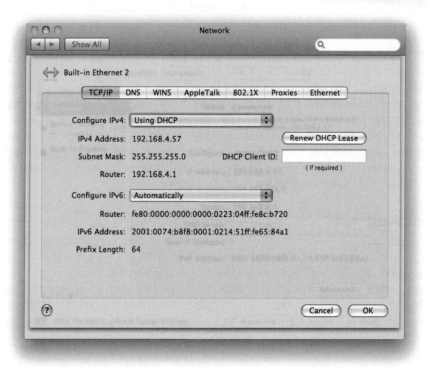

Figure 13-5 IPv6 configuration on Mac OS X

Let's look at this process in detail with an example:

1. An IPv6-capable computer boots up. As it boots, it sends out a router solicitation message (FF02::2).

2. An IPv6-configured router hears the request and then sends the prefix to the computer. In this example, let's say it is 2001:470:b8f9:1/64.

3. The computer takes the prefix and adds the EUI-64 address to the end of the prefix. If the MAC address is 00-0C-29-53-45-CA, then the EUI-64 address is 20C:29FF:FE53:45CA.

4. Putting the prefix with the EUI-64 address, you get the global address: 2001:470:b8f9:1:20C:29FF:FE53:45CA.

NOTE At the moment, IANA only passes out global addresses that begin with the number 2 (for example, 2001::, 2002::, and so on). As demand increases, this will certainly change, but for now, it sure makes recognizing a global address easy.

A global address is a true Internet address. If another computer is running IPv6 and also has a global address, it can access your system unless you have some form of firewall.

EXAM TIP Computers using IPv6 need a global address to access the Internet.

Aggregation

Routers need to know where to send every packet they encounter. Most routers have a default path on which they send packets that aren't specifically defined to go on any other route. As you get to the top of the Internet, the tier-one routers that connect to the other tier-one routers can't have any default route (Figure 13-6). We call these the *no-default routers*.

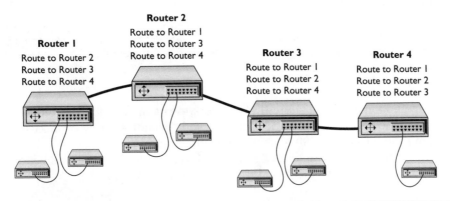

Figure 13-6 No-default routers

The current state of the Internet's upper tiers is rather messy. A typical no-default router has somewhere around 30,000 to 50,000 routes in its routing table, requiring a router with massive firepower. But what would happen if the Internet was organized as shown in Figure 13-7? Note how every router underneath one router always uses a subset of that router's existing routes. This is called *aggregation*.

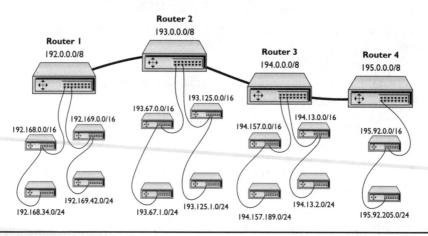

Figure 13-7   Aggregation

Aggregation would drastically reduce the size and complexity of routing tables and make the Internet faster. Aggregation would also give a more detailed, geographic picture of how the Internet is organized—you could get a good idea of where a person is physically located just by looking at the IP address.

It's way too late for IPv4 to use aggregation. Many organizations that received class licenses 20 to 30 years ago simply will not relinquish them, and the amount of effort necessary to make aggregation work would require a level of synchronization that would bring the entire Internet to its knees for days if not weeks.

But aggregation is part and parcel with IPv6. Remember, your computer gets the first 64 bits of its Internet address from your default gateway. The router, in turn, gets a (usually) 48-bit prefix from its upstream router and adds its own 16-bit subnet.

 NOTE   Keep this formula in mind: A 48-bit prefix from upstream router + 16-bit subnet from default gateway + 64-bit unique number = 128-bit IPv6 address.

This method enables the entire IPv6 network to change IP addresses on-the-fly to keep aggregation working. Imagine you have your default gateway connected to an upstream router from your ISP, as shown in Figure 13-8.

Your PC's IPv6 address is 2001:d0be:7922:1:fc2d:aeb2:99d2:e2b4. Let's cut out the last 64 bits and look at the prefix and see where this comes from:

Your network's prefix: 2001:d0be:7922:1/64

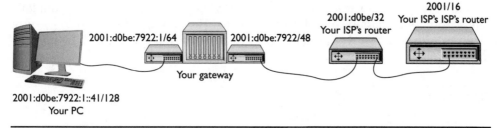

Figure 13-8   An IPv6 group of routers

IPv6 addresses begin at the very top of the Internet with the no-default servers. We'll assume your ISP's ISP is one of those routers. Your ISP gets (usually) a 32-bit prefix from IANA or from its ISP if it is small.

NOTE   The IANA doesn't actually pass out IPv6 prefixes. This job is delegated to the five Regional Internet Registries (RIRs):

- American Registry for Internet Numbers (ARIN) supports North America.

- RIPE Network Coordination Centre (RIPE NCC) supports Europe, the Middle East, and Central Asia.

- Asia-Pacific Network Information Centre (APNIC) supports Asia and the Pacific region.

- Latin American and Caribbean Internet Addresses Registry (LACNIC) supports Central and South America and parts of the Caribbean.

- African Network Information Centre (AfriNIC) supports Africa.

In this case, the prefix is 2001:d0be/32. This prefix comes from the upstream router, and your ISP has no control over it. The person setting up the ISP's router, however, will add a 16-bit subnet to the prefix, as shown in Figure 13-9.

Figure 13-9
Adding the first prefix

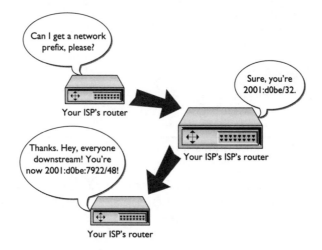

Your router receives a 48-bit prefix (in this case, 2001:d0be:7922/48) from your ISP's router. Your router has no control over that prefix. The person setting up your gateway, however, adds your own 16-bit subnet (in this case, :0001 or :1) to the 48-bit prefix to make the 64-bit prefix for your network (Figure 13-10).

Figure 13-10
Adding the second prefix

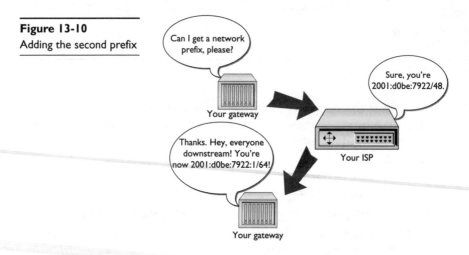

What makes all this particularly interesting is that any router upstream of anyone else may change the prefix it sends downstream, keeping aggregation intact. To see this in action, let's watch what happens if your ISP decides to change to another upstream ISP (Figure 13-11). In this case, your ISP moves from the old ISP (ISP1) to a new ISP (ISP2). When your ISP makes the new connection, the new ISP passes out a different 32-bit prefix (in this example, 2AB0:3C05/32). As quickly as this change takes place, all of the downstream routers make an "all nodes" multicast and all clients get new IP addresses.

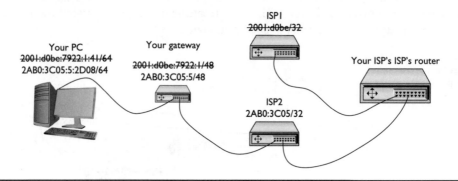

Figure 13-11   New IP address updated downstream

Aggregation is an intrinsic but for the most part completely transparent part of IPv6. Know that your IPv6 Internet addresses may suddenly change from time to time and that the address changes are a fairly rare but normal aspect of using IPv6.

Using IPv6

Once IPv6 fully replaces IPv4, we will find ourselves in a very different world from the one we left in terms of configuration. In this section, you will see what it takes to turn on IPv6 for your network. This section also assumes you've turned off IPv4—which isn't a realistic option right now because IPv4 is still prevalent, but it makes understanding some aspects of using IPv6 much easier. You'll also learn how IPv6 works (or doesn't work, as the case may be) with NAT, DHCP, and DNS. We'll cover the idea of running IPv6 and IPv4 at the same time in the next section.

Enabling IPv6

Enabling IPv6 is very easy because, in most cases, it is already running on your operating system. Table 13-2 lists the popular operating systems and their IPv6 statuses.

Operating System	IPv6 Status
Windows 2000	Windows 2000 came with "developmental" IPv6 support. Microsoft does not recommend using Windows 2000 for IPv6.
Windows XP	Originally, Windows XP came with a rudimentary but fully functional IPv6 stack that had to be installed from the command prompt. SP1 added the ability to add the same IPv6 stack under the Install | Protocols menu.
Windows Vista/Windows 7	Complete IPv6 support. IPv6 is active on default installs.
Windows Server 2003	Complete IPv6 support. IPv6 is not installed by default but is easily installed via the Install | Protocols menu.
Windows Server 2008	Complete IPv6 support. IPv6 is active on default installs.
Linux	Complete IPv6 support from Kernel 2.6. IPv6 is active on most default installs.
Mac OS X	Complete IPv6 support on all versions. IPv6 is active on default installs.

Table 13-2 IPv6 Adoption by Operating System

The fastest way to verify if your system runs IPv6 is to check the IP status for your OS. In Windows, go to a command prompt and type **ipconfig** (Figure 13-12). In Linux or Mac OS X, go to a terminal and type **ifconfig** (Figure 13-13). Remember that you will have a link-local address only if your router isn't configured for IPv6.

Figure 13-12
IPv6 enabled
in Windows
Vista

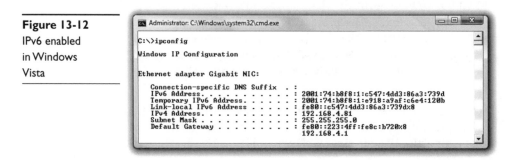

```
┌─────────────────────────────────────────────────────────────────────┐
│ ▣              vmuser@ubuntuvm-Ibex: ~                  _ □ ✕         │
├─────────────────────────────────────────────────────────────────────┤
│ File  Edit  View  Terminal  Tabs  Help                               │
│ vmuser@ubuntuvm-Ibex:~$ ifconfig                                     │
│ eth0      Link encap:Ethernet  HWaddr 00:0c:29:53:45:ca              │
│           inet addr:192.168.4.97  Bcast:192.168.4.255  Mask:255.255.255.0 │
│           inet6 addr: 2001:74:b8f8:1:20c:29ff:fe53:45ca/64 Scope:Global │
│           inet6 addr: fe80::20c:29ff:fe53:45ca/64 Scope:Link         │
│           UP BROADCAST RUNNING MULTICAST  MTU:1500  Metric:1         │
│           RX packets:57093 errors:0 dropped:0 overruns:0 frame:0     │
│           TX packets:2720 errors:0 dropped:0 overruns:0 carrier:0    │
│           collisions:0 txqueuelen:1000                               │
│           RX bytes:6704626 (6.7 MB)  TX bytes:424587 (424.5 KB)      │
│           Interrupt:19 Base address:0x2024                           │
│                                                                       │
│ lo        Link encap:Local Loopback                                  │
│           inet addr:127.0.0.1  Mask:255.0.0.0                        │
│           inet6 addr: ::1/128 Scope:Host                             │
│           UP LOOPBACK RUNNING  MTU:16436  Metric:1                   │
│           RX packets:4 errors:0 dropped:0 overruns:0 frame:0         │
│           TX packets:4 errors:0 dropped:0 overruns:0 carrier:0       │
│           collisions:0 txqueuelen:0                                  │
│           RX bytes:200 (200.0 B)  TX bytes:200 (200.0 B)             │
│                                                                       │
│ vmuser@ubuntuvm-Ibex:~$                                              │
│                                                                       │
└─────────────────────────────────────────────────────────────────────┘
```

Figure 13-13   IPv6 enabled in Ubuntu 8.10

NAT in IPv6

The folks pushing IPv6 forward are a vocal group with some pretty strong feelings about how IPv6 should work. If you want to get some really nasty e-mail, just go to one of the many IPv6 sites and ask this question: "How do I set up NAT on IPv6?" I know they will get mad because I asked that question. Here are some of the answers as I saw them:

> "NAT was developed a long time ago as a way to avoid running out of IP addresses. It was never meant to be a type of firewall."
> "NAT messes up IPsec."
> "Only jerks use NAT!"

If you're going to use IPv6, you're not going to use NAT. That means every one of your IP addresses will be exposed to the Internet, and that's not good. The answer is: count on IPv6 to make life hard on hackers and use a good firewall.

 EXAM TIP   There is a version of NAT for IPv6 called *NAPT-PT* (an earlier version was called NAT-PT). This solution tries to get an IPv6 network to use a single IPv4 address and it does not work well.

One big problem with IPv4 is how easy it is to sniff networks. Using tools like Anton Keks' popular Angry IP Scanner (www.angryziber.com), you can scan an entire subnet looking for active IP addresses, as shown in Figure 13-14.

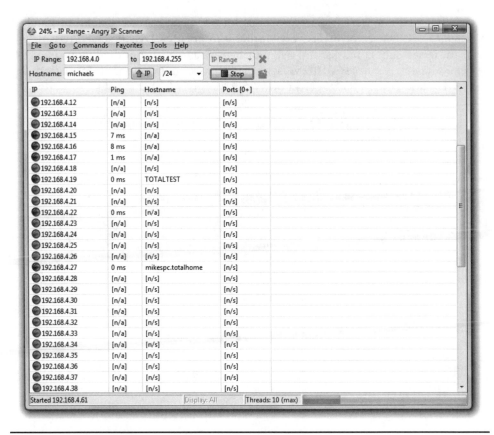

Figure 13-14   Angry IP Scanner at work

IPv6's huge address space makes such scanning programs obsolete. Let's say you knew my subnet was 2001:d0be:7922:1/64. There are 2^{64} different possible IP addresses on this subnet. Assuming a scanner could check one million addresses per second, it would take something like 580,000 years to check them all.

If a bad guy knows your address, the hope is that you're using IPsec to prevent other people from reading your information. You also have a number of other security options that aren't specific to IPv6 that you can use. You've seen some of these (like encryption) in earlier chapters. Others, like good firewalling, you'll see in Chapter 16.

DHCP in IPv6

DHCP is alive and well in the IPv6 world but works very differently than IPv4's DHCP. At first glance, you'd think you wouldn't need DHCP anymore. IPv6 clients get their IP address and subnet from their gateway router's advertisements (so they also know the default gateway). Although this is true, IPv6 router advertisements do not pass out a number of other very important bits of information that clients need, such as DNS server information, giving DHCP a very important place in IPv6.

A fully functional DHCPv6 server works in one of two modes: stateful or stateless. A *stateful* DHCPv6 server works very similarly to an IPv4 DHCP server, passing out IPv6 addresses, subnet masks, and default gateways as well as optional items like DNS server addresses. A *stateless* DHCPv6 server only passes out optional information. Figure 13-15 shows the DHCPv6 server on Windows Server 2008.

NOTE We call IPv6's DHCP servers DHCPv6 to separate them from IPv4 DHCP servers.

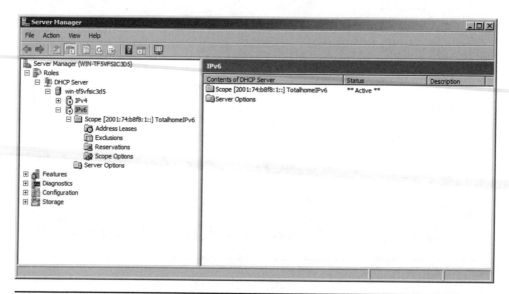

Figure 13-15 DHCPv6 server in action

Most IPv6 installations should take advantage of IPv6's auto-configuration and only run stateless DHCPv6 servers. But if you really want to skip aggregation, you may certainly go stateful. Be careful about going stateful, however: as long as you're using an intranet or your upstream router knows what to do with your non-aggregated network ID, you're okay. Stateful DHCPv6 might be helpful for internal networks that do strange things like try to use subnets greater than /64 but, for the most part, expect stateless to be the norm.

EXAM TIP There's a push to get DNS server information added to IPv6 router advertisements. If this happens, the need for DHCPv6 might fall dramatically.

DNS in IPv6

DNS with IPv6 is trivial. Just about every DNS server made in the last five to six years or so supports IPv6 addresses. All IPv6 addresses use an AAAA nomenclature. Figure 13-16 shows some IPv6 addresses in Windows Server 2008.

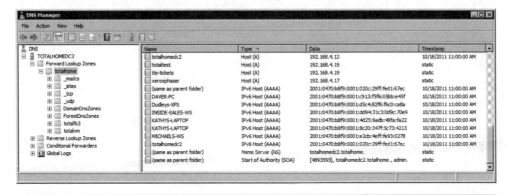

Figure 13-16   IPv6 addresses on DNS server

A common trick to get around using DHCPv6 is to add DNS server information manually to IPv6 clients. You do this exactly the same as you do it with IPv4, as shown in Figure 13-17. This isn't the best long-term solution, but until all the IPv6 DNS details are worked out, it works well.

Figure 13-17
Manually adding
an IPv6 DNS
server in
Windows Vista

Moving to IPv6

There's no reason for you *not* to try running IPv6 today—like right now! At the very least, a whole world of IPv6-only Web sites are out there for you to explore. At the most, you may very well become the IPv6 expert in your organization. You almost certainly have an operating system ready to do IPv6; the only trick is to get you connected to the rest of us fun-loving IPv6-capable folks.

This section is designed to help you get connected. If you can, grab an IPv6-capable system, fire up IPv6 as shown earlier, and make sure you're connected to the Internet. We are going someplace you've never been before: the IPv6 Internet.

NOTE IPv6 is just now gaining wide support, so there are issues in connecting to the IPv6 world. IPv6 has potential security risks as well as less-than-perfect support with operating systems. Don't connect to the IPv6 Internet on a mission-critical computer.

IPv4 and IPv6

The first and most important point to make right now is that you can run both IPv4 and IPv6 on your computers and routers at the same time, just as my computer does, as shown in Figure 13-18. This ability is a critical part of the process enabling the world to migrate slowly from IPv4 to IPv6.

Figure 13-18
IPv4 and IPv6
on one computer

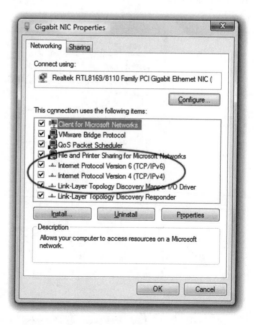

Almost all operating systems support IPv6, and almost all serious routers support IPv6, but very few of the small home routers support IPv6. Plus, not all routers on the Internet have their IPv6 support turned on.

In order for IPv6 to work, every router and every computer on the Internet needs to support IPv6, but the Internet is not yet there. Two critical parts of the Internet are ready, however:

- All of the root DNS servers now support IPv6 resolution.

- Almost all of the tier-one ISP routers properly forward IPv6 packets.

The problem is that the routers and DNS servers between your IPv6-capable computer and the other IPv6-capable computers to which you would like to connect are not yet IPv6-ready. How do you get past this IPv6 gap (Figure 13-19)?

Figure 13-19
The IPv6 gap

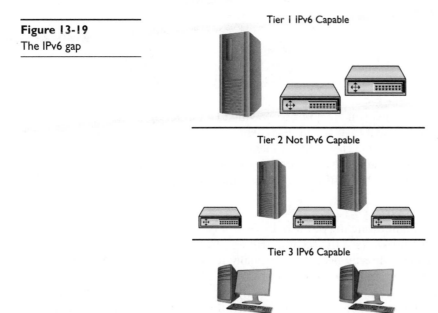

Tier 1 IPv6 Capable

Tier 2 Not IPv6 Capable

Tier 3 IPv6 Capable

Tunnels

To get on the IPv6 network, you need to leap over this gap. The folks who developed IPv6 have a number of ways for you to do this using one of many IPv4-to-IPv6 tunneling standards. An IPv4-to-IPv6 tunnel works like any other tunnel, encapsulating one type of data into another. In this case, you are encapsulating your IPv6 traffic into an IPv4 tunnel to get to an IPv6-capable router, as shown in Figure 13-20.

Figure 13-20
The IPv4-to-IPv6 tunnel

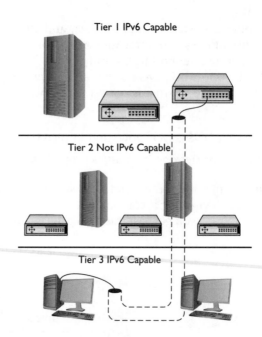

To make this tunnel, you are going to download a tunneling client and install it on your computer. You will then fire up the client and make the tunnel connection—it's very easy to do. Before you create this tunnel, however, you need to appreciate that this is only one way to make an IPv6 connection—I'll show you other ways in a moment. I describe four popular IPv4-to-IPv6 tunneling standards next.

6to4

6to4 is the dominant tunneling protocol because it is the only IPv6 tunnel that doesn't require a tunnel broker (see the section "Tunnel Brokers"). 6to4 is generally used to connect two routers directly because it normally requires a public IPv4 address. 6to4 addresses always start with 2002::/16. If you have an IPv6-capable router, or if you have a computer directly connected to the Internet, you can set up a 6to4 tunnel. 6to4 uses public relay routers all around the world. Search the Web for **"public 6to4 relays"** to find one close to you. One IPv4 address, 192.88.99.1, is called the *6to4 anycast address* and works everywhere.

Setting up a 6to4 tunnel can be more challenging than setting up the tunnels that use tunnel brokers. If you're feeling adventurous, just do a Web search on **"6to4 setup"** and the name of your operating system. You'll find hundreds of Web sites to show you how to set up a 6to4 tunnel.

6in4

6in4 (also called IPv6-in-IPv4) is one of the most popular IPv6 tunneling standards and the one I'll use in the tunneling example. 6in4 is one of only two IPv6 tunneling protocols that can go through a NAT (called *NAT traversal*).

Teredo

Teredo is the second NAT-traversal IPv6 tunneling protocol. Teredo is built into Microsoft Windows and, as a result, sees some adoption. Teredo addresses start with 2001:0000:/32. Most people prefer to skip Windows built-in support and instead get a third-party tool that supports 6to4 or 6in4.

If you're using Windows XP (with Service Pack 1 or later) or Windows Vista/7, you have nothing to lose but your chains, so try this! You can use Teredo to access the IPv6 Internet as long as you have access to the Internet normally and your computer is not part of a Windows domain; it's possible to use Teredo on a domain, but the process gets a little ugly in my opinion.

Beware! Some home routers can't handle Teredo, and many high-end routers are specifically designed to prevent this traffic (it's a great way to get around many network defenses), so if Teredo doesn't work, blame the router.

Here are the steps in Windows Vista or later:

1. Make sure the Windows Firewall is enabled. If you have a third-party firewall, turn it off.

2. Go to the Start menu and type **cmd** in the Start Search box, but don't press ENTER yet. Instead, right-click the command prompt option above and select **Run as administrator**.

3. From the command prompt, type these commands, followed by ENTER each time:
```
netsh
interface
teredo
set state client
exit
```

4. Test by typing **ipconfig /all**. You should see an adapter called "Tunnel adapter Teredo tunneling pseudo-interface" (or something close to that) with an IP address starting with 2001.

5. Then type **ping ipv6.google.com** to make sure you can reach the Internet.

6. Open a Web browser and go to an IPv6 Web site, like www.sixxs.com or ipv6.google.com.

7. Remember, Microsoft loves to change things. If these steps don't work, search for new instructions on the Microsoft Web site.

ISATAP

Intra-Site Automatic Tunnel Addressing Protocol (ISATAP) is designed to work within an IPv4 network by actually adding the IPv4 address to an IPv6 prefix to create a rather interesting but nonstandard address for the endpoints. One example of an ISATAP address is 2001:DB8::98CA:200:131.107.28.9. ISATAP has a strong following, but other tunneling standards are gaining ground because they use a more common IPv6 addressing structure.

 NOTE You rarely have a choice of tunneling protocol. The tunneling protocol you use is the one your tunnel broker provides and is usually invisible to you.

Tunnel Brokers

Setting up an IPv6 tunnel can be a chore. You have to find someone willing to act as the far endpoint; you have to connect to them somehow; and then you have to know the tunneling standard they use. To make life easier, those who provide the endpoints have created the idea of the *tunnel broker*. Tunnel brokers create the actual tunnel and (usually) offer a custom-made endpoint client for you to use, although more advanced users can often make a manual connection. Many tunnel brokers take advantage of one of two automatic configuration protocols, called *Tunnel Setup Protocol (TSP)* and *Tunnel Information and Control protocol (TIC)*. These protocols set up the tunnel and handle configuration as well as login. If it wasn't for TSP and TIC, there would be no such thing as automatic third-party tunnel endpoint clients for you to use. Here's a short list of the most popular IPv6 tunnel brokers around the world. For a more complete list, go to www.sixxs.net/tools/aiccu/brokers.

Tunnel Broker	URL
Freenet/gogo6	http://gogonet.gogo6.com/
SixXS	www.sixxs.net
Hurricane Electric (no TSP/TIC)	www.tunnelbroker.net
AARNet	http://broker.aarnet.net.au

Setting Up a Tunnel

Every tunnel broker has its own setup, so you should always read the instructions carefully. In this example, you'll install the gogoCLIENT onto Windows Vista. Go to www.gogo6.com and register for an account (look for the "Sign Up" link). You'll then be led to a download page where you can download the client. Gogo6 is always updating this client so be sure to download the latest version. Install the client to see the screen shown in Figure 13-21. Enter the Gateway6 address and your user name and password. You can log on anonymously, but I think it works more reliably if you log in.

Click **Connect**, and, assuming you have a good connection, you should be on the IPv6 Internet. Go to the **Status** tab to see your IP information (Figure 13-22).

Figure 13-21
Gateway6 Client Utility

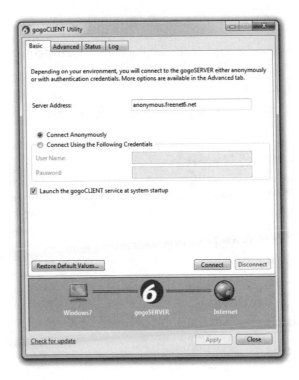

Figure 13-22
Gateway6 Client
Utility Status tab

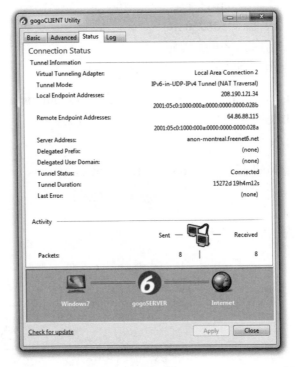

Excellent! Now let's check out the IPv6 Internet. Try these IPv6-only Web pages:

- www.ipv6.sixxs.net (click the **Enter website** hyperlink to see your IPv6 address on the bottom left of the page)
- http://ipv6.google.com
- http://ipv6.sunny.ch (shows your IPv6 address)

IPv6 Is Here, Really!

Depending on who you talk to, IPv6 is either happening now or going to happen soon, and when it does happen, it'll happen very quickly. IPv4 addresses are already all but exhausted, and the time is coming when new devices simply will have to move to IPv6. The people who know IPv6 will be in a unique place to leap into the insanity of what will invariably be called "The Big Switchover" and will find themselves making a lot of money. Take some time to learn IPv6. You'll be glad you did.

Chapter Review

Questions

1. Which of the following is a valid IPv6 address?

   A. 2001:beacd:beef::1

   B. 2001:30f5::3d62::04ffe

   C. 192.168.1.4:ff45:129g:48fd:1

   D. 2001.0470.b33e.23f4.27de.d34a.aed2.1827

2. DHCP is required to receive an IPv6 address automatically.

   A. True

   B. False

3. What kind of DNS records do IPv6 addresses use?

   A. A

   B. SIX

   C. AAAA

   D. NSSIX

4. Is NAT needed with IPv6?

    A. No, because NAT has been replaced with a new version called NAT6.

    B. No, the address space is so large that rationing routable addresses is unnecessary.

    C. Yes, because it is the only way to protect against hackers.

    D. Yes, because of the limited nature of IPv6 addressing.

5. How do IPv6 multicasts differ from broadcasts?

    A. Broadcasts are sent to all network nodes; multicasts are sent only to specific network nodes.

    B. Both broadcasts and multicasts are sent to all network nodes, but in a multicast, only the destination nodes process the incoming packets.

    C. Broadcasts can cross over a router, whereas multicasts cannot.

    D. Broadcasts are used on local networks; multicasts are used on the Internet.

6. What is the /16 prefix for all 6to4 address?

    A. 2001

    B. 2003

    C. 2002

    D. 2021

7. Which of the following operating systems have Teredo built in? (Select two.)

    A. Windows XP

    B. Macintosh OS X

    C. Windows Vista

    D. Windows 2000

8. What service do tunnel brokers provide?

    A. A way for users to jump the gap between their computers and the IPv6 Internet routers.

    B. They provide no useful service.

    C. Access to IPv6 DNS records.

    D. A second connection for multihoming.

9. What is the /48 prefix of the address 2001:0480:b6f3:0001::0001?

    A. 2001:480:b6f3:1

    B. 2001:480:b6f3

    C. 2001:480:b6f3:1:0000::1

    D. 2001:480:b6f3:1:0000:0000:0000:1

10. Which of the following is the valid reduced version of the address 2001:0489:000f:0000:0000:1f00:0000:000d?

   A. 2001:489:f::1f:0:d

   B. 2001:489:f::1f00::d

   C. 2001:0489:000f::1f00:0000:000d

   D. 2001:489:f::1f00:0:d

Answers

1. **A.** B has two sets of double colons. C is using IPv4 numbers. D is using periods instead of colons.

2. **B.** Router advertisements allow clients to receive a valid IPv6 address without a DHCP server.

3. **C.** The DNS system uses AAAA for IPv6 records.

4. **B.** NAT is no longer needed because of the massive size of the IPv6 address space.

5. **B.** While multicasts, like broadcasts, are sent to every network node, only the target nodes actually process the multicast packets.

6. **C.** The /16 prefix designated by IANA for all 6to4 addresses is 2002.

7. **A and C.** Teredo is built into Windows XP and Vista.

8. **A.** Tunnel brokers provide a way to jump the gap between users and the IPv6 Internet.

9. **B.** The /48 prefix consists of only the first three groups of the address.

10. **D.** Leading zeroes can be dropped and only one group of contiguous zeroes can be represented by a double colon.

Remote Connectivity

The CompTIA Network+ certification exam expects you to know how to

- 1.5 Identify common TCP and UDP default ports: RDP
- 1.6 Explain the function of common networking protocols: SIP, RTP
- 3.1 Categorize standard media types and associated properties: T1 crossover, broadband over powerline
- 3.4 Categorize WAN technology types and properties
- 3.5 Describe different network topologies: MPLS
- 3.6 Given a scenario, troubleshoot common physical connectivity problems: split cables, dB loss
- 3.8 Identify components of wiring distribution: CSU/DSU
- 5.2 Explain the methods of network access security: RAS, RDP, PPPoE, ICA

To achieve these goals, you must be able to

- Describe WAN telephony technologies, such as SONET, T1, and T3
- Compare last-mile connections for connecting homes and businesses to the Internet
- Discuss and implement various remote access connection methods

Computers connect to other computers locally in a local area network (LAN)—you've read about LAN connections throughout this book—and remotely through a number of different methods. This chapter takes both an historical and a modern look at ways to interconnect a local computer or network with distant computers, what's called *remote connectivity*.

Historical/Conceptual

Remote connections have been around for a long time. Before the Internet, network users and developers created ways to take a single system or network and connect it to another faraway system or network. This wasn't the Internet! These were private interconnections of private networks. These connections were very expensive and, compared to today's options, pretty slow.

As the Internet developed, most of the same technologies used to make the earlier private remote connections became the way the Internet itself interconnects. Before the Internet was popular, many organizations used dedicated lines, called *T1 lines* (discussed in more detail later in this chapter), to connect far-flung offices. Some people still use T1 lines privately, but more often you'll see them used as an Internet connection to a company's local ISP. Private interconnections are only used today by organizations that need massive bandwidth or high security.

This chapter shows you all the ways you can make remote connections. You'll see every type of remote connection currently in popular use, from good-old telephone lines to advanced fiber-optic carriers, and even satellites. There are so many ways to make remote connections that this chapter is broken into three parts. The first part, "Telephony and Beyond," gives you a tour of the technologies that originally existed for long-distance voice connections that now also support data. The next part, "The Last Mile," goes into how we as individual users connect to those long-distance technologies and demonstrates how wireless technologies come into play in remote connectivity. Last, "Using Remote Access" shows you the many different ways to use these connections to connect to another, faraway computer.

Telephony and Beyond

We've already discussed the tier 1 ISPs of the Internet, but let's look at them once again in a different way. Describing the tier 1 Internet is always an interesting topic. Those of us in the instruction business invariably start this description by drawing a picture of the United States and then adding lines connecting big cities, as shown in Figure 14-1.

Figure 14-1
The tier 1 Internet

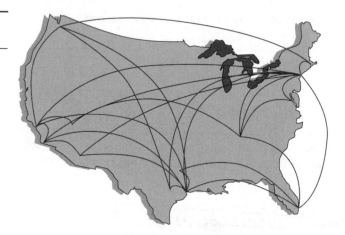

But what are these lines and where did they come from? If the Internet is just a big TCP/IP network, wouldn't these lines be Ethernet connections? Maybe copper, maybe fiber, but surely they're Ethernet? Well, traditionally they're not (with one exception; see the following Note). The vast majority of the long-distance connections that make up the Internet use a unique type of signal called SONET. SONET was originally designed to handle special heavy-duty circuits with names like T1. Never heard of SONET or T1? Don't worry—you're about to learn quite a bit.

NOTE Even as you read this, more and more of the Internet interconnections are moving toward Gigabit and 10 Gigabit Ethernet. Telephone technologies, however, continue to dominate.

Most of the connections that make up the high-speed backbone of the Internet use technologies designed at least 20 years ago to support telephone calls. We're not talking about your cool, cell phone–type calls here, but rather the old-school, wire-runs-up-to-the-house, telephone-connected-to-a-phone-jack connections. (See "Public Switched Telephone Network" later in this chapter for more on this subject.) If you want to understand how the Internet connects, you have to go way back to the 1970s and 1980s, before the Internet really took off, and learn how the U.S. telephone system developed to support networks.

NOTE This section is just the lightest of overviews to get you through the CompTIA Network+ exam. The full history of long-distance communication is an incredible story, full of good guys, bad guys, crazy technology, and huge fortunes won and lost.

The Dawn of Long Distance

Have you ever watched one of those old-time movies in which someone makes a phone call by picking up the phone and saying, "Operator, get me Mohawk 4, 3-8-2-5!" Suddenly, the scene changes to some person sitting at a switchboard like the one shown in Figure 14-2.

Figure 14-2
Old-time telephone operator (photo courtesy of the Richardson Historical and Genealogical Society)

This was the telephone operator. The telephone operator made a physical link between your phone and the other phone, making your connection. The switchboard acted as a *circuit switch*, where plugging in the two wires created a physical circuit between the two phones. This worked pretty well in the first few years of telephones, but it quickly became a problem as more and more phone lines began to fill the skies overhead (Figure 14-3).

Figure 14-3
Now that's a lot of telephone lines!

These first generations of long-distance telephone systems (think 1930s here) used analog signals, because that was how your telephone worked—the higher and lower the pitch of your voice, the lower or greater the voltage. If you graphed out a voice signal, it looked something like Figure 14-4. This type of transmission had issues, however, because analog signals over long distances, even if you amplified them, lost sound quality very quickly.

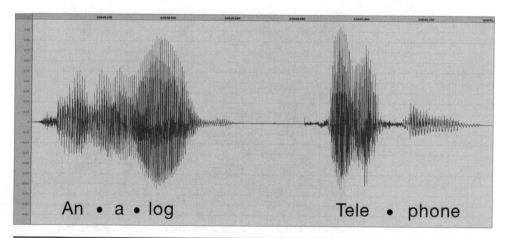

Figure 14-4   Another problem of early long-distance telephone systems

The first problem to take care of was the number of telephone wires. Individual wires were slowly replaced with special boxes called multiplexers. A *multiplexer* took a circuit and combined it with a few hundred other circuits into a single complex circuit on one wire. A *demultiplexer* (devices were both multiplexers and demultiplexers) on the other end of the connection split the individual connections back out (Figure 14-5).

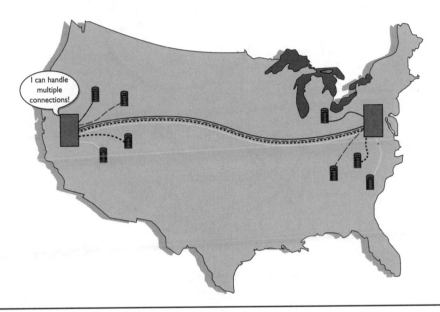

Figure 14-5 Multiplexers combine multiple circuits.

Over time, the entire United States was divided into hundreds, eventually thousands, of local exchanges. *Local exchanges* were a defined grouping of individual phone circuits served by a single multiplexer (calls within the exchange were handled first by human operators who were replaced, eventually, with dial tones and special switches that interpreted your pulses or tones for a number). One or more exchanges were (and still are) housed in a physical building called a *central office* (Figure 14-6) where individual voice circuits all came together. Local calls were still manually connected (although dial-up began to appear in earnest by the 1950s, after which many operators lost their jobs), but any connection between exchanges was carried over these special multiplexed trunk lines. Figure 14-7 shows a very stylized example of how this worked.

Figure 14-6
A central office
building

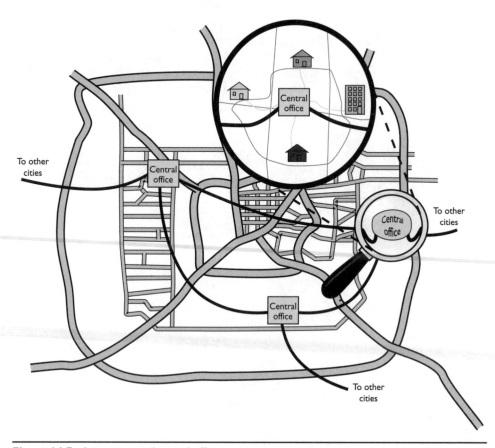

Figure 14-7 Interconnected central offices

These old-style trunk lines were fascinating technology. How did they put a bunch of voice calls on a single piece of cable, yet still somehow keep them separate? To understand this trick you need to appreciate a little bit about frequency. A typical telephone only detects a fairly limited frequency range—from around 350 Hz to around 4000 Hz. This range covers enough of the human speech range to make a decent phone call. As the individual calls came into the multiplexer, it added a certain frequency multiplier to each call, keeping every separate call in its own unique frequency range (Figure 14-8). This process is called *frequency division multiplexing (FDM)*.

This analog network still required a physical connection from one phone to the other, even if those phones were on opposite sides of the country. Long distance used a series of trunk lines, and at each intersection of those lines an operator had to connect the calls. When you physically connect two phones together on one circuit, you are using something called *circuit switching*. As you might imagine, circuit switching isn't that great for long distance, but it's your only option when you use analog.

Figure 14-8
Multiplexed FDM

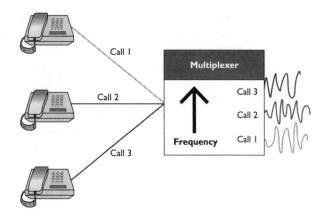

NOTE The long-distance lines used for voice calls are the same ones that carry our Internet data. There is no difference as far as the carriers are concerned.

This analog system worked pretty well through the 1930s to the 1950s, but telephones became so common and demand so heavy that the United States needed a new system to handle the load. The folks developing this new system realized that they had to dump analog and replace it with a digital system—sowing the seeds for the remote connections that eventually became the Internet.

Digital data transmits much easier over long distances than analog data because you can use repeaters. (You cannot use repeaters on analog signals.) If you remember from earlier chapters, a repeater is not an amplifier. An amplifier just increases the voltage and includes all the pops and hisses created by all kinds of interferences. A repeater takes the entire digital signal and re-creates it out the other end (Figure 14-9).

Figure 14-9
Repeater vs.
amplifier

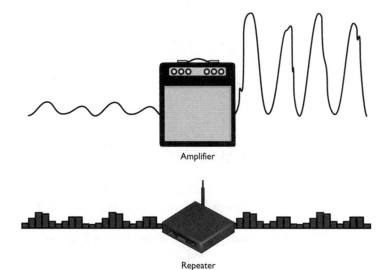

Amplifier

Repeater

The downside to adopting a digital system was that the entire telephone system was analog: every telephone, every switch, every multiplexer. The task of converting the entire analog voice system to digital was a massive undertaking. Luckily, virtually the entire U.S. phone system at that time was a monopoly run by a company called AT&T. A single company could make all of its own decisions and its own standards—one of the few times in history where a monopoly was probably a good thing. The AT&T folks had a choice here: completely revamp the entire U.S. phone system, including replacing every single telephone in the United States, or just make the trunk lines digital and let the central offices convert from analog to digital. They chose the latter.

Even today, a classic telephone line in your home or small office uses analog signals—the rest of the entire telephone system is digital. The telecommunications industry calls the connection from a central office to individual users the *last mile*. The telephone company's decision to keep the last mile analog has had serious repercussions that still challenge us even in the 21st century (Figure 14-10)

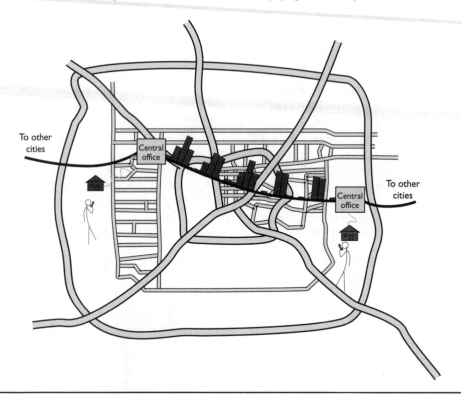

Figure 14-10   Analog and digital

NOTE   Attempts were made to convert the entire telephone system, including your telephones, to digital, but these technologies never took off (except in a few niches). See "ISDN" later in this chapter.

Test Specific

Digital Telephony

You'll find digital telephony easy to understand, because most of the aspects you've already learned about computer networking work roughly the same way in a telephone network. In fact, most of the concepts that created computer networking came from the telephone industry. For example, the telephone industry was the first technology to adopt heavily the idea of digital packets. It was the first to do what is now called switching. Heck, the telephone industry even made the first working topologies! Let's take advantage of what you already know about how networks work to learn about how the telephone industry invented the idea of digital networks.

When you learned about networks in the first few chapters of this book, you learned about cabling, frame types, speeds, switching, and so on. All of these are important for computer networks. Well, let's do it again (in a much simpler format) to see the cabling, frame types, speed, and switching used in telephone systems. Don't worry—unlike computer networks, in which a certain type of cable might run different types of frames at different speeds, most of the remote connections used in the telephony world tend to have one type of cable that only runs one type of frame at one speed.

Let's begin with the most basic data chunk you get in the telephone world: DS0.

It All Starts with DS0

When AT&T decided to go digital, it knew all phone calls had to be broken into a digital sample. AT&T decided (some people say "guessed" or "compromised") that if it took an analog signal of a human voice and converted it into 8-bit chunks 8000 times a second, it would be good enough to re-create the sound later. Figure 14-11 shows an example of the analog human voice seen earlier being converted into a digital sample.

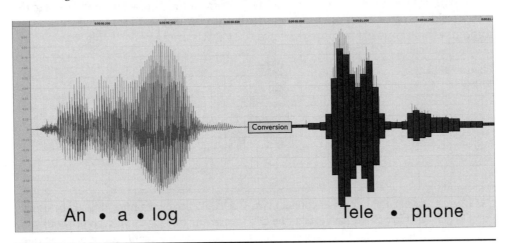

Figure 14-11 Analog to digital

NOTE A modulator takes a digital signal and converts it into an analog signal. A demodulator takes an analog signal and converts it into a digital signal. You call a device that does both a *modulator-demodulator*, better known as a *modem*.

Converting analog sound into 8-bit chunks 8000 times a second creates a data stream (called a *digital signal*) of 8 × 8000 = 64 kilobits per second (Kbps). This digital signal rate, known as *DS0*, makes up the simplest data stream (and the slowest rate) of the digital part of the telephone system. Each analog voice call gets converted into a DS0 signal at the telephone company's central office. From there, they are multiplexed into larger circuits.

Now that we have our voice calls converted to digital data, we need to get them to the right telephone. First, we need network technologies to handle the cabling, frames, and speed. Second, we need to come up with a method to switch the digital voice calls across a network. To handle the former, we need to define the types of interconnections, with names like T1 and OC3. To handle the latter, we no longer connect via multiplexed circuit switching, as we did back with analog, but rather are now switching packets. I'll show you what I mean as I discuss the digital lines in use today.

Copper Carriers: T1 and T3

The first (and still popular) digital trunk carriers used by the telephone industry are called *T-carriers*. There are a number of different versions of T-carriers and the CompTIA Network+ exam expects you to know something about them. Let's begin with the most common and most basic, the venerable T-carrier level 1 (T1).

T1 has several meanings. First, it refers to a high-speed digital networking technology called a *T1 connection*. Second, the term *T1 line* refers to the specific, shielded, two-pair cabling that connects the two ends of a T1 connection (Figure 14-12). Two wires are for sending data and two wires are for receiving data. At either end of a T1 line, you'll find an unassuming box called a *Channel Service Unit/Digital Service Unit (CSU/DSU)*. The CSU/DSU has a second connection that goes from the phone company (where the boxes reside) to a customer's equipment (usually a router). A T1 connection is point-to-point—you cannot have more than two CSU/DSUs on a single T1 line.

Figure 14-12
T1 line

 EXAM TIP You can connect two CSU/DSU boxes together directly by using a T1 crossover cable. Like the UTP crossover cables you've seen previously in the book, the *T1 crossover cable* simply reverses the send/receive pairs on one end of the cable. You'll only see this in use to connect older routers together. The CSU/DSU connections provide convenient link points.

T1 uses a special signaling method called a *digital signal 1 (DS1)*.

DS1 uses a relatively primitive frame—the frame doesn't need to be complex because with point-to-point no addressing is necessary. Each DS1 frame has 25 pieces: a framing bit and 24 channels. Each DS1 channel holds a single 8-bit DS0 data sample. The framing bit and data channels combine to make 193 bits per DS1 frame. These frames are transmitted 8000 times/sec, making a total throughput of 1.544 Mbps (Figure 14-13). DS1 defines, therefore, a data transfer speed of 1.544 Mbps, split into twenty-five 64-Kbps DS0 channels. The process of having frames that carry a portion of every channel in every frame sent on a regular interval is called *time division multiplexing (TDM)*.

NOTE Each 64-Kbps channel in a DS1 signal is a DS0.

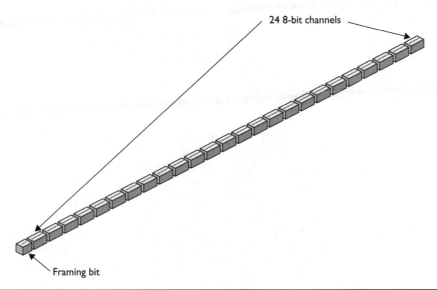

24 8-bit channels

Framing bit

Figure 14-13 DS1 frame

When discussing T1 technology in class, I like to use an analogy of a conveyor belt in a milk-bottling factory. At regular intervals, big crates with 24 bottles come rolling down the belt. When they reach the filling machine, the bottles get filled with milk, and the crate keeps rolling down to the other end where two machines take over: the labeling and sorting machines. The labeling machine plucks out the bottles and applies a label to each, appropriate to the contents. The sorting machine sorts the bottles into cases of each type.

This is pretty simple if the filling machine uses only one type of milk. All 24 bottles fill with whole milk, all are labeled as whole milk, and all go into the case marked "Whole Milk." Once enough full bottles of milk arrive, the case gets completed, and you have a product.

That's pretty much how an Ethernet frame works, right? The whole frame encapsulates a single set of data, such as an IP packet that, in turn, encapsulates a single type of TCP segment or UDP datagram. It generally takes multiple frames to get the data to the recipient, where the frames are removed, the IP packet is removed, and the segment or datagram gets put together to make the data transfer complete.

The cool thing about the DS1 frame, though, is that you don't have to use the whole frame for a single set of data. With the right CSU/DSU at either end, you can specify which channels go with a specific thread of data. Sloshing back into the analogy, the milk company produces four types of milk: whole milk, low-fat milk, chocolate milk, and strawberry milk. The strawberry milk is seasonal; the whole milk sells the most, followed by chocolate, and then low fat.

To accommodate the different products, the factory master might designate channels 1–10 for whole milk, 11–18 for chocolate milk, 19–22 for low-fat milk, and 23–24 for strawberry. Now the labeling and sorting machines are going to have to work for a living! When a crate reaches the filling machine, the bottles get filled with the various types of milk, and then the crate trundles on down the belt. The labeling machine knows the numbering system, so it labels bottles 1–10 as whole milk, 11–18 as chocolate, and so on. The sorting machine also knows the system and has four cases at hand, one for each product. As the bottles arrive, it places them into the appropriate cases. Note that the cases will fill at different rates of speed. The strawberry milk case will take longer to fill, especially compared to the whole milk case, because only two channels in each crate carry strawberry.

What happens if the cows temporarily stop producing chocolate milk? Will the whole factory need to be reordered so the filling machine's eight chocolate dispensers can dispense some other kind of milk? Not in this factory. The crates continue to roll down the conveyor belt at regular intervals. The filling machine fills the bottles in channels 1–10 with whole milk, leaves the bottles in channels 11–18 empty, and puts low fat and strawberry in channels 19–22 and 23–24, respectively.

DS1/T1 work the same way. The frame just keeps jetting down the line, even if some of the channels contain no data. The CSU/DSU at the other end collects the data streams and keeps them separate. To paraphrase the immortal words of Professor Egon, "Never cross the streams." (You have seen *Ghostbusters*, right?) Otherwise you'd lose data.

NOTE People rarely use the term "DS1." Because T1 lines only carry DS1 signals, you usually just say T1 when describing the signal, even though the term DS1 is more accurate.

To bring the milk bottling–factory analogy completely into the realm of networking and T1 connections, keep in mind that two conveyor belts are running in opposite directions. Milk flows in; milk flows out. You can both send and receive on T1 connections.

A T1 line is a dedicated phone connection that you lease, usually on a monthly basis, from the telephone company. It has no telephone number, and it's always connected. An entire T1 bundle is expensive, so many telephone companies let you buy just some of these individual channels, a practice known as *fractional T1 access*.

A *T3 line* supports a data rate of about 45 Mbps on a dedicated telephone connection. It consists of 672 individual DS0 channels. T3 lines (sometimes referred to as *DS3 lines*) are mainly used by regional telephone companies and ISPs connecting to the Internet.

Similar to the North American T1 line, E-carrier level 1 (*E1*) is the European format for digital transmission. An E1 line carries signals at 2.048 Mbps (32 channels at 64 Kbps), compared to the T1's 1.544 Mbps (24 channels at 64 Kbps). E1 and T1 lines can interconnect for international use. There are also E3 lines, which carry 16 E1 lines, with a bandwidth of about 34 Mbps.

EXAM TIP E1 and SONET use a derivative of the *High-Level Data Link Control (HDLC)* protocol as the control channel.

A CSU/DSU, as mentioned earlier, connects a leased T1 or T3 line from the telephone company to a customer's equipment. A CSU/DSU has (at least) two connectors, one that goes to the T1/T3 line running out of your demarc and another connection that goes to your router. It performs line encoding and conditioning functions and often has a loopback function for testing. Many newer routers have CSU/DSUs built into them. Figure 14-14 shows the front of a Juniper Networks router with two T1 interfaces.

Figure 14-14 CSU/DSU on a Juniper router (photo courtesy of Juniper Networks, Inc.)

Many routers feature two interfaces on one router, with the dual links providing redundancy if one link goes down. The CSU part of a CSU/DSU protects the T1 or T3 line and the user equipment from lightning strikes and other types of electrical interference. It also stores statistics and has capabilities for loopback testing. The DSU part supplies timing to each user port, taking the incoming user's data signals and converting the input signal into the specified line code and then framing the format for transmission over the provided line.

Make sure you know the four T-carriers shown in Table 14-1!

	Carrier	Channels	Speed
Table 14-1 T-carriers	TI	24	1.544 Mbps
	T3	672	44.736 Mbps
	E1	32	2.048 Mbps
	E3	512	34.368 Mbps

Fiber Carriers: SONET/SDH and OC

T-carriers were a great start into the digital world, but in the early 1980s, fiber-optic cabling became the primary tool for long-distance communication all over the world. By now, AT&T was gone, replaced by a number of competing carriers. Competition was strong and everyone was making their own fiber transmission standards. In an incredible moment of corporate cooperation, in 1987, all of the primary fiber-optic carriers decided to drop their own standards and move to a new international standard called *Synchronous Optical Network (SONET)* in the United States and *Synchronous Digital Hierarchy (SDH)* in Europe.

NOTE Students often wonder why two separate names exist for the same technology. In reality, SONET and SDH vary a little in their signaling and frame type, but routers and other magic boxes on the Internet handle the interoperability between the standards. The American National Standards Institute (ANSI) publishes the standard as SONET; the International Telecommunication Union (ITU) publishes the standard as SDH, but includes SONET signaling. For simplicity's sake and because SONET is the more common term in the United States, this book uses SONET as the term for this technology.

All of these carriers adopting the same standard created a world of simple interconnections between competing voice and data carriers. This adoption defined the moment that truly made the Internet a universal network. Before SONET, interconnections happened, but they were outlandishly expensive, preventing the Internet from reaching many areas of the world.

SONET remains the primary standard for long-distance, high-speed, fiber-optic transmission systems. SONET, like Ethernet, defines interface standards at the Physical and Data Link layers of the OSI seven-layer model. The physical aspect of SONET is partially covered by the Optical Carrier standards, but it also defines a ring-based topology that most SONET adopters now use. SONET does not require a ring, but a SONET ring has fault tolerance in case of line loss. As a result, most of the big long-distance optical pipes for the world's telecommunications networks are SONET rings.

EXAM TIP SONET is one of the most important standards for making all WAN interconnections—and it's also the least likely standard you'll ever see because it's hidden away from all but the biggest networks.

The real beauty of SONET lies in its multiplexing capabilities. A single SONET ring can combine multiple DS1, DS3, even European E1 signals, and package them into single, huge SONET frames for transmission. Clearly, SONET needs high-capacity fiber optics to handle such large data rates. That's where the Optical Carrier standards come into play!

The *Optical Carrier (OC)* standards denote the optical data-carrying capacity (in bps) of fiber-optic cables in networks conforming to the SONET standard. The OC standard describes an escalating series of speeds, designed to meet the needs of medium-to-large corporations. SONET establishes OC speeds from 51.8 Mbps (OC-1) to 39.8 Gbps (OC-768).

Still want more throughput? Many fiber devices now use a very clever feature called *Wavelength Division Multiplexing (WDM)* or its newer and more popular version, *Dense WDM (DWDM)*. DWDM enables an individual single-mode fiber to carry multiple signals by giving each signal a different wavelength. The result varies, but a single DWDM fiber can support ~150 signals, enabling, for example, a 51.8-Mbps OC-1 line run at 51.8 Mbps × 150 signals = 7.77 *gigabytes per second!* DWDM has become very popular for long-distance lines as it's usually less expensive to replace older SONET/OC-*x* equipment with DWDM than it is to add more fiber lines.

 NOTE DWDM isn't just upgrading SONET lines; DWDM works just as well on long-distance fiber Ethernet.

SONET uses the *Synchronous Transport Signal (STS)* signal method. The STS consists of two parts: the *STS payload* (which carries data) and the *STS overhead* (which carries the signaling and protocol information). When folks talk about STS, they add a number to the end of "STS" to designate the speed of the signal. For example, STS-1 runs a 51.85 Mbps signal on an OC-1 line. STS-3 runs at 155.52 Mbps on OC-3 lines, and so on. Table 14-2 describes the most common optical carriers.

SONET Optical Level	Line Speed	Signal Method
OC-1	51.85 Mbps	STS-1
OC-3	155.52 Mbps	STS-3
OC-12	622.08 Mbps	STS-12
OC-24	1.244 Gbps	STS-24
OC-48	2.488 Gbps	STS-48
OC-192	9.955 Gbps	STS-192
OC-256	13.22 Gbps	STS-256
OC-768	39.82 Gbps	STS-768

Table 14-2 Common Optical Carriers

Packet Switching

All of these impressive connections that start with *T*s and *O*s are powerful, but they are not in and of themselves a complete WAN solution. These WAN connections with their unique packets (DS0, STS, and so on) make up the entire mesh of long-range connections called the Internet, carrying both packetized voice data and TCP/IP data packets. All of these connections are point-to-point, so you need to add another level of devices to enable you to connect multiple T1s, T3s, or OC connections together to make that mesh. That's where packet switching comes into play.

EXAM TIP The first generation of packet-switching technology was called *X.25*. It enabled remote devices to communicate with each other across high-speed digital links without the expense of individual leased lines. CompTIA also refers to X.25 as the *CCITT Packet Switching Protocol*.

Packets, as you know, need some form of addressing scheme to get from one location to another. The telephone industry came up with its own types of packets that run on T-carrier and OC lines to get data from one central office to another. These packet-switching protocols are functionally identical to routable network protocols like TCP/IP. Today's WAN connections predominantly use two different forms of packet switching: Frame Relay and ATM.

 EXAM TIP Machines that forward and store packets using any type of packet switching protocol are called *packet switches*.

Frame Relay

Frame Relay is an extremely efficient packet-switching standard, designed for and used primarily with T-carrier lines. It works especially well for the off-again/on-again traffic typical of most LAN applications. Frame Relay switches packets quickly, but without any guarantee of data integrity at all. You can't even count on it to deliver all the frames, because it will discard frames whenever there is network congestion. At first this might sound problematic—what happens if you have a data problem? In practice, however, a Frame Relay network delivers data quite reliably because T-carrier digital lines that use Frame Relay have very low error rates. It's up to the higher-level protocols to error-check as needed. Frame Relay was extremely popular in its day, but newer technologies such as ATM and especially MPLS are beginning to replace it. If you decide to go with a T1 line in the United States, you'll get a T1 line running Frame Relay, although many companies use the newer ATM standard as their packet-switching solution with T-carrier lines.

ATM

Don't think automatic teller machine here! *Asynchronous Transfer Mode (ATM)* is a network technology originally designed for high-speed LANs in the early 1990s. ATM only saw limited success in the LAN world, but became extremely popular in the WAN world. In fact, until the recent advent of MPLS (see "MPLS" next), most of the SONET rings that moved voice and data all over the world used ATM for packet switching. ATM integrated voice, video, and data on one connection, using short and fixed-length packets called *cells* to transfer information. Every cell sent with the same source and destination traveled over the same route.

ATM existed because data and audio/video transmissions have different transfer requirements. Data tolerates a delay in transfer, but not signal loss (if it takes a moment for a Web page to appear, you don't care). Audio and video transmissions, on the other hand, tolerate signal loss but not delay (delay makes phone calls sound choppy and clipped). Because ATM transferred information in cells of one set size (53 bytes long), it handled both types of transfers well. ATM transfer speeds ranged from 155.52 to 622.08 Mbps and beyond. If your location was big enough to order an OC line from your ISP, odds were good that OC line connected to an ATM switch.

NOTE Referring to ATM in the past tense might seem a bit premature. Plenty of ISPs still use ATM, but it's definitely on the way out due to MPLS.

MPLS

Frame Relay and ATM were both fantastic packet-switching technologies, but they were designed to support any type of traffic that might come over the network. Today, TCP/IP, the predominant data technology, has a number of issues that neither Frame Relay nor ATM address. For example, ATM uses a very small frame, only 53 bytes, which adds quite a bit of overhead to 1500-byte Ethernet frames. To address this and other issues, many ISPs (and large ISP clients) use an improved technology called *Multiprotocol Label Switching (MPLS)* as a replacement for Frame Relay and ATM switching.

MPLS adds an MPLS label that sits between the Layer 2 header and the Layer 3 information. Layer 3 is always IP, so MPLS labels sit between Layer 2 and the IP headers. Figure 14-15 shows the structure of an MPLS header.

Figure 14-15
MPLS header

The MPLS header consists of four parts:

- **Label** A unique identifier, used by MPLS-capable routers to determine how to move data.
- **Cost of Service (CoS)** A relative value used to determine the importance of the labeled packet.
- **S** In certain situations, a single packet may have multiple MPLS labels. This single bit value is set to 1 for the initial label.
- **Time to Live (TTL)** A value that determines the number of hops the label can make before it's eliminated

Figure 14-16 shows the location of the MPLS header.

Figure 14-16 MPLS header inserted in a frame

The original idea for MPLS was to give individual ISPs a way to move traffic through their morass of different interconnections and switches more quickly and efficiently by providing network-wide quality of service. MPLS-capable routers avoid running IP packets through their full routing tables and instead use the header information to route packets quickly. Where "regular" routers use QoS on an individual basis, MPLS routers use their existing dynamic routing protocols to send each other messages about their overhead, enabling QoS to span an entire group of routers (Figure 14-17).

Figure 14-17 MPLS routers talk to each other about their overhead.

Let's see how the MPLS-labeled packets, combined with MPLS-capable routers, create improved throughput. To see this happen, I need to introduce a few MPLS terms:

- **Forwarding Equivalence Class (FEC)** FEC is a group of devices (usually computers) that tend to send packets to the same place, such as a single broadcast domain of computers connected to a router.

- **Label switching router (LSR)** An LSR looks for and forwards packets based on their MPLS label. These are the "MPLS routers" mentioned previously.

- **Label edge router (LER)** An LER is an MPLS router that has the job of adding MPLS labels to incoming packets that do not yet have a label.

- **Label Distribution Protocol (LDP)** LSRs and LERs use the LDP to communicate dynamic information about their state. Figure 14-17 shows an example of LDP in action.

Figure 14-18 shows a highly simplified MPLS network. Note the position of the LERs and LSRs.

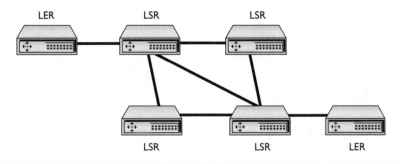

Figure 14-18 Sample MPLS network

When an MPLS network comes online, administrators will configure initial routing information, primarily setting metrics to routes (Figure 14-19).

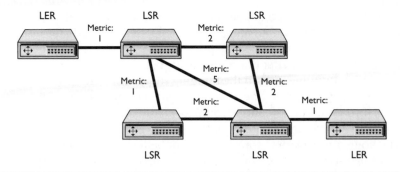

Figure 14-19 MPLS initial routes added

LERs have the real power in determining routes. Because LERs are the entrances and exits for an MPLS network, they talk to each other to determine the best possible routes. As data moves from one FEC, the LERs add an MPLS label to every packet. LSRs strip away incoming labels and add their own. This progresses until the packets exit out the opposing LER (Figure 14-20).

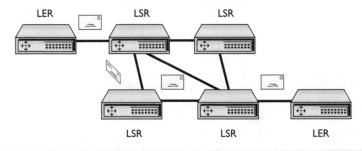

Figure 14-20 Data routing through an MPLS network

Although MPLS was originally used just to move data quickly between LERs, MPLS's label-stacking ability makes it a perfect candidate for end-user VPNs. Instead of having to set up your own VPN, an ISP using MPLS can set up and lease you a fully functional connection to your network. The ISP makes the VPN for you; you just insert an RJ-45 plug into the switch in your office and it works. This feature of MPLS is called a *permanent virtual circuit (PVC)* and is a popular product sold by ISPs to connect two customer locations.

Real-World WAN

There are two reasons to use a telephony WAN connection: to get your LAN on the Internet or to make a private connection between two or more of your private LANs. How you go about getting one of these lines changes a bit depending on which you want to do. Let's start with connecting to the Internet.

Traditionally, getting a WAN Internet connection was a two-step process: you talked to the telephone company to get the line physically installed and then talked to an ISP to provide you with Internet access. Today, almost every telephone company is also an ISP, so this process is usually simple. Just go online and do a Web search of ISPs in your area and give them a call. You'll get a price quote, and, if you sign up, the ISP will do the installation.

You can use a few tricks to reduce the price, however. If you're in an office building, odds are good that a T1 or better line is already installed and that an ISP is already serving people in your building. Talk to the building supervisor. If there isn't a T1 or better line, you have to pay for a new line. If an interconnect is nearby, this option might be inexpensive. If you want the telephone company to run an OC line to your house, however, brace for a quote of thousands of dollars just to get the line.

The telephone company runs your T-carrier (or better) line to a demarc. This demarc is important because this is where the phone company's responsibility ends! Everything on "your" side of the demarc is your responsibility. From there, you or your ISP installs a CSU/DSU (for T-carriers) and that device connects to your router.

Depending on who does this for you, you may encounter a tremendous amount of variance here. The classic example (sticking with T-carrier) consists of a demarc, CSU/DSU, and router setup, as shown in Figure 14-21.

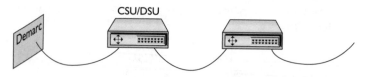

CSU/DSU

Figure 14-21 Old-school T-carrier setup

T-carriers have been around so long that many of these parts are combined. You'll often see a single box that combines the CSU/DSU and the router in one handy device, such as the Juniper router shown earlier in Figure 14-14.

WAN telephony carriers are incredibly dependable—far more dependable than inexpensive alternatives (like cable modems)—and that's one of the main reasons people still use them. But you should definitely know how to test your end of the connection if you ever suspect a problem. The single most important test is called the *Bit Error Rate Test*

(BERT). A BERT test verifies the T-carrier connection from end to end. Every CSU/DSU has a different way to BERT test. Just make sure you know how to perform the test on yours!

Alternative to Telephony WAN

Telephony WANs were the first big connections. They're still the core of what makes up most of the Internet backbone and private connections, but they've given way to more advanced technologies. The three biggest newer technologies for Internet connections are Ethernet, DSL, and cable modems. I need to give them a quick mention here.

Over the last few years, many ISPs started replacing their T1, T3, and OC*x* equipment with good-old Ethernet. Well, not "good-old" Ethernet—rather, superfast 10 Gbps Ethernet running on single-mode fiber and connected to DWDM-capable switches. As a result, in many areas—especially metropolitan areas—you can get native Ethernet right to your office. Anyone want 10 Gbps to their router? If you've got the money and you're in a larger city, you can get it now. These Ethernet connections also work great for dedicated connections. A good friend of mine leases a dedicated 10 Gbps Ethernet connection from his company's data center in Houston, Texas, to his office in London, England. It costs roughly $15,000/month. DSL and cable have been around for quite a while and deserve some serious discussion. You can't install your own DSL or cable modem connection, however, as you can with telephony WAN carriers. For example, you can't have your own private cable modem connection between two of your offices. DSL and cable modems are only for Internet connections and, as a result, are really more of a last-mile issue—let's discuss DSL and cable in the next section.

 NOTE OCx refers to the Optical Carrier standards collectively.

The Last Mile

Speed is the key to the Internet, but historically there's always been one big challenge: getting data from central offices to individual users. Although this wasn't a problem for larger companies that could afford their own WAN connections, what about individuals and small companies that couldn't or wouldn't pay hundreds of dollars a month for a T1? This area, the infamous last mile, was a serious challenge early on for both Internet connections and private connections because the only common medium was standard telephone lines. A number of last-mile solutions have appeared over the years, and the CompTIA Network+ exam tests you on the most popular ones—and a few obscure ones as well. Here's the list:

- Dial-up
- DSL
- Cable
- Satellite
- Cellular
- Fiber
- BPL

Dial-Up

Many different types of telephone lines are available, but all the choices break down into two groups: dedicated and dial-up. *Dedicated lines* are always off the hook (that is, they never hang up on each other).

A dedicated line (like a T1) does not have a phone number. In essence, the telephone company creates a permanent, hard-wired connection between the two locations, rendering a phone number superfluous. *Dial-up lines*, by contrast, have phone numbers; they must dial each other up to make a connection. When they're finished communicating, they hang up. Two technologies make up the overwhelming majority of dial-up connections: PSTN and ISDN.

Public Switched Telephone Network

The oldest, slowest, and most common original phone connection is the *public switched telephone network (PSTN)*. PSTN is also known as *plain old telephone service (POTS)*. PSTN is just a regular phone line, the same line that used to run into everybody's home telephone jacks from the central office of your *Local Exchange Carrier (LEC)*. The LEC is the telephone company (telco) that provides local connections and usually the one that owns your local central office).

 EXAM TIP A company that provides local telephone service to individual customers is called a *Local Exchange Carrier (LEC)*. A company that provides long-distance service is called an *Interexchange Carrier (IXC)*. Classically, LECs owned the central offices and IXCs owned the lines and equipment that interconnected them. Over time, the line between LECs and IXCs has become very blurred.

Because PSTN was designed long before computers were common, it was designed to work with only one type of data: sound. Here's how it works. The telephone's microphone takes the sound of your voice and translates it into an electrical analog waveform. The telephone then sends that signal through the PSTN line to the phone on the other end of the connection. That phone translates the signal into sound on the other end using its speaker. Note the word *analog*. The telephone microphone converts the sounds into electrical waveforms that cycle 2400 times a second. An individual cycle is known as a *baud*. The number of bauds per second is called the *baud rate*. Pretty much all phone companies' PSTN lines have a baud rate of 2400. PSTN connections use a connector called RJ-11. It's the classic connector you see on all telephones (Figure 14-22).

Figure 14-22
RJ-11 connectors
(top and side views)

When you connect your modem to a phone jack, the line then runs to your *network interface unit (NIU)*, or demarc. The term "network interface unit" is more commonly used to describe the small box on the side of a home that accepts the incoming lines from the telephone company and then splits them to the different wall outlets. "Demarc" more commonly describes large connections used in businesses. The terms are interchangeable and always describe the interface between the lines the telephone company is responsible for and the lines for which you are responsible (Figure 14-23).

Figure 14-23
Typical home demarc

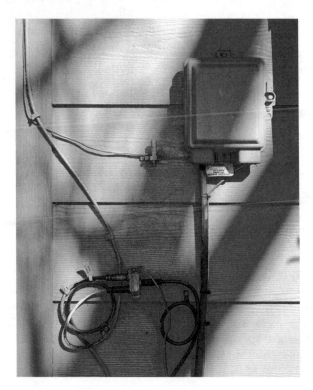

Computers, as you know, don't speak analog—only digital/binary (0 or 1) will do. In addition, the people who invented the way PCs communicate decided to divide any digital signal going in and out of your computer into 8 bits at a time. To connect over phone lines, PCs need two devices: one that converts this 8-bit-wide (parallel) digital signal from the computer into serial (1-bit -wide) digital data and then another device to convert (modulate) the data into analog waveforms that can travel across PSTN lines. You already know that the device that converts the digital data to analog and back is called a *modulator-demodulator (modem)*. The modem in your PC (assuming you still have one) also contains a device called a *Universal Asynchronous Receiver/Transmitter (UART)*. The UART takes the 8-bit-wide digital data and converts it into 1-bit-wide digital data and hands it to the modem for conversion to analog. The process is reversed for incoming data. Even though internal modems are actually both a UART and a modem, we just say the word "modem" (Figure 14-24).

Figure 14-24

Internal modem

NOTE Internal modems are both a UART and a modem. External modems use a serial or USB port. The serial or USB port contains the UART, so the external modem truly is just a modem.

Baud vs. Bits per Second

Modems use phone lines to transmit data at various speeds. These speeds cause a world of confusion and problems for computer people. This is where a little bit of knowledge becomes dangerous. Standard modems you can buy for your home computer normally transmit data at speeds up to 56 Kbps. That's 56 kilobits per second, *not* 56 kilobaud! Many people confuse the terms *baud* and *bits per second*. This confusion arises because the baud rate and bits per second are the same for modems until the data transfer rate surpasses 2400 bps.

A PSTN phone line takes analog samples of sound 2400 times a second. This standard was determined a long time ago as an acceptable rate for sending voice traffic over phone lines. Although 2400-baud analog signals are fine for voice communication, they are a big problem for computers trying to send data because computers only work with digital signals. The job of the modem is to take the digital signals it receives from the computer and send them out over the phone line in an analog form, using the baud cycles from the phone system. A 2400-bps modem—often erroneously called a 2400-baud modem—uses 1 analog baud to send 1 bit of data.

As technology progressed, modems became faster and faster. To get past the 2400-baud limit, modems modulated the 2400-baud signal multiple times in each cycle. A 4800-bps modem modulated 2 bits per baud, thereby transmitting 4800 bps. All PSTN modem speeds are a multiple of 2400, with the latest (and last) generation of modems achieving 2,400 × 24 = 57,600 bps (56 Kbps).

V Standards

For two modems to communicate with each other at their fastest rate, they must modulate signals in the same fashion. The two modems must also negotiate with, or *query*, each other to determine the fastest speed they share. The modem manufacturers themselves originally standardized these processes as a set of proprietary protocols. The downside to these protocols was that unless you had two modems from the same manufacturer, modems often would not work together. In response, the International Telegraph and Telephone Consultative Committee (*CCITT*), a European standards body, established standards for modems. These standards, known generically as the *V standards*, define the speeds at which modems can modulate. The most common of these speed standards are as follows:

- **V.22**   1,200 bps
- **V.22bis**   2,400 bps
- **V.32**   9,600 bps
- **V.32bis**   14,400 bps
- **V.34**   28,000 bps
- **V.90**   57,600 bps
- **V.92**   57,600 bps

The current modem standard now on the market is the *V.92 standard*. V.92 has the same download speed as the V.90, but upstream rates increase to as much as 48 Kbps. If your modem is having trouble getting 56-Kbps rates with V.90 in your area, you will not notice an improvement. V.92 also offers a Quick Connect feature that implements faster handshaking to cut connection delays. Finally, the V.92 standard offers a Modem On Hold feature that enables the modem to stay connected while you take an incoming call-waiting call or even initiate an outgoing voice call. This feature only works if the V.92 server modem is configured to enable it.

In addition to speed standards, the CCITT, now known simply as the International Telecommunication Union (ITU), has established standards controlling how modems compress data and perform error checking when they communicate. These standards are as follows:

- **V.42**   Error checking
- **V.42bis**   Data compression
- **V.44**   Data compression
- **MNP5**   Both error checking and data compression

 EXAM TIP   Do not memorize these V standards—just know what they do.

The beauty of these standards is that you don't need to do anything special to enjoy their benefits. If you want 56-Kbps data transfers, for example, you simply need to ensure that the modems in the local system and the remote system both support the V.90 standard. Assuming you have good line quality, the connections will run at or at least close to 56 Kbps.

ISDN

PSTN lines traditionally just aren't that good. While the digital equipment that connects to a PSTN supports a full 64-Kbps DS0 channel, the combination of the lines themselves and the conversion from analog to digital means that most PSTN lines rarely go faster than 33 Kbps—and, yes, that includes the 56 Kbps connections.

A PSTN telephone connection has many pieces. First, there's the modem in your computer that converts the digital information to analog. Then there's the phone line that runs from your phone out to your NIU and into the central office. The central office stores the modems that convert the analog signal back to digital and the telephone switches that interconnect multiple individual local connections into the larger telephone network. A central office switch connects to long-distance carriers via high-capacity *trunk lines* (at least a T1) and also connects to other nearby central offices. The analog last mile was an awful way to send data, but it had one huge advantage: most everyone owned a telephone line.

During this upgrade period, customers continued to demand higher throughput from their phone lines. The phone companies were motivated to come up with a way to generate higher capacities. Their answer was fairly straightforward: make the last mile digital. Since everything but the last mile was already digital, by adding special equipment at the central office and the user's location, phone companies felt they could achieve a true, steady, dependable throughput of 64 Kbps per line over the same copper wires already used by PSTN lines. This process of sending telephone transmission across fully digital lines end-to-end is called *Integrated Services Digital Network (ISDN)* service.

 NOTE ISDN also supports voice but requires special ISDN telephones.

ISDN service consists of two types of channels: *Bearer channels (B channels)* carry data and voice information using standard DS0 channels (64 Kbps), whereas *Delta channels (D channels)* carry setup and configuration information at 16 Kbps. Most ISDN providers let the user choose either one or two B channels. The more common setup is two B/one D, called a *Basic Rate Interface (BRI)* setup. A BRI setup uses only one physical line, but each B channel sends 64 Kbps, doubling the throughput total to 128 Kbps.

Another type of ISDN is called *Primary Rate Interface (PRI)*. ISDN PRI is actually just a full T1 line, carrying 23 B channels.

The physical connections for ISDN bear some similarity to PSTN modems. An ISDN wall socket is usually something that looks like a standard RJ-45 network jack. This line runs to your demarc. In home installations, many telephone companies install a second demarc separate from your PSTN demarc. The most common interface for your computer is a device called a *terminal adapter (TA)*. TAs look like regular modems and, like modems, come in external and internal variants. You can even get TAs that also function as hubs, enabling your system to support a direct LAN connection (Figure 14-25).

Figure 14-25
A TeleWell ISDN
terminal adapter

 EXAM TIP   Remember, a B channel is a DS0 channel.

You generally need to be within approximately 18,000 feet of a central office to use ISDN. When you install an ISDN TA, you must configure the other ISDN telephone number you want to call, as well as a special number called the *Service Profile ID (SPID)*. Your ISP provides the telephone number, and the telephone company gives you the SPID. (In many cases, the telephone company is also the ISP.) Figure 14-26 shows a typical installation screen for an internal ISDN TA in an old version of Windows. Note that each channel has a phone number in this case.

Figure 14-26
ISDN settings in an
old version of Windows

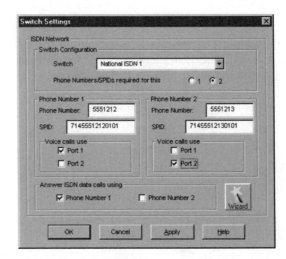

ISDN continues to soldier on in today's networking world, but with the exception of a few unique markets, such as automated teller machines (ATMs), ISDN has been replaced by faster and less expensive methods such as DSL and cable modems. Nevertheless, every major telephone company still provides ISDN.

DSL

Many telephone companies offer a *digital subscriber line (DSL)* connection, a fully digital, dedicated (no phone number) connection. DSL represented the next great leap forward past ISDN for telephone lines. A physical DSL connection manifests as just another PSTN connection, using the same telephone lines and RJ-11 jacks as any regular phone line. DSL comes in a number of versions, but the three most important to know for the CompTIA Network+ exam are *Symmetric DSL (SDSL)*, *Asymmetric DSL (ADSL)*, and the newer *Very High Bitrate DSL (VDSL)*. SDSL lines provide the same upload and download speeds, making them excellent for those who send as much data as they receive, although SDSL is relatively expensive (VDSL is a new form of SDSL—see "VDSL" later in this section). ADSL uses different upload and download speeds. ADSL download speeds are much faster than the upload speeds. Most small office and home office (SOHO) users are primarily concerned with fast *downloads* for things like Web pages and can tolerate slower upload speeds. ADSL is always much less expensive than SDSL, and VDSL is usually the most expensive.

 NOTE To use DSL, you must be within 18,000 feet of a central switch. The closer you are, the faster your connection will be. Several companies offer a service called *Extended DSL (XDSL)* that can go much farther away from the central switch, but that's not a standard. Depending on the implementation, Extended DSL is a rebranded T1 or partial T1 line or something completely proprietary to the telecommunications company offering the service. Buyer beware!

SDSL

SDSL provides equal upload and download speed and, in theory, provides speeds up to 15 Mbps, although the vast majority of ISPs provide packages ranging from 192 Kbps to 9 Mbps. A recent tour of some major DSL providers in my hometown of Houston, Texas, revealed the following SDSL speed options:

- 192 Kbps
- 384 Kbps
- 768 Kbps
- 1.1 Mbps
- 1.5 Mbps

As you might imagine, the pricing for the faster services was higher than for the lower services!

ADSL

ADSL provides theoretical maximum download speeds up to 15 Mbps and upload speeds up to 1 Mbps. All ADSL suppliers "throttle" their ADSL speeds, however, and provide different levels of service. Real-world ADSL download speeds vary from 384 Kbps to 15 Mbps, and upload speeds go from as low as 128 Kbps to around 768 Kbps. Touring the same DSL providers in Houston, Texas, here's a few speed options:

- 384 Kbps download/128 Kbps upload
- 1.5 Mbps download/384 Kbps upload
- 6 Mbps download/768 Kbps upload

NOTE The one potentially costly aspect of ADSL service is the ISP link. Many ISPs add a significant surcharge to use ADSL. Before you choose ADSL, make sure your ISP provides ADSL links at a reasonable price. Most telephone companies bundle ISP services with their ADSL service for a relatively low cost.

VDSL

VDSL is the latest version of DSL to appear. Although not as many people use it as regular DSL (at least in the United States), its ability to provide speeds up to 100 Mbps in both directions makes it an attractive option. VDSL achieves these speeds by adding very advanced methods to encode the data. Don't get too excited about these great speed increases. They are very distance dependent: you won't get 100 Mbps unless you're around 300 meters from the DSLAM (see "DSL Features"). VDSL is designed to run on copper phone lines, but many VDSL suppliers use fiber-optic cabling to increase distances. In the United States, these fiber VDSL services are fiber-to-the-home solutions. The two most popular carriers are AT&T's U-verse and Verizon's Fiber Optic Service (FiOS).

EXAM TIP The CompTIA Network+ objectives offer *Variable* Digital Subscriber Line as the words that match the VDSL initials. No such DSL variant exists. VDSL stands for *Very High Bitrate* DSL. You'll probably only see the initials on the exam, so no worries on that score.

DSL Features

One nice aspect of DSL is that you don't have to run new phone lines. The same DSL lines you use for data can simultaneously transmit your voice calls.

All versions of DSL have the same central office–to–end user distance restrictions as ISDN—around 18,000 feet from your demarc to the central office. At the central office, your DSL provider has a device called a *DSL Access Multiplexer (DSLAM)* that connects multiple customers to the Internet.

NOTE No DSL provider guarantees any particular transmission speed and will only provide service as a "best efforts" contract—a nice way to say that DSL lines are notorious for substantial variations in throughput.

Comparing Options in Your Neighborhood

So what do your local providers offer in terms of higher-speed service, if any? Call your local phone company or shop them on the Web (www.dslreports.com is an excellent reference). Does the company offer DSL? What about ISDN? What speed options do you have? If you want to compare with other parts of the United States, check one of the national services, such as Speakeasy (www.speakeasy.net).

Installing DSL

DSL operates using your preexisting telephone lines (assuming they are up to specification). This is wonderful but also presents a technical challenge. For DSL and your run-of-the-mill POTS line to coexist, you need to filter out the DSL signal on the POTS line. A DSL line has three information channels: a high-speed downstream channel, a medium-speed duplex channel, and a POTS channel. Segregating the two DSL channels from the POTS channel guarantees that your POTS line will continue to operate even if the DSL fails. You accomplish this by inserting a filter on each POTS line, or a splitter mechanism that allows all three channels to flow to the DSL modem but sends only the POTS channel down the POTS line. The DSL company should provide you with a few POTS filters for your telephones. If you need more, most computer/electronics stores stock DSL POTS filters.

NOTE If you install a telephone onto a line in your home with DSL and you forget to add a filter, don't panic. You won't destroy anything, although you won't get a dial tone either! Just insert a DSL POTS filter and the telephone will work.

The most common DSL installation consists of a *DSL modem* connected to a telephone wall jack and to a standard NIC in your computer (Figure 14-27). A DSL modem is not an actual modem—it's more like an ISDN terminal adapter—but the term stuck, and even the manufacturers of the devices now call them DSL modems.

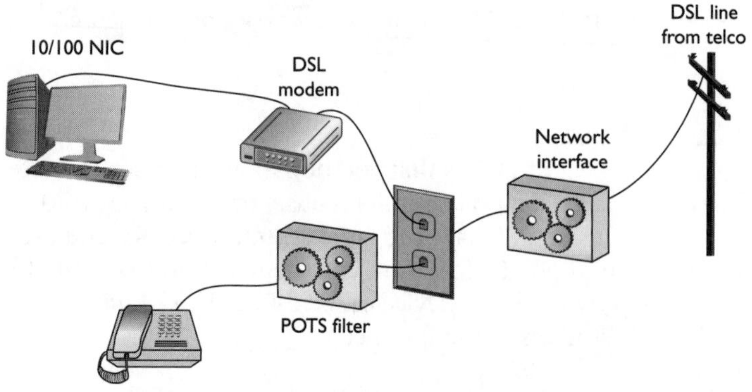

Figure 14-27
A DSL modem connection between a PC and telco

10/100 NIC

DSL modem

DSL line from telco

Network interface

POTS filter

Many offices use DSL. In my office, we use a special DSL line (we use a digital phone system, so the DSL must be separate) that runs directly into our equipment room (Figure 14-28).

Figure 14-28
DSL line into
equipment room

This DSL line runs into our DSL modem via a standard phone line with RJ-11 connectors. The DSL modem connects to our gateway router with a CAT 5e patch cable, which, in turn, connects to the company's switch. Figure 14-29 shows an ADSL modem and a router, giving you an idea of the configuration in our office.

Figure 14-29
DSL connection

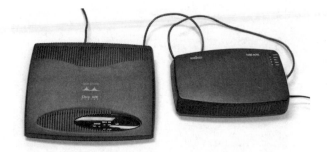

Home users often connect the DSL modem directly to their PC's NIC. Either way, you have nothing to do in terms of installing DSL equipment on an individual system—just make sure you have a NIC. The person who installs your DSL will test the DSL line, install the DSL modem, connect it to your system, and verify that it all works. With DSL, be aware that you might run into an issue with something called *Point-to-Point Protocol over Ethernet (PPPoE)*.

The first generation of DSL providers used a *bridged connection*; once the DSL line was running, it was as if you had snapped an Ethernet cable into your NIC. You were on the network. Those were good days for DSL. You just plugged your DSL modem into your NIC and, assuming your IP settings were whatever the DSL folks told you to use, you were running.

The DSL providers didn't like that too much. There was no control—no way to monitor who was using the DSL modem. As a result, the DSL folks started to use PPPoE, a protocol that was originally designed to encapsulate PPP frames into Ethernet frames. The DSL people adopted it to make stronger controls over your DSL connection. In particular, you could no longer simply connect; you now had to log on with an account and a password to make the DSL connection. PPPoE is now predominant on DSL. If you get a DSL line, your operating system has software to enable you to log onto your DSL network. Most SOHO routers come with built-in PPPoE support, enabling you to enter your user name and password into the router itself (Figure 14-30).

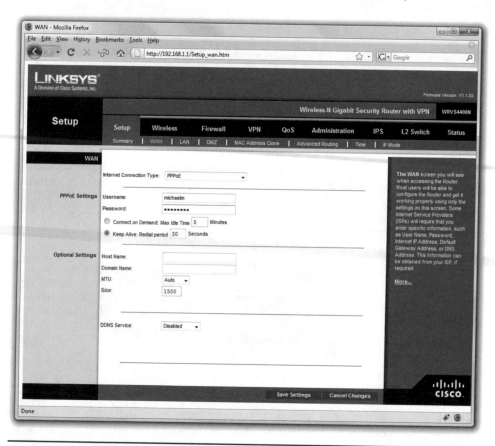

Figure 14-30 PPPoE settings in SOHO router

Cable Modems

The first big competition for ADSL came from the cable companies. Almost every house in America has a coax cable running into it for cable TV. In a moment of genius, the cable industry realized that if it could put the Home Shopping Network and the History Channel into every home, why not provide Internet access? The entire infrastructure of the cabling industry had to undergo some major changes to deal with issues like bidirectional communication, but cable modem service quickly became common in the United States. Cable modems are now as common as cable TV boxes.

Cable modems have the impressive benefit of phenomenal top speeds. These speeds vary from cable company to cable company, but most advertise speeds in the (are you sitting down?) *5 to 100 megabits per second* range. Many cable modems provide a throughput speed of 5 to 30 Mbps for downloading and 2 Mbps to 10 Mbps for uploading—there is tremendous variance among different providers.

A cable modem installation consists of a cable modem connected to a cable. The cable modem gets its own cable connection, separate from the one that goes to the television. It's the same cable line, just split from the main line as if you were adding a second cable outlet for another television. As with ADSL, cable modems connect to PCs using a standard NIC (Figure 14-31).

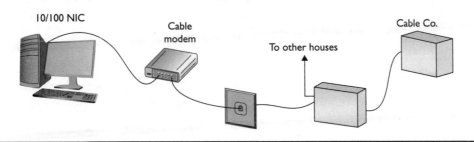

Figure 14-31   Cable modem

Cable modems connect using coax cable to a head end, similar to a telephone company's central office. Head ends, in turn, connect to the cable company's network. This network uses a unique protocol called *Data Over Cable Service Interface Specification (DOCSIS)*. Most recently, the specification was revised (DOCSIS 3.0) to increase transmission speeds significantly (this time both upstream and downstream) and introduce support for Internet Protocol version 6 (IPv6).

   NOTE   Many companies sell routers with a built-in cable modem.

You'll have a hard time telling a cable modem from a DSL modem. The only difference, other than the fact that one will have "cable modem" printed on it whereas the other will say "DSL modem," is that the cable modem has a coax BNC connector and an RJ-45 connector; the DSL modem has an RJ-11 connector and an RJ-45 connector.

Cable modems have proven themselves to be reliable and fast and have surpassed DSL as the broadband connection of choice in homes. Cable companies are also aggressively marketing to business customers with high-speed packages, making cable a viable option for businesses.

Satellite

Living in the countryside may have its charms; but you'll have a hard time getting high-speed Internet out on the farm. For those too far away to get anything else, satellite may be your only option. Satellite access comes in two types: one-way and two-way. *One-way* means that you download via satellite but you must use a PSTN/dial-up modem connection for uploads. *Two-way* means the satellite service handles both the uploading and downloading.

Satellite isn't as fast as DSL or cable modems, but it's still faster than PSTN. Both one-way and two-way satellite connections provide around 500 Kbps download and 50 Kbps upload.

 NOTE Companies that design satellite communications equipment haven't given up on their technology. At the time of this writing, at least one company, HughesNet, offered speeds up to 2 Mbps download. You can surf with that kind of speed!

Satellite requires a small satellite antenna, identical to the ones used for satellite television. This antenna connects to a satellite modem, which, in turn, connects to your PC or your network (Figure 14-32).

Figure 14-32
Satellite connection

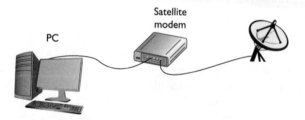

 EXAM TIP Neither cable modems nor satellites use PPP, PPPoE, or anything else that begins with three Ps.

Cellular WAN

Anyone with a smartphone these days appreciates the convenience of using wireless cellular technology on the road. Who doesn't love firing up an Android phone and cruising the Internet from anywhere? The Network+ exam expects you to know a few abbreviations. I'll divide these into two groups: mobile data services and 802.16 (WiMAX).

Mobile Data Services

Mobile data services have names like GSM, GRPS, EDGE, and HSPDA (there are many more standards). These services use the cellular telephone network to provide access.

Primarily used with cell phones and smartphones, most mobile data services have wireless NICs that you can plug into laptops and desktop computers (Figure 14-33).

Figure 14-33
Mobile wireless NIC

802.16

Products that use the *802.16* wireless standard—often called *WiMAX*—are appearing in select markets everywhere. Although speed for 802.16-compliant devices is about the same as 802.11b, manufacturers claim a range of up to 30 miles. This kind of range makes 802.16 perfect for so-called metropolitan area networks (MANs). Before you get too excited, though, keep in mind that the speed of the network will almost certainly decrease the farther away from the base station (the WAP) the nodes are. Effective range could be as little as three miles, but that still beats 300 feet in my book.

If you want WiMAX access right now, you'll probably end up going to CLEAR or Sprint (currently the biggest WiMAX ISPs in America) for a WiMAX home router that plugs directly into your own router (Figure 14-34). They even sell WiMAX/802.11 wireless hot spots, although they limit the number of concurrent connections you can have.

Figure 14-34
CLEAR home modem
(photo courtesy of
CLEAR)

LTE

WiMAX has only one serious competitor—*Long Term Evolution (LTE)*. LTE marks the latest evolution of the popular High-Speed Packet Access (HSPA), better known to the cellular world as GSM or 3G technology. LTE has some heavy-hitter companies behind it, such as AT&T, Verizon, and Sprint. LTE has become quite popular for portable Internet access (see Figure 14-33 for an example), but CLEAR's inexpensive and well-entrenched service should make the next few years interesting in terms of which cellular WAN technology will eventually reign.

Fiber

DSL was the first popular last-mile WAN option but over the years cable modems have taken the lead. In an attempt to regain market share, telephone providers are now rolling out fiber-to-the-home/fiber-to-the-premises options that are giving the cable companies a scare. In the United States, two companies, AT&T (U-verse) and Verizon (FiOS), are offering very attractive ISP, television, and phone services at speeds that will eventually increase above 100 Mbps. These services are quickly gaining in popularity and giving cable companies a run for their money.

To make rollouts affordable, most fiber-to-the-home technologies employ a version of *passive optical network (PON)* architecture that uses a single fiber to the neighborhood switch and then individual fiber runs to each final destination. PON uses WDM to enable multiple signals to travel on the same fiber and then passively splits the signal at the switch to send traffic to its proper recipient.

BPL

With the exception of fiber, most wired networks use electrical signaling to enable systems to interconnect. Rather than running all new wiring dedicated to networks, why not use the vast infrastructure of wiring already in place in just about every home and office in the developed world? Enterprising engineers have been working to provide networking over electrical power lines for many years now with varying degrees of success. The overall field is called *powerline communications (PLC)* and encompasses everything from voice transmission to home automation to high-speed Internet access.

 NOTE The most successful PLC technology is HomePlug, a collection of standards for creating LANs in houses, running smart meters for more efficient electrical use, and home automation. The HomePlug Powerline Alliance, with a membership of over 60 companies, actively promotes the various HomePlug standards and devices.

Broadband over Power Line (BPL) is one specific field of technologies that tries to bring usable Internet access to homes and businesses through the electrical power grid. The various companies that have rolled this out, such as Ambient Corporation, Current Technologies, and Motorola, have had some success, though the electrical grid poses serious challenges to networking because of noise and interference from other devices. Most BPL rollouts to date have failed, but companies continue to explore the possibilities.

Which Connection?

With so many connection options for homes and small offices, making a decision is often a challenge. Your first question is availability: Which services are available in your area? The second question is, How much bandwidth do you need? The latter is a question of great debate. Most services are more than happy to increase service levels if you find that a certain level is too slow. I usually advise clients to start with a relatively slow level and then increase if necessary. After all, once you've tasted the higher speeds, going slower is hard, but the transition to faster is relatively painless!

Going Connection Shopping

You've already checked the availability of DSL and ISDN in your neighborhood, but now you have more choices! Do you have cable or satellite available? A great Web site to start your search is www.dslreports.com. It has a handy search feature that helps you determine the types of service and the costs for DSL, cable, and other services. Which one makes sense for you?

Using Remote Access

Because most businesses are no longer limited to a simple little shop like you would find in a Dickens novel, many people need to be able to access files and resources over a great distance. Enter remote access. *Remote access* uses WAN and LAN connections to enable a computer user to log onto a network from the other side of a city, a state, or even the globe. As people travel, information has to remain accessible. Remote access enables users to connect a server at the business location and log into the network as if they were in the same building as the company. The only problem with remote access is that there are so many ways to do it! I've listed the six most common forms of remote access here:

- **Dial-up to the Internet**   Using a dial-up connection to connect to your ISP
- **Private dial-up**   Using a dial-up connection to connect to your private network
- **Virtual private network**   Using an Internet connection to connect to a private network
- **Dedicated connection**   Using a non-dial-up connection to another private network or the Internet
- **Remote terminal**   Using a terminal emulation program to connect to another computer
- **VoIP**   Voice over IP

In this section, I discuss the issues related to configuring these six types of connections. After seeing how to configure these types of remote connections, I move into observing some security issues common to every type of remote connection.

NOTE You'll see the term *extranet* more in books than in the day-to-day workings of networks and network techs. So what is an extranet? Whenever you allow authorized remote users to access some part of your private network, you have created an extranet.

Dial-Up to the Internet

Dialing up to the Internet is the oldest and least expensive method to connect to the Internet and is still somewhat common. Even with broadband and wireless so prevalent, every self-respecting network tech (or maybe just old network techs like me) keeps a dial-up account as a backup. You buy a dial-up account from an ISP (many wireless and broadband ISPs give free dial-up—just ask). All operating systems come with dial-up support programs, but you'll need to provide:

- A modem (most operating systems check for a modem before setting up a dial-up connection)
- The telephone number to dial (provided to you by the ISP)
- User name and password (provided to you by the ISP)
- Type of connection (dial-up always uses PPP)
- IP information (provided to you by the ISP—usually just DHCP)

Every operating system comes with the software to help you set up a dial-up connection. In Windows Vista or Windows 7, you go to the **Set up a dial-up connection** option in the Network and Sharing Center (Figure 14-35). Whatever the name, this tool is what you use to create dial-up connections.

Private Dial-Up

A private dial-up connection connects a remote system to a private network via a dial-up connection. Private dial-up does not use the Internet! Private dial-up requires two systems. One system acts as a *remote access server (RAS)*. The other system, the client, runs a connection tool (usually the same tool you just read about in the previous section).

In Windows, a RAS is a server running Remote Access Service (RAS), dedicated to handling users who are not directly connected to a LAN but who need to access file and print services on the LAN from a remote location. For example, when a user dials into a network from home using an analog modem connection, she is dialing into a RAS. Once the user authenticates, she can access shared drives and printers as if her computer were physically connected to the office LAN.

NOTE When you run Microsoft's Remote Access Service on a server, you turn that server into a remote access server.

Figure 14-35
Dial-up on
Windows Vista

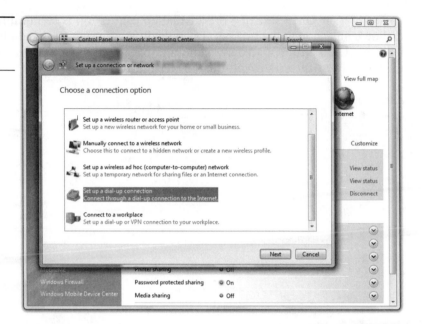

You must set up a server in your LAN as a RAS server. That RAS server, which must have at least one modem, accepts incoming calls and handles password authentication. RAS servers use all the standard authentication methods (PAP, CHAP, EAP, 802.1X, and so on) and have separate sets of permissions for dial-in users and local users. You must also configure the RAS to set the rights and permissions for all of the dial-in users. Configuring a RAS system is outside the scope of this book, however, because each one is different. (Figure 14-36).

Figure 14-36
Windows RAS
in action

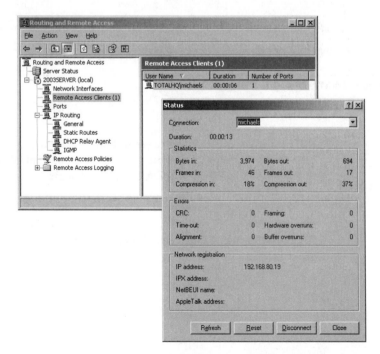

Creating the client side of a private dial-up connection is identical to setting up a dial-up connection to the Internet. The only difference is that instead of having an ISP tell you what IP settings, account name, and password to use, the person who sets up the RAS server tells you this information (Figure 14-37).

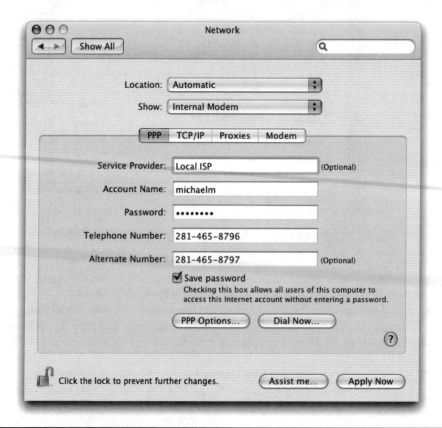

Figure 14-37 Dial-up on Mac OS X

 NOTE *Remote access server* refers to both the hardware component (servers built to handle the unique stresses of a large number of clients calling in) and the software service component of a remote access solution. You might call it a catchall phrase.

Most techs call RAS "razz," rather than using the initials, "R-A-S." This creates a seemingly redundant phrase used to describe a system running RAS: "RAS server." This helps distinguish servers from clients and makes geeks happier.

VPNs

A VPN enables you to connect through a tunnel from a local computer to a remote network securely, as you'll recall from the in-depth discussion in Chapter 12. Refer back to that chapter for the details.

Dedicated Connection

Dedicated connections are remote connections that are never disconnected. Dedicated connections can be broken into two groups: dedicated private connections between two locations and dedicated connections to the Internet. Dedicated private connections manifest themselves as two locations interconnected by a (usually high-speed) connection such as a T1 line (Figure 14-38).

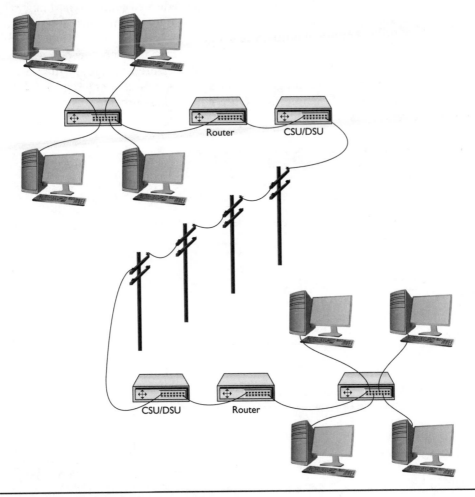

Figure 14-38   Dedicated private connection

Each end of the T1 line goes into a router (after going through a CSU/DSU, of course). Note that this connection does not use the Internet in any way—it is not a VPN connection. Private dedicated connections of this type are expensive and are only used by organizations that need the high bandwidth and high security these connections provide. These connections are invisible to the individual computers on each network. There is no special remote connection configuration of the individual systems, although you may have to configure DHCP, DNS, and WINS servers to ensure that the network runs optimally.

DSL and Cable

Dedicated connections to the Internet are common today. Cable modems and DSL have made dedicated connections to the Internet inexpensive and very popular. In most cases, you don't have to configure anything in these dedicated connections. Many cable and DSL providers give you a CD-ROM that installs different items, such as testing software, PPPoE login support, and little extras like e-mail clients and software firewalls. Personally, I prefer not to use these (they add a lot of stuff you don't need) and instead use the operating system's tools or a hardware router. Figure 14-39 shows the DSL wizard built into Windows 7. This program enables you to connect by entering your PPPoE information for your ADSL connection. Once started, these programs usually stay running in the system tray until your next reboot.

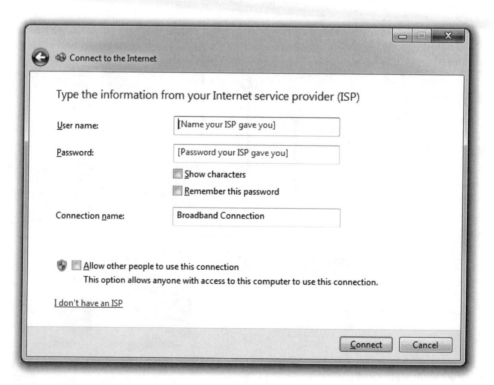

Figure 14-39 PPPoE connection

Cable Issues

Dedicated cable connections provide the only exception to the "plug them in and they work" rule because most cable networks bring television and often voice communication into the same line. This complicates things in one simple way: *splitters*.

If you have a cable connection coming to your house and you have a television set in two rooms, how do you get cable in both rooms? Easy, right? Just grab a two-way splitter from Radio Shack and run an extra pair of cables, one to each room. The problem comes from the fact that every time you split a cable signal, the signal degrades by half. This is called, logically, a *split cable* problem.

The quality of a signal can be measured in *decibels (dB)*, a unit that describes a ratio between an ideal point—a reference point—and the current state of the signal. When discussing signal strength, a solid signal is 0 dB. When that signal degrades, it's described as a *dB loss* and a negative number. An increase in signal is *gain* and gets a positive number. Decibels are logarithmic units, which, if you've forgotten the high school math, means that going up or down the scale in a simple number translates into a huge number in a percentage scale.

For example, when you split a cable signal into two, you get half the signal strength into each new cable. That's described as a –3 dB signal. Split it again and you've got a –6 dB signal. Although 6 isn't a big number in standard units, it's horribly huge in networking. You might have a 20-Mbps cable connection into your house, but split it twice and you're left with a 5-Mbps connection. Ouch!

The standard procedure with cable connections is to split them once: one cable goes to the cable modem and the other to the television. You can then split the television cable into as many connections as you need or can tolerate as far as reception quality.

Remote Terminal

You can use a terminal emulation program to create a *remote terminal*, a connection on a faraway computer that enables you to control that computer as if you were sitting in front of it, logged in. Terminal emulation has been a part of TCP/IP from its earliest days, in the form of good-old Telnet. Because it dates from pre-GUI days, Telnet is a text-based utility; all modern operating systems are graphical, so there was a strong desire to come up with graphical remote terminal tools. Citrix Corporation made the first popular terminal emulation products—the *WinFrame/MetaFrame* products (Figure 14-40).

Remote terminal programs all require a server and a client. The server is the computer to be controlled. The client is the computer from which you do the controlling. Citrix created a standard called *Independent Computing Architecture (ICA)* that defined how terminal information was passed between the server and the client. Citrix made a breakthrough product—so powerful that Microsoft licensed the Citrix code and created its own product called Windows Terminal Services. Not wanting to pay Citrix any more money, Microsoft then created its own standard called *Remote Desktop Protocol (RDP)* and unveiled a new remote terminal called *Remote Desktop Connection (RDC)* starting with Windows XP. Figure 14-41 shows Windows Remote Desktop Connection running on a Windows 7 system, connecting to a Windows 2008 Server.

Figure 14-40   Citrix MetaFrame

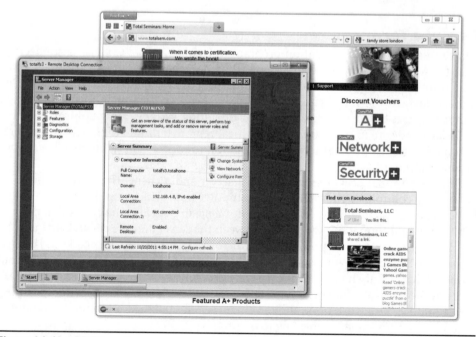

Figure 14-41   RDC in action

NOTE All RDP applications run on port 3389 by default.

Unfortunately, Terminal Services only works in the Windows environment; however, a number of third parties make absolutely amazing terminal emulation programs that run on any operating system. The best of these, *VNC* (VNC stands for Virtual Network Computing) doesn't let you share folders or printers because it is only a terminal emulator (Figure 14-42), but it runs on every operating system, is solid as a rock, and even runs from a Web browser. It works nicely in Secure Shell (SSH) tunnels for great security, plus it comes, by default, with every copy of Mac OS X and almost every Linux distro. Why bother sharing if you can literally be at the screen? Oh, and did I mention that VNC is completely free?

Figure 14-42 VNC in action

VoIP

Voice over IP (VoIP) uses an IP network to transfer voice calls. VoIP works so well because it uses an existing network you're already paying for (your Internet connection) to replace another network you're also paying for (PSTN lines). The technology needed for VoIP isn't very challenging, but making a VoIP system that's standardized so everyone can use it (and still contact those who choose to use PSTN) requires international standards, making it quite a bit harder. VoIP is still a very fractured world, but it's getting closer to universally adopted standards—one day everyone will be able to contact everyone else, no matter what brand of VoIP they use. To do this, you need to know three important standards: RTP, SIP, and H.323.

RTP

The *Real-time Transport Protocol (RTP)*, the heavily adopted bedrock of VoIP standards, defines the type of packets used on the Internet to move voice or data from a server to clients. The vast majority of VoIP solutions available today use RTP.

EXAM TIP The CompTIA Network+ objectives inexplicably drop the word "Transport" from this protocol and call it the *Real Time Protocol.* There's no such thing. It's the *Real-time Transport Protocol.*

SIP and H.323

Session Initiation Protocol (SIP) and *H.323* handle the initiation, setup, and delivery of VoIP sessions. VoIP requires a lot of special features that are not very common in many other Internet protocols. The biggest one is multicasting. You don't ever really use multicasting, unless you want to show a number of people a video or want to make a conference call. SIP and H.323 both have methods for handling multicasting.

EXAM TIP SIP and H.323 both run on top of RTP. Most VoIP solutions are either SIP/RTP or H.323/RTP

Skype

Almost every VoIP solution available today uses SIP or H.323 running on top of RTP, with one huge exception: the very famous and incredibly popular Skype. Skype was unveiled in 2003 by Niklas Zennström, a Swedish computer guy famous for inventing the Kazaa peer-to-peer file-sharing system. Skype is completely different from and completely incompatible with any other type of VoIP solution: Skype doesn't use servers, but instead uses a peer-to-peer topology that is identical to the old Kazaa network. Skype calls are also encrypted using a proprietary encryption method. No one has a standard method for VoIP encryption at this time, although many smart people are working hard on the issue.

Streaming Media with RTSP

VoIP isn't the only thing that takes advantage of protocols such as RTP. Streaming video is now mainstream and many streaming video severs (Windows Media Player, Quick-Time, and many others) use a popular protocol called Real Time Streaming Protocol (RTSP). Like SIP and H.323, RTSP runs on top of RTP. RTSP has a number of features that are perfect for video streaming such as the ability to run, pause, and stop videos. RTSP runs on TCP port 554.

Chapter Review

Questions

1. What is the signal rate for DS0?

   A. 1.544 Mbps

   B. 64 Kbps

   C. 2.048 Mbps

   D. 128 Kbps

2. Which of the following provides the fastest throughput?

   A. PSTN

   B. ISDN BRI

   C. VDSL

   D. POTS

3. What is the popular Microsoft remote access server program called?

   A. RAS

   B. Dial-Up Networking

   C. Dial-Up Server

   D. Microsoft Client for Networks

4. What device do you use to connect to a T1 line?

   A. Router

   B. CSU/DSU

   C. Modem

   D. WIC-2T

5. BRI ISDN uses

   A. 1 B channel and 24 D channels

   B. 24 B channels and 1 D channel

   C. 1 B channel and 2 D channels

   D. 2 B channels and 1 D channel

6. The V.90 standard defines a modem speed of

    A. 56 Kbps

    B. 33.6 K baud

    C. 28.8 Kbps

    D. 2400 baud

7. You have just had DSL installed at your house and while the Internet connection is fast, your phones no longer work. What is the problem?

    A. The installer failed to install the POTS filters on the phones.

    B. Nothing; the phones can't function at the same time as the Internet.

    C. The house phone lines can't handle the bandwidth of both the phone and DSL.

    D. The DSL modem is missing the filter and is causing line interference.

8. What protocol do cable modems use?

    A. ACMSIS

    B. CMAS

    C. DOCSIS

    D. CCSIP

9. What is SONET used for?

    A. Short-distance, high-speed, fiber-optic transmission

    B. Long-distance, high-speed, fiber-optic transmission

    C. Long-distance, low-speed, copper cable transmission

    D. Short-distance, low-speed, copper cable transmission

10. What does SIP stand for?

    A. Standard Initiation Protocol

    B. System Internetworking Protocol

    C. Session Initiation Protocol

    D. Sector Information Protocol

Answers

1. **B.** DS0 operates at a constant rate of 64 Kbps.

2. **C.** VDSL can run up to 100 Mbps.

3. **A.** The popular Microsoft remote access server is called Remote Access Service, or RAS.

4. **B.** A CSU/DSU is required to connect to a T1 line.

5. **D.** BRI ISDN uses two B channels and one D channel.

6. **A.** The V.90 standard defines a 56-Kbps modem speed.

7. **A.** The problem is the installer did not install the POTS filters on the jacks with phones attached.

8. **C.** Cable modems use DOCSIS, Data Over Cable Service Interface Specification.

9. **B.** SONET is used for long-distance, high-speed, fiber-optic transmission.

10. **C.** Session Initiation Protocol; SIP is one of the main protocols for VoIP.

## CHAPTER 15

Wireless Networking

The CompTIA Network+ certification exam expects you to know how to

- 2.1 Given a scenario, install and configure routers and switches: MAC filtering, PoE
- 2.2 Given a scenario, install and configure a wireless network
- 2.4 Given a scenario, troubleshoot common wireless problems
- 3.3 Compare and contrast different wireless standards
- 3.7 Compare and contrast different LAN technologies: CSMA/CA, speed, distance
- 5.1 Given a scenario, implement appropriate wireless security measures
- 5.2 Explain the methods of network access security: MAC filtering

To achieve these goals, you must be able to

- Explain wireless networking standards
- Describe the process for implementing Wi-Fi networks
- Describe troubleshooting techniques for wireless networks

Every type of network covered thus far in the book assumes that your PCs connect to your network with some kind of physical cabling. Now it's time to cut the cord and look at one of the most exciting developments in network technology: wireless networking.

Historical/Conceptual

Instead of a physical set of wires running among networked PCs, servers, printers, or what-have-you, a *wireless network* uses radio frequency (RF) waves to enable these devices to communicate with each other. Wireless offers great promise to the folks who've spent time pulling cable up through ceiling spaces and down behind walls and, therefore, know how time consuming that job can be.

But wireless networking is more than just convenient—sometimes it's the only networking solution that works. I have a client, for example, whose offices are housed in a building designated as a historic landmark. Guess what? You can't go punching holes in historic landmarks to make room for network cable runs. Wireless networking is the only solution.

NOTE Because the networking signal is freed from wires, you'll sometimes hear the term *unbounded media* to describe wireless networking.

Wireless networks operate at the same OSI layers and use the same protocols as wired networks. The thing that differs is the type of media—radio waves instead of cables—and the methods for accessing the media. Different wireless networking solutions have come and gone in the past, but the wireless networking market these days is dominated by the most common implementation of the IEEE 802.11 wireless Ethernet standard, *Wi-Fi*.

NOTE The CompTIA Network+ objectives draw a clear distinction between wireless technologies that enable devices to *access the Internet*, such as WiMAX and LTE, and wireless technologies that you use to *create a network*. You read about the former in Chapter 14; now you're going to learn about the latter: Wi-Fi.

This chapter looks first at the standards for modern wireless networks and then turns to implementing those networks. The chapter finishes with a discussion on troubleshooting Wi-Fi.

Test Specific

Wi-Fi Standards

Wi-Fi is by far the most widely adopted wireless networking type today. Not only do thousands of private businesses and homes have wireless networks, but also many public places, such as coffee shops and libraries, offer Internet access through wireless networks.

NOTE Wi-Fi originally stood for *wireless fidelity* to make it cutely equated with *high fidelity (Hi-Fi)*, but it doesn't really stand for anything anymore.

Technically, only wireless devices that conform to the extended versions of the 802.11 standard—802.11a, 802.11b, 802.11g, and 802.11n—are Wi-Fi certified. Wi-Fi certification comes from the Wi-Fi Alliance, a nonprofit industry group made up of over 300 member companies that design and manufacture wireless networking products. Wi-Fi certification ensures compatibility between wireless networking devices made by different vendors. That's the way it's *supposed* to work, anyway, but see the last section of this chapter on troubleshooting for the real-world scoop.

802.11

The *802.11* standard defines both how wireless devices communicate and how to secure that communication. The communication standards take on the name of the IEEE sub-committee that sets those standards, such as 802.11b and 802.11n. The original 802.11 standard established the baseline features common to all subsequent Wi-Fi standards. I'll discuss the almost unused, original 802.11 before exploring the variations in 802.11b, 802.11a, 802.11g, and 802.11n. The section wraps up with a discussion on security standards, from authentication to encryption.

All Wi-Fi standards share certain features, such as a wireless network card, special configuration software, and the capability to run in multiple styles of networks. In addition, Wi-Fi implementations require a shared network name and channel for communication. Each standard has a certain top speed and range of networking capability. Finally, 802.11 defines how transmissions work, so we'll look at frequencies of radio signals, transmission methods, and collision avoidance.

Hardware

Wireless networking hardware serves the same function as hardware used on wired PCs. Wireless Ethernet NICs take data passed down from the upper OSI layers, encapsulate it into frames, send the frames out on the network media in strings of ones and zeroes, and receive frames sent from other PCs. The only difference is that instead of charging up a network cable with electrical current or firing off pulses of light, these devices transmit and receive radio waves.

Wireless networking capabilities of one form or another are built into many modern computing devices. Almost all portable devices have built-in wireless capabilities. Desktop computers can easily go wireless by adding an expansion card. Figure 15-1 shows a wireless PCIe Ethernet card.

Figure 15-1
Wireless PCIe NIC

You can also add wireless network capabilities using external USB wireless network adapters, as shown in Figure 15-2. The USB NICs have the added benefit of being *placeable*—that is, you can move them around to catch the wireless signal as strongly as possible, akin to moving the rabbit ears on old precable television sets.

Figure 15-2
External USB
wireless NIC

 NOTE   Many USB Wi-Fi NICs these days come as little USB sticks, similar in looks to a flash drive. You can still position this type of NIC, though, by using a USB extender cable, with a male USB A connector on one end and a female USB A connector on the other.

Is the wireless network adapter all the hardware you need to connect wirelessly? Well, if your needs are simple—for example, if you're connecting a small group of computers into a decentralized workgroup—then the answer is yes. If, however, you need to extend the capabilities of a wireless Ethernet network—say, connecting a wireless network segment to a wired network—you need additional equipment. This typically means a wireless access point.

A *wireless access point (WAP)* connects wireless network nodes to wireless or wired networks. A basic WAP operates like a hub and works at OSI Layer 1. Many WAP manufacturers combine multiple devices into one box, however, to create a high-speed hub or switch, bridge, and router, all rolled into one and working at many different OSI layers. The Linksys device shown in Figure 15-3 is an example of this type of combo device.

Figure 15-3
Linksys device that acts
as wireless access point,
switch, and DSL router

NOTE Some manufacturers drop the word "wireless" from wireless access points and simply call them access points. Furthermore, many sources abbreviate both forms, so you'll see the former written as *WAP* and the latter as *AP*.

Software

Every wireless network adapter needs two pieces of software to function with an operating system: a driver and a configuration utility. Installing drivers for wireless networking devices is usually no more difficult than for any other hardware device, but you should always consult your vendor's instructions before popping that card into a slot. Most of the time, you simply have to let Plug and Play (PnP) work its magic and put in the driver disc when prompted, but some devices (particularly USB devices) require that you install the drivers beforehand. All modern operating systems come well equipped for wireless networking. Even so, it's always a good idea to use the manufacturer's drivers and configuration utilities.

You also need a utility for configuring how the wireless hardware connects to other wireless devices. Windows XP, Windows Vista, Windows 7, and Mac OS X have built-in tools for configuring these settings, but for previous versions of Windows, you needed to rely on wireless client configuration tools provided by the wireless network adapter vendor. Figure 15-4 shows a typical wireless network adapter's client configuration utility. Using this utility, you can determine important things like your *link state* (whether your wireless device is connected) and your *signal strength* (a measurement of how well your wireless device is connecting to other devices); you can also configure items such as your wireless networking *mode*, security encryption, power-saving options, and so on. I'll cover each of these topics in detail later in this chapter.

Figure 15-4

Wireless client configuration utility

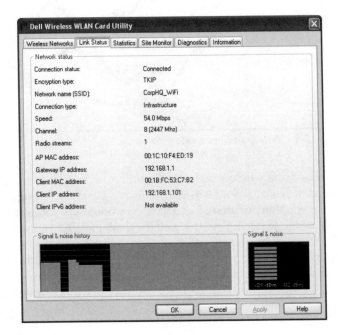

You configure WAPs and routers through browser-based setup utilities. The section "Implementing Wi-Fi" covers this process a bit later in this chapter. Let's look at the different modes that wireless networks use.

Wireless Network Modes

Wireless networks work in two ways. In *ad hoc* mode, two or more PCs communicate directly without cabling or any other intermediary hardware. The more common way, known as *infrastructure* mode, uses an access point that, in essence, acts as a hub for all wireless clients. A WAP also bridges wireless network segments to wired network segments.

Ad Hoc Mode   *Ad hoc mode* is sometimes called *peer-to-peer mode*, with each wireless node in direct contact with each other node in a decentralized free-for-all, as shown in Figure 15-5. Ad hoc mode does not use an access point and instead uses a *mesh* topology, as discussed in Chapter 3.

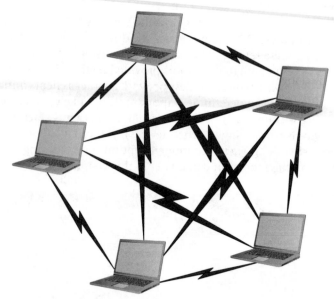

Figure 15-5   Wireless ad hoc mode network

Two or more wireless nodes communicating in ad hoc mode form what's called an *Independent Basic Service Set (IBSS)*. This is a basic unit of organization in wireless networks. If you think of an IBSS as a wireless workgroup, you wouldn't be far off the mark.

Ad hoc mode networks work well for small groups of computers (fewer than a dozen or so) that need to transfer files or share printers. Ad hoc networks are also good for temporary networks, such as study groups or business meetings.

Hardly anyone uses ad hoc networks for day-to-day work, simply because you can't use an ad hoc network to connect to other networks unless one of the machines is running Internet Connection Sharing (ICS) or some equivalent. More commonly, you'll find wireless networks configured in infrastructure mode.

NOTE Infrastructure mode is so much more commonly used than ad hoc mode that most wireless NICs come preconfigured to run on an infrastructure mode network. Getting them to run in ad hoc mode usually requires reconfiguration.

Infrastructure Mode   Wireless networks running in *infrastructure mode* use one or more WAPs to connect the wireless network nodes centrally, as shown in Figure 15-6. This configuration is similar to the physical *star* topology of a wired network. You also use infrastructure mode to connect wireless network segments to wired segments. If you plan to set up a wireless network for a large number of PCs, or you need to have centralized control over the wireless network, infrastructure mode is what you need.

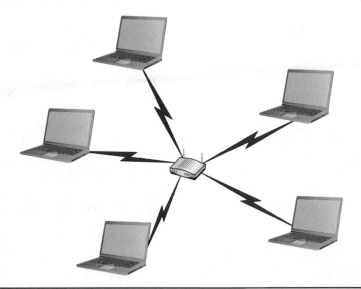

Figure 15-6   Wireless infrastructure mode network

A single WAP servicing a given area is called a *Basic Service Set (BSS)*. This service area can be extended by adding more access points. This is called, appropriately, an *Extended Service Set (ESS)*.

NOTE   Many techs have dropped the word "basic" from the Extended Basic Service Set, the early name for an infrastructure-mode wireless network with more than one WAP. Accordingly, you'll see the initials for the Extended Basic Service Set as ESS. Using either EBSS or ESS is correct.

Wireless networks running in infrastructure mode require a little more planning—such as where you place the WAPs to provide adequate coverage—than ad hoc mode networks, and they provide a stable environment for permanent wireless network installations. Infrastructure mode is better suited to business networks or networks that need to share dedicated resources such as Internet connections and centralized databases. (See "Implementing Wi-Fi" later in this chapter.)

Range

Wireless networking range is hard to define. You'll see most descriptions listed with qualifiers such as *"around* 150 feet" and *"about* 300 feet." 802.11 networks fall into the former category. Like throughput speed, wireless range is greatly affected by environmental factors. Interference from other wireless devices and solid objects affects range.

The maximum ranges listed in the sections that follow are those presented by wireless manufacturers as the *theoretical* maximum ranges. In the real world, you'll achieve these ranges only under the most ideal circumstances. Cut the manufacturer's listed range in half to find the true effective range.

BSSID, SSID, and ESSID

Wireless devices connected together into a network, whether ad hoc or infrastructure, require some way to identify that network. Frames bound for computers within the network need to go where they're supposed to go, even when you have more than one Wi-Fi network overlapping. The jargon gets a little crazy here, especially because marketing has come into the mix.

The *Basic Service Set Identifier (BSSID)* defines the most basic infrastructure mode network—a BSS of one WAP and one or more wireless nodes. With such a simple network, the Wi-Fi folks didn't see any reason to create some new numbering or naming scheme, so they made the BSSID the same as the MAC address for the WAP. Simple! Ah, but what do you do about ad hoc networks that don't have a WAP? The nodes that connect in an IBSS randomly generate a 48-bit string of numbers that looks and functions just like a MAC address, and that BSSID goes in every frame.

You could, if required, discover the MAC address for the WAP in a BSS and manually type that into the network name field when setting up a wireless computer. But that causes two problems. First, people don't want to remember strings of 48 digits, even if translated out as six hexadecimal octets, like A9–45–F2–3E–CA–12. People want names. Second, how do you connect two or more computers together into an IBSS when the BSSID has to be randomly generated?

The Wi-Fi folks created another level of naming called a *Service Set Identifier (SSID)*, a standard name applied to the BSS or IBSS to help the connection happen. The SSID—sometimes called a *network name*—is a 32-bit identification string that's inserted into the header of each frame processed by a WAP. Every Wi-Fi device must share the same SSID to communicate in a single network.

So let's take it one step further into a Wi-Fi network that has multiple WAPs, an ESS. How do you determine the network name at this level? You just use the SSID, only you apply it to the ESS as an *Extended Service Set Identifier (ESSID)*.

Unfortunately, most Wi-Fi devices just use the term *SSID*, not *ESSID*. When you configure a wireless device to connect to an ESS, you're technically using the ESSID rather than just the SSID, but the manufacturer often tries to make it simple for you by using only the term *SSID*.

 EXAM TIP The CompTIA Network+ certification exam uses the two terms—*SSID* and *ESSID*—interchangeably. Concentrate on these two terms for the exam.

Broadcasting Frequency

One of the biggest issues with wireless communication is the potential for interference from other wireless devices. To solve this, different wireless devices must operate in specific broadcasting frequencies. Knowing these wireless frequency ranges will assist you in troubleshooting interference issues from other devices operating in the same wireless band. The original 802.11 standards use the 2.4-GHz frequency band. Later standards use either 2.4-GHz or 5.0-GHz frequencies.

Broadcasting Methods

The original IEEE 802.11 wireless Ethernet standard defined methods by which devices may communicate using *spread-spectrum* radio waves. Spread-spectrum broadcasts data in small, discrete chunks over the different frequencies available within a certain frequency range.

The 802.11 standard defines three different spread-spectrum broadcasting methods: *direct-sequence spread-spectrum (DSSS)*, *frequency-hopping spread-spectrum (FHSS)*, and *orthogonal frequency-division multiplexing (OFDM)*. DSSS sends data out on different frequencies at the same time, whereas FHSS sends data on one frequency at a time, constantly shifting (or *hopping*) frequencies. DSSS uses considerably more bandwidth than FHSS—around 22 MHz as opposed to 1 MHz. DSSS is capable of greater data throughput, but it's also more prone to interference than FHSS. OFDM is the latest method and combines the multiple frequencies of DSSS with FHSS's hopping capability. The 802.11 wireless networking implementation used DSSS and later OFDM.

Channels

Every Wi-Fi network communicates on a *channel*, a portion of the spectrum available. The 802.11 standard defined 14 channels, but different countries may limit exactly which channels may be used. In the United States, for example, a WAP may only use channels 1 through 11. These channels have some overlap, so two nearby WAPs should not use close channels like 6 and 7. Most WAPs use channel 1, 6, or 11 by default because these are the only nonoverlapping channels. You can fine-tune a network by moving WAPs to other channels to avoid overlap with other nearby WAPs. This capability is especially important in environments with many wireless networks sharing the same physical space.

CSMA/CA

Because only a single device can use any network at a time in a physical bus topology, network nodes must have a way to access the network media without stepping on each other's frames. Wired Ethernet networks use *carrier sense multiple access with collision detection (CSMA/CD)*, as you'll recall from previous chapters, but Wi-Fi networks use *carrier sense multiple access with collision avoidance (CSMA/CA)*. Let's compare both methods.

 EXAM TIP Wired Ethernet networks use CSMA/CD. Wi-Fi networks use CSMA/CA.

How do multiple devices share network media, such as a cable? Sharing is fairly simple: Each device listens in on the network media by measuring the level of voltage currently on the wire. If the level is below the threshold, the device knows that it's clear to send data. If the voltage level rises above a preset threshold, the device knows that the line is busy and it must wait before sending data. Typically, the waiting period is the length of the current frame plus a short, predefined silence period called an *interframe gap (IFG)*. So far, so good—but what happens when two devices both detect that the wire is free and try to send data simultaneously? As you probably guessed, frames transmitted on the network from two different devices at the same time will corrupt each other, canceling each other out. This is called a *collision*. Collisions are a fact of networking life. So how do network nodes deal with collisions? They both react to collisions after they happen, and they take steps to avoid collisions in the first place.

Modern wired networks use switches running in full-duplex mode, so they don't have to worry about collisions. You'll recall that from back in Chapter 2. CSMA/CD is disabled with full-duplex. Wireless networks don't have this luxury.

With CSMA/CD, each sending node detects the collision and responds by generating a random timeout period for itself, during which it doesn't try to send any more data on the network—this is called a *backoff*. Once the backoff period expires (remember that I'm talking about only milliseconds here), the node goes through the whole process again. This approach may not be very elegant, but it gets the job done.

CSMA/CD won't work for wireless networking because wireless devices simply can't detect collisions for two reasons. First, radio is a half-duplex transmission method. A wireless device cannot listen and send at the same time. Second, wireless clients may not know about the existence of another client due to signal strength. Wireless networks need another way to deal with potential collisions. The CSMA/CA access method, as the name implies, proactively takes steps to avoid collisions, as does CSMA/CD. The difference comes in the collision avoidance.

The 802.11 standard defines two methods for collision avoidance: *Distributed Coordination Function (DCF)* and *Point Coordination Function (PCF)*. Currently, only DCF is implemented. DCF specifies rules for sending data onto the network media. For instance, if a wireless network node detects that the network is busy, DCF defines a backoff period on top of the normal IFG wait period before a node can try to access the network again. DCF also requires that receiving nodes send an acknowledgement (ACK) for every frame that they process. The ACK also includes a value that tells other wireless nodes to wait a certain duration before trying to access the network media. This period is calculated to be the time that the data frame takes to reach its destination based on the frame's length and data rate. If the sending node doesn't receive an ACK, it retransmits the same data frame until it gets a confirmation that the packet reached its destination.

 EXAM TIP Current CSMA/CA devices use the Distributed Coordination Function (DCF) method for collision avoidance.

The 802.11 standard was the very oldest wireless standard (see Table 15-1). Over time, more detailed additions to 802.11 came along that improved speeds and took advantage of other frequency bands.

Standard	Frequency	Spectrum	Speed	Range	Compatibility
802.11	2.4 GHz	DSSS	2 Mbps	~300'	802.11

Table 15-1 802.11 Summary

802.11b

The first widely adopted Wi-Fi standard—*802.11b*—supports data throughput of up to 11 Mbps and a range of up to 300 feet under ideal conditions. The main downside to using 802.11b is its frequency. The 2.4-GHz frequency is a crowded place, so you're more likely to run into interference from other wireless devices. Table 15-2 gives you the 802.11b summary.

Standard	Frequency	Spectrum	Speed	Range	Compatibility
802.11b	2.4 GHz	DSSS	11 Mbps	~300'	802.11b

Table 15-2 802.11b Summary

802.11a

Despite the *a* designation for this extension to the 802.11 standard, *802.11a* was available on the market *after* 802.11b. The 802.11a standard differs from the other 802.11-based standards in significant ways. Foremost is that it operates in a different frequency range, 5.0 GHz. The 5.0-GHz range is much less crowded than the 2.4-GHz range, reducing the chance of interference from devices such as telephones and microwave ovens. Too much signal interference can increase *latency*, making the network sluggish and slow to respond. Running in the 5.0-GHz range greatly reduces this problem.

The 802.11a standard also offers considerably greater throughput than 802.11b, with speeds up to 54 Mbps. Range, however, suffers somewhat and tops out at about 150 feet. Despite the superior speed of 802.11a, it has never enjoyed the popularity of 802.11b.

Although you can find NICs and WAPs that support both 802.11b and 802.11a, the standards are not compatible with each other because of the different frequency bands. A computer with an 802.11b NIC, for example, can't connect to a WAP that's only 802.11a, but it could connect to an 802.11a/b WAP. Table 15-3 gives you the 802.11a summary.

Standard	Frequency	Spectrum	Speed	Range	Compatibility
802.11a	5.0 GHz	DSSS	54 Mbps	~150'	802.11a

Table 15-3   802.11a Summary

802.11g

The *802.11g* standard offers data transfer speeds equivalent to 802.11a—up to 54 Mbps—and the wider 300-foot range of 802.11b. More importantly, 802.11g is backward-compatible with 802.11b, so the same 802.11g WAP can service both 802.11b and 802.11g wireless nodes.

If an 802.11g network only has 802.11g devices connected, the network runs in *native mode*—at up to 54 Mbps—whereas when 802.11b devices connect, the network drops down to *mixed mode*—all communication runs up to only 11 Mbps. Table 15-4 gives you the 802.11g summary.

Standard	Frequency	Spectrum	Speed	Range	Compatibility
802.11g	2.4 GHz	OFDM	54 Mbps	~300'	802.11b/g

Table 15-4   802.11g Summary

Later 802.11g manufacturers incorporated *channel bonding* into their devices, enabling the devices to use two channels for transmission. Channel bonding is not part of the 802.11g standard, but rather proprietary technology pushed by various companies to increase the throughput of their wireless networks. Both the NIC and WAP, therefore, had to be from the same company for channel bonding to work.

802.11n

The *802.11n* standard brings several improvements to Wi-Fi networking, including faster speeds and new antenna technology implementations.

The 802.11n specification requires all but handheld devices to use multiple antennas to implement a feature called *multiple in/multiple out (MIMO)*, which enables the devices to make multiple simultaneous connections. With up to four antennas, 802.11n devices can achieve amazing speeds. They also can implement channel bonding to increase throughput even more. (The official standard supports throughput of up to 600 Mbps, although practical implementation drops that down substantially.)

Many 802.11n WAPs employ *transmit beamforming*, a multiple-antenna technology that helps get rid of dead spots—or at least make them not so bad. The antennas adjust the signal once the WAP discovers a client to optimize the radio signal.

Like 802.11g, 802.11n WAPs can support earlier, slower 802.11b/g devices. The so-called dual-band WAPs can run at both 5.0 GHz and 2.4 GHz simultaneously; some support 802.11a devices as well as 802.11b/g devices. Nice! Table 15-5 gives you the 802.11n summary.

Standard	Frequency	Spectrum	Speed	Range	Compatibility
802.11n	2.4 GHz[1]	OFDM	100+ Mbps	~300'	802.11b/g/n[2]

[1] Dual-band 802.11n devices can function simultaneously at both 2.4- and 5.0-GHz bands.
[2] Many dual-band 802.11n WAPs support 802.11a devices as well as 802.11b/g/n devices. This is not part of the standard, but something manufacturers have implemented.

Table 15-5 802.11n Summary

Wireless Networking Security

One of the biggest problems with wireless networking devices is that right out of the box they provide *no* security. Vendors go out of their way to make setting up their devices easy, so usually the only thing that you have to do to join a wireless network is turn your wireless devices on and let them find each other. Sure, this is great from a configuration point of view—but from a security point of view, it's a disaster!

You also need to consider that your network's data frames float through the air on radio waves instead of zipping safely along wrapped up inside network cabling. What's to stop an unscrupulous network tech with the right equipment from grabbing those frames out of the air and reading that data?

To address these issues, wireless networks use three methods: MAC address filtering, authentication, and data encryption. The first two methods secure access to the network itself, and the third secures the data that's moving around the network. All three of these methods require you to configure the WAPs and wireless devices. Let's take a look.

MAC Address Filtering

Most WAPs support *MAC address filtering*, a method that enables you to limit access to your network based on the physical addresses of wireless NICs. MAC address filtering creates a type of "accepted users" list to limit access to your wireless network. A table stored in the WAP lists the MAC addresses that are permitted to participate in the wireless network. Any network frames that don't contain the MAC address of a node listed in the table are rejected.

 EXAM TIP WAPs use an *access control list (ACL)* to enable or deny specific MAC addresses. Note that a WAP's ACL has *nothing* to do with ACL in NTFS; it's just the same term used for two different things.

Many WAPs also enable you to deny specific MAC addresses from logging onto the network. This works great in close quarters, such as apartments or office buildings, where your wireless network signal goes beyond your perimeter. You can check the WAP and see the MAC addresses of every node that connects to your network. Check that list against the list of your computers, and you can readily spot any unwanted interloper. Putting an offending MAC address in the "deny" column effectively blocks that system from piggybacking onto your wireless connection.

EXAM TIP MAC filtering with a *whitelist* means you allow only specific computers to join the network. When you deny specific computers, you create a *blacklist*.

While address filtering works, a hacker can very easily *spoof* a MAC address—make the NIC report a legitimate address rather than its own—and access the network. Worse, a hacker doesn't have to connect to your network to grab your network traffic out of thin air! If you have data so important that a hacker would want to get at it, you should seriously consider using a wired network or separating the sensitive data from your wireless network in some fashion.

Wireless Authentication

Implementing authentication enables you to secure a network so only users with the proper credentials can access network resources. It's not an all-or-nothing deal, of course; you can use authentication to restrict or enable what a specific user can do once inside the network as well.

Authentication in a wired network, as you'll recall from Chapter 11, generally takes the form of a centralized security database that contains user names, passwords, and permissions, like the Active Directory in a Windows Server environment. Wireless network clients can use the same security database as wired clients, but getting the wireless user authenticated takes a couple of extra steps.

The IEEE *802.1X* standard enables you to set up a network with some seriously secure authentication using a RADIUS server and passwords encrypted with *Extensible Authentication Protocol (EAP)*. Let's look at the components and the process.

A *RADIUS server* enables remote users to connect to a network service. It provides authentication through a user name and password and enables you to set a user's rights once in the network. A RADIUS server functions like a typical server, but the remote aspect of it requires you to learn new jargon. The terms "client" and "server" are *so* Active Directory, after all.

NOTE RADIUS stands for *Remote Authentication Dial In User Service*. Say that five times.

Here's how it works. The client computer, called a *supplicant*, contacts the WAP, called a *Network Access Server (NAS)*, and requests permission to access the network. The NAS contacts the RADIUS server to see if the supplicant appears in the RADIUS server's security database. If the supplicant appears and the user name and password are correct, the RADIUS server sends a packet back to the supplicant, through the WAP, with an Access-Accept code and an Authenticator section that proves the packet actually came from the RADIUS server. Then the remote user gets access to the network resources. That's some serious security! See Figure 15-7.

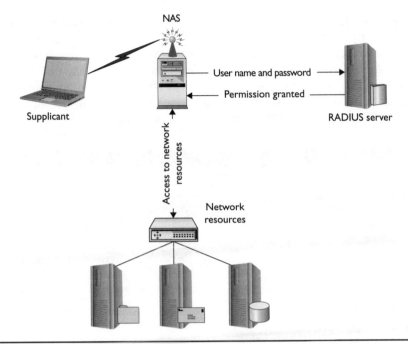

Figure 15-7 Authenticating using RADIUS

But here's where it gets tricky. What are the points of potential security failure here? All over the place, right? The connection between each of these devices must be secure; several protocols make certain of that security. PPP, for example, provides a secure dial-up connection between the supplicant and the NAS.

IPsec often provides security between the NAS and the RADIUS server. Finally, the RADIUS server needs to use a protocol, such as one of the many implementations of the Extensible Authentication Protocol (EAP), for the authentication part of the deal. See Figure 15-8.

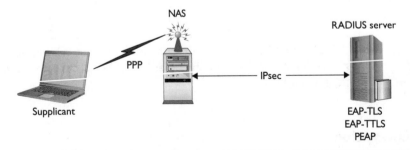

Figure 15-8 Authentication using RADIUS with protocols in place

EAP defines a framework for authentication but does not specify how the authentication happens. Developers have, therefore, come up with many ways to handle the specifics, such as EAP-TLS, EAP-TTLS, and PEAP, to name just a few. The differences among the many flavors of EAP cause countless hours of argument among geeks, but from a technician's perspective, you simply use the scheme that your network hardware supports. Both the WAP and the wireless NICs have to use the same EAP authentication scheme. You set this in the firmware or software, as you can see in Figure 15-9.

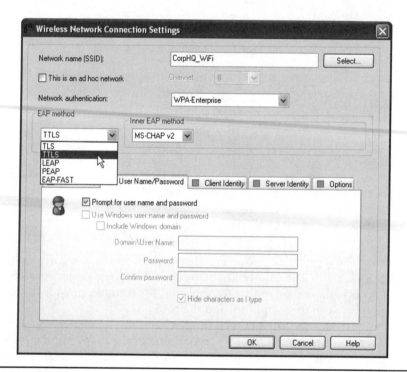

Figure 15-9 Setting EAP authentication scheme

NOTE EAP and RADIUS servers for authentication paint half the picture on 802.1X security implementation. The other half is WPA2, discussed in "Data Encryption Using WPA2."

Data Encryption

The final step in securing a wireless network is encrypting the data packets that are floating around. *Encryption* electronically scrambles data packets and locks them with a private encryption key before transmitting them onto the wireless network. The receiving network device has to possess the encryption key to unscramble the packet and process the data. Thus, a hacker who grabs any data frames out of the air can't read those frames unless he or she has the encryption key. Enabling wireless encryption through WPA2 provides a good level of security to data packets in transit.

Data Encryption Using WEP The granddaddy of wireless security, *Wired Equivalent Privacy (WEP)*, uses a 64- or 128-bit encryption algorithm to scramble data frames. But even with the strongest encryption enabled, WEP isn't a particularly robust security solution. In fact, WEP can be cracked in under a minute with just a regular laptop and open source software!

Hackers can easily crack WEP for two reasons: the size of the encryption key and the way the key is updated. First, the WEP keys were never really 64- and 128-bit. WEP uses an encryption protocol called *RC4*. There's nothing inherently wrong with RC4, but RC4 is a streaming protocol and needs a little code to start the encryption process, just like a water pump needs some water in the pump before it works. This extra code is stored in the key in the form of what's called an *initialization vector (IV)*. The IV with WEP is 24 bits, which means the encryption part of a WEP key is only 40-bit or 104-bit.

 NOTE RC4 officially stands for *Rivest Cipher 4*, named after its creator, Ron Rivest. Unofficially, but possibly more likely, the RC stands for *Ron's Code*.

The second problem with WEP is that the encryption key is both static (never changes from session to session) and shared (the same key is used by all network nodes). This means it's not that hard to crack assuming you can capture enough WEP-encrypted packets to figure out the code. WEP is simply a disaster.

WEP also fails to provide a mechanism for performing user authentication. That is, network nodes that use WEP encryption are identified by their MAC address, and no other credentials are offered or required. With just a laptop and some open source software, MAC addresses are very easy to sniff out and duplicate, thus opening you up to a possible spoofing attack.

The key thing to remember about WEP is that it is outdated and should never be used. The only security WEP provides today is to prevent casual people from connecting to your WAP. Its encryption is so easily cracked that you might as well be transmitting plaintext.

Data Encryption Using WPA *Wi-Fi Protected Access (WPA)* addresses some of the weaknesses of WEP and acts as a security protocol upgrade to WEP-enabled devices. WPA offers security enhancements such as dynamic encryption key generation (keys are issued on a per-user and per-session basis) and an encryption key integrity-checking feature.

WPA works by using an extra layer of security, called the *Temporal Key Integrity Protocol (TKIP)*, around the WEP encryption scheme. It's not, therefore, a complete replacement protocol for WEP. TKIP added a 128-bit encryption key that seemed unbreakable when first introduced. Within a couple of years of introduction, however, hackers could waltz through WPA security almost as quickly as through WEP security. Another solution had to be found.

Data Encryption Using WPA2   The IEEE *802.11i* standard amended the 802.11 standard to add much-needed security features. I already discussed the 802.1X authentication measure using EAP to provide secure access to Wi-Fi networks. Another key feature, *Wi-Fi Protected Access 2 (WPA2)*, changes the encryption algorithm used in WEP and WPA to the *Advanced Encryption Standard (AES)*, a 128-bit block cipher that's much tougher to crack than the 128-bit TKIP wrapper. WPA2 is not hack proof, but it definitely offers a much tougher encryption standard that stops the casual hacker cold.

When you use a RADIUS server for authentication with WPA2 to create an amazingly secure wireless network, it gets a fancy name: *WPA2-Enterprise*.

Power over Ethernet

Wireless access points need electrical power, but they're invariably placed in strange locations (like ceilings or high up on walls) where providing electrical power is not convenient. No worries! Better WAPs now support a standard called *Power over Ethernet (PoE)*, which enables them to receive their power from the same Ethernet cables that transfer their data. The switch that connects the WAPs must support PoE, but as long as both the WAP and the switches to which they connect support PoE, you don't have to do anything other than just plug in Ethernet cables. PoE works automatically. As you might imagine, it costs extra to get WAPs and switches that support PoE, but the convenience of PoE for wireless networks makes it a popular option.

Implementing Wi-Fi

To install and configure a Wi-Fi network requires a number of discrete steps. You should start with a site survey to determine any obstacles you need to overcome. All wireless networks require clients, so that's your next step. That's all the hardware you'll need for an ad hoc network, but an infrastructure network takes a few more pieces, such as installing an access point and configuring both the access point and clients. Unless you have a small, personal network, you need to look at ways to extend the network so you have the coverage you want. Finally, you should put your network to the test, verifying that it works as you intended.

Performing a Site Survey

A *site survey* enables you to determine any obstacles to creating the wireless network you want. You should discover any other wireless networks in the area and create a drawing with interference sources clearly marked. This enables you to get the right kind of hardware you need and makes it possible to get the proper network coverage.

What Wireless Is Already There?

Discovering any wireless network signals other than your own in your space enables you to set both the SSID and channel to avoid networks that overlap. Wireless networks send out radio signals along the 2.4- or 5.0-GHz band and use channels 1–11. If you have an 802.11g WAP and clients, for example, those devices would use the 2.4-GHz band and could be set to channel 1. A quick scan of the Wi-Fi networks in my neighborhood, for instance, shows five Wi-Fi networks, two with the SSID of Linksys, three using Channel 6, and two with both distinctive nondefault names and channels. If my network SSID were set to Linksys, which WAP have I used when I log onto the Linksys network?

Even if you change the SSID, why run on the same channel as other Wi-Fi networks? You'll see better performance if your Wi-Fi network uses a unique channel.

Interference Sources

It might seem like overkill in a small network, but any network beyond a simple ad hoc one should have a sketched-out site survey with any potential interference sources clearly marked (Figure 15-10). Refrigerators, reinforced walls, metal plumbing, microwave ovens; all of these can create horrible dead spots where your network radio wave can't easily penetrate. With a difficult or high-interference area, you might need to move up to 802.11n equipment with three or four antennas just to get the kind of coverage you want. Or you might need to plan a multiple WAP network to wipe out the dead zones. A proper site survey gives you the first tool for implementing a network that works.

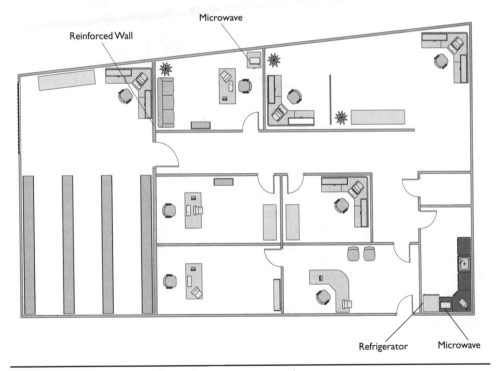

Figure 15-10 Site survey with interference sources noted

Installing the Client

Because every Wi-Fi network needs clients (otherwise, what's the point?), you need to install Wi-Fi client hardware and software. With a PCI or PCI Express NIC, power down the PC, disconnect from the AC source, and open the case. Following good CompTIA A+ technician procedures, locate a free slot on the motherboard, remove the slot cover, remove the NIC from its antistatic bag, install the NIC, and affix the retaining screw. See Figure 15-11. Often you'll need to attach the antenna. Button everything up, plug it in, and start the computer. If prompted, put in the disc that came from the manufacturer and install drivers and any other software necessary.

Figure 15-11
Wi-Fi NIC installed

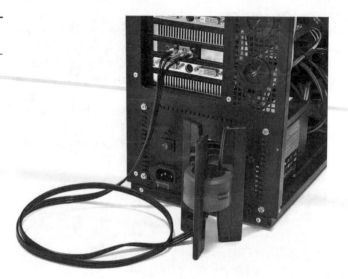

With a USB NIC, you should install the drivers and software before you connect the NIC to the computer. This is standard operating procedure for any USB device, as you most likely recall from your CompTIA A+ certification training (or from personal experience).

Setting Up an Ad Hoc Network

Configuring NICs for ad hoc mode networking requires you to address four things: SSID, IP addresses, channel, and sharing. (Plus, of course, you have to set the NICs to function in ad hoc mode!) Each wireless node must use the same network name (SSID). Also, no two nodes can use the same IP address—although this is unlikely with modern versions of Windows and the Automatic Private IP Addressing (APIPA) feature that automatically selects a Class B IP address in the 169.254.0.0 network for any node not connected to a DHCP server or assigned a static IP address. Finally, ensure that the File and Printer Sharing service is running on all nodes. Figure 15-12 shows a wireless network configuration utility with ad hoc mode selected.

Figure 15-12

Selecting ad hoc mode in a wireless configuration utility

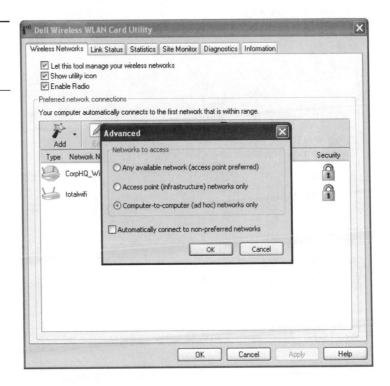

Setting Up an Infrastructure Network

Site survey in hand and Wi-Fi technology selected, you're ready to set up a wireless network in infrastructure mode. You need to determine the optimal location for your WAP, configure the WAP, and then configure any clients to access that WAP. Seems pretty straightforward, but the devil, they say, is in the details.

Placing the Access Point

The optimal location for an access point depends on the area you want to cover and whether you care if the signal bleeds out beyond the borders. You also need to use antennas that provide enough signal and push that signal in the proper direction.

Omnidirectional and Centered   For a typical network, you want blanket coverage and would place a WAP with an omnidirectional antenna in the center of the area (Figure 15-13). With an omnidirectional antenna, the radio wave flows outward from the WAP. This has the advantage of ease of use—anything within the signal radius can potentially access the network. Most wireless networks use this combination, especially in the consumer space. The standard straight-wire antennas that provide the most omnidirectional function are called *dipole antennas*.

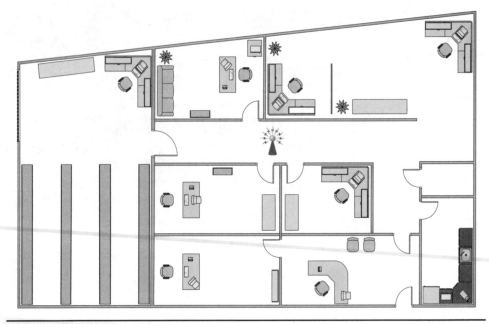

Figure 15-13 Room layout with WAP in the center

The omnidirectional and centered approach does not work for every network for three reasons. First, if the signal exceeds the size of the network space, that signal bleeds out. The signal can bleed out a lot in some cases, particularly if your specific space doesn't allow you to put the WAP in the center, but rather off-center. This presents a security risk as well, because someone outside your network space could lurk, pick up the signal, and run software to try to hack into your network. Or, a hacker might use your wireless signal for purposes that you might not condone. Second, if your network space exceeds the signal of your WAP, you'll need to get some sort of signal booster (see "Gaining Gain"). Third, any obstacles will produce glaring dead spots in network coverage. Too many dead spots make a less-than-ideal solution. To address these issues, you might need to turn to other solutions.

Gaining Gain An antenna strengthens and focuses the radio frequency (RF) output from a WAP. The ratio of increase—what's called *gain*—is measured in decibels (dB). The gain from a typical WAP is 2 dB, enough to cover a reasonable area but not a very large room. Increasing the signal requires a bigger antenna. Many WAPs have removable antennas that you can replace. To increase the signal in an omnidirectional and centered setup, simply replace the factory antennas with one or more bigger antennas (Figure 15-14). Get a big enough antenna and you can crank it all the way up to 11!

 NOTE Proper *device placement* promotes better security!

Figure 15-14
Replacement antenna
on a WAP

Focusing the Wave   When you don't necessarily want to broadcast to the world, you can use one or more directional antennas to create a nicely focused network. A *directional antenna*, as the name implies, focuses a radio wave into a beam of sorts. Directional antennas come in a variety of flavors, such as parabolic, dish, and Yagi, to name a just a few. A parabolic antenna looks like a satellite dish. A Yagi antenna (named for one of its Japanese inventors) is often called a *beam antenna* and can enable a focused radio wave to travel a long way, even miles!

NOTE   *Patch antennas* are flat, plate-shaped antennas that generate a half-sphere beam. Patch antennas are always placed on walls. The half-sphere is perfect for indoor offices where you want to fill the room with a strong signal but not broadcast to the room behind the patch.

Configuring the Access Point

Wireless access points have a browser-based setup utility. Typically, you fire up the Web browser on one of your network client workstations and enter the access point's default IP address, such as 192.168.1.1, to bring up the configuration page. You need to supply an administrative password, included with your access point's documentation, to log in (Figure 15-15).

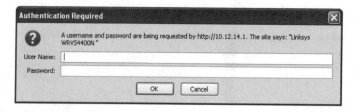

Figure 15-15 Security login for Linksys WAP

Once you've logged in, you'll see configuration screens for changing your basic setup, access point password, security, and so on. Different access points offer different configuration options. Figure 15-16 shows the initial setup screen for a popular Linksys WAP/router.

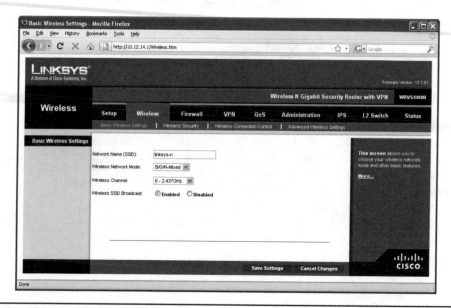

Figure 15-16 Linksys WAP setup screen

Configuring the SSID (ESSID) and Beacon The SSID option is usually located somewhere obvious on the configuration utility. On the Linksys model shown in Figure 15-16, this option on the Setup tab. Configure your SSID to something unique.

You can choose not to broadcast the SSID, but this only stops casual users. Sophisticated wireless intruders have tools to detect networks that do not broadcast their SSIDs.

EXAM TIP One of the great benefits of SSIDs in the wild is the ability to configure multiple wireless networks in close proximity, even using the same frequency and channel, and still not conflict. For tight locations, such as dorm rooms, office complexes, and apartments, choose a unique SSID for each wireless network to avoid the potential for overlap problems.

Aside from the SSID (or ESSID in an extended network), broadcast traffic includes the *beacon*, essentially a timing frame sent from the WAP at regular intervals. The beacon frame enables Wi-Fi networks to function, so this is fairly important. Beacon traffic also makes up a major percentage of network traffic because most WAPs have beacons set to go off every 100 ms! You can adjust the rate of the beacon traffic down and improve your network traffic speeds, but you lower the speed at which devices can negotiate to get on the network, among other things. Figure 15-17 shows the Beacon Interval setting on a Linksys router.

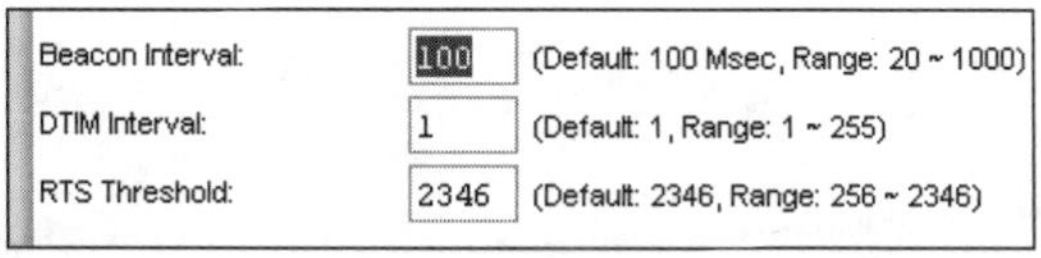

Figure 15-17
Setting the beacon interval

Beacon Interval:	100	(Default: 100 Msec, Range: 20 ~ 1000)
DTIM Interval:	1	(Default: 1, Range: 1 ~ 255)
RTS Threshold:	2346	(Default: 2346, Range: 256 ~ 2346)

Configuring MAC Address Filtering Increase security even further by using MAC address filtering to build a list of wireless network clients that are permitted or denied access to your wireless network based on their unique MAC addresses. Figure 15-18 shows the MAC address filtering configuration screen on a Linksys WAP. Simply enter the MAC address of a wireless node that you want to allow or deny access to your wireless network.

Figure 15-18 MAC address filtering configuration screen for a Linksys WAP

Configuring Encryption Enabling encryption ensures that data frames are secured against unauthorized access. To set up encryption, you turn on encryption at the WAP and generate a unique security key. Then you configure all connected wireless nodes on the network with the same key information. Figure 15-19 shows the WEP key configuration dialog box for a Linksys WAP.

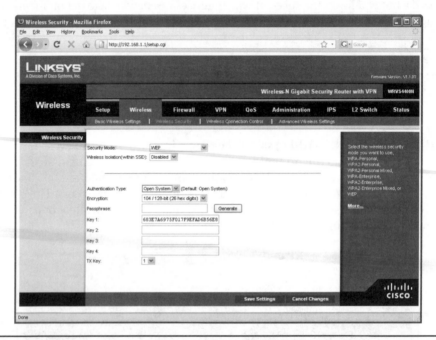

Figure 15-19 Encryption key configuration screen on Linksys WAP

You can either generate a set of encryption keys automatically or do it manually. You can save yourself a certain amount of effort by using the automatic method. Select an encryption level—the usual choices are either 64-bit or 128-bit—and then enter a unique *passphrase* and click the **Generate** button (or whatever the equivalent button is called in your WAP's software). Then select a default key and save the settings.

The encryption level, key, and passphrase must match on the wireless client node or communication fails. Many access points have the capability to export the encryption key data onto removable media for easy importing onto a client workstation, or you can configure encryption manually using the vendor-supplied configuration utility, as shown in Figure 15-20.

WPA encryption, if supported by your wireless equipment, is configured in much the same way. You may be required to input a valid user name and password to configure encryption using WPA.

If you have the option, choose WPA2 encryption for both the WAP and the NICs in your network. You configure WPA2 the same way you would WPA. Note that the settings such as WPA2 for the Enterprise assume you'll enable authentication using a

RADIUS server (Figure 15-21). Always use the strongest encryption you can. If you have WPA2, use it. If not, use WPA. WEP is always a terrible choice.

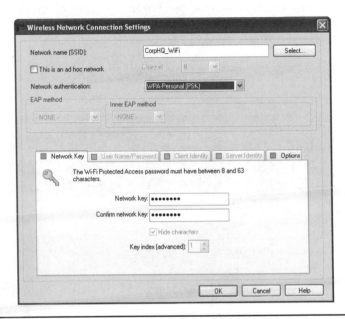

Figure 15-20 Encryption screen on client wireless network adapter configuration utility

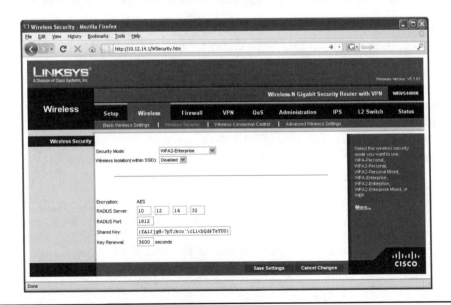

Figure 15-21 Encryption screen with RADIUS option

Configuring Channel and Frequency   With most home networks, you can simply leave the channel and frequency of the WAP at the factory defaults, but in an environment with overlapping Wi-Fi signals, you'll want to adjust one or both features. To adjust the channel, find the option in the WAP configuration screens and simply change it. Figure 15-22 shows the channel option in a Linksys WAP.

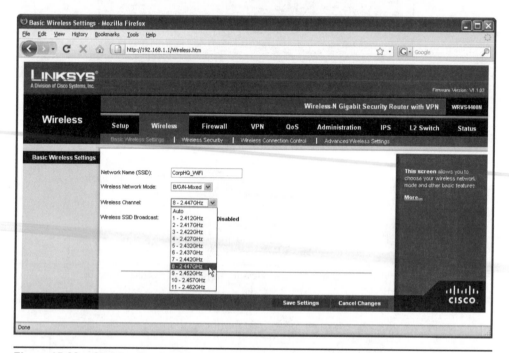

Figure 15-22   Changing the channel

With dual-band 802.11n WAPs, you can choose which band to put 802.11n traffic on, either 2.4 GHz or 5.0 GHz. In an area with overlapping signals, most of the traffic will be on the 2.4-GHz frequency because most devices are either 802.11b or 802.11g. You can avoid any kind of conflict with your 802.11n devices by using the 5.0-GHz frequency band instead. Figure 15-23 shows the configuration screen for a dual-band 802.11n WAP.

Configuring the Client

As with ad hoc mode wireless networks, infrastructure mode networks require that the same SSID be configured on all nodes and access points. Normally, the client would pick up a broadcast SSID and all you need to do is type in the security passphrase or encryption key. With nonbroadcasting networks, on the other hand, you need to type in a valid SSID as well as the security information (Figure 15-24).

Figure 15-23 Selecting frequency

Figure 15-24
Typing in an SSID
manually

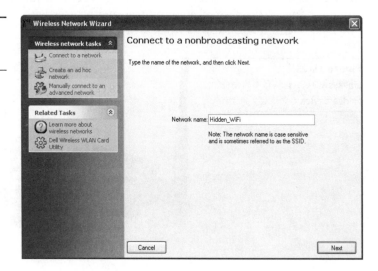

Extending the Network

Creating a Basic Service Set network with a single WAP and multiple clients works in a relatively small area, but you can extend a Wi-Fi network in a couple of ways if you have difficult spaces—with lots of obstructions, for example—or a need to communicate beyond the ~300-foot range of the typical wireless network. Most commonly, you'd add one or more WAPs to create an Extended Service Set. You can also install a wireless bridge to connect two or more segments.

NOTE Some manufacturers market special Wi-Fi extenders or repeaters that pick up the Wi-Fi signal wirelessly and repeat it into a wider space.

Adding a WAP

To add a WAP to a Wi-Fi network, you'll need to run a cable from a switch on the network to where you want to install it. Configuration is pretty straightforward. Both WAPs require the same ESSID, and if the WAPs are near each other, use separate channels. You can vary the frequency if they are 802.11n WAPs.

Wireless Bridges

Dedicated *wireless bridges* are used to connect two wireless network segments together, or to join wireless and wired networks together in the same way that wired bridge devices do. You can also use wireless bridges to join wireless networks with other networked devices, such as printers.

Wireless bridges come in two different flavors: point-to-point and point-to-multipoint. *Point-to-point* bridges can only communicate with a single other bridge and are used to connect two wireless network segments. *Point-to-multipoint* bridges can talk to more than one other bridge at a time and can connect multiple network segments. Some vendors also offer repeating bridges and bridges with access point and router functions. Figure 15-25 shows a wireless bridge.

Figure 15-25
Linksys wireless
bridge device

Verify the Installation

Once you've completed the initial installation of a Wi-Fi network, test it. Move some traffic from one computer to another using the wireless connection. Never leave a job site without verifying the installation.

Troubleshooting Wi-Fi

Wireless networks are a real boon when they work right, but they can also be one of the most vexing things to troubleshoot when they don't. Let's turn to some practical advice on how to detect and correct wireless hardware, software, and configuration problems.

As with any troubleshooting scenario, your first step in troubleshooting a wireless network is to break down your tasks into logical steps. Your first step should be to figure out the scope of your wireless networking problem. Ask yourself *who, what,* and *when:*

- Who is affected by the problem?
- What is the nature of the network problem?
- When did the problem start?

The answers to these questions dictate at least the initial direction of your troubleshooting.

So who's affected? If all machines on your network—wired and wireless—have lost connectivity, you have bigger problems than the wireless machines being unable to access the network. Troubleshoot this situation the way you'd troubleshoot any network failure. Once you determine which wireless nodes are affected, you'll find it easier to pinpoint whether the problem lies in one or more wireless clients or in one or more access points.

After you narrow down the number of affected machines, your next task is to figure out specifically what type of error the users are experiencing. If they can access some, but not all, network services, then it's unlikely the problem is limited to their wireless equipment. If they can browse the Internet but can't access any shared resources on a server, for example, then they're probably experiencing a permissions-related issue rather than a wireless one.

Finally, determine when the problem started. What has changed that might explain your loss of connectivity? Did you or somebody else change the wireless network configuration? If the network seems to disappear after you change the WEP key on the access point, for example, you have your solution—or at least your culprit! Did your office experience a power outage, power sag, or power surge? Any of these might cause a WAP to fail.

Once you figure out the who, what, and when, you can start troubleshooting in earnest. Typically, your problem is going to center on your hardware, software, connectivity, or configuration.

NOTE As with all things computing, don't forget to do the standard PC troubleshooting thing and reboot the computer before you do any configuration or hardware changes!

Hardware Troubleshooting

Wireless networking hardware components are subject to the same kind of abuse and faulty installation as any other hardware component. Troubleshooting a suspected hardware problem should bring out the CompTIA A+ certified technician in you.

Open Windows Device Manager and check to see if there's an error or conflict with the wireless adapter. If you see a big yellow exclamation point or a red *X* next to the device, you have either a driver error or a resource conflict. Reinstall the device driver or manually reset the IRQ resources as needed.

Software Troubleshooting

Because you've already checked to confirm that your hardware is using the correct drivers, what kind of software-related problems are left to check? Two things come immediately to mind: the wireless adapter configuration utility and the WAP's firmware version.

As mentioned earlier, some wireless devices won't work correctly unless you install the vendor-provided drivers and configuration utility before plugging in the device. This is particularly true of wireless USB devices. If you didn't do this, go into Device Manager and uninstall the device and then start again from scratch.

Some WAP manufacturers are notorious for shipping devices without the latest firmware installed. This problem often manifests as a device that enables clients to connect, but only at such slow speeds that the devices experience frequent timeout errors. The fix for this is to update the access point's firmware. Go to the manufacturer's Web site and follow the support links until you find the latest version. You need the device's exact model and serial number—this is important, because installing the wrong firmware version on your device is a guaranteed way to render it unusable!

Again, follow the manufacturer's instructions for updating the firmware to the letter. Typically, you need to download a small executable updating program along with a data file containing the firmware software. The process takes only minutes, and you'll be amazed at the results.

Connectivity Troubleshooting

Properly configured wireless clients should automatically and quickly connect to the desired SSID. If this isn't taking place, it's time for some troubleshooting. Most wireless connectivity problems come down to an incorrect configuration (like an incorrect password), low signal strength, or interference.

Without a strong signal, even a properly configured wireless client isn't going to work. Wireless clients use a multibar graph (usually five bars) to give an idea of signal strength: zero bars indicates no signal, and five bars indicates maximum signal.

Whether configuration or signal strength is the issue, the process to diagnose and repair the problem uses the same methods that you would use for a wired network. First, check the wireless NIC's link light to see whether it's passing data packets to and from the network. Second, check the wireless NIC's configuration utility. Typically, the utility has an icon in your System Tray that shows the strength of your wireless signal. Figure 15-26 shows Windows XP Professional's built-in wireless configuration utility—called Wireless Zero Configuration (or just Zeroconf)—displaying the link state and signal strength.

Figure 15-26

Windows XP Professional's wireless configuration utility

NOTE If you have a laptop with an internally installed NIC (instead of a USB NIC, for example), your device may not have a link light.

The link state defines the wireless NIC's connection status to a wireless network: connected or disconnected. If your link state indicates that your computer is currently disconnected, you may have a problem with your WAP. If your signal is too weak to receive a signal, you may be out of range of your access point, or a device may be causing interference. The interference can be caused by a device blocking the signal, like a metal object—think refrigerator or water heater. Because Wi-Fi uses radio waves, it's also subject to *radio frequency interference (RFI)*, where the Wi-Fi signal is disrupted by a radio signal from another device.

You can fix these problems in a number of ways. Because Wi-Fi signals *bounce* off objects, you can try small adjustments to your antennas to see if the signal improves. You can swap out the standard antenna for one or more higher-gain antennas. You can relocate the PC or access point. If you've just set up the network and find dead spots, you might have incorrect WAP placement. Move the WAP.

EXAM TIP The CompTIA Network+ exam might use the phrase "incorrect switch placement" even though, technically, the WAP function in a typical Wi-Fi box is not a switch.

Other wireless devices that operate in the same frequency range as your wireless nodes can cause interference and increased latency as well, making the network seem sluggish. Look for wireless telephones, intercoms, and so on, as possible culprits.

EXAM TIP Wi-Fi signals bounce when they strike solid objects and the powerful radio frequency (RF) signals generated by omnidirectional antennas make this problem much worse. This bounce can result in *multipath*, where multiple versions of a single signal hit the node, some stronger than others. If you get bad enough overlap of strong signals in a particular spot, a receiving node in that spot won't be able to detect *any* proper traffic, thus the spot is a *multipath null* (as opposed to a null spot created by some blocking object).

Another problem can occur when you have overlapping WAP signals sent by WAPs that aren't broadcasting their SSIDs. If you have one of these wireless networks saved in your system, your computer could attempt to log into the other WAP, resulting in an *SSID mismatch error*.

One fix for interference caused by other wireless devices is to change the channel your network uses. Another is to change the channel the offending device uses, if possible. If you can't change channels, try moving the interfering device to another area, or replacing it with a different device.

NOTE One trick that works for wireless networks that seem a bit flaky with a Windows XP client is to disable the Wireless Zero Configuration service on the client. To do this, simply open the Services applet in Administrative Tools and change the **Startup Type** option from **Automatic** to **Disabled**. Document your change, of course, so you'll remember to turn Zeroconf back on in case disabling it doesn't provide the fix you want.

Configuration Troubleshooting

With all due respect to the fine network techs in the field, the most common type of wireless networking problem is misconfigured hardware or software. That's right—the dreaded *user error!* Given the complexities of wireless networking, this isn't so surprising. All it takes is one slip of the typing finger to throw off your configuration completely. The things that you're most likely to get wrong are the SSID and security configuration.

Verify the SSID configuration on your access point first, and then check the affected wireless nodes. Most wireless devices enable you to use any characters in the SSID, including blank spaces. Be careful not to add blank characters where they don't belong, such as trailing blank spaces behind any other characters typed into the name field.

If you're using MAC address filtering, make sure the MAC address of the client that's attempting to access the wireless network is on the list of accepted users. This is particularly important if you swap out NICs on a PC or if you introduce a new PC to your wireless network.

Check the security configuration to make sure all wireless nodes and access points match. Mistyping an encryption key prevents the affected node from talking to the wireless network, even if your signal strength is 100 percent! Remember that many access points have the capability to export encryption keys onto a flash drive. Then you simply import the encryption key onto the PC using the wireless NIC's configuration utility. Remember the encryption level must match on access points and wireless nodes. If your WAP is configured for 128-bit encryption, all nodes must also use 128-bit encryption.

Chapter Review

Questions

1. Which wireless networking technology used the 5.0-GHz frequency range?

   A. 802.11

   B. 802.11a

   C. 802.11b

   D. 802.11g

2. The original 802.11 wireless specification enables a maximum throughput speed of _____.

   A. 2 Mbps

   B. 11 Mbps

   C. 54 Mbps

   D. 4 Mbps

3. What function does CSMA/CD provide that CSMA/CA does not?

   A. Data packet collision detection

   B. End-to-end data packet encryption

   C. Data packet collision avoidance

   D. Data packet error checking

4. Why should you configure a unique SSID for your wireless network?

   A. A unique SSID enables backward-compatibility between 802.11g and 802.11b.

   B. A unique SSID boosts wireless network range.

   C. A unique SSID boosts wireless network data throughput.

   D. A unique SSID prevents access by any network device that does not have the same SSID configured.

5. Which of these consumer electronics may cause interference with 802.11b wireless networks? (Select two.)

   A. Wireless telephones

   B. Wireless baby monitors

   C. Cellular telephones

   D. Television remote controls

6. Which of the following advantages does WPA have over WEP? (Select three.)

   A. End-to-end data packet encryption

   B. EAP user authentication

   C. Encryption key integrity checking

   D. 128-bit data encryption

7. What hardware enables wireless PCs to connect to resources on a wired network segment in infrastructure mode? (Select two.)

   A. An access point

   B. A router

   C. A hub

   D. A wireless bridge

8. What do you call a wireless Ethernet network in infrastructure mode with more than one access point?

   A. BSS

   B. EBSS

   C. WBSS

   D. ExNet

9. What type of server supports EAP-encrypted passwords in accordance with the 802.1X standard?

   A. WAP server

   B. WEP server

   C. RADIUS server

   D. NAS server

10. Which of the following is the most secure method of wireless encryption?

   A. WEP

   B. WEP2

   C. WPA

   D. WPA2

Answers

1. **B.** 802.11a operates in the 5.0-GHz frequency range.

2. **A.** Early 802.11 wireless networks ran at a maximum of 2 Mbps.

3. **A.** CSMA/CD offers collision detection. Wireless networks use collision avoidance instead.

4. **D.** A unique SSID prevents wireless devices that do not have the same SSID from accessing the network.

5. **A and B.** Many wireless telephones and baby monitors operate in the same 2.4-GHz frequency range as 802.11b wireless networking equipment and may cause interference. Bluetooth devices operate in the same frequency but are unlikely to cause interference because they use FHSS instead of DSSS. Television remote controls use infrared signals.

6. **A, B, and C.** WPA upgrades WEP to provide end-to-end data packet encryption, user authentication via EAP, and encryption key integrity checking.

7. **A and D.** A wireless access point or wireless bridge enables you to connect wireless PCs to a wired network segment.

8. **B.** A wireless network with more than one access point is called an EBSS, or Extended Basic Service Set.

9. **C.** A RADIUS server provides authentication through a user name and password encrypted with EAP.

10. **D.** WPA2 is the most secure because it uses Advanced Encryption Standard (AES), a 128-bit cipher that is harder to crack than the 128-bit TKIP wrapper used by WPA. Both WPA and WPA2 are stronger than WEP. WEP2 was never fully developed.

Protecting Your Network

The CompTIA Network+ certification exam expects you to know how to

- 5.2 Explain the methods of network access security: IP filtering, port filtering
- 5.3 Explain methods of user authentication: network access control, two-factor authentication, multifactor authentication, single sign-on
- 5.4 Explain common threats, vulnerabilities, and mitigation techniques
- 5.5 Given a scenario, install and configure a basic firewall
- 5.6 Categorize different types of network security appliances and methods: vulnerability scanners, honeypots, honeynets

To achieve these goals, you must be able to

- Discuss the common security threats in network computing
- Describe methods for securing user accounts
- Explain how firewalls, NAT, port filtering, and packet filtering protect a network from threats

The very nature of networking makes networks vulnerable to a dizzying array of threats. By definition, a network must allow multiple users to access serving systems, but at the same time, you must protect the network from harm. Who are the people creating this threat?

The news may be full of tales about *hackers* and other malicious people with nothing better to do than lurk around the Internet and trash the peace-loving systems of good folks like us, but in reality, hackers are only one of many serious network threats. You will learn how to protect your networks from hackers, but first I want you to appreciate that the average network faces many more threats from the folks who are authorized to use it than those who are not authorized. Users with good intentions are far more likely to cause you trouble than any hacker.

 NOTE Be aware that in some circles the term "hacker" describes folks who love the challenge of overcoming obstacles and perceived limitations—and that's a positive thing! At least for this chapter, I will define a "hacker" as an unauthorized person who is intentionally trying to access resources on your network. That's the way the term is generally used today.

Additionally, don't think all network threats are people. Let's not forget natural disasters like floods and hurricanes. Even third parties can unintentionally wreak havoc—what will you do if your building suddenly lacks electricity? A *network threat* can be any number of factors or elements that share one essential feature: the potential to damage network data, machines, or users.

To protect your network, you need to implement proper *network access control (NAC)*, which means control over information, people, access, machines, and everything in between.

The first order of business, therefore, is to stop and think about the types of threats that face the average network. As I define the threats, I'll also discuss the many tools and methods used to protect your precious networks from intentional harm.

NOTE Assessing threats in complicated networks can be daunting, but several companies can assess the threats for you. Cisco has a program, for example, called Cisco Security Posture Assessment Service that will analyze your network, run simulated attacks, and more, just to see where potential problems lie. Then you can find solutions before the bad guys discover the flaws.

Test Specific

Common Threats

The threats to your network are real and widespread. Here's a list of some of the more common potential threats to your network. The sections that follow give details on these threats and explain how to deal with them.

- System crashes and other hardware failures
- Administrative access control weaknesses
- Malware, such as viruses and worms
- Social engineering
- Man in the middle attacks
- Denial of service attacks
- Physical intrusion
- Attacks on wireless connections

System Crash/Hardware Failure

Like any technology, computers can and will fail—usually when you can least afford for it to happen. Hard drives crash, servers lock up, the power fails—it's all part of the joy of working in the networking business. Because of this, you need to create redundancy in areas prone to failure (like installing backup power in case of electrical failure) and performing those all-important data backups. Beyond that, the idea is to deploy redundant hardware to provide *fault tolerance*. Take advantage of technologies like Redundant Array of Independent Disks (RAID) to spread data across multiple drives. Buy a server case with multiple power supplies, or add a second NIC.

 NOTE See Chapter 18 for more information on RAID.

Administrative Access Control

All operating systems and many TCP applications come with some form of access control list (ACL) that defines what users can do with the server's shared resources. An access control might be a file server giving a user read-only privileges to a particular folder or an FTP server only allowing certain user IDs to use certain folders. Every operating system—and many Internet applications—are packed with administrative tools and functionality. You need these tools to get all kinds of work done, but by the same token, you need to work hard to keep these capabilities out of the reach of those who don't need them.

 EXAM TIP The CompTIA Network+ exam does not test you on the details of file system access controls. In other words, don't bother memorizing details like NTFS permissions, but do appreciate that you have fine-grained controls available.

Make sure you know the "super" accounts native to Windows (administrator), Linux (root), and Mac OS X (root). You must carefully control these accounts. Clearly, giving regular users administrator/root access is a bad idea, but far more subtle problems can arise. I once gave a user the Manage Documents permission for a busy laser printer in a Windows network. She quickly realized she could pause other users' print jobs and send her print jobs to the beginning of the print queue—nice for her but not so nice for her co-workers. Protecting administrative programs and functions from access and abuse by users is a real challenge and one that requires an extensive knowledge of the operating system and of users' motivations.

 NOTE Administering your super accounts is only part of what's called *user account control*. See "Controlling User Accounts" later in this chapter for more details.

Malware

The term *malware* defines any program or code (macro, script, and so on) that's designed to do something on a system or network that you don't want to have happen. Malware comes in quite a variety of guises, such as viruses, worms, macros, Trojans, rootkits, adware, and spyware. Let's examine all these malware flavors and then finish with how to deal with them.

Virus

A *virus* is a program that has two jobs: to replicate and to activate. *Replication* means it makes copies of itself, often as code stored in boot sectors or as extra code added to the end of executable programs. *Activation* is when a virus does something like erase the boot sector of a drive. A virus only replicates to other drives, such as thumb drives or optical media. It does not replicate across networks. Plus, a virus needs human action to spread.

Worm

A *worm* functions similarly to a virus, though it replicates exclusively through networks. A worm, unlike a virus, doesn't have to wait for someone to use a removable drive to replicate. If the infected computer is on a network, a worm will immediately start sending copies of itself to any other computers on the network it can locate. Worms can exploit inherent flaws in program code like *buffer overflows*, where a buffer cannot hold all the data sent to it.

Macro

A *macro* is any type of virus that exploits application macros to replicate and activate. A *macro* is also programming within an application that enables you to control aspects of the application. Macros exist in any application that has a built-in macro language, such as Microsoft Excel, that users can program to handle repetitive tasks (among other things).

Trojan

A *Trojan* is a piece of malware that looks or pretends to do one thing while, at the same time, doing something evil. A Trojan may be a game, like poker, or a free screensaver. The sky is the limit. The more "popular" Trojans turn an infected computer into a server and then open TCP or UDP ports so a remote user can control the infected computer. They can be used to capture keystrokes, passwords, files, credit card information, and more. This type of Trojan is called a *remote administration tool (RAT)*, although you don't need to know that for the CompTIA Network+ exam. Trojans do not replicate.

Rootkit

For a virus or Trojan to succeed, it needs to come up with some method to hide itself. As awareness of malware has grown, anti-malware programs make it harder to find new locations on a computer to hide. A *rootkit* is a Trojan that takes advantage of very low-level operating system functions to hide itself from all but the most aggressive of anti-malware tools. Worse, a rootkit, by definition, gains privileged access to the computer. Rootkits can strike operating systems, hypervisors, and even firmware.

The most infamous rootkit appeared a few years ago as an antipiracy attempt by Sony on its music CDs. Unfortunately for the media giant, the rootkit software installed when you played a music CD and opened a backdoor to an infected computer that could be used for malicious intent.

Adware/Spyware

There are two types of programs that are similar to malware in that they try to hide themselves to an extent. *Adware* is a program that monitors the types of Web sites you frequent and uses that information to generate targeted advertisements, usually pop-up windows. Many of these programs use Adobe Flash. Adware isn't, by definition, evil, but many adware makers use sneaky methods to get you to use adware, such as using deceptive-looking Web pages ("Your computer is infected with a virus—click here to scan NOW!"). As a result, adware is often considered malware. Some of the computer-infected ads actually install a virus when you click them, so avoid these things like the plague.

Spyware is a function of any program that sends information about your system or your actions over the Internet. The type of information sent depends on the program. A spyware program will include your browsing history. A more aggressive form of spyware may send keystrokes or all of the contacts in your e-mail. Some spyware makers bundle their product with ads to make them look innocuous. Adware, therefore, can contain spyware.

Dealing with Malware

You can deal with malware in several ways: anti-malware programs, training and awareness, policies and procedures, patch management, and incident response.

At the very least, every computer should run an anti-malware program. If possible, add an appliance that runs anti-malware programs against incoming data from your network. Many such appliances exist, but they are most common in proxy servers. Also remember that an anti-malware program is only as good as its updates—keep everyone's definition file up to date with, literally, nightly updates! Users must be trained to look for suspicious ads, programs, and pop-ups, and understand that they must not click these things. The more you teach users about malware, the more aware they'll be of potential threats. Your organization should have policies and procedures in place so everyone knows what to do if they encounter malware. Finally, a good network administrator maintains proper incident response records to see if any pattern to attacks emerges. He or she can then adjust policies and procedures to mitigate these attacks.

 EXAM TIP One of the most important malware mitigation procedures is to keep systems under your control patched and up to date through proper *patch management*. Microsoft does a very good job of putting out bug fixes and patches as soon as problems occur. If your systems aren't set up to update automatically, then perform manual updates regularly.

Scoring Excellent Anti-Malware Programs

You can download many excellent anti-malware programs for free, either for extended trial periods or for indefinite use. Since you need these programs to keep your systems happy, try this! Download one or more anti-malware programs, such as the following:

- **Malwarebytes Anti-Malware** (www.malwarebytes.org)   Malwarebytes' Anti-Malware program rocks the house in terms of dealing with malicious software. They offer both a free version that scans your computer for malware and quarantines it and a PRO version that actively protects against any incoming malware. Anti-Malware is my first choice in dealing with malware on a client's computer.

- **Lavasoft Ad-Aware** (www.lavasoft.com)   Ad-Aware is an excellent anti-spyware program. Ad-Aware will root out all sorts of files and programs that can cause your computer to run slowly (or worse).

- **Spybot Search&Destroy** (www.safer-networking.org)   Spybot Search&Destroy from Safer Networking Ltd. is another superb anti-spyware program. Many folks use both Ad-Aware and Spybot—though sometimes the two programs detect each other as spyware!

- **AVG Anti-Virus** (http://free.avg.com)   AVG offers a free version of their anti-virus software for noncommercial use. Updated regularly to add the latest virus signatures, the software will keep your system clean and bug free.

Social Engineering

A nice percentage of attacks against your network come under the heading of *social engineering*—the process of using or manipulating people inside the networking environment to gain access to that network from the outside. The term "social engineering" covers the many ways humans can use other humans to gain unauthorized information. This unauthorized information may be a network login, a credit card number, company customer data—almost anything you might imagine that one person or organization may not want a person outside of that organization to access.

Social engineering attacks aren't hacking—at least in the classic sense of the word—although the goals are the same. Social engineering is where people attack an organization through the people in the organization or physically access the organization to get the information they need.

The most classic form of social engineering is the telephone scam in which someone calls a person and tries to get him or her to reveal his or her user name/password combination. In the same vein, someone may physically enter your building under the guise of having a legitimate reason for being there, such as a cleaning person, repair technician, or messenger. The attacker then snoops around desks, looking for whatever he or she has come to find (one of many good reasons not to put passwords on your desk or monitor). The attacker might talk with people inside the organization, gathering names, office numbers, or department names—little things in and of themselves, but powerful tools when combined later with other social engineering attacks.

These old-school social engineering tactics are taking a backseat to a far more nefarious form of social engineering: phishing.

 CAUTION All these attacks are commonly used together, so if you discover one of them being used against your organization, it's a good idea to look for others.

Phishing

In a *phishing* attack, the attacker poses as some sort of trusted site, like an online version of your bank or credit card company, and solicits you to update your financial information, such as a credit card number. You might get an e-mail message, for example, that purports to be from PayPal telling you that your account needs to be updated and provides a link that looks like it goes to http://www.paypal.com. Clicking the link, however, you end up at a site that resembles the PayPal login but is actually http://100.16.49.21/2s82ds.php, a phishing site.

Man in the Middle

In a *man in the middle* attack, a person inserts him- or herself into a conversation between two others, covertly intercepting traffic thought to be only between those other people. The man in the middle might gather those conversations to gain access to passwords or other sensitive data or to the shared keys in an encrypted conversation. The attacker might then use a rogue access point to get into the network or social engineering techniques to gain access to a wired network.

Denial of Service

Denial of service (DoS) attacks are the work of hackers whose only interest is in bringing a network to its knees. They accomplish this by flooding the network with so many requests that it becomes overwhelmed and ceases functioning. These attacks are most commonly performed on Web and e-mail servers, but virtually any part of a network can be attacked via some DoS method.

The secret to a successful DoS attack is to send as many packets as possible to the victim. Not only do you want to send a lot of packets, you want the packets to contain some kind of request that the victim must process as long as possible to force the victim to deal with each attacking packet for as long as possible. You can employ one of several methods to get a good DoS going, but the CompTIA Network+ objectives expressly mention a *smurf* attack. A *smurf attack* is when an attacker floods a network with ping packets sent to the broadcast address. The trick that makes this attack special is that the return address of the pings is spoofed to that of the intended victim. When all the computers on the network respond to the initial ping, they send their response to the intended victim. The attacker can then amplify the effect of the attack by the number of responding machines on the network. Due to modern network management procedures and controls built into modern operating systems, the danger of the smurf attack has been largely mitigated.

EXAM TIP A smurf attack is a form of DoS that sends broadcast pings to the victim.

Far more menacing than a simple DoS attack are *distributed denial of service (DDoS) attacks*. A DDoS uses multiple (as in hundreds or up to hundreds of thousands of) computers under the control of a single operator to launch a devastating attack. DDoS operators don't own these computers, but instead use malware to take control of computers. A single computer under the control of an operator is called a *zombie*. A group of computers under the control of one operator is called a *botnet*.

NOTE Zombified computers aren't obvious. DDoS operators often wait weeks or months after a computer's been infected to take control of it.

To take control of your network's computers, someone has to install malware on the computer. Again, anti-malware, training, and procedures will keep you safe from zombification (but feel free to make some joke about eating human brains).

Physical Intrusion

You can't consider a network secure unless you provide some physical protection to your network. I separate physical protection into two different areas: protection of servers and protection of clients.

Server protection is easy. Lock up your servers to prevent physical access by any unauthorized person. Large organizations have special server rooms, complete with card-key locks and tracking of anyone who enters or exits. Smaller organizations should at least have a locked closet. While you're locking up your servers, don't forget about any network switches! Hackers can access networks by plugging into a switch, so don't leave any switches available to them.

Physical server protection doesn't stop with a locked door. One of the most common mistakes made by techs is walking away from a server while still logged in. Always log off your server when it's not in use! As a backup, add a password-protected screensaver (Figure 16-1).

Locking up all of your client systems is difficult, but your users should be required to perform some physical security. First, all users should lock their computers when they step away from their desks. Instruct them to press the WINDOWS KEY-L combination to perform the lock. Hackers take advantage of unattended systems to get access to networks.

Figure 16-1

Applying a
password-protected
screensaver to a server

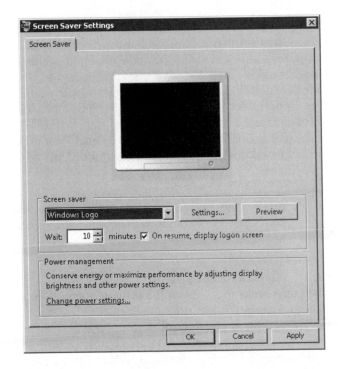

Second, make users aware of the potential for dumpster diving and make paper shredders available. Last, tell users to mind their work areas. It's amazing how many users leave passwords readily available. I can go into any office, open a few desk drawers, and will invariably find little yellow sticky notes with user names and passwords. If users must write down passwords, tell them to put them in locked drawers!

EXAM TIP A Windows PC should be locked down when not actively used. The simplest thing to teach your users to do is to press the WINDOWS KEY-L combination when they get up from their desks. The effects from the key combination vary according to both the version of Windows and whether a system is a member of a workgroup or domain, but all will require the user to log in to access his or her account (assuming the account is password protected in the first place, of course!).

Attacks on Wireless Connections

With more and more wireless networks coming online every day, it shouldn't be much of a surprise that they've drawn the attention of the bad guys. Attacks on wireless connections come in several forms, such as leeching, cracking wireless encryption, rogue access points, and evil twin attacks.

Leeching

Leeching is using another person's wireless network without that person's permission. Leeching takes some of the bandwidth the other person has paid for, so it's simply theft with another name.

In the heady early days of Wi-Fi networks, people would seek out unprotected networks by using sniffer hardware and cruising neighborhoods. This process, called *war driving*, often resulted in marks or symbols stenciled onto a nearby fence, gate, door, wall, or whatever, marking the open Wi-Fi signal. The marking was called *war chalking*. Neither practice is common today, but you might see the terms on the CompTIA Network+ exam.

 NOTE Many people concatenate the terms, so *wardriving* and *warchalking*. Be prepared to see them with or without the space.

Cracking Wireless Encryption

Most Wi-Fi networks today use some form of encryption to stop casual leeching, but that doesn't necessarily stop the sophisticated thief. Wi-Fi networks use one of three types of encryption, as you'll recall from the previous chapter: WEP, WPA, and WPA2. All three are crackable, though WPA2 offers more security than WEP or WPA.

The techniques for *WEP cracking* and *WPA cracking* are simple: run a sniffer program, capture packets in the air with a *packet sniffing* program, and then run a program to sniff out the password or preshared key. WEP networks can be cracked in under a minute; WPA, with a very strong key using letters, numbers, and symbols, will take hours or longer to crack, depending on the computing power of the machine running the hacking software.

Rogue Access Points

A *rogue access point* is an unauthorized wireless access point (WAP) installed in a computer network. Rogue access points are a huge problem today. Anyone can easily purchase an inexpensive WAP and just plug it into a network. To make the issue even worse, almost all WAPs are designed to work using the preinstalled configuration, giving bad guys easy access to your network from a location physically outside your network.

The biggest reason rogue access points exist is that members of an organization install them for convenience. Users like their own wireless networks and, due to lack of training, don't appreciate the danger they pose. Bad guys getting into your physical location and installing rogue access points is less common.

Locating rogue access points is a challenge, especially if the person installing the rogue access point is clever enough to turn off SSID broadcasting. There are wireless sniffing programs designed to find any wireless network, but they must be run often.

Evil Twin

Hackers can use an *evil twin* attack to fool people into logging into a rogue access point that looks very similar to a legitimate access point. The evil twin access point might have an SSID that matches a legitimate SSID, for example, only it's off by a letter or a character. People who log into the evil twin will have their keystrokes recorded in the hopes of stealing passwords and other valuable information. An evil twin is basically a *wireless phishing attack.*

Securing User Accounts

Even the smallest network will have a number of user accounts and groups scattered about with different levels of permissions. Every time you give a user access to a resource, you create potential loopholes that can leave your network vulnerable to unauthorized access, data destruction, and other administrative nightmares. You can categorize all of these potential dangers as *internal threats.* To protect your network from these threats, you need to implement the right controls over passwords, user accounts, groups, and permissions. The whole process begins with authentication.

Authentication

Properly authenticating users is the first step in securing user accounts. *Authentication* means that a person can prove his or her identity.

You can categorize ways to authenticate into three broad areas: ownership factors, knowledge factors, and inherent factors. A *knowledge factor* is something the user knows, like a password or personal identification number (PIN). An *ownership factor* is something the user has, like an ID card or security token. An *inherent factor* is something that is part of the user, like a fingerprint or retinal pattern.

Multifactor authentication provides the best authentication, where a user must use two or more factors to prove his or her identity. Note that multifactor means more than one factor, not just more than one *thing.* Logging in with a user name and password is two things, for example, but because both fall into the category of what a user knows, it's not multifactor authentication.

Many organizations use *two-factor authentication,* typically some sort of physical token that, when inserted, prompts for a password. That way, the user authenticates with both what she has and what she knows.

Passwords

Passwords are the ultimate key to protecting your network. Anyone with access to a user account with a valid password will get into any system. Even if the user account only has limited permissions, you still have a security breach. Remember: for a hacker, just getting into the system is half the battle.

Protect your passwords. Never give out passwords over the phone. If a user loses a password, an administrator should reset the password to a complex combination of letters and numbers and then allow the user to change the password to something he or she wants.

All of the stronger network operating systems have this capability. Windows Server, for example, provides a setting called **User must change password at next logon**, as shown in Figure 16-2.

Figure 16-2

Windows Server option for requiring a user to change a password

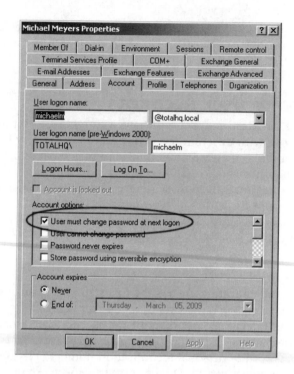

Make your users choose good passwords. I once attended a network security seminar, and the speaker had everyone stand up. She then began to ask questions about our passwords—if we responded positively to the question we were to sit down. She began to ask questions like "Do you use the name of your spouse as a password?" and "Do you use your pet's name?"

By the time she was done asking about 15 questions, only 6 people out of some 300 were still standing! The reality is that most of us choose passwords that are amazingly easy to hack. Make sure you use strong passwords: at least eight characters in length (more than eight characters is better), including letters, numbers, and special characters.

Using nonalphanumeric characters makes any password much more difficult to crack for two reasons. First, the most common password-cracking programs use a *brute-force* approach, basically running through combinations of letters until something works. Adding nonalphanumeric characters forces the hacker to consider many more possible characters than just letters and numbers. This doesn't stop brute-force cracking, but it makes it more difficult.

Second, many password crackers use combinations of common words and numbers to try to hack a password. Because nonalphanumeric characters don't fit into common words or numbers, including a character such as an exclamation point will defeat these common-word hacks. Not all serving systems let you use characters such as @, $, %, or \, however, so you need to experiment to see if a particular server will accept them.

Once you've forced your users to choose strong passwords, you should make them change passwords at regular intervals. While this concept sounds good on paper and for the CompTIA Network+ exam, you should remember that, although regular password changing is a good idea, in the real world it is a hard policy to maintain. For starters, users tend to forget passwords when they change them often. One way to remember passwords if your organization forces you to change them is to use a numbering system. I worked at a company that required me to change my password at the beginning of each month, so I did something simple. I took a root password—let's say it was "m3y3rs5"—and simply added a number to the end representing the current month. So when June rolled around, for example, I would change my password to "m3y3rs56." It worked pretty well!

No matter how well your password implementation goes, using passwords always creates administrative problems. First, users forget passwords and someone (usually you) has to access their account and reset their passwords. Second, users will write down passwords, giving hackers an easy way into the network if those bits of paper fall into the wrong hands. If you've got the cash, you have two alternatives to passwords: smart devices and biometrics.

Smart devices are cards with magnetic stripes, USB keys, or other small devices that you insert into your PC in lieu of entering a password. They work extremely well and are incredibly difficult to bypass. The downside is that they might be lost or stolen.

 NOTE Many companies use smart devices for *single sign-on*, a method of authentication that, in one shot, both authenticates the user and gives the user access (authorization) to all the resources he or she has permission to access. That way the user only has to do the sign-on stuff once.

If you want to go seriously space-age, then biometrics are the way to go. *Biometric devices* scan fingerprints, retinas, or even the sound of the user's voice to provide a foolproof replacement for both passwords and smart devices. Biometrics have been around for quite a while, but were relegated to extremely high-security networks due to their high cost (thousand of dollars per device). That price has dropped substantially, making biometrics worthy of consideration for some networks.

Controlling User Accounts

A user account is just information: nothing more than a combination of a user name and password. Like any important information, it's critical to control who has a user account and to track what these accounts can do. Access to user accounts should be restricted to the assigned individuals (no sharing, no stealing), and those accounts should have permission to access only the resources they need, no more. This control over what a legitimate account can do is called the *principle of least privilege* approach to network security and is, by far, the most common approach used in networks.

Tight control of user accounts is critical to preventing unauthorized access. Disabling unused accounts is an important part of this strategy, but good user account control goes far deeper than that. One of your best tools for user account control is groups. Instead of giving permissions to individual user accounts, give them to groups; this makes keeping track of the permissions assigned to individual user accounts much easier. Figure 16-3 shows an example of giving permissions to a group for a folder in Windows Server. Once a group is created and its permissions set, you can then add user accounts to that group as needed. Any user account that becomes a member of a group automatically gets the permissions assigned to that group. Figure 16-4 shows an example of adding a user to a newly created group in the same Windows Server system.

Figure 16-3

Giving a group permissions for a folder in Windows

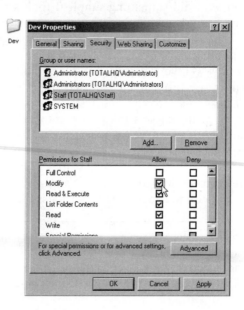

Groups are a great way to get increased complexity without increasing the administrative burden on network administrators because all network operating systems combine permissions. When a user is a member of more than one group, which permissions does he or she have with respect to any particular resource? In all network operating systems, the permissions of the groups are *combined*, and the result is what is called the *effective permissions* the user has to access the resource. Let's use an example from Windows Server. If Timmy is a member of the Sales group, which has List Folder Contents permission to a folder, and he is also a member of the Managers group, which has Read and Execute permissions to the same folder, Timmy will have List Folder Contents *and* Read and Execute permissions to that folder.

Combined permissions can also lead to *conflicting permissions*, where a user does not get access to a needed resource because one of his groups has Deny permission to that resource. Deny always trumps any other permission.

Watch out for *default* user accounts and groups—they can become secret backdoors to your network! All network operating systems have a default Everyone group, and it can easily be used to sneak into shared resources. This Everyone group, as its name implies, literally includes anyone who connects to that resource. Some versions of Windows give full control to the Everyone group by default. All of the default groups—Everyone, Guest, Users—define broad groups of users. Never use them unless you intend to permit all those folks to access a resource. If you use one of the default groups, remember to configure it with the proper permissions to prevent users from doing things you don't want them to do with a shared resource!

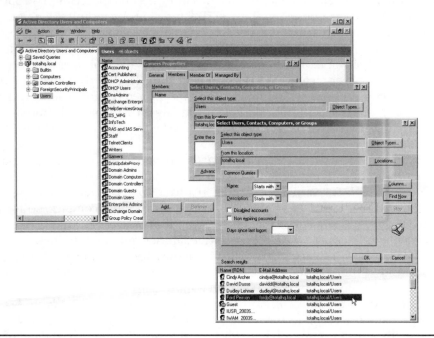

Figure 16-4 Adding a user to a newly created group

All of these groups only do one thing for you: they enable you to keep track of your user accounts. That way you know resources are only available for users who need those resources, and users only access the resources you want them to use.

Before I move on, let me add one more tool to your kit: diligence. Managing user accounts is a thankless and difficult task, but one that you must stay on top of if you want to keep your network secure. Most organizations integrate the creating, disabling/enabling, and deleting of user accounts with the work of their human resources folks. Whenever a person joins, quits, or moves, the network admin is always one of the first to know!

The administration of permissions can become incredibly complex—even with judicious use of groups. You now know what happens when a user account has multiple sets of permissions to the same resource, but what happens if the user has one set of permissions to a folder and a different set of permissions to one of its subfolders? This brings up a phenomenon called *inheritance*. I won't get into the many ways different network operating systems handle inherited permissions. Luckily for you, the CompTIA Network+ exam doesn't test you on all the nuances of combined or inherited permissions—just be aware they exist. Those who go on to get more advanced certifications, on the other hand, must become extremely familiar with the many complex permutations of permissions.

Firewalls

I always fear the moment when technical terms move beyond the technical people and start to find use in the nontechnical world. The moment any technical term becomes part of the common vernacular, you can bet that its true meaning will become obscured because without a technical background people are reduced to simplistic descriptions of what is invariably a far more complex idea. I submit the term *firewall* as a perfect example of this phenomenon. Most people with some level of computer knowledge think of a firewall as some sort of thingamabob that protects an internal network from unauthorized access to and from the Internet at large. That type of definition might work for your VP as you explain why you need to get a firewall, but as techs, we need a deeper understanding.

Firewalls protect networks from *external threats*—potential attacks from outside your network—by filtering packets using a number of methods, such as hiding IP addresses using NAT, selectively blocking TCP/UDP ports, or even filtering traffic based on MAC addresses. From there, things get much more complex, so for now, let's define a firewall as a device that filters IP traffic to protect networks and computers. But a firewall doesn't have to be a dedicated device. You run into firewalls in two very different places. The first place is a device at the edge of your network. Given that there's already a router at the edge of your network, you'd be hard pressed to find a router today that does not also act as a firewall. Because the firewall is in a box on the network, these are called *network-based* firewalls (also called *hardware firewalls,* although many use software too). The second place is software installed on your computer that does the same job but only firewalls packets coming in and out of your system. These are called *host-based* firewalls (also called *software firewalls*). In a perfect world, your network has a network-based firewall at the edge of your network and all of your systems run a host-based firewall.

Hiding the IPs

The first and most common technique for protecting a network is to hide the real IP addresses of the internal network systems from the Internet. If a hacker gets a real IP address, he or she can begin to probe that system, looking for vulnerabilities. If you can prevent a hacker from getting an IP address to probe, you've stopped most hacking techniques cold. You already know how to hide IP addresses using *Network Address Translation (NAT).* That's why most routers have built-in NAT capability. Not only does NAT reduce the need for true IANA-supplied public IP addresses, but it also does a great job protecting networks from hackers because it is difficult to access a network using private IP addresses hidden behind a NAT-enabled router.

 NOTE Many sources challenge the idea that NAT is a firewall feature. Granted, NAT wasn't originally designed to act as a firewall, but it sure does protect your network.

Port Filtering

The second most common firewall tool is *port filtering*, also called *port blocking*. Hackers often try less commonly used port numbers to get into a network. Port filtering simply means preventing the passage of any TCP or UDP segments or datagrams through any ports other than the ones prescribed by the system administrator. Port filtering is effective, but it requires some serious configuration to work properly. The question is always, "Which ports do I allow into the network?"

When you open your browser and access a Web page, your Web browser sends out TCP segments to the Web server with the destination port of 80. Web servers require this, and it's how TCP/IP works. No one has problems with the well-known ports like 80 (HTTP), 20/21 (FTP), 25 (SMTP), and 110 (POP3), but there are a large number of lesser-known ports that networks often want opened.

 EXAM TIP   One early exploit of open ports came in the form of an *FTP bounce attack*, where a malicious user could run the port command on an FTP server to discover any open ports on the FTP server. Modern FTP servers block this kind of attack, but you get the idea. Open ports can be dangerous.

I recently installed port filtering on my personal firewall and everything worked great—until I decided to play the popular game World of Warcraft on the Internet. (Note to WoW nerds: on the Blackwater Raiders server, I'm "Pelape.") I simply could not connect to the Internet servers until I discovered that World of Warcraft requires TCP port 3724 open to work over the Internet. After reconfiguring my port filter (I reopened port 3724), I was able to play WoW, but when I tried to help one of my friends using Microsoft Remote Desktop, I couldn't access his system! Want to guess where the problem was? Yup, I needed to open port 3389. How did I figure these out? I didn't know which ports to open, but I suspected that my problem was in the port arena so I fired up my Web browser (thank goodness that worked!) and went to the World of Warcraft and Microsoft Web sites, which told me which ports I needed to open. This constant opening and closing of ports is one of the prices you pay for the protection of port filtering, but it sure stops hackers if they can't use certain ports to gain access.

Most routers that provide port blocking manifest it in one of two ways. The first way is to have port filtering close *all* ports until you open them explicitly. The other port filtering method is to leave all ports open unless you explicitly close them. The gotcha here is that most types of IP sessions require *dynamic port* usage. For example, when my system makes a query for a Web page on HTTP port 80, the Web server and my system establish a session using a *different* port to send the Web pages to my system. Figure 16-5 shows the results of running the `netstat  -n` switch while I have a number of Web pages open—note the TCP ports used for the incoming Web pages (the Local Address column). Dynamic ports can cause some problems for older (much older) port filtering systems, but almost all of today's port filtering systems are aware of this issue and handle it automatically.

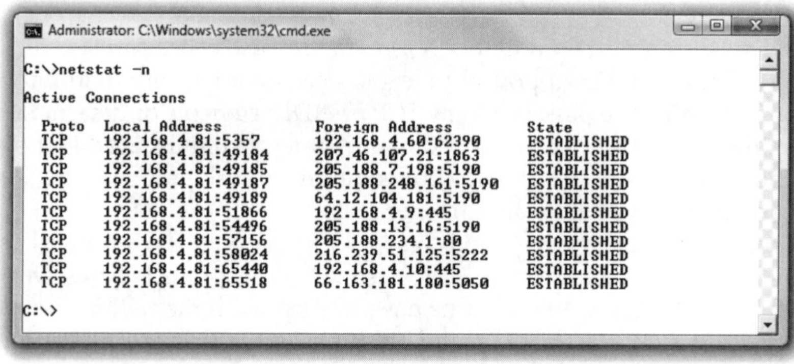

Administrator: C:\Windows\system32\cmd.exe
C:\>netstat -n
Active Connections
Proto Local Address Foreign Address State
TCP 192.168.4.81:5357 192.168.4.60:62390 ESTABLISHED
TCP 192.168.4.81:49184 207.46.107.21:1863 ESTABLISHED
TCP 192.168.4.81:49185 205.188.7.198:5190 ESTABLISHED
TCP 192.168.4.81:49187 205.188.248.161:5190 ESTABLISHED
TCP 192.168.4.81:49189 64.12.104.181:5190 ESTABLISHED
TCP 192.168.4.81:51866 192.168.4.9:445 ESTABLISHED
TCP 192.168.4.81:54496 205.188.13.16:5190 ESTABLISHED
TCP 192.168.4.81:57156 205.188.234.1:80 ESTABLISHED
TCP 192.168.4.81:58024 216.239.51.125:5222 ESTABLISHED
TCP 192.168.4.81:65440 192.168.4.10:445 ESTABLISHED
TCP 192.168.4.81:65518 66.163.181.180:5050 ESTABLISHED
C:\>

Figure 16-5 The `netstat -n` command showing HTTP connections

Port filters have many different interfaces. On my little gateway router, the port filtering uses the pretty, Web-based interface shown in Figure 16-6. Linux systems use either iptables or netfilter for their firewall work. Like most Linux tools, these programs are rather dull to look at directly and require substantial skill manipulating text files to do your filtering chores. Most Linux distributions come with handy graphical tools, however, to make the job much easier. Figure 16-7 shows the firewall configuration screen from the popular YaST utility, found on the SuSE Linux distribution.

Service - Mozilla Firefox
File Edit View History Bookmarks Tools Help
http://192.168.1.1/setup.cgi
LINKSYS
Firewall
Wireless-N Gigabit Security Router with VPN
Setup
Wireless
Firewall
VPN
QoS
Administration
IPS
L2 Switch
Status
Services
Service Definition
Name :
policy2
Type :
TCP/UDP
Start Port :
2551
Finish Port :
4400
Save
Delete
Index
Name
Type
Start Port
End Port
1
policy1
TCP
1044
2550
Edit
Cancel Changes
cisco
Done

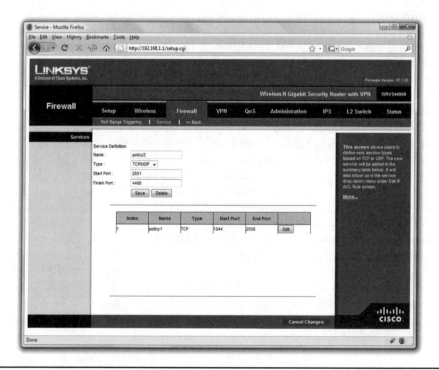

Figure 16-6 Web-based port filtering interface

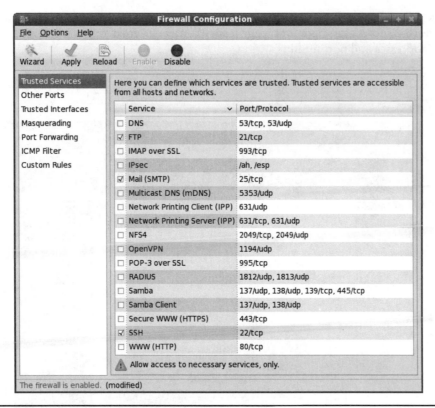

Figure 16-7 YaST configuration program

So can one router have both NAT and port filtering? You bet it can! Most gateway routers come with both—you just need to take the time to configure them and make them work! You need to implement proper *port security*.

 EXAM TIP The CompTIA Network+ exam expects you to know that NAT, proxy serving, and port filtering are typical firewall functions!

Packet Filtering

Port filtering deals only with port numbers; it completely disregards IP addresses. If an IP packet comes in with a filtered port number, the packet is blocked, regardless of the IP address. *Packet filtering* or *IP filtering* works in the same way, except it blocks packets based on IP addresses. *Packet filters*, also known as *IP filters*, will block any incoming or outgoing packet from a particular IP address or range of IP addresses. Packet filters are far better at blocking outgoing IP addresses because the network administrator knows and can specify the IP addresses of the internal systems. Blocking outgoing packets is a good way to prevent users on certain systems from accessing the Internet. Figure 16-8 shows a configuration page from a router designed to block different ranges of IP addresses and port numbers.

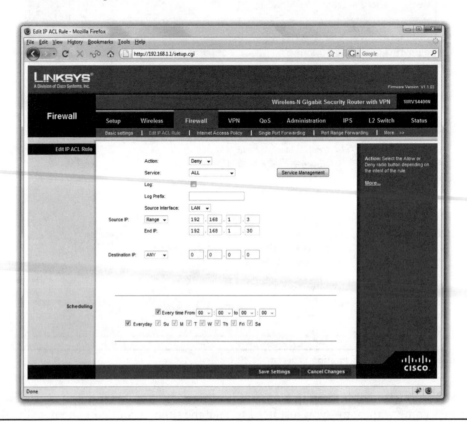

Figure 16-8   Blocking IP addresses

This type of filtering is called *stateless filtering* because the device that does the filtering just checks the packet for IP addresses and port numbers and blocks or allows accordingly. Each packet is judged as an individual entity to determine whether it should be allowed into the network. Stateless filtering works at Layer 3 of the OSI seven-layer model. Stateless filtering is inexpensive and easy to implement, but has one issue: once you've opened a particular path into your network, that path is open. Someone spoofing IP information could get in.

A more secure method of filtering is to use devices that do *stateful filtering* or *stateful inspection*, where all packets are examined as a stream. Stateful devices can do more than allow or block; they can track when a stream is disrupted or packets get corrupted and act accordingly. The best of the stateful filtering devices are application proxies, working at Layer 7 of the OSI seven-layer model. The only real problems with application proxies are that they tend to be slower than stateless filters and more expensive.

MAC Filtering

Similar to packet filtering, some firewall devices can allow or deny access to the network according to the MAC address of the client; what's called *MAC filtering*. Because every network device has a unique 48-bit MAC address, MAC filtering should make for a very secure network. It's often one of the implemented security measures in wireless networks, for example, because setting it up is quick.

Many programs enable you to spoof or mimic a MAC address, though, so MAC filtering is not a strong deterrent for a determined hacker. Plus it gets a little tedious to add a new MAC address every time a friend drops by with a new smartphone or tablet and wants to use your Wi-Fi.

Personal Firewalls

Back in the days of dial-up connections, the concept of protection from external threats wasn't very interesting. The concept of dial-up alone was more than enough protection for most users. First, systems using dial-up connections were, by definition, only periodically on the Internet, making them tough for hackers to detect. Second, all dial-up connections use DHCP-assigned IP addresses, so even if a hacker could access a dial-up user during one session, that dial-up user would almost certainly have a different IP address the next time he or she accessed the Internet. As long as the user installs a good antivirus program, dial-up users have nothing to fear from hackers.

The onset of high-speed, always-connected Internet links has changed the security picture completely. The user who dumps his or her dial-up connection for ADSL or a cable modem immediately becomes a prime target for hackers. Even though most ADSL and cable modems use DHCP links, the IP address almost never changes, even after disconnecting for several hours. When the router reconnects, it almost always receives the same address again. Such long-lived addresses give attackers all the time in the world to try to break in.

One of the first items on the agenda of Windows users with high-bandwidth connections is to turn off File and Print Sharing. Because NetBIOS can run over TCP/IP (NetBT), sharing a folder or printer makes it available to anyone on the Internet unless your ISP helps you out by filtering NetBIOS traffic. Some hacker groups run port scanner programs looking for systems with File and Print Sharing enabled and post these IP addresses to public sites (no, I will not tell you where to find them!). When I first got my cable modem many years ago, I absentmindedly clicked the My Network Places icon on my Desktop and discovered that four of my fellow cable users had their systems shared, and two of them were sharing printers! Being a good neighbor and not a hacker, I made sure they changed their erroneous ways!

Although you can (and should) buy a hardware firewall to place between your system and the Internet, a single user should, at the very least, employ a personal software firewall program. Every operating system comes with some form of built-in personal firewall. Every copy of Windows comes with Windows Firewall (which I will discuss in detail in a moment). There are also third-party software firewalls like ZoneAlarm Pro (Figure 16-9). These personal firewall programs are quite powerful and have the added benefit of being easy to use. These days, an individual Internet user has no excuse not to use a personal firewall.

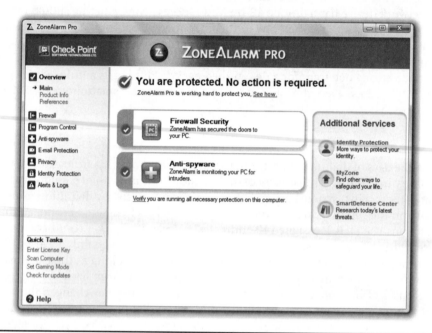

Figure 16-9   ZoneAlarm Pro

Every version of Windows comes with the handy Internet Connection Sharing (ICS), but ICS alone doesn't provide any level of support other than NAT. Starting with Windows XP, Microsoft included Internet Connection Firewall (ICF), renamed in Windows XP Service Pack 2 as *Windows Firewall*. Windows Firewall works with ICS to provide basic firewall protection for your network. Windows Firewall is often used without ICS to provide protection for single machines connected to the Internet. Figure 16-10 shows the screen where you'd turn on Windows Firewall in Windows Vista.

By default, Windows Firewall *blocks* all incoming IP packets that attempt to initiate a session. This is great for networks that only use the Internet to browse the Web or grab e-mail but will cause problems in circumstances where you want to provide any type of Internet server on your network. You can, however, manually open ports through the firewall (Figure 16-11).

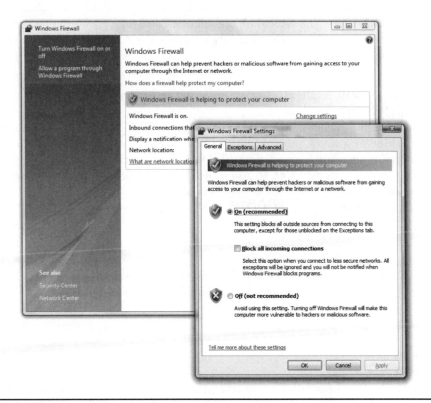

Figure 16-10   Enabling Windows Firewall

Figure 16-11
Opening TCP/IP
ports in Windows
Firewall

EXAM TIP The settings on firewalls are called *rules*. Many firewalls use the term *implicit deny any* to describe a rule like Windows Firewall's block setting for inbound traffic.

Windows Firewall is set to *allow* all outgoing traffic by default, though you can change this behavior.

Products such as ZoneAlarm and Windows Firewall do a fine job of protecting a single machine or a small network. But software firewalls run on your system, taking CPU processing away from your system. This firewall overhead doesn't strain your individual system, but once you start to add more than three or four systems, or you need to add advanced functions like a VPN, you'll need a more robust solution. That's where small office and home office (SOHO) connections come into play (which I'll discuss in Chapter 19).

EXAM TIP Look for the CompTIA Network+ exam to refer to network setups where the firewall resides in a dedicated box as a *network-based firewall*. The exam calls firewall programs installed on your computer, such as Windows Firewall, *host-based firewalls*.

Network Zones

Large networks need heavy-duty protection that not only protects from external threats, but also does so without undue restriction on the overall throughput of the network. To do this, large networks often use dedicated firewall boxes, which usually sit between the gateway router and the protected network. These firewalls are designed to filter IP traffic (including NAT and proxy functions), as well as to provide high-end tools to track and stop incoming threats. Some of the firewall systems even contain a rather interesting feature called a honeypot. A *honeypot* is a device (or a set of functions within a firewall) that creates a fake network called a *honeynet*, which seems attackable to a hacker. Instead of trying to access the real network, hackers are attracted to the honeypot, which records their actions and keeps them away from the true network. Plus, you can study the hackers' methods to help shore up your vulnerabilities.

Once you start to add publicly accessible servers to your network, like Web and e-mail servers, you're going to have to step up to a more serious network protection configuration. Because Web and e-mail servers must have exposure to the Internet, you will need to create what's called a *demilitarized zone (DMZ)*, a lightly protected network positioned between your firewall and the Internet. You can configure a DMZ in a number of ways. Figure 16-12 shows one classic example using an external and an internal router.

Figure 16-12
A DMZ configuration

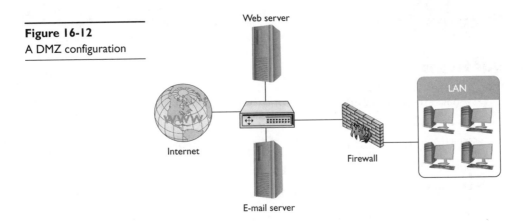

A private, protected network is called an *intranet*. Compare this term to the term *extranet* you learned in Chapter 14, and make sure you understand the difference!

Securing Remote Access

The mad proliferation of high-speed Internet connections to most households in the United States has enabled a lot of workers to work partly from home. Although this provides one cost-effective solution to the rising price of gasoline and of physical commuting, from a network security standpoint, it opens up a potential can of worms. Network techs and administrators must strike a fine balance between making resources readily available over the Internet and making certain that only authorized users get access to those resources.

Vulnerability Scanners

A number of fine utility programs can scan a network to determine things like open ports, passive applications, and more. *Nmap*, for example, has been around since 1997, is updated regularly, and made available as open source software. It was designed initially to do what its name would suggest—map a network so a system administrator doesn't have to walk from room to room, creating a physical map of all the computers. In numerous updates, features have been added, and Nmap is now used heavily as a *vulnerability scanner*. You can find Nmap here at

    http://nmap.org/

Another excellent tool is *Nessus,* also free for noncommercial use. Tenable Network Security maintains and updates the Nessus products. You can download Nessus from www.nessus.org.

Chapter Review

Questions

1. What is the most common technique for protecting a network?

   A. Port filtering

   B. Hiding IP addresses

   C. Packet filtering

   D. Encryption

2. Which of the following blocks IP packets using any port other than the ones prescribed by the system administrator?

   A. Hiding IP addresses

   B. Port filtering

   C. Packet filtering

   D. Encryption

3. Which of the following blocks any incoming or outgoing packets from a particular IP address or range of IP addresses?

   A. Hiding IP addresses

   B. Port filtering

   C. Packet filtering

   D. Encryption

4. What are the names of the administrative accounts on Windows and Linux?

   A. "Administrator" on both

   B. "Administrator" on Windows, "admin" on Linux

   C. "Admin" on Windows, "root" on Linux

   D. "Administrator" on Windows, "root" on Linux

5. Which type of packet filtering is the most powerful?

   A. IP filtering

   B. Stateful filtering

   C. Stateless filtering

   D. Port filtering

6. You receive a call at your desk from someone claiming to be the new supervisor for the sales department. The caller says he forgot his password and asks if you can kindly remind him of what it is. How can this call be categorized? (Select three.)

   A. Internal threat

   B. External threat

   C. Social engineering

   D. Denial of service

7. RAID is an implementation of what concept?

   A. Phishing prevention

   B. Fault tolerance

   C. Network encryption

   D. User account control

8. John is a member of the Sales group, which has Read permissions on a file. He is also a member of the Tech group, which has Write permissions on the same file. What are John's effective permissions on the file?

   A. Read only

   B. Write only

   C. Read and Write

   D. No access

9. Which are examples of malware? (Select all that apply.)

   A. Virus

   B. Worm

   C. Trojan

   D. Rootkit

10. What is the difference between a DoS and a DDoS?

    A. A DoS uses a single zombie whereas a DDoS uses a botnet to attack a single system.

    B. A DoS uses a botnet whereas a DDoS uses a zombie to attack a single system.

    C. A DoS attacks a single system whereas a DDoS attacks multiple systems.

    D. A DoS attacks systems on the Internet whereas a DDoS attacks systems in a DMZ.

Answers

1. **B.** Hiding IP addresses is the most common technique for protecting a network.

2. **B.** Port filtering blocks IP packets using any ports other than the ones prescribed by the system administrator.

3. **C.** Packet filtering blocks any incoming or outgoing packets from a particular IP address or range of IP addresses.

4. **D.** The "administrator" and "root" account are the administrative accounts on Windows and Linux, respectively.

5. **B.** IP filtering is another name for packet filtering whereas port filtering is a totally different concept. Stateful filtering is more powerful than stateless filtering.

6. **A, B,** and **C.** Because there is no way to determine if the caller is an employee or someone external to the organization, it may be an internal or external threat. It is also a form of social engineering.

7. **B.** RAID is an implementation of fault tolerance for data stored on hard drives.

8. **C.** The effective permissions will be a combination of Read and Write.

9. **A, B, C,** and **D.** All of these are types of malware.

10. **A.** A DoS attack uses a single infected computer (zombie) whereas a DDoS attack uses multiple infected computers (botnet) to attack a single system.

Virtualization

The CompTIA Network+ certification exam expects you to know how to

- 1.9 Identify virtual network components

To achieve these goals, you must be able to

- Describe the concepts of virtualization
- Explain why PC and network administrators have widely adopted virtualization
- Describe how virtualization manifests in modern networks

Virtualization takes your everyday notion of computing and turns it on its head. Left becomes right. Red becomes blue. Physical computers become virtual computers. It might sound complicated—properly configuring a real computer is hard enough—but once you see it in action, it makes perfect sense. In the simplest terms, *virtualization* is the process of using special software—a class of programs called *hypervisors* or *virtual machine managers*—to create a complete environment in which a guest operating system can function as though it were installed on its own computer. That guest environment is called a *virtual machine (VM)*. Figure 17-1 shows one such example: a system running Windows 7 using a program called VMware Workstation to host a virtual machine running Ubuntu Linux.

This chapter begins by explaining the ideas behind virtualization. The chapter then explores the motivating factors behind the widespread adoption of virtualization throughout the IT industry. The chapter concludes with an in-depth look at how modern networks implement virtualization.

Historical/Conceptual

What Is Virtualization?

Ask 100 people what the term *virtual* means and you'll get a lot of different answers. Most people define *virtual* with words like "fake" or "pretend," but these terms only begin to describe it. Let's try to zero in on virtualization using a term that hopefully you've heard: *virtual reality*. For most of us, the idea of virtual reality starts with someone wearing headgear and gloves, as shown in Figure 17-2.

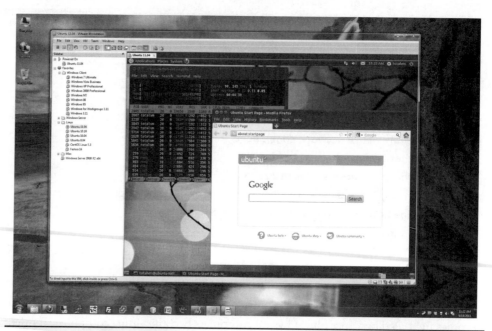

Figure 17-1   VMware running Linux

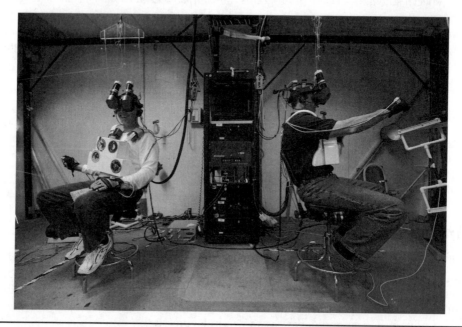

Figure 17-2   Virtual reality training (Image courtesy of NASA)

The headgear and the gloves work together to create a simulation of a world or environment that appears to be real, even though the person wearing them is located in a room that doesn't resemble the simulated space. Inside this virtual reality you can see the world by turning your head, just as you do in the real world. Software works with the headset's inputs to emulate a physical world. At the same time, the gloves enable you to touch and move objects in the virtual world.

To make virtual reality effective, the hardware and software need to work together to create an environment convincing enough for a human to work within it. Virtual reality doesn't have to be perfect—it has limitations—but it's pretty cool for teaching someone how to fly a plane or do a spacewalk, for example, without having to start with the real thing (Figure 17-3).

Figure 17-3   Using virtual reality to practice spacewalking (Image courtesy of NASA)

Virtualization on a computer is virtually (sorry, can't pass up the pun) the same as virtual reality for humans. Just as virtual reality creates an environment that convinces humans they're in a real environment, virtualization convinces an operating system it's running on its own hardware.

Meet the Hypervisor

A normal operating system uses programming called a *supervisor* to handle very low-level interaction among hardware and software, such as task scheduling, allotment of time and resources, and so on.

Because virtualization enables one machine—called the *host*—to run multiple operating systems simultaneously, full virtualization requires an extra layer of sophisticated programming to manage the vastly more complex interactions. One common method calls this extra programming a *hypervisor* or *virtual machine manager (VMM)*.

A hypervisor has to handle every input and output that the operating system would request of normal hardware. With a good hypervisor like VMware Workstation, you can easily add and remove virtual hard drives, virtual network cards, virtual RAM, and so on. Figure 17-4 shows the Hardware Configuration screen from VMware Workstation.

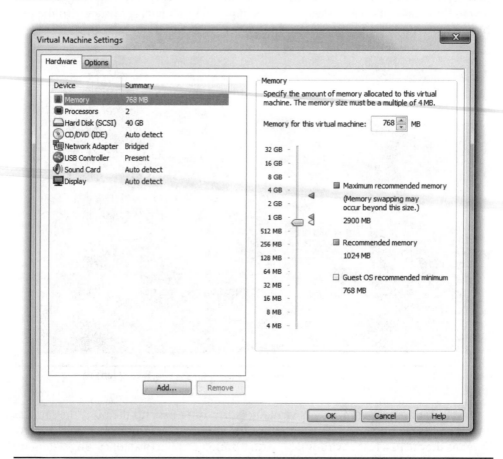

Figure 17-4   Configuring virtual hardware in VMware Workstation

Virtualization even goes so far as to provide a virtualized BIOS and System Setup for every virtual machine. Figure 17-5 shows VMware Workstation displaying the System Setup, just like you'd see it on a regular computer.

```
                     PhoenixBIOS Setup Utility
    Main      Advanced    Security    Boot     Exit

                                               ┌─────────────────────┐
                                               │  Item Specific Help │
        System Time:           [14:46:17]      │                     │
        System Date:           [09/19/2011]    │                     │
                                               │ <Tab>, <Shift-Tab>, or│
        Legacy Diskette A:     [1.44/1.25 MB  3½"] │ <Enter> selects field.│
        Legacy Diskette B:     [Disabled]      │                     │
                                               │                     │
      ▶ Primary Master         [None]          │                     │
      ▶ Primary Slave          [None]          │                     │
      ▶ Secondary Master       [VMware Virtual ID] │                 │
      ▶ Secondary Slave        [None]          │                     │
                                               │                     │
      ▶ Keyboard Features                      │                     │
                                               │                     │
        System Memory:         640 KB          │                     │
        Extended Memory:       785408 KB       │                     │
        Boot-time Diagnostic Screen:  [Disabled] │                   │
                                               │                     │
                                               └─────────────────────┘

    F1   Help    ↑↓  Select Item   -/+   Change Values    F9   Setup Defaults
    Esc  Exit    ↔   Select Menu    Enter  Select ▶ Sub-Menu  F10  Save and Exit
```

Figure 17-5   System Setup in VMware Workstation

NOTE   The host machine allocates real RAM and CPU time to every running virtual machine. If you want to run a number of virtual machines at the same time, make sure your host machine has plenty of CPU power and, more importantly, plenty of RAM to support all the running virtual machines!

Emulation vs. Virtualization

Virtualization takes the hardware of the host system and segments it into individual virtual machines. If you have an Intel system, a hypervisor creates a virtual machine that acts exactly like the host Intel system. It cannot act like any other type of computer. For example, you cannot make a virtual machine on an Intel system that acts like a Sony PlayStation 3. Hypervisors simply pass the code from the virtual machine to the actual CPU.

Emulation is very different from virtualization. An *emulator* is software or hardware that converts the commands to and from the host machine into an entirely different platform. Figure 17-6 shows a Super Nintendo Entertainment System emulator, Snes9X, running a game called Donkey Kong Kountry on a Windows system.

Figure 17-6 Super Nintendo emulator running on Windows

Sample Virtualization

You can perform virtualization in a number of ways; this chapter will show you several of them. Before I go any further, though, let's take the basic pieces you've learned about virtualization and put them together in one of its simpler forms. In this example, I'll use the popular VMware Workstation on a Windows 7 system and create a virtual machine running Ubuntu Linux.

Begin by obtaining a copy of VMware Workstation. This program isn't free, but VMware will give you a 30-day trial. Go to www.vmware.com to get a trial copy. A freshly installed copy of VMware Workstation looks like Figure 17-7.

NOTE Microsoft's Virtual PC is a free competitor to VMware Workstation. Virtual PC works well, but it lacks some of the more interesting features included in VMware Workstation.

Clicking **New Virtual Machine** prompts you for a typical or custom setup (Figure 17-8). These settings are only for backward-compatibility with earlier versions of VMware, so just click **Next**.

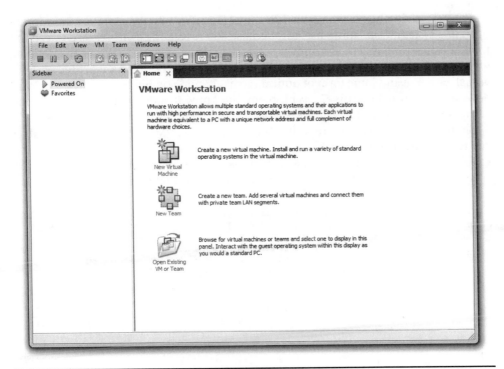

Figure 17-7 VMware Workstation

Figure 17-8
Selecting a
Typical or
Custom setup

The next dialog box is where the fun starts. Here, VMware Workstation asks for an operating system installation disc. Just because you're creating a virtual machine, don't think the operating system and applications aren't real. You need to install an operating system on that virtual machine. You do this just as you would on a machine without virtualization, using some form of optical media. Would you like to use Microsoft Windows in your virtual machine? No problem, but know that every virtual machine you create on which you install Windows requires a separate, legal copy of Windows.

Because virtual machines are so flexible on hardware, VMware Workstation enables you to use either the host machine's optical drive or an ISO file. I'm installing Ubuntu, so I downloaded the latest ISO image from the Ubuntu Web site (www.ubuntu.com), and as Figure 17-9 shows, I've pointed the dialog box to that image.

Figure 17-9

Selecting the installation media

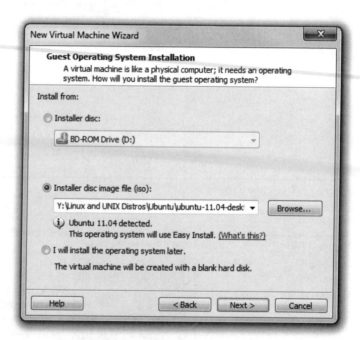

Compared to some other virtualization programs, VMware Workstation is a powerful, easy-to-use program. If you look closely at Figure 17-9, you'll see that VMware reads the installation media (note the "Ubuntu 11.04 Detected"). Because VMware knows this operating system, it configures all of the virtual hardware settings automatically: amount of RAM, virtual hard drive size, and so on. You can change any of these settings, either before or after the virtual machine is created. Refer to Figure 17-5 to see these settings. Next, you need to accept the size of the virtual drive, as shown in Figure 17-10.

You also need to give the virtual machine a name. By default, VMware Workstation uses a simple name. For this overview, accept the default name: Ubuntu. This dialog box also lets you decide where you want to store the files that comprise the virtual machine. Note that VMware uses a folder in the user's Documents folder called Virtual Machines (Figure 17-11).

Figure 17-10
Setting the
virtual drive size

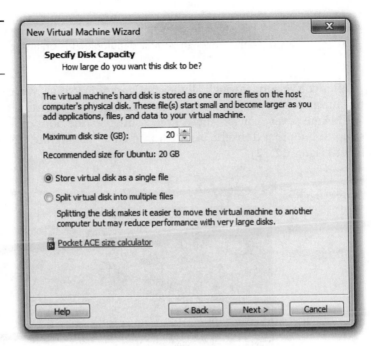

Figure 17-11
Entering VM
name and location

EXAM TIP Use descriptive names for virtual machines. This will save you a lot of confusion when you have multiple VMs on a single hypervisor.

After you've gone through all the configuration screens, you can start using your virtual machine. You can start, stop, pause, add, or remove virtual hardware.

VMware is very convenient; it even configures the boot order in the virtual system setup to boot first from the installation media, making the Ubuntu installation automatic (Figure 17-12).

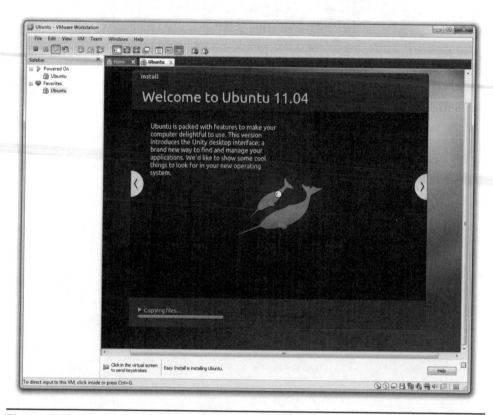

Figure 17-12 Ubuntu installing into the new virtual machine

After the virtual machine installs, you then treat the VM exactly as though it were a real machine. The only big difference is that VMware replaces CTRL-ALT-DELETE with CTRL-ALT-INSERT. Figure 17-13 shows VMware Workstation with the single VM installed but not running. A VM goes through a POST process just like any computer, as shown in Figure 17-14. If you wish, you can even access a complete virtual System Setup by pressing the DELETE key just like on a real system.

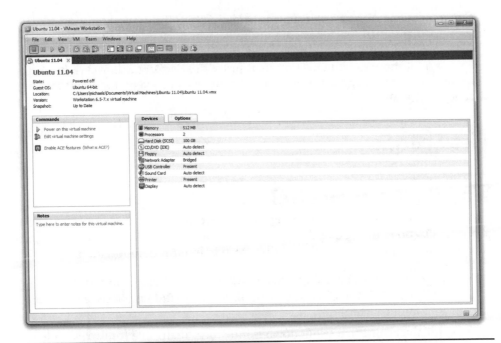

Figure 17-13 VMware Workstation with a single VM

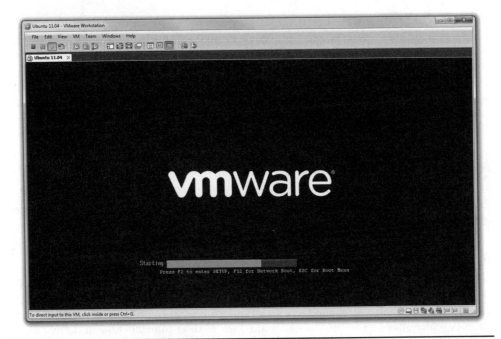

Figure 17-14 POST in a virtual machine

Congratulations! You've just installed a *virtual desktop*. Virtual desktops were the first type of popular virtual machines seen in the PC world, championed by VMware and quickly copied by other virtualization programs.

There's a lot more to virtualization than just virtual desktops, however, but before I dive in too far, let's step back a moment and understand a very important question: Why do we virtualize?

Test Specific

Why Do We Virtualize?

Virtualization has taken the networking world by storm, but for those who have never seen virtualization, the big question has got to be: Why? Let's talk about the benefits of virtualization. While your read this section, keep in mind two important things:

- A single hypervisor on a single system will happily run as many virtual machines as its RAM, CPU, and drive space allow. (RAM is almost always the main limiting factor.)
- A virtual machine that's shut down is little more than a file (or two) sitting on a hard drive.

Power Saving

Before virtualization, each server OS needed to be on a unique physical system. With virtualization, you can place multiple virtual servers on a single physical system, reducing electrical power use substantially. Rather than one machine running Windows 2008 and acting as a file server and DNS server, and a second machine running Linux for a DHCP server, for example, the same computer can handle both operating systems simultaneously. Expand this electricity savings over an enterprise network or on a data server farm and the savings—both in terms of dollars spent and electricity used—are tremendous.

Hardware Consolidation

Similar to power saving, why buy a high-end server, complete with multiple processors, RAID arrays, redundant power supplies, and so on, and only run a single server? With virtualization, you can easily beef up the RAM and run a number of servers on a single box.

System Recovery

Possibly the most popular reason for virtualizing is to keep uptime percentage as high as possible. Let's say you have a Web server installed on a single system. If that system goes down—due to hacking, malware, or so on—you need to restore the system from a backup, which may or may not be easily at hand. With virtualization, you merely need to shut down the virtual machine and reload an alternative copy of it.

Think of virtual machines like you would a word processing document. Virtual machines don't have a "File | Save" equivalent, but they do have something called a *snapshot* that enables you to save an extra copy of the virtual machine as it is exactly at the moment the snapshot is taken. Figure 17-15 shows VMware Workstation saving a snapshot.

Figure 17-15   Saving a snapshot

System Duplication

Closely tied to system recovery, system duplication takes advantage of the fact that VMs are simply files, and like any file, they can be copied. Let's say you want to teach 20 students about Ubuntu Linux. Depending on the hypervisor you choose (VMware does this extremely well), you can simply install a hypervisor on 20 machines and copy a single virtual machine to all the computers. Equally, if you have a virtualized Web server and need to add another Web server (assuming your physical box has the hardware to support it), why not just make a copy of the server and fire it up as well?

Research

Here's a great example that happens in my own company. I sell my popular Total Tester test banks: practice questions for you to test your skills on a broad number of certification topics. As with any distributed program, I tend to get a few support calls. Running a problem through the same OS, even down to the service pack, helps me solve the problem.

In the previrtualization days, I commonly had seven to ten PCs, using dual-boot, each keeping copies of a particular Windows version. Today, a single hypervisor enables me to support a huge number of Windows versions on a single machine (Figure 17-16).

Figure 17-16
Lots of VMs
used for research

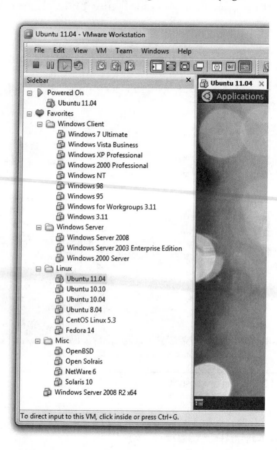

 NOTE The system shown in Figure 17-16 could obviously never run all those VMs at the same time.

Clearly there are a number of good reasons to virtualize some of the computers in a network. Let's look at implementation now.

Virtualization in Modern Networks

You've already seen virtualization in action with the example shown using VMware Workstation earlier in this chapter. Many networks use a few virtual machines to augment and refine a traditional network closet. VMware Workstation is how I first performed virtualization on PCs, but the technology and power have grown dramatically over the last few years.

VMware Workstation requires an underlying operating system, so it functions essentially like a very powerful desktop application. What if you could remove the OS altogether and create a bare-metal implementation of virtualization?

VMware introduced ESX in 2001 to accomplish this goal. ESX is a hypervisor that's powerful enough to replace the host operating system on a physical box, turning the physical machine into a machine that does nothing but support virtual machines. ESX, by itself, isn't much to look at; it's a tiny operating system/hypervisor that's usually installed on something other than a hard drive. Figure 17-17 shows how I loaded my copy of ESX: via a small USB thumb drive. Power up the server; the server loads ESX off the thumb drive; and in short order, a very rudimentary interface appears where I can input essential information, such as a master password and a static IP address.

 NOTE For all you abbreviation lovers, I have some good news and some bad news about "ESX." Officially, it means nothing. Unofficially, it stands for "Elastic Sky," which is probably why it officially means nothing.

Figure 17-17
USB drive on
server system

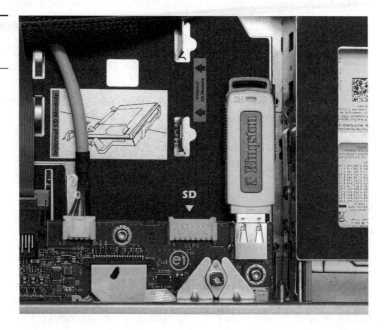

 NOTE A free version of ESX is available. Called ESXi, it lacks a number of ESX's features but is still quite powerful.

Don't let ESX's small size fool you. It's small because it only has one job: to host virtual machines. ESX is an extremely powerful operating system/hypervisor.

 NOTE Some writers will use the term *virtual machine manager* to describe virtual machine software that runs on top of a host operating system. They'll use the term *hypervisor* to describe only software that does not need a host operating system. Using this terminology, VMware Workstation is a virtual machine manager and ESX is a hypervisor.

Other writers call both the hosted and bare-metal—or *native—* virtualization software products *hypervisors*, but make a distinction in other descriptive words (such as *hosted* or *native*).

Notice the built-in USB port shown in Figure 17-17. The popularity of hypervisors on dedicated servers makes these ports extremely common in a serious server box like the Dell system shown.

Powerful hypervisors like ESXi are rarely administered directly at the box. Instead you use tools such as VMware's vSphere Client, so you can create, configure, and maintain virtual machines on the hypervisor server from the comfort of a client computer running this program. Once the VM is up and running, you can close the vSphere client, but the VM will continue to run happily on the server. For example, let's say you create a VM and install a Web server on that VM. As long as everything is running well on the Web server, you will find yourself using the vSphere client only to check on the Web server for occasional maintenance and administration.

So you now really have two different ways to virtualize: using virtual machine managers like VMware's Workstation to manage virtual desktops and using powerful hypervisors like ESX to manage virtual servers. Granted, you could run a server like a Web browser in VMware Workstation, and you also could run a copy of Windows 7 Ultimate from an ESX system. Nothing is wrong with doing either of these.

 EXAM TIP For the scope of the CompTIA Network+ exam, remember that virtual servers run on hypervisors like ESX whereas virtual desktops run on virtual machine managers.

Thus far, this chapter sounds like an advertisement for VMware. VMware really brought virtualization to the PC world and still holds a strong presence, but there are a number of alternatives to VMware products. Let's see what else is available.

Virtual Machine Managers

When it comes to the more basic virtual machine managers, you have a huge number of choices. The one you use is going to be based on features and prices.

VMware Workstation

The granddaddy and front leader for virtualization, VMware Workstation, comes in both Windows and Linux versions. VMware Workstation runs virtually (PUN!) on any operating system you'll ever need and is incredibly stable and proven. Too bad it's not free.

One of the more interesting features of VMware Workstation is VMTools. VMTools adds useful features such as copy/cut and paste between the virtual desktop and the real desktop.

Virtual PC

Microsoft has offered a few different virtual machine managers over the years, with the current mainstream product being Windows Virtual PC (Figure 17-18). Windows Virtual PC is free, but has some serious limitations. First, it only works on Windows 7 Professional, Ultimate, and Enterprise. Second, it only officially supports Windows VMs, although a few intrepid souls have managed to get Linux working.

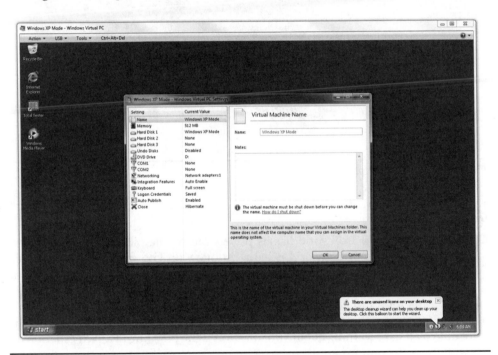

Figure 17-18 Windows Virtual PC

Parallels

Parallels is the most popular virtualization manager for Mac OS X (Figure 17-19), although VMware Fusion is a close second. Parallels supports all popular operating systems, and even has a fair degree of 3-D graphics support; more so than even the mighty VMware. Parallels also offers Windows and Linux versions.

Figure 17-19 Parallels for Mac

KVM

Of course, the open source world has its players too. While picking a single product to represent the Linux/UNIX world is hard, no one who knows virtualization would disagree that KVM from Redhat is a dominant player. Unlike the other virtual machine managers discussed, KVM also supports a few non-x86 processors.

Don't think for a moment that this list is complete! There are lots of other virtual machine options for your desktop, especially if your host machine runs Linux. The most fun you'll have learning about virtualization is the playtime involved experimenting with the many options available.

Hypervisors

While you have lots of choices when it comes to virtual machine managers, your choices for real embedded hypervisors are limited to the two biggies: VMware's ESX and

Microsoft's Hyper-V. There are others such as Oracle's VM Server but nothing has the market share of ESX or Hyper-V.

ESX

I've already discussed a few aspects of ESX, so instead I'll delve into the features that make ESX so popular. When it comes to real server virtualization, VMware truly leads the pack with a host of innovations (some of which are add-on products) that make ESX almost unstoppable. Here are a few examples:

- **Interface with large storage**   ESX virtual machines easily integrate with network attached storage (NAS) and storage area networks (SANs) to handle massive data storage.

- **Transparent fault tolerance**   ESX can monitor and automatically recover failed VMs with little or no input.

- **Transparent server transfer**   You can move a *running* VM from one machine to another. How cool is that?

- **High virtual CPUs**   Most hypervisors support a limited number of virtual CPUs, usually two at most. ESX can support up to 32 CPUs, depending on the vSphere product version you purchase to support it.

Hyper-V

Although Hyper-V can't stand toe-to-toe with ESX, it has a few aces up its sleeve that give it some intrigue. First, it's free. This is important in that ESX, with only a few extra add-ons, can cost thousands of dollars. Second, it comes as a stand-alone product or as part of Windows Server 2008 and even on some versions of Windows 7, making it easy for those who like to play to access it. Third, its simplicity makes it easier to learn for those new to using hypervisors. Watch Hyper-V. If Microsoft does one thing well, it's taking market share away from arguably better, more powerful competitors, while slowly making its product better.

Virtual Switches

Imagine for a moment that you have three virtual machines running as virtual desktops. You want all of these machines to have access to the Internet. Therefore, you need to give them all legitimate IP addresses. The physical server, however, only has a single NIC. There are two ways in which virtualization gives individual VMs valid IP addresses. The oldest and simplest way is to bridge the NIC. Each virtual NIC is given a bridged connection to the real NIC (Figure 17-20). This bridge works at Layer 2 of the OSI model, so each virtual NIC gets a legitimate, unique MAC address.

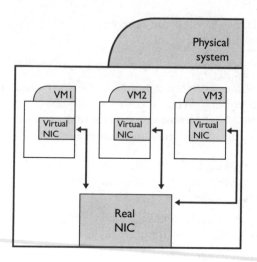

Figure 17-20

Bridged NICs

A subset of this type of bridging is to give every VM its own physical NIC (Figure 17-21). In this case, you're still bridging, but every virtual NIC goes straight to a dedicated physical NIC.

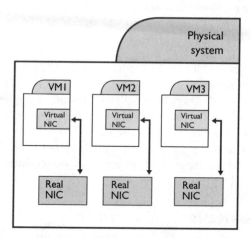

Figure 17-21

Dedicated bridged NICs

Your second option is to create a *virtual switch*, which is special software that enables VMs to communicate with each other, without going outside of the host system. A good hypervisor (like ESX and Hyper-V) enables you to connect all of your virtual machines to their own virtual switch. Depending on your hypervisor, this switch can do everything you'd expect from a typical managed Layer 2 switch, including VLANs (Figure 17-22).

If you really want to go crazy on virtual switches (and have lots of money), Cisco will sell you an appliance like the Cisco Nexus 1000V that offloads all of the virtual switching from the hypervisor and adds higher-layer features such as firewalls/ACLs, DHCP servers, and many other features.

Figure 17-22
Virtual switch

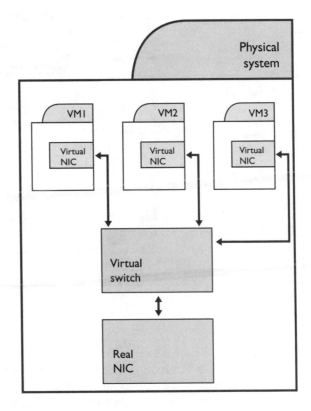

Virtual PBX

The ancient PBX telephone systems used in offices since the 1970s have gone through many transformations over the last 40 years. One of the more common upgrades is to replace ancient PBX hardware with a single PC running many of the popular PBX programs like Asterisk (www.asterisk.org) or Virtual PBX (www.virtualpbx.com). Figure 17-23 shows Asterisk. These create a *virtual PBX,* software that functionally replaces a physical PBX.

Typically this requires a dedicated single system to run the PBX software. Why not stop wasting a dedicated computer and instead just place all this on a virtual machine? That's the power of a virtual PBX system. All of the power that makes virtualization attractive is perfect for PBX systems.

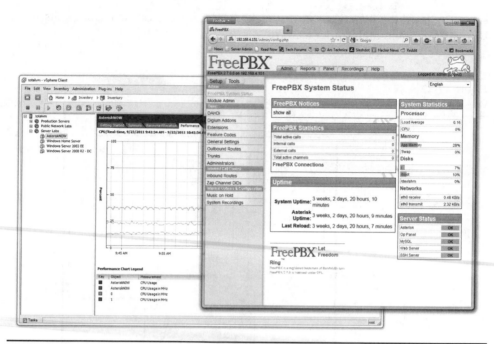

Figure 17-23   Asterisk running on a system

NOTE   You will hear the term *virtual PBX* used as a form of cloud computing, but one dedicated to routing telephone numbers to the proper location for a business person on the go or a decentralized business. You can subscribe to this type of service, for example, so phone calls to one of your phone numbers go to the proper voicemail. Or you can have a single phone number with multiple extensions, where each extension directs to a completely different telephone. The telephones don't have to be in the same location, but to the end users, the single number gives the impression of a single location.

Network as a Service

With hypervisor-based virtualization, you don't need to worry about where the virtualized server is physically located—you just want it to serve your data. If a virtual computer is at your location, you call it *onsite*. If a virtual server is somewhere other than at your location, you call it *offsite*. Does it really matter? No! In fact, some companies rent virtual servers to others. Why pay thousands of dollars for a server when you can rent an equivalent server for a few dollars a month? This is, by definition, *Network as a Service (NaaS)*, a small division of what is called *cloud computing*. Virtualization didn't invent the concept of cloud computing, but it made it cheap and practical.

NOTE Cloud computing is a huge industry these days that encompasses far more than just NaaS. Another big area for cloud computing is in *application service providers (ASPs)*. As the name implies, an ASP provides an application as a service. This might be a broad selection of applications, such as Google Docs, or a single application like the payment services of PayPal. A common term for this use of the cloud is *Software as a Service (SaaS)*.

Chapter Review

Questions

1. Upgrading which component of a host machine would most likely enable you to run more virtual machines simultaneously?

   A. CPU

   B. Hard drive

   C. RAM

   D. Windows

2. What enables two VMs hosted on the same physical machine to communicate without leaving the machine itself?

   A. NaaS

   B. Virtual LAN

   C. Virtual PBX

   D. Virtual switch

3. What is the difference between a virtual machine (VM) and an emulator?

   A. A VM converts commands to and from a host machine to an entirely different platform, whereas an emulator creates an environment based on the host machine and does no converting.

   B. An emulator converts commands to and from a host machine to an entirely different platform, whereas a VM creates an environment based on the host machine and does no converting.

   C. An emulator requires a host OS, whereas a VM runs on bare-metal servers without an OS.

   D. A VM requires a host OS whereas an emulator runs on bare-metal servers without an OS.

4. Which program handles telephone switching in software rather than hardware?

A. Virtual LAN

B. Virtual PBX

C. Virtual switch

D. Virtual 64 block

5. What do you make when you save a copy of a VM?

A. Replacement

B. Save

C. Snapshot

D. Zip

6. What do you need to install a legal copy of Windows 7 Professional into a virtual machine using VMware Workstation?

A. A valid VM key

B. A valid Windows 7 Professional installation media

C. A valid ESX key

D. A second NIC

7. What is a key benefit of Network as a Service?

A. The network hardware is managed locally.

B. The network service is managed by someone else.

C. The network service is managed locally.

D. The monthly subscription fee reduces cost.

8. What is one benefit of ESX over VMware Workstation?

A. ESX costs less.

B. ESX is easier to set up.

C. ESX uses less electricity.

D. You can move a running VM from one machine to another with ESX.

9. Which of the following is *not* a good reason for virtualization?

A. Power saving

B. Hardware consolidation

C. System recovery

D. Reduced hardware costs

10. VMware Workstation replaces CTRL-ALT-DELETE with

    A. A mouse click

    B. CTRL-ALT-INSERT

    C. CTRL-ALT-TAB

    D. CTRL-ALT-SHIFT

Answers

1. **C.** Adding more RAM will enable you to run more simultaneous VMs. Upgrading a hard drive could help, but it's not the best answer here.

2. **D.** Hypervisors come with virtual switching capability to enable the VMs to communicate.

3. **B.** An emulator converts from one platform to another, whereas a virtual machine mirrors the host machine.

4. **B.** Virtual PBX software enables you to leave the punchdown block behind.

5. **C.** A copy or saved version of a VM is called a snapshot.

6. **B.** You need a copy of the Windows installation media to install Windows.

7. **B.** One great benefit of NaaS is that you don't have to manage all the network services. Someone else handles that end.

8. **D.** Among the many benefits of ESX over its little brother is the capability of moving a running VM from one machine to another.

9. **D.** Switching to virtual machines may or may not save money on hardware. A good virtual machine server can cost a lot more than a series of PCs, but operating costs are reduced.

10. **B.** VMware uses CTRL-ALT-INSERT for login.

18

Network Management

The CompTIA Network+ certification exam expects you to know how to

- 4.1 Explain the purpose and features of various network appliances: Load balancer
- 4.4 Given a scenario, use the appropriate network monitoring resource to analyze traffic: Syslog, system logs, history logs, general logs, traffic analysis
- 4.5 Describe the purpose of configuration management documentation
- 4.6 Explain different methods and rationales for network performance optimization

To achieve these goals, you must be able to

- Describe how configuration management documentation enables you to manage and upgrade a network efficiently
- Conduct network monitoring to identify performance and connectivity issues
- Explain how to optimize network performance

Managing a network well on-the-fly can challenge even very advanced network techs, so it won't come as any surprise to you that most techs use an array of techniques and tools to make it all . . . well . . . manageable. This chapter looks first at documentation for networks, including how the network is put together and how you go about making changes that don't disrupt the network. I'll then turn to tools and techniques for monitoring performance and connectivity. The chapter concludes with a section on optimizing network performance.

 EXAM TIP Managing each aspect of a network, from documentation to performance to hardware, falls into a broad category called *asset management*.

Test Specific

Network Configuration Management

The more complicated a network becomes, the more vulnerable it becomes in terms of security, efficiency, duplication or unnecessary redundancy, and unnecessary cost.

Chapter 16 covered many of the security issues, but left a major component for coverage here, configuration management. *Configuration management* is a set of documents, policies, and procedures designed to help you maintain and update your network in a logical, orderly fashion, so you may lessen the risks of these vulnerabilities. Your network should standardize on types of NICs, cabling, network operating systems, and network applications, to make certain that when upgrades need to happen, they do so with the utmost efficiency.

If you want to upgrade your users from Windows XP to Windows 7, for example, you neither want to create a huge security risk for your network, nor waste a lot of money, time, and effort by realizing *after the fact* that an important application wasn't compatible with the new OS. That's not the way to do it in the real world!

Configuration Management Documentation

The *configuration management documentation* enables you to see many things about your network quickly. Good documentation helps you to troubleshoot a network efficiently. You can also determine as quickly as possible both how to upgrade components of that network and what effects such an upgrade might have. Configuration management documentation covers everything, from the wires used to how the people using the network should be trained. You can think about the configuration management documentation in four broad categories:

- Network connectivity
- Baselines
- Policies, procedures, and configurations
- Regulations

Network Connectivity

Documentation on network connectivity describes the many details about both the machines on the network and how they connect. The documentation can be hard copy or electronic and falls into three categories:

- Wiring schemes
- Network diagrams
- Network maps

Wiring Schemes   A *wiring scheme* describes the cabling and connectors used in the network. In this documentation you find the specific types of UTP used, such as CAT 5e or CAT 6, and the TIA/EIA standard used in the RJ-45 crimps (Figure 18-1). You'll discover multimode or single-mode fiber (or both, depending on the run) and which connectors plug into the PCs, switches, and routers. CompTIA shortens the category name for this type of documentation to *wire schemes*.

Figure 18-1

Wiring scheme detail on the TIA/EIA standard used throughout the network

For the San Francisco office, make sure we use TIA/EIA 568B connectors.

All connections must be TIA/EIA 568B. Sample below

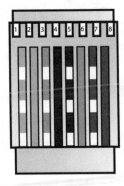

Sample 568B connection

 EXAM TIP CompTIA Network+ refers to a *wiring scheme* as a *wire scheme* in the current exam objectives and as *wiring schematics* in the previous objectives. Expect to see any of the three terms on the exam.

Network Diagrams A *network diagram* shows devices on the network and how they connect. It shows the physical runs and defines the type of connection, such as Gigabit Ethernet, T1, and so on. A network diagram includes every router, switch, server, CSU/DSU, cable modem, and wireless access point, including the make and model and firmware upgrade. Figure 18-2 shows a typical network diagram.

The network administrator creates the network diagram. Lucky for you, two critical tools make your job easier. First are standardized icons. As you look at Figure 18-2, you might notice the icons are somewhat cryptic. That's because many years ago Cisco developed this shorthand to represent any type of networking device you might imagine.

Cisco generally calls these "network topology icons," and they are the accepted standard to use whenever you're drawing a network. Figure 18-3 shows some examples of the more common topology icons.

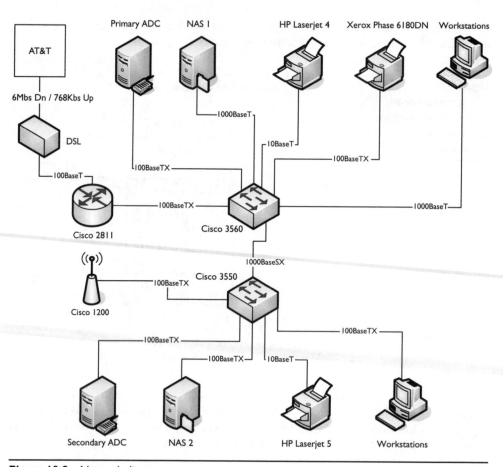

Figure 18-2 Network diagram

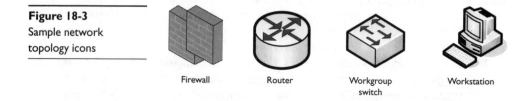

Figure 18-3
Sample network
topology icons

Firewall   Router   Workgroup   Workstation
                                  switch

NOTE New network devices show up all the time, so there's no single place
to see every network topology icon available. That said, Cisco keeps a fairly
complete list here: www.cisco.com/web/about/ac50/ac47/2.html.

Your second tool is one of the many drawing programs that support network topology icons. You can use a presentation tool like Microsoft PowerPoint, but Microsoft

Visio is the most famous tool for drawing any type of network diagram. Visio adds a number of extras that make putting together any type of diagram a snap. Figure 18-4 shows how I made Figures 18-2 and 18-5: with Visio!

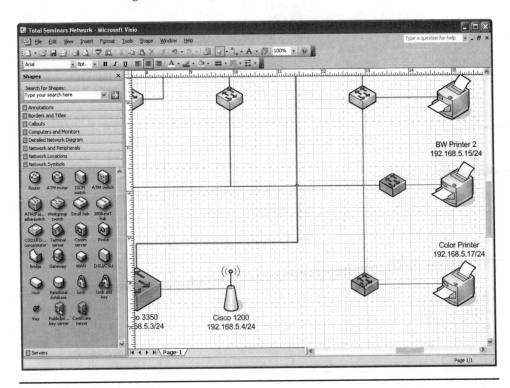

Figure 18-4 Visio in action

Network Maps A *network map* goes deeper into the individual components of the network, documenting IP addresses, ports, protocols, and more. You can create a network map manually using tools like Visio. Figure 18-5 shows such a network map.

EXAM TIP Most techs and companies use the terms *network diagram* and *network map* interchangeably or have strict definitions that reverse what you read here. Don't sweat the differences for the exam. Just know that part of your configuration management documentation involves mapping out the nodes and including IP address, connection speed, and so forth.

Alternatively, you can create a network map with powerful programs such as Nmap. You know about Nmap from Chapter 16, where you saw it scanning for unusual open ports. It offers many configuration features, including telling you whether an open port is using TCP or UDP, for example. Plus this sort of application can create stunning graphical representations of your network.

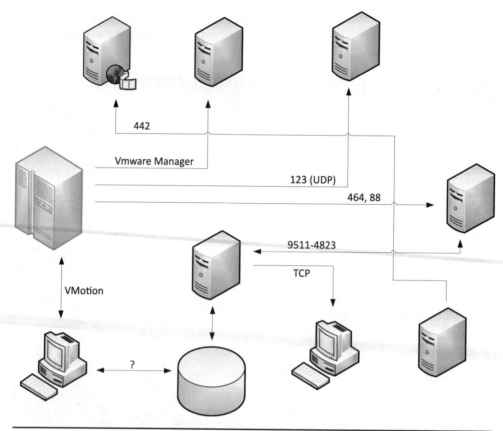

Figure 18-5   Network map

Figure 18-6 shows a graphic of my office network. Figure 18-7 has zeroed in on a single router, examining open protocols and TCP/IP applications in use. Both screens are from Zenmap, a graphical interface for Nmap.

 EXAM TIP   Make updating your network documentation the last step of any changes you make to the network.

Baselines

The best way to know when a problem is brewing is to know how things perform when all's well with the system. Part of any proper configuration management documentation is a *baseline*: a log of performance indicators such as CPU usage, network utilization, and other values to give you a picture of your network and servers when they are working correctly. A major change in these values can point to problems on a server or the network as a whole.

Figure 18-6
My network
in pictures

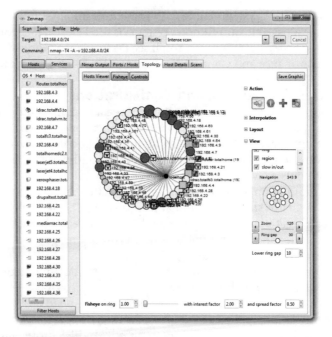

Figure 18-7
Router close up

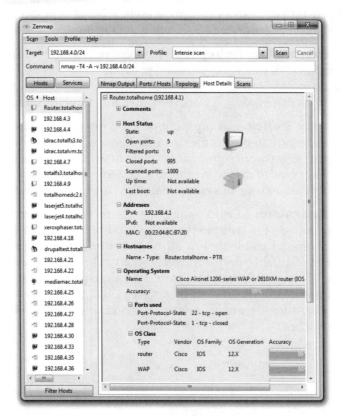

All operating systems come with some form of baseline tools. A common tool used to create a baseline on Windows systems is the Performance Monitor utility that comes with all versions of Windows. You'll see Performance Monitor at work in the "Monitoring Performance and Connectivity" section later in this chapter.

Policies, Procedures, and Configurations

Network security, costs, time, and employee and management frustration—all of these things matter when managing a complex network. As part of any good documentation, therefore, you'll find policies about what people can and cannot do with network hardware and software. You'll see procedures outlined for what to do when upgrading components or adding new user accounts. You'll also get down-to-the-user-interface-level information about how software and hardware should be configured.

Much of this should be familiar from a CompTIA A+ certification level. For example, what's a great way to keep a Windows PC from becoming vulnerable to a new piece of malware floating around the Internet? C'mon, one guess! Keep it patched and up to date with Windows Update, right? Exactly.

Properly created configuration management documentation will inform network folks what to do with user training. Who gets it? Which departments? What level of access should you give new employees versus seasoned and trusted veterans?

Many of the policies and procedures help protect your network from harm. In CompTIA terms, they *mitigate security risks* like those outlined in gory detail in Chapter 16! Two policies affect most users: acceptable use and security. After explaining these polices, I'll also give you a configuration example.

Acceptable Use Policy   An *acceptable use policy* defines exactly what you can and cannot do with your computers and network. Some classic areas defined by an acceptable use policy include personal computer use and adding personal software. Can a user access Facebook on a work computer, for example, or install a game?

Security Policy   An organization's *security policy* defines procedures employees should perform to protect the network's security. Security policies cover a wide gamut. They define password complexity, explain to users how to deal with social engineering, and clarify how to deal with virus attacks. Security policies almost always define action plans to deal with serious events that might threaten your network.

Configuration   *Configurations* are the results of the procedures. Documenting configurations for critical systems is important. Imagine if a carefully configured gateway router suddenly lost all of its settings and no one had made a backup! Every configurable device in today's networking world comes with some tool to document its configuration. Figure 18-8 shows a part of one of the most common of all network configuration files, Cisco's IOS startup configuration. It can be displayed by running `show startup-config` on all of Cisco's IOS-based routers and switches.

Regulations

Very few people profess to like *regulations*, the rules that govern behavior in the workplace. Nevertheless, regulations help keep networks and people safe and productive. Every decent configuration management documentation talks about regulations, such as what to do when you have a safety violation or some sort of potentially bad accident.

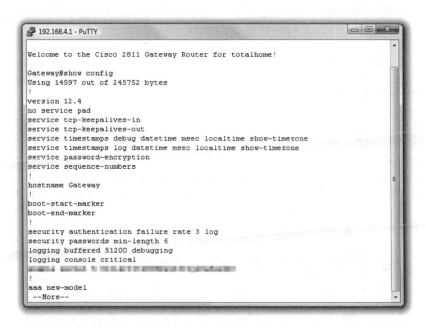

```
Welcome to the Cisco 2811 Gateway Router for totalhome!

Gateway#show config
Using 14597 out of 245752 bytes
!
version 12.4
no service pad
service tcp-keepalives-in
service tcp-keepalives-out
service timestamps debug datetime msec localtime show-timezone
service timestamps log datetime msec localtime show-timezone
service password-encryption
service sequence-numbers
!
hostname Gateway
!
boot-start-marker
boot-end-marker
!
security authentication failure rate 3 log
security passwords min-length 6
logging buffered 51200 debugging
logging console critical
!
aaa new-model
--More--
```

Figure 18-8   Section of show startup-config

Change Management Documentation

Although CompTIA seems to separate the detailed overview of the network from how to upgrade it, most networking professionals use the term *change management documentation* to describe this single body of knowledge. An example will make this clear. Let's say you want to change your network by adding a demilitarized zone (DMZ) because you want to add a server that people outside the network can access easily.

The change management documentation shows you network diagrams, so you can verify where to place the DMZ, and what other machines are potentially affected by the change. Plus, it gives you the detailed information on what to do to get approval from supervisors, get through the budgeting office, and so on.

Change management documentation details the procedures and policies to update the documentation so after each network change, your master documents are accurate. This information is extremely important! Failure to update the correct document will eventually result in you looking really bad when an otherwise minor troubleshoot turns into a nightmare.

Monitoring Performance and Connectivity

Networking technicians need to know how to use the tools that are available to monitor network performance and connectivity. A network administrator sets up the tools you use, but a tech needs to know how to use those tools to create baselines, monitoring utilities, and logs of various sorts. The tools vary from operating system to operating system, but let's look at the two most commonly in use: Performance Monitor and Event Viewer, both Windows utilities.

EXAM TIP Windows Vista calls the tool *Reliability and Performance Monitor*. It functions similarly to the Windows XP and Windows 7 tools, although the screens differ a little.

Performance Monitor

Administrators use *Performance Monitor* (also called PerfMon) to view the behavior of hardware and other resources on Windows machines, either locally or remotely. Performance Monitor can both monitor real-time performance and display historical data about the performance of your systems. Figure 18-9 shows the default Performance Monitor in Windows XP.

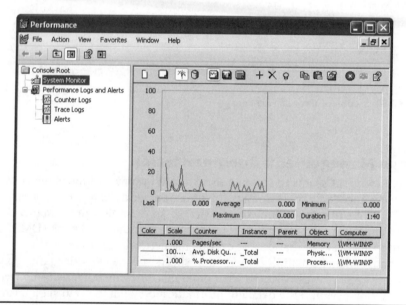

Figure 18-9 The real-time monitoring tool in Performance Monitor in Windows XP

EXAM TIP The CompTIA Network+ exam is not going to test you on using Performance Monitor or any other baselining tool. Just make sure you understand what a baseline does for you.

Windows 2000/XP calls the real-time monitoring section of Performance Monitor the System Monitor, as you can see in Figure 18-9. Windows Vista/7 calls it Performance Monitor (Figure 18-10). Regardless of the name, this is the tool that enables you to view network performance.

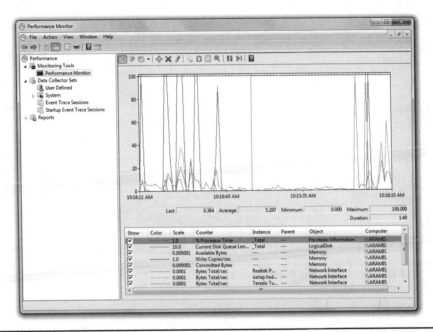

Figure 18-10   The real-time monitoring tool in Performance Monitor in Windows 7

Objects, Counters, and Views

Once you access Performance Monitor, you need to configure it to display data. To do that accurately, you add objects, counters, and views.

An *object*, in Performance Monitor terms, is a system component that you want to monitor, such as the processor, memory, or network connection. Each object has different measurable features called *counters*.

Counters, in other words, are the aspects of an object that you want to track. As you decide which object(s) to monitor, you can also select specific counters for each object. If the network seems sluggish on a specific computer, for example, you can open Performance Monitor, right-click in the data display pane, and select **Add Counters** (Figure 18-11).

In the Add Counters dialog box, select an object from the left pane—click the **arrow** next to an object to see all the counters available for that object. Select a counter from the menu options under the object. Figure 18-12 shows the Network Interface object with the Current Bandwidth selected. To complete the process, click the **Add** button and then the **OK** button. Performance Monitor immediately shows you the new real-time information on the selected counter.

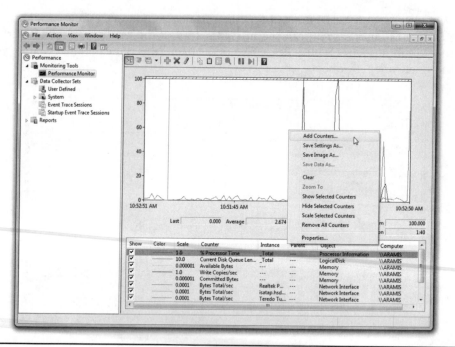

Figure 18-11   Adding a counter in Windows 7

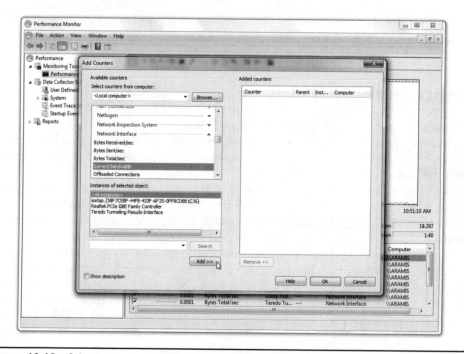

Figure 18-12   Selecting a counter object in the Add Counters dialog box

Performance Monitor can organize and display selected counter information using a variety of *views*, each of which provides a different way of presenting information. The Line view is the default, similar to what you saw in Figure 18-10. Figure 18-13 shows the Histogram bar view of the same counters. The third view, Report, provides statistics. Click the **Change graph type** button—third from the left above the graph area—or press CTRL-G to cycle through the three views.

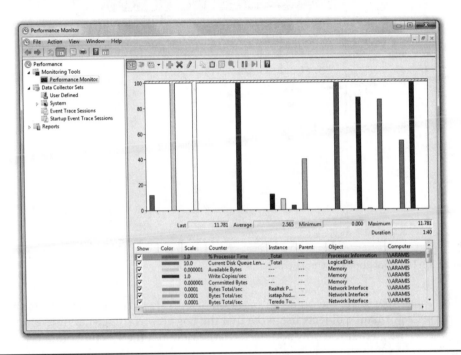

Figure 18-13   Real-time monitoring in Histogram bar view

Creating Logs

In addition to showing you real-time information about the system, Performance Monitor enables you to create logs, data recorded over time that you can save for later review. This is the option you use to create a baseline. The process of creating a log differs between Windows XP and Windows Vista/7, so let's look at both. Windows XP has a more complicated process, so I'll start there and then briefly examine the much simpler process in the later versions of Windows.

Creating a Log in Windows XP   To create a new log in Windows XP, expand the **Performance Logs and Alerts** tree in the left pane and click **Counter Logs**. Click **Action | New Log Settings** and give the new log a name such as Domain Controller. To add objects to the new log, click the **Add Objects** button in the middle of the dialog box. In the Add Objects dialog box, first select the computer you want to monitor. You can choose either the local machine (the default) or a remote machine. To monitor a remote machine, type the Universal Naming Convention (UNC) name of the computer

in question. To monitor a machine named HOUBDC1, for example, you would type \\
HOUBDC1 in the **Select counter objects from computer** field (Figure 18-14).

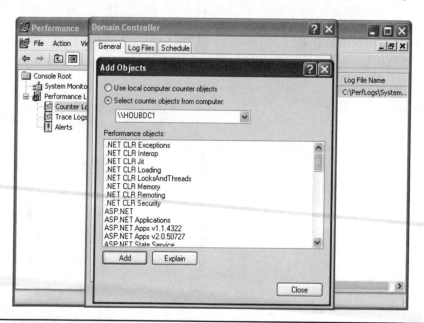

Figure 18-14   Monitoring a remote computer

You must now select the object to monitor. Select one or more objects to monitor
from the **Performance objects** list. Note that the Log view is somewhat different from
the other views, in that you only add *objects* to the view, not the specific counters for the
objects, as shown in the Add Objects dialog box in Figure 18-15.

Figure 18-15
Selecting performance
objects

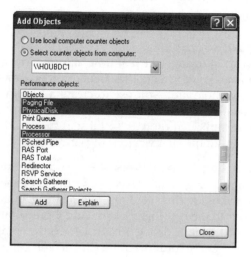

After you select the objects for Performance Monitor to track and log, click the **Add** button and then the **Close** button. Click **OK** to close the Domain Controller dialog box. Select your new log—in this case, the one labeled Domain Controller. By default, logging begins immediately upon closing the Domain Controller dialog box. With the newly created log selected, you can easily start and stop logging by clicking the play and pause buttons, as shown in Figure 18-16.

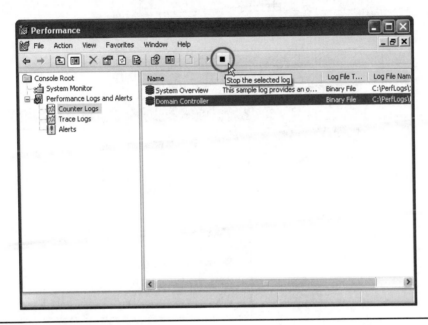

Figure 18-16   Logging data

After you have configured the log settings and captured data for a minute or so, you can then view the results in System Monitor. Click the **System Monitor** item in the console tree on the left. In System Monitor, click the **View Log Data** button, and then select the **Log files** radio button on the Source tab of the System Monitor Properties dialog box. From there you can click the **Add** button and select the log file created earlier (Figure 18-17).

These directions walked you through the process of creating a simple log, letting it run for a minute, and then viewing it. That's not an accurate or effective baseline.

To create a good baseline log, you need to set it to run for extended periods of time, like a week, three weeks, or even three months. Creating a baseline over an extended time enables you to find patterns of peak usage and idle times that you can use to fine-tune a workstation or server.

It also enables you to return to a system at some later date, run another log using the same parameters, and then compare the two. If you find problems in the new log, like performance spikes that affect user productivity, you can then discover what's different on the machine now as opposed to when you ran the baseline on the "clean" (and assumedly optimized) machine.

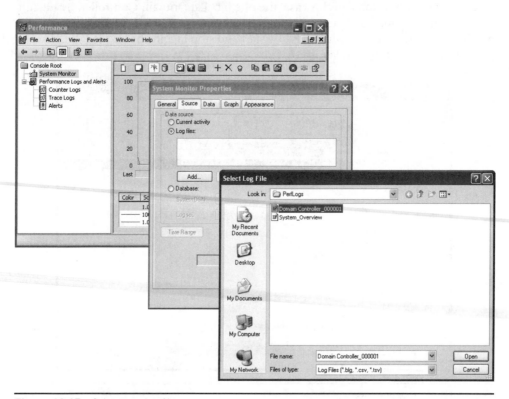

Figure 18-17   Selecting a log file

Creating a Log in Windows 7   To create a new log in Windows 7, right-click **User Defined** under the Data Collector Sets option in the left pane. (Windows Vista and Windows 7 refer to log files as *data collector sets*, which, I guess, is more descriptive.) Select **New | Data Collector Set** (Figure 18-18).

In the Create new Data Collector Set dialog box, name the new data collector set with something memorable and then select either to use one of the few templates or to create one that's as simple or complex as you like (Figure 18-19). Once you click **Next**, you'll follow the wizard and select counters to include or which template to use, where to save the log, and the user account. Eventually the wizard finishes running.

NOTE   Performance Monitor saves new logs in a subfolder in the Windows folder: %systemdrive%\PerfLogs\Admin\<new log file here>.

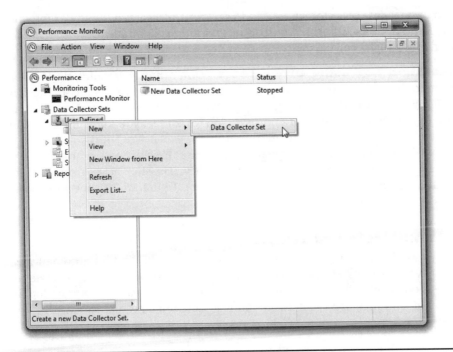

Figure 18-18 Starting the wizard to create a new data collector set

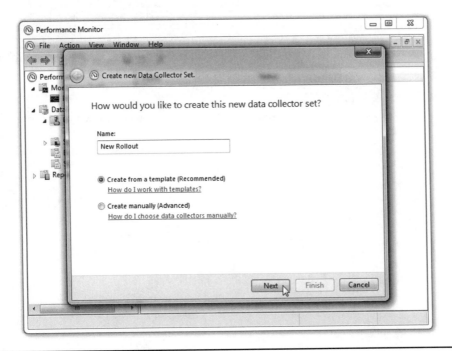

Figure 18-19 Creating a new data collector set using the wizard

To open a data collector set in Windows 7, just navigate to the folder in which it's stored and double-click it. It will load in Performance Monitor with all the data collected in the main viewing pane.

Creating a Log Using Other Tools   Don't limit your thinking to operating system tools when you think about baselining. A number of third-party network monitoring tools are available that not only generate baselines on almost any criteria you wish, but also stay online and monitor the network to let you know if any parameters have been exceeded. These network monitors are expensive, but if you want superior real-time monitoring, they are a great option. Since these network monitors are always online and always checking for certain items, they also often act as network intrusion detection system (IDS) devices at the same time. Figure 18-20 shows one example, IPSentry by RGE, Inc.

Logs and Network Traffic

Every operating system and many applications generate log files automatically that record events, actions, errors, and more. You can also use programs to generate custom logs. A skilled network administrator or technician can use various tools on log files to, among other things, analyze network traffic to determine problem areas.

Figure 18-20

IPSentry at work

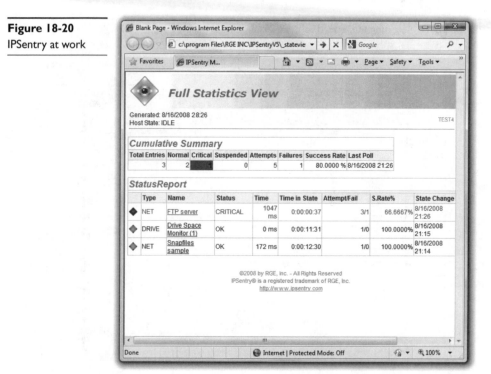

EXAM TIP Most UNIX/Linux distributions and many Windows applications use *syslog* as the basic building block for logging messages and doing custom logs. Eric Allman developed Syslog in the 1980s as a logging program for e-mail, but it has grown into a general logging tool today.

Logs fall into several categories, such as general, system, and history. You see *general logs* in tools like Windows Event Viewer (Figure 18-21). These record updates to applications, for example, and aren't terribly interesting from a networking standpoint. Linux systems tend to have lots of logs, but most versions have a directory called /var/log where all of your logs (usually) reside. Mac OS X has roughly the same logs as Linux.

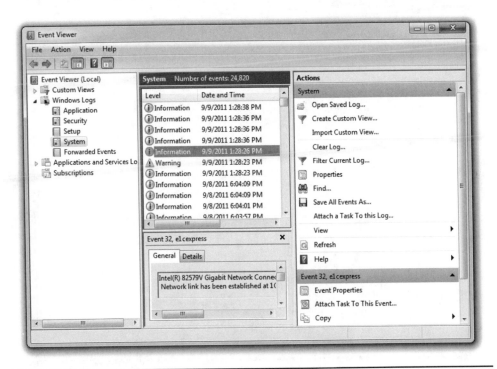

Figure 18-21 Event Viewer in Windows 7

System logs display events such as login attempts, reboots needed for changes to OS files, and similar things. System logs (and security logs in Windows) can be important for finding security problems, but like general logs, they don't do much for network optimization.

History logs track the history of how a user or users access network resources, or how network resources are accessed throughout the network. Generically, you can use *network sniffer programs* or *traffic analysis* tools to chart HTTP use, for example, or discover when your network gets a spike in BitTorrent traffic.

Most of this "logging" happens in a relationship between a router and a management server. Figure 18-22 shows a screenshot from Cacti that displays information gleaned from my gateway router. Several programs handle the requests for information and the aggregation of that information, but the Cacti program creates a nice graph displaying all the traffic analyzed for me.

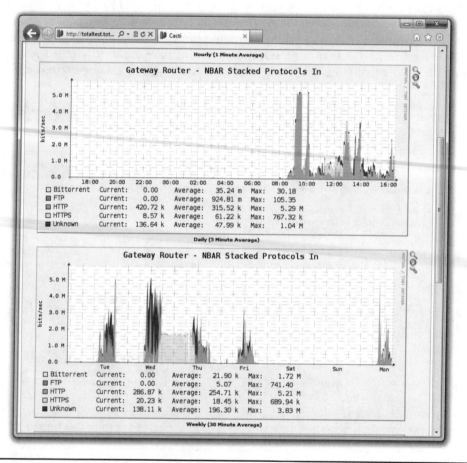

Figure 18-22   Traffic analysis in Cacti

Network Performance Optimization

It's a tough, ugly world when you're a network administrator. You get very little praise when the network runs well and all the blame when the network isn't running in the fashion that users expect. The situation in which you'll get the most complaints from users is when the network isn't running as fast as they're used to experiencing. We work hard to keep users from contacting us, and the best way to keep them at bay is to make sure the network runs at optimal performance at all times.

Okay, maybe fear of users yelling at us isn't the best rationale. On a more professional basis, as network administrators, we need our networks to deliver their resources as quickly as possible. A Web site that keeps users waiting for long loads or a file server that drags along, leaving users staring at status bars, is contrary to efficiency. Network administrators need to do everything they can to optimize network performance.

Luckily hundreds, if not thousands, of strategies and technologies are designed to optimize network performance. The CompTIA Network+ exam objectives define a short but well-considered list of topics that this section addresses. Some of these you've seen in earlier chapters, so I'll not belabor them here, but merely mention them and point you to those chapters. Others are topics new to the book. To make learning easier, I've broken them into three distinct groups: caching, controlling data throughput, and keeping resources available.

Caching

Caching is the process of storing data that someone asks for in the hope that someone else will ask for it again. Generally, odds are incredibly good that anytime anyone asks for anything on the Internet, either they or other folks on your LAN will ask for the same thing again—and that's why caching works so well in so many different ways. Caching reduces network workload by eliminating the processes required to reacquire data. Caching reduces network traffic and server workloads.

The challenge to caching is identifying all the diverse places one can cache. Different caching methods and devices have already been discussed in the book. Refer to Chapter 10 (DNS caching) and Chapter 12 (proxy servers) for two examples.

You can also employ dedicated cache servers on your network. These network appliances—CompTIA calls them *caching engines*—can work at just about any level, such as LAN or WAN, and reduce overall network traffic dramatically. One example is EngageIP Cache Server. Cisco has also produced these appliances, though now caching is part of boxes with more integrated functions.

More commonly today, you'll find caching server functions as part of software services. Squid, for example, is a proxy and caching server that handles HTTP traffic, DNS, FTP, and more. You can deploy Squid on multiple servers and use the *Cache Array Routing Protocol (CARP)* to load balance among them all, optimizing network performance (at least for HTTP).

Controlling Data Throughput

A certain U.S. senator got a lot of teasing a few years ago by describing the Internet as "a series of tubes," but there's actually a strong argument for the idea of tubes when discussing the amount of data per second any given Internet connection may need. Unless your budget allows you to buy a "big tube" connection to the Internet, every network suffers from a limited amount of bandwidth that's rarely truly sufficient for everything your users need. Even if you're lucky enough to have good bandwidth today, ongoing network growth guarantees you'll eventually run into network slowdowns as demand grows.

There's no magic point at which a network goes from working well to working slowly. Most people are used to having to wait a bit for a Web page or a file transfer. Certain applications, called *latency-sensitive* applications, do not perform well when they lack adequate bandwidth. Some latency-sensitive applications require high bandwidth. Streaming video is a great example. Have you ever watched a video on YouTube that constantly stops and starts? At least YouTube enables you to pause the video so it can load more before you continue watching (Figure 18-23).

Figure 18-23
Pausing a video on YouTube

Try watching a video on Hulu.com (Figure 18-24) over a highly busy or slow connection. Hulu, unlike YouTube but like most other video sites, only caches a few seconds (to prevent people from stealing the video) and is all but unwatchable if there are constant stops and starts. Voice over IP (VoIP) applications are another great example. If every conversation is clipped . . . and . . . chopped . . . the beauty of VoIP falls apart.

Latency sensitivity takes on a whole new level of importance when you get into *unified communications (UC)*, where you roll all kinds of these services into one box: VoIP, instant messaging (IM), telephone service, video conferencing, and more. If you can't control the bandwidth, your network won't function properly.

When the size of your Internet pipe is limited, you need some method to throttle bandwidth, so that in high-demand times, latency-sensitive applications get more bandwidth at the cost of reducing bandwidth to those applications that don't mind the wait. The CompTIA Network+ exam mentions two of the most common: quality of service (QoS) and traffic shaping, both of which you learned about in Chapter 12. Here's a quick recap and some extra details.

Figure 18-24

Hulu.com

(I love this site!)

Quality of Service

Quality of service (QoS) is a procedure used almost exclusively on gateway devices to give certain applications priority when a connection reaches a certain amount of utilization. QoS works at Layer 2 of the OSI model and works with 802.1Q trunks to prioritize traffic. QoS applies a *Class of Service (CoS)* priority (0 to 7) to a certain port. As traffic from that port goes through a trunk line, its priority defines how much bandwidth is allocated. The higher the priority of traffic, the more bandwidth it gets. This form of QoS is specialized when you have high-priority file server or VoIP server systems connected to your network.

NOTE QoS can also reduce jitter on VoIP connections.

Traffic Shaping

Traffic shaping (also called *bandwidth shaping*) prioritizes traffic in various ways, such as by analyzing TCP/UDP port numbers or by examining the Application layer information in packets. Traffic shaping works in either of two ways: by giving certain packets a priority or by directly assigning a fixed amount of bandwidth (in bits/sec) to packets from a particular application based on port number.

NOTE When ISPs limit traffic based on applications to customers, it is called *bandwidth throttling.*

A typical setup of traffic shaping first requires you to tell the router the total upstream and downstream bandwidth of your connection. From there, you assign bandwidth to a particular application, as shown in Figure 18-25.

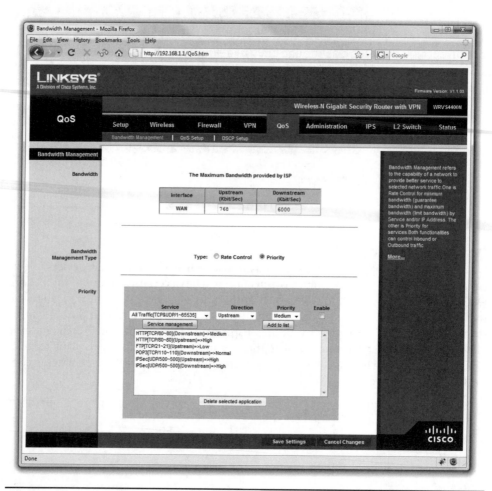

Figure 18-25   Traffic shaping on a SOHO router

QoS and traffic shaping give you a number of tools to control traffic. You can control or prioritize traffic based on port/MAC address (QoS), IP address, or application. The choice depends on the equipment you choose and the needs of your network.

Keeping Resources Available

No throttling or QoS does you a bit of good if the resource itself isn't available due to problems with the hardware. There are two areas where hardware limitations come into play. First is some form of hardware failure. Anyone who has worked on a PC for more than a few months knows one thing: hardware fails. Second, the design of the Internet dictates that a single IP address be given to a resource. Every Web server has a single IP address; every e-mail server eventually goes back to one IP address. This creates a problem when a resource becomes popular, because no single machine could ever handle the demands of a www.yahoo.com or a www.google.com. No worries, though, because many techniques exist to make multiple physical servers look as though they're a single IP address. Collectively, these techniques ensure a shared resource is available in a timely manner when clients request it: we call this *high availability*.

Proper network management requires *fault tolerance*: systems that can continue to provide network functions even in the face of catastrophic hardware failure. Ensuring fault tolerance begins with a plain-old *data backup*, where you make a copy of all important files and folders, but then quickly goes into redundant hardware, real-time load balancing, and more. The key thing you want to achieve is guaranteed *uptime*—each of these options helps avoid any unplanned server downtime, thus making your users happier.

Data Backup

Without a solid data backup, you're sunk if too much hardware goes down too quickly. Proper backup routines require both software and hardware to create, preferably, removable or remote backups of all data.

Most operating systems come with some type of backup program, plus developers offer many third-party tools. Figure 18-26 shows the Windows Server Backup in Windows Server 2008. Third-party tools include Veritas NetBackup from Symantec and CA ARCserve Backup (from the company formerly known as Computer Associates), both of which offer enterprise-level backup and recovery tools.

Most backup software looks first to tape backup devices and then to hard drive or networked storage for backup. Use of tape drives seemed to be on the wane a few years ago, but they have made a strong comeback as a storage medium. Tape is relatively inexpensive and quite reliable over a long period of time. Some of the big players in tape drives include Dell, HP, IBM, and Qualstar.

The goal of backing up data is to ensure that when a system dies, you will have an available, recent copy you can use to restore the system. You could simply back up the complete system at the end of each day—or whatever interval you feel is prudent to keep the backups fresh—but complete backups can be a tremendous waste of time and materials.

Instead of backing up the entire system, take advantage of the fact that all the files won't be changed in any given period; much of the time you only need to back up what's changed since your last backup. Recognizing this, many backup software solutions have a series of options available beyond the old complete (usually called Full or Normal) backup.

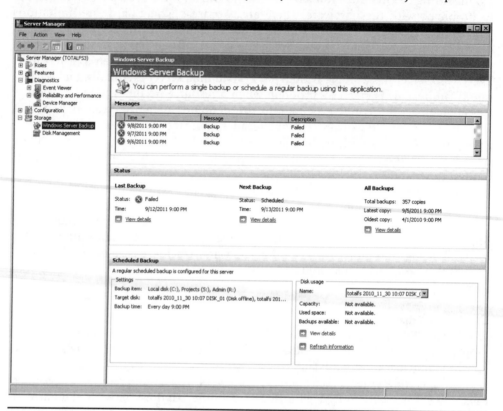

Figure 18-26 Windows Server Backup (Hmm ... is "failed" a good thing?)

The key to understanding backups other than the full backup is *attributes,* 1-bit storage areas that all files have. The most common attributes are Hidden (don't show the file in Windows Explorer or when typing `dir` at the command line), System (a critical file for the system), Read-Only (can't edit or erase it), and Archive. Archive needs a more detailed explanation. These attributes were first used in FAT-formatted drives in the DOS era, but they are still completely supported today by all file formats. The *archive bit* works like this: whenever a file is saved, the archive bit is turned on. Simply opening a file will affect the current state of the archive bit. Backup programs usually turn off a file's archive bit when the file is backed up. In theory, if a file's archive bit is turned off (set to 0), it means there's a good backup of that file on some tape. If the archive bit is turned on (set to 1), it means the file has been changed since it was last backed up (see Figure 18-27).

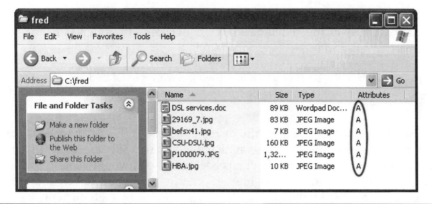

Figure 18-27 The archive bit on these files is on.

 NOTE Windows Explorer (My Computer in Windows XP, Computer in Vista/7), by default, does not show much about files in any view, even when you select Details from the View menu. The Details view is highly customizable, however, and can reveal a phenomenal amount and variety of information about files.

To customize your view, right-click the column bar (the gray bar that says Name, Size, Type, Date Modified, and so forth) to look at the default choices. You'll see everything from Attributes, Owner, Author, and Title, to file-type specific information such as Genre, Duration, and Bit Rate (for music files). If the default extra view options don't get your motor revving, selecting the More option brings up a menu offering many more view options! For the purposes of this section, click the **Attribute** box to display file and folder attributes.

Archive bits are used to perform backups that are not full backups. The following backup types are most often supported:

- A *normal backup* is a full backup. Every file selected will be backed up, and the archive bit will be turned off for every file backed up. This type is the standard "back it all up" option.

- A *copy backup* is identical to a normal backup, with the important distinction being that the archive bits are *not* changed. This backup is used (although not often) for making extra copies of a previously completed backup.

- An *incremental backup* includes only files with the archive bit turned on. In other words, it copies only the files that have been changed since the last backup. This backup turns off the archive bits.

- A *differential backup* is identical to an incremental backup, except that it doesn't turn off the archive bits.

- A *daily backup*, also known as a daily copy backup, makes copies of all the files that have been changed that day. It does not change the archive bits.

 EXAM TIP Be sure you know the different types of backups, including which ones change the archive bits and which ones do not.

The motivation for having both the incremental and differential backups may not be clear at first glance—they seem so similar as to be basically the same. Incremental seems the better option at first. If a file is backed up, you would want to turn off the archive bit, right? Well, maybe. But in one scenario, that might not be too attractive. Most backups do a big weekly normal backup, followed by daily incremental or differential backups at the end of every business day. Figure 18-28 shows the difference between incremental and differential backups.

Figure 18-28
Incremental vs. differential

Incremental

MON	TUE	WED	THU	FRI
Full Backup	All Tuesday Changes	All Wednesday Changes	All Thursday Changes	All Friday Changes

Differential

MON	TUE	WED	THU	FRI
Full Backup	All Changes Through Tuesday	All Changes Through Wednesday	All Changes Through Thursday	All Changes Through Friday

Notice that a differential backup is a *cumulative* backup. Because the archive bits are not cleared, it keeps backing up all changes since the last normal backup. This means the backup files will get progressively larger throughout the week (assuming a standard weekly normal backup). The incremental backup, by contrast, only backs up files changed since the last backup. Each incremental backup file will be relatively small and also totally different from the previous backup file.

Let's assume that the system is wiped out on a Thursday morning. How can you restore the system to a useful state?

If you're using an incremental backup, you will first have to restore the last weekly backup you ran on Monday, then the Tuesday backup, and then the Wednesday backup before the system is restored to its Thursday morning state. The longer the time between normal backups, the more incremental backups you must restore.

Using the same scenario, but assuming you're doing differential instead of incremental backups, you'll only need the weekly backup and then the Wednesday backup to restore your system. A differential backup always requires only two backups to restore a system (see Figure 18-29). Suddenly, the differential backup looks better than the incremental! On the other hand, one big benefit of incremental over differential is backup file size. Differential backup files will be massive compared to incremental ones.

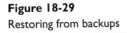

Figure 18-29
Restoring from backups

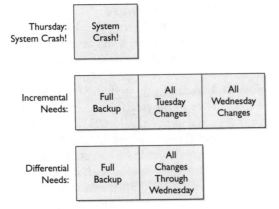

One of the typical regimens, or rotations, for backing up to tape or to external hard drive and rotating media is called *grandfather, father, son (GFS)*, and it works like this. Typically, you have a weekly and daily backup. You run a full backup once a week and store the tape offsite. Then you run a differential backup each day. The full backup is the father and the differential backups are the son. The grandfather is the last full backup of the month that then gets stored offsite. Using such a strategy enables you to restore by previous months, weeks, or days.

Choosing between incremental backups and differential backups is only one factor in choosing how you back up your data. You must also consider your business, your data, your backup hardware, your operating systems, and other factors to create a backup strategy.

UPS

During a power failure, an *uninterruptible power supply (UPS)* keeps the power on long enough to shut down the servers properly. Without a good UPS, you risk an ugly shutdown with the potential for serious data loss. A UPS enables a computer to function for a short period of time, so for extended outages, there's only one answer: backup generators.

NOTE Uninterruptible power supplies differ a lot in how they work and in the quality of electricity they provide. The standard device called a UPS is actually a *standby power supply (SPS)* because it takes a few milliseconds to bring the power online. These are fine, and they are much less expensive than a true UPS.

Backup Generators

For extended blackouts, such as when Hurricane Ike took down my office (and much of the Gulf Coast) for several weeks in 2008, you need to have backup generators to guarantee any hope of uninterrupted uptime. A *backup generator* runs on some sort of fuel (often diesel or gasoline) to provide electricity.

RAID and Redundant Hardware

Once you've secured the electricity for your servers, you need to make sure that individual components within the system don't take out your entire server. Most commonly, these redundant pieces of hardware include multiple hard drives, power supplies, and network connections.

As you most likely recall from studying for your CompTIA A+ exams, you can use two or more hard drives to provide fault tolerance through one of the several levels of *Redundant Array of Independent Disks (RAID)*. Several RAID levels are commonly used in networks for data redundancy, such as RAID 1, RAID 5, and RAID 6.

RAID 1 is *mirroring* or *duplexing* (if two controllers are used). Requiring at least two drives, RAID 1 writes the same data to each drive. RAID 1 arrays have great fault tolerance, but because each drive contains the full file, they are about as fast as a single drive when writing. Read times are faster, though, because the controller can access both drives together.

RAID 5 is *disk striping with distributed parity*. RAID 5 requires at least three drives. RAID 5 takes stripes, performs a parity calculation, and then stores the stripes and the parity across the drives in the array. If a single drive fails, the RAID array can rebuild the data. RAID 5 is fast and provides good fault tolerance.

RAID 6 takes one step beyond RAID 5 to add another parity block to the scheme. This enables you to create an array of four or more drives of which you can lose two and still recover. Now that's fault tolerance!

 EXAM TIP The CompTIA Network+ exam doesn't require you to know the different levels of RAID.

Redundant power supplies and network connections provide exactly what their names suggest. The spare power supply should kick on automatically if the main power supply dies for some reason. The spare network connection can do the same for either a dead NIC or a dead connection.

 NOTE You might recall another use for a second network connection—bonding, using multiple NICs to increase your throughput. Bonding provides no fault tolerance, but can be very useful if you have an overly busy server!

Cluster Servers and Load Balancing

If you're not content with duplicating hardware components inside a server, you're not alone. Many network installations reproduce entire servers or use multiple servers that act as a cluster server, so if any server goes down, the rest just pick up the slack and keep on chugging. Clustering servers requires cluster-aware operating systems, such as Windows Server Enterprise edition.

Clustered servers can also balance the load when dealing with heavy usage, as you'll recall from the discussion of busy Web servers in Chapter 12. When scaled up and done right, the end user sees there's only one identity. Google.com's home page might be balanced on 20 giant servers, for example, but you merely type in www.google.com and away you go.

Finally, you can use multiple servers to provide a single network or Internet service, such as a popular database, like the Internet Movie Database (www.imdb.com). When you access IMDB, you're accessing a Web site, certainly, but then interacting with an enormous database (Figure 18-30). That database could be placed onto a *server farm*—another name for a cluster—that harnesses the power of multiple servers acting as a *load balancer* to handle both the processing and the traffic.

Figure 18-30 The Internet Movie Database

Chapter Review

Questions

1. Which of the following describes standards for physical wiring in a network?

   A. Baseline

   B. Demarc

   C. Network diagram

   D. Wiring scheme

2. Which of the following defines the type of connection or technology used in a network and maps how each machine connects?

   A. Baseline

   B. Demarc

   C. Network diagram

   D. Wiring scheme

3. John wants to analyze the procedure for adding a new file server on his network. What should he do?

   A. Ask his supervisor.

   B. Check the change management documentation.

   C. Redraw the network diagram.

   D. Redraw the wiring diagram.

4. What defines the performance of the network when everything is working properly?

   A. Baseline

   B. Demarc

   C. Network diagram

   D. Wiring diagram

5. What tool enables you to view the behavior of hardware and other resources on a computer?

   A. Baseline

   B. Network Monitor

   C. Performance Monitor

   D. System Monitor

6. What is a record of data about your system?

   A. Counter

   B. Log

   C. Node

   D. Object

7. How can you ensure that your servers will continue to run during a blackout?

   A. Implement load balancing.

   B. Implement network monitoring.

   C. Install a backup generator.

   D. Install a traffic shaper.

8. Grandfather, father, son is an example of what?

   A. Backup rotation

   B. Log file entries

   C. RAID array

   D. Bandwidth shaping

9. What is the minimum number of drives required for a RAID 5 array?

   A. One

   B. Two

   C. Three

   D. Four

10. What tool in Windows enables you to look at log files?

    A. Baseline Viewer

    B. Event Viewer

    C. Network Monitor

    D. Performance Monitor

Answers

1. **D.** The wiring scheme describes specific standard used for the wiring, such as TIA/EIA 568A.

2. **C.** The network diagram describes the type of connections used in a network, such as Gigabit Ethernet, T1, and so on, and maps out the connections among machines.

3. **B.** Although consulting a supervisor will certainly happen at some point in the process, the change management documentation will give John a quick idea of the procedures and policies involved in doing an upgrade of this magnitude.

4. **A.** The baseline is a snapshot of the properly functioning network.

5. **C.** Performance Monitor enables you to view the behavior of hardware and other resources on a computer.

6. **B.** You can view logs to see details of your system performance.

7. **C.** This one's pretty straightforward. Without the juice, your servers go down.

8. **A.** Grandfather, father, son (GFS) is a common regimen for dealing with tape backups.

9. **C.** RAID 5 arrays require at least three drives; a RAID 1 array can get away with only two.

10. **B.** Event Viewer enables you to view log files.

## CHAPTER 19

Building a SOHO Network

The CompTIA Network+ certification exam expects you to know how to

- 2.5 Given a scenario, troubleshoot common router and switch problems: Bad cables/improper cable types, mismatched MTU/MUT black hole, power failure, bad modules (SFPs, GBICs)
- 2.6 Given a set of requirements, plan and implement a basic SOHO network: list of requirements, cable length, device types/requirements, environment limitations, equipment limitations, compatibility requirements

To achieve these goals, you must be able to

- Describe the major steps to consider when designing a SOHO network
- Describe and implement a SOHO network, including solving assorted problems
- Explain how security comes into play while building a SOHO network

The time has come for you to take what you learned in previous chapters and apply that knowledge to creating a product: a real, functioning network. This chapter walks you through the steps for building a typical small office/home office (SOHO) network from the ground up, using the tools provided in earlier chapters to handle the entire process. This network needs to include structured cabling, wireless, operating systems, Internet connectivity, and network/system security. The network must have servers, workstations, and printers installed. I'll also add a few troubleshooting tips beyond what was discussed in other chapters.

Historical/Conceptual

Building a SOHO network is a big job, so let's break it into three discrete steps. First, you need to plan the process. To do this, I've created my own checklist to help you think about what needs planning. Second, there's the actual process of building the SOHO network. I'll walk you through this process, from running the cables to installing anti-malware software. Third, I'll discuss security and you'll see that, although security isn't on the checklist, it's actually part of almost every section of the checklist.

This chapter is unique. I want you to look at an entire network and see it as a whole so you gain a broad understanding of how it all works. I won't rehash procedures or technologies already covered in earlier chapters. Instead, I'll cover the building of a SOHO network from a higher level, dealing with individual scenarios that you might encounter as you build the network after it's running. Be warned! You'll probably find yourself jumping back to earlier chapters to consider issues in this chapter.

The chapter also offers about a dozen sections where I suggest you take some kind of action, like drawing a diagram or visiting a computer store. I think that if you do the exercises while studying the chapter, you'll come away with a fundamentally more solid understanding of the components and processes.

Test Specific

Designing a SOHO Network

The CompTIA Network+ exam doesn't define a list titled "The x Steps to Design and Build a Network." As you've read this book, however, you've probably discovered what needs to happen. For this chapter, I'll use the following list. It may not be perfect, but I've built hundreds of networks using these steps.

1. **List of requirements**   Define the network's needs. Why are you installing this network? What primary features do you need?

2. **Network design**   What equipment do you need to build this network? How should you organize the network?

3. **Compatibility issues**   Are you using existing equipment, applications, or cabling that have compatibility issues?

4. **Internal connections**   What type of structured cabling do you need? Does this network need wireless?

5. **External connections**   How do you connect to the Internet?

6. **Peripherals**   How will peripherals come into play? Are you connecting any printers, fax machines, or scanners?

7. **Security**   How will you deal with computer, data, and network security?

Although I've numbered them here, these steps might come in any order. Even though network security is in the seventh position, for example, you might make a decision concerning the firewall as early as Step 2. Don't be afraid to jump around a bit as needed to construct the network. Let's start building a network using this list. For each point on the list, I'll use a scenario or two to consider some of the pitfalls and issues that might pop up.

NOTE   This list happily ignores a few important issues such as costs vs. budget, time to install, and so on. While you should definitely consider these when constructing your own network, the CompTIA Network+ exam isn't very interested in them.

Remember being introduced to MHTechED back in Chapter 2? Well, the prosperous folks over there have hired you to bring their network up to speed (Figure 19-1). It seems that MHTechEd's grown from 2 computers to about 15 (including servers) over the years, but the network itself is a mess. Now they want to move into new offices. They even have a new floor plan (Figure 19-2).

Figure 19-1
MHTechED's
gotten bigger

Figure 19-2
Floor plan for
the new MHTechEd

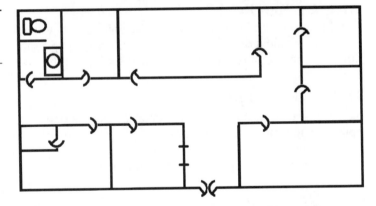

So grab some boxes and let's move MHTechED into their new home.

Building the Network

Designing a SOHO network isn't too terribly challenging. There simply aren't enough computers, switches, routers, printers, or servers to overwhelm the design process. The challenge comes in the actual implementation of the network. Here, the "gotchas" come hot and heavy, no matter how well you think you've planned ahead. The secret is to stick with your checklist and, above all, be patient!

Define the Network Needs

MHTechED is a typical small office. They need a single file server to store marketing, accounting, and sales data. They want a second file server that only supports their current projects. They also have a few individual servers running a number of different operating systems used for research. Every employee will get a computer running Windows 7 Ultimate and the latest version of Microsoft Office. Employees need access to shared folders on the file server for personal storage as well as shared access to customer information. All employees need to print documents as well as send and receive faxes. All employees need access to a telephone.

Two of the employees work full time on graphics, including photography and video. They need cameras, scanners, and a high-quality color printer. The nature of their work compels them to have an Apple Mac Pro computer running the latest version of OS X, in addition to their Windows systems.

Defining network needs never actually ends. All networks are highly evolving entities and new ideas, applications, and equipment appear on an ongoing basis.

 NOTE Network needs are tough to quantify. Don't try to dig too deeply here, because many issues can be assumed such as "everyone will want a mouse on their PC." Try to stay with job functions and what the network needs to do to support those functions.

What Are *Your* Needs?

Imagine the coolest home network you've ever desired. What would that network look like? What would it do for you? Go ahead and sketch up a sample floor plan. Keep this floor plan handy for other action-oriented sections in this chapter.

Network Design

Now you need to work on the finer details. Network design quantifies the equipment, operating systems, and applications used by the network. This step ties closely with Step 3, compatibility issues.

You need to address the following equipment:

- Workstations
- Servers
- Equipment room
- Peripherals

Workstations

The company has eight employees. Each needs a late-generation Windows system (Windows 7) running Microsoft Office 2010. Additionally, two employees need a late-generation Mac running OS X; these machines will not have Office.

Servers

The network needs three file servers. You have a lot of flexibility here, as the users simply need two places to store data and some way to run multiple research and development (R&D) systems. The R&D machines are perfect candidates for virtualization, so you can add a third server for storing these.

Most people really enjoy the single sign-on convenience of a Windows domain, so you'll use a single Windows Server domain controller. Granted, if you really wanted to do things right, you would add a second domain controller, so why not virtualize the two file servers? You can get two copies of VMware's ESX Hypervisor.

The network now has three file servers, all virtualized with the following virtual machines:

- **Server #1**   Windows Server 2008
- **Server #2**   Windows Server 2008
- **Server #3**   A number of virtualized operating systems from Windows 95 through Windows 7. Also two versions of Linux: Ubuntu and Debian.

NOTE   Many small networks avoid using a full-blown file server and instead take advantage of inexpensive and reliable *network attached storage (NAS)* devices. Technically, an NAS is a computer that's preconfigured to offer file storage for just about any type of client. Most NAS systems use the Common Internet File System (CIFS) configuration to create a plug and play (PnP) type of device. These devices include features such as RAID to make storage safer.

Equipment Room

An equipment room will act as the intermediate distribution frame (IDF) for the network. (See Chapter 6 for the details on the IDF.) All systems will tie into a single, managed, 24-port gigabit switch on a rack mount. The rack will be a floor-to-ceiling rack with a rack-mounted UPS.

Peripherals

MHTechEd has a small office, so you'll purchase a single high-capacity, networked laser printer and a color inkjet printer. The graphics folks picked a printer that doesn't have a NIC, so you'll just install the printer onto one of the Macs and share the printer.

The office doesn't do a lot of faxing or scanning, so a typical All-in-One device should work perfectly. I found one that shares the fax system across the network (sweet!), enabling anyone to convert almost any document into a fax. This groovy machine connects to the network via Gigabit Ethernet or wirelessly over 802.11g (Figure 19-3). Scanning isn't quite as handy. All scanned documents go straight to the machine's built-in storage, where it is shared as a folder on the network. It's not perfect, but for $249, the company is happy.

Figure 19-3
MHTechEd's
cool All-in-One
machine

Your Network, Your Equipment

Continuing from the previous exercise, decide what equipment you want for your own home network. Surely you're going to add a home theater PC, but what about a separate media server? Do you want a computer in the kitchen? Would you like a rack in your house? Can you find a smaller rack online? Can you wall-mount it? Make a list similar to the one in this section and keep it handy for more action-oriented sections.

Compatibility Issues

MHTechED's new building recently added more rooms to their office. The equipment room still has runs going to rooms 1, 2, and 6, but these runs are only CAT 5e. Three new rooms have been added, but they need CAT 6. You could run CAT 6 into the old rooms, but the boss said "No" to save money (Figure 19-4). MHTechED has a very nice Cisco 802.11g WAP. The boss wasn't happy when you bought a new 802.11n WAP for almost $1,000, because the old one still works fine.

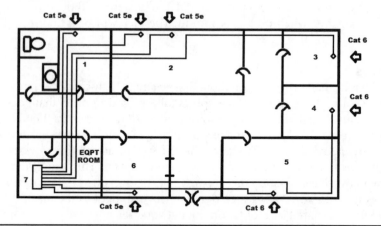

Figure 19-4 CAT 5e and CAT 6 drops in the MHTechED office

The few existing applications the company needs to bring along will work perfectly on the new PCs and Macs: namely Peachtree 2012, Adobe Illustrator CS5, and Final Cut Studio.

What's Compatible?

If you were building a new home network from scratch, which of your existing parts could work in the new network? Do you have older equipment that might have compatibility issues, like an old 10BaseT switch or router?

If you needed to use all of your old equipment, visualize your new network connecting to it and how you might get around some of these issues. Does your old printer have a way to connect to the network directly? Where would you connect your Xbox 360? What if you have older TVs? Will they work with a powerful, HDMI-equipped video card?

Create an inventory of your old equipment and jot down any compatibility issues you might imagine taking place.

Internal Connections

Now that you have an idea of your equipment and what you want to do with it, you need to get everything properly connected using structured cabling. You should also begin to install your 802.11 network. Once you connect all your equipment, configure your internal VLANs, IP address scheme, DHCP/DNS servers, gateway, and so on.

The Switch

MHTechED is small enough to use a single switch to handle all the interconnections. Their switch needs two features: VLAN support and Power over Ethernet (PoE) to support the WAP. They have a Cisco 3750 switch that handles all of this quite nicely, so they'll stick with what they have.

NOTE You learned about CAT levels in Chapter 5, so check your memory as you read about the mixed CAT 5e and CAT 6 runs. What is the maximum throughput for CAT 5e and CAT 6? How might these different cable runs affect your network? What would be the fastest backbone switch to use in this network?

Structured Cabling

Setting up good structured cabling for MHTechED is a breeze. Like most office buildings, this building has plenum space over everything for horizontal runs and simple sheetrock walls for installing drops. You shouldn't run into any fire stops or heavy machinery.

Don't forget what you learned in Chapter 6. Now is the time to verify the exact location of your drops as well as where all horizontal runs come into the equipment room. Estimate the distances so you don't go over the cable length limits.

Although you can probably do the work yourself, hiring a professional can save on time and stress. Get a good floor layout, get on the phone, and call a professional installer. When he or she finishes the job, make sure you have

- Clearly labeled runs
- The length of all runs
- CAT ratings on all runs
- The floor plan showing all runs

Since you've hired an installer, you might as well look at your phone lines as well. Want the fax machine in the hall? No problem, but MHTechED needs to make sure it has access to an RJ-11 outlet. Running a PBX system? Verify all the phone lines and PBX lines run to a patch panel.

Electrical and Environmental Limits

You've got to be careful when installing racks in places where no rack has ever been. Watch out for electricity and environment issues. It's never a good idea to run your network equipment on anything other than a very high-amperage dedicated circuit. Figure 19-5 shows the dedicated circuit in MHTechEd's equipment room. Those plugs are not in circuit with any other plugs!

Figure 19-5
Dedicated circuit

Environment is an equally big "gotcha." Don't turn a typical closet into rack space without making serious environmental changes first. For very small single racks, you can get away with the existing air conditioning. Keep in mind, however, that the same ventilation that keeps a single person cool will not be enough to keep the rack cool. If you're making a new rack, call building services and get them to dump extra air into that room!

Wireless

MHTechED has lots of customers who walk in and need to see products online while in the office. To make this easier, MHTechED is going to create a well-locked-down 802.11 network. Because the boss won't let them upgrade to 802.11n, they choose to place the single WAP centrally in the office, as shown in Figure 19-6. Given the small size of the office, this single WAP should do well.

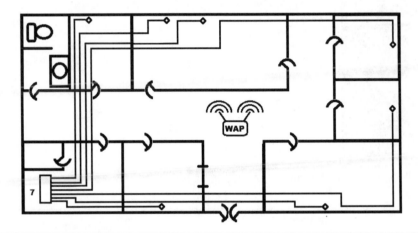

Figure 19-6   Placement of WAP in network

There's no power or network drop here, however. Good thing you hired those installers! It's time to add another drop. Power won't be a problem because the WAP supports PoE.

VLANs

These days, you won't find many networks that don't use VLANs. Even though MHTechED uses a small network, the company plans to separate the wireless devices, the virtual R&D machines and special server, the switch, and the router management tools into separate VLANs from the main network VLAN. The wireless VLANs will make it substantially harder to hack into the main network wirelessly.

Placing all of the R&D virtual machines into a VLAN will help prevent anyone "playing" on these test machines from hurting the main network. Figure 19-7 shows a *lights-out management (LOM)* program running on a Dell server being configured for VLAN200. These LOMs are special "computer within a computer" features built into better servers, designed to give you access to a server even when the server itself is shut off.

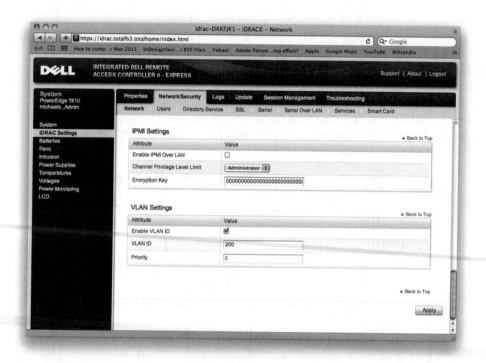

Figure 19-7   Lights-out management

Most managed devices have the ability to place their management screens into separate VLANs, as shown in Figure 19-7. This tool keeps people out of the most critical parts of your network.

The VLAN configuration for MHTechED is

- **Main VLAN**   VLAN1
- **Wireless VLAN**   VLAN2
- **R&D VLAN**   VLAN3
- **Management VLAN**   VLAN200

Set Up the Network IP Address Scheme

Long before you start plugging in RJ-45s, you need to decide on your internal IP addressing scheme. For most SOHO networks, this means picking an arbitrary, unique, internal private IP network ID and then preassigning static IP addresses to servers and WAPs. Plus, pick a DHCP server and preassign DHCP scope IP address ranges.

   NOTE   Try to avoid the overused 192.168.1.0/24 network ID. Bad guys look for mistakes like these.

MHTechED chooses four different network IDs for the four VLANs:

- **VLAN1**   10.11.12.0/24
- **VLAN2**   10.11.13.0/24
- **VLAN3**   10.11.14.0/24
- **VLAN200**   10.11.15.0/24

Sure, the company will never need a full Class C range and could have gone with a CIDR range like /28, but they're lazy people, and remembering subnets like 255.255.255.224 is harder than remembering 255.255.255.0. Here's the rest of the IP organization:

- **Gateway router**   10.11.12.1
- **Switches/WAP/router management**   10.11.15.2–10.11.15.20
- **Server 1 virtual machines**   10.11.12.10–10.11.12.19
- **Server 2 virtual machines**   10.11.12.20–10.11.12.29
- **R&D server virtualized**   10.11.14.1–10.11.14-254
- **Wired DHCP clients**   10.11.12.100–10.11.12.130
- **Wireless DHCP clients**   10.11.13.100–10.11.13.120

If MHTechEd is using Windows Server, then picking a DHCP server is easy because the company will just use one of the two DHCP servers that come with Windows Server 2008.

Setting up the IP addressing scheme beforehand saves you a lot of time and effort once you start installing the systems. Be sure to make multiple copies of this scheme. Print out a copy and put it in the equipment room. Put a copy in your network documentation. Even put a copy in your wallet or in your phone. Having this information at your fingertips is a huge benefit.

Setting Up an IP Address Scheme

Now it's your turn to set up your dream home network's IP address scheme. List all of the IP address assignments for your network just like you did for MHTechEd. Here's the big question: Which computers get static addresses and which get DHCP? What would you use for a DHCP server?

External Connections

No network is an island anymore. At the very least, MHTechEd needs an ISP so folks can Google and update their Facebook pages—er, I mean, get work done online. In a SOHO network like MHTechEd, you don't have to deal with many of the issues you'd see in larger networks. A typical home-type ISP (DSL or cable) should be more than enough for them in terms of bandwidth. On the other hand, MHTechEd needs to be connected to the Internet all the time (or pay the price in lost business), so the company should consider a second ISP as a fallback plan in case the primary ISP fails.

Paper Router Table

Assume MHTechEd has two static Internet connections:

ISP A	ISP B
IP Address: 1.5.4.3	IP Address: 11.45.27.3
Subnet Mask: 255.255.255.192	Subnet Mask: 255.255.255.0
Default Gateway: 1.5.4.1	Default Gateway: 11.45.27.1

Using the internal IP address scheme discussed earlier in this chapter (10.11.12.0/24) and the predefined default gateway (10.11.12.1), write up a four-line paper routing table.

Using the Cisco naming conventions, your router has three Ethernet ports: Fa0/0 connects to the local network; Fa0/1 connects to ISP A; and Fa0/2 connects to ISP B. Run `route print` from a Windows command prompt to remind you of the data needed to make a routing table. Make sure you have at least three routes:

- Default route to the Internet when ISP A is working
- Default route when ISP A is *not* working (clue: metrics)
- Local traffic route

Choose a Gateway Router

A serious business can't get away with a cheap home router. It needs something that fires up quickly, runs dependably, and never locks up. That's why MHTechEd chose a real battleship of a router: the Cisco 2811. This router comes with two fixed 100BaseT Ethernet ports (Figure 19-8) and plenty of extra slots to add even more NICs. It's a good firewall, too, and supports NAT. Unfortunately, the Cisco 2811 only supports 100BaseT. Depending on what's available in your area, that router might need an upgrade soon.

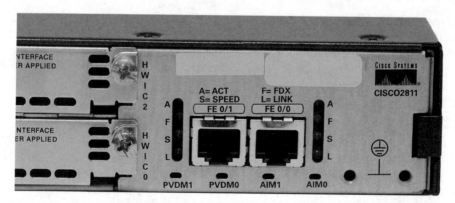

Figure 19-8   Fixed 100BaseT ports on Cisco 2811

EXAM TIP Cisco would prefer that small businesses use their ASA series of "security appliances" over the 2800 series of routers. Go to www.cisco.com and compare a Cisco ASA 5540 to the Cisco 2811.

As you'll see in the next section, MHTechEd wants to connect to two different ISPs as a safety feature. To support this, the company needs to add an extra port to the 2811. Luckily, the 2811 is designed to accept special *high-speed WAN interface cards (HWICs)*, router expansion cards that make adding the third port easy (Figure 19-9).

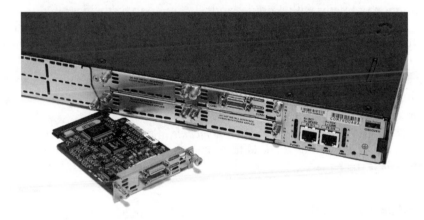

Figure 19-9 Cisco HWIC card and router

Most good routers and switches come with interchangeable components, enabling manufacturers to make a base model device and then offer components to address each customer's individual needs. These components come in a number of different shapes and sizes. In Chapter 5, you saw a gigabit interface converter (GBIC) that gives customers the ability to match their router and switch connections to whatever type of fiber already exists in their location. You've now seen the Cisco HWIC as well. Another popular module used by Cisco is their *Small Form-Factor Pluggable (SFP)* connector, used in many Cisco and other brand switches (Figure 19-10). Note that the SFP is designed exclusively for fiber networks.

Figure 19-10
NETGEAR SFP

You can easily install these modules. Turn off the router or switch, remove a protective plate (if one exists), plug in the module, and turn the switch/router back on. Assuming the device is in good working order, the switch or router will automatically recognize the new connectors and you'll be able to do whatever you'd do with any connector: add it to a VLAN, configure its speed/duplex, apply an IP address (on router ports), and so on.

If you install a module that doesn't work, use the same tests that you'd perform on any port on a switch or router. The fact that these are modules doesn't change the troubleshooting tools you've learned about in earlier chapters. I've listed some of the most common problems with modules and what to do to fix them:

- *Did you plug the wrong type of cable into the new port (single-mode into multimode, for example)?* Make sure you use the right cabling for the new connection.

- *Are the link lights working? Is the new port properly connected?* It's just as easy to plug a bad cable into a module as it is to plug it into a regular port. Make sure the device on the other end of the cable works, too!

- *Does the switch/router recognize the new module in the maintenance Web page/utility/ whatever?* If it doesn't, you need to contact the manufacturer. In most cases, you can "fix it" by replacing the module.

Customizing Your 2811

Do some research to see how many different types of HWICs are available for the 2811. You'll find quite a few! Also check out a single series of Cisco router. Try the 2800 series, if you'd like, but also consider investigating another series such as the 3800 line. Pick three routers in the series and determine the difference among the three. Answer this question: What is the significance of the last two digits of a router's model number?

Choose an ISP

Before you choose an Internet service provider, ask yourself, "What is available at my location?" If you're constructing a network in an existing office building, also ask, "What's already installed that I can tap into?" Once an ISP makes some form of endpoint in a building, you can easily (and inexpensively) connect to that ISP as opposed to finding your own. Additionally, many office buildings offer Internet connectivity as part of the lease agreement or at least tell you what ISP already connects to the building.

After making a few calls to building management, MHTechEd learns that an ISP already provides 100BaseT, Metro Ethernet service. The ISP promises 5 Mbps throughput and is prepared to get them up and running in just a few days (they need to run a 100BaseT connection from the demarc in the basement up to MHTechED). Additionally, MHTechEd is also purchasing a commercial account from the local cable provider.

What's Available in Your Building?

Home networks won't have a preexisting ISP. You need to determine which ISPs provide service in your neighborhood. Fortunately, there's a great Web site designed to help you see what you can get: www.broadbandreports.com. Go the site, select the **Find Service** menu, and enter your ZIP code (sorry—USA only). Even if you already have an Internet connection at your house, see if you can find a better deal than the one you have. How much money can you save per month?

ISPs and MTUs

I discussed the Maximum Transmission Unit (MTU) in Chapter 8. Back in the dark ages (before Windows Vista), Microsoft users often found themselves with terrible connection problems due to the fact that IP packets were too big to fit into certain network protocols. The largest Ethernet packet is 1500 bytes, so some earlier versions of Windows set their MTU size to a value less than 1500 to minimize the fragmentation of packets. The problem cropped up when you tried to connect to a technology other than Ethernet, such as DSL. Some DSL carriers couldn't handle an MTU size greater than 1400. When your network's packets are so large that they must be fragmented to fit into your ISPs packets, we call it an *MTU mismatch*.

As a result, techs would tweak their MTU settings to improve throughput by matching up the MTU sizes between the ISP and their own network. This usually required a manual registry setting adjustment, although some older versions of Windows used third-party programs like Dr. TCP (Figure 19-11). This process is called "matching up" mismatched MTU settings.

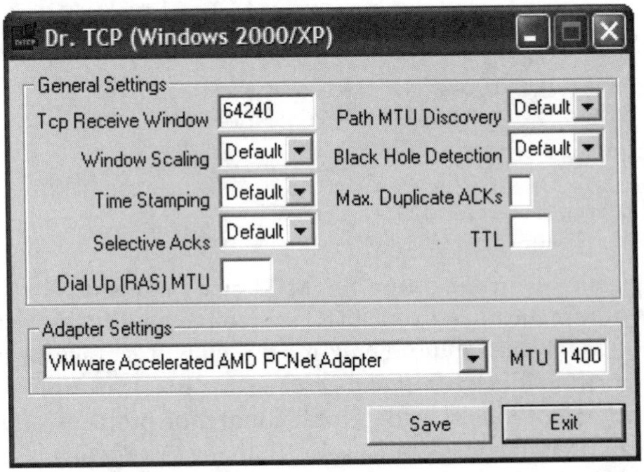

Figure 19-11   Adjusting the MTU settings in Dr. TCP

NOTE Dr. TCP is an old program and does not work on Windows Vista or 7. Don't use it anymore; you don't have to, either, because of Path MTU Discovery.

Around 2007, *Path MTU Discovery (PMTU)*, a new method to determine the best MTU setting automatically, was created. PMTU works by adding a new feature called the "Don't Fragment (DF) flag" to the IP packet. A PMTU-aware operating system can automatically send a series of fixed-size ICMP packets (basically just pings) with the DF flag set to another device to see if it works. If it doesn't work, the system lowers the MTU size and tries again until the ping is successful.

You can imitate this feature by running a ping yourself. Open a command prompt and run the following command:

```
ping www.totalsem.com -f -l 1500
```

You should get results similar to the following:

```
Pinging www.totalsem.com [216.40.231.195] with 1500 bytes of data:
Packet needs to be fragmented but DF set.
Packet needs to be fragmented but DF set.
Packet needs to be fragmented but DF set.
Packet needs to be fragmented but DF set.

Ping statistics for 216.40.231.195:
    Packets: Sent = 4, Received = 0, Lost = 4 (100% loss),
```

Try running the ping command again, this time setting the MTU size smaller:

```
C:\>ping www.totalsem.com -f -l 1400

Pinging www.totalsem.com [216.40.231.195] with 1400 bytes of data:
Reply from 216.40.231.195: bytes=1400 time=81ms TTL=51
Reply from 216.40.231.195: bytes=1400 time=85ms TTL=51
Reply from 216.40.231.195: bytes=1400 time=134ms TTL=51
Reply from 216.40.231.195: bytes=1400 time=144ms TTL=51

Ping statistics for 216.40.231.195:
    Packets: Sent = 4, Received = 4, Lost = 0 (0% loss),
Approximate round trip times in milli-seconds:
    Minimum = 81ms, Maximum = 144ms, Average = 111ms
```

Imagine the hassle of incrementing the MTU size manually. That's the beauty of PMTU—you can automatically set your MTU size to the perfect amount.

Unfortunately, PMTU runs under ICMP; most routers have firewall features that, by default, are configured to block ICMP requests, making PMTU worthless. This is called a *PMTU* or *MTU black hole*. If you're having terrible connection problems and you've checked everything else, you need to consider this issue. In many cases, going into the router and turning off ICMP blocking in the firewall is all you need to do to fix the problem.

EXAM TIP The CompTIA Network+ objectives use the term *MUT/MTU black holes*. There's no such thing as "MUT" so, hopefully, CompTIA will have fixed this by the time you're reading this book.

Peripherals

The MHTechEd requirement list defined the following peripherals:

- One high-speed laser printer hooked directly to the network
- One color printer connected to a machine to be determined
- A combined fax/copier/printer (All-in-One) device primarily used for faxes
- A single scanner connected to a system

This doesn't mean that other printers won't be installed, but these are the base needs in terms of peripherals.

Since the color printer and the All-in-One have already been purchased, or at least already decided upon, MHTechEd only needs to purchase the big laser printer. MHTechEd chooses a Hewlett-Packard M9050 like the one shown in Figure 19-12. These are very popular, high-speed, and network-capable out of the box. They're also built like tanks and will last a long time.

Figure 19-12
HP M9050

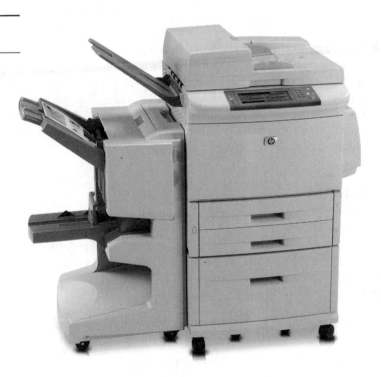

Only the big laser printer and the All-in-One box will connect directly to the network. To make things convenient, install both of these in Office 2 (Figure 19-13). Oops! I forgot yet another drop for a run to the laser printer. Even though the fax machine can run wirelessly, let's go ahead and just run a second drop for the fax machine.

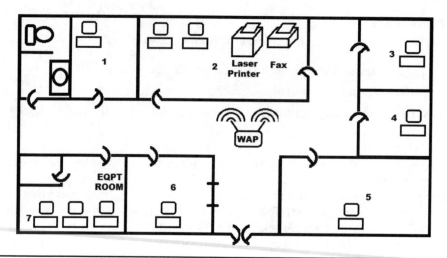

Figure 19-13 Location of fax machine and printer

Make Your Own Networked Printer

Putting a printer directly onto the network as opposed to sharing it through a PC has some big benefits. First, the printer doesn't need a running PC to be accessed. Second, heavy print jobs won't slow down any PCs. Third, less running equipment saves purchase costs and energy. But what if your printer on your home network doesn't have an Ethernet connection? Go online and see if you can find devices that enable you to interconnect a USB printer to an Ethernet network.

Security

Thinking about network security is like thinking about network electricity: security is not really a single step but an integral part of all the steps. Two chapters of this book, Chapter 11 and Chapter 16, already do a great job of covering these issues. Now I need to describe how to secure the MHTechED network. Going forward with that idea, here are the previous six steps with some of the security issues that come into play during each step:

1. **List of requirements** What are MHTechED's security needs? Here's a small subset:

   A. Anti-malware on all systems

   B. Firewall with ACL capacity

   C. Security from equipment theft

D. Wireless encryption

E. Wireless network isolation

2. **Network design** You need to make sure MHTechEd has the equipment that satisfies the requirements listed in Step 1.

A. Microsoft Security Essentials on all systems

B. A built-in firewall on the Cisco 2811

C. Door locks, deadbolts, motion sensors all tied to a security monitoring company

D. WPA Personal Shared Key

E. WAPs that support isolation

3. **Compatibility issues** Will there be security issues with the older equipment? Can the old WAP support WPA2 PSK?

4. **Internal connections** What do you need to do to protect the internal network from threats and failures?

A. Verify anti-malware is installed and updated—install Microsoft Security Essentials and configure for automatic updates.

B. Document the location of all PCs and their associated connections.

C. Configure servers to use RAID 5.

D. For power failure, use four 5000-joule, rack-mounted standby power supplies in the equipment room: three for servers and one for all routers, switches, and so on.

E. Install removable hard drives for backup. Contract for offsite backup.

F. Configure domain for strict password security.

5. **External connections** How do you connect to the Internet?

A. The network uses the 2811 router's firewall features, but how exactly do you keep it up to date? What, if any, manual ACLs must you configure?

6. **Peripherals** Not a traditional security issue.

EXAM TIP Be ready for some fairly complex scenario questions on the CompTIA Network+ exams. CompTIA does a great job giving you some clues about the scenario questions you'll encounter with the details of Domain 2.6, as shown at the beginning of this chapter. Like any CompTIA question, take your time when reading the scenario questions. In many cases, the question itself hinges completely on a single word or statement, making the entire scenario actually incredibly simple to answer.

Chapter Review

Questions

1. What's the first step needed when building a SOHO network?

   A. Define the network needs.

   B. Design the network.

   C. Select network infrastructure.

   D. Pull cable.

2. When you have a cable pulled, what should the installer provide you in terms of documentation?

   A. The documentation should show the length of all runs, labeling, CAT ratings, and a floor plan.

   B. The installer only needs to label the cables.

   C. The installer only needs to pull the cables.

   D. The documentation should show the width of the cables and the cost of the runs.

3. What issues should you consider when setting up a server closet?

   A. Make certain the server closet has adequate cooling.

   B. Make certain the server closet has a solid electrical circuit.

   C. Make certain the server closet has a dedicated electrical circuit.

   D. Make certain the server closet has adequate cooling and a dedicated electrical circuit.

4. What program enables you to access a server when the server is turned off?

   A. GBIC

   B. LOM

   C. PBX

   D. Virtual PBX

5. Which of the following block of IP addresses would be best for a private network that has an Internet connection through a gateway router?

   A. 10.200.65.0 /8

   B. 135.10.0.0 /16

   C. 192.168.1.0 /24

   D. 225.1.1.0 /16

6. Which of the following devices would enable you to add, not replace, a port on a typical Cisco switch?

    A. GBIC

    B. HWIC

    C. PBX

    D. SFP

7. John installed a new router that's running more slowly than it should. He suspects some type of mismatch between the Ethernet frame and the frame needed by the DSL. When he tries to ping the router, though, he gets no response. He can access the router through its Web interface just fine. What could the problem be?

    A. The connection between his system and the router is down.

    B. The router is an MTU black hole.

    C. The MTU mismatch has blocked ping.

    D. The router is running PMTU.

8. Melissa replaced a faulty SFP with another one from the server room. The new one doesn't enable a connection. What's an option to fix the problem?

    A. Replace the router.

    B. Replace the server.

    C. Replace the new SFP.

    D. Reinstall Windows Server.

9. Which of the following is a dedicated computer that's preconfigured to offer file storage for many types of client computers?

    A. Active Directory

    B. NAS

    C. PAN

    D. SPAN

10. What type of electrical setup is ideal for a network closet?

    A. Circuits shared with no more than two other locations

    B. Dedicated circuit

    C. High-voltage circuit

    D. Any circuit will do.

Answers

1. **A.** The first thing to do when designing a network is to define the needs of that network. Everything else should follow.

2. **A.** The installer needs to label the cable runs, certainly, but in terms of documentation, he or she should show the length of the runs, the cable type used, and the floor plan.

3. **D.** The server closet must have proper cooling and a dedicated circuit.

4. **B.** A lights-out management program enables you to access a server that's powered down.

5. **A.** Both A and C are valid for private IP addresses, but the more unusual number is the better option.

6. **B.** A high-speed WAN interface card enables you to add a port to router.

7. **B.** The router is refusing ICMP packets, thus it's an MTU black hole.

8. **C.** The simplest solution is to replace the SFP, preferably with a known good device.

9. **B.** A network access server (NAS) is a dedicated computer that's preconfigured to offer file storage for many types of client computers.

10. **B.** Ideally, you want the server closet to have a dedicated, high-amperage circuit.

Network Troubleshooting

The CompTIA Network+ certification exam expects you to know how to

- 1.8 Given a scenario, implement the following network troubleshooting methodology:
  - Identify the problem
  - Establish a theory of probable cause
  - Test the theory to determine cause
  - Establish a plan of action to resolve the problem and identify potential effects
  - Implement the solution or escalate as necessary
  - Verify full system functionality and if applicable implement preventative measures
  - Document findings, actions and outcomes
- 2.5 Given a scenario, troubleshoot common router and switch problems: switching loop
- 3.6 Given a scenario, troubleshoot common physical connectivity problems: open short
- 4.2 Given a scenario, use appropriate hardware tools to troubleshoot connectivity issues: cable tester, cable certifier, protocol analyzer
- 4.3 Given a scenario, use appropriate software tools to troubleshoot connectivity issues

To achieve these goals, you must be able to

- Describe appropriate troubleshooting tools and their functions
- Analyze and discuss the troubleshooting process
- Tackle a variety of troubleshooting scenarios

Have you ever seen a tech walk up to a network and seem to know all the answers, effortlessly typing in a few commands and magically making the system or network work? I've always been intrigued by how they do this. Observing such techs over the years, I've noticed that they tend to follow the same steps for similar problems—looking in the same places, typing the same commands, and so on.

When someone performs a task the same way every time, I figure they're probably following a plan. They understand what tools they have to work with, and they know where to start and what to do second and third and fourth until they find the problem.

This chapter's lofty goal is to consolidate my observations on how these "übertechs" fix networks. I'll show you the primary troubleshooting tools and help you formulate a troubleshooting process and learn where to look for different sorts of problems. At the end of the chapter, you'll apply this knowledge to some common troubleshooting scenarios.

Test Specific

Troubleshooting Tools

While working through the process of finding a problem's cause, you sometimes need tools. These tools are the software and hardware tools that provide information about your network and enact repairs. I covered a number of tools already: hardware tools like cable testers and crimpers, plus software utilities like ping and tracert. The trick is knowing when and how to use these tools to solve your network problems.

 CAUTION No matter what the problem, always consider the safety of your data first. Ask yourself this question before performing any troubleshooting action: "Can what I'm about to do potentially damage my data?"

Almost every new networking person I teach will, at some point, ask me: "What tools do I need to buy?" My answer shocks them: "None. Don't buy a thing." It's not so much that you don't need tools, but more that different networking jobs require wildly different tools. Plenty of network techs never crimp a cable. An equal number never open a system. Some techs do nothing all day but pull cable. The tools you need are defined by your job. You'll know by the end of the first day what you'll need.

This answer is especially true with software tools. Almost all the network problems I encounter in established networks don't require me to use any tools other than the classic ones provided by the operating system. I've fixed more network problems with ping than with any other single tool. As you gain skill in this area, you'll find yourself hounded by vendors trying to sell you the latest and greatest networking diagnostic tools. You may like these tools. All I can say is that I've never needed a software diagnostics tool that I had to purchase.

Hardware Tools

In multiple chapters in this book, you've read about a few hardware tools used to configure a network. These *hardware tools* include cable testers, TDRs, OTDRs, certifiers, voltage event recorders, protocol analyzers, cable strippers, multimeters, tone probes/ generators, butt sets, and punchdown tools. Some of these tools can also be used in troubleshooting scenarios to help you eliminate or narrow down the possible causes of certain problems. Let's review the tools as listed in the CompTIA Network+ exam objectives.

EXAM TIP Read this section! The CompTIA Network+ exam is filled with repair scenarios, and you must know what every tool does and when to use it.

Cable Testers, TDRs, and OTDRs

The vast majority of cabling problems occur when the network is first installed or when a change is made. Once a cable has been made, installed, and tested, the chances of it failing are pretty small compared to all of the other network problems that might take place. Imagine what happens when you can't connect to a resource and ask yourself, "Could the cable be bad?" Broken cables don't make intermittent problems, and they don't slow down data. They make permanent disconnects.

Network techs define a "broken" cable in numerous ways. First, a broken cable might have an *open circuit*, where one or more of the wires in a cable simply don't connect from one end of the cable to the other. The signal lacks *continuity*. Second, a cable might have a *short*, where one or more of the wires in a cable connect to another wire in the cable. (Within a normal cable, no wires connect to other wires.) Third, a cable might have a *wire map problem*, where one or more of the wires in a cable don't connect to the proper location on the jack or plug. This can be caused by improperly crimping a cable, for example. Fourth, the cable might experience *crosstalk*, where the electrical signal bleeds from one wire pair to another, creating interference. Fifth, a broken cable might pick up *noise*, spurious signals usually caused by faulty hardware or poorly crimped jacks. Finally, a broken cable might have *impedance mismatch*. Impedance is the natural electrical resistance of a cable. When cables of different types—think thickness, composition of the metal, and so on—connect and the flow of electrons is not uniform, it can cause a unique type of electrical noise, called an *echo*.

EXAM TIP The CompTIA Network+ objectives use the term *open short* at the time of this writing. There should be a comma after "open," however, so you know you're looking at two different types of broken cable issues.

Network technicians use three different devices to deal with broken cables. *Cable testers* can tell you if you have a continuity problem or if a wire map isn't correct (Figure 20-1). *Time domain reflectometers (TDRs)* and *optical time domain reflectometers (OTDRs)* can tell you where the break is on the cable (Figure 20-2). A TDR works with copper cables and an OTDR works with fiber optics, but otherwise they share the same function. If a problem shows itself as a disconnect and you've first checked easier issues that would manifest as disconnects, such as loss of permissions, an unplugged cable, or a server shut off, then think about using these tools.

Figure 20-1

Typical cable tester

Figure 20-2

An EXFO AXS-100 OTDR (photo courtesy of EXFO)

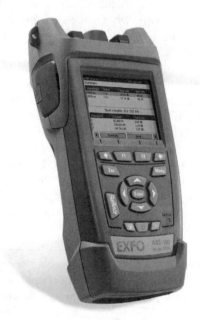

Cable Certifiers

Certifiers test a cable to ensure that it can handle its rated amount of capacity. When a cable is unbroken but not moving data the way it should, turn to a certifier. Look for problems that cause a cable to underperform. A bad installation might increase crosstalk, attenuation, or interference. A certifier can pick up an impedance mismatch as well. Most of these problems show up at installation, but running a certifier to eliminate cabling as a problem is never a bad idea. Don't use a certifier for disconnects, only slowdowns. All certifiers need some kind of loopback on the other end of the cable run.

Voltage Event Recorder/Temperature Monitor

Networks need the proper temperature and adequate power, but most network techs tend to view these issues as outside of the normal places to look for problems. That's too bad, because both heat and power problems invariably manifest themselves as intermittent problems. Look for problems that might point to heat or power issues: server rooms that get too hot at certain times of the day, switches that fail whenever an air conditioning system kicks on, and so on. You can use a *voltage event recorder* and a *temperature monitor* to monitor server rooms over time to detect and record issues with electricity or heat, respectively. They're great for those "something happened last night" types of issues.

Protocol Analyzers

Protocol analyzers monitor the different protocols running at different layers on the network. A good protocol analyzer will give you Application, Session, Transport, Network, and Data Link layer information on every frame going through your network. Even though the CompTIA Network+ exam places protocol analyzers in a hardware category, they aren't necessarily always hardware. Some of the best and most useful protocol analyzers, like Wireshark, are software.

Use a protocol analyzer when being able to see the data on the network will help you answer these questions: Is something trying to start a session and not getting an answer? Maybe a DNS server isn't responding. Is some computer on the network placing confusing information on the network? Is a rogue DHCP server sending out responses to DHCP requests? In the same vein, a protocol analyzer helps you determine slowdowns on a network by giving you an idea of excess or unexpected traffic (see the "Packet Sniffer" subsection under "Software Tools" later in this chapter).

Cable Strippers/Snips

A *cable stripper* or *snip* (Figure 20-3) helps you to make UTP cables. Even though the CompTIA Network+ competencies don't mention crimpers, don't forget you'll need them, too. You don't need these tools to punch down 66- or 110-blocks. You would use a punchdown tool for that.

Figure 20-3
A cable stripping and crimping tool

Multimeters

Multimeters test voltage (both AC and DC), resistance, and continuity. They are the unsung heroes of cabling infrastructures because no other tool can tell you how much voltage is on a line. They are also a great fallback for continuity testing when you don't have a cable tester handy.

EXAM TIP There's an old adage used by carpenters and other craftspeople that goes, "Never buy cheap tools." Cheap tools save you money at the beginning, but they often break more readily than higher-quality tools and, more importantly, make it harder to get the job done. This adage definitely applies to multimeters! You might be tempted to go for the $10 model that looks pretty much like the $25 model, but chances are the leads will break or the readings will lie on the cheaper model. Buy a decent tool, and you'll never have to worry about it.

Tone Probes and Tone Generators

Tone probes and their partners, *tone generators,* have only one job: to help you locate a particular cable. You'll never use a tone probe without a tone generator.

EXAM TIP The CompTIA Network+ exam and many techs refer to the probe as a *toner probe* rather than a *tone probe* or simply a *probe*. Don't be surprised by this terminology on the exam. You always need both a probe and a tone generator to use this tool properly.

Butt Sets

Butt sets are the telephone person's best friend. Use a butt set to tap into a 66- or 110-block to see if a particular line is working.

Punchdown Tools

Punchdown tools (Figure 20-4) put UTP wires into 66- and 110-blocks. The only time you would use a punchdown tool in a diagnostic environment is a quick repunch of a connection to make sure all the contacts are properly set.

Figure 20-4
A punchdown
tool in action

Software Tools

Make the CompTIA Network+ exam (and real life) easier by separating your software tools into two groups: those that come built into every operating system and those that are third-party tools. Typical built-in tools are tracert/traceroute, ipconfig/ifconfig, ping, arping, nslookup/dig, hostname, route, nbtstat, and netstat. Third-party tools fall into the categories of packet sniffers, port scanners, and throughput testers.

 EXAM TIP The CompTIA Network+ exam tests your ability to recognize the output from all of the built-in tools. Take some time to memorize example outputs from all of these tools.

The tracert/traceroute Commands

The *traceroute* command (the actual command in Windows is *tracert*) is used to trace all of the routers between two points. Use traceroute to diagnose where the problem lies when you have problems reaching a remote system. If a traceroute stops at a certain router, you know the problem is either the next router or the connections between them. Because many routers block the ICMP packets containing traceroute information, traceroute isn't perfect. Here's sample traceroute output:

```
Tracing route to adsl-208-190-121-38.dsl.hstntx.swbell.net

[208.190.121.38] over a maximum of 30 hops:

   1     1 ms     <1 ms     1 ms    Router.totalhome
[192.168.4.1]

   2    38 ms     41 ms     70 ms   adsl-208-190-121-
38.dsl.hstntx.swbell.net [208.190.121.38]
```

 NOTE This section contains many command-line tools that you've seen earlier in the book in various places. Now is a great time to refresh your memory about how each one works, so after I review each command, run it yourself. Then type **help** followed by the command to see the available switches for that command. Run the command with some of the switches to see what they do. Running them is more fun than just reading about it; plus, you'll solidify the knowledge you need to master.

The ipconfig/ifconfig Commands

The *ipconfig* (Windows) and *ifconfig* (UNIX/Linux/Mac) commands tell you almost anything you want to know about a particular computer's IP settings. Make sure you know that typing `ipconfig` alone only gives basic information. Typing `ipconfig /all` gives detailed information (like DNS servers and MAC addresses).

Here's sample ipconfig output:

```
Ethernet adapter Main:

    Connection-specific DNS Suffix  . :
    IPv6 Address. . . . . . . . . . . : 2001:470:bf88:1:fc2d:aeb2:99d2:e2b4
    Temporary IPv6 Address. . . . . . : 2001:470:bf88:1:5e4:c1ef:7b30:ddd6
    Link-local IPv6 Address . . . . . : fe80::fc2d:aeb2:99d2:e2b4%8
    IPv4 Address. . . . . . . . . . . : 192.168.4.27
    Subnet Mask . . . . . . . . . . . : 255.255.255.0
    Default Gateway . . . . . . . . . : fe80::223:4ff:fe8c:b720%8
                                        192.168.4.1

Tunnel adapter Local Area Connection* 6:

    Media State . . . . . . . . . . . : Media disconnected
    Connection-specific DNS Suffix  . :
```

And here's sample ifconfig output:

```
eth0    Link encap:Ethernet  HWaddr 00:02:b3:8a:7d:ae
        inet addr:192.168.4.19  Bcast:192.168.4.255  Mask:255.255.255.0
        inet6 addr: 2001:470:bf88:1:202:b3ff:fe8a:7dae/64 Scope:Global
        inet6 addr: fe80::202:b3ff:fe8a:7dae/64 Scope:Link
        UP BROADCAST RUNNING MULTICAST  MTU:1500  Metric:1
        RX packets:2206320 errors:0 dropped:0 overruns:0 frame:0
        TX packets:925034 errors:0 dropped:0 overruns:0 carrier:0
        collisions:0 txqueuelen:1000
        RX bytes:292522698 (292.5 MB)  TX bytes:132985596 (132.9 MB)

lo      Link encap:Local Loopback
        inet addr:127.0.0.1  Mask:255.0.0.0
        inet6 addr: ::1/128 Scope:Host
        UP LOOPBACK RUNNING  MTU:16436  Metric:1
        RX packets:15414 errors:0 dropped:0 overruns:0 frame:0
        TX packets:15414 errors:0 dropped:0 overruns:0 carrier:0
        collisions:0 txqueuelen:0
        RX bytes:1006671 (1.0 MB)  TX bytes:1006671 (1.0 MB)
```

The ping and arping Commands

The *ping* command uses Internet Message Control Protocol (ICMP) packets to query by IP or by name. It works across routers, so it's generally the first tool used to check if a system is reachable. Unfortunately, many devices block ICMP packets, so a failed ping doesn't always point to an offline system.

If ping doesn't work you can try *arping*, which uses Address Resolution Protocol (ARP) frames instead of ICMP. The only downside to arping is that ARP frames do not cross routers because they only consist of frames and never IP packets, so you can only use it within a broadcast domain. Windows does not have arping. UNIX and UNIX-like systems, on the other hand, support the arping utility. Here's sample ping output:

```
Pinging 192.168.4.19 with 32 bytes of data:
Reply from 192.168.4.19: bytes=32 time<1ms TTL=64
Reply from 192.168.4.19: bytes=32 time<1ms TTL=64
Reply from 192.168.4.19: bytes=32 time<1ms TTL=64
Reply from 192.168.4.19: bytes=32 time<1ms TTL=64
```

```
Ping statistics for 192.168.4.19:
    Packets: Sent = 4, Received = 4, Lost = 0 (0% loss),
Approximate round trip times in milli-seconds:
    Minimum = 0ms, Maximum = 0ms, Average = 0ms
```

Next is sample arping output:

```
ARPING 192.168.4.27 from 192.168.4.19 eth0
Unicast reply from 192.168.4.27 [00:1D:60:DD:92:C6]   0.875ms
Unicast reply from 192.168.4.27 [00:1D:60:DD:92:C6]   0.897ms
Unicast reply from 192.168.4.27 [00:1D:60:DD:92:C6]   0.924ms
Unicast reply from 192.168.4.27 [00:1D:60:DD:92:C6]   0.977ms
```

EXAM TIP The ping command has the word `Pinging` in the output. The arping command has the word `ARPING`. Don't assume that the CompTIA Network+ exam will include those words in its sample outputs, however.

NOTE The ping (along with traceroute) commands are excellent examples of *connectivity software*, applications that enable you to determine if a connection can be made between two computers.

The nslookup/dig Commands

The *nslookup* (all operating systems) and *dig* (UNIX/Linux/Mac) commands are used to diagnose DNS problems. These tools are very powerful, but the CompTIA Network+ exam won't ask you more than basic questions, such as how to use them to see if a DNS server is working. The nslookup command is a poor tool that most everyone considers obsolete. The dig command is far more powerful. The dig example shows the output of this command:

```
dig mx totalsem.com
```

This command says, "Show me all the MX records for the totalsem.com domain."
    Here's the output for that dig command:

```
; <<>> DiG 9.5.0-P2 <<>> mx totalsem.com
;; global options:  printcmd
;; Got answer:
;; ->>HEADER<<- opcode: QUERY, status: NOERROR, id: 6070
;; flags: qr rd ra; QUERY: 1, ANSWER: 3, AUTHORITY: 0, ADDITIONAL: 1
;; QUESTION SECTION:
;totalsem.com.                  IN      MX
;; ANSWER SECTION:
totalsem.com.   86400           IN      MX      10      mx1c1.megamailservers.com.
totalsem.com.   86400           IN      MX      100     mx2c1.megamailservers.com.
totalsem.com.   86400           IN      MX      110     mx3c1.megamailservers.com.
```

EXAM TIP Running the networking commands several times will help you memorize the functions of the commands as well as the syntax. The CompTIA Network+ exam is also big on the switches available for various commands, such as `ipconfig /all`.

The hostname Command

The *hostname* command is the simplest of all the utilities shown here. When you run it, it returns with the host name of the computer you are on. Here's what it looked like when I ran it on my Windows 7 box:

```
C:\>
C:\>hostname
mike-win7
```

The mtr Command

My traceroute (mtr) is a dynamic (keeps running) equivalent to traceroute. Windows does not support mtr.

Here's a sample of mtr output:

```
                          My traceroute  [v0.73]
totaltest (0.0.0.0)
Keys:  Help  Display mode  Restart statistics  Order of fields  quit
                                 Packets              Pings
Host                          Loss%  Snt  Last  Avg  Best  Wrst  StDev
1. Router.totalhome           0.0%    5   0.8   0.8  0.7   0.9   0.1
2. adsl-208-190-121-38.dsl.hstntx.s 0.0%  4  85.7  90.7 69.5 119.2  20.8
```

The route Command

The *route* command gives you the capability to display and edit the local system's routing table. To show the routing table, just type **route print** or **netstat -r**.

Here's a sample of route print output:

```
===========================================================================

Interface List

8 ...00 1d 60 dd 92 c6 ...... Marvell 88E8056 PCI-E Ethernet Controller
1 ......................... Software Loopback Interface 1
===========================================================================
IPv4 Route Table
===========================================================================
Active Routes:
Network Destination        Netmask          Gateway        Interface  Metric
        0.0.0.0            0.0.0.0      192.168.4.1     192.168.4.27     10
      127.0.0.0          255.0.0.0        On-link         127.0.0.1    306
      127.0.0.1    255.255.255.255        On-link         127.0.0.1    306
127.255.255.255    255.255.255.255        On-link         127.0.0.1    306
    169.254.0.0        255.255.0.0        On-link      192.168.4.27    286
169.254.214.185    255.255.255.255        On-link   169.254.214.185    276
169.254.255.255    255.255.255.255        On-link      192.168.4.27    266
    192.168.4.0      255.255.255.0        On-link      192.168.4.27    266
```

```
     192.168.4.27       255.255.255.255     On-link        192.168.4.27      266
    192.168.4.255       255.255.255.255     On-link        192.168.4.27      266
        224.0.0.0           240.0.0.0       On-link          127.0.0.1       306
        224.0.0.0           240.0.0.0       On-link     169.254.214.185      276
        224.0.0.0           240.0.0.0       On-link        192.168.4.27      266
  255.255.255.255       255.255.255.255     On-link          127.0.0.1       306
  255.255.255.255       255.255.255.255     On-link     169.254.214.185      276
  255.255.255.255       255.255.255.255     On-link        192.168.4.27      266
===========================================================================
Persistent Routes:

None
```

The nbtstat Command

The *nbtstat* command is a Windows-only program that can best be described as a command-line pseudo-equivalent to Window's My Network Places or Network icon. Always run nbtstat with a switch. The most useful switch is −n, which shows the local NetBIOS names. All versions of Windows include nbtstat. Running nbtstat is a handy way to see what systems are on your Windows network. Any systems running Samba will also appear here.

Here's an example of running nbtstat −n from the command prompt:

```
Main:
Node IpAddress: [192.168.4.27] Scope Id: []
                 NetBIOS Local Name Table
         Name              Type          Status
--------------------------------------------------
       MIKESPC     <00>  UNIQUE      Registered
     TOTALHOME     <00>  GROUP       Registered
       MIKESPC     <20>  UNIQUE      Registered
     TOTALHOME     <1E>  GROUP       Registered
```

The netstat Command

The *netstat* command is a very handy tool that displays information on the current state of all of your running IP processes. It shows what sessions are active and can also provide statistics based on ports or protocols (TCP, UDP, and so on). Typing netstat by itself only shows current sessions. Typing netstat −r shows the routing table (100 percent identical to route print). If you want to know about your current sessions, netstat is the tool to use.

Here's sample netstat output:

```
Active Connections

  Proto   Local Address            Foreign Address         State
  TCP     127.0.0.1:27015          MikesPC:51090           ESTABLISHED
  TCP     127.0.0.1:51090          MikesPC:27015           ESTABLISHED
  TCP     127.0.0.1:52500          MikesPC:52501           ESTABLISHED
  TCP     192.168.4.27:54731       72-165-61-141:27039     CLOSE_WAIT
  TCP     192.168.4.27:55080       63-246-140-18:http      CLOSE_WAIT
  TCP     192.168.4.27:56126       acd4129913:https        ESTABLISHED
  TCP     192.168.4.27:62727       TOTALTEST:ssh           ESTABLISHED
  TCP     192.168.4.27:63325       65.54.165.136:https     TIME_WAIT
  TCP     192.168.4.27:63968       209.8.115.129:http      ESTABLISHED
```

Packet Sniffer

Packet sniffer, protocol analyzer, or *packet analyzer:* All of these names are used to define a tool that intercepts and logs network packets. You have many choices when it comes to packet sniffers. Some sniffers come as programs you run on a computer, while others manifest as dedicated hardware devices. Arguably, the most popular is *Wireshark* (Figure 20-5). You've already seen Wireshark in the book, but here's a screen to jog your memory.

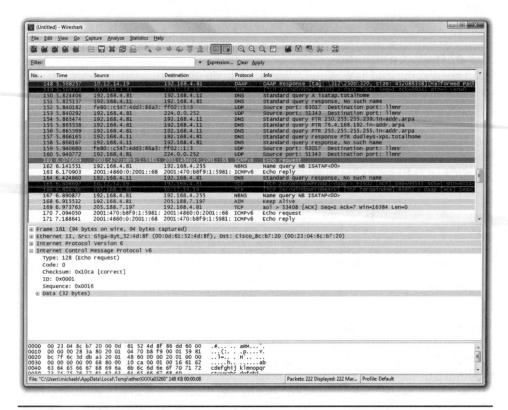

Figure 20-5 Wireshark in action!

You can get the latest version of Wireshark at www.wireshark.org, so I suggest firing up your favorite Web browser and trying this program. Download the executable, and install it on a networked computer. Don't forget to look at the extensive documentation on the Web site to get a sense of all the coolness that is Wireshark.

Port Scanners

A *port scanner* is a program that probes ports on another system, logging the state of the scanned ports. These tools are used to look for unintentionally opened ports that might make a system vulnerable to attack. As you might imagine, they also are used by hackers to break into systems. The most famous of all port scanners is probably the powerful and free Nmap. Nmap was originally designed to work on UNIX systems, so Windows folks looked for alternatives like Angry IP Scanner by Anton Keks (Figure 20-6). Nmap has been ported to just about every operating system these days, however, so you can find it for Windows.

Figure 20-6

Angry IP Scanner

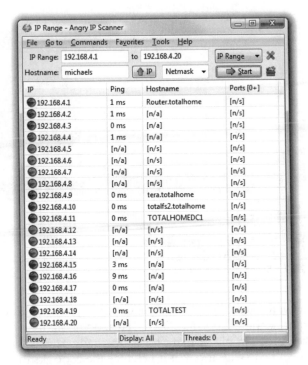

Throughput Testers

Throughput testers enable you to measure the data flow in a network. Which tool is appropriate depends on the type of network throughput you want to test. Most techs use one of several speed-testing Web sites for checking an Internet connection's throughput, such as Speed Test at Speakeasy (Figure 20-7): www.speakeasy.net/speedtest.

The Troubleshooting Process

Troubleshooting is a dynamic, fluid process that requires you to make snap judgments and act on them to try and make the network go. Any attempt to cover every possible scenario would be futile at best, and probably also not in your best interest, because any reference that tried to list every troubleshooting problem would be obsolete the moment it was created. If an exhaustive listing of all network problems is impossible, then how do you decide what to do and in what order?

Figure 20-7   Speed Test results from Speakeasy

Before you touch a single console or cable, you should remember two basic rules: To paraphrase the Hippocratic Oath, "First, do no harm." If at all possible, don't make a network problem bigger than it was originally. This is a rule I've broken thousands of times, and you will, too. But if I change the good doctor's phrase a bit, it's possible to formulate a rule you can actually live with: "First, do not trash the data!" My gosh, if I had a dollar for every megabyte of irreplaceable data I've destroyed, I'd be rich! I've learned my lesson, and you should learn from my mistakes. The second rule is: "Always make good backups!" Computers can be replaced; data that is not backed up is, at best, expensive to recover and, at worst, gone forever.

No matter how complex and fancy, any troubleshooting process can be broken down into simple steps. Having a sequence of steps to follow makes the entire trouble-shooting process simpler and easier, because you have a clear set of goals to achieve in a specific sequence.

The CompTIA Network+ objectives contain a detailed troubleshooting methodology that provides a good starting point for our discussion. Here are the basic steps in the troubleshooting process:

1. Identify the problem.

    A. Gather information.

    B. Identify symptoms.

C. Question users.

D. Determine if anything has changed.

2. Establish a theory of probable cause.

A. Question the obvious.

3. Test the theory to determine cause.

A. Once theory is confirmed, determine next steps to resolve the problem.

B. If theory is not confirmed, reestablish new theory or escalate.

4. Establish a plan of action to resolve the problem and identify potential effects.

5. Implement and test the solution or escalate as necessary.

6. Verify full system functionality and, if applicable, implement preventative measures.

7. Document findings, actions, and outcomes.

Identify the Problem

First, identify the problem. That means grasping the true problem, rather than what someone tells you. A user might call in and complain that he can't access the Internet from his workstation, for example, which could be the only problem. But the problem could also be that the entire wing of the office just went down and you've got a much bigger situation on your hands. You need to gather information, identify symptoms, question users, and determine if anything has changed on the network. Doing this will help you get to the root of the problem.

Gather Information, Identify Symptoms, and Question Users

If you are working directly on the affected system and not relying on somebody on the other end of a telephone to guide you, you will establish the symptoms through your observation of what is (or isn't) happening. If you're troubleshooting over the telephone (always a *joy*, in my experience), you will need to ask questions based on what the user is telling you. These questions can be *closed-ended*, which is to say there can only be a yes-or-no-type answer, such as, "Can you see a light on the front of the monitor?" You can also ask *open-ended* questions, such as, "Tell me what you see on the screen." The type of question you use at any given moment depends on what information you need and on the user's knowledge level. If, for example, the user seems to be technically oriented, you will probably be able to ask more closed-ended questions because they will know what you are talking about. If, on the other hand, the user seems to be confused about what's happening, open-ended questions will allow him or her to explain in his or her own words what is going on.

One of the first steps in trying to determine the cause of a problem is to understand the extent of the problem—is it specific to one user or is it network-wide? Sometimes this entails trying the task yourself, both from the user's machine and from your own or another machine.

For example, if a user is experiencing problems logging into the network, you might need to go to that user's machine and try to use his or her user name to log in. Doing this tells you whether the problem is a user error of some kind, as well as enables you to see the symptoms of the problem yourself. Next, you probably want to try logging in with your own user name from that machine, or have the user try to log in from another machine. In some cases, you can ask other users in the area if they are experiencing the same problem to see if the issue is affecting more than one user. Depending on the size of your network, you should find out whether the problem is occurring in only one part of your company or across the entire network.

What does all of this tell you? Essentially, it tells you how big the problem is. If nobody in an entire remote office can log in, you may be able to assume that the problem is the network link or router connecting that office to the server. If nobody in any office can log in, you may be able to assume the server is down or not accepting logins. If only that one user in that one location can't log in, the problem may be with that user, that machine, or that user's account.

 EXAM TIP Eliminating variables is one of the first tools in your arsenal of diagnostic techniques.

Determine If Anything Has Changed

The goal of this step is to identify if anything has changed that might have caused the problem. You may not have to ask many questions before the person using the problem system can tell you what has changed, but, in some cases, establishing if anything has changed can take quite a bit of time and involve further work behind the scenes. Here are some examples of questions to ask:

- "Tell me exactly what was happening when the problem occurred."
- "Has anything been changed on the system recently?"
- "Has the system been moved recently?"

Notice the way I've tactfully avoided the word *you*, as in "Have *you* changed anything on the system recently?" This is a deliberate tactic to avoid any implied blame on the part of the user. Being nice never hurts, and it makes the whole troubleshooting process more friendly.

You should also *internally* ask yourself some isolating questions, such as "Was that machine involved in the software push last night?" or "Didn't a tech visit that machine this morning?" Note you will only be able to answer these questions if *your* documentation is up to date. Sometimes, isolating a problem may require you to check system and hardware logs (such as those stored by some routers and other network devices), so make sure you know how to do this.

 EXAM TIP Avoid aggressive or accusatory questions.

Establish a Theory of Probable Cause

This step comes down to experience—or good use of the support tools at your disposal, such as your knowledge base. You need to select the most *probable* cause from all the *possible* causes, so the solution you choose fixes the problem the first time. This may not always happen, but whenever possible, you want to avoid spending a whole day stabbing in the dark while the problem snores softly to itself in some cozy, neglected corner of your network.

Don't forget to question the obvious. If Bob can't print to the networked printer, check to see that the printer is plugged in and turned on, for example.

Test the Theory to Determine Cause

With the third step, you need to test the theory, but do so without changing anything or risking any repercussions. If you have determined that the probable cause for Bob not being able to print is that the printer is turned off, go look. If that's the case, then you should plan out your next step to resolve the problem. Do not act yet! That comes next.

If the probable cause doesn't pan out, you need to go back to step two and determine a new probable cause. Once you have another idea, test it.

The reason you should hesitate to act at this third step is that you might not have permission to make the fix or the fix might cause repercussions you don't fully understand yet. For example, if you walk over to the print server room to see if the printer is powered up and online and find the door padlocked, that's a whole different level of problem. Sure, the printer is turned off, but management has done it for a reason. In this sort of situation, you need to escalate the problem.

To *escalate* has two meanings: either to inform other parties about a problem for guidance or to pass the job off to another authority who has control over the device/issue that's most probably causing the problem. Let's say you have a server with a bad NIC. This server is used heavily by the accounting department, and taking it down may cause problems you don't even know about. You need to inform the accounting manager to consult with them. Alternatively, you'll come across problems over which you have no control or authority. A badly acting server across the country (hopefully) has another person in charge to whom you need to hand over the job.

Establish a Plan of Action and Identify Potential Effects

By this point, you should have some ideas as to what the problem might be. It's time to "look before you leap." An action plan defines how you are going to fix this problem. Most problems are simple, but if the problem is complex, you need to write down the steps. As you do this, think about what else might happen as you go about the repair. If you take out a switch without a replacement switch at hand, the users might experience excessive downtime while you hunt for a new switch and move them over. If you replace a router, can you restore all the old router's settings to the new one or will you have to rebuild from scratch?

Implement and Test the Solution or Escalate as Necessary

Once you think you have isolated the cause of the problem, you should decide what you think is the best way to fix it and then try your solution, whether that's giving advice over the phone to a user, installing a replacement part, or adding a software patch. All the way through this step, try only one likely solution at a time. There's no point in installing several patches at once because then you can't tell which one fixed the problem. Similarly, there's no point in replacing several items of hardware (such as a hard disk and its controller cable) at the same time, because then you can't tell which part (or parts) was faulty.

As you try each possibility, always *document* what you do and what results you get. This isn't just for a future problem either—during a lengthy troubleshooting process, it's easy to forget exactly what you tried two hours before or which thing you tried produced a particular result. Although being methodical may take longer, it will save time the next time—and it may enable you to pinpoint what needs to be done to stop the problem from recurring at all, thereby reducing future call volume to your support team—and as any support person will tell you, that's definitely worth the effort!

Then you need to test the solution. This is the part everybody hates. Once you think you've fixed a problem, you should try to make it happen again. If you can't, great! But sometimes you will be able to re-create the problem, and then you know you haven't finished the job at hand. Many techs want to slide away quietly as soon as everything seems to be fine, but trust me on this, it won't impress your customer when her problem flares up again 30 seconds after you've left the building—not to mention that you get the joy of another two-hour car trip the next day to fix the same problem, for an even more unhappy client! In the scenario where you are providing support to someone else rather than working directly on the problem, you should make *her* try to re-create the problem. This tells you whether she understands what you have been telling her and educates her at the same time, lessening the chance that she'll call you back later and ask, "Can we just go through that one more time?"

 EXAM TIP Always test a solution before you walk away from the job!

Verify Full System Functionality and Implement Preventative Measures

Okay, now that you have changed something on the system in the process of solving one problem, you must think about the wider repercussions of what you have done. If you've replaced a faulty NIC in a server, for instance, will the fact that the MAC address has changed (remember, it's built into the NIC) affect anything else, such as the logon security controls or your network management and inventory software? If you've installed a patch on a client PC, will this change the default protocol or any other default settings that may affect other functionality? If you've changed a user's security settings, will this affect his or her ability to access other network resources? This is part of testing your solution to make sure it works properly, but it also makes you think about the impact of your work on the system as a whole.

Make sure you test the full system so you don't have to have a second tech call to resolve an outstanding issue. This saves time and money and helps your customer do his or her job better. Everybody wins.

Also at this time, if applicable, implement measures to avoid a repeat of the problem. If that means you need to educate the user to do or not do something, teach him or her tactfully. If you need to install software or patch a system, do it now.

Document Findings, Actions, and Outcomes

It is *vital* that you document the problem, symptoms, and solutions of all support calls for two reasons: First, you're creating a support database to serve as a knowledge base for future reference, enabling everyone on the support team to identify new problems as they arise and know how to deal with them quickly, without having to duplicate someone else's research efforts. Second, documentation enables you to track problem trends and anticipate future workloads, or even to identify a particular brand or model of an item, such as a printer or a NIC, that seems to be less reliable or that creates more work for you than others. Don't skip this step—it *really* is essential!

EXAM TIP   Memorize these problem analysis steps:

1. Identify the problem.
    A. Gather information.
    B. Identify symptoms.
    C. Question users.
    D. Determine if anything has changed.

2. Establish a theory of probable cause.
    A. Question the obvious.

3. Test the theory to determine cause.
    A. Once the theory is confirmed, determine the next steps to resolve the problem.
    B. If a theory is not confirmed, reestablish a new theory or escalate.

4. Establish a plan of action to resolve the problem and identify potential effects.

5. Implement and test the solution or escalate as necessary.

6. Verify full system functionality and, if applicable, implement preventative measures.

7. Document findings, actions, and outcomes.

Troubleshooting Scenarios

I want to end this chapter with some good troubleshooting scenarios. Take some time and think about these situations and how you would handle them. What questions would you ask? What tests would you do first? The CompTIA Network+ exam absolutely *loves* to ask scenario questions. The knowledge from the previous chapters combined with the methods you've learned in this chapter should enable you to fix any network!

"I Can't Log In!"

One of the most complex troubleshooting issues is that one set of symptoms, in this case a user's inability to log in, can have many causes. Suppose Woody has called complaining that he cannot log into the company's intranet. Tina Tech first tries accessing the intranet site from her system and finds she has no problem. Tina might also want to have other users try to log in or confirm that other users are not having the same problem. Next, Tina should have Woody try to log in from another machine. This helps Tina determine whether the problem lies with Woody's user account's capability to log in, with Woody's system, or with some connectivity issue.

If Woody is unable to log in from another machine, Tina should probably check to be sure Woody is using the correct login ID, password, and procedure when he logs in. On the other hand, if Woody can log in from another user's system, Tina should probably focus on determining whether Woody's system is working properly and connecting to the network. One step she could try here is to ping Woody's system. If Tina can ping Woody's machine successfully, she knows that the machine is up, the TCP/IP protocol is configured correctly, and the system is connected to the network. Tina might then check the configuration of the network client on Woody's system. If Tina is not able to ping the system, however, she might need to test the cables and NIC using cable testers or loopback devices, and verify that TCP/IP was correctly configured using ipconfig.

"I Can't Get to This Web Site!"

Reaching external Web sites requires that a variety of components be configured correctly. Some of these components are within your company's internal control; many of them are not. When Fatima calls and tells Tina Tech that she cannot reach www.comptia.org, Tina's first step is to try to reach that site herself. In this case, Tina was also unable to get a response from the comptia.org site. One of her next steps is to ping the site, first by name, and then by IP address. In this case, she gets no response by name, but she does get a normal response when she pings the site by IP address. This immediately indicates to her that the problem is name resolution; in this case, its DNS.

On the other hand, had Tina been unable to ping successfully using either the IP address or domain name, she should consider two possibilities. First, if her company uses a firewall or proxy server to reach the Internet, she should ping that machine. This machine usually has the same IP address as the default gateway TCP/IP setting. If Tina can successfully ping her default gateway, she can be almost certain that the problem is not something she or her company has any control over. To verify this, Tina should attempt to reach some other external sites, both by using ping and a Web browser. If she can reach other sites successfully, the problem is most likely with the comptia.org site.

"Our Web Server Is Sluggish!"

Slow response from a server can be related to a variety of things. Usually, however, the problem can be traced to a connection to the server or to the server itself. When Wanda calls in from working at home and tells Tina Tech that she is getting a slow response from the company's Web site, Tina Tech leaps into action. Tina tries to reach the offending server and is immediately connected; this indicates a connectivity problem for that user. She asks Wanda to execute a tracert command from her system to the slow server. This reveals to Tina that the slowdown stems from one of the intermediate steps through which Wanda's system connects to the server. Because of this, the problem is out of Tina's hands, unless she can offer a direct dial-up option for Wanda.

If Tina finds she cannot reach the offending server quickly when she tries from her system, then the problem may lie with the server itself. Tina checks the Change Log for the Web server to see if anyone has changed anything recently. She discovers that a new antivirus component was recently added, so she checks the vendor's Web site to make sure there are no known problems or patches for that piece of software. She also uses Performance Monitor to compare the server's current responses to the baseline that she previously recorded. This shows her that the bottleneck is related to excessive paging, indicating that the server may need more physical memory, or RAM.

"I Can't See Anything on the Network!"

When a user is completely cut off from the network, the problem is usually limited to that user's system or network connection. When Tina gets a call from Johnny saying his Windows machine is on, but that he can't log in and can't see any other machines on the company's TCP/IP network, Tina goes to Johnny's office to run some tests. The first test Tina runs is to ping an external machine. She doesn't expect it to work, but tests just to be certain. Next, she tries to ping Johnny's machine using either `ping localhost` or `ping 127.0.0.1` (remember the loopback address?). When this ping doesn't work, Tina guesses that the problem is in the TCP/IP configuration. To view the machine's TCP/IP configuration, Tina uses ipconfig, and notices the IP address is blank. After checking her network documentation to verify what IP address Johnny's machine should have, she adds the IP address, and he is able to connect to the network.

If Tina's `ping 127.0.0.1` had worked, she would have had to assume the TCP/IP and networking configuration of Johnny's machine was correct. She should then check the hardware, using a network card utility to verify that the NIC itself is working correctly, and a cable tester to verify that the cable from Johnny's system is operating properly. In this case, the cable tester shows the cable is bad, so she replaces the cable between Johnny's system and the patch panel, and he is able to connect.

"It's Time to Escalate!"

No single person is truly in control of an entire Internet-connected network. Large organizations split network support duties into very skill-specific areas: routers, cable infrastructure, user administration, and so on. Even in a tiny network with a single network support person, problems will arise that go beyond the tech's skill level or that involve equipment the organization doesn't own (usually it's their ISP's gear). In these situations, the tech needs to identify the problem and, instead of trying to fix it on his or her own, escalate the issue.

In network troubleshooting, problem escalation should occur when you face a problem that falls outside the scope of your skills and you need help. In large organizations, escalation problems have very clear procedures, such as who to call and what to document. In small organizations, escalation often is nothing more than a technician realizing that he or she needs help. The CompTIA Network+ competencies define some classic networking situations that CompTIA feels should be escalated. Here's how to recognize broadcast storms, switching loops, routing problems, routing loops, and proxy ARP.

Broadcast Storms

A *broadcast storm* is the result of one or more devices sending a nonstop flurry of broadcast frames on the network. The first sign of a broadcast storm is when every computer on the broadcast domain suddenly can't connect to the rest of the network. There are usually no clues other than network applications freezing or presenting "can't connect to…" types of error messages. Every activity light on every node is solidly on. Computers on other broadcast domains work perfectly well.

The trick is to isolate; that's where escalation comes in. You need to break down the network quickly by unplugging devices until you can find the one causing trouble. Getting a packet analyzer to work can be difficult, but at least try. If you can scoop up one packet, you'll know what node is causing the trouble. The second the bad node is disconnected, the network returns to normal. But if you have a lot of machines to deal with and a bunch of users who can't get on the network yelling at you, you need help. Call a supervisor to get support to solve the crisis as quickly as possible.

Switching Loops

Also known as a *bridge loop*, a *switching loop* is when you connect multiple switches together to cause a loop to appear. Switching loops are rare because most switches use the Spanning Tree Protocol (STP), but they do happen. The symptoms are identical to a broadcast storm: every computer on the broadcast domain can no longer access the network.

The good part about switching loops is that they rarely take place on a well-running network. Someone had to create that loop and that means someone, somewhere is messing with patch cables. Escalate the problem, and get the team to help you find the person making changes to the switches.

Routing Problems

Improperly configured routers aren't going to send packets to the proper destination. The symptoms are clear: every system that uses the misconfigured router as a default gateway is either not able to get packets out or not able to get packets in, or sometimes both. Web pages don't come up, FTP servers suddenly disappear, and e-mail clients can't access their servers. In these cases, you need to verify first that everything in your area of responsibility works. If that is true, then escalate the problem and find the person responsible for the router.

 EXAM TIP If you want to prevent downtime due to a failure on your default gateway, you should consider buying Cisco routers with *Hot Standby Router Protocol (HSRP)*. This Cisco-only feature enables you to configure two or more routers—one router acting as the primary router and one or more routers acting as backup routers. If the primary router fails, one of the backup routers automatically takes over. The power of HSRP is transparency and quick response. When properly configured, your users will never know if the primary router fails.

Routing Loops

A *routing loop* occurs when interconnected routers loop traffic, causing the routers to respond slowly or not respond at all. Dynamic routing protocols sometimes cause routing loops when a router goes down, but most routing loops are caused by static routes. Your big clue is a huge amount of traffic—far more than your usual traffic—on the links between the routers. Router loops never cause individual computers to stop responding (unless they happen to be on the same broadcast domain as the looping packets). As with any routing problem, be able to recognize the symptoms and escalate.

Proxy ARP

Proxy ARP is the process of making remotely connected computers truly act as though they are on the same LAN as local computers. Proxy ARPs are done in a number of different ways, with a Virtual Private Network (VPN) as the classic example. If a laptop in an airport connects to a network through a VPN, that computer takes on the network ID of your local network. In order for all this to work, the VPN concentrator needs to allow some very LAN-type traffic to go through it that would normally never get through a router. ARP is a great example. If your VPN client wants to talk to another computer on the LAN, it has to ARP to get the IP address. Your VPN device is designed to act as a proxy for all that type of data.

Almost all proxy ARP problems take place on the VPN concentrator. With misconfigured proxy ARP settings, the VPN concentrator can send what looks like a denial of service (DoS) attack on the LAN. (A DoS attack is usually directed at a server exposed on the Internet, like a Web server. See Chapter 16 for more details on these and other malicious attacks.) If your clients start receiving a large number of packets from the VPN concentrator, assume you have a proxy ARP problem and escalate by getting the person in charge of the VPN to fix it.

Troubleshooting Is Fun!

The art of network troubleshooting can be a fun, frolicsome, and frequently frustrating feature of your network career. By applying a good troubleshooting methodology and constantly increasing your knowledge of networks, you too can develop into a great troubleshooting artist. Developing your artistry takes time, naturally, but stick with it. Begin the training. Use the Force. Learn new stuff, document problems and fixes, talk to other network techs about similar problems. Every bit of knowledge and experience you gain will make things that much easier for you when crunch time comes and a network disaster occurs—and as any experienced network tech can tell you, it will occur, even on the most robust network.

Chapter Review

Questions

1. When should you use a cable tester to troubleshoot a network cable?

   A. When you have a host experiencing a very slow connection

   B. When you have an intermittent connection problem

   C. When you have a dead connection and you suspect a broken cable

   D. When you are trying to find the correct cable up in the plenum

2. What are tone probes and tone generators used for?

   A. Locating a particular cable

   B. Testing the dial tone on a PBX system

   C. A long-duration ping test

   D. As safety equipment when working in crawl spaces

3. What does nslookup do?

   A. Retrieves the name space for the network

   B. Queries DNS for the IP address of the supplied host name

   C. Performs a reverse IP lookup

   D. Lists the current running network services on localhost

4. What is Wireshark?

   A. Protocol analyzer

   B. Packet sniffer

   C. Packet analyzer

   D. All of the above

5. What will the command `route print` return on a Windows system?

   A. The results of the last tracert

   B. The gateway's router table

   C. The routes taken by a concurrent connection

   D. The current system's route table

6. When trying to establish symptoms over the phone, what kind of questions should you ask of a novice or confused user?

   A. You should ask open-ended questions and let the user explain the problem in his or her own words.

   B. You should ask detailed, closed-ended questions to try and narrow down the possible causes.

   C. Leading questions are your best choice for pointing the user in the right direction.

   D. None; ask the user to bring the machine in because it is useless to trouble-shoot over the phone.

7. While you are asking the user problem-isolating questions, what else should you be doing?

   A. Asking yourself if there is anything on your side of the network that could be causing the problem.

   B. Nothing; just keep asking the user questions.

   C. Using an accusatory tone with the user.

   D. Playing solitaire.

8. Once you have implemented your solution, you should always _____.

   A. Close the ticket.

   B. Verify full system functionality.

   C. Return the machine.

   D. Reboot.

9. What is the last step in the troubleshooting process?

   A. Implementing the solution

   B. Testing the solution

   C. Documenting the solution

   D. Closing the help ticket

10. One of your users calls you with a complaint that he can't reach the site www.google.com. You try and access the site and discover you can't connect either, but you can ping the site with its IP address. What is the most probable culprit?

    A. The workgroup switch is down.

    B. Google is down.

    C. The gateway is down.

    D. The DNS server is down.

Answers

1. **C.** Cable testers can only show that you have a broken or miswired cable, not if the cable is up to proper specification.

2. **A.** Tone probes are only used for locating individual cables.

3. **B.** The nslookup command queries DNS and returns the IP address of the supplied host name.

4. **D.** All of the above; Wireshark can sniff and analyze all the network traffic that enters the computer's NIC.

5. **D.** The `route print` command returns the local system's routing table.

6. **A.** With novice or confused users, ask open-ended questions so the user can explain the problem in his or her own words.

7. **A.** Ask yourself if anything could have happened on your side of the network.

8. **B.** Although it's not fun, you should always verify full system functionality after you have implemented a fix.

9. **C.** Documenting the solution is the last and, in many ways, the most important step in the troubleshooting process.

10. **D.** In this case, the DNS system is probably at fault. By pinging the site with its IP address, you have established that the site is up and your LAN and gateway are functioning properly.

Objectives Map: CompTIA Network+

Topic	Chapter(s)	Page(s)
1.0 Networking Concepts		
1.1 Compare the layers of the OSI and TCP/IP models.		
OSI model:		
Layer 1 – Physical	2	17
Layer 2 – Data Link	2	17
Layer 3 – Network	2	31
Layer 4 – Transport	2	36
Layer 5 – Session	2	37
Layer 6 – Presentation	2	40
Layer 7 – Application	2	42
TCP/IP model:		
Network Interface Layer	2	44
Internet Layer	2	45
Transport Layer	2	45
Application Layer	2	48
Also described as: Link Layer, Internet Layer, Transport Layer, Application Layer	2	44
1.2 Classify how applications, devices, and protocols relate to the OSI model layers.		
MAC address	2	20
IP address	2	31
EUI-64	13	436
Frames	2	22
Packets	2	33
Switch	4	100

Topic	Chapter(s)	Page(s)
Router	2	32
Multilayer switch	12	419
Hub	2	17
Encryption devices	11	368
Cable	2	17
NIC	2	18
Bridge	4	99
1.3 Explain the purpose and properties of IP addressing.		
Classes of addresses		
A, B, C, and D	7	200
Public vs. Private	7	223
Classless (CIDR)	7	202, 211
IPv4 vs. IPv6 (formatting)	7, 13	180, 434
MAC address format	2	20
Subnetting	7	202
Multicast vs. unicast vs. broadcast	7	201
APIPA	7	220
1.4 Explain the purpose and properties of routing and switching.		
EIGRP	8	259
OSPF	8	254
RIP	8	251
Link state vs. distance vector vs. hybrid	8	247, 254, 259
Static vs. dynamic	8	245
Routing metrics	8	246
Hop counts	8	245, 247
MTU, bandwidth	8	246, 247
Costs	8	247
Latency	8	247
Next hop	8	231
Spanning-Tree Protocol	4	102
VLAN (802.1q)	12	412, 414
Port mirroring	12	427
Broadcast domain vs. collision domain	4	102

Topic	Chapter(s)	Page(s)
IGP vs. EGP	8	253
Routing tables	8	230
Convergence (steady state)	8	251
1.5 Identify common TCP and UDP default ports.		
SMTP – 25	9	305
HTTP – 80	9	294
HTTPS – 443	9	298
FTP – 20, 21	9, 11	309, 396
TELNET – 23	9	299
IMAP – 143	9	305
RDP – 3389	14	501, 503
SSH – 22	9	300
DNS – 53	10	317, 320
DHCP – 67, 68	7, 9	216, 278
1.6 Explain the function of common networking protocols.		
TCP	9	277
FTP	9	309
UDP	9	278
TCP/IP suite	2, 7, 9	31, 179, 276-277
DHCP	7	216
TFTP	9	278
DNS	10	320
HTTPS	9, 11	298, 394
HTTP	9	294
ARP	7	197
SIP (VoIP)	14	504
RTP (VoIP)	14	504
SSH	9, 11	300, 388
POP3	9	305
NTP	9, 11	278, 398
IMAP4	9	305
Telnet	9	299
SMTP	9	305

Topic	Chapter(s)	Page(s)
SNMP2/3	11	396
ICMP	9	297
IGMP	9	208
TLS	11	392
1.7 Summarize DNS concepts and its components.		
DNS servers	10	320
DNS records (A, MX, AAAA, CNAME, PTR)	10	339-341
Dynamic DNS	10	345
1.8 Given a scenario, implement the following network troubleshooting methodology:		
Identify the problem:	20	671
Information gathering	20	671
Identify symptoms	20	671
Question users	20	671
Determine if anything has changed	20	672
Establish a theory of probable cause	20	673
Question the obvious	20	673
Test the theory to determine cause:	20	673
Once theory is confirmed determine next steps to resolve problem.	20	673
If theory is not confirmed, re-establish new theory or escalate.	20	673
Establish a plan of action to resolve the problem and identify potential effects	20	673
Implement the solution or escalate as necessary	20	674
Verify full system functionality and if applicable implement preventative measures	20	674
Document findings, actions, and outcomes	20	675
1.9 Identify virtual network components.		
Virtual switches	17	593
Virtual desktops	17	580, 586
Virtual servers	17	590, 593
Virtual PBX	17	595
Onsite vs. offsite	17	596
Network as a Service (NaaS)	17	596

Topic	Chapter(s)	Page(s)
2.0 Network Installation and Configuration		
2.1 Given a scenario, install and configure routers and switches.		
Routing tables	8	269
NAT	8	244
PAT	8	240
VLAN (trunking)	12	412, 413
Managed vs. unmanaged	12	414
Interface configurations		
Full duplex	4	92
Half duplex	4	92
Port speeds	5	108
IP addressing	7	212, 216
MAC filtering	15	521, 533
PoE	15	526
Traffic filtering	12	423
Diagnostics	9	289
VTP configuration	12	417
QoS	12	423
Port mirroring	12	427
2.2 Given a scenario, install and configure a wireless network.		
WAP placement	15	529
Antenna types	15	529
Interference	15	541
Frequencies	15	517
Channels	15	517
Wireless standards	15	510, 519
SSID (enable/disable)	15	516, 532
Compatibility (802.11 a/b/g/n)	15	519
2.3 Explain the purpose and properties of DHCP.		
Static vs. dynamic IP addressing	7	212
Reservations	7	218
Scopes	7	217

Topic	Chapter(s)	Page(s)
Leases	7	219
Options (DNS servers, suffixes)	10	320, 336, 345
2.4 Given a scenario, troubleshoot common wireless problems.		
Interference	15	517
Signal strength	15	513
Configurations	15	513
Incompatibilities	15	519
Incorrect channel	15	542
Latency	15	519
Encryption type	15	525
Bounce	15	541
SSID mismatch	15	542
Incorrect switch placement	15	541
2.5 Given a scenario, troubleshoot common router and switch problems.		
Switching loop	4, 20	102-103, 678
Bad cables/improper cable types	4	103
Port configuration	12	416
VLAN assignment	12	416
Mismatched MTU/MUT black hole	19	650
Power failure	19	639
Bad/missing routes	8	270
Bad modules (SFPs, GBICs)	19	648
Wrong subnet mask	8	270
Wrong gateway	8	270
Duplicate IP address	2	32
Wrong DNS	10	347-348
2.6 Given a set of requirements, plan and implement a basic SOHO network.		
List of requirements	19	636, 638
Cable length	19	642
Device types/requirements	19	636, 639
Environment limitations	19	636, 642
Equipment limitations	19	636, 646
Compatibility requirements	19	636, 640

Topic	Chapter(s)	Page(s)
3.0 Network Media and Topologies		
3.1 Categorize standard media types and associated properties.		
Fiber:		
Multimode	3	72
Single mode	3	73
Copper:		
UTP	3	68
STP	3	68
CAT3	3	69
CAT5	3	69
CAT5e	3	69
CAT6	3	69
CAT6a	3	69
Coaxial	3	63
Crossover	4	98
T1 Crossover	14	468
Straight-through	4	96
Plenum vs. non-plenum	3	76
Media converters:	4	95
Single mode fiber to Ethernet	5	116
Multimode fiber to Ethernet	5	116
Fiber to coaxial	5	116
Single mode to multimode fiber	5	116
Distance limitations and speed limitations	4, 5	94, 117-119
Broadband over powerline	14	494
3.2 Categorize standard connector types based on network media.		
Fiber:		
ST	3, 5	73, 114
SC	3, 5	73, 114
LC	3, 5	73, 114
MTRJ	5	114

Topic	Chapter(s)	Page(s)
Copper:		
RJ-45	3, 4	71, 91
RJ-11	3, 14	71, 480
BNC	3	64
F-connector	3	65
DB-9 (RS-232)	3	74
Patch panel	6	134
110 block (T568A, T568B)	6	135
3.3 Compare and contrast different wireless standards.		
802.11 a/b/g/n standards	15	519-521
Distance	15	519-521
Speed	15	519-521
Latency	15	519
Frequency	15	519-521
Channels	15	517
MIMO	15	520
Channel bonding	15	520
3.4 Categorize WAN technology types and properties.		
Types:		
T1/E1	14	468, 471
T3/E3	14	471
DS3	14	471
OCx	14	479
SONET	14	472
SDH	14	472
DWDM	14	473
Satellite	14	492
ISDN	14	484
Cable	14	490
DSL	14	486
Cellular	14	492
WiMAX	14, 15	492, 510
LTE	14	494
HSPA+	14	494

Topic	Chapter(s)	Page(s)
Fiber	14	494
Dial-up	14	480
PON	14	484
Frame relay	14	474
ATMs	14	474
Properties:		
Circuit switch	14	462
Packet switch	14	474
Speed	14	473, 483, 486-487, 491
Transmission media	14	486, 490, 492
Distance	14	485-486, 493
3.5 Describe different network topologies.		
MPLS	14	475
Point to point	3	62
Point to multipoint	3	62
Ring	3	56
Star	3	58
Mesh	3	61
Bus	3	56
Peer-to-peer	12, 15	404, 514
Client/server	12	402
Hybrid	3	59
3.6 Given a scenario, troubleshoot common physical connectivity problems.		
Cable problems:		
Bad connectors	6	169
Bad wiring	6	170
Open short	20	659
Split cables	14	488, 491
DB loss	14	501
TXRX reversed	6	135
Cable placement	6	154
EMI/Interference	6	155
Distance	6	159
Cross-talk	6	157

Topic	Chapter(s)	Page(s)
3.7 Compare and contrast different LAN technologies.		
Types:		
Ethernet	4, 5	82, 107, 113
10BaseT	4	89
100BaseT	5	108
1000BaseT	5	113
100BaseTX	5	108
100BaseFX	5	108
1000BaseX	5	113
10GBaseSR	5	117
10GBaseLR	5	118
10GBaseER	5	118
10GBaseSW	5	117
10GBaseLW	5	118
10GBaseEW	5	118
10GBaseT	5	119
Properties:		
CSMA/CD	4	87
CSMA/CA	15	518
Broadcast	4	102
Collision	4	87
Bonding	6	165
Speed	4, 5	94, 115, 117-118
Distance	4, 5	94, 115, 117-118
3.8 Identify components of wiring distribution.		
IDF	6	132
MDF	6	144
Demarc	6	141
Demarc extension	6	143
Smart jack	6	143
CSU/DSU	14	468
4.0 Network Management		
4.1 Explain the purpose and features of various network appliances.		
Load balancer	12, 18	421, 631
Proxy server	12	427

Topic	Chapter(s)	Page(s)
Content filter	12	422-423
VPN concentrator	12	411
4.2 Given a scenario, use appropriate hardware tools to troubleshoot connectivity issues.		
Cable tester	6, 20	155, 659
Cable certifier	6, 20	159, 660
Crimper	6	151
Butt set	6	173
Toner probe	6	172-173
Punchdown tool	6	135
Protocol analyzer	20	661
Loopback plug	6	169
TDR	6	157, 659
OTDR	6, 20	161, 659
Multimeter	6, 20	156, 662
Environmental monitor	6, 20	171
4.3 Given a scenario, use appropriate software tools to troubleshoot connectivity issues.		
Protocol analyzer	20	661
Throughput testers	20	669
Connectivity software	20	665
Ping	7, 10, 20	180-181, 319, 664
Tracert/traceroute	20	663
Dig	10, 20	349, 665
Ipconfig/ifconfig	10, 20	333, 663
Nslookup	10, 20	348, 665
Arp	7, 20	197, 664
Nbtstat	10, 20	352, 667
Netstat	10, 20	354, 667
Route	20	666
4.4 Given a scenario, use the appropriate network monitoring resource to analyze traffic.		
SNMP	11	396
SNMPv2	11	396
SNMPv3	11	396
Syslog	18	619
System logs	18	619

Topic	Chapter(s)	Page(s)
History logs	18	619
General logs	18	619
Traffic analysis	18	619
Network sniffer	18	619
4.5 Describe the purpose of configuration management documentation.		
Wire schemes	18	603
Network maps	18	605
Documentation	18	602
Cable management	6	148
Asset management	18	601
Baselines	18	606, 610
Change management	18	609
4.6 Explain different methods and rationales for network performance optimization.		
Methods:		
QoS	12, 18	423, 623
Traffic shaping	12, 18	423, 623
Load balancing	18	630
High availability	18	625
Caching engines	18	621
Fault tolerance	18	625
CARP	18	621
Reasons:		
Latency sensitivity	18	622
High bandwidth applications (VoIP, video applications, unified communications)	18	622
Uptime	18	625
5.0 Network Security		
5.1 Given a scenario, implement appropriate wireless security measures.		
Encryption protocols:		
WEP	15	525
WPA	15	525
WPA2	15	526
WPA Enterprise	15	526
MAC address filtering	15	521

Topic	Chapter(s)	Page(s)
Device placement	15	530
Signal strength	15	529-530
5.2 Explain the methods of network access security.		
ACL:		
MAC filtering	15, 18	521
IP filtering	16	565
Port filtering	16	563
Tunneling and encryption:		
SSL VPN	12	408, 411
VPN	12	406
L2TP	12	408, 411
PPTP	12	408
IPsec	11	368, 392
ISAKMP	11	394
TLS	11	368, 392
TLS1.2	11	392
Site-to-site and client-to-site	12	410-411
Remote access:		
RAS	14	496
RDP	14	501
PPPoE	14	489
PPP	11	376
ICA	14	501
SSH	11	388
5.3 Explain methods of user authentication.		
PKI	11	370
Kerberos	11	382
AAA (RADIUS, TACACS+)	11	379, 381-382
Network access control (802.1x, posture assessment)	11, 16	375, 386, 548
CHAP	11	378
MS-CHAP	11	379
EAP	11	384
Two-factor authentication	16	557

Topic	Chapter(s)	Page(s)
Multifactor authentication	16	557
Single sign-on	16	559
5.4 Explain common threats, vulnerabilities, and mitigation techniques.		
Wireless:		
War driving	16	556
War chalking	16	556
WEP cracking	16	556
WPA cracking	16	556
Evil twin	16	556
Rogue access point	16	556
Attacks:		
DoS	16	553
DDoS	16	554
Man in the middle	16	553
Social engineering	16	552
Virus	16	550
Worms	16	550
Buffer overflow	16	550
Packet sniffing	16	556
FTP bounce	16	563
Smurf	16	553
Mitigation techniques:		
Training and awareness	16	551
Patch management	16	551
Policies and procedures	16	551
Incident response	16	551
5.5 Given a scenario, install and configure a basic firewall.		
Types:		
Software and hardware firewalls	16	562, 567
Port security	16	565
Stateful inspection vs. packet filtering	16	565-566
Firewall rules:		
Block/allow	16	565, 568, 570
Implicit deny	16	570
ACL	16	549

Topic	Chapter(s)	Page(s)
NAT/PAT	8, 16	238, 240, 562
DMZ	16	570

5.6 Categorize different types of network security appliances and methods.

IDS and IPS:		
Behavior based	12	426
Signature based	12	426
Network based	12	425
Host based	12	425
Vulnerability scanners:		
NESSUS	16	571
NMAP	16	571
Methods:		
Honeypots	16	570
Honeynets	16	570

About the CD-ROM

The CD-ROM included with this book comes with an introduction video from the author, Mike Meyers; Total Tester practice exam software with two complete practice exams; a sample of LearnKey's Network+ video training, featuring Mike Meyers; a collection of Mike's current favorite tools and utilities for network management; and a link to download the Secure PDF copy of the book. The software can be installed on any Windows 98/NT/2000/XP/Vista/7 computer and must be installed to access the Total Tester practice exam and LearnKey video training software. The CD also includes a sample version of the Boson NetSim Network Simulator with a free lab.

Playing the Mike Meyers Introduction Video

If your computer CD-ROM drive is configured to auto-run, the CD-ROM will automatically start upon inserting the disc. If the auto-run feature did not launch the CD, browse to the CD and click the **Launch.exe** icon.

From the opening screen, you can launch the video message from Mike by clicking the **Mike Meyers Introduction Video** button. This launches the video file using your system's default video player.

System Requirements

The software requires Windows 98 or higher, Internet Explorer 5.5 or higher, or Firefox with Flash Player, and 30 MB of hard disk space for full installation.

The Boson NetSim requires Windows 7, Windows Vista, or Windows XP. NetSim also requires Microsoft .NET Framework Version 3.5, a 1-GHz Pentium processor or equivalent (minimum) or a 3-GHz Pentium processor or equivalent (recommended), 512 MB of RAM (minimum); 2 GB of RAM (recommended), up to 100 MB of available hard disk space; display capabilities for 1024 × 768, 256 colors (minimum) or 1024 × 768, high color, 32-bit (recommended). The NetSim demo also requires an active Internet connection. NetSim is a Windows-based product. Complete system requirements and product activation instructions can be found on the Boson Web site. A user guide is also available on the CD-ROM.

Installing and Running Total Tester

From the main screen, you may install the Total Tester by clicking the **Software Installers** button, and then selecting the **Total Tester Network+ Practice Exams** button. This begins the installation process. An icon will appear on your desktop and in your Start menu. To run Total Tester, navigate to **Start | (All) Programs | Total Seminars** or double-click the icon on your desktop.

To uninstall the Total Tester software, go to **Start | Settings | Control Panel | Add/ Remove Programs** (XP) or **Programs and Features** (Vista/7), and then select the **Network+ Total Tester** program. Select **Remove** and Windows will completely uninstall the software.

Total Tester

Total Tester provides you with a simulation of the CompTIA Network+ exam. There are two complete CompTIA Network+ practice exams. The exams can be taken in either Practice or Final mode. Practice mode provides an assistance window with hints, references to the book, an explanation of the answer, and the option to check your answer as you take the test. Both Practice and Final modes provide an overall grade and a grade broken down by certification objective. To take a test, launch the program, select a suite from the menu at the top, and then select an exam from the menu.

LearnKey Video Training

To install the LearnKey training demo from the CD in the back of the book, click the **Software Installers** button on the main screen. Then click the **LearnKey Training Demo** button to begin the installation program. After completing the installation, the program should automatically open. You must create a user name and password to run the Network+ Training Demo. Additional sessions for this course may be purchased from Total Seminars at www.totalsem.com or by calling 800-446-6004.

The LearnKey Network+ Training Demo requires Windows XP or later and a Web browser with Adobe Flash Player installed. If you do not have Flash Player installed, you can download it from get.adobe.com/flashplayer.

Mike's Cool Tools

Mike loves freeware/open source networking tools! Most of the utilities mentioned in the text are right here on the CD in the Mike's Cool Tools folder. You can access the folder from the menu by clicking the **Software Installers** button and then selecting **Mike's Cool Tools** from the list.

Please read the Cool Tools Descriptions.pdf file for a description of the utilities.

 CAUTION Although all of the tools are "Mike Meyers Approved," there is no guarantee they will work for you. Read any and all documentation that comes with each utility before using that program.

Secure PDF Copy of the Book

The contents of this book are available as a free download in the form of a secured Adobe Digital Editions PDF file, the Secure PDF. To download your copy, please visit http://books.mcgraw-hill.com/ebookdownloads/9780071789196. The menu on the disc contains links to both Adobe Digital Editions and to the book itself.

You are required to provide your name, a valid e-mail address, and a unique access code. The unique access code can be found on the label that is adhered to the flap of the CD envelope bound into the sleeve in the back of this book. Upon submitting this information, an e-mail message will be sent to the e-mail address you provided. Follow the instructions included in the e-mail message to download your Secure PDF.

NOTE The unique access code entitles you to download one copy of the Secure PDF to one personal computer. The unique access code can only be used once and the Secure PDF is only usable on the computer on which it was downloaded. Be sure to download the Secure PDF to the computer you intend to use.

Adobe Digital Editions is required to open, view, and navigate the Secure PDF. Adobe Digital Editions is available as a free download from Adobe's Web site, www.adobe.com, and is also included on the CD. It is highly recommended that you download and install Adobe Digital Editions before attempting to download the Secure PDF.

Boson's NetSim Network Simulator

This book includes a free demonstration version of Boson's NetSim network simulation software. Click the **Software Installers** button and then the **Boson NetSim network simulation** button on the CD interface to install the NetSim demo. You will need to register for a free online account with Boson by visiting *www.boson.com* before you can complete the activation process.

The Boson NetSim Network Simulator® is an application that simulates Cisco Systems' networking hardware and software and is designed to aid the user in learning the Cisco IOS command structure. The NetSim labs do not directly address the CompTIA Network+ objectives, but all the labs/features/functions/components of NetSim enable you to view simulated networks in a practice environment. Try the demo lab for free and see why NetSim stands in a class of its own.

NetSim uses Boson's proprietary Network Simulator, Router Simulator®, and EROUTER® software technologies, along with the Boson Virtual Packet Technology® engine, to create individual packets. These packets are routed and switched through the simulated network, allowing NetSim to build an appropriate virtual routing table and simulate true networking. Other simulation products on the market do not support this level of functionality.

Boson offers a NetSim for CCENT, CCNA, and CCNP. Each supports the technologies and skills you will need for these respective certifications.

Boson NetSim provides more versatility and support than any other network simulation software on the market. NetSim software also includes a comprehensive lab menu that contains lessons and labs covering routing protocols, Cisco devices, switching, topological design, and much more.

NetSim is a Windows-based product and requires Windows XP, Windows Vista, or Windows 7 to run. System requirements and product activation instructions can be found on the Boson Web site. For technical support related to the Boson NetSim, please visit www.boson.com or e-mail supportissues@boson.com.

Technical Support

For questions regarding the Total Tester software, visit www.totalsem.com, e-mail support@totalsem.com, or e-mail customer.service@mcgraw-hill.com. For customers outside the United States, e-mail international_cs@mcgraw-hill.com.

LearnKey Technical Support

For technical support with the online training, contact techsupport@learnkey.com.

Boson Technical Support

For technical support related to the Boson NetSim, please visit www.boson.com or e-mail supportissues@boson.com.

6in4   One of the most popular of all the IPv6 tunneling standards, and one of only two IPv6 tunneling protocols that can go through a NAT.

6to4   The dominant IPv6 tunneling protocol because it is the only IPv6 tunnel that doesn't require a tunnel broker. It is generally used to directly connect two routers because it normally requires a public IPv4 address.

10BaseFL   Fiber-optic implementation of Ethernet that runs at 10 megabits per second (Mbps) using baseband signaling. Maximum segment length is 2 km.

10BaseT   An Ethernet LAN designed to run on UTP cabling. Runs at 10 Mbps and uses baseband signaling. Maximum length for the cabling between the NIC and the hub (or the switch, the repeater, and so forth) is 100 m.

10GBaseER/10GBaseEW   A 10 GbE standard using 1550-nm single-mode fiber. Maximum cable length up to 40 km.

10GBaseLR/10GBaseLW   A 10 GbE standard using 1310-nm single-mode fiber. Maximum cable length up to 10 km.

10GBaseSR/10GBaseSW   A 10 GbE standard using 850-nm multimode fiber. Maximum cable length up to 300 m.

10GBaseT   A 10 GbE standard designed to run on CAT 6a UTP cabling. Maximum cable length of 100 m.

10 Gigabit Ethernet (10 GbE)   Currently (2012) the fastest Ethernet designation available, with a number of fiber-optic and copper standards.

100BaseFX   An Ethernet LAN designed to run on fiber-optic cabling. Runs at 100 Mbps and uses baseband signaling. Maximum cable length is 400 m for half-duplex and 2 km for full-duplex.

100BaseT   An Ethernet LAN designed to run on UTP cabling. Runs at 100 Mbps, uses baseband signaling, and uses two pairs of wires on CAT 5 or better cabling.

100BaseT4 An Ethernet LAN designed to run on UTP cabling. Runs at 100 Mbps and uses four-pair CAT 3 or better cabling. Made obsolete by 100BaseT.

100BaseTX The technically accurate but little-used name for 100BaseT.

110-Punchdown Block The most common connection used on the back of an RJ-45 jack and patch panels.

110-Punchdown Tool *See* Punchdown Tool.

802 Committee The IEEE committee responsible for all Ethernet standards.

802.1X A port-authentication network access control mechanism for networks.

802.3 (Ethernet) *See* Ethernet.

802.3ab The IEEE standard for 1000BaseT.

802.3z The umbrella IEEE standard for all versions of Gigabit Ethernet other than 1000BaseT.

802.11 *See* IEEE 802.11.

802.11a A wireless standard that operates in the frequency range of 5 GHz and offers throughput of up to 54 Mbps.

802.11b The first popular wireless standard, which operates in the frequency range of 2.4 GHz and offers throughput of up to 11 Mbps.

802.11g Currently (2012) the wireless standard with the widest use, 802.11g operates on the 2.4-GHz band with a maximum throughput of 54 Mbps.

802.11i A wireless standard that added security features.

802.11n An updated 802.11 standard that increases transfer speeds and adds support for multiple in/multiple out (MIMO) by using multiple antennas. 802.11n can operate on either the 2.4- or 5-GHz frequency band and has a maximum throughput of 400 Mbps.

802.16 A wireless standard (also known as WiMax) with a range of up to 30 miles.

1000BaseCX A Gigabit Ethernet standard using unique copper cabling, with a 25-m maximum cable distance.

1000BaseLX A Gigabit Ethernet standard using single-mode fiber cabling, with a 220- to 500-m maximum cable distance.

1000BaseSX A Gigabit Ethernet standard using multimode fiber cabling, with a 5-km maximum cable distance.

1000BaseT A Gigabit Ethernet standard using CAT 5e/6 UTP cabling, with a 100-m maximum cable distance.

1000BaseX An umbrella Gigabit Ethernet standard. Also known as 802.3z. Comprises all Gigabit standards with the exception of 1000BaseT, which is under the 802.3ab standard.

A Records A list of the IP addresses and names of all the systems on a DNS server domain.

AAA (Authentication, Authorization, and Accounting) *See* Authentication, Authorization, and Accounting (AAA).

Acceptable Use Policy A document that defines what a person may and may not do on an organization's computers and networks.

Access Control List (ACL) A clearly defined list of permissions that specifies what actions an authenticated user may perform on a shared resource.

Active Directory A form of directory service used in networks with Windows servers. Creates an organization of related computers that share one or more Windows domains.

Activity Light An LED on a NIC, hub, or switch that blinks rapidly to show data transfers over the network.

Ad Hoc Mode A wireless networking mode where each node is in direct contact with every other node in a decentralized free-for-all. Ad hoc mode is similar to the *mesh topology*.

Address Resolution Protocol (ARP) A protocol in the TCP/IP suite used with the command-line utility of the same name to determine the MAC address that corresponds to a particular IP address.

ADSL (Asymmetric Digital Subscriber Line) *See* Asymmetric Digital Subscriber Line (ADSL).

Advanced Encryption Standard (AES) A block cipher created in the late 1990s that uses a 128-bit block size and a 128-, 192-, or 256-bit key size. Practically uncrackable.

Adware A program that monitors the types of Web sites you frequent and uses that information to generate targeted advertisements, usually pop-up windows.

Aggregation A router hierarchy in which every router underneath a higher router always uses a subnet of that router's existing routes.

Algorithm A set of rules for solving a problem in a given number of steps.

Anycast A method of addressing groups of computers as though they were a single computer. Anycasting starts by giving a number of computers (or clusters of computers) the same IP address. Advanced routers then send incoming packets to the closest of the computers.

Apache HTTP Server An open-source HTTP server program that runs on a wide variety of operating systems.

Application Layer *See* Open System Interconnection (OSI) Seven-Layer Model.

Application Log Tracks application events, such as when an application opens or closes. Different types of application logs record different events.

Archive Bit An attribute of a file that shows whether the file has been backed up since the last change. Each time a file is opened, changed, or saved, the archive bit is turned on. Some types of backups turn off this archive bit to indicate that a good backup of the file exists on tape.

Area ID Address assigned to routers in an OSPF network to prevent flooding beyond the routers in that particular network. *See also* Open Shortest Path First (OSPF).

arping A command used to discover hosts on a network, similar to ping, but that relies on ARP rather than ICMP. The arping command won't cross any routers, so it will only work within a broadcast domain. *See also* Address Resolution Protocol (ARP) and ping.

Asset Management Managing each aspect of a network, from documentation to performance to hardware.

Asymmetric Digital Subscriber Line (ADSL) A fully digital, dedicated connection to the telephone system that provides download speeds of up to 9 Mbps and upload speeds of up to 1 Mbps.

Asymmetric-Key Algorithm An encryption method in which the key used to encrypt a message and the key used to decrypt it are different, or asymmetrical.

Asynchronous Transfer Mode (ATM) A network technology that runs at speeds between 25 and 622 Mbps using fiber-optic cabling or CAT 5 or better UTP.

Attenuation The degradation of signal over distance for a networking cable.

Authentication A process that proves good data traffic truly came from where it says it originated by verifying the sending and receiving users and computers.

Authentication, Authorization, and Accounting (AAA) A security philosophy wherein a computer trying to connect to a network must first present some form of credential in order to be authenticated and then must have limitable permissions within the network. The authenticating server should also record session information about the client.

Authentication Server (AS) In Kerberos, a system that hands out Ticket-Granting Tickets to clients after comparing the client hash to its own. *See also* Ticket-Granting Ticket (TGT).

Authoritative DNS Servers   DNS servers that hold the IP addresses and names of systems for a particular domain or domains in special storage areas called *forward lookup zones*.

Authorization   A step in the AAA philosophy during which a client's permissions are decided upon. *See also* Authentication, Authorization, and Accounting (AAA).

Automatic Private IP Addressing (APIPA)   A networking feature in operating systems that enables DHCP clients to self-configure an IP address and subnet mask automatically when a DHCP server isn't available.

Autonomous System (AS)   One or more networks that are governed by a single protocol within that AS, which provides routing for the Internet backbone.

Back Up   To save important data in a secondary location as a safety precaution against the loss of the primary data.

Backup Designated Router (BDR)   A second router set to take over if the designated router fails. *See also* Designated Router (DR).

Backup Generator   An onsite generator that provides electricity if the power utility fails.

Bandwidth   A piece of the spectrum occupied by some form of signal, whether it is television, voice, fax data, and so forth. Signals require a certain size and location of bandwidth to be transmitted. The higher the bandwidth, the faster the signal transmission, thus allowing for a more complex signal such as audio or video. Because bandwidth is a limited space, when one user is occupying it, others must wait their turn. Bandwidth is also the capacity of a network to transmit a given amount of data during a given period.

Baseband   Digital signaling that has only one signal (a single signal) on the cable at a time. The signals must be in one of three states: one, zero, or idle.

Baseline   Static image of a system's (or network's) performance when all elements are known to be working properly.

Basic NAT   A simple form of NAT that translates a computer's private or internal IP address to a global IP address on a one-to-one basis.

Basic Rate Interface (BRI)   The basic ISDN configuration, which consists of two *B* channels (which can carry voice or data at a rate of 64 Kbps) and one *D* channel (which carries setup and configuration information, as well as data, at 16 Kbps).

Basic Service Set (BSS)   In wireless networking, a single access point servicing a given area.

Basic Service Set Identifier (BSSID)   Naming scheme in wireless networks.

Baud   One analog cycle on a telephone line.

Baud Rate The number of bauds per second. In the early days of telephone data transmission, the baud rate was often analogous to bits per second. Due to advanced modulation of baud cycles as well as data compression, this is no longer true.

Bearer Channel (B Channel) A type of ISDN channel that carries data and voice information using standard DS0 channels at 64 Kbps.

Biometric Devices Devices that scan fingerprints, retinas, or even the sound of the user's voice to provide a foolproof replacement for both passwords and smart devices.

Bit Error Rate Test (BERT) An end-to-end test that verifies a T-carrier connection.

Block Cipher An encryption algorithm in which data is encrypted in "chunks" of a certain length at a time. Popular in wired networks.

BNC Connector A connector used for 10Base2 coaxial cable. All BNC connectors have to be locked into place by turning the locking ring 90 degrees.

Bonding Two or more NICs in a system working together to act as a single NIC to increase performance.

Bootstrap Protocol (BOOTP) A component of TCP/IP that allows computers to discover and receive an IP address from a DHCP server prior to booting the OS. Other items that may be discovered during the BOOTP process are the IP address of the default gateway for the subnet and the IP addresses of any name servers.

Border Gateway Protocol (BGP-4) An exterior gateway routing protocol that enables groups of routers to share routing information so that efficient, loop-free routes can be established.

Botnet A group of computers under the control of one operator, used for malicious purposes.

Bps (Bits Per Second) A measurement of how fast data is moved across a transmission medium. A Gigabit Ethernet connection moves 1,000,000,000 bps.

Bridge A device that connects two networks and passes traffic between them based only on the node address, so that traffic between nodes on one network does not appear on the other network. For example, an Ethernet bridge only looks at the MAC address. Bridges filter and forward frames based on MAC addresses and operate at Layer 2 (Data Link layer) of the OSI seven-layer model.

Bridge Loop A negative situation in which bridging devices (usually switches) are installed in a loop configuration, causing frames to loop continuously. Switches using Spanning Tree Protocol (STP) prevent bridge loops by automatically turning off looping ports.

Bridged Connection An early type of DSL connection that made the DSL line function the same as if you snapped an Ethernet cable into your NIC.

Broadband Analog signaling that sends multiple signals over the cable at the same time. The best example of broadband signaling is cable television. The zero, one, and idle states exist on multiple channels on the same cable. *See also* Baseband.

Broadcast A frame or packet addressed to all machines, almost always limited to a broadcast domain.

Broadcast Address The address a NIC attaches to a frame when it wants every other NIC on the network to read it. In TCP/IP, the general broadcast address is 255.255.255.255. In Ethernet, the broadcast MAC address is FF-FF-FF-FF-FF-FF.

Broadcast Domain A network of computers that will hear each other's broadcasts. The older term *collision domain* is the same, but rarely used today.

Broadcast Storm The result of one or more devices sending a nonstop flurry of broadcast frames on the network.

Browser A software program specifically designed to retrieve, interpret, and display Web pages.

Building Entrance Location where all the cables from the outside world (telephone lines, cables from other buildings, and so on) come into a building.

Bus Topology A network topology that uses a single bus cable that connects all of the computers in line. Bus topology networks must be terminated to prevent signal reflection.

Butt Set Device that can tap into a 66- or 110-punchdown block to see if a particular line is working.

Byte Eight contiguous bits, the fundamental data unit of personal computers. Storing the equivalent of one character, the byte is also the basic unit of measurement for computer storage. Bytes are counted in powers of two.

CAB Files Short for "cabinet files." These files are compressed and most commonly used during Microsoft operating system installation to store many smaller files, such as device drivers.

Cable Certifier A very powerful cable testing device used by professional installers to test the electrical characteristics of a cable and then generate a certification report, proving that cable runs pass TIA/EIA standards.

Cable Drop Location where the cable comes out of the wall at the workstation location.

Cable Modem A bridge device that interconnects the cable company's DOCSIS service to the user's Ethernet network. In most locations, the cable modem is the demarc.

Cable Stripper   Device that enables the creation of UTP cables.

Cable Tester   A generic name for a device that tests cables. Some common tests are continuity, electrical shorts, crossed wires, or other electrical characteristics.

Cable Tray   A device for organizing cable runs in a drop ceiling.

Cache   A special area of RAM that stores frequently accessed data. In a network there are a number of applications that take advantage of cache in some way.

Cache-Only DNS Servers (Caching-Only DNS Servers)   DNS servers that do not have any forward lookup zones. They resolve names of systems on the Internet for the network, but are not responsible for telling other DNS servers the names of any clients.

Cached Lookup   The list kept by a DNS server of IP addresses it has already resolved, so it won't have to re-resolve an FQDN it has already checked.

Caching Engine   A server dedicated to storing cache information on your network. These servers can reduce overall network traffic dramatically.

Canonical Name (CNAME)   Less common type of DNS record that acts as a computer's alias.

Capturing a Printer   A process by which a printer uses a local LPT port that connects to a networked printer. This is usually only done to support older programs that are not smart enough to know how to print directly to a UNC-named printer; it's quite rare today.

Card   Generic term for anything that you can snap into an expansion slot.

Carrier Sense Multiple Access with Collision Avoidance (CSMA/CA)   *See* CSMA/CA (Carrier Sense Multiple Access with Collision Avoidance).

Carrier Sense Multiple Access with Collision Detection (CSMA/CD)   *See* CSMA/CD (Carrier Sense Multiple Access with Collision Detection).

CAT 3   Category 3 wire, a TIA/EIA standard for UTP wiring that can operate at up to 16 Mbps.

CAT 4   Category 4 wire, a TIA/EIA standard for UTP wiring that can operate at up to 20 Mbps. This wire is not widely used, except in older Token Ring networks.

CAT 5   Category 5 wire, a TIA/EIA standard for UTP wiring that can operate at up to 100 Mbps.

CAT 5e   Category 5e wire, a TIA/EIA standard for UTP wiring with improved support for 100 Mbps using two pairs and support for 1000 Mbps using four pairs.

CAT 6   Category 6 wire, a TIA/EIA standard for UTP wiring with improved support for 1000 Mbps.

Category (CAT) Rating   A grade assigned to cable to help network installers get the right cable for the right network technology. CAT ratings are officially rated in megahertz (MHz), indicating the highest-frequency bandwidth the cable can handle.

CCITT (Comité Consultatif International Téléphonique et Télégraphique)   European standards body that established the V standards for modems.

Central Office   Building that houses local exchanges and a location where individual voice circuits come together.

Certificate   A public encryption key signed with the digital signature from a trusted third party called a *certificate authority (CA)*. This key serves to validate the identity of its holder when that person or company sends data to other parties.

Certifier   A device that tests a cable to ensure that it can handle its rated amount of capacity.

Challenge Handshake Authentication Protocol (CHAP)   A remote access authentication protocol. It has the serving system challenge the remote client, which must provide an encrypted password.

Change Management Documentation   A set of documents that defines procedures for changes to the network.

Channel   A portion of the wireless spectrum on which a particular wireless network operates. Setting wireless networks to different channels enables separation of the networks.

Channel Bonding   Wireless technology that enables WAPs to use two channels for transmission.

Channel Service Unit/Digital Service Unit (CSU/DSU)   *See* CSU/DSU (Channel Service Unit/Data Service Unit).

Chat   A multiparty, real-time text conversation. The Internet's most popular version is known as Internet Relay Chat (IRC), which many groups use to converse in real time with each other.

Checksum   A simple error-detection method that adds a numerical value to each data packet, based on the number of data bits in the packet. The receiving node applies the same formula to the data and verifies that the numerical value is the same; if not, the data has been corrupted and must be re-sent.

Cipher   A series of complex and hard-to-reverse mathematics run on a string of ones and zeroes in order to make a new set of seemingly meaningless ones and zeroes.

Ciphertext   The output when cleartext is run through a cipher algorithm using a key.

Circuit Switching   The process for connecting two phones together on one circuit.

Cisco IOS   Cisco's proprietary operating system.

Cladding   The part of a fiber-optic cable that makes the light reflect down the fiber.

Class License   Contiguous chunk of IP addresses passed out by the Internet Assigned Numbers Authority (IANA).

Classless Inter-Domain Routing (CIDR)   Method of categorizing IP addresses in order to distribute them. *See also* Subnetting.

Classless Subnet   A subnet that does not fall into the common categories such as Class A, Class B, and Class C.

Cleartext   *See* Plaintext.

Client   A computer program that uses the services of another computer program; software that extracts information from a server. Your autodial phone is a client, and the phone company is its server. Also, a machine that accesses shared resources on a server.

Client/Server   A relationship in which client software obtains services from a server on behalf of a user.

Client/Server Application   An application that performs some or all of its processing on an application server rather than on the client. The client usually only receives the result of the processing.

Client/Server Network   A network that has dedicated server machines and client machines.

Client-to-Site   A type of VPN connection where a single computer logs into a remote network and becomes, for all intents and purposes, a member of that network.

Cloud Computing   Using the Internet to store files and run applications. For example, Google Documents is a cloud computing application that enables you to run productivity applications over the Internet from your Web browser.

Coaxial Cable   A type of cable that contains a central conductor wire surrounded by an insulating material, which in turn is surrounded by a braided metal shield. It is called coaxial because the center wire and the braided metal shield share a common axis or centerline.

Collision   The result of two nodes transmitting at the same time on a multiple access network such as Ethernet. Both frames may be lost or partial frames may result.

Collision Domain   *See* Broadcast Domain.

Collision Light   A light on some older NICs that flickers when a network collision is detected.

Command   A request, typed from a terminal or embedded in a file, to perform an operation or to execute a particular program.

Common Internet File System (CIFS) The protocol that NetBIOS used to share folders and printers. Still very common, even on UNIX/Linux systems.

Compatibility Issue When different pieces of hardware or software don't work together correctly.

Complete Algorithm A cipher and the methods used to implement that cipher.

Concentrator A device that brings together at a common center connections to a particular kind of network (such as Ethernet) and implements that network internally.

Configuration Management A set of documents, policies, and procedures designed to help you maintain and update your network in a logical, orderly fashion.

Configuration Management Documentation Documents that define the configuration of a network. These would include wiring diagrams, network diagrams, baselines, and policy/procedure/configuration documentation.

Configurations The settings stored in devices that define how they are to operate.

Connection A term used to refer to communication between two computers.

Connection-Oriented Communication A protocol that establishes a connection between two hosts before transmitting data and verifies receipt before closing the connection between the hosts. TCP is an example of a connection-oriented protocol.

Connectionless Communication A protocol that does not establish and verify a connection between the hosts before sending data; it just sends the data and hopes for the best. This is faster than connection-oriented protocols. UDP is an example of a connectionless protocol.

Content Switch Advanced networking device that works at least at Layer 7 (Application layer) and hides servers behind a single IP.

Continuity The physical connection of wires in a network.

Continuity Tester Inexpensive network tester that can only test for continuity on a line.

Convergence Point at which the routing tables for all routers in a network are updated.

Copy Backup A type of backup similar to Normal or Full, in that all selected files on a system are backed up. This type of backup does *not* change the archive bit of the files being backed up.

Core The central glass of the fiber-optic cable that carries the light signal.

Cost Routers can use a connection's monetary cost when determining a route's metric.

Counter   A predefined event that is recorded to a log file.

CRC (Cyclic Redundancy Check)   A mathematical method that is used to check for errors in long streams of transmitted data with high accuracy. Before data is sent, the main computer uses the data to calculate a CRC value from the data's contents. If the receiver calculates a different CRC value from the received data, the data was corrupted during transmission and is re-sent. Ethernet frames have a CRC code.

Crimper   Also called a *crimping tool*, the tool used to secure a crimp (or an RJ-45 connector) onto the end of a cable.

Cross-Platform Support   Standards created to enable terminals (and now operating systems) from different companies to interact with one another.

Crossover Cable   A special UTP cable used to interconnect hubs/switches or to connect network cards without a hub/switch. Crossover cables reverse the sending and receiving wire pairs from one end to the other.

Crossover Port   Special port in a hub that crosses the sending and receiving wires, thus removing the need for a crossover cable to connect the hubs.

Crosstalk   Electrical signal interference between two cables that are in close proximity to each other.

CSMA/CA (Carrier Sense Multiple Access with Collision Avoidance)   Access method used mainly on wireless networks. Before hosts send out data, they send out a signal that checks to make sure the network is free of other signals. If data is detected on the wire, the hosts wait a random time period before trying again. If the wire is free, the data is sent out.

CSMA/CD (Carrier Sense Multiple Access with Collision Detection)   Access method that Ethernet systems use in LAN technologies, enabling frames of data to flow through the network and ultimately reach address locations. Known as a *contention* protocol, hosts on CSMA/CD networks send out data without checking to see if the wire is free first. If a collision occurs, then both hosts wait a random time period before retransmitting the data.

CSU/DSU (Channel Service Unit/Data Service Unit)   A piece of equipment that connects a T-carrier leased line from the telephone company to a customer's equipment (such as a router). It performs line encoding and conditioning functions, and it often has a loopback function for testing.

Daily Backup   Also called a *daily copy backup*, makes a copy of all files that have been changed on that day without changing the archive bits of those files.

Daisy-chain   A method of connecting together several devices along a bus and managing the signals for each device.

Data Backup The process of creating extra copies of data to be used in case the primary data source fails.

Data Encryption Standard (DES) A symmetric-key algorithm developed by the U.S. government in the 1970s and formerly in use in a variety of TCP/IP applications. DES used a 64-bit block and a 56-bit key. Over time, the 56-bit key made DES susceptible to brute-force attacks.

Data Link Layer *See* Open Systems Interconnection (OSI) Seven-Layer Model.

Data Over Cable Service Interface Specification (DOCSIS) The unique protocol used by cable modem networks.

Datagram A connectionless transfer unit created with User Datagram Protocol designed for quick transfers over a packet-switched network.

Decibel (dB) A measurement of the quality of a signal.

Dedicated Circuit A circuit that runs from a breaker box to specific outlets.

Dedicated Line A telephone line that is an always open, or connected, circuit. Dedicated telephone lines usually do not have telephone numbers.

Dedicated Server A machine that does not use any client functions, only server functions.

Default A software function or operation that occurs automatically unless the user specifies something else.

Default Gateway In a TCP/IP network, the IP address of the router that interconnects the LAN to a wider network, usually the Internet. This router's IP address is part of the necessary TCP/IP configuration for communicating with multiple networks using IP.

Delta Channel (D Channel) A type of ISDN line that transfers data at 16 Kbps.

Demarc A device that marks the dividing line of responsibility for the functioning of a network between internal users and upstream service providers.

Demarc Extension Any cabling that runs from the network interface to whatever box is used by the customer as a demarc.

Demilitarized Zone (DMZ) A lightly protected or unprotected subnet network positioned between an outer firewall and an organization's highly protected internal network. DMZs are used mainly to host public address servers (such as Web servers).

Denial of Service (DoS) Attack An attack that floods a networked server with so many requests that it becomes overwhelmed and ceases functioning.

Designated Router (DR) The main router in an OSPF network that relays information to all other routers in the area.

Destination Port A fixed, predetermined number that defines the function or session type in a TCP/IP network.

Device Driver A subprogram to control communications between the computer and some peripheral hardware.

Device ID The last six digits of a MAC address, identifying the manufacturer's unique serial number for that NIC.

DHCP Lease Created by the DHCP server to allow a system requesting DHCP IP information to use that information for a certain amount of time.

DHCP Scope The pool of IP addresses that a DHCP server may allocate to clients requesting IP addresses or other IP information like DNS server addresses.

Dial-up Lines Telephone lines with telephone numbers; they must dial to make a connection, as opposed to a dedicated line.

Differential Backup Similar to an incremental backup in that it backs up the files that have been changed since the last backup. This type of backup does not change the state of the archive bit.

DIG (Domain Information Groper) *See* Domain Information Groper.

Digital Signature A string of characters, created from a private encryption key, that verifies a sender's identity to those who receive encrypted data or messages.

Digital Subscriber Line (DSL) A high-speed Internet connection technology that uses a regular telephone line for connectivity. DSL comes in several varieties, including Asymmetric (ADSL) and Symmetric (SDSL), and many speeds. Typical home-user DSL connections are ADSL with a download speed of up to 9 Mbps and an upload speed of up to 1 Kbps.

Dipole Antenna The standard straight-wire antenna that provides most omni-directional function.

Direct Current (DC) A type of electric circuit where the flow of electrons is in a complete circle.

Direct-Sequence Spread-Spectrum (DSSS) A spread-spectrum broadcasting method defined in the 802.11 standard that sends data out on different frequencies at the same time.

Directional Antenna An antenna that focuses its signal into a beam of sorts.

Discretionary Access Control (DAC) Authorization method based on the idea that there is an owner of a resource who may at his or her discretion assign access to that resource. DAC is considered much more flexible than MAC.

Disk Mirroring   Process by which data is written simultaneously to two or more disk drives. Read and write speed is decreased, but redundancy, in case of catastrophe, is increased. Also known as RAID level 1. *See also* Duplexing.

Disk Striping   Process by which data is spread among multiple (at least two) drives. It increases speed for both reads and writes of data, but provides no fault tolerance. Also known as RAID level 0.

Disk Striping with Parity   Process by which data is spread among multiple (at least three) drives, with parity information as well to provide fault tolerance. The most commonly implemented type is RAID 5, where the data and parity information is spread across three or more drives.

Dispersion   Diffusion over distance of light propagating down fiber cable.

Distance Vector   Set of routing protocols that calculates the total cost to get to a particular network ID and compares that cost to the total cost of all the other routes to get to that same network ID.

Distributed Coordination Function (DCF)   One of two methods of collision avoidance defined by the 802.11 standard and the only one currently implemented. DCF specifies strict rules for sending data onto the network media.

Distributed Denial of Service (DDoS) Attack   A DoS attack that uses multiple (as in hundreds or up to hundreds of thousands) of computers under the control of a single operator to conduct a devastating attack.

DLL (Dynamic Link Library)   A file of executable functions or data that can be used by a Windows application. Typically, a DLL provides one or more particular functions, and a program accesses the functions by creating links to the DLL.

DNS Domain   A specific branch of the DNS name space. First-level DNS domains include .com, .gov, and .edu.

DNS Resolver Cache   A cache used by Windows DNS clients to keep track of DNS information.

DNS Root Servers   The highest in the hierarchy of DNS servers running the Internet.

DNS Server   A system that runs a special DNS server program.

DNS Tree   A hierarchy of DNS domains and individual computer names organized into a tree-like structure, the top of which is the root.

Document   A medium and the data recorded on it for human use; for example, a report sheet or book. By extension, any record that has permanence and that can be read by a human or a machine.

Documentation   A collection of organized documents or the information recorded in documents. Also, instructional material specifying the inputs, operations, and outputs of a computer program or system.

Domain   A term used to describe a grouping of users, computers, and/or networks. In Microsoft networking, a domain is a group of computers and users that shares a common account database and a common security policy. For the Internet, a domain is a group of computers that shares a common element in their DNS hierarchical name.

Domain Controller   A Microsoft Windows Server system specifically configured to store user and server account information for its domain. Often abbreviated as "DC." Windows domain controllers store all account and security information in the *Active Directory* directory service.

Domain Information Groper (DIG)   Command-line tool in non-Windows systems used to diagnose DNS problems.

Domain Name System (DNS)   A TCP/IP name resolution system that resolves host names to IP addresses.

Domain Users and Groups   Users and groups that are defined across an entire network domain.

Dotted Decimal Notation   Shorthand method for discussing and configuring binary IP addresses.

Download   The transfer of information from a remote computer system to the user's system. Opposite of *upload*.

Drive Duplexing   *See* Duplexing.

Drive Mirroring   The process of writing identical data to two hard drives on the same controller at the same time to provide data redundancy.

DS0   The digital signal rate created by converting analog sound into 8-bit chunks 8000 times a second, with a data stream of 64 Kbps. This is the simplest data stream (and the slowest rate) of the digital part of the phone system.

DS1   The signaling method used by T1 lines, which uses a relatively simple frame consisting of 25 pieces: a framing bit and 24 channels. Each DS1 channel holds a single 8-bit DS0 data sample. The framing bit and data channels combine to make 193 bits per DS1 frame. These frames are transmitted 8000 times/sec, making a total throughput of 1.544 Mbps.

DSL Access Multiplexer (DSLAM)   A device located in a telephone company's central office that connects multiple customers to the Internet.

DSL Modem A device that enables customers to connect to the Internet using a DSL connection. A DSL modem isn't really a modem—it's more like an ISDN terminal adapter—but the term stuck, and even the manufacturers of the devices now call them DSL modems.

DSP (Digital Signal Processor) A specialized microprocessor-like device that processes digital signals at the expense of other capabilities, much as the floating-point unit (FPU) is optimized for math functions. DSPs are used in such specialized hardware as high-speed modems, multimedia sound cards, MIDI equipment, and real-time video capture and compression.

Duplexing Also called *disk duplexing* or *drive duplexing*, similar to mirroring in that data is written to and read from two physical drives for fault tolerance. In addition, separate controllers are used for each drive, for both additional fault tolerance and additional speed. Considered RAID level 1. *See also* Disk Mirroring.

Dynamic Addressing A way for a computer to receive IP information automatically from a server program. *See also* Dynamic Host Configuration Protocol (DHCP).

Dynamic DNS (DDNS) A protocol that enables DNS servers to get automatic updates of IP addresses of computers in their forward lookup zones, mainly by talking to the local DHCP server.

Dynamic Host Configuration Protocol (DHCP) A protocol that enables a DHCP server to set TCP/IP settings automatically for a DHCP client.

Dynamic Link Library (DLL) *See* DLL (Dynamic Link Library).

Dynamic NAT Type of NAT in which many computers can share a pool of routable IP addresses that number fewer than the computers.

Dynamic Port Numbers Port numbers 49152–65535, recommended by the IANA to be used as ephemeral port numbers.

Dynamic Routing Process by which routers in an internetwork automatically exchange information with other routers. Requires a dynamic routing protocol, such as OSPF or RIP.

Dynamic Routing Protocol A protocol that supports the building of automatic routing tables, such as OSPF or RIP.

E1 The European counterpart of a T1 connection that carries 32 channels at 64 Kbps for a total of 2.048 Mbps—making it slightly faster than a T1.

E3 The European counterpart of a T3 line that carries 16 E1 lines (512 channels), for a total bandwidth of 34.368 Mbps—making it a little bit slower than an American T3.

Edge Router Router that connects one automated system (AS) to another.

Effective Permissions   The permissions of all groups combined in any network operating system.

Electromagnetic Interference (EMI)   Interference from one device to another, resulting in poor performance in the device's capabilities. This is similar to having static on your TV while running a hair dryer, or placing two monitors too close together and getting a "shaky" screen.

E-mail (Electronic Mail)   Messages, usually text, sent from one person to another via computer. E-mail can also be sent automatically to a large number of addresses, known as a *mailing list.*

E-mail Client   Program that runs on a computer and enables you to send, receive, and organize e-mail.

E-mail Server   Also known as *mail server,* a server that accepts incoming mail, sorts the mail for recipients into mailboxes, and sends mail to other servers using SMTP.

Emulator   Software or hardware that converts the commands to and from the host machine to an entirely different platform. For example, a program that enables you to run Nintendo games on your PC.

Encapsulation   The process of putting the packets from one protocol inside the packets of another protocol. An example of this is TCP/IP encapsulation in Ethernet, which places TCP/IP packets inside Ethernet frames.

Encryption   A method of securing messages by scrambling and encoding each packet as it is sent across an unsecured medium, such as the Internet. Each encryption level provides multiple standards and options.

Endpoint   In the TCP/IP world, the session information stored in RAM. *See also* Socket.

Endpoints   Correct term to use when discussing the data each computer stores about the connection between two computers' TCP/IP applications. *See also* Socket Pairs.

Enhanced Interior Gateway Routing Protocol (EIGRP)   Cisco's proprietary hybrid protocol that has elements of both distance vector and link state routing.

Environmental Monitor   Device used in telecommunications rooms that keeps track of humidity, temperature, and more.

Ephemeral Port   In TCP/IP communication, an arbitrary number generated by a sending computer that the receiving computer uses as a destination address when sending a return packet.

Ephemeral Port Numbers   *See* Ephemeral Port.

Equipment Rack   A metal structure used in equipment rooms to secure network hardware devices and patch panels. Most racks are 19" wide. Devices designed to fit in such a rack use a height measurement called *units*, or simply *U*.

ESD (Electro-Static Discharge)   The movement of electrons from one body to another. ESD is a real menace to PCs because it can cause permanent damage to semiconductors.

Ethernet   Name coined by Xerox for the first standard of network cabling and protocols. Ethernet is based on a bus topology. The IEEE 802.3 subcommittee defines the current Ethernet specifications.

Evil Twin   An attack that lures people into logging into a rogue access point that looks similar to a legitimate access point.

Executable Viruses   Viruses that are literally extensions of executables and that are unable to exist by themselves. Once an infected executable file is run, the virus loads into memory, adding copies of itself to other EXEs that are subsequently run.

Extended Service Set (ESS)   A single wireless access point servicing a given area that has been extended by adding more access points.

Extended Service Set ID (ESSID)   An SSID applied to an Extended Service Set as a network naming convention.

Extended Unique Identifier, 64-bit (EUI-64)   The last 64 bits of the IPv6 address, which are determined based on a device's MAC address.

Extensible Authentication Protocol (EAP)   Authentication wrapper that EAP-compliant applications can use to accept one of many types of authentication. While EAP is a general-purpose authentication wrapper, its only substantial use is in wireless networks.

External Connections   A network's connection to the wider Internet. Also a major concern when setting up a SOHO network.

External Data Bus (EDB)   The primary data highway of all computers. Everything in your computer is tied either directly or indirectly to the EDB.

External Network Address   A number added to the MAC address of every computer on an IPX/SPX network that defines every computer on the network; this is often referred to as a *network number*.

External Threats   Threats to your network through external means; examples include virus attacks and the exploitation of users, security holes in the OS, or the network hardware itself.

FAQ (Frequently Asked Questions)   Common abbreviation coined by BBS users and spread to Usenet and the Internet. This is a list of questions and answers that pertains to a particular topic, maintained so that users new to the group don't all bombard the group with similar questions. Examples are "What is the name of the actor who plays *X* on this show, and was he in anything else?" or "Can anyone list all of the books by this author in the order that they were published so that I can read them in that order?" The common answer to this type of question is "Read the FAQ!"

Far-End Crosstalk (FEXT)   Crosstalk on the opposite end of a cable from the signal's source.

Fast Ethernet   Nickname for the 100-Mbps Ethernet standards. Originally applied to 100BaseT.

Fault Tolerance   The capability of any system to continue functioning after some part of the system has failed. RAID is an example of a hardware device that provides fault tolerance for hard drives.

Federal Communications Commission (FCC)   In the United States, regulates public airwaves and rates PCs and other equipment according to the amount of radiation emitted.

Fiber-Optic Cable   A high-speed physical medium for transmitting data that uses light rather than electricity to transmit data and is made of high-purity glass fibers sealed within a flexible opaque tube. Much faster than conventional copper wire.

File Server   A computer designated to store software, courseware, administrative tools, and other data on a local or wide area network. It "serves" this information to other computers via the network when users enter their personal access codes.

File Transfer Protocol (FTP)   A set of rules that allows two computers to talk to one another as a file transfer is carried out. This is the protocol used when you transfer a file from one computer to another across the Internet.

Fire Ratings   Ratings developed by Underwriters Laboratories (UL) and the National Electrical Code (NEC) to define the risk of network cables burning and creating noxious fumes and smoke.

Firewall   A device that restricts traffic between a local network and the Internet.

FireWire   An IEEE 1394 standard to send wide-band signals over a thin connector system that plugs into TVs, VCRs, TV cameras, PCs, and so forth. This serial bus developed by Apple and Texas Instruments enables connection of 60 devices at speeds ranging from 100 to 800 Mbps.

Flat Name Space   A naming convention that gives each device only one name that must be unique. NetBIOS uses a flat name space. TCP/IP's DNS uses a hierarchical name space.

Forward Lookup Zone   The storage area in a DNS server to store the IP addresses and names of systems for a particular domain or domains.

FQDN (Fully Qualified Domain Name)   The complete DNS name of a system, from its host name to the top-level domain name.

Fractional T1 Access   A service provided by many telephone companies wherein customers can purchase a number of individual channels in a T1 line in order to save money.

Frame   A defined series of binary data that is the basic container for a discrete amount of data moving across a network. Frames are created at Layer 2 of the OSI model.

Frame Check Sequence (FCS)   A sequence of bits placed in a frame that is used to check the primary data for errors.

Frame Relay   An extremely efficient data transmission technique used to send digital information such as voice, data, LAN, and WAN traffic quickly and cost-efficiently to many destinations from one port.

FreeRADIUS   Free RADIUS server software for UNIX/Linux systems.

Freeware   Software that is distributed for free with no license fee.

Frequency Division Multiplexing (FDM)   A process of keeping individual phone calls separate by adding a different frequency multiplier to each phone call, making it possible to separate phone calls by their unique frequency range.

Frequency-Hopping Spread-Spectrum (FHSS)   A spread-spectrum broadcasting method defined in the 802.11 standard that sends data on one frequency at a time, constantly shifting (or *hopping*) frequencies.

FUBAR   Fouled Up Beyond All Recognition.

Full Duplex   Any device that can send and receive data simultaneously.

Fully Meshed Topology   A mesh network where every node is directly connected to every other node.

Gain   The strengthening and focusing of radio frequency output from a wireless access point (WAP).

Gateway Router   A router that acts as a default gateway in a TCP/IP network.

General Logs   Logs that record updates to applications.

Giga-   The prefix that generally refers to the quantity 1,073,741,824. One gigabyte is 1,073,741,824 bytes. With frequencies, in contrast, giga- often refers to one billion. One gigahertz is 1,000,000,000 hertz.

Gigabit Ethernet   *See* 1000BaseT.

Gigabyte   1024 megabytes.

Global Unicast Address   A second IPv6 address that every system needs in order to get on the Internet.

Grandfather, Father, Son (GFS)   A tape rotation strategy used in data backups.

Group Policy   A feature of Windows Active Directory that allows an administrator to apply policy settings to network users *en masse*.

Group Policy Object (GPO)   Enables network administrators to define multiple rights and permissions to entire sets of users all at one time.

Groups   Collections of network users who share similar tasks and need similar permissions; defined to make administration tasks easier.

H.323   A VoIP standard that handles the initiation, setup, and delivery of VoIP sessions.

Hackers   People who break into computer systems with malicious intent.

Half Duplex   Any device that can only send or receive data at any given moment.

Hardware Tools   Tools such as cable testers, TDRs, OTDRs, certifiers, voltage event recorders, protocol analyzers, cable strippers, multimeters, tone probes/generators, butt sets, and punchdown tools used to configure and troubleshoot a network.

Hash   A mathematical function used in cryptography that is run on a string of binary digits of any length that results in a value of some fixed length.

Hex (Hexadecimal)   Hex symbols based on a numbering system of 16 (computer shorthand for binary numbers), using 10 digits and 6 letters to condense 0s and 1s to binary numbers. Hex is represented by digits 0 through 9 and alpha *A* through *F*, so that 09h has a value of 9, and 0Ah has a value of 10.

Hierarchical Name Space   A naming scheme where the full name of each object includes its position within the hierarchy. An example of a hierarchical name is www.totalseminars.com, which includes not only the host name, but also the domain name. DNS uses a hierarchical name space scheme for fully qualified domain names (FQDNs).

High Availability   A collection of technologies and procedures that work together to keep an application available at all times.

High-Speed WAN Internet Cards   A type of router expansion card that enables connection to two different ISPs.

History Logs   Logs that track the history of how a user or users access network resources, or how network resources are accessed throughout the network.

Home Page   Either the Web page that your browser is set to use when it starts up or the main Web page for a business, organization, or person. Also, the main page in any collection of Web pages.

Honeynet   The network created by a honeypot in order to lure in hackers.

Honeypot   An area of a network that an administrator sets up for the express purpose of attracting a computer hacker. If a hacker takes the bait, the network's important resources are unharmed and network personnel can analyze the attack to predict and protect against future attacks, making the network more secure.

Hop   The passage of a packet through a router.

Horizontal Cabling   Cabling that connects the equipment room to the work areas.

Host   A single device (usually a computer) on a TCP/IP network that has an IP address; any device that can be the source or destination of a data packet. Also, a computer running multiple virtualized operating systems.

Host ID   The portion of an IP address that defines a specific machine in a subnet.

Host Name   An individual computer name in the DNS naming convention.

hostname   Command-line tool that returns the host name of the computer it is run on.

HOSTS File   The predecessor to DNS, a static text file that resides on a computer and is used to resolve DNS host names to IP addresses. The HOSTS file is checked before the machine sends a name resolution request to a DNS name server. The HOSTS file has no extension.

HTML (Hypertext Markup Language)   An ASCII-based script-like language for creating hypertext documents like those on the World Wide Web.

HTTP (Hypertext Transfer Protocol)   Extremely fast protocol used for network file transfers on the World Wide Web.

HTTP over SSL (HTTPS)   A secure form of HTTP, used commonly for Internet business transactions or any time where a secure connection is required. *See also* Hypertext Transfer Protocol (HTTP) *and* Secure Sockets Layer (SSL).

Hub   An electronic device that sits at the center of a star topology network, providing a common point for the connection of network devices. In a 10BaseT Ethernet network, the hub contains the electronic equivalent of a properly terminated bus cable. Hubs are rare today and have been replaced by switches.

Hybrid Topology   A mix or blend of two different topologies. A star-bus topology is a hybrid of the star and bus topologies.

Hypertext A document that has been marked up to enable a user to select words or pictures within the document, click them, and connect to further information. The basis of the World Wide Web.

Hypervisor An extra layer of sophisticated programming to manage the vastly more complex interactions required for virtualization.

ICF (Internet Connection Firewall) The software firewall built into Windows XP that protects your system from unauthorized access from the Internet. Microsoft changed the name to the Windows Firewall in Windows XP Service Pack 2.

ICS (Internet Connection Sharing) Also known simply as *Internet sharing*, the technique of enabling more than one computer to access the Internet simultaneously using a single Internet connection. When you use Internet sharing, you connect an entire LAN to the Internet using a single public IP address.

IEEE (Institute of Electrical and Electronics Engineers) The leading standards-setting group in the United States.

IEEE 802.2 IEEE subcommittee that defined the standards for Logical Link Control (LLC).

IEEE 802.3 IEEE subcommittee that defined the standards for CSMA/CD (a.k.a. *Ethernet*).

IEEE 802.11 IEEE subcommittee that defined the standards for wireless.

IEEE 802.14 IEEE subcommittee that defined the standards for cable modems.

IEEE 1284 The IEEE standard for the now obsolete parallel communication.

IEEE 1394 IEEE standard for FireWire communication.

IETF (Internet Engineering Task Force) The primary standards organization for the Internet.

ifconfig A command-line utility for Linux servers and workstations that displays the current TCP/IP configuration of the machine, similar to ipconfig for Windows systems.

IMAP (Internet Message Access Protocol) An alternative to POP3. IMAP retrieves e-mail from an e-mail server like POP3; IMAP uses TCP port 143.

Impedance The amount of resistance to an electrical signal on a wire. It is used as a relative measure of the amount of data a cable can handle.

Incremental Backup Backs up all files that have their archive bits turned on, meaning they have been changed since the last backup. This type of backup turns the archive bits off after the files have been backed up.

Independent Basic Service Set (IBSS) A basic unit of organization in wireless networks formed by two or more wireless nodes communicating in ad hoc mode.

Independent Computing Architecture (ICA) A Citrix-created standard that defines how a server and a client exchange terminal information.

Infrastructure Mode Mode in which wireless networks use one or more wireless access points to connect the wireless network nodes centrally. This configuration is similar to the *star topology* of a wired network.

Inheritance A method of assigning user permissions, in which folder permissions flow downward into subfolders.

Insulating Jacket The external plastic covering of a fiber-optic cable.

Integrated Services Digital Network (ISDN) *See* ISDN (Integrated Services Digital Network).

Interframe Gap (IFG) A short, predefined silence used in CSMA/CA.

Interframe Space (IFS) Short, predefined period of silence in CSMA/CA appended to the waiting time when a device detects activity on the line.

Intermediate Distribution Frame (IDF) The room where all the horizontal runs from all the work areas on a given floor in a building come together.

Intermediate System to Intermediate System (IS-IS) Protocol similar to, but not as popular as, OSPF, but with support for IPv6 since inception.

Internal Connections The connections between computers in a network.

Internal Network A private LAN, with a unique network ID, that resides behind a router.

Internal Threats All the things that a network's own users do to create problems on the network. Examples include accidental deletion of files, accidental damage to hardware devices or cabling, and abuse of rights and permissions.

Internet Assigned Numbers Authority (IANA) The organization responsible for assigning public IP addresses. IANA no longer directly assigns IP addresses, having delegated this to the five Regional Internet Registries. *See* Regional Internet Registries.

Internet Authentication Service (IAS) Popular RADIUS server for Microsoft environments.

Internet Connection Firewall (ICF) *See* ICF (Internet Connection Firewall).

Internet Connection Sharing (ICS) *See* ICS (Internet Connection Sharing).

Internet Control Message Protocol (ICMP) Protocol in which messages consist of a single packet and are connectionless. ICMP packets determine connectivity between two hosts.

Internet Group Management Protocol (IGMP)   Protocol that routers use to communicate with hosts to determine a "group" membership in order to determine which computers want to receive a multicast.

Internet Information Services (IIS)   Microsoft's Web server program for managing Web servers.

Internet Message Access Protocol Version 4 (IMAP4)   An alternative to POP3 for receiving e-mail from an e-mail server. Supports searching through messages stored on a server and supports using folders to organize e-mail.

Internet Protocol (IP)   The Internet standard protocol that handles the logical naming for the TCP/IP protocol using IP addresses.

Internet Protocol Version 4 (IPv4)   Protocol in which addresses consist of four sets of numbers, each number being a value between 0 and 255, using a period to separate the numbers. Often called *dotted decimal* format. No IPv4 address may be all 0s or all 255s. Examples include 192.168.0.1 and 64.176.19.164.

Internet Protocol Version 6 (IPv6)   Protocol in which addresses consist of eight sets of four hexadecimal numbers, each number being a value between 0000 and FFFF, using a colon to separate the numbers. No IP address may be all 0s or all FFFFs. An example is FEDC:BA98:7654:3210:0800:200C:00CF:1234.

InterNIC   The organization that maintained the DNS services, registrations, and so forth run by Network Solutions, General Atomics, and AT&T in the early days of the Internet. ICANN assumed these roles in 1998, so the only time you'll see this organization mentioned currently is on certification exams.

InterVLAN Routing   A feature on some switches to create virtual routers.

Intra-Site Automatic Tunnel Addressing Protocol (ISATAP)   An IPv6 tunneling protocol that adds the IPv4 address to an IPv6 prefix.

Intranet   A private TCP/IP network inside a company or organization.

Intrusion Detection System (IDS)/Intrusion Prevention System (IPS)   An application (often running on a dedicated IDS box) that inspects incoming packets, looking for active intrusions. The difference between an IDS and an IPS is that an IPS can react to an attack.

IP Address   The numeric address of a computer connected to a TCP/IP network, such as the Internet. IPv4 addresses are 32 bits long, written as four octets of 8-bit binary. IPv6 addresses are 128 bits long, written as eight sets of four hexadecimal characters. IP addresses must be matched with a valid subnet mask, which identifies the part of the IP address that is the network ID and the part that is the host ID.

IP Filtering   A method of blocking packets based on IP addresses.

IP Security (IPsec) A IP packet encryption protocol. IPsec is the only IP encryption protocol to work at Layer 3 of the OSI seven-layer model. IPsec is most commonly seen on virtual private networks. *See* Virtual Private Network (VPN).

ipconfig A command-line utility for Windows that displays the current TCP/IP configuration of the machine; similar to UNIX/Linux's ifconfig.

IRC (Internet Relay Chat) An online group discussion. Also called *chat*.

ISDN (Integrated Services Digital Network) The CCITT (Comité Consultatif International Téléphonique et Télégraphique) standard that defines a digital method for telephone communications. Originally designed to replace the current analog telephone systems. ISDN lines have telephone numbers and support up to 128-Kbps transfer rates. ISDN also allows data and voice to share a common phone line. Never very popular, ISDN is now relegated to specialized niches.

ISP (Internet Service Provider) An institution that provides access to the Internet in some form, usually for a fee.

IT (Information Technology) The business of computers, electronic communications, and electronic commerce.

Java A network-oriented programming language invented by Sun Microsystems and specifically designed for writing programs that can be safely downloaded to your computer through the Internet and immediately run without fear of viruses or other harm to your computer or files. Using small Java programs (called *applets*), Web pages can include functions such as animations, calculators, and other fancy tricks.

Just a Bunch of Disks (JBOD) An array of hard drives that are simply connected with no RAID implementations.

K- Most commonly used as the suffix for the binary quantity 1024. For instance, 640 K means 640 × 1024 or 655,360. Just to add some extra confusion to the IT industry, *K* is often misspoken as "kilo," the metric value for 1,000. For example, 10 KB, spoken as "10 kilobytes," means 10,240 bytes rather than 10,000 bytes. Finally, when discussing frequencies, K means 1,000. So, 1 KHz = 1,000 kilohertz.

Kbps (Kilobits Per Second) Data transfer rate.

Kerberos An authentication standard designed to allow different operating systems and applications to authenticate each other.

Key Distribution Center (KDC) System for granting authentication in Kerberos.

Key Pair Name for the two keys generated in asymmetric-key algorithm systems.

Kilohertz (KHz) A unit of measure that equals a frequency of 1000 cycles per second.

LAN (Local Area Network) A group of PCs connected together via cabling, radio, or infrared that use this connectivity to share resources such as printers and mass storage.

Last Mile The connection between a central office and individual users in a telephone system.

Latency A measure of a signal's delay.

Layer A grouping of related tasks involving the transfer of information. Also, a particular level of the OSI seven-layer model, for example, Physical layer, Data Link layer, and so forth.

Layer 2 Switch Any device that filters and forwards frames based on the MAC addresses of the sending and receiving machines. What is normally called a "switch" is actually a "Layer 2 switch."

Layer 2 Tunneling Protocol (L2TP) A VPN protocol developed by Cisco that can be run on almost any connection imaginable. LT2P has no authentication or encryption, but uses IPsec for all its security needs.

Layer 3 Switch Also known as a *router*, filters and forwards data packets based on the IP addresses of the sending and receiving machines.

LC A duplex type of Small Form Factor (SFF) fiber connector, designed to accept two fiber cables.

LEDs (Light Emitting Diodes) Solid-state devices that vibrate at luminous frequencies when current is applied.

Leeching Using another person's wireless connection to the Internet without that person's permission.

Light Leakage The type of interference caused by bending a piece of fiber-optic cable past its maximum bend radius. Light bleeds through the cladding, causing signal distortion and loss.

Lights-out Management Special "computer within a computer" features built into better servers, designed to give you access to a server even when the server itself is shut off.

Lightweight Directory Access Protocol (LDAP) The tool that programs use to query and change a database used by the network. LDAP uses TCP port 389 by default.

Lightweight Extensible Authentication Protocol (LEAP)
A proprietary EAP authentication used almost exclusively by Cisco wireless products. LEAP is an interesting combination of MS-CHAP authentication between a wireless client and a RADIUS server.

Link Light An LED on NICs, hubs, and switches that lights up to show good connection between the devices.

Link-Local Address   The address that a computer running IPv6 gives itself after first booting. The first 64 bits of a link-local address are always FE80::/64.

Link Segments   Segments that link other segments together, but are unpopulated or have no computers directly attached to them.

Link State   Type of dynamic routing protocol that announces only changes to routing tables, as opposed to entire routing tables. Compare to distance vector routing protocols. *See also* Distance Vector.

Linux   The popular open source UNIX-clone operating system.

List of Requirements   A list of all the things you'll need to do to set up your SOHO network, as well as the desired capabilities of the network.

Listening Port   A socket that is prepared to respond to any IP packets destined for that socket's port number.

LMHOSTS File   A static text file that resides on a computer and is used to resolve NetBIOS names to IP addresses. The LMHOSTS file is checked before the machine sends a name resolution request to a WINS name server. The LMHOSTS file has no extension.

Load Balancing   The process of taking several servers and making them look like a single server.

Local   Refers to the computer(s), server(s), and/or LAN that a user is physically using or that is in the same room or building.

Local Connector (LC)   One popular type of Small Form Factor (SFF) connector, considered by many to be the predominant fiber connector.

Local User Accounts   The accounts unique to a single Windows system. Stored in the local system's registry.

Localhost   The HOSTS file alias for the loopback address of 127.0.0.1, referring to the current machine.

Logical Address   A programmable network address, unlike a physical address that is burned into ROM.

Logical Link Control (LLC)   The aspect of the NIC that talks to the operating system, places data coming from the software into frames, and creates the FCS on each frame. The LLC also deals with incoming frames—processing those that are addressed to this NIC and erasing frames addressed to other machines on the network.

Logical Network Diagram   A document that shows the broadcast domains and individual IP addresses for all devices on the network. Only critical switches and routers are shown.

Logical Topology   A network topology defined by signal paths as opposed to the physical layout of the cables. *See also* Physical Topology.

Loopback Address   Sometimes called the localhost, a reserved IP address used for internal testing: 127.0.0.1.

Loopback Plug   Network connector that connects back into itself, used to connect loopback tests.

Loopback Test   A special test often included in diagnostic software that sends data out of the NIC and checks to see if it comes back.

MAC (Media Access Control) Address   Unique 48-bit address assigned to each network card. IEEE assigns blocks of possible addresses to various NIC manufacturers to help ensure that each address is unique. The Data Link layer of the OSI seven-layer model uses MAC addresses for locating machines.

MAC Address Filtering   A method of limiting access to a wireless network based on the physical addresses of wireless NICs.

MAC Filtering   *See* MAC Address Filtering.

Macro   A specially written application macro (collection of commands) that performs the same functions as a virus. These macros normally autostart when the application is run and then make copies of themselves, often propagating across networks.

Mailbox   Special holding area on an e-mail server that separates out e-mail for each user.

Main Distribution Frame (MDF)   The room in a building that stores the demarc, telephone cross-connects, and LAN cross-connects.

Malware   Any program or code (macro, script, and so on) that's designed to do something on a system or network that you don't want to have happen.

Man in the Middle   A hacking attack where a person inserts him- or herself into a conversation between two others, covertly intercepting traffic thought to be only between those other people.

Managed Device   Networking devices, such as routers and advanced switches, that must be configured to use.

Managed Switch   *See* Managed Device.

Management Information Base (MIB)   SNMP's version of a server. *See* Simple Network Management Protocol (SNMP).

Mandatory Access Control (MAC)   A security model in which every resource is assigned a label that defines its security level. If the user lacks that security level, they do not get access.

Maximum Transfer Unit (MTU)   Specifies the largest size of a data unit in a communications protocol, such as Ethernet.

MB (Megabyte)   1,048,576 bytes.

MD5 (Message-Digest Algorithm Version 5)   Arguably the most popular hashing function.

Mechanical Transfer Registered Jack (MT-RJ)   The first type of Small Form Factor (SFF) fiber connector, still in common use.

Media Access Control (MAC)   The part of a NIC that remembers the NIC's own MAC address and attaches that address to outgoing frames.

Media Converter   A device that lets you interconnect different types of Ethernet cable.

Mega-   A prefix that usually stands for the binary quantity 1,048,576. One megabyte is 1,048,576 bytes. One megahertz, however, is 1,000,000 hertz. Sometimes shortened to *meg*, as in "a 286 has an address space of 16 megs."

Mesh Topology   Topology in which each computer has a direct or indirect connection to every other computer in a network. Any node on the network can forward traffic to other nodes. Popular in cellular and many wireless networks.

Metric   Relative value that defines the "cost" of using a particular route.

Metropolitan Area Network (MAN)   Multiple computers connected via cabling, radio, leased phone lines, or infrared that are within the same city. A typical example of a MAN is a college campus. No firm dividing lines dictate what is considered a WAN, MAN, or LAN.

MHz (Megahertz)   A unit of measure that equals a frequency of 1 million cycles per second.

MIME (Multipurpose Internet Mail Extensions)   A standard for attaching binary files, such as executables and images, to the Internet's text-based mail (24-Kbps packet size).

Mirroring   Also called *drive mirroring*, reading and writing data at the same time to two drives for fault-tolerance purposes. Considered RAID level 1.

Modal Distortion   A light distortion problem unique to multimode fiber-optic cable.

Modem (Modulator-Demodulator)   A device that converts both digital bit streams into analog signals (modulation) and incoming analog signals back into digital signals (demodulation). Most commonly used to interconnect telephone lines to computers.

Mounting Bracket Bracket that acts as a holder for a faceplate in cable installations.

MS-CHAP Microsoft's dominant variation of the CHAP protocol, uses a slightly more advanced encryption protocol.

MTU (Maximum Transfer Unit) *See* Maximum Transfer Unit (MTU).

MTU Black Hole When a router's firewall features block ICMP requests, making MTU worthless.

MTU Mismatch The situation when your network's packets are so large that they must be fragmented to fit into your ISP's packets.

Multicast Method of sending a packet in which the sending computer sends it to a group of interested computers.

Multicast Addresses In IPv6, a set of reserved addresses designed to go only to certain systems.

Multifactor Authentication A form of authentication where a user must use two or more factors to prove his or her identity.

Multilayer Switch A switch that has functions that operate at multiple layers of the OSI seven-layer model.

Multimeter A tool for testing voltage (AC and DC), resistance, and continuity.

Multimode Fiber (MMF) Type of fiber-optic cable that uses LEDs.

Multiple In/Multiple Out (MIMO) A feature in 802.11 WAPs that enables them to make multiple simultaneous connections.

Multiplexer A device that merges information from multiple input channels to a single output channel.

Multiprotocol Label Switching (MPLS) A router feature that labels certain data to use a desired connection. It works with any type of packet switching (even Ethernet) to force certain types of data to use a certain path.

Multisource Agreement (MSA) Interchangeable modular transceivers used in 10 GbE networking devices.

Multispeed Hub Any hub that supports more than one network speed for otherwise similar cabling systems. Multispeed hubs come in two flavors: one has mostly dedicated slower ports, with a few dedicated faster ports, whereas the other has only special auto-sensing ports that automatically run at either the faster or the slower speed.

MX Records Records used by SMTP servers to determine where to send mail.

My Traceroute (mtr)   Terminal command in Linux that dynamically displays the route a packet is taking. Similar to traceroute.

Name Resolution   A method that enables one computer on the network to locate another to establish a session. All network protocols perform name resolution in one of two ways: either via *broadcast* or by providing some form of *name server*.

Name Server   A computer whose job is to know the name of every other computer on the network.

NAT Translation Table   Special database in a NAT router that stores destination IP addresses and ephemeral source ports from outgoing packets and compares them against returning packets.

nbtstat   A command-line utility used to check the current NetBIOS name cache on a particular machine. The utility compares NetBIOS names to their corresponding IP addresses.

Near-End Crosstalk (NEXT)   Crosstalk at the same end of a cable from which the signal is being generated.

NetBEUI (NetBIOS Extended User Interface)   Microsoft's first networking protocol, designed to work with NetBIOS. NetBEUI is long obsolesced by TCP/IP. NetBEUI did not support routing.

NetBIOS (Network Basic Input/Output System)   A protocol that operates at the Session layer of the OSI seven-layer model. This protocol creates and manages connections based on the names of the computers involved.

NetBIOS Name   A computer name that identifies both the specific machine and the functions that machine performs. A NetBIOS name consists of 16 characters: the first 15 are an alphanumeric name, and the 16th is a special suffix that identifies the role the machine plays.

netstat   A universal command-line utility used to examine the TCP/IP connections open on a given host.

Network   A collection of two or more computers interconnected by telephone lines, coaxial cables, satellite links, radio, and/or some other communication technique. A computer *network* is a group of computers that are connected together and communicate with one another for a common purpose. Computer networks support "people and organization" networks, users who also share a common purpose for communicating.

Network Access Control (NAC)   Control over information, people, access, machines, and everything in between.

Network Access Server (NAS)   Systems that control the modems in a RADIUS network.

Network Address Translation (NAT)   A means of translating a system's IP address into another IP address before sending it out to a larger network. NAT manifests itself by a NAT program that runs on a system or a router. A network using NAT provides the systems on the network with private IP addresses. The system running the NAT software has two interfaces: one connected to the network and the other connected to the larger network.

The NAT program takes packets from the client systems bound for the larger network and translates their internal private IP addresses to its own public IP address, enabling many systems to share a single IP address.

Network as a Service (NaaS)   The act of renting virtual server space over the Internet. *See* Cloud Computing.

Network Design   The process of gathering together and planning the layout for the equipment needed to create a network.

Network Diagram   An illustration that shows devices on a network and how they connect.

Network ID   A number used in IP networks to identify the network on which a device or machine exists.

Network Interface   A device by which a system accesses a network. In most cases, this is a NIC or a modem.

Network Interface Card (NIC)   Traditionally, an expansion card that enables a PC to link physically to a network. Modern computers now use built-in NICs, no longer requiring physical cards, but the term "NIC" is still very common.

Network Interface Unit (NIU)   Another name for a demarc. *See* Demarc.

Network Layer   Layer 3 of the OSI seven-layer model. *See* Open Systems Interconnection (OSI) Seven-Layer Model.

Network Management Software (NMS)   Tools that enable you to describe, visualize, and configure an entire network.

Network Map   A highly detailed illustration of a network, down to the individual computers. A network map will show IP addresses, ports, protocols, and more.

Network Name   Another name for the SSID.

Network Protocol   Special software that exists in every network-capable operating system that acts to create unique identifiers for each system. It also creates a set of communication rules for issues like how to handle data chopped up into multiple packets and how to deal with routers. TCP/IP is the dominant network protocol today.

Network Share   A shared resource on a network.

Network Threat Any number of things that share one essential feature: the potential to damage network data, machines, or users.

Network Time Protocol (NTP) Protocol that gives the current time.

Network Topology Refers to the way that cables and other pieces of hardware connect to one another.

Newsgroup The name for a discussion group on Usenet.

Next Hop The next router a packet should go to at any given point.

NFS (Network File System) A TCP/IP file system–sharing protocol that enables systems to treat files on a remote machine as though they were local files. NFS uses TCP port 2049, but many users choose alternative port numbers. Though still somewhat popular and heavily supported, NFS has been largely replaced by Samba/CIFS. *See also* Samba *and* Common Internet File System (CIFS).

Nmap A network utility designed to scan a network and create a map. Frequently used as a vulnerability scanner.

Node A member of a network or a point where one or more functional units interconnect transmission lines.

Noise Undesirable signals bearing no desired information and frequently capable of introducing errors into the communication process.

Non-Discovery Mode A setting for Bluetooth devices that effectively hides them from other Bluetooth devices.

Nonrepudiation The process that guarantees the data is as originally sent and that it came from the source you think it should have come from.

Normal Backup A full backup of every selected file on a system. This type of backup turns off the archive bit after the backup.

Novell NetWare A powerful, unique, and once dominant network operating system that operated on a client/server model.

Ns (Nanosecond) A billionth of a second. Light travels a little over 11 inches in 1 ns.

NS Records Records that list the DNS servers for a Web site.

nslookup A once handy tool that advanced techs used to query the functions of DNS servers. Most DNS servers now ignore all but the most basic nslookup queries.

NTFS (NT File System)   A file system for hard drives that enables object-level security, long filename support, compression, and encryption. NTFS 4.0 debuted with Windows NT 4.0. Windows 2000 offered NTFS 5.0; Windows XP saw the debut of NTFS 5.1. Later Windows versions continued the updates, so Windows Vista uses NTFS 6.0 and Windows 7 uses NTFS 6.1.

NTFS Permissions   Groupings of what Microsoft calls special permissions that have names like Execute, Read, and Write, and that allow or disallow users certain access to files.

NTLDR   A Windows NT/2000/XP/2003 boot file. Launched by the MBR or MFT, NTLDR looks at the BOOT.INI configuration file for any installed operating systems.

Object   A group of related counters used in Windows logging utilities.

OEM (Original Equipment Manufacturer)   Contrary to the name, does not create original hardware, but rather purchases components from manufacturers and puts them together in systems under its own brand name. Dell, Inc. and Gateway, Inc., for example, are for the most part OEMs. Apple, Inc., which manufactures most of the components for its own Macintosh-branded machines, is not an OEM. Also known as *VARs (value-added resellers)*.

Offsite   The term for a virtual computer accessed and stored remotely.

Ohm Rating   Electronic measurement of a cable's or an electronic component's impedance.

Onsite   The term for a virtual computer stored at your location.

Open Port   *See* Listening Port.

Open Shortest Path First (OSPF)   An interior gateway routing protocol developed for IP networks based on the *shortest path first* or *link-state algorithm*.

Open Source   Applications and operating systems that offer access to their source code; this enables developers to modify applications and operating systems easily to meet their specific needs.

Open Systems Interconnection (OSI)   An international standard suite of protocols defined by the International Organization for Standardization (ISO) that implements the OSI seven-layer model for network communications between computers.

Open Systems Interconnection (OSI) Seven-Layer Model   An architecture model based on the OSI protocol suite, which defines and standardizes the flow of data between computers. The following lists the seven layers:

- **Layer 1**   The *Physical layer* defines hardware connections and turns binary into physical pulses (electrical or light). Repeaters and hubs operate at the Physical layer.

- **Layer 2**   The *Data Link layer* identifies devices on the Physical layer. MAC addresses are part of the Data Link layer. Bridges operate at the Data Link layer.

- **Layer 3**   The *Network layer* moves packets between computers on different networks. Routers operate at the Network layer. IP and IPX operate at the Network layer.

- **Layer 4**   The *Transport layer* breaks data down into manageable chunks. TCP, UDP, SPX, and NetBEUI operate at the Transport layer.

- **Layer 5**   The *Session layer* manages connections between machines. NetBIOS and Sockets operate at the Session layer.

- **Layer 6**   The *Presentation layer*, which can also manage data encryption, hides the differences among various types of computer systems.

- **Layer 7**   The *Application layer* provides tools for programs to use to access the network (and the lower layers). HTTP, FTP, SMTP, and POP3 are all examples of protocols that operate at the Application layer.

OpenSSH   A series of secure programs developed by the OpenBSD organization to fix SSH's limitation of only being able to handle one session per tunnel.

Operating System (OS)   The set of programming that enables a program to interact with the computer and provides an interface between the PC and the user. Examples are Microsoft Windows 7, Apple Macintosh OS X, and SUSE Linux.

Optical Carrier (OC)   Specification used to denote the optical data carrying capacity (in Mbps) of fiber-optic cables in networks conforming to the SONET standard. The OC standard is an escalating series of speeds, designed to meet the needs of medium-to-large corporations. SONET establishes OCs from 51.8 Mbps (OC-1) to 39.8 Gbps (OC-768).

Optical Time Domain Reflectometer (OTDR)   Tester for fiber-optic cable that determines continuity and reports the location of cable breaks.

Organizationally Unique Identifier (OUI)   The first 24 bits of a MAC address, assigned to the NIC manufacturer by the IEEE.

Orthogonal Frequency-Division Multiplexing (OFDM)   A spread-spectrum broadcasting method that combines the multiple frequencies of DSSS with FHSS's hopping capability.

OS (Operating System)   *See* Operating System (OS).

Oscilloscope   A device that gives a graphical/visual representation of signal levels over a period of time.

Packet   Basic component of communication over a network. A group of bits of fixed maximum size and well-defined format that is switched and transmitted as a complete whole through a network. It contains source and destination address, data, and control information. *See also* Frame.

Packet Filtering A mechanism that blocks any incoming or outgoing packet from a particular IP address or range of IP addresses. Also known as *IP filtering*.

Packet Sniffer A tool that intercepts and logs network packets.

Pad Extra data added to an Ethernet frame to bring the data up to the minimum required size of 64 bytes.

Path MTU Discovery (PMTU) A method for determining the best MTU setting that works by adding a new feature called the "Don't Fragment (DF) flag" to the IP packet.

Partially Meshed Topology A mesh topology in which not all of the nodes are directly connected.

Passive Optical Network (PON) A fiber architecture that uses a single fiber to the neighborhood switch and then individual fiber runs to each final destination.

Password A series of characters that enables a user to gain access to a file, a folder, a PC, or a program.

Password Authentication Protocol (PAP) The oldest and most basic form of authentication and also the least safe because it sends all passwords in cleartext.

Patch Cables Short (2 to 5 foot) UTP cables that connect patch panels to the hubs.

Patch Panel A panel containing a row of female connectors (ports) that terminate the horizontal cabling in the equipment room. Patch panels facilitate cabling organization and provide protection to horizontal cabling.

PBX (Private Branch Exchange) A private phone system used within an organization.

PDA (Personal Digital Assistant) A hand-held computer that blurs the line between the calculator and computer. Earlier PDAs were calculators that enabled the user to program in such information as addresses and appointments. Newer machines, such as the Palm Pilot, are fully programmable computers. Most PDAs use a pen/stylus for input rather than a keyboard. A few of the larger PDAs have a tiny keyboard in addition to the stylus.

Peer-to-Peer A network in which each machine can act as either a client or a server.

Peer-to-Peer Mode *See* Ad Hoc Mode.

Performance Monitor (PerfMon) The Windows XP logging utility.

Peripherals Noncomputer devices on a network, for example, fax machines, printers, or scanners.

Permissions Sets of attributes that network administrators assign to users and groups that define what they can do to resources.

Persistent Connection   A connection to a shared folder or drive that the computer immediately reconnects to at logon.

Personal Area Network (PAN)   The network created among Bluetooth devices such as smartphones, tablets, printers, keyboards, mice, and so on.

Phishing   A social engineering technique where the attacker poses as a trusted source in order to obtain sensitive information.

Physical Address   An address burned into a ROM chip on a NIC. A MAC address is an example of a physical address.

Physical Layer   *See* Open Systems Interconnection (OSI) Seven-Layer Model.

Physical Network Diagram   A document that shows all of the physical connections on a network. Cabling type, protocol, and speed are also listed for each connection.

Physical Topology   The manner in which the physical components of a network are arranged.

PING (Packet Internet Groper)   A small network message sent by a computer to check for the presence and response of another system. A ping uses ICMP packets. *See* Internet Control Message Protocol (ICMP).

Plain Old Telephone Service (POTS)   *See* Public Switched Telephone Network (PSTN).

Plaintext   Data that is in an easily read or viewed industry-wide standard format.

Platform   Hardware environment that supports the running of a computer system.

Plenum   Usually a space between a building's false ceiling and the floor above it. Most of the wiring for networks is located in this space. Plenum is also a fire rating for network cabling.

Point Coordination Function (PCF)   A method of collision avoidance defined by the 802.11 standard, which has yet to be implemented.

Point-to-Multipoint   Topology in which one device communicates with more than one other device on a network.

Point-to-Point Protocol (PPP)   A protocol that enables a computer to connect to the Internet through a dial-in connection and to enjoy most of the benefits of a direct connection. PPP is considered to be superior to SLIP because of its error detection and data compression features, which SLIP lacks, and the capability to use dynamic IP addresses.

Point-to-Point Protocol over Ethernet (PPPoE)   A protocol that was originally designed to encapsulate PPP frames into Ethernet frames. Used by DSL providers to force customers to log into their DSL connections instead of simply connecting automatically.

Point-to-Point Topology   A network of two single devices communicating with each other.

Point-to-Point Tunneling Protocol (PPTP)   A protocol that works with PPP to provide a secure data link between computers using encryption.

Pointer Record (PTR)   A record that points to canonical names. *See also* Reverse Lookup Zone.

Polyvinyl Chloride (PVC)   A material used for the outside insulation and jacketing of most cables. Also a fire rating for a type of cable that has no significant fire protection.

Port   That portion of a computer through which a peripheral device may communicate. Often identified with the various plug-in jacks on the back of your computer. On a network hub, it is the connector that receives the wire link from a node. In TCP/IP, ports are 16-bit numbers between 0 and 65535 assigned to a particular TCP/IP session.

Port Address Translation (PAT)   The most commonly used form of Network Address Translation, where the NAT uses port numbers to map traffic from specific machines in the network. *See* Network Address Translation.

Port Authentication   Function of many advanced networking devices that authenticates a connecting device at the point of connection.

Port Blocking   Preventing the passage of any TCP or UDP segments or datagrams through any ports other than the ones prescribed by the system administrator.

Port Filtering   *See* Port Blocking.

Port Forwarding   Preventing the passage of any IP packets through any ports other than the ones prescribed by the system administrator.

Port Mirroring   The capability of many advanced switches to mirror data from any or all physical ports on a switch to a single physical port. Useful for any type of situation where an administrator needs to inspect packets coming to or from certain computers.

Port Number   Number used to identify the requested service (such as SMTP or FTP) when connecting to a TCP/IP host. Some example port numbers include 80 (HTTP), 20 (FTP), 69 (TFTP), 25 (SMTP), and 110 (POP3).

Post Office Protocol Version 3 (POP3)   One of the two protocols that receive e-mail from SMTP servers. POP3 uses TCP port 110. Most e-mail clients use this protocol, although some use IMAP4.

PostScript   A language defined by Adobe Systems, Inc., for describing how to create an image on a page. The description is independent of the resolution of the device that will create the image. It includes a technology for defining the shape of a font and creating a raster image at many different resolutions and sizes.

Power over Ethernet (PoE)   A standard that enables WAPs to receive their power from the same Ethernet cables that transfer their data.

Power Users   A user account that has the capability to do many, but not all, of the basic administrator functions.

PPPoE (PPP over Ethernet)   *See* Point-to-Point Protocol over Ethernet (PPPoE).

Preamble   A 64-bit series of alternating 1s and 0s, ending with 11, that begins every Ethernet frame. The preamble gives a receiving NIC time to realize a frame is coming and to know exactly where the frame starts.

Presentation Layer   *See* Open Systems Interconnection (OSI) Seven-Layer Model.

Primary Lookup Zone   A forward lookup zone stored in a text file. *See* Forward Lookup Zone.

Primary Rate Interface (PRI)   A type of ISDN that is actually just a full T1 line carrying 23 B channels.

Private Port Numbers   *See* Dynamic Port Numbers.

Program   A set of actions or instructions that a machine is capable of interpreting and executing. Used as a verb, it means to design, write, and test such instructions.

Promiscuous Mode   A mode of operation for a NIC in which the NIC processes all frames that it sees on the cable.

Prompt   A character or message provided by an operating system or program to indicate that it is ready to accept input.

Proprietary   Term used to describe technology that is unique to, and owned by, a particular vendor.

Protected Extensible Authentication Protocol (PEAP)   An authentication protocol that uses a password function based on MS-CHAPv2 with the addition of an encrypted TLS tunnel similar to EAP-TLS.

Protocol   An agreement that governs the procedures used to exchange information between cooperating entities; usually includes how much information is to be sent, how often it is sent, how to recover from transmission errors, and who is to receive the information.

Protocol Analyzer   A tool that monitors the different protocols running at different layers on the network and that can give Application, Session, Network, and Data Link layer information on every frame going through a network.

Protocol Stack   The actual software that implements the protocol suite on a particular operating system.

Protocol Suite   A set of protocols that are commonly used together and operate at different levels of the OSI seven-layer model.

Proxy ARP   The process of making remotely connected computers act as though they are on the same LAN as local computers.

Proxy Server   A device that fetches Internet resources for a client without exposing that client directly to the Internet. Most proxy servers accept requests for HTTP, FTP, POP3, and SMTP resources. The proxy server often caches, or stores, a copy of the requested resource for later use.

PSTN (Public Switched Telephone Network)   *See* Public Switched Telephone Network (PSTN).

Public-Key Cryptography   A method for exchanging digital keys securely.

Public-Key Infrastructure (PKI)   The system for creating and distributing digital certificates using sites like VeriSign, Thawte, or GoDaddy.

Public Switched Telephone Network (PSTN)   Also known as *Plain Old Telephone Service (POTS)*. The most common type of phone connection, which takes your sounds, translated into an analog waveform by the microphone, and transmits them to another phone.

Punchdown Tool   A specialized tool for connecting UTP wires to a 110-block.

Quality of Service (QoS)   Policies that control how much bandwidth a protocol, PC, user, VLAN, or IP address may use.

Raceway   Cable organizing device that adheres to walls, making for a much simpler, though less neat, installation than running cables in the walls.

Radio Frequency Interference (RFI)   The phenomenon where a Wi-Fi signal is disrupted by a radio signal from another device.

Radio Grade (RG) Ratings   Ratings developed by the U.S. military to provide a quick reference for the different types of coaxial cables.

RADIUS Server   A system that enables remote users to connect to a network service.

Real-Time Processing   The processing of transactions as they occur, rather than batching them. Pertaining to an application, processing in which response to input is fast enough to affect subsequent inputs and guide the process, and in which records are updated immediately. The lag from input time to output time must be sufficiently small for acceptable timeliness. Timeliness is a function of the total system: missile guidance requires output within a few milliseconds of input, whereas scheduling of steamships requires a response time in days. Real-time systems are those with a response time of milliseconds; interactive systems respond in seconds; and batch systems may respond in hours or days.

Real-Time Transport Protocol (RTP) Protocol that defines the type of packets used on the Internet to move voice or data from a server to clients. The vast majority of VoIP solutions available today use RTP.

Redundant Array of Independent [or Inexpensive] Devices [or Disks] (RAID) A way to create a fault-tolerant storage system. RAID has six levels. Level 0 uses byte-level striping and provides no fault tolerance. Level 1 uses mirroring or duplexing. Level 2 uses bit-level striping. Level 3 stores error-correcting information (such as parity) on a separate disk and data striping on the remaining drives. Level 4 is level 3 with block-level striping. Level 5 uses block-level and parity data striping.

REGEDIT.EXE A program used to edit the Windows registry.

Regional Internet Registries (RIRs) Entities under the oversight of the Internet Assigned Numbers Authority (IANA), which parcels out IP addresses.

Registered Ports Port numbers from 1024 to 49151. Anyone can use these port numbers for their servers or for ephemeral numbers on clients.

Regulations Rules of law or policy that govern behavior in the workplace, such as what to do when a particular event occurs.

Remote Refers to the computer(s), server(s), and/or LAN that cannot be physically used due to its distance from the user.

Remote Access The capability to access a computer from outside a building in which it is housed. Remote access requires communications hardware, software, and actual physical links.

Remote Access Server (RAS) Refers to both the hardware component (servers built to handle the unique stresses of a large number of clients calling in) and the software component (programs that work with the operating system to allow remote access to the network) of a remote access solution.

Remote Authentication Dial-In User Service (RADIUS) An AAA standard created to support ISPs with hundreds if not thousands of modems in hundreds of computers to connect to a single central database. RADIUS consists of three devices: the RADIUS server that has access to a database of user names and passwords, a number of network access servers (NASs) that control the modems, and a group of systems that dial into the network.

Remote Copy Protocol (RCP) Provides the capability to copy files to and from the remote server without the need to resort to FTP or Network File System (NFS, a UNIX form of folder sharing). RCP can also be used in scripts and shares TCP port 514 with RSH.

Remote Desktop Protocol (RDP) A Microsoft-created remote terminal protocol.

Remote Installation Services (RIS)   A tool introduced with Windows 2000 that can be used to initiate either a scripted installation or an installation of an image of an operating system onto a PC.

Remote Login (rlogin)   Program in UNIX that enables you to log into a server remotely. Unlike Telnet, rlogin can be configured to log in automatically.

Remote Shell (RSH)   Allows you to send single commands to the remote server. Whereas rlogin is designed to be used interactively, RSH can be easily integrated into a script.

Remote Terminal   A connection on a faraway computer that enables you to control that computer as if you were sitting in front of it and logged in. Remote terminal programs all require a server and a client. The server is the computer to be controlled. The client is the computer from which you do the controlling.

Repeater   A device that takes all of the frames it receives on one Ethernet segment and re-creates them on another Ethernet segment. This allows for longer cables or more computers on a segment. Repeaters operate at Layer 1 (Physical) of the OSI seven-layer model.

Replication   A process where multiple computers might share complete copies of a database and constantly update each other.

Resistance   The tendency for a physical medium to impede electron flow. It is classically measured in a unit called *ohms*. *See also* Impedance.

Resource   Anything that exists on another computer that a person wants to use without going to that computer. Also an online information set or an online interactive option. An online library catalog and the local school lunch menu are examples of information sets. Online menus or graphical user interfaces, Internet e-mail, online conferences, Telnet, FTP, and Gopher are examples of interactive options.

Reverse Lookup Zone   A DNS setting that resolves IP addresses to FQDNs. In other words, it does exactly the reverse of what DNS normally accomplishes using forward lookup zones.

Ring Topology   A network topology in which all the computers on the network attach to a central ring of cable.

RIPv1   The first version of RIP, which had several shortcomings, such as a maximum hop count of 15 and a routing table update interval of 30 seconds, which was a problem because every router on a network would send out its table at the same time.

RIPv2   The current version of RIP. Fixed many problems of RIPv1, but the maximum hop count of 15 still applies.

Riser   Fire rating that designates the proper cabling to use for vertical runs between floors of a building.

Rivest Cipher 4 (RC4)   A popular streaming symmetric-key algorithm.

Rivest Shamir Adleman (RSA)   An improved public-key cryptography algorithm that enables secure digital signatures.

RJ (Registered Jack)   Connectors used for UTP cable on both telephone and network connections.

RJ-11   Type of connector with four-wire UTP connections; usually found in telephone connections.

RJ-45   Type of connector with eight-wire UTP connections; usually found in network connections and used for 10/100/1000BaseT networking.

Rogue Access Point   An unauthorized wireless access point (WAP) installed in a computer network.

Role-Based Access Control (RBAC)   The most popular authentication model used in file sharing, defines a user's access to a resource based on the roles the user plays in the network environment. This leads to the idea of creation of groups. A group in most networks is nothing more than a name that has clearly defined accesses to different resources. User accounts are placed into various groups.

ROM (Read-Only Memory)   The generic term for nonvolatile memory that can be read from but not written to. This means that code and data stored in ROM cannot be corrupted by accidental erasure. Additionally, ROM retains its data when power is removed, which makes it the perfect medium for storing BIOS data or information such as scientific constants.

Root Directory   The directory that contains all other directories.

Rootkit   A Trojan that takes advantage of very low-level operating system functions to hide itself from all but the most aggressive of anti-malware tools.

route   A command that enables a user to display and edit the local system's routing table.

Router   A device that connects separate networks and forwards a packet from one network to another based only on the network address for the protocol being used. For example, an IP router looks only at the IP network number. Routers operate at Layer 3 (Network) of the OSI seven-layer model.

Routing and Remote Access Service (RRAS)   A special remote access server program, originally only available on Windows Server, on which a PPTP endpoint is placed in Microsoft networks.

Routing Information Protocol (RIP)   Distance vector routing protocol that dates from the 1980s.

Routing Loop   A situation where interconnected routers loop traffic, causing the routers to respond slowly or not respond at all.

Routing Table   A list of paths to various networks required by routers. This table can be built either manually or automatically.

RS-232   The recommended standard (RS) upon which all serial communication takes place on a PC.

Run   A single piece of installed horizontal cabling.

Samba   An application that enables UNIX systems to communicate using Server Message Blocks (SMBs). This, in turn, enables them to act as Microsoft clients and servers on the network.

SC Connector   One of two special types of fiber-optic cable used in 10BaseFL networks.

Scalability   The capability to support network growth.

Scanner   A device that senses alterations of light and dark. It enables the user to import photographs, other physical images, and text into the computer in digital form.

Secondary Lookup Zone   A backup lookup zone stored on another DNS server. *See also* Forward Lookup Zone.

Secure Copy Protocol (SCP)   One of the first SSH-enabled programs to appear after the introduction of SSH. SCP was one of the first protocols used to transfer data securely between two hosts and thus might have replaced FTP. SCP works well but lacks features such as a directory listing.

Secure FTP (SFTP)   Designed as a replacement for FTP after many of the inadequacies of SCP (such as the inability to see the files on the other computer) were discovered.

Secure Hash Algorithm (SHA)   A popular cryptographic hash.

Secure Shell (SSH)   A terminal emulation program that looks exactly like Telnet but encrypts the data. SSH has replaced Telnet on the Internet.

Secure Sockets Layer (SSL)   A protocol developed by Netscape for transmitting private documents over the Internet. SSL works by using a public key to encrypt sensitive data. This encrypted data is sent over an SSL connection and then decrypted at the receiving end using a private key.

Security   A network's resilience against unwanted access or attack.

Security Log   A log that tracks anything that affects security, such as successful and failed logons and logoffs.

Security Policy A set of procedures defining actions employees should perform to protect the network's security.

Segment The bus cable to which the computers on an Ethernet network connect.

Sendmail A popular e-mail server program.

Sequential A method of storing and retrieving information that requires data to be written and read sequentially. Accessing any portion of the data requires reading all the preceding data.

Server A computer that shares its resources, such as printers and files, with other computers on the network. An example of this is a Network File System Server that shares its disk space with a workstation that has no disk drive of its own.

Server-Based Network A network in which one or more systems function as dedicated file, print, or application servers, but do not function as clients.

Service Set Identification (SSID) A 32-bit identification string, sometimes called a *network name*, that's inserted into the header of each data packet processed by a wireless access point.

Session A networking term used to refer to the logical stream of data flowing between two programs and being communicated over a network. Many different sessions may be emanating from any one node on a network.

Session Initiation Protocol (SIP) A signaling protocol for controlling voice and video calls over IP. SIP competes with H.323 for VoIP dominance.

Session Layer *See* Open Systems Interconnection (OSI) Seven-Layer Model.

Session Software Handles the process of differentiating among various types of connections on a PC.

Share Level Security A security system in which each resource has a password assigned to it; access to the resource is based on knowing the password.

Share Permissions Permissions that only control the access of other users on the network with whom you share your resource. They have no impact on you (or anyone else) sitting at the computer whose resource is being shared.

Shareware Software that is protected by copyright, but the copyright holder allows (encourages!) you to make and distribute copies, under the condition that those who adopt the software after preview pay a fee. Derivative works are not allowed, and you may make an archival copy.

Shell Generally refers to the user interface of an operating system. A shell is the command processor that is the actual interface between the kernel and the user.

Shielded Twisted Pair (STP)   A cabling for networks composed of pairs of wires twisted around each other at specific intervals. The twists serve to reduce interference (also called *crosstalk*). The more twists, the less interference. The cable has metallic shielding to protect the wires from external interference. *See also* Unshielded Twisted Pair (UTP) for the more commonly used cable type in modern networks.

Short Circuit   Allows electricity to pass between two conductive elements that weren't designed to interact together. Also called a *short*.

Shortest Path First   Networking algorithm for directing router traffic. *See also* Open Shortest Path First (OSPF).

Signal Strength   A measurement of how well your wireless device is connecting to other devices.

Signaling Topology   Another name for logical topology. *See* Logical Topology.

Simple Mail Transfer Protocol (SMTP)   The main protocol used to send electronic mail on the Internet.

Simple Network Management Protocol (SNMP)   A set of standards for communication with devices connected to a TCP/IP network. Examples of these devices include routers, hubs, and switches.

Single-Mode Fiber (SMF)   Fiber-optic cables that use lasers.

Site Survey   A process that enables you to determine any obstacles to creating the wireless network you want.

Site-to-Site   A type of VPN connection using two Cisco VPN concentrators to connect two separate LANs permanently.

Small Form Factor (SFF)   A description of later-generation, fiber-optic connectors designed to be much smaller than the first iterations of connectors. *See also* LC *and* Mechanical Transfer Registered Jack (MT-RJ).

Small Form Factor Pluggable (SFP)   A Cisco module that enables you to add additional features to its routers.

Smart Device   Devices (such as credit cards, USB keys, etc.) that you insert into your PC in lieu of entering a password.

Smart Jack   Type of NIU that enables ISPs or telephone companies to test for faults in a network, such as disconnections and loopbacks.

SMB (Server Message Block)   Protocol used by Microsoft clients and servers to share file and print resources.

Smurf A type of hacking attack in which an attacker floods a network with ping packets sent to the broadcast address. The trick that makes this attack special is that the return address of the pings is spoofed to that of the intended victim. When all the computers on the network respond to the initial ping, they send their response to the intended victim.

Snap-Ins Small utilities that can be used with the Microsoft Management Console.

Snapshot A tool that enables you to save an extra copy of a virtual machine as it is exactly at the moment the snapshot is taken.

Sneakernet Saving a file on a portable medium and walking it over to another computer.

Sniffer Diagnostic program that can order a NIC to run in promiscuous mode. *See* Promiscuous Mode.

Snip *See* Cable Stripper.

Social Engineering The process of using or manipulating people inside the networking environment to gain access to that network from the outside.

Socket A combination of a port number and an IP address that uniquely identifies a connection.

Socket Pairs *See* Endpoints.

Software Programming instructions or data stored on some type of binary storage device.

Solid Core A cable that uses a single solid wire to transmit signals.

SONET (Synchronous Optical Network) A standard for connecting fiberoptic transmission systems. SONET was proposed in the mid-1980s and is now an ANSI standard. SONET defines interface standards at the Physical layer of the OSI seven-layer model.

Source Address Table (SAT) An electronic table of the MAC addresses of each computer connected to a switch.

Spanning Tree Protocol (STP) A protocol that enables switches to detect and repair bridge loops automatically.

Spyware Any program that sends information about your system or your actions over the Internet.

SQL (Structured Query Language) A language created by IBM that relies on simple English statements to perform database queries. SQL enables databases from different manufacturers to be queried using a standard syntax.

SSL (Secure Sockets Layer) *See* Secure Sockets Layer (SSL).

SSL VPN   A type of VPN that uses SSL encryption. Clients connect to the VPN server using a standard Web browser, with the traffic secured using SSL. The two most common types of SSL VPNs are SSL portal VPNs and SSL tunnel VPNs.

ST Connector   One of two special types of fiber-optic cable used in 10BaseFL networks.

Star Topology   A network topology in which all computers in the network connect to a central wiring point.

Star-Bus Topology   A hybrid of the star and bus topologies that uses a physical star, where all nodes connect to a single wiring point such as a hub and a logical bus that maintains the Ethernet standards. One benefit of a star-bus topology is *fault tolerance*.

Star-Ring Topology   A hybrid of the Token Ring topology and the physical star.

Stateful   Describes a DHCPv6 server that works very similarly to an IPv4 DHCP server, passing out IPv6 addresses, subnet masks, and default gateways as well as optional items like DNS server addresses.

Stateful Filtering/Stateful Inspection   A method of filtering in which all packets are examined as a stream. Stateful devices can do more than allow or block; they can track when a stream is disrupted or packets get corrupted and act accordingly.

Stateless   Describes a DHCPv6 server that only passes out optional information.

Stateless Filtering   A method of filtering where the device that does the filtering just checks the packet for IP addresses and port numbers and blocks or allows accordingly.

Static Addressing   The process of assigning IP addresses by manually typing them into client computers.

Static NAT (SNAT)   A type of NAT that maps a single routable IP address to a single machine, allowing you to access that machine from outside the network.

Static Routing   A process by which routers in an internetwork obtain information about paths to other routers. This information must be supplied manually.

Storage   A device or medium that can retain data for subsequent retrieval.

STP (Spanning Tree Protocol)   *See* Spanning Tree Protocol (STP).

Straight-through Cable   A cable that enables you to connect the uplink ports of two hubs together.

Stranded Core   A cable that uses a bundle of tiny wire strands to transmit signals. Stranded core is not quite as good a conductor as solid core, but it will stand up to substantial handling without breaking.

Stream Cipher   An encryption method that encrypts a single bit at a time. Popular when data comes in long streams (such as with older wireless networks or cell phones).

Stripe Set   Two or more drives in a group that are used for a striped volume.

Structured Cabling   Standards defined by the Telecommunications Industry Association/Electronic Industries Alliance (TIA/EIA) that define methods of organizing the cables in a network for ease of repair and replacement.

STS Overhead   Carries the signaling and protocol information in Synchronous Transport Signal (STS).

STS Payload   Carries data in STS.

Subnet   Each independent network in a TCP/IP internetwork.

Subnet Mask   The value used in TCP/IP settings to divide the IP address of a host into its component parts: network ID and host ID.

Subnetting   Taking a single class of IP addresses and chopping it into multiple smaller groups.

Supplicant   A client computer in a RADIUS network.

Switch   A device that filters and forwards traffic based on some criteria. A bridge and a router are both examples of switches.

Switching Loop   When you connect multiple switches together to cause a loop to appear.

Symmetric DSL (SDSL)   Type of DSL connection that provides equal upload and download speed and, in theory, provides speeds up to 15 Mbps, although the vast majority of ISPs provide packages ranging from 192 Kbps to 9 Mbps.

Symmetric-Key Algorithm   Any encryption method that uses the same key for both encryption and decryption.

Synchronous   Describes a connection between two electronic devices where neither must acknowledge (ACK) when receiving data.

Synchronous Digital Hierarchy (SDH)   European fiber carrier standard equivalent to SONET.

Synchronous Optical Network (SONET)   American fiber carrier standard. *See also* SONET (Synchronous Optical Network).

Synchronous Transport Signal (STS)   Signal method used by SONET. It consists of the STS payload and the STS overhead. A number is appended to the end of STS to designate signal speed.

System Log A log file that records issues dealing with the overall system, such as system services, device drivers, or configuration changes.

System Restore A Windows utility that enables you to return your PC to a recent working configuration when something goes wrong. System Restore returns your computer's system settings to the way they were the last time you remember your system working correctly—all without affecting your personal files or e-mail.

T1 A leased-line connection capable of carrying data at 1,544,000 bps.

T1 Line The specific, shielded, two-pair cabling that connects the two ends of a T1 connection.

T3 Line A leased-line connection capable of carrying data at 44,736,000 bps.

TCP Segment The connection-oriented payload of an IP packet. A TCP segment works on the Transport layer.

TCP/IP Model An architecture model based on the TCP/IP protocol suite, which defines and standardizes the flow of data between computers. The following lists the four layers:

- **Layer 1** The *Link layer (Network Interface layer)* is similar to OSI's Data Link and Physical layers. The Link layer consists of any part of the network that deals with frames.

- **Layer 2** The *Internet layer* is the same as OSI's Network layer. Any part of the network that deals with pure IP packets—getting a packet to its destination—is on the Internet layer.

- **Layer 3** The *Transport layer* combines the features of OSI's Transport and Session layers. It is concerned with the assembly and disassembly of data, as well as connection-oriented and connectionless communication.

- **Layer 4** The *Application layer* combines the features of the top three layers of the OSI model. It consists of the processes that applications use to initiate, control, and disconnect from a remote system.

Telecommunications Room A central location for computer or telephone equipment and, most importantly, centralized cabling. All cables usually run to the telecommunications room from the rest of the installation.

Telephony The science of converting sound into electrical signals, moving those signals from one location to another, and then converting those signals back into sounds. This includes modems, telephone lines, the telephone system, and any products used to create a remote access link between a remote access client and server.

Telnet A program that enables users on the Internet to log onto remote systems from their own host systems.

Temperature Monitor   Device for keeping a telecommunications room at an optimal temperature.

Temporal Key Integrity Protocol (TKIP)   The extra layer of security that WPA adds on top of WEP.

Teredo   A NAT-traversal IPv6 tunneling protocol, built into Microsoft Windows.

Terminal Access Controller Access Control System Plus (TACACS+) A proprietary protocol developed by Cisco to support AAA in a network with many routers and switches. It is similar to RADIUS in function, but uses TCP port 49 by default and separates authorization, authentication, and accounting into different parts.

Terminal Adapter (TA)   The most common interface used to connect a computer to an ISDN line.

Terminal Emulation   Software that enables a PC to communicate with another computer or network as if it were a specific type of hardware terminal.

TIA/EIA (Telecommunications Industry Association/ Electronics Industry Association)   The standards body that defines most of the standards for computer network cabling. Many of these standards are defined under the TIA/EIA 568 standard.

TIA/EIA 568A   One of two four-pair UTP crimping standards for 10/100/1000BaseT networks. Often shortened to T568A. The other standard is TIA/EIA 568B.

TIA/EIA 568B   One of two four-pair UTP crimping standards for 10/100/1000BaseT networks. Often shortened to T568B. The other standard is TIA/EIA 568A.

TIA/EIA 606   Official methodology for labeling patch panels.

Ticket-Granting Ticket (TGT)   Sent by an Authentication Server in a Kerberos setup if a client's hash matches its own, signaling that the client is authenticated but not yet authorized.

Time Division Multiplexing (TDM)   The process of having frames that carry a bit of every channel in every frame sent at a regular interval in a T1 connection.

Time Domain Reflectometer (TDR)   Advanced cable tester that tests the length of cables and their continuity or discontinuity, and identifies the location of any discontinuity due to a bend, break, unwanted crimp, and so on.

Tone Generator   *See* Toners.

Tone Probe   *See* Toners.

Toners   Generic term for two devices used together—a tone generator and a tone locator (probe)—to trace cables by sending an electrical signal along a wire at a particular frequency. The tone locator then emits a sound when it distinguishes that frequency. Also referred to as *Fox and Hound*.

Top-Level Domain Servers   A set of DNS servers—just below the root servers—that handle the top-level domain names, such as .com, .org, .net, and so on.

Topology   The pattern of interconnections in a communications system among devices, nodes, and associated input and output stations. Also describes how computers connect to each other without regard to how they actually communicate.

tracert (also traceroute)   A command-line utility used to follow the path a packet takes between two hosts.

Traffic Analysis   Tools that chart a network's traffic usage.

Traffic Shaping   Controlling the flow of packets into or out of the network according to the type of packet or other rules.

Transceiver   The device that transmits and receives signals on a cable.

Transmission Control Protocol (TCP)   Part of the TCP/ IP protocol suite, operates at Layer 4 (Transport) of the OSI seven-layer model. TCP is a connection-oriented protocol.

Transmission Control Protocol/Internet Protocol (TCP/IP)   A set of communication protocols developed by the U.S. Department of Defense that enables dissimilar computers to share information over a network.

Transmit Beamforming   A multiple-antenna technology in 802.11n WAPs that helps get rid of dead spots.

Transport Layer   *See* Open System Interconnection (OSI) Seven-Layer Model.

Transport Layer Security (TLS)   A robust update to SSL that works with almost any TCP application.

Trivial File Transfer Protocol (TFTP)   A protocol that transfers files between servers and clients. Unlike FTP, TFTP requires no user login. Devices that need an operating system, but have no local hard disk (for example, diskless workstations and routers), often use TFTP to download their operating systems.

Trojan   A virus that masquerades as a file with a legitimate purpose, so that a user will run it intentionally. The classic example is a file that runs a game, but also causes some type of damage to the player's system.

Trunk Port   A port on a switch configured to carry all data, regardless of VLAN number, between all switches in a LAN.

Trunking   The process of transferring VLAN data between two or more switches.

Tunnel   An encrypted link between two programs on two separate computers.

Tunnel Broker   In IPv6, a service that creates the actual tunnel and (usually) offers a custom-made endpoint client for you to use, although more advanced users can often make a manual connection.

Tunnel Information and Control Protocol (TIC)   One of the protocols that set up IPv6 tunnels and handle configuration as well as login.

Tunnel Setup Protocol (TSP)   One of the protocols that set up IPv6 tunnels and handle configuration as well as login.

Twisted Pair   Twisted pairs of cables, the most overwhelmingly common type of cabling used in networks. The two types of twisted pair cabling are UTP (unshielded twisted pair) and STP (shielded twisted pair). The twists serve to reduce interference, called *crosstalk*; the more twists, the less crosstalk.

Two-Factor Authentication   A method of security authentication that requires two separate means of authentication, for example, some sort of physical token that, when inserted, prompts for a password.

U (Units)   The unique height measurement used with equipment racks; 1 U equals 1.75 inches.

UART (Universal Asynchronous Receiver/Transmitter)   A device that turns serial data into parallel data. The cornerstone of serial ports and modems.

UDP (User Datagram Protocol)   Part of the TCP/IP protocol suite, a connectionless protocol that is an alternative to TCP.

UDP Datagram   A connectionless networking container used in UDP communication.

UNC (Universal Naming Convention)   Describes any shared resource in a network using the convention *<server name>**<name of shared resource>*.

Unicast   A message sent from one computer to one other computer.

Unicast Address   A unique IPv6 address that is exclusive to a system. Link-local addresses are unicast addresses.

Unified Communication (UC)   A system that rolls many different network services into one, for example, instant messaging (IM), telephone service, video conferencing, and more.

Uninterruptible Power Supply (UPS)   A device that supplies continuous clean power to a computer system the whole time the computer is on. Protects against power outages and sags. The term *UPS* is often used mistakenly when people mean stand-by power supply or system (SPS).

Universal Asynchronous Receiver/Transmitter (UART)   A device inside a modem that takes the 8-bit-wide digital data and converts it into 1-bit-wide digital data and hands it to the modem for conversion to analog data. The process is reversed for incoming data.

UNIX   A popular computer software operating system used on many Internet host systems.

Unshielded Twisted Pair (UTP)   A popular cabling for telephone and networks composed of pairs of wires twisted around each other at specific intervals. The twists serve to reduce interference (also called *crosstalk*). The more twists, the less interference. The cable has *no* metallic shielding to protect the wires from external interference, unlike its cousin, *STP*. 10BaseT uses UTP, as do many other networking technologies. UTP is available in a variety of grades, called categories, as defined in the following:

- **Category 1 UTP**   Regular analog phone lines, not used for data communications
- **Category 2 UTP**   Supports speeds up to 4 Mbps
- **Category 3 UTP**   Supports speeds up to 16 Mbps
- **Category 4 UTP**   Supports speeds up to 20 Mbps
- **Category 5 UTP**   Supports speeds up to 100 Mbps
- **Category 5e UTP**   Supports speeds up to 100 Mbps with two pairs and up to 1000 Mbps with four pairs
- **Category 6 UTP**   Improved support for speeds up to 10 Gbps
- **Category 6a UTP**   Extends the length of 10-Gbps communication to the full 100 meters commonly associated with UTP cabling.

Uplink Port   Port on a hub that enables you to connect two hubs together using a straight-through cable.

Upload   The transfer of information from a user's system to a remote computer system. Opposite of download. *See also* Download.

URL (Uniform Resource Locator)   An address that defines the type and the location of a resource on the Internet. URLs are used in almost every TCP/IP application. A typical HTTP URL is http://www.totalsem.com.

Usenet   The network of UNIX users, generally perceived as informal and made up of loosely coupled nodes, that exchanges mail and messages. Started by Duke University and UNC-Chapel Hill. An information cooperative linking around 16,000 computer sites and millions of people. Usenet provides a series of "news groups" analogous to online conferences.

User   Anyone who uses a computer. You.

User Account A container that identifies a user to the application, operating system, or network, including name, password, user name, groups to which the user belongs, and other information based on the user and the OS or NOS being used. Usually defines the rights and roles a user plays on a system.

User Datagram Protocol (UDP) A protocol used by some older applications, most prominently TFTP (Trivial FTP), to transfer files. UDP datagrams are both simpler and smaller than TCP segments, and they do most of the behind-the-scenes work in a TCP/IP network.

User-Level Security A security system in which each user has an account, and access to resources is based on user identity.

User Profiles A collection of settings that corresponds to a specific user account and may follow the user, regardless of the computer at which he or she logs on. These settings enable the user to have customized environment and security settings.

V Standards Standards established by CCITT for modem manufacturers to follow (voluntarily) to ensure compatible speeds, compression, and error correction.

V.92 Standard The current modem standard, which has a download speed of 57,600 bps and an upload speed of 48 Kbps. V.92 modems have several interesting features, such as Quick Connect and Modem on Hold.

Vertical Cross-Connect Main patch panel in a telecommunications room. *See also* Patch Panel.

Very High Bitrate DSL (VDSL) The latest form of DSL with download and upload speeds of up to 100 Mbps. VDSL was designed to run on copper phone lines, but many VDSL suppliers use fiber-optic cabling to increase effective distances.

View The different displays found in Performance Monitor.

Virtual Local Area Network (VLAN) A LAN that, using VLAN-capable switches, places some (or any on the more expensive VLANs) systems on virtual broadcast domains.

Virtual Machine (VM) A virtual computer accessed through a class of program called a hypervisor or virtual machine manager. A virtual machine runs *inside* your actual operating system, essentially enabling you to run two or more operating systems at once.

Virtual Machine Manager (VMM) *See* Hypervisor.

Virtual PBX Software that functionally replaces a physical PBX telephone system.

Virtual Private Network (VPN) A network configuration that enables a remote user to access a private network via the Internet. VPNs employ an encryption methodology called *tunneling*, which protects the data from interception.

Virtual Switch   Special software that enables VMs to communicate with each other without going outside of the host system.

Virtual Trunk Protocol (VTP)   A proprietary Cisco protocol to automate the updating of multiple VLAN switches.

Virus   A program that can make a copy of itself without you necessarily being aware of it. Some viruses can destroy or damage files, and generally the best protection is always to maintain backups of your files.

Virus Definition or Data Files   Enables the virus protection software to recognize the viruses on your system and clean them. These files should be updated often. Also called *signature files*, depending on the virus protection software in use.

Voice over IP (VoIP)   Using an IP network to transfer voice calls.

Voltage   The pressure of the electrons passing through a wire.

Voltage Event Recorder   Tracks voltage over time by plugging into a power outlet.

Volts (V)   Units of measurement for voltage.

VPN Concentrator   The new endpoint of the local LAN in L2TP.

Vulnerability Scanner   A tool that scans a network for potential attack vectors.

WAN (Wide Area Network)   A geographically dispersed network created by linking various computers and LANs over long distances, generally using leased phone lines. There is no firm dividing line between a WAN and a LAN.

Warm Boot   A system restart performed after the system has been powered and operating. This clears and resets the memory, but does not stop and start the hard drive.

Wattage (Watts or W)   The amount of amps and volts needed by a particular device to function.

Web Server   A server that enables access to HTML documents by remote users.

Well-Known Port Numbers   Port numbers from 0 to 1204 that are used primarily by client applications to talk to server applications in TCP/IP networks.

Wi-Fi   The most widely adopted wireless networking type in use today. Technically, only wireless devices that conform to the extended versions of the 802.11 standard—802.11a, 802.11b, and 802.11g—are Wi-Fi certified.

Wi-Fi Protected Access (WPA)   A wireless security protocol that addresses the weaknesses and acts as a sort of upgrade to WEP. WPA offers security enhancements such as dynamic encryption key generation (keys are issued on a per-user and per-session basis), an encryption key integrity-checking feature, user authentication through the industry-standard Extensible Authentication Protocol (EAP), and other advanced features that WEP lacks.

Wi-Fi Protected Access 2 (WPA2) An update to the WPA protocol that uses the Advanced Encryption Standard algorithm, making it much harder to crack.

WiMax *See* 802.16.

Windows Domain A group of computers controlled by a computer running Windows Server, which is configured as a domain controller.

Windows Firewall The firewall that has been included in Windows operating systems since Windows XP; originally named Internet Connection Firewall (ICF) but renamed in XP Service Pack 2.

Windows Internet Name Service (WINS) A name resolution service that resolves NetBIOS names to IP addresses.

winipcfg A graphical program used on Windows 95, Windows 98, and Windows Me machines to display the current TCP/IP configuration of the machine; similar to more modern Windows's ipconfig and UNIX/ Linux's ifconfig.

WINS Proxy Agent A WINS relay agent that forwards WINS broadcasts to a WINS server on the other side of a router to keep older systems from broadcasting in place of registering with the server.

Wire Scheme *See* Wiring Diagram.

Wired Equivalent Privacy (WEP) A wireless security protocol that uses a 64-bit encryption algorithm to scramble data packets.

Wireless Access Point (WAP) Connects wireless network nodes to wireless or wired networks. Many WAPs are combination devices that act as high-speed hubs, switches, bridges, and routers, all rolled into one.

Wireless Bridge Device used to connect two wireless network segments together, or to join wireless and wired networks together in the same way that wired bridge devices do.

Wireless Network *See* Wi-Fi.

Wiremap Term that techs use to refer to the proper connectivity of wires in a network.

Wireshark A popular packet sniffer.

Wiring Diagram A document, also known as a *wiring schematic*, that usually consists of multiple pages and that shows the following: how the wires in a network connect to switches and other nodes, what types of cables are used, and how patch panels are configured. It usually includes details about each cable run.

Wiring Schematic *See* Wiring Diagram.

Work Area In a basic structured cabling network, often simply an office or cubicle that potentially contains a PC attached to the network.

Workgroup A convenient method of organizing computers under Network/My Network Places in Windows operating systems.

Workstation A general-purpose computer that is small enough and inexpensive enough to reside at a person's work area for his or her exclusive use.

Worm A very special form of virus. Unlike other viruses, a worm does not infect other files on the computer. Instead, it replicates by making copies of itself on other systems on a network by taking advantage of security weaknesses in networking protocols.

WPA2-Enterprise A version of WPA2 that uses a RADIUS server for authentication.

WWW (World Wide Web) The (graphical) Internet that can be accessed using Gopher, FTP, HTTP, Telnet, Usenet, WAIS, and some other tools.

X.25 The first generation of packet-switching technology, enables remote devices to communicate with each other across high-speed digital links without the expense of individual leased lines.

Yost Cable Cable used to interface with a Cisco device.

Zombie A single computer under the control of an operator that is used in a botnet attack. *See also* Botnet.

INDEX

Numbers

10/100 NICs, 109
10 GbE (Gigabit Ethernet)
    copper-based, 119
    fiber-based, 117–119
    overview of, 116
    physical connections, 119–120
    summary, 119
100-megabit Ethernet
    100Base T4, 108
    100BaseFX, 110–111
    100BaseTX (100BaseT), 108–110
    full-duplex Ethernet, 111–112
    overview of, 107
1000BaseCX, Gigabit Ethernet, 113
1000BaseLX, Gigabit Ethernet, 114
1000BaseSX, Gigabit Ethernet, 113
100BaseFX Ethernet, 110–111
100BaseT Ethernet, 108–110
10Base2, 82, 90
10Base5, 82, 90
10BaseFL, 94–95
10BaseT
    as early Ethernet implementation, 89–90
    inadequacy of, 107
    limits and specifications, 93–94
    requiring UTP, 90–93
    upgrading to 100BaseT, 108–110
10GBase1.4, 119
10GBaseER, 118
10GBaseEW, 117
10GBaseLR, 118
10GBaseLW, 117–118
10GBaseRM, 119
10GBaseSR, 117
10GBaseSW, 117–118
10GBaseZR, 119
110-blocks
    patch panels, 135
    punchdown tools for, 662
    troubleshooting with butt sets, 662
128-bit addressing. *See* IPv6 (Internet Protocol
    version 6)
255 characters, DNS names, 322
32 binary digits
    calculating hosts, 204
    IP addresses, 186
    subnet masks, 196, 200, 205–206

32-bit addressing. *See* IPv4 (Internet Protocol
    version 4)
3G technology, LTE, 494
5.0 GHz range, 802.11a, 518
66-blocks
    patch panels, 136
    punchdown tools for, 662
    troubleshooting with butt sets, 662
6in4 tunneling protocol, IPv6, 452
6to4 tunneling protocol, IPv6, 452
802 Working Group, IEEE, 76–77
802.11 Wi-Fi standard
    802.11a, 519–520
    802.11b, 519
    802.11g, 520
    802.11i, 526
    802.11n, 520–521
    ad hoc mode, 514–515
    broadcasting frequency, 517
    broadcasting methods, 517
    BSSID, SSID and ESSID, 516–517
    channels, 517
    CSMA/CA, 517–519
    hardware, 511–513
    IEEE and, 77
    infrastructure mode, 515–516
    overview of, 511
    range, 516
    software, 513–514
    SOHO network design, 643
802.16 (WiMAX), 493
802.1Q trunks, and QoS, 623
802.1X standard
    overview of, 386–387
    port authentication, 428–429
    wireless authentication, 522–524
802.3 standard, 77
8P8C (8 Position 8 Contact), 92

A

A records
    adding manually to DNS server, 341
    DNS forward lookup zones and, 338–339
    DNS load balancing and, 421–422
    Dynamic DNS and, 345
AAA (Authentication, Authorization, and Accounting)
    802.1X combining with EAP and, 387
    overview of, 379–381

RADIUS, 381–382
TACACS+, 382–387
AAAA records, IPv6, 340, 449
acceptable use policy,
    documentation, 608
access control
    location of telecommunications
        room, 147
    to user accounts, 559
access token, Kerberos, 383–384
accounting, AAA authentication, 381
ACK/NACK process, TCP, 182
ACK number field, TCP header, 183
ACLs (access control lists)
    administrative access control, 549
    authorization, 375
    WAPs enabling/denying MAC
        addresses, 521
activation, virus, 550
Active Directory, 344, 396
Active Directory-integrated zones,
    344–345
active FTP, 312–313
activity light, NICs, 166
ad hoc mode
        infrastructure mode vs., 515–516
        wireless networks, 514–515
ad hoc network, Wi-Fi set up, 528
Add Counters dialog box, Performance
    Monitor, 611–612
Add Objects dialog box, logs in
    Windows XP, 614–615
address notation, IPv6, 434–435
Address Resolution Protocol (ARP),
    197–199, 664
administrative access control, 549
administrative problems, with
    passwords, 559
ads, free Web hosts and, 294
ADSL (Asymmetric DSL)
    cable modems competing with,
        490–491
    defined, 486
    overview of, 486
    as prime target for hackers, 567
Advanced Encryption Standard. See AES
    (Advanced Encryption Standard)
advanced networking devices
    client/servers, classic, 402–404
    client/servers, today, 405–406
    multilayer switches, 419–422
    network protection. See network
        protection devices
    overview of, 401–402
    peer-to-peer, classic, 404–405
    peer-to-peer, today, 405–406
    QoS and traffic shaping, 423–424
    review Q & A, 430–432
    virtual private networks, 408–412
adware, 551

AES (Advanced Encryption Standard)
    data encryption using WPA2
        and, 526
    SSH using, 389
    for symmetric key encryption,
        364–365
AfriNIC (African Network Information
    Center), 443
agents, SNMP, 396
aggregation, IPv6, 441–444
AH (Authentication Header), IPsec, 394
algorithms
    asymmetric-key standards,
        365–367
    overview of, 361–363
    symmetric-key standards, 363–365
All-In-One device, SOHOs,
    639–640, 651
AM (amplitude modulation), and
    networks today, 82
American National Standards Institute
    (ANSI), 69, 472
American Registry for Internet Numbers
    (ARIN), 200–201, 443
amplifiers, repeaters vs., 465
analog signals, PSTN, 480–485
analog system, long-distance telephone
    systems
        converting to digital, 465–466
        converting to digital with DS0,
            467–468
        history of, 462–465
        keeping "the last mile", 466
Angry IP Scanner, 446–447, 669
anonymous access, FTP sites, 309, 311
ANSI (American National Standards
    Institute), 69, 472
antennas
    802.11n using multiple, 518
    focusing wave, 530
    placing WAP for infrastructure
        network, 529–530
    satellite, 492
    troubleshooting wireless
        connectivity, 541
    WAP replacement, 530–531
anti-malware programs, 551–552
anycast addresses
    6to4, 452
    IPv6, 439
Apache HTTP Web Server, 295–296
APIPA (Automatic Private IP
    Addressing), IPv4, 220–221, 436
APIs (Application Programming
    Interfaces), 42–43
APNIC (Asia-Pacific Network
    Information Center), 443
Application layer (Layer 7) OSI
    load balancing with content
        switch, 422–423

overview of, 42–43
    TCP/IP protocol suite, 183–185
    TCP/IP Transport layer vs., 45–46
Application layer, TCP/IP model, 48–50
Application Programming Interfaces
    (APIs), 42–43
application proxies, 566–567
application service providers (ASPs),
    cloud computing, 597
applications
    of client/servers and P2P today,
        405–406
    latency-sensitive, 622
    TCP/IP. See TCP/IP applications
APs (access points), 513. See also WAPs
    (wireless access points)
archive bits, data backups, 626–629
ARCserve Backup, 625
Area IDs, OSPF, 255
ARIN (American Registry for Internet
    Numbers), 200–201, 443
ARP (Address Resolution Protocol),
    197–199, 664
arping utility, troubleshooting tool,
    664–665
AS (Authentication Server),
    Kerberos, 383
AS (Autonomous Systems)
    protocols communicating
        between, 252–254
    using OSPF internally, 254–259
Asia-Pacific Network Information
    Center (APNIC), 443
ASN (Autonomous System
    Number), 253
ASPs (application service providers),
    cloud computing, 597
assembly, Transport layer OSI, 36–37
Asymmetric DSL. See ADSL
    (Asymmetric DSL)
asymmetric-key algorithm
    defined, 363
    digital certificates linked to, 374
    standards, 365–367
AT&T, converting telephones to digital,
    466–468
ATM (Asynchronous Transfer Mode)
    connecting Ethernet to, 237–238
    MPLS replacing, 475–478
    packet switching technology,
        474–475
attenuation of signals, 159, 161–162
attributes, data backup, 626
authentication. See also AAA
    (Authentication, Authorization,
    and Accounting); authentication
    standards
        CRAM-MD5, 369
        defined, 360
        DNS Security Extensions, 346

hashes, 369
L2TP VPNs lacking, 411
OSPF, 258
port, 428–429
RIPv1 lacking, 251
RIPv2, 251
standards combining encryption
and, 391–394
TCP/IP, 375
user account, 557
wireless, 522–524
World Wide Web, 297–298
Authentication Header (AH), IPsec, 394
Authentication phase, PPP, 377
Authentication Server (AS),
Kerberos, 383
authentication standards
802.1X, 386–387
AAA, 379–381
EAP, 384–386
Kerberos, 382–384
overview of, 376
PPP, 376–379
RADIUS, 381–382
TACACS+, 382
authenticator, PPP, 377, 379–380
authoritative DNS servers, 327, 338
authorization
AAA, 381
certificate, 373
defined, 360
DNS Security Extensions, 346
TCP/IP security and, 375–376
auto-sensing NICs, 100BaseT, 108–110
Automatic Private IP Addressing
(APIPA), 220–221, 436
Autonomous System Number
(ASN), 253
Autonomous Systems (AS)
protocols communicating
between, 252–254
using OSPF internally, 254–259
AVG Anti-Virus, 552

B

B (Bearer) channels, ISDN, 484
backbones
1000BaseLX as long-distance, 114
for building-wide networks, 141
Gigabit Ethernet, 120–121
backup designated router (BDR), OSPF,
256–257
backup power
in case of electrical failure, 549
generators for, 629
backup, restoring router configuration,
269–270

backups, data
providing fault tolerance, 625–629
for system crash/hardware
failure, 549
bandwidth
bridges preserving, 99
calculating hop cost of OSPF, 255
controlling with separate
network, 202
determining routing metric, 247
full-duplex network doubling use
of, 112
latency-sensitive applications
and, 622
link state dynamic routing
protocols optimizing, 254
QoS and traffic shaping
optimizing, 423–424
QoS optimizing, 623
switched Ethernet optimizing,
99–103
bandwidth-efficient encoding schemes,
CAT ratings, 69
bandwidth (traffic) shaping
bandwidth management, 423–424
performance optimization,
623–624
barrel connectors, coaxial cable, 67
baseband, broadband vs., 90
baseline
creating logs with Performance
Monitor, 613–618
documentation, 606–608
basic NAT, 240
Basic Rate Interface (BRI), ISDN, 484
Basic Service Set (BSS), 515–517
Basic Service Set Identifier (BSSID),
516–517
batteries, for diagnosing cabling, 173
baud, 480, 482
baud rate, PSTN, 480
BDPU (Bridge Protocol Data Unit), 103
BDR (backup designated router), OSPF,
256–257
beacon, Wi-Fi, 532–533
beam antennas, 530
BERT (Bit Error Rate Test), 479
BGP (Border Gateway Protocol),
252–254, 439
BICSI organization, 128
binary numbers
converting IPv4 dotted decimals
to, 186–188
in cryptographic hash functions,
368–369
in subnet masks, 196–200
subnetting with, 203–206
BIND DNS server tool, 422
biometrics, 559

BIOS, virtualized for VMs, 578–579
Bit Error Rate Test (BERT), 479
bits per second, baud vs., 482
BitTorrent standard, 405–406
black holes, PMTU or MTU, 650
blacklist, MAC filtering with, 522
block ciphers
Advanced Encryption Standard,
364–365
Data Encryption Standard, 364
overview of, 363
blueprint, structured cabling, 145
BNC connectors, coaxial cable, 64–65
bonding, adding using identical NICs,
165–166
boot, after making patch cable, 153
BOOTP (Bootstrap Protocol), 219–222
BOOTPS (Bootstrap Protocol
Server), 221
Border Gateway Protocol (BGP),
252–254, 439
botnets, 554
BPL (Broadband over Power Line),
494–495
Brainiacs group, in this book, 7–8
BRI (Basic Rate Interface), ISDN, 484
bridge loops (switching loops)
defined, 102
eliminating accidental, 103
escalation for problem of, 678
Bridge Protocol Data Unit (BDPU), 103
bridged connections, first generation
DSL providers, 489
bridges
connecting Ethernet segments,
98–99
wireless, 538
broadband, baseband vs., 90
Broadband over Power Line (BPL),
494–495
broadcast addresses, 25
broadcast domains
creating VLANs, 412
defined, 102
interVLAN routing, 417–418
broadcast storms, escalation for
problem of, 678
broadcasts
IP packet, 201
IPv6 as end of, 437–439
MAC address, 185–186
name resolution, 331
NetBIOS, 349–351
WINS server reducing
overhead from, 350–351
wireless networking, 517
broken cables, troubleshooting,
659–660
brokers, IPv6 tunnel, 454

brute force attacks
 breaking code with, 362–363
 DES vulnerability to, 364
 with password-cracking
  programs, 558
BSS (Basic Service Set), 515–517
BSSID (Basic Service Set Identifier),
 516–517
buffer overflows, worms exploiting, 550
buffers, fiber-optic cabling, 71–72
bus topology, 12–14
 bus-ring topology, 58–59
 coaxial cable in early, 64
 original Ethernet based on, 82
 overview of, 56–58
 star topology vs., 58
butt sets, 173, 658–659

C

cable certifiers, 159–160, 660–661
cable drops, mapping cable runs,
 145–146
cable modems
 coaxial cable for, 65–66
 connecting using RG-6 or RG-59
  cable, 66
 as dedicated connections, 500–501
 IP packets in frames for, 35
 network diagram documentation,
  603–605
 popular for last-mile WANs,
  490–491
 as prime targets for hackers, 567
 replacing telephony WANs, 479
cable strippers/snips
 making UTP cables, 661
 rolling own patch cables, 151
cable testers
 fat probes, 157–160
 network support with, 173
 testing cable runs, 155–157
 troubleshooting broken cables,
  659–660
 troubleshooting log in, 676
 troubleshooting problems in work
  area, 170–171
cabling
 classic serial, 74
 coaxial cable, 63–67
 diagnosing and repairing physical,
  168–173
 fiber-optic, 71–73
 fire ratings, 75–76
 FireWire, 75
 in Link layer TCP/IP, 44–45
 network connectivity
  documentation, 602–603
 overview of, 63

parallel, 74–75
patch, 138
in Physical layer OSI, 17–19, 28
pulling for entire building,
 147–150
review Q & A, 78–80
shielded twisted pair, 68
twisted pair, 67–68
unshielded twisted pair, 68–71
upgrading 10BaseT to
 100BaseT, 108
cache
 checking DNS, 334
 for performance optimization, 621
 proxy server updating, 428
 recently resolved FQDNs, 336
Cache Array Routing Protocol (CARP),
 deploying Squid, 621
cache-only DNS servers, 338
Cached Lookups folder, DNS server,
 336–337
caching engines, 621
Cacti, enabling SNMP, 396–397
Caesar ciphers, 362
calculator utility, 187–188, 209–210
canonical name (CNAME) DNS
 records, 340
CARP (Cache Array Routing Protocol),
 deploying Squid, 621
carrier sense multiple access/collision
 detection. See CSMA/CD (carrier
 sense multiple access/collision
 detection)
carrier sense multiple access with
 collision avoidance (CSMA/CD),
 Wi-Fi networks, 517–519
case sensitivity
 DNS name space, 324
 UNIX, Linux and Mac
  commands, 222
CAT (category) ratings, UTP cables
 10BaseT, 90–93
 horizontal cabling, 130–132
 network connectivity
  documentation, 602–603
 overview of, 69–71
 patch panels, 137
 RJ-45 jacks in work area
  outlets, 140
 SOHO compatibility issues,
  640–641
 SOHO structured cabling design,
  641–642
 upgrading 10BaseT to
  100BaseT, 108
cat /etc/resolve.conf, UNIX/Linux, 333
CCITT (International Telegraph and
 Telephone Consultative Committee),
 472, 483–484

CCITT Packet Switching Protocol
 (X.25), 474
CDs, installing driver for NIC from, 165
ceilings, pulling cable in, 148–149
cellular WANs, 492–493
central office buildings, telephones
 converting to digital, 466
 DSL features, 487–488
 history of long distance, 463–464
certificates
 creating unsigned, 374
 HTTPS, 394–395
 PKI, 370–373
 providers offering Web-of-
  Trust, 374
 SSL, 392
certifiers
 of standards for cable runs,
  159–160
 troubleshooting cables with,
  660–661
chadding, fiber-optic cabling, 71–72
Challenge Handshake Authentication
 Protocol. See CHAP (Challenge
 Handshake Authentication Protocol)
Challenge Handshake Authentication
 Protocol (MS-CHAPv2), 379, 382
Challenge-Response Authentication
 Mechanism-Message Digest 5
 (CRAM-MD5), 369
Change Log for the Web Server,
 troubleshooting sluggish server, 677
change management
 documentation, 609
channel bonding, 802.11g, 518
Channel Service Unit/Digital Service
 Unit. See CSU/DSU (Channel Service
 Unit/Digital Service Unit)
channels
 configuring NICs for ad hoc
  network, 528
 configuring Wi-Fi, 536
 DS1/T1, 468–470
 wireless connectivity,
  troubleshooting, 542
 wireless networking, 517
CHAP (Challenge Handshake
 Authentication Protocol)
 EAP-MS-CHAPv2, 386
 MS-CHAPv2, 379, 382
 PPP authentication, 378–379
 RADIUS supporting, 382
checksum field, TCP header, 183
checksum (or digest), cryptographic
 hashes, 368–369
Chinese-only Web server, 297
CIDR (Classless Inter-Domain Routing)
 dropping trailing zeros for
  notation, 204

generating blocks of IP
addresses, 202
IPv6 using nomenclature of, 435
and subnetting. *See* subnetting
CIFS (Common Internet File System)
defined, 342
legacy of, 342–344
making NetBIOS compatible with
DNS, 350
NAS systems using, 639
ciphers
defined, 361
overview of, 361–363
SSH encryption, 388–390
ciphertext, 362–363
circuit switching, old-time telephones,
462, 464
Cisco 2811 router, 411
customizing, 648
port authentication, 429
SOHO network design, 646–648
Cisco 3550 interVLAN-routing-capable
switch, 418–419
Cisco console cable, connecting to
routers, 260–261
Cisco Network Assistant, 265–267,
414–415
Cisco routers
Cisco 2600 Series, 228
configuring, 260–263
diagram, 229
Cisco Security Posture Assessment
Service, 548
Citrix, terminal emulation program,
501–502
class licenses, IP, 201–202
classic serial cables, 74
Classless Inter-Domain Routing. *See*
CIDR (Classless Inter-Domain
Routing)
CLEAR, WiMAX ISP, 493
cleartext (or plaintext) encryption,
360–361
client configuration utility, wireless, 513
client/server topologies, 402–406
client-to-site connections
L2TP VPNs, 411
PPTP VPNs, 410
clients
configuring Wi-Fi, 536–537
connection-oriented session on
TCP, 277–278
DHCP, 216–219, 220–221
e-mail, 304, 307–309
FTP, 311–312
installing for Wi-Fi, 528
installing Wi-Fi network, 528
Novell NetWare model, 404
peer-to-peer applications today,
405–406

peer-to-peer network model,
404–405
physical protection of, 554–555
port numbers and Web, 281–282
private dial-up connection, 498
proxy servers and, 427–428
Telnet, 301–302
troubleshooting DNS, 346–347
VPN, 408–412
Web, 295–297
WINS, 351–352
wireless authentication, 522–524
clocks, protocols synchronizing
device, 221
close-ended questions, troubleshooting
process, 671–672
cloud computing
with application service
providers, 597
with Network as a Service, 596
clustered servers, 630–631
CNAME (canonical name) DNS
records, 340
coaxial cable
cable modem connections, 491
original Ethernet based on, 82
overview of, 63–67
collision avoidance, Wi-Fi networks,
517–519
collision detection
on Ethernet networks, 87–89
full-duplex eliminating
collisions, 112
switches vs. hubs, 101
collision domains, 102
collision light, NICs, 167
colons (::), IPv6 address notation, 435
color-coded pairs, UTP cable, 92
color printer, SOHO network
design, 651
commands, UNIX, Linux and Mac case
sensitivity, 222
Common Internet File System. *See* CIFS
(Common Internet File System)
common-word hackers, defeating, 558
communications, determining good vs.
bad, 291
compatibility, in SOHO network design,
640–641
complete algorithms, 361
CompTIA A+ certification, 2–3
CompTIA (Computing Technology
Industry Association), 2–3
CompTIA Network+ certification,
introduction
becoming certified, 3
exam preparation, 6–8
exam structure and contents, 4–5
historical/conceptual data, 8–9
learning about networking and, 2

overview of, 1
understanding, 2–3
configuration management
baselines documentation,
606–608
change management
documentation, 609
network connectivity
documentation, 602–606
overview of, 601–602
policies, procedures,
and configurations
documentation, 608
regulations documentation, 609
review Q & A, 632–634
troubleshooting Wi-Fi, 542–543
configurations documentation, 608
conflicting permissions, user
accounts, 560
connection-oriented communication
example of people, 276
TCP enabling, 277–278
TCP/IP Transport layer, 45–47
TCP segments and, 47–48
using TCP for TCP/IP Transport
layer, 182–183
connectionless communication
example of people, 276
ICMP using, 279
TCP/IP Transport layer, 45–47
using UDP for TCP/IP, 182–183
connections
defined, 283
determining good vs. bad, 291
determining status of, 286–291
inside demarc, 143–144
installing cable throughout
building, 150–151
interconnecting TCP/IP LANS
using routers, 192–194
patch panels within entire
building, 153–155
routing table information on, 232
viewing active, 283–285
VPN client-to-site, 410
wireless, attacks on, 555–557
wireless, troubleshooting, 540–541
between work areas in large
building, 151
connections, router
other methods f, 266
overview of, 260–263
troubleshooting problems, 270
understanding, 228
using Network Management
Software, 265–267
for Web access, 263–265
connectors
10 GbE physical, 119–120
1000BaseLX, 114

1000BaseSX and 100BaseFX, 113
coaxial cables, 63–67
documentation of network,
    602–603
fiber-optic cabling, 73,
    114–115, 167
FireWire, 75
parallel connectors, 74–75
patch cable, 138
serial ports, 74
UTP cable, 71
console port, 261
content switches, 422
Continuing Education Program,
    CompTIA, 3
continuity
    broken cables lacking, 659
    testing cable runs for, 156–157
    testing with medium-priced
        testers, 157
    testing with multimeter, 662
convergence
    limitations of RIP, 251–252
    with OSPF, 258–259
    routers in, 251
cooling, telecommunications room,
    146–147
copper-based 10 GbE, 119
copper carriers
    T1 and T3, 468–471
    VDSL running on, 486
copy backup, 627
core, fiber-optic cabling, 71–72
CoS (cost of service) value
    MPLS header, 475
    QoS applying, 623
cost
    buying NICs, 163
    of cable drops, 146
    calculating routing metric, 247
    of CompTIA Network+ exam, 5
    distance vector routing protocols
        calculating, 247–251
    of ISP link for ADSL, 487
counters, Performance Monitor,
    611–613
CPUs
    benefits of virtualization, 586
    ESX support for multiple, 593
    host machine for virtualization
        and, 579
CRAM-MD5 (Challenge-Response
    Authentication Mechanism-Message
    Digest 5), 369
CRC (cyclic redundancy check)
    defined, 23
    frame check sequence and
        Ethernet frames, 87
    processing frames, 24–25

crimping
    connecting work areas, 151
    crosstalk increasing after, 158
    defined, 92
    making UTP cables, 661
    rolling own patch cables, 151–153
crossover cables
    connecting Ethernet segments, 98
    connecting to new router, 264
    T1, 468
crosstalk
    in broken cables, 659
    threatening cable runs, 157–158
    twisted pair cabling reducing, 68
cryptographic hash functions, 368–369
CSMA/CA (carrier sense multiple access
    with collision avoidance), Wi-Fi,
    517–519
CSMA/CD (carrier sense multiple
    access/collision detection)
    10BaseT, 91
    Ethernet, 87
    full-duplex disabling, 112
    limitations of hubs, 99–100, 484
    not working for Wi-Fi
        networks, 518
CSU/DSU (Channel Service Unit/
    Digital Service Unit)
    connecting T1 or T3 lines, 471
    network diagram documentation,
        603–605
    T1 lines, 468
    telephony WAN and, 478
CTRL-ALT-INSERT, VMware, 584
cumulative backups, 628
current time, with NTP, 221, 398
cyclic redundancy check. See CRC (cyclic
    redundancy check)

D

D-rings, patch panel cables, 153–154
DAC (discretionary access control)
    security model, 375
daily backups, 627
daisy-chained hubs, 96–98
data backups
    performance optimization,
        625–629
    for system crash/hardware
        failure, 549
data collector sets, 616–618
data conversion, 40–41
Data Encryption Standard (DES), 364
data, Ethernet frames, 86
Data Link layer (Layer 2) OSI
    defined, 28
    MPLS labels between Layer 3 and,
        475–478

NICs operating at, 29–30
QoS working at, 623
routers stripping packets of
    data, 230
routing and freedom from,
    237–238
SONET at, 472
Data-Over-Cable Service Interface
    Specification (DOCSIS)
    cable modems, 35, 491
    connecting Ethernet to, 237–238
data throughput, and performance
    optimization, 621–623
databases, using LDAP, 396
datagrams, UDP, 183
dB (decibels)
    measuring gain, 530
    measuring NEXT and FEXT, 159
    in split cable problem, 501
DCF (Distributed Coordination
    Function), CSMA/CD devices,
    518–519
DDNS (Dynamic DNS), 345–346
DDoS (distributed denial of service)
    attacks, 554
dead spots
    802.11n transmit beamforming
        for, 520
    placing access point, 530
    site survey to locate, 527
    troubleshooting wireless
        connectivity, 541
DEC (Digital Equipment Corporation),
    and Ethernet, 82
decibels. See dB (decibels)
dedicated connections, 499–501
dedicated FTP client, 312
dedicated lines, 480
default gateways
    getting IPv6 global address from,
        439–440
    overview of, 192–194
    sending ARP to, 198
    sending packet remotely to, 196
    in static IP addressing, 212–216
default routes, routers, 232–233
default user accounts and groups, 560
demarc (demarcation point)
    connections inside, 143–144
    DSL features, 487
    ISDN, 484–485
    PSTN connections, 481
    in structured cabling for home/
        office, 141–143
demarc extension, 141–142, 143
demilitarized zone (DMZ)
    configuration, 570–571
demultiplexers, telephones, 463
Denial of Service (DoS) attacks, 295,
    553–554

Dense WDM (Dense Wavelength Division Multiplexing), fiber devices, 473
DES (Data Encryption Standard), 364
designated router (DR), OSPF, 256–257
Destination LAN IP column, routing tables, 231–232
Details view, customizing in Windows Explorer, 627
devices. See advanced networking devices
DF (Don't Fragment) flag, PMTU, 650
DHCP acknowledge, 219
DHCP (Dynamic Host Configuration Protocol)
    client, 216–219, 220–221
    Discover message, 216–217, 220–221
    as dynamic IP addressing, 216
    for home routers, 267–268
    how it works, 216–219
    in IPv6, 447–448
    living with, 219–222
    SOHO network IP address scheme, 644–645
    supporting Dynamic DNS, 345
DHCP lease
    defined, 219
    releasing, 222
    troubleshooting DHCP, 221
DHCP offer, 217
DHCP request, 219
DHCP reservations, 218
DHCP scope, 217
DHCPv6 servers, 448
dial-up
    defined, 480
    to Internet for remote access, 495–497
    ISDN, 484–486
    protection from external threats using, 567
    PSTN, 480–484
    remote access with private, 496–498
differential backup, 627–629
Differentiated Services Code Point (DSCP) field, IP packet header, 181
Diffie-Hellman key exchange, 365
dig (domain information groper) tool, troubleshooting DNS, 349, 665–666
Digital Equipment Corporation (DEC), and Ethernet, 82
Digital-Intel-Xerox (DIX) standard, 82
digital signal (DS1), T1, 35, 468–470
digital signal (DS3), T3, 471
digital signal rate (DSo), telephones, 469

Digital Signature Algorithm (DSA) keys, SSH, 389
digital signatures
    certificates as standardized, 371–373
    for nonrepudiation, 370
digital subscriber line. See DSL (digital subscriber line)
digital telephony
    conversion to, 465–466
    converting from analog to, 465–466
    ISDN, 484–486
    SONET/SDH and OC fiber carriers, 472–473
    starting with DSo, 467–468
    T1 and T3 copper carriers, 468–471
diligence, user account management, 561
dipole antennas, placing WAP, 529–530
direct-sequence spread-spectrum (DSSS), Wi-Fi, 517
directional antennas, 530
directories, hierarchical file name space, 323
disassembly, Transport layer OSI, 36–37
discretionary access control (DAC) security model, 375
disk striping with distributed parity (RAID 5), 630
dispersion, testing fiber runs for, 161–162
distance limitation, UTP, 110
distance, location of telecommunications room, 146
distance vector routing protocols
    BGP, 252–254
    overview of, 247–251
    RIPv1, 251
    RIPv2, 251–252
Distributed Coordination Function (DCF), CSMA/CD devices, 518–519
distributed denial of service (DDoS) attacks, 554
DIX (Digital-Intel-Xerox) standard, 82
DMZ (demilitarized zone)
    configuration, 570–571
DNS (Domain Name System)
    Active Directory-integrated zones, 344–345
    anycast addressing in, 439
    dynamic, 345–346
    dynamic, on the Web, 346
    historical/conceptual information, 318–320
    how it works, 320–321
    in IPv6, 449
    load balancing, 421–422

    name resolution, 330–336
    name servers, 326–330
    name spaces, 321–326
    root servers or root, 320–321
    security extensions, 346
    servers, 336–341
    servers, and migrating to IPv6, 451
    troubleshooting, 346–349
    Web site text addresses using, 294
DNS Security Extensions (DNSSEC), 346
DNS suffix, 345
DNSSEC (DNS Security Extensions), 346
DOCSIS (Data-Over-Cable Service Interface Specification)
    cable modems, 35, 491
    connecting Ethernet to, 237–238
document findings, troubleshooting process, 675
documentation
    basic router configuration, 269–270
    configuration. See configuration management
    troubleshooting process, 675
domain controllers
    in Active Directory-integrated zone, 345
    as DNS servers, 344
Domain Name System. See DNS (Domain Name System)
domain names
    dynamic DNS mapping router to, 346
    hierarchical aspect of DNS and, 328–330
    registering with ICANN, 330
    top-level, 321
domains
    CompTIA Network+ exam, 4
    DNS name space, 324
    multiple DNS servers for single, 327
    Windows vs. DNS, 344
Don't Fragment (DF) flag, PMTU, 650
DoS (Denial of Service) attacks, 295, 553–554
dotted decimal notation
    converting IP addresses to binary and back, 186–188
    converting to binary and back, 209–211
    IP addresses, 31–32
    manual conversion to binary and back, 210–211
    subnet masks represented by, 196–200
DR (designated router), OSPF, 256–257

drivers
    installing NICs, 165
    installing wireless networking
        devices, 514
    replacing on name-brand
        NICs, 163
drives
    benefits of virtualization, 586
    setting size of virtual, 582–583
    viruses replicating only to, 550
drop ceiling, pulling cable in, 148–149
DS1 (digital signal), T1, 35, 468–470
DS3 (digital signal), T3, 471
DSA (Digital Signature Algorithm) keys,
    SSH, 389
DSCP (Differentiated Services Code
    Point) field, IP packet header, 181
DSL (digital subscriber line)
    ADSL, 487
    as dedicated connection, 500
    into equipment room, 489
    features, 487–488
    installing, 488–490
    neighborhood options for, 488
    overview of, 486
    replacing telephony WANs, 479
    SDSL, 486
    use of cable modems
        surpassing, 491
    VDSL, 487
DSLAM (DSL Access Multiplexer),
    486–487
DSo (digital signal rate), telephones,
    467–469
DSSS (direct-sequence spread-
    spectrum), Wi-Fi, 517
dumb terminals, 261, 298–299
dumpster diving, 555
duplex fiber-optic cable, 72
Dynamic DNS (DDNS), 345–346
dynamic encryption key generation,
    WPA, 525
Dynamic Host Configuration
    Protocol. See DHCP (Dynamic Host
    Configuration Protocol)
dynamic IP addressing, 212, 216–222
dynamic NAT, 240
dynamic (private) port numbers
    defined, 282
    handling, 563
    list of, 283
dynamic routing
    BGP protocol, 252–254
    determining metrics, 246–247
    distance vector protocols, 247–251
    EIGRP, 259
    Internet and, 259
    IS-IS protocol, 259
    link state protocol, 254–255
    OSPF protocol, 254–259
    overview of, 245–246
    review Q & A, 272–274
    RIPv1 protocol, 251
    RIPv2 protocol, 251–252
dynamic VLANs, 416

E

e-mail
    clients, 307–308
    configuring client, 308–309
    IMAP4, 305
    overview of, 304–305
    POP3, 305
    public-key cryptography for,
        365–367
    servers, 306–307
    SMTP, 305
    Web-based services, 305–306
    Web-of-Trust option for, 374
E1 (E-carrier level), 471
E3 (E-carrier level), 471
EAP (Extensible Authentication
    Protocol)
    802.1x for Ethernet networks,
        386–387
    EAP-MS-CHAPv2, 386
    EAP-PSK, 385
    EAP-TLS, 385, 523–524
    EAP-TTLS, 386, 523–524
    overview of, 384–386
    wireless authentication, 522–524
eBGP (external BGP), 254
echo replys, ICMP, 279
echo requests, ICMP, 279
echos, in broken cables, 659
edge routers, 253
EDNS (extension mechanisms for
    DNS), 346
effective permissions, user accounts, 560
EGP (Exterior Gateway Protocol), 253
EIA (Electronic Industries Alliance), 69
EIGRP (Enhanced Interior Gateway
    Routing Protocol), 259
Elastic Sky (ESX) hypervisor,
    589–590, 593
electrical power. See also EMI
    (electromagnetic interference)
    benefits of virtualization, 586
    creating redundancy for failure of,
        548–549, 629
    limits of SOHO network
        design, 642
    location of telecommunications
        room, 146
electrical pulses, NICs, 21–22
electrical signaling, wired networks, 494
Electronic Industries Alliance (EIA), 69
electronic mail. See e-mail

EMI (electromagnetic interference)
    coaxial cable shielding, 64
    installing networks in places of
        high, 110
    shielded twisted pair cabling
        shielding, 68
emulation, virtualization vs., 579–580
Encapsulating Security Payload (ESP),
    IPsec, 394
encryption
    asymmetric-key algorithm
        standards, 365–367
    configuring Wi-Fi, 534–535
    cracking wireless, 556
    encryption, 360–363
    hashes used, 369
    L2TP VPNs lacking, 411
    OSI model and, 367
    SSH replacing Telnet, 304
    standards combining
        authentication and, 391–394
    symmetric-key algorithm
        standards, 363–365
    troubleshooting Wi-Fi
        configuration, 543
    wireless networking security,
        524–526
    World Wide Web security,
        297–298
endpoints, tunnel
    defined, 283
    L2TP VPNs, 411
    PPTP VPNs, 408–410
    viewing active TCP/IP connections,
        283–285
    VPNs, 408–409
Enhanced Interior Gateway Routing
    Protocol (EIGRP), 259
environmental limits, SOHO network
    design, 642–643
environmental monitors,
    telecommunications room, 171
ephemeral port numbers, 282
equipment racks
    SOHO network design, 639, 642
    telecommunications room,
        133–134
equipment room, SOHO network
    design, 639
escalation, problem
    classic situations of, 677–679
    determining cause or, 673
    testing solution or, 674
ESP (Encapsulating Security Payload),
    IPsec, 394
ESS (Extended Service Set), 515–517
ESSID (Extended Service Set Identifier)
    configuring Wi-Fi, 532–533
    wireless networking, 516–517

ESX (Elastic Sky) hypervisor,
589–590, 593
ESXi (free version), 589–590
/etc/resolve.conf file, Linux, 333
Ethernet
10BaseFL, 94–95
10BaseT limits and specifications,
93–94
connecting segments with bridges,
98–99
connecting segments with
crossover cables, 98
connecting segments with uplink
ports, 96–97
frames, 84–89
historical/conceptual data, 82–83
interconnecting different types
of, 95
IOBaseT, 89–90
overview of, 81
replacing telephony WANs, 479
review Q & A, 104–106
switched, 99–103
topology, 83
troubleshooting hubs and
switches, 103
UTP, 90–93
Ethernet, modern
100BaseFX, 110–111
100BaseTX (100BaseT), 108–110
full-duplex Ethernet, 111–112
Gigabit Ethernet. See GbE (Gigabit
Ethernet)
inadequacy of 10BaseT leading
to, 107
knowing for exam, 121
review Q & A, 122–124
EUI-48 numbering name space, 21
EUI-64 bit (Extended Unique
Identifier), IPv6, 436–437, 441
Everyone group, user account control,
560–561
evil twin attacks, 556–557
eXclusive OR, 362
expandability, telecommunications
room, 147
expansion cards, wireless desktop
computers, 511
experience, CompTIA Network+
certification, 3
experimental (reserved) addresses, 201
Extended DSL (XDSL), 486
Extended Service Set (ESS), 515–517
Extended Service Set Identifier (ESSID),
516–517, 532–533
Extended Unique Identifier (EUI-64
bit), IPv6, 436–437, 441
Extensible Authentication Protocol.
See EAP (Extensible Authentication
Protocol)

extension mechanisms for DNS
(EDNS), 346
Exterior Gateway Protocol (EGP), 253
external BGP (eBGP), 254
external connections, SOHO network
design, 645–649
extranet, 496

F

F-connector, coaxial cable, 65
far-end crosstalk (FEXT)
interference, 159
Fast Ethernet. See 100-megabit Ethernet
Fast Track group, in this book, 7–8
fat probes, 157–160
fault tolerance
with data backup, 625–629
ESX, 593
in proper network
management, 625
redundant hardware for, 549
SONET, 472
of star topology, 58
FCS (frame check sequence)
defined, 23
Ethernet frames, 87
frame movement process, 26
processing frames, 24–25
FDM (frequency division multiplexing),
telephones, 464–465
FEC (Forwarding Equivalence Class),
MPLS, 476
FEXT (far-end crosstalk)
interference, 159
FHSS (frequency-hopping spread-
spectrum), Wi-Fi, 517
fiber-based 10 GbE, 117–119
fiber-optic cabling
100BaseFX, 110–111
10BaseFL, 93–94
checking connectors on, 167
fiber-to-the-home
technologies, 494
overview of, 71–73
SONET/SDH and OC carriers for,
472–473
testing for entire building, 161–162
VDSL running on, 486
fiber-optic NICs, 163
File and Print Sharing, turning off, 567
file format standardization, 40–41
File Transfer Protocol. See FTP (File
Transfer Protocol)
files
flat name space for, 323
hierarchical name space for,
322–323
sharing with MD5, 369

filter traffic, bridges, 99
filters, DSL coexistence with PSTN,
488–490
FIN, ACK (finish, acknowledge) packet,
TCP, 277
fire ratings, 75–76
Firefox, 311–312
FireFTP, 312
firewalls
defined, 279
hiding IP addresses, 562
host-based (software), 562
IDS vsl, 425
MAC filtering, 567
network-based (hardware), 562
network zones, 570–571
overview of, 562
packet filtering, 565–567
personal, 567–570
port filtering, 563–565
review Q & A, 572–574
FireWire, 75–76
flags field, TCP header, 183
flat name space
file name space as, 323
HOSTS file using, 321
flooding, OSPF, 255–256
floor plan, cabling entire building, 145
FM (frequency modulation), not in
networks today, 82
folders
configuring DNS server, 338
hierarchical file name space
and, 323
Windows DNS server, 336–337
forward lookup zones, DNS
Active Directory-integrated zones
and, 344–345
overview of, 338–339
types of, 340
forward slash (/), IP address and subnet
mask, 198
forward traffic, bridges, 99
Forwarding Equivalence Class (FEC),
MPLS, 476
Fox and Hound devices, 172
FQDNs (fully qualified domain names),
DNS
authoritative vs. cache-only DNS
servers, 338
cache of, 336
cached lookups for, 336–337
determining with reverse lookup
zone, 340
DNS load balancing, 421–422
name servers, 326–329
overview of, 325–326
resolving into IP address, 335–336
fractional T1 access, 470

fragmentation, avoiding or reducing, 247

frame check sequence. *See* FCS (frame check sequence)

Frame Relay packet-switching technology
    MPLS replacing, 475–478
    overview of, 474

frames
    Ethernet, 84–89
    switches vs. hubs, 101
    TCP/IP model, 49–50

frames, OSI model
    IP packets within, 33–35
    send-receive process, 25–28
    understanding, 22–25

framing bit, DS1/T1, 468–470

free version (ESXi), 589–590

free Web hosting, 294

freeSSHd, Telnet server, 301

frequency analysis, breaking code with, 362–363

frequency, configuring Wi-Fi, 536

frequency division multiplexing (FDM), telephones, 464–465

frequency-hopping spread-spectrum (FHSS), Wi-Fi, 517

frequency modulation (FM), not in networks today, 82

FTP bounce attack, 563

FTP (File Transfer Protocol)
    clients, 311–312
    overview of, 309
    passive vs. active, 312–313
    Secure FTP, 396
    servers, 309–311
    TFTP vs., 313

full-duplex Ethernet, 111–112

full-duplex mode, NICs, 92, 101–102

full or normal backups, 626–629

fully meshed topology network, 61

fully qualified domain names. *See* FQDNs (fully qualified domain names), DNS

G

gain, antennas for higher, 530–531, 541

Gateway column, routing tables, 231–236

gateway router
    choosing for SOHO network, 646–648
    defined, 239
    diagnosing TCP/IP networks, 354–355
    SOHO network IP address scheme, 645

Gateway6 client, setting up IPv6 tunnel, 454–455

GbE (Gigabit Ethernet)
    10 GbE, 116
    10 GbE physical connections, 119–120
    1000BaseCX, 113
    1000BaseLX, 114
    1000BaseSX, 113
    backbones, 120–121
    copper-based 10 GbE, 119
    fiber-based 10 GbE, 117–118
    implementing multiple types of, 115–116
    knowing for exam, 121
    new fiber connectors, 114–115
    other fiber-based 10 GbE standards, 118–119
    overview of, 112–113
    regulations for pulling cable in ceilings, 148
    replacing telephony WANs, 479
    review Q & A, 122–124
    summary, 115

GBIC (gigabit interface converter), 116, 647

general logs, 619

GFS (grandfather, father, son) rotation, data backups, 629

Gigabit Ethernet. *See* GbE (Gigabit Ethernet)

gigabit interface converter (GBIC), 116, 647

global unicast address, IPv6, 439–441

Gmail, 305–306

Google's Gmail, 305–306

GPG (GNU Privacy Guard), 374

grandfather, father, son (GFS) rotation, data backups, 629

groups
    beware of default user, 560
    CIFS organizing computers into, 343
    user account control, 559–561

GSM technology, LTE, 494

GUIs (graphical user interfaces), Apache HTTP Server, 296

GWS (Google Web Server), 296–297

H

H.323
    Skype, 504
    VoIP, 504

hackers
    defeating with strong passwords, 558
    easily cracking WEP, 525

    spoofing MAC addresses, 522
    use of term in this book, 547

half-duplex mode, NICs
    10BaseT, 92
    collisions in, 101–102
    full-duplex Ethernet vs., 111–112

hand-drawn network floor plan, 145

hard drive volumes, hierarchical file name space for, 322–323

hardware firewalls, 562, 567–568

hardware, network
    diagnosing cabling by checking, 168
    failure, 548–549, 625
    mounting into equipment racks, 134
    at Network layer of OSI, 31–35
    NICs. *See* NICs (network interface cards)
    patch panel cable management, 153–155
    at Physical layer of OSI, 17–20
    redundancy, 630
    routers. *See* routers
    wireless, 511–513
    wireless, troubleshooting, 540

hardware troubleshooting tools
    butt sets, 662
    cable strippers/snips, 661
    cable testers, TDRs, and OTDRs, 659–660
    certifiers, 660
    multimeters, 662
    overview of, 658–659
    protocol analyzers, 661
    punchdown tools, 662
    tone probes/generators, 662
    voltage event recorders/ temperature monitors, 661

hardware, virtual
    benefits of, 586
    configuring in VMware Workstation, 578
    sample virtualization, 584
    understanding, 577

hashes, for nonrepudiation, 368–369

header length field, IP packet header, 181

headers
    IP packet, 180–181
    MPLS, 475–476
    TCP, 182–183
    UDP, 183

Hello packets, OSPF, 255–256

Hewlett-Packard (HP) M9050 laser printer, 651

hexadecimal characters, IPv6 addresses, 434–435

Hidden attribute, data backups, 626

HIDS (host-based IDS), 425–426
hierarchical name space
 DNS, 324–326
 overview of, 321–323
high availability, of resources, 625
High-Speed Packet Access (HSPA),
 LTE, 494
high-speed WAN interface cards
 (HWICs), Cisco, 647
higher gain antennas, 530–531, 541
Histogram bar view, monitoring in, 613
historical/conceptual data
 building SOHO network, 635 636
 client/server model, 402–403
 DNS, 318–320
 Ethernet, 82–83
 how routers work, 228–229
 network models, 12–14
 peer-to-peer model, 404–406
 remote connectivity, 459–466
 routing, 228–229
 SOHO networks, 635–636
 standardizing networking
  technology, 178
 structured cabling, 127–128
 TCP/IP, 178
 in this book, 8–9
 Transport and Network layer
  protocols, 276
 virtualization, 575–588
 wireless networking, 509–510
history logs, 619
home office network. *See* SOHO (small
 office/home office) network
home router
 basic configuration, 267–268
 configuring NAT on, 244
 connection methods, 266
 overview of, 228–229
 routing table from, 231–232
 setting RIP in, 252
HomePlug Powerline Alliance, 494
honeynets, 570
honeypots, 570
hop cost, RIP vs. OSPF, 255
hop count
 distance vector routing
  protocols, 247
 RIPv1, 251
 routers and, 245–246
horizontal cabling
 choosing, 132
 diagnosing network problems in
  work area, 170–171
 number of pairs, 131
 solid core vs. stranded core, 131
 as structured cabling network
  component, 129–130
 for telecommunications room,
  132–138

host-based IDS (HIDS), 425–426
host-based (software) firewalls, 562, 570
host IDs
 calculating subnet, 204
 class licenses for, 201
 creating first subnet, 205–206
 with network IDs in IP
  addresses, 192
 subnet masks and, 196
host machine
 defined, 577
 emulation vs. virtualization,
  579–580
 sample virtualization, 582–586
host names
 configuring Telnet client, 302–303
 DNS name space, 324
hostname command, 666
HOSTS file, DNS
 LMHOSTS file in NetBIOS vs., 350
 name resolution with,
  318–320, 331
 using flat name space, 321
HP (Hewlett-Packard) M9050 laser
 printer, 651
HSPA (High-Speed Packet Access),
 LTE, 494
HTML (HyperText Markup Language)
 publishing web pages, 294
 source code, 292–293
HTTP (HyperText Transfer Protocol)
 proxy servers, 427–428
 at TCP/IP Application layer,
  183–185
 underlying World Wide Web, 294
HTTP, port 80
 connection status in TCP/IP
  applications, 287, 289
 defined, 294
 TCP header, 182
 TCP/IP port numbering system, 48
 using netstat, 284
 using port forwarding, 242
 Web servers listening on, 295
https://, HTTPS documents, 394
HTTPS (HyperText Transfer Protocol
 over SSL)
 as secure TCP/IP application,
  394–395
 World Wide Web and, 297–299
hubs
 10BaseT, 89–90
 bridges acting like repeaters or, 99
 connecting Ethernet segments,
  96–99
 defined, 16
 Ethernet, 83
 limitations of, 99–100
 in Link layer of TCP/IP, 44–45
 link lights on, 166

 at Physical layer of OSI, 17, 28
 processing frames with, 24
 switches replacing, 18
 switches vs., 100–101
 troubleshooting, 103
 upgrading to 100BaseT and,
  108–110
HughesNet, 492
Hulu.com, 622–623
humidity, telecommunications room
 and, 146
HWICs (high-speed WAN interface
 cards), Cisco, 647
hybrid topology, 59–60, 83
Hyper-V, 593
HyperTerminal, 261
HyperText Markup Language (HTML)
 publishing web pages, 294
 source code, 292–293
HyperText Transfer Protocol. *See* HTTP
 (HyperText Transfer Protocol)
HyperText Transfer Protocol over SSL
 (HTTPS)
 as secure TCP/IP application,
  394–395
 World Wide Web and, 297–299
hypervisors
 benefits of virtualization, 586
 choosing, 592–593
 defined, 575
 emulation vs. virtualization,
  579–580
 ESX, 589–590
 use of term, 590
 in virtualization, 577–579

I

IANA (Internet Assigned Numbers
 Authority)
 assigning Autonomous System
  Number, 253
 assigning IP addresses in class
  licenses, 200–202
 assigning IPv6 subnets, 437
 ephemeral port numbers, 282
 registering ports for less common
  TCP/IP applications, 282–283
 standardizing dynamic routing
  protocol, 252
IAS (Internet Authentication Service),
 RADIUS, 381
iBGP (internal BGP), 254
IBSS (Independent Basic Service Set), 514
ICA (Independent Computing
 Architecture), 501–502
ICANN (Internet Corporation for
 Assigned Names and Numbers),
 321, 330

ICF (Internet Connection Firewall), 568
ICMP (Internet Control Message Protocol)
 blocking PMTU, 650
 at Internet layer of TCP/IP model, 180–181
 ping command using, 664
 TCP/IP applications, 279
IDF (intermediate distribution frame)
 defined, 132
 main distribution frame vs., 144
 SOHO network design, 639
IDS (intrusion detection system)
 network monitors often acting as, 618
 overview of, 425–427
 port mirroring in, 427
IEEE (Institute of Electrical and Electronics Engineers)
 developing 802.3, 82
 issuing MAC addresses, 20
 networking industry standards, 76–77
 numbering name spaces, 21
 parallel communication standards, 74
IETF (Internet Engineering Task Force)
 IPsec protocol suite, 393
 standardizing dynamic routing protocol, 252
ifconfig command
 releasing/renewing DHCP lease, 222
 running in Ubuntu, 191
 software troubleshooting tool, 663–664
 static IP addressing with, 214–215
IFG (interframe gap), and collisions, 518
IGMP (Internet Group Management Protocol), TCP/IP, 280
IGP (Interior Gateway Protocol), 253
IGRP (Interior Gateway Routing Protocol), 258
IIS (Internet Information Services), 295–296
IKE and IKEv2 (Internet Key Exchange), IPsec, 394
IMAP4 (Internet Message Access Protocol version 4), e-mail, 305, 307–308
impedance
 certifiers picking up mismatch in, 660
 Ohm rating describing cable, 66
implement and test solution, troubleshooting process, 674
incident response records, malware mitigation, 551

incremental backups, 627–629
Independent Basic Service Set (IBSS), 514
Independent Computing Architecture (ICA), 501–502
information gathering, troubleshooting process, 671–672
infrastructure mode wireless network
 BSSID describing basic, 516
 overview of, 515–516
 setting up, 529–531
inherent factor, user authentication, 557
inherited permissions, 561
initialization vector (IV), WEP, 525
installation and configuration domain, CompTIA Network+ exam, 4
installation media, virtualization, 582
Institute of Electrical and Electronics Engineers. See IEEE (Institute of Electrical and Electronics Engineers)
Integrated Services Digital Network. See ISDN (Integrated Services Digital Network)
Intel, and Ethernet, 82
Interexchange Carrier (IXC), 480
interface
 adding to routers, 238
 port filter, 564
 using router's Web, 263–365
Interface column, routing tables, 232–236
interference sources, site survey for Wi-Fi, 527
interframe gap (IFG), and collisions, 518
Interior Gateway Protocol (IGP), 253
Interior Gateway Routing Protocol (IGRP), 258
intermediate distribution frame. See IDF (intermediate distribution frame)
internal BGP (iBGP), 254
internal connections, SOHO network design, 641–645
International Organization for Standardization. See ISO (International Organization for Standardization)
International Telecommunications Unit (ITU)
 SDH standard, 472
 V standards for modems, 483–484
International Telegraph and Telephone Consultative Committee (CCITT), 472, 483–484
Internet
 class IDs for IP addresses, 200–202
 dedicated connections to, 499–501

diagnosing TCP/IP networks to, 355
 dynamic routing and, 259
 generating IPv6 global address for, 439–441
 governance of network IDs on, 194
 private dial-up not using, 496
 standardizing dynamic routing protocol, 252
 using DNS to access, 330
Internet applications
 e-mail, 305–311
 FTP, 309–313
 summary of, 313
 Telnet, 299–304
 World Wide Web. See World Wide Web
Internet Assigned Numbers Authority. See IANA (Internet Assigned Numbers Authority)
Internet Authentication Service (IAS), RADIUS, 381
Internet Connection Firewall (ICF), 568
Internet Control Message Protocol. See ICMP (Internet Control Message Protocol)
Internet Corporation for Assigned Names and Numbers (ICANN), 321, 330
Internet Engineering Task Force (IETF)
 IPsec protocol suite, 393
 standardizing dynamic routing protocol, 252
Internet Group Management Protocol (IGMP), TCP/IP, 280
Internet Information Services (IIS), 295–296
Internet Key Exchange (IKE and IKEv2), IPsec, 394
Internet layer, TCP/IP model
 encapsulation at, 50
 IP working at, 180–181
 IPsec working at, 393–394
 overview of, 44–45
 protocols, 180–181
Internet Message Access Protocol version 4 (IMAP4), e-mail, 305, 307–308
Internet Movie Database, 631
Internet Protocol, instead of term TCP/IP, 276
Internet Protocol Security. See IPsec (Internet Protocol Security)
Internet Protocol version 4. See IPv4 (Internet Protocol version 4)
Internet Protocol version 6. See IPv6 (Internet Protocol version 6)

Internet Security Association and Key
    Management Protocol (ISAKMP),
    IPsec, 394
Internet service providers. *See* ISPs
    (Internet service providers)
Internet Society (ISOC), 252
interVLAN routing, 417–419
Intra-Site Automatic Tunnel Addressing
    Protocol (ISATAP), IPv6, 453–454
intranets
    defined, 571
    setting up DNS for private, 324
intrusion detection system. *See* IDS
    (intrusion detection system)
intrusion prevention system (IPS),
    425–427
IOS, configuring Cisco routers, 262–263
IP addresses
    Autonomous Systems not using,
        253
    class IDs and, 200–202
    configuring managed switches
        with preset, 414–415
    configuring NICs for ad hoc
        network, 528
    connecting to routers for Web
        access, 263–365
    conserving with NAT. *See* NAT
        (Network Address Translation)
    diagnosing TCP/IP networks, 354
    displaying, 189–190
    DNS load balancing using
        multiple, 421–422
    Dynamic DNS and, 345
    endpoints requiring own, 408
    hiding with firewalls, 562
    interconnecting, 192–194
    as logical addressing protocol for
        TCP/IP, 31–33
    loopback, 222–223
    name resolution with HOSTS file,
        318–320
    network IDs for, 191–192
    network maps documentation,
        605–606
    overview, 185–191
    packet filters blocking outgoing,
        565–567
    packet headers, 180
    packets within frames, 33–35
    part of TCP/IP protocol suite,
        180–181
    power of HOSTS file, 319–320
    private, 223
    public, 223
    resolving names to, 330–336
    risks with ADSL and cable
        modems, 567
    routing tables and, 230–237

sending packets locally vs.
    remotely, 196
SOHO network design, 644–645
static, 212–216
at TCP/IP Internet layer, 45
TCP/IP overcoming limitations in
    LANs with, 186
troubleshooting network
    connectivity, 677
troubleshooting with ipconfig/
    ifconfig, 663–664
using multilayer or content switch,
    422–423
using subnet masks, 194–200
using text addresses in browsers
    vs., 293–294
ways to send packets, 201
ipconfig /all
    configuring Teredo tunneling
        protocol, 452
    displaying TCP/IP settings, 190
    MAC address output, 20–21
    troubleshooting DNS, 348
    troubleshooting IP with ifconfig,
        663–664
    verifying DNS server settings,
        333–334
ipconfig command
    checking IP status for OS, 445
    releasing/renewing DHCP
        lease, 222
    software troubleshooting tools,
        663–664
    troubleshooting DHCP
        problems, 221
IPS (intrusion prevention system),
    425–427
IPsec (Internet Protocol Security)
    in IPv6, 434
    L2TP VPNs using, 411
    overview of, 393–394
    VPN options, 412
    wireless authentication, 523–524
IPv4 (Internet Protocol version 4)
    development of, 433
    dotted decimal notation, 186–187
    at Internet layer of TCP/IP model,
        180–181
    migrating to IPv6. *See* IPv6
        (Internet Protocol version 6),
        moving to
    static IP addressing in, 213–216
    subnetting. *See* subnetting
IPv4-to-IPv6 tunnel, 451–454
IPv6 (Internet Protocol version 6)
    128-bit addressing, 442
    address notation in, 434–435
    aggregation in, 441–444
    anycast addresses, 439
    DHCP in, 447–448

DNS in, 449
    enabling, 445–446
    global unicast address in, 439–441
    at Internet layer of TCP/IP model,
        180–181
    IPsec for, 393–394
    IS-IS working with, 258
    link-local address in, 435–437
    multicast addresses, 437–439
    NAT in, 446–447
    OSPF only recently
        supporting, 258
    overview of, 433–434
    as really here, 456
    review Q & A, 456–458
    RIRs passing out IPv6 prefixes, 443
    subnet masks in, 437
    unicast addresses, 437
IPv6 (Internet Protocol version 6),
    moving to
    6in4 tunneling protocol, 452
    6to4 tunneling protocol, 452
    IPv4 and, 450–451
    ISATAP, 453–454
    overview of, 450
    setting up tunnel, 454–456
    Teredo tunneling protocol, 453
    tunnel brokers, 454
    tunnels, 451–452
IS (Intermediate System to Intermediate
    System), 259
IS-IS (Intermediate System to
    Intermediate System), 259
ISAKMP (Internet Security Association
    and Key Management Protocol),
    IPsec, 394
ISATAP (Intra-Site Automatic Tunnel
    Addressing Protocol), IPv6, 453–454
ISDN (Integrated Services Digital
    Network)
    cable modems often replacing,
        490–491
    DSL often replacing, 485–490
    overview of, 484–486
ISO (International Organization for
    Standardization)
    cabling and networking
        standards, 69
    file format standardization, 40–41
    OSI seven-layer model of, 14
ISOC (Internet Society), 252
ISPs (Internet service providers)
    choosing for SOHO network,
        648–649
    connecting cable modems to, 65
    and MTUs for SOHO network,
        649–650
    offering e-mail as free service, 304
    setting up NAT, 239–240
    telephony WAN and, 478

Web hosting service
companies, 294
WiMAX, 493
ITU (International
Telecommunications Unit)
SDH standard, 472
V standards for modems, 483–484
IV (initialization vector), WEP, 525
IXC (Interexchange Carrier), 480

J

jacket, fiber-optic cabling, 71–72

K

KDC (Key Distribution Center),
Kerberos, 383–384
Kerberos authentication, 382–384
KINK (Kerberized Internet Negotiation
of Keys), IPsec, 394
knowledge factor, user
authentication, 557

L

L2F (Layer 2 Forwarding), 411
L2TP (Layer 2 Tunneling Protocol)
VPNs, 411
Label Distribution Protocol (LDP),
MPLS, 476
label edge routers (LERs), MPLS,
476–478
label switching routers (LSRs), MPLS,
476–477
labels
block panel, 136–137
for cable connections in large
buildings, 150
MPLS header, 475–478
work area outlet, 140
LACNIC (Latin America and Caribbean
Internet Addresses Registry), 443
LACP (Link Aggregation Control
Protocol), 166
LAN Ethernet
10GBaseER for, 118
10GBaseLR for, 118
10GBaseSR for, 117–118
creating with TCP/IP, 185–186
SONET vs., 117
LANs (large area networks)
basic router configuration, 269
interconnecting TCP/IP, 192–194
private dial-up, 496–498
subnet masks and, 194–200
virtual. See VLANs (virtual LANs)

laptops
connecting to new router, 264
replacing onboard NICs, 170
laser printers, SOHO network
design, 651
lasers, in fiber-optic cables, 73
"the last mile" analog
BPL, 494–495
cable modems, 490–491
cellular WAN, 492–494
choosing connection option, 495
decision to keep, 466
dial-up, 480–486
DSL, 486–490
fiber, 494
satellite, 492
latency, calculating routing metrics, 247
latency-sensitive applications, 622
Latin America and Caribbean Internet
Addresses Registry (LACNIC), 443
Lavasoft Ad-Aware, 552
Layer 1 OSI. See Physical layer
(Layer 1) OSI
Layer 2 Forwarding (L2F), 411
Layer 2 OSI. See Data Link layer
(Layer 2) OSI
Layer 2 Tunneling Protocol (L2TP)
VPNs, 411
Layer 3 OSI. See Network layer
(Layer 3) OSI
Layer 4 (Transport layer) OSI,
36–37, 422
Layer 5 OSI, 48. See also Session layer
(Layer 5) OSI
Layer 6 (Presentation layer) OSI,
40–41, 48
Layer 7 OSI. See Application layer
(Layer 7) OSI
LC (Local Connector)-type fiber
connector
1000BaseSX using, 113
overview of, 73
predominance of, 114–115
LCP (Link Control Protocol), PPP
authentication, 377
LDAP (Lightweight Directory Access
Protocol), 397–398
LDP (Label Distribution Protocol),
MPLS, 476
LEAP (Lightweight Extensible
Authentication Protocol), 386
LEC (Local Exchange Carrier),
PSTN, 480
LEDs (light-emitting diodes)
1000BaseSX using, 113–114
fiber-optic cables using, 72
as link lights of UTP NICs,
166–168
leeching, 556

LERs (label edge routers), MPLS,
476–478
light-emitting diodes. See LEDs (light-
emitting diodes)
light leakage, testing fiber runs for, 161
lights-out management (LOM), SOHO
network design, 643–644
Lightweight Directory Access Protocol
(LDAP), 397–398
Lightweight Extensible Authentication
Protocol (LEAP), 386
Link Aggregation Control Protocol
(LACP), 166
link aggregation, identical NICs for,
165–166
Link Control Protocol (LCP), PPP
authentication, 377
Link dead phase, PPP, 377
Link establishment phase, PPP, 377
Link layer (Network Interface layer),
TCP/IP model
encapsulation at, 50
not part of TCP/IP protocol
suite, 179
overview of, 44–45
TCP/IP model, 44–45
link lights
connecting to routers for Web
access, 264
diagnosing cabling, 168
NICs, 166–168
troubleshooting wireless
connectivity, 541
link-local address, IPv6, 435–437
link state advertisements (LSAs), OSPF,
255–257
link state, determining, 513
link state dynamic routing protocol
defined, 254
IS-IS, 259
OSPF, 254–259
Linksys home router diagram, 229
Linksys WAP
configuring MAC address
filtering, 533
encryption key configuration, 534
setup screen, 531–532
Linksys wireless bridge device, 538
listening (or open) ports, 287–288
LLC (Logical Link Control), NICs,
28–29
LMHOSTS file, NetBIOS, 350
load balancer, 421
load balancing
overview of, 420–421
performance optimization with,
630–631
using DNS for, 421–422
using multilayer or content switch,
422–423

Local Connector-type fiber connector. See LC (Local Connector)-type fiber connector
Local Exchange Carrier (LEC), PSTN, 480
local exchanges, old-time telephones, 463
lock icon, on secure Web pages, 298
locked doors, physical server protection, 554
locking client systems, when not in use, 554–555
log in, troubleshooting, 676
log off, physical server protection, 554
logical addresses
    IP addresses as, 31–35
    overview of, 30–31
Logical Link Control (LLC), NICs, 28–29
logical (signaling) topology, 60
logs
    categories of, 619–620
    creating with other tools, 618
    creating with Performance Monitor, 613–618
    network traffic and custom, 618–620
LOM (lights-out management), SOHO network design, 643–644
long distance, history of, 461
Long Term Evolution (LTE), 494
loopback IP addresses, 222–223
loopback plug/test
    diagnosing cabling, 169
    troubleshooting logs, 676
LSAs (link state advertisements), OSPF, 255–257
LSRs (label switching routers), MPLS, 476–477
LTE (Long Term Evolution), 494

M

MAC-48 numbering name space, 21
MAC address filtering
    configuring Wi-Fi, 533
    firewall tool, 567
    troubleshooting Wi-Fi, 542
    wireless networking security, 521–522
MAC addresses
    broadcast addresses, 25
    broadcasting for, 185–186
    displaying, 189–190
    dynamic VLANs based on, 416
    Ethernet frames and, 85–86
    in frame movement process, 27–28

generating IPv6 global address, 440–441
generating IPv6 ink-local address, 436–437
NICs, 29
processing frames, 23–25
review Q & A, 50–53
segments, 196
switches tracking, 100–103
in TCP/IP network, 32, 188–189
TCP/IP using ARP to figure out, 197–198
understanding, 20
using logical addresses vs., 31
MAC (mandatory access control) security model, 375
Mac OS X
    administrative access control, 549
    case sensitivity of commands, 222
    displaying IP and MAC address, 189–191
    displaying routing table, 234
    enabling IPv6, 445–446
    entering static IP information, 214
    Parallels VMM for, 591–592
    troubleshooting DHCP, 221
    troubleshooting IP with ifconfig, 663–664
macros, 550
Mail eXchanger (MX) DNS records, 340
mailboxes, e-mail servers and, 307
main distribution frame (MDF), 144
mainframes, replaced by PCs, 300
malware
    dealing with, 551
    excellent anti-malware programs, 552
    types of, 550–551
Malwarebytes Anti-Malware, 552
man in the middle attacks, 553
managed devices, 260
managed switches, 414
management
    bandwidth, 423–424
    change m documentation, 609
    CompTIA Network+ exam domain, 4
    configuration. See configuration management
    network. See network management
    patch panel cable, 153–155
Management Information Base (MIB), SNMP, 396
mandatory access control (MAC) security model, 375
MANs (metropolitan area networks), WiMAX for, 493
maximum transmission units (MTUs)

calculating routing metric, 246–247
    SOHO network design, 651
MD5 (Message-Digest Algorithm version 5), 369
MDF (main distribution frame), 144
MDI (media dependent interface), 97
MDIX (media dependent interface crossover), 97
Mechanical Transfer Registered Jack (MT-RJ) connector, 114–115
media access control addresses. See MAC addresses
media and topologies domain, CompTIA Network+ exam, 4
media converter(s), 95, 116
media dependent interface crossover (MDIX), 97
media dependent interface (MDI), 97
medium-priced testers, 157
megahertz (MHz), CAT ratings, 69–71
mesh topology, 60–61, 514
Message-Digest Algorithm version 5 (MD5), 369
Metric column, routing tables, 234–236
metrics
    dynamic routing, 246–247
    routing, 234–235
metropolitan area networks (MANs), WiMAX for, 493
MHTechEd, introduction to, 16
MHz (megahertz), CAT ratings, 69–71
MIB (Management Information Base), SNMP, 396
Microsoft Exchange Server
    as dedicated server, 405
    e-mail, 307
Microsoft IPX/SPX Protocol, as obsolete, 178
Microsoft Outlook, e-mail client, 308, 405
Microsoft Visio, 605–606
Microsoft's Windows Mail, e-mail client, 308–309
Microtest OMNIScanner, 160
MIMO (multiple in/multiple out), 802.11n, 518
mirroring or duplexing (RAID 1), 630
mixed mode, 802.11g, 518
MMF (multimode fiber)
    1000BaseSX using, 113–114
    10BaseFL using, 94
    defined, 72
    preventing modal distortion, 73
mnemonics, for memorizing OSI layers, 14
mobile data services, cellular WANs
    802.16 (WiMAX), 493
    LTE, 494
    overview of, 492–493

modal distortion
  preventing using SMF cables, 73
  testing fiber runs for, 161
models
  biography of, 13
  network, 14
  working with, 12
modems (modulator-demodulator)
  baud vs. bits per second and, 482
  cable. *See* cable modems
  defining speed with V standards, 483–484
  dial-up to Internet with, 496–497
  DSL, 488–489
  internal, 481–482
modern Ethernet. *See* Ethernet, modern
mounting brackets, pulling cable through, 149–150
Mouse Gestures, Firefox add-on, 312
Mozilla Thunderbird, e-mail client, 308
Mozilla's FileZilla, FTP, 310, 312
MPLS (Multiprotocol Label Switching), 475–478
MS-CHAP (Challenge Handshake Authentication Protocol), 379, 382
MSAs (multisource agreements), 119–120
MT-RJ (Mechanical Transfer Registered Jack) connector, 114–115
µTorrent, 405–406
mtr (My traceroute) command, 271–272, 666
MTU black holes, 650
MTU mismatch, 649
MTUs (maximum transmission units)
  calculating routing metric, 246–247
  SOHO network design, 651
multicast addresses
  defined, 438
  IGMP and, 280
  IPv6, 437–439
  overview of, 201
multicast class licenses, 201
multifactor authentication, 557
multihomed computers, 233
multilayer switches
  DNS load balancing, 421–422
  load balancing, 420–421
  overview of, 419–420
  QoS and traffic shaping, 423–424
  using content switches or, 422
multimeters
  testing cable runs, 156–157
  troubleshooting with, 662
multimode fiber. *See* MMF (multimode fiber)
multiple access, CSMA/CD, 88

multiple in/multiple out (MIMO), 802.11n, 518
multiplexers, telephone
  connections inside demarc, 143
  converting to digital, 466
  history of long distance, 463–465
multiplexing, SONET features, 472
Multiprotocol Label Switching (MPLS), 475–478
multispeed lights, NICs, 166–167
multispeed NICs, 100BaseT, 108–110
mutual authentication, SSL/TLS, 392
MX (Mail eXchanger) DNS records, 340
My traceroute (mtr) command, 271–272, 666

N

NaaS (Network as a Service), 596
NAC (Network Access Control), 375, 548
name-brand NICs, buying, 163
name resolution
  DNS, 330–336
  DNS and CIFS, 342–343
  DNS load balancing, 422
  how DNS works, 320–321
  overview of, 317–318
  WINS enabling, 350–351
name servers, DNS, 326–330, 338
name spaces
  DNS, 324–326
  hierarchical vs. flat, 321–323
naming conventions
  10BaseT, 90
  DNS, 325–326
  name servers, 326
  virtual machines, 582
NAPT-PT, 446
NAS (Network Access Server)
  RADIUS setup, 381–382
  wireless authentication, 522–524
NAS (network attached storage)
  and ESX, 593
  SOHO network design, 639
NAT (Network Address Translation)
  configuring, 244
  hiding IP addresses, 562
  IPv6 and, 446–447
  overview of, 238
  Port Address Translation, 240–242
  port forwarding, 242–243
  review Q & A, 272–274
  setup, 239–240
NAT traversal, 452
National Electrical Code (NEC)
  cabling fire ratings, 76
  pulling cable in ceilings, 148
native mode, 802.11g, 518

nbstat command
  software troubleshooting tools, 667
  troubleshooting WINS, 352
NCP (Network Control Protocol), PPP, 377
near-end crosstalk (NEXT) interference, testing, 158–159
NEC (National Electrical Code)
  cabling fire ratings, 76
  pulling cable in ceilings, 148
Nessus, vulnerability scanner, 571
Net Activity Viewer, Linux, 286–287
net view command, 353
NetBEUI, 341
NetBIOS
  diagnosing TCP/IP networks, 353
  enabling in routed network with WINS, 349–352
  overview of, 341
  turning off File and Print Sharing for security, 567
NetBIOS over TCP/IP (NetBT), 342
NetBT (NetBIOS over TCP/IP), 342
Netmask column, routing tables, 234–236
Netscape Navigator, 392
netstat command
  diagnosing computer, 291
  diagnosing TCP/IP networks, 354
  discovering process ID, 288–289
  software troubleshooting tool, 667
  understanding connection status, 286–291
  viewing active TCP/IP connections, 283–285
  viewing all listening ports, 287–288
  viewing HTTP connections, 563–564
  viewing routing table, 234
  viewing sessions, 38
Network Access Control (NAC), 375, 548
Network Access Server (NAS)
  RADIUS setup, 381–382
  wireless authentication, 522–524
Network Address Translation. *See* NAT (Network Address Translation)
Network as a Service (NaaS), 596
network attached storage (NAS)
  ESX and, 593
  SOHO network design, 639
network-based (hardware) firewalls, 562, 567–568
Network Configuration utility, Ubuntu, 214–215, 333
network connectivity
  documentation, 602–606

monitoring with Performance
Monitor. *See* Performance
Monitor
troubleshooting, 677
Network Control Protocol (NCP),
PPP, 377
network design, SOHO network,
638–640
Network Destination column, routing
tables, 234–236
network diagrams
change management
documentation, 609
network connectivity
documentation, 603–605
terminology of, 606
network IDs
breaking into subnets. *See*
subnetting
class licenses for IP addresses
and, 201
creating IP addresses, 191–192
router configuration, 267–269
routers determining traffic with,
193–194
routing tables and, 231–236
in static IP addressing, 212–216
VPNs, 408–412
network interface cards. *See* NICs
(network interface cards)
Network Interface layer. *See* Link layer
(Network Interface layer), TCP/IP
model
network interface units. *See* NIUs
(network interface units)
network intrusion prevention system
(NIPS), 426
Network layer (Layer 3) OSI
ICMP working at, 279
IPsec working at, 393–394
load balancing with multilayer
switch, 422
MPLS labels between Layer 2 and,
475–478
overview of, 31–35
PPP working at, 377
switches based on IP addresses
at, 419
TCP/IP Internet layer vs., 45
Network layer protocol phase, PPP, 377
network management
configuration. *See* configuration
management
with Event Monitor, 618–620
with Performance Monitor. *See*
Performance Monitor
performance optimization. *See*
performance optimization
review Q & A, 632–634

Network Management Software (NMS),
265–267
network maps, connectivity
documentation, 605–606
network models
historical/conceptual data, 12–14
OSI. *See* OSI seven-layer model
overview of, 11–12
review answers, 53
review Q & A, 51–53
TCP/IP model. *See* TCP/IP model
network monitors, 618
network name (SSID), 516–517
network naming
Active Directory-integrated zones,
344–345
DNS security extensions, 346
DNS servers, 336–341
dynamic DNS, 345–346
historical/conceptual data,
318–320
legacy of CIFS, 342–344
name resolution, 330–336
name servers, 326–330
name spaces, 321–326
overview of, 317–318
review Q & A, 355–357
TCP/IP networks, 352–355
troubleshooting DNS, 346–349
understanding DNS, 320–321
Windows, 341–342
WINS, 349–352
network needs, SOHO network design,
638–639
Network News Transfer Protocol
(NNTP), accessing USENET, 294
network operating system (NOS)
software, frame movement, 25
network protection devices
IDS/IPS, 425–427
port authentication, 428–429
port mirroring, 427
proxy serving, 427–428
network protocols
defined, 31
naming conventions, 31–32
TCP/IP, 31
network technologies, 63
Network Time Protocol (NTP), using
UDP, 221
network topology icons, network
diagrams, 603–605
network traffic, and custom logs,
618–620
Network utility, Mac
displaying IP and MAC
addresses, 189
entering static IP information, 214
troubleshooting DHCP
problems, 221

network zones, 570–571
networking, defined, 1
next hop router, routing tables, 231–232
NEXT (near-end crosstalk) interference,
testing, 158–159
NICs (network interface cards)
100BaseT upgrade, 108–110
bonding used by, 165–166
bridged or dedicated bridged,
593–594
buying, 163
collision detection on Ethernet
networks, 88–89
configuring for ad hoc
network, 528
creating virtual switches, 594
diagnosing cabling by checking,
169–170
diagnosing TCP/IP networks, 353
expansion card, 511
frame movement and, 25–28,
34–35
frames and, 22–25
frames, Ethernet and, 85–86
function of, 17–19
getting data onto the wire, 25
Gigabit Ethernet and. *See* GbE
(Gigabit Ethernet)
installing drivers, 165
installing DSL, 489
installing Wi-Fi network
clients, 528
at Layer 1 and 2 of OSI, 29–30
at Link layer of TCP/IP, 44–45
link lights, 166–168
Logical Link Control and, 28–29
MAC addresses and, 20–21, 29
mobile wireless, 493
multihomed computers using
multiple, 233
overview of, 162–163
physically connecting, 163–165
PPTP VPNs, 409
sending broadcast addresses, 25
sending/receiving electrical pulses,
21–22
troubleshooting wireless
connectivity, 541
USB wireless, 511–512
VPN client tunnel endpoints
and, 408
NIDS (network-based IDS), 425–426
NIPS (network intrusion prevention
system), 426
NIUs (network interface units)
connections inside demarc,
143–144
PSTN connections, 481
in structured cabling for home/
office, 141–143

Nmap
creating network map with, 606
port scanner, 669
vulnerability scanner, 571
NMS (Network Management Software), 265–267
NNTP (Network News Transfer Protocol), accessing USENET, 294
no-default routers, 441
noise, in broken cables, 659
nonalphanumeric characters, passwords, 558
nonrepudiation
defined, 360, 368
digital signatures for, 370
hashes for, 368–369
PKI for, 370–374
for World Wide Web security, 297–298
NOS (network operating system) software, frame movement, 25
Novell NetWare, 403–404
nslookup
diagnosing DNS problems, 665–666
querying DNS server, 348
NTP (Network Time Protocol), using UDP, 221
numbering system, remembering passwords with, 559
NWLINK, as obsolete, 178

O

objects
creating log in Windows XP, 613–615
Performance Monitor, 611–613
OC (Optical Carrier Standards), 472–473, 478
octets. *See* IPv4 (Internet Protocol version 4)
OEM tools, Network Management Software, 265–267
OFDM (orthogonal frequency-division multiplexing), Wi-Fi, 517
Ohm ratings, coax cabling, 66
omnidirectional antenna, placing WAPs, 529–530
On Hold feature, V.92 standard, 483
online resources
anti-malware programs, 552
cabling certification, 128
CompTIA Network, 3
CompTIA Network+ exam, 4
CompTIA website, 9
downloading TCPView, 285–286
DSL options in your neighborhood, 488

Ethernet basics, 82
GNU Privacy Guard, 374
Internet Movie Database, 631
IPv6 tunnel brokers, 454
ISPs in your neighborhood, 649
Prometric and Pearson VUE testing centers, 5
terminal emulation programs, 261
VMware Workstation, 580
vulnerability scanners, 571
Wireshark, 668
Yost cable, 260
open circuits, in broken cables, 659
open-ended questions, troubleshooting process, 671–672
open (or listening) ports, 287–288
Open Shortest Path First (OSPF) protocol, 254–259
Open Systems Interconnection. *See* OSI (Open Systems Interconnection)
OpenNMS, 266–267
OpenSSH, 396
OpenVPN, 412
operating system
converting IPv4 dotted decimal to binary and back, 187–188
crash, 548–549
displaying IP and MAC addresses, 189–190
enabling IPv6, 445–446
forcing speed/duplex, 112
installing on virtual machine, 582
verifying computer recognizes NIC, 165
operators, old-time telephone, 461–462
Optical Carrier Standards (OC), 472–473, 478
optical connection tester, 167–168
optical time domain reflectometers (OTDRs), 161, 658–659
orthogonal frequency-division multiplexing (OFDM), Wi-Fi, 517
oscilloscope of data, 22
OSI (Open Systems Interconnection)
on CompTIA Network+ exam, 4
seven-layer model. *See* OSI seven-layer model
OSI seven-layer model
encryption and, 367
history of, 14
Layer 1 (Physical), 17–20
Layer 2 (Data Link), 17–20
Layer 3 (Network), 31–35
Layer 4 (Transport), 36–37
Layer 5 (Session), 37–39
Layer 6 (Presentation), 40–41
Layer 7 (Application), 42–43
network hardware, 17–20
network software, 30–31

NICs. *See* NICs (network interface cards)
overview of, 15–16
review Q & A, 51–53
TCP/IP model compared to, 49
as troubleshooting tool, 11–12, 50–51
wireless networks and, 510
OSPF (Open Shortest Path First) protocol, 254–259
OTDRs (optical time domain reflectometers), 161, 658–659
outlet, work area, 138–140
overhead, STS, 473
ownership factor, user authentication, 557

P

P2P (peer-to-peer) topologies, 404–406
packet analyzers, 668
packet (or IP) filtering, firewall tool, 565–567
packet sniffers
cracking wireless encryption with, 556
troubleshooting network packets, 668
packet switches, 474
packet switching technologies
ATM for, 474–475
Frame Relay, 474
MPLS, 475–478
overview of, 473–474
packets
in OSI model, 33–37
in TCP/IP model, 49–50
pad, Ethernet frames, 86
PAP (Password Authentication Protocol)
PPP authentication, 378
RADIUS supporting, 382
paper shredders, and dumpster diving, 555
parabolic antennas, 530
parallel cables
IEEE 1284-compliant, 76
overview of, 74–75
parameters, topology, 63
partially meshed topology network, 61
passive FTP, 313
passive optical network (PON), fiber-to-the-home, 494
password-protected screensavers, 554–555
passwords
AAA authentication and, 381
adding to FTP server, 310–311
changing at intervals, 558–559
configuring Telnet client, 302–303

connecting to routers for Web access, 264
dial-up to Internet, 496–497
Novell NetWare model, 403
physical client protection, 555
PPP authentication methods, 377–379
providing authentication via, 374
RADIUS authentication, 382
securing user accounts, 557–559
smart devices in lieu of, 559
strong, 558
troubleshooting log in, 676
PAT (Port Address Translation), 240–242
patch antennas, 530
patch cables
connecting PC to wall outlet, 140
connecting to patch panels, 153–155
diagnosing cabling with, 169
overview of, 138
rolling own, 151–153
patch management, malware mitigation, 551
patch panels
connecting inside demarc, 143–144
connecting within entire building, 153–155
telecommunications room, 134–138
Path MTU Discovery (PMTU), 650
payload, STS, 473
PBX, virtual, 594–595
PC Card NICs, 164
PCF (Point Coordination Function), 802.11 collision avoidance, 518
PCI Express (PCIe) NIC, 164, 511
PCI (Peripheral Component Interconnect) NIC, 164
PCIe (PCI Express) NIC, 164, 511
PCs
connecting NICs, 163–164
connecting over phone lines, 481–482
connecting to wall outlet, 140
Novell NetWare popularizing networks, 404
on peer-to-peer networks, 404
replacing mainframes, 300
star topology for structured cabling, 127–128
PDF (Portable Document Format), 40–41
PEAP (Protected Extensible Authentication Protocol), 386, 523–524
Pearson VUE testing centers, CompTIA Network+ exam, 5–6

peer to peer mode, wireless networks, 514–515
peer-to-peer (P2P) topologies, 404–406
performance, baselines documentation of, 606–608
Performance Logs and Alerts tree, Windows XP, 613
Performance Monitor
creating baseline in Windows, 608
creating log in Windows 7, 616–618
creating log in Windows XP, 613–616
creating log using other tools, 618
objects, counters, and views, 611–613
overview of, 610–611
troubleshooting sluggish server, 677
performance optimization
backup generators, 629
caching, 621
cluster servers and load balancing, 630–631
controlling data throughput, 621–623
data backup, 625–629
keeping resources available, 625
overview of, 620–621
with Performance Monitor. *See* Performance Monitor
quality of service, 623
RAID and redundant hardware, 630
review Q & A, 632–634
traffic shaping (or filtering), 623–624
UPS, 629
Peripheral Component Interconnect (PCI) NIC, 164
peripherals, SOHO network design, 639, 651
permanent virtual circuit (PVC), MPLS, 478
permissions
access control lists as, 375
administering user accounts, 559–561
Novell NetWare model, 403
on peer-to-peer networks, 405
personal firewalls, 567–570
Personal Shared Key (PSK), EAP-PSK, 385
PGP (Pretty Good Privacy) encryption, 374
phishing attacks
evil twins as wireless, 557
overview of, 553
physical address
at Link layer of TCP/IP, 44–45
MAC address as, 20

physical intrusion attacks, 554–555
Physical layer (Layer 1) OSI
NICs operating at, 29–30
overview of, 17–19
SONET at, 472
physical network installation
diagnostics and repair of physical cabling, 168–173
historical/conceptual data, 127–128
NICs, 162–168
overview of, 125–126
review Q & A, 173–176
structured cabling. *See* structured cabling
structured cabling for entire building. *See* structured cabling for entire building
PID (process ID), 289, 291
ping utility
determining best MTU setting, 650
diagnosing TCP/IP networks locally, 353
diagnosing TCP/IP networks to gateway, 355
ICMP used with, 180–181, 279
loopback address used with, 222–223
in smurf attacks, 553–554
as software troubleshooting tool, 664–665
troubleshooting DNS, 347–348
troubleshooting inability to reach Web site, 676
troubleshooting log in, 676
troubleshooting network connectivity, 677
verifying static IP addresses, 214–216
pins, on RJ-45 connectors, 91
PKI (public-key infrastructure)
digital certificates linked to, 374
for nonrepudiation, 370–374
SSH servers using, 388
placeable USB NICs, 511–512
plain-old telephone service. *See* PSTN (public switched telephone network)
plaintext (or cleartext) encryption, 360–361
plan of action, troubleshooting process, 673
PLC (powerline communications), for networking, 494
plenum fire-rated cable, 76
Plug and Play (PnP), 513
PMTU black holes, 650
PMTU (Path MTU Discovery), 650
PnP (Plug and Play), 513
PoE (Power over Ethernet), 526

Point Coordination Function (PCF),
802.11 collision avoidance, 518
point-to-multipoint bridges, Wi-Fi, 538
point-to-multipoint topology, 62
point-to-point bridges, Wi-Fi, 538
Point-to-Point Protocol. *See* PPP (Point-
to-Point Protocol)
Point-to-Point Protocol over Ethernet
(PPPoE), 489–490, 500
point-to-point topology networks
FireWire restricted to, 75
overview of, 60, 62
parallel connectors restricted to,
74–75
serial ports restricted to, 74
T1 connections, 468
Point-to-Point Tunneling Protocol
(PPTP) VPNs, 408–411
pointer records (PTRs), 340
policies
change management
documentation, 609
documentation, 608
polyvinyl chloride (PVC) cable, fire
rating, 76
PON (passive optical network), fiber-to-
the-home, 494
POP3 (Post Office Protocol version 3),
e-mail, 305–308
Port Address Translation (PAT),
240–242
port authentication, 428–429. *See also*
AAA (Authentication, Authorization,
and Accounting)
port filtering (or blocking), firewall tool,
563–565
port forwarding, NAT, 242–243
port mirroring, 427
port numbers, TCP
defined, 280
differentiating hubs by, 90
DNS servers, port 53, 320
filtering or blocking of, 563–565
FTP, ports 20 and 21, 312–313
HTTP, port 80. *See* HTTP, port 80
HTTPS, port 443, 298
IMAP4, port 143, 305
Kerberos, port 88, 383
PAT (Port Address Translation)
using, 240–242
POP3, port 110, 182, 305
power of, 280–282
RADIUS, port 49, 382–387
registered ports, 282–286
SMTP, port 25, 305
SSH, port 22, 313, 388–390
TCP/IP system for, 48–49
Telnet, port 23, 300

port numbers, UDP
BOOTP servers, ports 67 and
68, 221
DHCP servers, ports 67 and 68,
221, 278
DNS servers, port 53, 320
filtering or blocking of, 563–565
Kerberos, port 88, 383
NTP/SNTP, port 123, 278
power of, 280–282
SNMP, port 161, 396
TFTP, port 69, 278, 313
port scanners, software troubleshooting,
668–669
Portable Document Format (PDF),
40–41
ports
challenges of multilayer
switches, 420
good vs. bad communication
rules, 291
home router, 231
network maps documenting,
605–606
patch panel configurations,
134, 137
rack-mounted switch
configurations, 134
static VLANs based on, 416–417
switches with high-speed, add-on,
120–121
TCP header, 182–183
trunk, VLANs, 414
uplink, 96–97
viewing opening or listening,
287–288
what is normal on your OS, 291
POST, in virtual machine, 584–585
Post Office Protocol version 3 (POP3),
e-mail, 305–308
POTS (plain-old telephone service). *See*
PSTN (public switched telephone
network)
power. *See* electrical power
Power over Ethernet (POE), 526
powerline communications (PLC), 494
PPP (Point-to-Point Protocol)
authentication, 376–379
dial-up to Internet, 496–497
limitations of, 379–380
PPPoE (Point-to-Point Protocol over
Ethernet), 489–490, 500
PPTP (Point-to-Point Tunneling
Protocol) VPNs, 408–411
practice exams, in this book, 9
preamble, Ethernet frame, 84–85
preferences, Mac, 214, 221
Presentation layer (Layer 6) OSI,
40–41, 48

Pretty Good Privacy (PGP)
encryption, 374
preventative measures, troubleshooting
process, 674–675
PRI (Primary Rate Interface), ISDN, 484
Primary Rate Interface (PRI), ISDN, 484
primary zone, DNS server, 340, 344 345
principle of least privilege, user
accounts, 559
private dedicated connections, 498
private dial-up, remote access via,
496–498
private DNS networks, 324–325
private internetworks, 233
private IP addresses
overview, 223
SOHO network design, 644–645
probable cause, in troubleshooting
process, 673
problem identification, in
troubleshooting process, 671–672
procedures, documentation, 608–609
Process Explorer, 289–290
process ID (PID), 289, 291
Prometric testing centers, CompTIA
Network+ exam, 5–6
promiscuous mode, NIC in, 85
properties, static IP addressing in
Windows, 213
protected access, FTP sites, 309
Protected Extensible Authentication
Protocol (PEAP), 386, 523–524
protection of network. *See* security
protocol analyzers, 661, 667
protocol field, IP packet header, 181
protocol suites
CompTIA Network+ exam
questions on, 4
defined, 178
IPsec, 393–394
splitting up data at Transport
layer, 36
standardizing networking
technology, 178
TCP enabling communication for
TCP/IP, 277–278
TCP/IP. *See* TCP/IP protocol suite
TCP/IP model for TCP/IP. *See*
TCP/IP model
protocols
historical/conceptual data, 178
network maps documentation,
605–606
used by wireless networks, 510
protocols, dynamic routing, 247–249
BGP, 252–254
configuring for routers, 269
defined, 245
distance vector, 247–251

EIGRP, 259
  Internet and, 259
  IS-IS, 259
  link state, 254–255
  OSPF, 254–259
  RIPv1, 251
  RIPv2, 251–252
proxy agent, WINS, 351
proxy ARP problems, 679
proxy serving, 427–428
PSK (Personal Shared Key), EAP-PSK, 385
PSTN (public switched telephone network)
  baud vs. bits per second, 482
  DSL coexistence with, 488–490
  making last mile digital with ISDN, 484–486
  overview of, 480–482
  satellite faster than, 492
  V standards, 483–484
  VoIP using, 503–504
PTRs (pointer records), 340
public IP addresses, 223
public-key cryptography algorithm, 365–367
public-key infrastructure. *See* PKI (public-key infrastructure)
public keys, SSL, 297–298
public switched telephone network. *See* PSTN (public switched telephone network)
publishing Web pages, 294
pulling cable, 147–150
punchdown tools
  for 110 block, 135
  troubleshooting with, 658–659, 662
PuTTY utility, 261–262, 266
PuTTYgen, 389
PVC (permanent virtual circuit), MPLS, 478
PVC (polyvinyl chloride) cable, fire rating, 76

Q

QoS (quality of service)
  bandwidth management with, 423–424
  and traffic shaping, 623–624
QPopper, e-mail server, 307
Qualcomm's Eudora, e-mail client, 308
questions, in troubleshooting, 671–673
Quick Connect feature, V.92 standard, 483
QZHTTP server, 297

R

raceways, cable run, 146
radio frequency interference (RFI), 541
radio frequency (RF) waves, wireless networks, 509, 530
Radio Grade (RG) rating, coax cables, 66
RADIUS (RADIUS Remote Authentication Dial-In User Service) server
  configuring Wi-Fi encryption, 534–535
  overview of, 381–382
  port authentication, 428–429
  wireless authentication, 522–524
RAID (Redundant Array of Independent Disks)
  fault tolerance, 549
  performance optimization, 630
  SOHO network design, 639
railroad signaling racks, 134
RAM
  host machine for virtualization, 579
  limiting virtualization, 586
  troubleshooting sluggish server, 677
range, wireless networking, 516
RARP (Reverse Address Resolution Protocol), 198
RAS (remote access server), 496–498
RAS (Remote Access Service), 496–498
RAT (remote administration tool), Trojans, 550
RBAC (role-based access control) security model, 376
RC4 (Rivest Cipher 4) stream cipher
  data encryption using WEP, 525
  symmetric-key algorithm, 364
  symmetric-key algorithm standards, 364
RCP (Remote Copy Protocol), 304
RDC (Remote Desktop Connection), 501–502
RDP (Remote Desktop Protocol), 501
Read-Only attribute, data backups, 626
Real Time Streaming Protocol (RTSP), 504
Real-time Transport Protocol (RTP), VoIP, 504
real transfer time (RTT), 181
record types
  configuring DNS server, 338
  less common, 339–340
  name servers and, 326
Redhat, KVM, 592
redundancy, for fault tolerance, 549

Redundant Array of Independent Disks. *See* RAID (Redundant Array of Independent Disks)
Regional Internet Registries (RIRs)
  giving out IPv6 prefixes, 443
  IANA, 200–201
registered jack connectors. *See* RJ (registered jack) connectors
registered ports, 282–286
registration, CompTIA Network+ exam, 5
regulations documentation, 609
Reliability and Performance Monitor, 610
remote access
  dedicated connections, 499–501
  dial-up to Internet, 496
  dynamic DNS, 346
  overview of, 495–496
  private dial-up, 496–498
  remote terminal, 501–503
  securing, 571
  VoIP, 503–504
  VPNs, 499
remote access server (RAS), 496–498
Remote Access Service (RAS), 496–498
remote administration tool (RAT), Trojans, 550
remote connectivity
  alternative to telephony WAN, 479
  BPL, 494–495
  cable modems, 490–491
  cellular WAN, 492–494
  choosing option, 495
  dawn of long distance, 461–466
  dial-up, 480–486
  digital telephony, 467–468
  DSL, 486–490
  fiber, 494
  historical/conceptual, 459–460
  packet switching, 473–478
  real-world WAN, 478–479
  review Q & A, 505–507
  satellite, 492
  SONET/SDH and OC fiber carriers, 472–473
  T1 and T3 copper carriers, 468–471
  telephony and beyond, 460–461
  using remote access. *See* remote access
  using VPNs, 408–412
Remote Copy Protocol (RCP), 304
Remote Desktop Connection (RDC), 501–502
Remote Desktop Protocol (RDP), 501
Remote Shell (RSH), 304
remote terminals, remote access via, 501–503

repeaters
        for digital data over long distances,
            465–466
        Ethernet bridge acting as, 99
replication
        macro, 550
        virus, 550
        worm, 550
research, benefits of virtualization,
    587–588
reservations, DHCP, 218
resistance, testing with multimeter, 662
Reverse Address Resolution Protocol
    (RARP), 198
reverse lookup zones, DNS server, 340
review Q & A
        advanced networking devices,
            430–432
        cabling, 78–80
        configuration management,
            632–634
        dynamic routing, 272–274
        Ethernet basics, 104–106
        modern Ethernet, 122–124
        network models, 51–53
        network naming, 355–357
        performance optimization,
            632–634
        physical network installation,
            173–176
        protecting network, 572–574
        remote connectivity, 505–507
        routing, 272–274
        SOHO network design, 654–656
        TCP/IP applications, 314–316
        TCP/IP basics, 223–225
        TCP/IP security, 398–400
        topologies, 78–80
        virtualization, 597–599
        wireless networking, 543–545
RF (radio frequency) waves, wireless
    networks, 509, 530
RFI (radio frequency interference), 541
RG-59 cable, 66
RG-6 cable, 66
RG (Radio Grade) rating, coax cables, 66
ring topology
        benefit of star topology over, 58
        overview of, 56–58
        SONET defining, 472
        star-ring topology, 58–59
RIPE NCC (RIPE Network Coordination
    Center), 443
RIPv1 (Routing Information
    Protocol v1)
        hop cost of OSPF vs., 255
        OSPF convergence vs., 258
        overview of, 251

RIPv2 (Routing Information
    Protocol v2)
        hop cost of OSPF vs., 255
        OSPF convergence vs., 258
        overview of, 251–252
RIRs (Regional Internet Registries)
        giving out IPv6 prefixes, 443
        IANA, 200–201
riser fire rating, 76
Rivest Cipher 4 (RC4) stream cipher
        data encryption using WEP, 525
        symmetric-key algorithm, 364
Rivest, Ron, 364–365
Rivest Shamir Adelman (RSA)
        algorithm, 365, 388–389
RJ-11 connectors, telephones
        defined, 71
        DSL, 486
        PSTN, 480
RJ-45 connectors
        10BaseT, 91–93
        defined, 71
        for UTP in Ethernet NICs, 162
        work area outlets, 140
RJ-45 crimper, 151–153
RJ (registered jack) connectors
        MT-RJ, 114
        UTP cabling, 71
Rlogin (remote login), 303–304
rogue access points, 556–557
role-based access control (RBAC)
        security model, 376
rollover cable, connecting to routers,
    260–261
root, DNS, 324
root name servers, DNS
        name resolution process, 334–336
        overview of, 328–329
rootkits, 550–551
round trip time (RTT), 181
route command, troubleshooting,
    666–667
route print command, 234
router port, multilayer switches, 420
routers
        configuration interface of, 261
        configuring, 267–270
        connecting to, 260–267
        CSU/DSUs built into, 471
        destroying private IP
            addresses, 223
        dynamic routing. See dynamic
            routing
        freedom from Layer 2, 237–238
        how they work, 228–229
        improved in IPv6 with
            aggregation, 434, 441–445
        interVLAN, 417–419

at Layer 3 of OSI, 32–35
migrating to IPv6. See IPv6
    (Internet Protocol version 6),
    moving to
network diagram documentation,
    603–605
not forwarding broadcasts, 331
port blocking, 563–564
review Q & A, 272–274
routing tables, 230–237
TCP/IP LANS interconnecting
    with, 192–194
troubleshooting, 270–272,
    663, 679
understanding, 228–229
using NAT for wireless. See NAT
    (Network Address Translation)
using TACACS+ for networks with
    many, 382–387
VPN concentrator, 411
Routing and Remote Access Service
    (RRAS), PPTP VPNs, 408–410
Routing Information Protocol v1.
    See RIPv1 (Routing Information
    Protocol v1)
Routing Information Protocol v2.
    See RIPv2 (Routing Information
    Protocol v2)
routing loop problems, 679
routing tables
        for Cisco 2811, 236–237
        for distance vector routing
            protocols, 247–254
        interconnecting TCP/IP LANS, 193
        for multihomed computers,
            233–236
        overview of, 230
        SOHO network design, 646
        troubleshooting, 270, 666–667
        for typical home router, 231–233
RRAS (Routing and Remote Access
    Service), PPTP VPNs, 408–410
RSA (Rivest Shamir Adelman)
        algorithm, 365, 388–389
RSH (Remote Shell), 304
RTP (Real-time Transport Protocol),
    VoIP, 504
RTSP (Real Time Streaming
    Protocol), 504
RTT (round trip time or real transfer
    time), 181
runs, cable
        defined, 130
        diagnosing network in work area,
            170–171
        mapping, 145–146
        network diagram documentation,
            603–605

SOHO structured cabling
design, 642
testing fiber-optic, 160
testing UTP, 155–160

S

S value, MPLS header, 475
SaaS (Software as a Service), 597
Samba, 342
SAT (Source Address Table), switches,
100–101
satellite
coaxial cable used for, 65
latency in connections, 247
remote connectivity via, 492
SC fiber-optic connector
100BaseFX using, 113
10BaseFL using, 94
new fiber connectors
replacing, 114
overview of, 73
scanners, SOHO network design, 651
scheduling exam
paying when, 5
preparing for exam, 6
SCP (Secure Copy Protocol), 395–396
SDH (Synchronous Digital Hierarchy),
472–473
SDSL (Symmetric DSL), 486
secondary zone, DNS server, 340,
344–345
Secure Copy Protocol (SCP), 395–396
Secure FTP or SSH FTP (SFTP), 396
Secure Hash Algorithm (SHA), 369
Secure Shell. See SSH (Secure Shell)
Secure Sockets Layer. See SSL (Secure
Sockets Layer)
security
CompTIA Network+ exam
domain, 4
DNS Security Extensions, 346
firewalls for. See firewalls
FTP lacking, 310–311
IPsec for IPv6 improving, 434
NAT for. See NAT (Network
Address Translation)
network protection devices for. See
network protection devices
overview of, 547–548
review Q & A, 572–574
separate network for, 202
SOHO network requirements,
652–653
SSL and HTTPS providing Web,
297–298
troubleshooting Wi-Fi
configuration, 542–543

user account, 557–561
UTP limitations, 110
vulnerability scanners, 571
Security Identifier (SID), Windows, 384
security, network threats
administrative access control
weaknesses, 549
Denial of Service, 553–554
malware, 550–552
man in the middle attacks, 553
phishing attacks, 553
physical intrusion, 554–555
social engineering attacks,
552–553
system crash/hardware failures,
548–549
on wireless connections, 555–557
security policy documentation, 608
security, TCP/IP, also see authentication
standards
asymmetric-key algorithm
standards, 365–367
authentication, 375
authorization, 375–376
combining authentication and
encryption, 391–394
encryption and OSI model, 367
encryption, overview of, 360–363
encryption standards, 388–391
HTTPS, 394–395
LDAP, 397–398
nonrepudiation, 368–374
overview of, 359–360
SCP, 395–396
secure applications, 394–398
SFTP, 396
SNMP, 396–397
symmetric-key algorithm
standards, 363–365
security, wireless networking
authentication, 522–524
data encryption, 524–526
MAC address filtering, 521–522
overview of, 521
Power over Ethernet, 526
segments
bridges connecting Ethernet,
98–99
bus-ring topology, 58–59
crossover cables connecting
Ethernet, 98
of Ethernet frames, 84–89
TCP, 182–183
TCP/IP model, 49–50
uplink ports connecting Ethernet,
96–97
self-hosting web pages, 294
sendmail. e-mail server, 306–307
sequence number field, TCP header, 183

serial cabling, 74
serial connections, to routers, 260–261
serial ports
configuring VLAN-capable
switches, 414
connecting to routers, 261
overview of, 74
server clusters, load balancing, 421
server farm, 631
Server Message Block (SMB), 342
"server not found" errors,
troubleshooting DNS, 347–349
servers
clustered, 630–631
dedicated cache, 621
e-mail, 304, 306–307
FTP, 309–311
network diagram documentation,
603–605
Novell NetWare, 403
peer-to-peer network model,
404–406
physical protection of, 554–555
proxy, 427–428
RADIUS setup, 381–382
SOHO network design, 639
TCP, 277–278
Telnet, 301–302
troubleshooting sluggish, 676 677
Web. See Web servers
wireless authentication, 522–524
servers, DNS
in action, 336–341
authoritative, 327
defined, 326
DNS root, 320–321
how DNS works, 320–321
Internet DNS names and, 322
name servers, 327–329
overview of, 332–336
root, 328–329
troubleshooting, 348–349
Service Profile ID (SPID), ISDN, 485
Service Set Identifiers. See SSIDs (Service
Set Identifiers)
session ID, SSH, 389
Session Initiation Protocol (SIP), 504
Session layer (Layer 5) OSI
overview of, 37–39
TCP/IP Application layer vs., 48
TCP/IP Transport layer vs., 45–46
session tracking/naming, Layer 5
OSI, 38
sessions
defined, 276
TCP/IP applications, 283
troubleshooting with netstat
command, 667

setup
Cisco routers, 260–263
NAT, 239–240
routers, 267–270
SFF (Small Form Factor) connectors, 114–115
SFTP (Secure FTP or SSH FTP), 396
SHA (Secure Hash Algorithm), 369
shared encryption key, WEP, 525
sharing
configuring NICs for ad hoc network, 528
Windows 98 options, 404
shielded twisted pair (STP) cables, 68, 10
shortest-path-first method, OSPF, 258
shorts, troubleshooting cable, 659
show startup-config, 608–609
SID (Security Identifier), Windows, 384
signal strength, wireless configuration, 513
signaling (logical) topology, 60
signals
DS1/T1, 468–470
placing WAP for infrastructure network, 530
split cable problem, 501
troubleshooting wireless connectivity, 541
Simple Mail Transfer Protocol. See SMTP (Simple Mail Transfer Protocol)
Simple Network Management Protocol (SNMP), 396–397
Simple Network Time Protocol (SNTP), 221
single-mode fiber (SMF), 73
single sign-on, 559
SIP (Session Initiation Protocol), 504
site survey, implementing Wi-Fi, 526–527
Skype, 504
Small Form-Factor Pluggable (SPF) connector, 647
Small Form Factor (SFF) connectors, 114–115
small office/home office network. See SOHO (small office/home office) network
smart devices, 559
smart jacks, 143
smartphones, 492–494
SMB (Server Message Block), 342
SMF (single-mode fiber), 73
SMTP (Simple Mail Transfer Protocol)
e-mail clients, 307–308
MX records used by, 340
sending e-mail with, 305
sendmail only using, 307
using CRAM-MD5 for server authentication, 369

smurf attacks, 553–554
snapshots, virtual machine, 587
SNAT (Static NAT), 242
Sneakernet, 81, 82
sniffers, 85
snips, rolling own patch cables, 151
SNMP (Simple Network Management Protocol), 396–397
SNTP (Simple Network Time Protocol), 221
SOA (Start of Authority)
defined, 327
in DNS forward lookup zones, 338
root servers in DNS and, 328–329
social engineering attacks, 552–553
socket pairs, TCP/IP applications, 283
sockets, TCP/IP applications, 283
Software as a Service (SaaS), 597
software, network
diagnosing cabling by checking, 168
Layer 3 (Network) OSI, 31–35
Layer 4 (Transport) OSI, 36–37
Layer 5 (Session) OSI, 37–39
Layer 6 (Presentation) OSI, 40–41
Layer 7 (Application) OSI, 42–43
Layers 3-7 OSI, overview, 30–31
software troubleshooting tools
hostname command, 666
ipconfig/ifconfig commands, 663–664
mtr (My traceroute) command, 666
nbstat command, 667
netstat command, 667
nslookup/dig commands, 665–666
packet sniffers, 668
ping/arping commands, 664–665
port scanners, 668–669
route command, 666–667
throughput testers, 669
tracert/traceroute commands, 663
software, virtual, 577
software, wireless networking, 513–514
SOHO (small office/home office) network
ASDL and, 486–487
compatibility issues, 640–641
define network needs, 638
external connections, 645–649
historical/conceptual, 635–636
internal connections, 641–645
ISPs and MTUs, 649–650
network design, 638–640
peripherals, 651
PPPoE settings for DSL in router, 490
review Q & A, 654–656

security, 652–653
steps for designing, 636–637
traffic shaping on router, 624
solid core UTP, 131. See also horizontal cabling
solution to problem, troubleshooting process, 673–675
SONET (Synchronous Optical Network)
10GBaseEW for, 118
10GBaseLW for, 118
10GBaseSW for, 117
as fiber-optic carrier, 472–473
LAN Ethernet standard vs., 117
long-distance Internet connections using, 460
Sony rootkit, 551
Source Address Table (SAT), switches, 100–101
source code, HTML, 292–293
Spanning Tree Protocol (STP), 102–103
Speed Dial, Firefox add-on, 312
SPF (Small Form-Factor Pluggable) connector, 647
SPID (Service Profile ID), ISDN, 485
split cable problem, 501
splitters, 488
coaxial, 67
dedicated cable connections and, 501
installing DSL, 488
spoofing MAC addresses, 522
spread-spectrum radio waves, 802.11 broadcasting methods, 517
Sprint, WiMAX ISP, 493
SPS (standby power supply), 629
Spybot Search&Destroy, 552
spyware, 551
Squid, 621
SSH (Secure Shell)
connecting to routers using, 266
encryption standard, 388–390
OpenSSH, 396
OpenVPN using, 412
replacing Telnet, 300, 304
SSH FTP, 396
tunnels, 390–391
SSID mismatch error, 542
SSIDs (Service Set Identifiers)
configuring NICs for ad hoc network, 528
configuring Wi-Fi, 532–533
configuring Wi-Fi client, 536–537
evil twin attacks, 556–557
rogue access point problem, 556
troubleshooting Wi-Fi configuration, 542
wireless networking, 516–517
SSL (Secure Sockets Layer)
Netscape creating, 392
SSL portal VPNs, 412

SSL/TLS, 392, 394
SSL tunnel VPNs, 412
SSL VPNs, 411–412
World Wide Web and, 297–299
ST fiber-optic connector
    10BaseFL using, 94
    defined, 73
    limitations of, 114
standards
    10 GbE, 116
    asymmetric-key algorithm,
        365–367
    authentication. *See* authentication
        standards
    authentication with encryption,
        391–394
    cabling and networking, 69
    encryption, 388–391
    file formats at OSI Layer 6, 40–41
    history of networking, 178
    IEEE, 76–77
    IPv4-to-IPv6 tunneling, 452–454
    Link layer of TCP/IP model
        lacking, 44
    structured cabling. *See* structured
        cabling
    symmetric-key algorithm,
        363–365
standards, Wi-Fi
    802.11. *See* 802.11 Wi-Fi standard
    802.11a, 519–520
    802.11b, 519
    802.11g, 520
    802.11n, 520–521
standby power supply (SPS), 629
star topology
    equipment racks, 133–134
    horizontal cabling, 130–132
    overview of, 58
    patch panels and cables, 134–138
    point-to-multipoint topology
        vs., 62
    for structured cabling, 127–128
    structured cabling network
        components, 129–130
    telecommunications room, 132
Start of Authority. *See* SOA (Start of
    Authority)
stateful DHCPv6 server, IPv6, 448
stateful filtering (or inspection),
    566–567
stateless DHCPv6 server, IPv6, 448
stateless filtering, 566
static encryption key, WEP, 525
static IP addressing
    basic router configuration, 268
    defined, 212
    overview, 212–216
    SOHO network design, 644–645

Static NAT (SNAT), 242
static VLANs, 416–417
status of connections, TCP/IP
    applications, 286–291
steady state, routers in, 251
Steel-Belted RADIUS server, 381
STP (shielded twisted pair) cables,
    68, 110
STP (Spanning Tree Protocol), 102–103
straight-through cable, 96–98
stranded core UTP
    defined, 131
    patch cables using, 138
    rolling own patch cables, 151
stream ciphers, 364
streaming video, latency sensitivity
    of, 622
strong passwords, 558
structured cabling
    choosing horizontal cabling, 132
    equipment racks, 133–134
    horizontal cabling, 130–131
    network components, 129–130
    patch panels and cables, 134–138
    SOHO network design, 641–642
    with star network, 127–128
    telecommunications room, 132
    understanding, 127
    work area, 138–140
structured cabling for entire building
    connecting patch panels, 153–155
    connecting work areas, 151
    connections inside demarc,
        143–144
    determining location of
        telecommunications room,
        146–147
    getting floor plan, 145
    making connections, 150–151
    mapping runs, 145–146
    overview of, 140–141, 144
    pulling cable, 147–150
    rolling own patch cables, 151–153
    testing cable runs, 155–160
    testing fiber, 161–162
STS (Synchronous Transport Signal),
    SONET, 473
stud finder, 149
study time, setting aside, 6–7
subdomains, adding to DNS tree, 326
Subnet mask column, routing tables,
    231–236
subnet masks
    diagnosing TCP/IP networks, 354
    how DHCP works, 217
    IPv6, 437
    overview of, 194–200
    in static IP addressing, 212–216
    subnetting using, 202–203

subnetting
    calculating hosts, 204
    calculating subnets, 206–209
    CIDR and, 211
    making first subnet, 205–206
    manual dotted decimal to binary
        conversion in, 209–211
    overview of, 202–204
    routers connecting subnets, 32
    setting up network with, 30–31
super accounts, administering, 549
supervisors, 577
supplicants, wireless authentication,
    522–524
surfing Web, Web clients, 297
switchboards, old-time telephone,
    461–462
switches
    configuration interface of, 261
    configuring VLAN-capable,
        414–416
    with high-speed, add-on ports,
        120–121
    hubs replaced by, 18
    increasing speed of Ethernet,
        99–103
    interchangeable components for,
        647–648
    interVLAN routing, 417–419
    link lights on, 166–167,
        168–169
    multilayer, 419–422
    network diagram documentation,
        603–605
    physical server protection, 554
    port mirroring, 427
    rack-mounted, 134
    running nbstat command, 667
    SOHO network design, 641, 645
    star topology for structured
        cabling, 127–128
    STP-enabled, 102–103
    troubleshooting, 103
    trunking VLAN traffic between,
        413–414
    upgrading to 100BaseT, 108–110
    using TACACS+ for many,
        382–387
    VLAN, 412–413
switching loops (bridge loops)
    defined, 103
    STP eliminating problem of
        accidental, 103
    troubleshooting, 678
switchport, 420
Symmetric DSL (SDSL), 486
symmetric-key algorithm
    defined, 363
    SSL, 392

standards, 363–365
  weakness of, 365
SYN, ACK (synchronize, acknowledge)
  packet, TCP, 277
Synchronous Digital Hierarchy (SDH),
  472–473
Synchronous Optical Network. *See*
  SONET (Synchronous Optical
  Network)
Synchronous Transport Signal (STS),
  SONET, 473
syslog, for custom logs, 619
System attribute, data backups, 626
system duplication, with
  virtualization, 587
system logs, 619
System Monitor, 611, 615
system recovery, with virtualization,
  586–587
System Setup, VMs, 578–579, 584

T

T-carriers
  digital telephony copper, 468–471
  Frame Relay packet-switching
    for, 474
T1 carrier
  Frame Relay packet-switching
    for, 474
  interconnecting with E1
    carrier, 471
  overview of, 468–470
T3 (DS3) lines, 471
TA (Terminal Adapter), ISDN, 485
TACACS+ (Terminal Access Controller
  Access Control System Plus)
  port authentication, 428–429
  using Kerberos for authentication,
    382–384
tape drives, data backup, 625
Task Manager, 289
TCP/IP applications
  connection status, 286–291
  e-mail, 304–309
  FTP, 309–313
  good vs. bad communications, 291
  historical/conceptual data, 276
  ICMP, 279
  IGMP, 280
  overview of, 275
  power of port numbers, 280–282
  registered ports, 282–286
  review Q & A, 314–316
  TCP, 277–278
  Telnet, 299–304
  UDP, 278
  World Wide Web, 291–299

TCP/IP basics
  Application layer protocols,
    183–185
  CIDR and subnetting. *See*
    subnetting
  dynamic IP addresses, or DHCP,
    216–222
  historical/conceptual data, 178
  Internet layer protocols, 180–181
  IP addresses and class IDs,
    200–202
  IP addresses and interconnecting,
    192–194
  IP addresses and network IDs,
    191–192
  IP addresses and subnet masks,
    194–200
  IP addresses, overview of, 185–191
  loopback IP addresses, 222–223
  overview of, 177
  private IP addresses, 223
  public IP addresses, 223
  review Q & A, 223–225
  static IP addresses, 212–216
  TCP/IP protocol suite, overview,
    179–180
  Transport layer protocols, 182 183
TCP/IP model
  Application layer, 48–49
  frames, packets and segments,
    49–50
  history of, 14
  Internet layer, 45
  Link layer, 44–45
  overview of, 43–44
  review Q & A, 51–53
  Transport layer, 45–48
  as troubleshooting tool, 11–12,
    50–51
TCP/IP networks
  defined, 31
  diagnosing, 352–355
  IP packets within frames, 33–35
  Microsoft redesigning NetBIOS to
    work with, 350
  troubleshooting connectivity, 677
  unique identifiers in, 32
TCP/IP protocol suite
  Application layer protocols,
    183–185
  Internet layer protocols, 180–181
  overview, 179–180
  TCP enabling communication for
    networks using, 277–278
  Transport layer protocols, 182 183
TCP segments, 47–48
TCP three-way handshake, 277
TCP (Transmission Control Protocol)
  as connection-oriented
    protocol, 47

TCP/IP applications using,
    277–278
  at TCP/IP Transport layer, 182 183
TCPView, 285
TDM (time division multiplexing), 468
TDRs (time domain reflectometers),
  157, 658–659
technologies, CompTIA Network+ exam
  domain, 4
Telecommunications Industry
  Association (TIA), 69
telecommunications room
  diagnosing network problems,
    171–172
  equipment racks, 133–134
  horizontal cabling running to, 130
  location of, 146–147
  overview of, 132
  patch cables, 134–137, 138
  pulling cable by starting from, 148
  in structured cabling network, 129
telephone scam, social engineering,
  552–553
telephone systems
  66-block patch panels in, 136
  for entire buildings. *See* structured
    cabling for entire building
  RJ-11 connectors for, 71
  structured cabling for, 127
  TCP/IP authentication taken
    from, 376
  UTP cables for, 69
telephony
  dial-up. *See* dial-up
  digital, 467–468
  history of long distance, 461–466
  most Internet connections using,
    460–461
  WAN, 478–479
  WAN alternatives, 479
television, split cable problem, 501
Telnet
  configuring client, 302–303
  connecting to routers, 266
  limitations of, 300
  overview of, 299–301
  Rlogin, RSH and RCP, 303–304
  servers and clients, 301–302
  SSH and death of, 304
  terminal emulation, 501
telnetd server, 301
temperature monitor, server rooms, 661
Temporal Key Integrity Protocol (TKIP),
  WPA, 525
Teredo tunneling protocol, IPv6, 453
Terminal Access Controller Access
  Control System Plus (TACACS+)
  port authentication, 428–429
  using Kerberos for authentication,
    382–384

Terminal Adapter (TA), ISDN, 485
terminal emulation
  configuring routers, 261–262
  creating remote terminal with, 501–503
  SSH and Telnet as, 266, 300
  SSH replacing Telnet, 304
Termination phase, PPP authentication, 377
Test Specific sections, in this book, 8
testing
  cable runs, 155–160
  fiber, 161–162
  solution to problem, 674
  telephony WAN, 478
  theory of probably cause in troubleshooting, 673
TFTP (Trivial File Transfer Protocol)
  FTP vs., 313
  using UDP, 221–222
TGS (Ticket-Granting Service), Kerberos, 383–384
TGT (Ticket-Granting Ticket), Kerberos, 383
theory of probable cause, troubleshooting, 673
third-party tools
  creating logs, 618
  data backup, 625
  Dr. TCP for MTU mismatch, 649–650
  FTP servers, 310
  IDS, 425
  Network Management Software, 266
  network threats from, 548
  terminal emulation programs, 503
  threat assessments, 548
  ZoneAlarm Pro personal firewall, 568
threats, network
  administrative access control weaknesses, 549
  defined, 548
  Denial of Service attacks, 553–554
  firewalls protecting from external. See firewalls
  malware, 550–552
  man in the middle attacks, 553
  phishing attacks, 553
  physical intrusion, 554–555
  social engineering attacks, 552–553
  system crash/hardware failure, 548–549
  wireless connection attacks, 555–557
throughput testers, 669

TIA/EIA standards
  568A color code for UTP, 92–93
  568B color code for UTP, 98
  606 standard for block panel labeling, 136–137
  inserting wires on patch panels, 135
  pulling cable in ceilings, 148
  solid core for horizontal cabling, 131
  structured cabling, 127–128
  telecommunications room, 132
  testing cable runs, 159–160
  testing fiber runs, 161
TIA (Telecommunications Industry Association), 69
TIC (Tunnel Information and Control) protocol, 454
Ticket-Granting Service (TGS), Kerberos, 383–384
Ticket-Granting Ticket (TGT), Kerberos, 383
tier 1 ISPs, 451–452
Tier One backbone, 233
time division multiplexing (TDM), 468
time domain reflectometers (TDRs), 157, 658–659
time, NTP giving current, 221, 398
timeout period, connection status, 288
timestamped service ticket , Kerberos, 383–384
TKIP (Temporal Key Integrity Protocol), WPA, 525
TLD (top-level domain) names, 321
TLS (Transport Layer Security)
  EAP-TLS, 385, 523–524
  replacing SSL, 298
  SSL/TLS, 392, 394
token, Kerberos, 383–384
tone probes/generators, 172–173, 662
top-level domain servers, DNS, 321
top-level domain (TLD) names, 321
topology icons, network diagram documentation, 603–604
topology, network
  100BaseFX, 111
  100BaseT, 108
  bus and ring, 56–58
  defined, 55
  hybrids, 59–60
  mesh, 60–61
  parameters of, 63
  point-to-multipoint, 62
  point-to-point, 62
  review Q & A, 78–80
  star, 58
  used by Ethernet, 83
Total Seminars web site, 4

traceroute/tracert command
  mtr (My traceroute) command, 271–272, 666
  software troubleshooting tools, 663
  tracing routers between two points, 663
  troubleshooting sluggish server, 677
traffic (bandwidth) shaping
  bandwidth management, 423–424
  performance optimization, 623–624
Transmission Control Protocol. See TCP (Transmission Control Protocol)
transmit beamforming, 802.11n WAPs, 518
Transport layer (Layer 4) OSI, 36–37, 422
Transport Layer Security. See TLS (Transport Layer Security)
Transport layer, TCP, 45–48, 50, 182–183
Transport mode, IPsec, 393
traversal tunneling protocols, NAT, 452
tree, DNS, 324, 326
Trivial File Transfer Protocol (TFTP)
  FTP vs., 313
  using UDP, 221–222
Trojans, 550
troubleshooting
  CompTIA Network+ exam, 4
  as fun, 679
  with hardware tools. See hardware troubleshooting tools
  overview of, 657–658
  review Q & A, 680–682
  with software tools. See software troubleshooting tools
  with TCP/IP and OSI models, 11–12, 50–51
troubleshooting process
  basic steps, 669–671
  document findings, actions and outcomes, 675
  establish plan of action and identify potential effects, 673
  establish theory or probable cause, 673
  gather information, identify symptoms, question users, 671–672
  identify problem, 671–672
  implement and test solution or escalate, 674
  test theory to determine cause, 673
  verify full system functionality/implement preventative measures, 674–675

troubleshooting scenarios
  broadcast storms, 678
  DHCP, 220
  DNS, 346–349
  hubs and switches, 103
  log in, 676
  problem escalation, 677–678
  proxy ARP, 679
  reaching Web site, 676
  routing, 270–272
  routing loops, 679
  routing problems, 678–679
  sluggish Web server, 676–677
  structured cabling in work
    area, 140
  switching loops, 678
  TCP/IP networks, 352–355
  tools, overview, 658
  unable to see anything on
    network, 677
  Wi-Fi, 539–543
  WINS, 352
trunk carriers, T-carriers, 468–471
trunk lines, old-time telephones,
  463–464
trunk ports, VLAN, 414
trunking, VLAN traffic, 413–414
trust model
  Pretty Good Privacy
    encryption, 374
  Web-of-Trust option for, 374
TSP (Tunnel Setup Protocol), 454
TTL (Time to Live) field, IP packet
  header, 181
TTL (Time to Live) field, MPLS
  header, 475
TTLS (Tunneled TLS), EAP-TTLS, 386,
  523–524
tunnel brokers, IPv6, 454
Tunnel Information and Control (TIC)
  protocol, 454
tunnel mode, IPsec, 393
Tunnel Setup Protocol (TSP), 454
tunnels
  EAP-TTLS, 411
  IPv4-to-IPv6, 451–456
  IPv6. See IPv6 (Internet Protocol
    version 6), moving to
  L2TP VPNs, 411
  PPTP VPNs, 408–410
  Secure Shell, 390–391
twinaxial cables, 1000BaseCX, 113
twisted pair cabling
  10GBaseT standard, 119
  crossover cables, 98
  overview of, 67–68
  shielded twisted pair, 68
two-factor authentication, 557
Type field, Ethernet frames, 86
TZO provider, 346

U

UART (Universal Asynchronous
  Receiver/Transmitter), internal
  modems, 481–482
Ubuntu
  entering DNS information in, 333
  running ifconfig in, 191
  Samba on, 342
  setting static IP addresses, 214–215
  Telnet, 301–302
UC (unified communications), 622
UDP (User Datagram Protocol), 48
  as connectionless protocol, 47
  DHCP using, 278
  NTP and SNTP using, 221
  TCP/IP applications using, 278
  at TCP/IP Transport layer, 183
  TFTP using, 221–222
UNC (Universal Naming
  Convention), 614
Underwriters Laboratories, cabling fire
  ratings, 76
unicast addresses
  IP packets, 201
  IPv6, 437
  IPv6 global, 439–441
unified communications (UC), 622
uniform resource locators (URLs)
  changing in port forwarding,
    242–243
  Web clients surfing Web
    using, 297
uninterruptible power supplies. See
  UPSs (uninterruptible power
  supplies)
unique identifiers, TCP/IP networks, 32
Universal Asynchronous Receiver/
  Transmitter (UART), internal
  modems, 481–482
Universal Naming Convention
  (UNC), 614
UNIX/Linux systems
  administrative access control, 549
  BIND DNS server tool, 336
  built-in FTP servers, 310
  case sensitivity of commands, 222
  converting dotted decimal to
    binary and back, 187–188
  discovering process ID, 289
  displaying IP and MAC address,
    190–191
  displaying routing table, 234
  enabling IPv6, 445
  entering DNS information, 333
  entering static IP information, 214
  FreeRadius server in, 381
  KVM VMM, 591–592
  Net Activity Viewer, 286–287
  port filter interfaces, 564–565

running Apache HTTP Web Server,
  295–296
supporting arping utility, 664
Telnet server, 301
troubleshooting DNS with dig
  tool, 349
troubleshooting IP with ifconfig,
  663–664
using Samba, 342
verifying DNS server settings, 333
unshielded twisted pair. See UTP
  (unshielded twisted pair) cable
unused user accounts, disabling,
  559–560
updates, anti-malware, 551
uplink ports, 96–98
UPSs (uninterruptible power supplies)
  diagnosing in telecommunications
    room, 171
  performance optimization, 629
  rack-mounted, 134
URLs (uniform resource locators)
  changing in port forwarding,
    242–243
  Web clients surfing Web
    using, 297
USB NICs, 164–165
USB-to-serial adapter, 261
USB wireless network adapters, 511–512
USENET, 294
user accounts
  authentication, 557
  controlling, 549, 559–561
  overview of, 557
  passwords, 557–559
  securing, 557–561
User Datagram Protocol. See UDP (User
  Datagram Protocol)
usernames
  AAA authentication, 381
  authentication via, 374
  connecting to routers for Web
    access, 264
  dial-up to Internet, 496–497
  FTP server, 310–311
  Novell NetWare, 403
  PPP authentication, 377–379
  RADIUS authentication, 382
  SSH encryption, 388–390
  Telnet client, 302–303
users
  teaching about malware, 551
  troubleshooting process, 671–672
UTP (unshielded twisted pair) cable
  10BaseT using, 90–93
  concentrating on for exam, 75
  crosstalk in, 157–158
  fiber-optic cable vs., 110–111
  for horizontal cabling. See
    horizontal cabling

network connectivity
documentation, 602–603
network hardware, 17
overview of, 68–71
star topology for structured
cabling, 127–128

V

V standards, PSTN, 483–484
V.92 standard, PSTN, 483–484
vampire taps, early bus networks, 64
variable-length subnet masking
(VLSM), 251
VDSL (Very High Bitrate DSL), 486
verification, Wi-Fi installation, 539
VeriSign, certificate authority, 373
Veritas NetBackup, 625
version (Ver) field, IP packet header, 181
vertical cross-connects, inside demarc,
143–144
Very High Bitrate DSL (VDSL), 486
video conferencing, with structured
cabling, 127
views, Performance Monitor, 613
virtual desktops, 586, 590–592
virtual LANs. See VLANs (virtual LANs)
virtual machine manager. See VMM
(virtual machine manager)
virtual machines. See VMs (virtual
machines)
Virtual Network Computing (VNC), 503
virtual PBX, 595–596
Virtual PC, 591
virtual private networks. See VPNs
(virtual private networks)
virtual reality, 575–577
virtual servers
choosing hypervisor, 592–594
running on hypervisors, 590
transferring with ESX, 593
virtual switches, 593–595
Virtual Trunk Protocol (VTP),
VLANs, 417
virtualization
benefits of, 586–588
choosing hypervisor, 592–593
emulation vs., 579–580
in modern networks, 588–590
Network as a Service, 596
overview of, 575
review Q & A, 597–599
sample, 580–586
understanding, 575–577
using hypervisors, 577–579
using virtual machine managers,
590–592
virtual PBX, 595–596
virtual switches, 593–595

viruses, 550
VLAN-capable switches, 414–417
VLANs (virtual LANs)
configuring VLAN-capable switch,
414–417
interVLAN routing, 417–419
overview of, 412–413
SOHO network design, 643–644
SOHO network IP address
scheme, 645
trunking, 413–414
updating switches with VTP, 417
VLSM (variable-length subnet
masking), 251
VMM (virtual machine manager)
choosing, 590–592
defined, 575
emulation vs. virtualization,
579–580
user of term, 590
in virtualization, 578–579
VMware Workstation as. See
VMware Workstation
VMs (virtual machines)
defined, 575–576
sample virtualization, 580–586
SOHO network IP address
scheme, 645
VMware
ESX, 589–590
vSphere Client, 590
VMware Workstation
defined, 589
sample virtualization, 580–586
saving snapshot, 587
system setup in, 578–579
virtual hardware
configuration, 578
as virtual machine manager, 591
VNC (Virtual Network Computing), 503
VoIP (Voice over IP)
latency sensitivity on, 622
QoS reducing jitter on, 623
remote access via, 503–504
Skype, 504
standards used by, 504
voltage event recorders, 171–172, 661
voltage, testing with multimeter, 662
vouchers, CompTIA Network+ exam, 5
VPN concentrator, L2TP VPNs, 411
VPNs (virtual private networks)
L2TP VPNs, 411
overview of, 406–408
PPTP VPNs, 408–410
remote access via, 499
SSL VPNs, 411–412
virtual LANs. See VLANs
(virtual LANs)
vSphere Client, 590

VTP (Virtual Trunk Protocol),
VLANs, 417
vulnerability scanners, 571

W

WANs (wide area networks)
ATM popularity for, 474–475
cellular, 492–494
network IDs enabling, 194
setting up for router, 267–269
in TCP/IP networks, 185–186
telephony, 478–479
WAPs (wireless access points)
802.11n and, 518
BSSID, SSID and ESSID, 516–517
configuring encryption, 534
configuring for Wi-Fi, 531–532
configuring MAC address, 533–534
configuring SSID (ESSID) and
beacon, 532–534
configuring Wi-Fi channel and
frequency, 535–536
extending Wi-Fi with, 538
network diagram documentation,
603–605
overview of, 512–513
placing, 529–530
replacement antenna for, 530–531
rogue access point problem, 556
SOHO network design, 643
troubleshooting Wi-Fi, 540–543
using ACLs for MAC
addresses, 521
wireless authentication, 522–524
wireless infrastructure mode
network, 515–516
war chalking, 556
war driving, 556
WDM (Wavelength Division
Multiplexing), fiber devices, 473, 494
Web-based services, e-mail, 305–306
Web browsers
configuring VLAN-capable
switches, 414–416
name resolution, 330–336
requesting HTML pages from Web
servers, 293
troubleshooting with, 676
types of, 297
using as FTP client, 311
using TLS for HTTPS-secured
Web sites, 392
Web interface, for Web access, 263–365
Web-of-Trust option, certificates, 374
Web pages
publishing, 294
telling if site is secure, 298
Web servers delivering, 295–296

Web servers
    Dynamic DNS on, 346
    as FTP servers, 310
    publishing web pages, 294
    storing documents using HTML, 292–293
    understanding, 295–297
    using port number 80, 280–281
Web sites, inability to reach external, 676
Webmin
    Apache module, 296
    sendmail module, 306
well-known port numbers
    defined, 280–281
    list of, 283
    memorizing for TCP/IP applications, 291
    port filtering and, 563
WEP (Wired Equivalent Privacy), 525, 556
whitelist, MAC filtering with, 522
Wi-Fi (wireless networking)
    adding WAP, 538
    adding wireless bridges, 538
    attacks on connections, 555–557
    configuring access point, 531–532
    configuring channel and frequency, 536
    configuring client, 536–537
    configuring encryption, 534–535
    configuring MAC address filtering, 533
    configuring SSID (ESSID) and beacon, 532–533
    historical/conceptual data, 509–510
    installing client, 528
    performing site survey for, 526–527
    review Q & A, 543–545
    security, 521–526
    setting up ad hoc network, 528
    setting up infrastructure network, 529–531
    SOHO network design, 643
    standards. *See* standards, Wi-Fi
    troubleshooting, 539–543
    verifying installation, 539
wide area networks. *See* WANs (wide area networks)
Windows
    Active Directory. *See* Active Directory
    administrative access control, 549
    DDNS use in, 345
    Device Manager, 540
    DNS servers, 336–341
    entering DNS information, 332
    entering static IP information, 213
    Event Viewer, 619
    Explorer, 627
    Firewall, 568–570

IAS for RADIUS server, 381
IIS in, 295
IP and MAC address display, 190
IPv6, 445
Live Hotmail, 305
network naming, 341–342
peer-to-peer networks, 404–405
Performance Monitor. *See* Performance Monitor
Remote Desktop, 346
routing table, 233–234
routing table display, 234
Server Backup, 625–626
Telnet server in, 301–302
Teredo tunneling protocol, 452
Terminal Services, 501–503
troubleshooting DHCP, 221
troubleshooting IP with ipconfig, 663–664
Virtual PC VMM for, 591
Windows domain, CIFS, 343–344
Windows Internet Name Service (WINS), 349–352
WINDOWS KEY-L combination, locking client systems, 554–555
WinFrame/MetaFrame, terminal emulation products, 501–502
WINS (Windows Internet Name Service), 349–352
Wired Equivalent Privacy (WEP), 525, 556
wireless access points. *See* WAPs (wireless access points)
wireless adapter configuration utility
    troubleshooting Wi-Fi software, 540
    Wi-Fi encryption, 535
wireless bridges, 538
wireless configuration utility, 541
wireless connection attacks, 555–557
wireless networks. *See also* Wi-Fi (wireless networking)
    accessing Internet vs. creating network, 510
    mesh topology in, 60–61
    point-to-multipoint topology in, 60–61
    point-to-point topology in, 62
wireless phishing attacks, 557
wireless USB devices, 540
Wireless Zero Configuration (ZeroConf), 541–542
wiremap tests, 156, 157
Wireshark protocol analyzer, 661, 668
wiring schemes (wire schemes), documentation, 602–603
word patterns, cracking Caesar ciphers, 362–363
work areas
    connecting in large building, 151
    diagnosing network problems, 170–171

    horizontal cabling in, 130
    in structured cabling system, 129–130, 138–140
workgroup, CIFS, 343
workstations, SOHO network design, 638
World Wide Web
    HTTP for, 294
    overview of, 291–294
    publishing web pages, 294
    SSL and HTTPS, 297–299
    Web servers and Web clients, 295–297
worms, 550
WPA (Wi-Fi Protected Access)
    configuring Wi-Fi encryption, 534–535
    cracking wireless encryption, 556
    data encryption using, 525
WPA2-Enterprise, 526
WPA2 (Wi-Fi Protected Access 2)
    configuring Wi-Fi encryption, 534–535
    cracking wireless encryption, 556
WPAs (Wi-Fi Protected Access 2), 526

X

X.25 (CCIT Packet Switching Protocol), 474
X.25 (CCITT Packet Switching Protocol), 474
XDSL (Extended DSL), 486
XENPAK MSA, 120
XML (Extensible Markup Language), 292

Y

Yagi antennas, 530
Yahoo! Mail, 305
YaST configuration program, Linux, 564–565
Yost cable, connecting to routers, 260–261
YouTube, latency sensitivity on, 622

Z

ZeroConf (Wireless Zero Configuration), 541–542
zombies, 554
ZoneAlarm Pro, personal firewall, 570
zones
    name servers and, 326–329
    network, 570–571